Criminal Justice Organizations

Administration and Management

Sixth Edition

Stan Stojkovic
University of Wisconsin-Milwaukee

David Kalinich
Florida Atlantic University

John Klofas
Rochester Institute of Technology

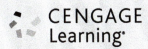

CENGAGE
Learning·

Australia · Brazil · Mexico · Singapore · United Kingdom · United States

CENGAGE
Learning·

Criminal Justice Organizations: Administration and Management, Sixth Edition

Stan Stojkovic, David Kalinich, John Klofas

Product Director: Marta Lee-Perriard

Product Manager: Carolyn Henderson Meier

Content Developer: Amy Hill

Product Assistant: Chelsea Meredith

Media Developer: Ting Jian Yap

Marketing Manager: Kara Kindstrom

Manufacturing Planner: Judy Inouye

Text Researcher: PreMedia Global

Art and Cover Direction, Production Management, and Composition: Integra Software Services Pvt. Ltd.

Cover Image Credit: moodboard / SuperStock

For product information and technology assistance, contact us at **Cengage Learning Customer & Sales Support, 1-800-354-9706.**

For permission to use material from this text or product, submit all requests online at **www.cengage.com/permissions.** Further permissions questions can be e-mailed to **permissionrequest@cengage.com.**

Library of Congress Control Number: 2014930393

ISBN 13: 978-1-285-45901-1

ISBN 10: 1-285-45901-6

Cengage Learning
200 First Stamford Place, 4th Floor
Stamford, CT 06902
USA

Cengage Learning is a leading provider of customized learning solutions with office locations around the globe, including Singapore, the United Kingdom, Australia, Mexico, Brazil, and Japan. Locate your local office at **www.cengage.com/global**.

Cengage Learning products are represented in Canada by Nelson Education, Ltd.

To learn more about Cengage Learning Solutions, visit **www.cengage.com**. Purchase any of our products at your local college store or at our preferred online store **www.cengagebrain.com**.

Printed in the United States of America
3 4 5 6 7 8 9   21 20 19 18 17

Brief Contents

Contents

Preface

Criminal justice administration and management has come a long way since the President's Commission in 1967 called for a closer look at the administration of criminal justice organizations. Concerns about effective management practices are still central to criminal justice professionals as well as to the academic researchers who must evaluate and question their methods. Since the initial statements and recommendations of the President's Commission, observers have seen the following become more prevalent in the criminal justice system: greater involvement of the courts in the administration of criminal justice agencies, the increased political nature of criminal justice administrations, a potential threat to criminal justice administrators from the private sector through the mechanism of privatization, and the creation of a Department of Homeland Security, designed to protect the country against terrorist attacks.

In short, our response to crime and terrorism is changing, and many are questioning the administration and management of criminal justice organizations. As we enter the early decades of the twenty-first century, new challenges are facing criminal justice administrators. The sixth edition of this book is being written at a time that a new sense of focus and direction exists in the nation and among criminal justice administrators. Terrorism has struck home, and the criminal justice system is being asked to provide greater security to the country and its citizens. In addition, the face of crime is also changing, with more use of the Internet and electronic means to commit crime. Criminal justice administrators are becoming more adept at addressing crime and rely on more analytical tools and strategies than ever before. Yet, the country is coming out of one of the worst economic times in our history, suffering massive deficits at all levels of government, and at the time of this writing, the government just came out of a shutdown due to political intransience and concerns over public spending.

The tough economic climate is forcing criminal justice administrators to critically examine their budgets, where once again, the mantra is doing more with less. In many communities across the country, criminal justice employees are being asked to take furlough days or significant cuts in pay and benefits. In some instances, cities are, for example, ending police services and are contracting with other agencies to meet their safety and security needs. In other areas, particularly at the state level, criminal justice agencies, as public entities, are being asked to cut back. In short, these are difficult times in our society, and criminal justice organizations are being asked to do things more efficiently and effectively, while facing budget cuts.

WHY A BOOK ON CRIMINAL JUSTICE ADMINISTRATION?

The context for criminal justice administrators is tense, to say the least. This sixth edition attempts to identify the basic structure and function of criminal justice organizations, while paying attention to *how* criminal justice organizations are managed and led. The book's primary market is both criminal justice practitioners, including managers and supervisors, and future criminal justice employees. This latter group represents students attending colleges and universities across the country, many of whom have no experience with criminal justice administrations. To students, the topic of criminal justice administration may seem boring. We hope to change that perception by providing the detail and discussion that illuminates key criminal justice administration concepts and ideas that will provide a framework for understanding the complexities of criminal justice administration. If we have begun this inquiry with students, we will have accomplished our primary goal of the book: the appreciation of the challenges and rewards that define criminal justice administration.

We began writing the first edition of this book in the late 1980s. As we progress into the twenty-first century, we still have the same purpose we had when we wrote the first edition: *to provide a book that summarizes what we know about criminal justice administration based on research and practice.* Our goal was to emulate the classic work written by Richard Hall, *Organizations: Structure, Processes, and Outcomes.* Based on the feedback provided by students, practitioners, and reviewers, we believe we have succeeded in our quest to emulate Hall's book and to provide both an academic and practical flavor that provides the best possible picture regarding criminal justice administration to our audiences.

As in the first five editions of the book, we provide an analysis of criminal justice administration by critically examining the research literature and applying it to this new world of the twenty-first century. Our primary concern is to provide students with a conceptual and theoretical basis upon which to consider criminal justice administration and management. To that end, we have included the most recent and relevant literature across topics. In addition, we have continued our focus on empirical research and its importance to the subject matter. This combination of theory and research literature allows students to appreciate the importance of these topics to criminal justice administration as well as to visualize its complexities.

The student requires an open mind and a willingness to appreciate the complexities of criminal justice administration from multiple perspectives. A legal examination, for example, of criminal justice administration would inundate students with laws and case precedents that guide and constrain criminal justice administrations, yet it is only one perspective on criminal justice administration— an important one, but nevertheless just one perspective. As the student reads through the book, it should become apparent that there are a number of ways to understand and examine criminal justice administration. Our expectation is that, regardless of perspective, a thorough understanding of criminal justice administration requires the appreciation of multiple perspectives, but more important, it also requires an awareness of the evidence we have concerning a particular topic or issue. It is common to ask: what are the "best practices" in criminal justice administration? The fact is that only recently have we been able to *minimally* answer this question. More often than not, we do not have an empirical basis to know whether or not a particular practice is actually a best practice. This will create uncertainty and anxiety among students. Welcome to criminal justice administration.

CENTRAL THEMES

As in the first five editions, we focus on three central themes in this edition: criminal justice; the system as a whole; and theory, research, and practice. Prior to the publication of the first edition, no texts on criminal justice administration emphasized the contributions of the growing number of scholars who were trained and educated in criminal justice. We have continued to integrate general notions of management and administration into this edition with the growing body of literature on criminal justice management and administration that has been produced by criminal justice scholars.

Because there has been a research explosion in the field of criminal justice over the past forty years, we now know more about the operations of criminal justice organizations than ever before. The disciplines of sociology, political science, psychology, and criminology have complemented research done in criminal justice to produce some valuable insights into the workings of the criminal justice system. We have integrated and applied these findings into this edition. Most important, we have relied heavily on what criminal justice practitioners have produced in the professional literature to guide us into a more comprehensive understanding of criminal justice administration and how it functions. We feel that the positive contributions of both criminal justice researchers and criminal justice professionals require more review and acceptance. More than ever before, their collaborative efforts will direct the future of the criminal justice system into the next century.

Our second focus is on the systemic nature of criminal justice administration. By this, we mean that our coverage of the subject matter includes how the various components of the criminal justice system—police, prosecution, courts, and corrections—work together. As noted in the first five editions, we see value in examining these components separately, yet we also see value in viewing the "big picture" to appreciate how the components interrelate. Our teaching experience and the research literature alike underscore the importance of understanding the perspective of each component of the criminal justice system. Through an exhaustive review of the research literature across all sectors, we hope to broaden students' perspectives on criminal justice administration.

Our final focus is on the integration of theory research and practice in understanding criminal justice administration. The chapters move through the various topics applying theories, testing them, reviewing research findings, and discussing practical relevance and consequences. The noted social psychologist Kurt Lewin once said, "There is nothing as practical as a good theory." We believe in this aphorism and think it has relevance for an examination of criminal justice administration and management.

We know that many students tend to be "practice-oriented" in their views, whereas instructors are often exclusively theoretical in their presentations. This edition, similar to the fifth edition, offers some middle ground in which theory and practice work together to produce an overview of criminal justice administration—all of its complexities as well as its simplicities. We hope to enhance the thought processes of students through theory research and practice. To this end, we seek to produce students who understand the central tenet upon which effective criminal justice administration is based: effective thinking. Good thinkers are good administrators. Our aim is to introduce students to good thinking skills through an integrative approach that appreciates theory, recognizes research, and identifies relevant practices among criminal justice administrators.

As you read the chapters, consider the empirical basis for statements being made, question the research and practical implications that emanate from the research, and, most important, *imagine* what criminal justice administration would be like if we either knew more or did more to address a specific issue. Einstein once stated that imagination is more important than intelligence. As you read the chapters, imagine a different criminal justice system. What would its primary goals be? How would we accomplish these goals? Are they attainable? Are they practical and politically acceptable and to whom? Are they affordable? In some of the chapters in this new edition, we imagine a new conceptualization of criminal justice. How will this new conceptualization alter the practices and processes within the criminal justice system and the behaviors of criminal justice administrators? Just think—imagining a new criminal justice system may be a fun and rewarding experience.

ORGANIZATION OF THIS EDITION

The organization of this book follows the same format as the first five editions. Part One examines the nature of criminal justice organizations. Chapter 1 explores basic concepts associated with criminal justice administration and management and offers an examination of the complexity of criminal justice organizations and administrations. Chapter 2 presents a description of the structure of criminal justice organizations. Chapter 3 examines the role of the environment in criminal justice organizations.

Part Two deals with the individual in criminal justice organizations and includes chapters on communication, motivation, job design, personnel supervision and evaluation, and leadership. Part Three focuses on group processes in criminal justice, including occupational socialization, power, and organizational conflict. Part Four, which looks at processes in criminal justice organizations, includes four chapters that explore decision making, organizational effectiveness, change and innovation, and research in criminal justice organizations.

In addition to the revised chapters, this edition also provides an introductory vignette that highlights some significant issue or topic in criminal justice administration that the chapter will address. Along with this new opening vignette, each chapter has bulleted learning objectives that students should attain after reading the chapter. At the end of each chapter, *case studies* written from the perspective of either a real or an imagined practitioner in the criminal justice system are provided. These case studies flesh out some point, issue, or concept presented in the chapter. The case studies are supplemented by *case study questions* designed to tease out significant issues found in the case studies. A new addition to each chapter is a section entitled *Think like an Administrator*, along with questions. These new sections provide thought-provoking examples of everyday situations faced by criminal justice administrators. The questions present points of view regarding the issues at hand and how a criminal justice administrator might address the concerns presented. We hope that students and instructors view these sections as illuminating and helpful in comprehending the material presented in the chapters.

Each chapter finishes with new *bulleted summaries, discussion questions,* and a *For Further Reading* section. These materials enable students to grasp significant points and issues presented in the chapter and provide other readings that expand on points raised in the chapter. Students are encouraged to go beyond the introductory views offered in the chapters and expand their horizons through these relevant readings. Terms are defined in the body of each chapter as a way to recognize and learn important concepts being offered in the chapters.

As in the first five editions, citations are found in the body of the chapters, and full references are found in a separate section at the end of the book. A perusal of the reference section can be useful to students who seek to expand their knowledge base because many of these references are the most recent and relevant to criminal justice administrations. We encourage all readers of the book to review these sources.

Our primary purpose in this edition is the same as in the first five editions: We seek to offer a comprehensive and thorough discussion of criminal justice administration through the presentation of theory, the examination of research findings, and the application of ideas to the practices of criminal justice organizations. We hope this integrated approach will provide students with a sound foundation to examine and question criminal justice administration from a number of diverse viewpoints. Such a reflective process will enhance a thorough examination of how criminal justice administration functions in our society, and questions about efficiency, effectiveness, efficacy, and equity within the criminal justice system can begin to be addressed.

NEW TO THIS EDITION

In the sixth edition, we maintain our focus on up-to-date research. But while this text was never meant to be a "how-to" book, we recognize that, for both students and faculty, such information is important to fully understand key concepts and principles. So, in recent editions, there has been an emphasis on including pedagogical tools to assist both instructors and students. We hope these additions will enable the student to comprehend the material and apply the concepts to criminal justice administration.

Key chapter-by-chapter updates in the sixth edition are as follows:

Chapter 1
- New discussion regarding the history of criminal justice administration
- New section "Think like an Administrator"

Chapter 2
- New discussion regarding the budget process for public agencies
- Expanded discussion of informal systems and informal work groups, the potential for unethical behaviors of informal group members, and the importance of executives to impose reasonable controls over organizational members
- New section on "Think like an Administrator"

Chapter 3
- New discussion of the 9/11 terrorist attacks and the resulting changes: creation of the Patriot Act, the Department of Homeland Security, and an increase in airport security
- Expanded section on technology to include consideration of cell phones and smartphones
- New discussion of the budgetary impact on criminal justice agencies resulting from the "great recession" of 2008
- New discussion of the impact of flight from the inner city to suburbs and the normalization of crime in the inner city
- Brief comments on the Mexican drug lords
- New discussion on the development of sex offender laws and the impact of legislators' personal opinions on legislation
- New discussion of the AMBER Alert system as symbolism
- New section on "Think like an Administrator"

Chapter 4
- Expanded introduction
- New addition of the importance of face-to-face communication
- Added consideration of the importance of networking for productivity and innovation and the value of building loose ties or casual relationships in order to develop networks

- New section on interorganizational communication and included in that discussion is a brief overview of Business Partners against Terrorism, a private sector effort to create a communication network with law enforcement
- New section on ethics and organizational communication
- New section on "Think like an Administrator"

Chapter 5
- New section on Public Service Motivation
- New section "Think like an Administrator"

Chapter 6
- New material in the section on the "New Criminal Justice" and job design
- New section "Think like an Administrator"

Chapter 7
- New section "Think like an Administrator"

Chapter 8
- New section "Rights of Criminal Justice Employees"
- New section "Think like an Administrator"

Chapter 9
- Overview of small-group socialization
- New discussion on differing socialization processes among traditional police compared to community police
- Brief comment of socialization and police relationships with news media
- New discussion of a fear and bias toward inmates in a maximum security prison as controlling correctional officers' socialization: a self-fulfilling prophecy at work
- New section on ethics and the socialization process
- New section on "Think like an Administrator"

Chapter 10
- New section "Think like an Administrator"

Chapter 11
- New section "Think like an Administrator"

Chapter 12
- New section on the framework for evidence-based decision making in criminal justice published by the National Institute of Justice in 2010
- New section on ethical decision making
- New section on "Think like an Administrator"

Chapter 13

- Expanded the introduction by adding a real-world example of politically based measures of effectiveness
- New discussion on using quality-of-life indicators as measures of effectiveness
- New section on COMPSTAT, a management tool that imposes responsibility for crime analysis and crime reduction upon district police commanders
- New section on ethics and measuring effectiveness
- New section on "Think like an Administrator"

Chapter 14

- New language in the introduction that links this chapter on organizational change to Chapter 3 on environmental forces
- New discussion on crisis and change and the urgency portrayed as a crisis leading to privatization efforts
- Comments on positive unintended consequences of change on correctional officers
- New section on ethics that discusses the need for executives to build an ethical framework to execute the change process
- New section on "Think like an Administrator"

Chapter 15

- New section "Think like an Administrator"

Each chapter also contains a *Work Perspective* section written by a current or former criminal justice administrator. These sections are meant to bring the chapter alive with the viewpoints of those who work or have worked in the criminal justice system as administrators. The Work Perspectives have been provided by a wide range of people: a former police chief, a prison social worker, an executive director of a federal drugs and gang initiative, the secretary of a department of corrections, a prison warden, and a current investigator for the Equal Employment Opportunity Commission, to mention a few. We hope these Work Perspectives enrich the text and provide the student with a practical perspective that shows integration of theory, research, and practice.

SUPPLEMENTS

Instructor's Companion Website

This book-specific website offers access to instructor resources, including an *Instructor's Manual*, **Test Bank**, and **PowerPoint Lecture Slides**. The *Instructor's Manual* will help you design your course, including learning objectives, key terms, a detailed chapter outline, a chapter summary, discussion topics, student activities, and a test bank. Each chapter's expanded test bank contains new questions in multiple-choice format as well as offers numerous critical thinking questions, all with a full answer key. The test bank is also coded to the learning objectives that appear in the main text. In addition, the Microsoft PowerPoint lecture slides for each chapter will assist you with your lecture by providing concept coverage using images, figures, and tables directly from the textbook.

The manual, test bank, and lecture slides are available for download on the password-protected instructor companion website and may also be obtained by e-mailing your local Cengage Learning representative.

Careers in Criminal Justice Website
Available bundled with this text at no additional charge. Featuring self-exploration and profiling activities, the interactive Careers in Criminal Justice website helps students investigate and focus on the criminal justice career choices that are right for them. It includes an interest assessment, video testimonials from career professionals, resume and interview tips, and links for reference.

About the Authors

Stan Stojkovic is dean and professor in the Helen Bader School of Social Welfare at the University of Wisconsin–Milwaukee. He has been teaching, writing, and providing training to criminal justice professionals over the past thirty years. He was co-coordinator of the California Leadership Institute for the California Department of Corrections from 1994–2004. He has published extensively on matters of criminal justice administration and management and has worked with criminal justice agencies around the world.

David Kalinich is school director and professor of the school of criminology/ criminal justice at Florida Atlantic University. In addition, he has taught at Michigan State University, Grand Valley State University, and Northern Michigan University. He has published extensively and provided cutting-edge training for jail operations and management and working with mentally ill offenders. He has broad experience in the criminal justice system, working as a probation and parole officer in the state of Ohio and trainer for a number of departments of corrections and local jails.

John Klofas is professor of criminal justice at the Rochester Institute of Technology. He is author and coauthor of numerous articles and books on criminal justice-related topics. His work, *The New Criminal Justice: American Communities and the Changing World of Crime Control,* coauthored with Natalie Kroovand-Hipple and Edmund McGarrell, explores what the "new" criminal justice looks like and its implications for communities. Dr. Klofas is also a former employee with the Massachusetts Department of Corrections.

Acknowledgments

This sixth edition of the book has received the assistance of a number of people. First and foremost, we appreciate the support and encouragement provided by Carolyn Henderson-Meier. Her patience in dealing with us is noteworthy. Very few people can put up with the rationalizations of three authors simultaneously and still show support; we appreciate her efforts more than she may know. In addition, we thank Amy Hill for her guidance and editorial work on the revisions of the chapters.

We benefited greatly from the expert opinions of our reviewers. The book has benefited from the work of others who are unknown to the authors. We would also like to thank all those criminal justice professionals, both past and present, who provided the Work Perspective sections at short notice; we appreciate their hard work. Finally, we would like to thank our families who supported us with their encouragement: Ilija Stojkovic, Carolyn Kalinich, and Mary Beth Klofas.

Stan Stojkovic (stojkovi@uwm.edu)

David Kalinich (kalinich@fau.edu)

John Klofas (klofas@mail.rit.edu)

Part I

The Nature of Criminal Justice Organizations

Criminal justice organizations (police, prosecution, courts, and corrections) are complex public entities. As you read the chapters in this part of the book, begin to think how you would understand the organization of criminal justice agencies. What is the best way, for example, to structure and manage a police department? Remember, police organizations are numerous in the United States. There are over 16,000 law enforcement agencies across the various levels of government, that is, federal, state, and local. Each one of them represents a constituency with specific expectations.

As you begin to examine these criminal justice organizations consider how you would best organize and manage them given diverse expectations. To begin you would have to consider basic concepts: methods of organization, purposes, complexity, and environment to mention a few. Once you have a basic understanding of criminal justice organizations, you then could elaborate further on how best to structure them. Questions of structure, however, would not precede questions of purposes. So, what do you expect criminal justice organizations to accomplish? Sounds simple? It is not.

Expectations are plentiful for criminal justice organizations. Outcomes, however, may be more challenging to achieve. For some, criminal justice organizations are to "protect and serve," yet for others, the expectation is that this goal is to be pursued within the framework of laws and due process. Some argue that the system should pursue "justice," yet this concept is elusive since no two people can agree on what this actually should be in the criminal justice system. At the end of the day, criminal justice administrators are called upon to pursue some sense of justice, all within the constraints of the law and the general will of the people. Chapter 1 will examine these issues.

Similarly problematic is the concept of structure. Once we agree on expectations and purposes for criminal justice organizations, how do we operationalize them in concrete terms? Chapter 2 examines the concept of structure of criminal justice organizations. Basic ideas are presented, but again, these ideas are always being changed and questioned. In a democracy this is a tedious process but necessary. Chapter 3 explores the environment of criminal justice organizations. Complexity reigns supreme in this analysis, but that is good, since it represents the complexity of expectations and purposes inherent in our society.

CHAPTER 1

Basic Concepts for Understanding Criminal Justice Organizations

LEARNING OBJECTIVES

After reading this chapter, the students will have achieved the following objectives:
- Comprehend criminal justice administration history.
- Understand a definition of an organization.
- Comprehend the concept of management.
- Know the concept of leadership.
- Comprehend the public context of both management and leadership.
- Define and comprehend open-system theory.
- Explain the importance of complex goals for criminal justice administration.
- Know the complex environment of criminal justice administration.
- Understand complex internal constituencies and criminal justice administration.

VIGNETTE

A broad-based movement to improve the quality of services provided in the public sector has been underway for almost thirty years. Yet, as we began the twenty-first century, an even greater call was made to make public agencies more efficient and effective in what they do. Criminal justice organizations were not beyond this call for change and improvement in the delivery of their services. In fact, in many criminal justice organizations, administrators had been asked to tighten their belts and provide more measurable outcomes regarding their activities. It might be said that this began with police agencies in the early 1990s when one large police department—the New York City Police Department, under the leadership of Michael Bratton—decided to guide and inform police decision making by collecting systematic information as a basis for the allocation of scarce resources.

Known as COMPSTAT, this effort was an attempt to utilize information for better decision making and to hold police supervisors accountable for crime in their districts. While this novel approach had its critics, it developed a whole genre of criminal justice administrators who began thinking differently about how they perform their duties and how they would show their constituents that they were serious about crime reduction and could prove it through the use of information and outcome measures. Administrators had started applying systematic information across the criminal justice system and included, for example, using classification and risk-assessment procedures in jails and prisons, case-management systems in courts, the use of integrated data systems in newly evolved drug treatment courts, and the application of basic data-analysis techniques to prosecutorial decision making.

As we experience profound changes in how criminal justice organizations perform their functions, consider how practices and behaviors might change based on employing evidence standards and research information in assessing performance. In addition, think about how these new standards can potentially change the very nature of criminal justice practices and how criminal justice administrators also will have to change their practices. Will the penchant and desire for more "evidence-based" practices in criminal justice alter how we practice and understand criminal justice administration?

Among the many organizations that touch our lives are those of the criminal justice system. Many Americans will be only indirectly involved in these organizations. They may find themselves fighting a traffic ticket in court or touring the local jail while serving on a grand jury. Other Americans will find themselves in the criminal justice system when they are processed as offenders. Still others will be employees of criminal justice organizations. This book is about the management and administration of those organizations, and the goal of this chapter is to lay a basic foundation from which to study them.

Our ties to organizations differ, as do the size, structure, and purpose of those organizations. The analysis of those differences forms a large part of the research and theory on organizations from which this book draws. Our approach to this material is eclectic. We do not intend either to introduce a new organizational theory as it applies to criminal justice or to reflect any single theoretical perspective in this book. Instead, our goal is to provide an overview of organizational theory and research as it applies to criminal justice.

CRIMINAL JUSTICE ADMINISTRATION: HISTORY

The historian Sam Walker noted back in 1980 that the history of American criminal justice is a visible tension between, on the one hand, the arbitrary and capricious practices of criminal justice officials, and on the other hand, the rule of law. Criminal justice administration as we know it in the beginning of the twenty-first century is much different from that of early America. In fact, criminal justice administration, as evidenced through police agencies, correctional institutions, prosecution offices, and courts, really did not exist until the beginning of the twentieth century (Walker, 1980). The tension that historian Walker describes is revealing and requires further elaboration.

Early administrative practices within criminal justice organizations are best understood as haphazard and uneven. More often than not, criminal justice "officials," those designated to manage criminal justice organizations, were political appointees or stood in favor with local political leaders. They served at the whim of these politicians. The early role of sheriffs, for example, was really not law enforcement per se, but instead was tax collecting and employing the authority of the sovereignty of the king or lord who held land title over the tenant or citizen, at least in England. Those who chose not to pay their taxes or could not pay their taxes faced the justice the sheriff meted out.

The role of the sheriff evolved into something different in America; they were elected and had broad powers to enforce the law. Nevertheless, as elected officials, sheriffs were inextricably linked to political leaders, which has engendered both good and bad results. Political patronage and poorly run jails were early examples of abuses by sheriffs and others acting in various criminal justice capacities. More often than not, accountability was limited until legislation was created to address abuses. Yet, early difficulties in criminal justice administration were not limited to sheriffs. Similar problems were evident in prisons as they evolved into institutions designed to address growing crime problems in burgeoning cities (Morris and Rothman, 1995; Rothman, 1980).

As a result of scandals and reform movements, the rule of law became the substitute standard over arbitrary and uneven practices as the country moved into the twenty-first century. More and more, legal decisions began to define criminal justice administration as dependent on objective rules and regulations and the adherence to them under the force of law if needed. The history of the twentieth century saw criminal justice administration become more formalized and rule bound, more akin to what we later will describe as the bureaucratization of criminal justice practices, particularly in the second half of the twentieth century (Kelling and Moore, 1983; Walker, 1999).

This reliance on laws, policies, and procedures to manage criminal justice organizations was unprecedented in our history. Again, historian Walker offers us the rubric of law as the standard on which criminal justice administration became assessed, and a new cadre of criminal justice administrators was born in the second half of the twentieth century. That cadre relied heavily on nascent management science and leadership programs to improve the operations of criminal justice organizations. This was most evident in the early 1950s in police organizations and was followed in correctional organizations beginning in the 1970s. Prosecution and court components were different and had developed rules, policies, and procedures consistent with the evolution of the legal profession.

This is not to suggest that arbitrary and capricious practices ended as we became more law oriented and rule bound in criminal justice organizations moving into the twentieth century. On the contrary, the tension described by Walker is a dynamic process or a give-and-take or push-pull between arbitrary actions of criminal justice personnel on the one hand and on the other hand, actions allowed and condoned by law and ultimately best professional practices promoted by criminal justice organizations today, legitimized through professional organizations, such as the International Association of Chiefs of Police and the American Correctional Association. The tension is ever present. So, we have come a long way in evolving into the criminal justice organizations we are today, yet we are constantly challenged by our past and its arbitrary nature and ultimately held accountable through the rule of law, something that is uniquely and distinctively American and not common throughout much of the world.

WHAT IS AN ORGANIZATION?

Organization: An entity defined by structure, purpose, and activity objectives.

This may seem like a straightforward question. We all know when we are part of an **organization**, and criminal justice organizations are no exception. The police officer, the probation officer, and the prison officer are certainly aware of their organizational attachments. But identifying organizations is not the same as defining them, and an adequate definition of the word *organization* continues to be the subject of debate among scholars (see Hall and Tolbert, 2005).

Definitions of the term *organization* hinge on three important issues: structure, purpose, and activity. The issue of structure was raised by Weber (1947), who first distinguished the corporate group from other forms of social organization. For Weber, the corporate group is marked by limited admission to the group and by a structure that usually involves a leader and a staff. Weber's ideas invite us to think of organizations as bureaucracies—that is, as entities requiring a particular formal structure. In Weber's bureaucratic model, the structure included a rigid hierarchy of offices, a clear division of labor, and formal rules that govern action. Many organizations, however, do not possess a bureaucratic structure. For example, Clynch and Neubauer (1981) point out that trial courts can be viewed as organizations, but they lack the attributes of bureaucracies. Trial courts are relatively autonomous units not closely tied to a larger structure. Their formal rules are often ignored, as demonstrated by the fact that the presumed adversarial nature of the courtroom has often been revealed to be much more cooperative than the rules would suggest.

Barnard dealt with the issue of structure in a way much more consistent with Clynch and Neubauer's view of the courts. His basic definition of an organization is "a system of consciously coordinated activities or forces of two or more persons" (Barnard, 1938:73). Such a definition suggests boundaries but also allows for a variety of organizational structures and makes it clear that courts, public defenders' offices, and other key components of the criminal justice system may be profitably studied as organizations.

Barnard's definition leaves the second issue, that of purpose, open. But other theorists have viewed the pursuit of goals as fundamental to organizations. Etzioni, for example, describes organizations as "social units deliberately constructed and reconstructed to seek specific goals" (1964:3). The question of goals is complicated, however. Although it seems clear that the police, courts, and corrections agencies all have goals, the waters quickly get murky when we try to spell out these goals. The police prevent and solve crimes, but they also maintain due process, reduce community conflicts, and seek to provide a good working environment for officers. Courts may pursue justice but temper that goal with mercy. They may also have retribution, deterrence, humaneness, or equity as goals. Among the goals of corrections organizations are punishment, rehabilitation, maintenance of order, and, perhaps, avoiding publicity. Even profit-making corporations must balance short- and long-run profit goals, quality and quantity concerns, and pollution or environmental interests. We see in the twenty-first century the changing purposes of criminal justice organizations that include new functions, such as those designated for the Department of Homeland Security (see the case study at the end of the chapter). This organization is not a traditional criminal justice organization, but it clearly has connections to the agencies of criminal justice. The threat of terrorism has changed how we understand criminal justice organizations and how they function. Thus, organizations have many goals, and their goals often conflict. It is important to avoid the oversimplified view of organizations as pursuing a single goal or even a most important goal.

The third issue is whether organizations act or are simply collections of individuals who act. We deal with this question in detail in several of the following chapters. At this time, however, we acknowledge that our view in this book is that organizations do act. In this view, leadership in organizations is more than simply the leadership of individuals. Likewise, socialization in organizations involves not just attitudes and values held by individuals but also an organizational ethos. Decision making, too, is shaped by influences beyond those of individual decision makers.

The three issues discussed here shape the view of organizations that underlies this book. According to that view, organizations require some boundaries and structure but are not limited to rigidly bureaucratic forms. Organizations pursue goals, but those goals are complex, multiple, and often conflicting. Finally, organizations act in that their influence extends beyond that of individual members. For this analysis, then, we may define an organization as a collective that has some identifiable boundaries and internal structures and that engages in activities related to some complex set of goals.

An organization is a fascinating beast. It develops cultures that guide the behaviors of its members as well as of the organization itself. Organizations are rich in politics: bargaining, negotiating, and intimidation by their members in search of resources, power, status, and influence. Members attempt to meet their psychological, emotional, and ego needs within an organization's range of opportunities for challenges and activities. A latent goal of an organization is survival, which usually translates into competition for resources and constant expansion. Organizations are complex and beyond complete understanding; they are surprising because outcomes of decisions are hard to predict; they are deceptive because they camouflage surprises; and they are ambiguous because events are disjointed, complex, and beyond coordination (Bolman and Deal, 1997).

Our focus in this book is on complex, surprising, deceptive, and ambiguous organizations related to criminal justice. Perspectives on criminal justice organizations are particularly unique, compared with other public sector organizations that carry the authority of government, because criminal justice agencies and their members may apply legitimate coercive force to control citizens.

WHAT IS MANAGEMENT?

Management: A process where elements of a group are coordinated, integrated, and utilized to effectively and efficiently achieve organizational objectives.

This, too, seems to be a straightforward question. Like organizations, however, **management** seems easier to identify than to define. The names of managers can be found high on the organizational chart. Their offices may give them away, as do their salaries. But the function of management is not as clear in criminal justice organizations as in many other types of organizations.

Management has been defined as the "process by which the elements of a group are integrated, coordinated, and/or utilized so as to effectively and efficiently achieve organizational objectives" (Carlisle, 1976). In this definition, management is a process in the sense that it is ongoing; it does not constitute an end in and of itself. Instead, management is directed at attaining organizational goals. We have little trouble with this view as long as the complexity of those goals is appreciated.

This definition, however, ignores the notion of office. It does not say whether management is a function of a specific office or is spread throughout an organization. Usually, we associate management with a particular office or point on the organizational chart. In this book, however, we prefer to view management as a function that may not be the sole responsibility of any one office. Although we recognize that wardens, chiefs of police, and others are managers, we also believe that even frontline police and corrections officers exercise some management responsibility. We have two reasons for holding this view. First, frontline staff supervise others. Whether police are directing citizens at the scene of a crime or corrections officers are controlling the routine of inmates, frontline staff manage people. Their positions are at the bottom of the organizational hierarchy, although their work requires that they manage many people in difficult situations.

Lipsky (1980) discusses a second reason for viewing the management function as not limited to particular offices. He argues that frontline staff in street-level bureaucracies, which include most of those working in criminal justice, determine organizational policy. They do so because the nature of their work requires that they exercise a great deal of discretion, and the collective use of that discretion reveals organizational policy. In these street-level bureaucracies, then, it may be productive at times to consider the hierarchy as inverted. Front-line staff may exercise considerable power in influencing the direction of the organization.

Management of organizations, thus, is not the sole province of executives. It is best thought of as only the process by which organizational members are directed toward organizational goals. This view of management suggests that many workers in criminal justice influence the direction of their organizations and that, consequently, the study of management is important to anyone interested in criminal justice.

As Hall and Tolbert (2005) warn, "Discussions of definitions can be quite deadly." Still, some appreciation of the complexity of the terms *organization* and *management* is necessary for understanding this book. Organizational theory also provides several other concepts that are central to understanding administration and management in criminal justice. We discuss them in the following sections.

WHAT IS LEADERSHIP?

Leadership "refers to a process that helps direct and mobilize people and their ideas" (Kotter, 1990). Leadership is tribal in nature (Dupree, 1989) and focuses on an organization's symbols, rituals, and culture. By contrast, managers create, maintain, protect, and perpetuate systems. They focus on planning and budgeting, setting short-term goals, and developing procedures to reach those goals. Moreover, managers concern themselves with developing organizational

Leadership: A process that helps to direct and mobilize people and their ideas, with an emphasis on the creation of a vision and inspiring people.

structures, implementing controls, and problem solving. In that context, management sciences create and perpetuate the mythology of achieving rationality in organizations based on goals, rules and regulations, and control. Leaders establish direction by developing a vision of the future, align people through shared values and vision, and motivate and inspire people to move them toward the shared vision (Kotter, 1990). Leaders challenge existing processes and systems, focus on the future of the tribe, and immerse themselves in the culture of their organization. They also challenge basic assumptions, values, and beliefs, and they identify and alter organizational principles to create the basis for structural or programmatic change. Leaders manipulate and evoke symbols to create change and practice the art of statesmanship. Planning documents usually gather dust in organizations that lack leadership.

Leaders are primarily concerned with motivating organizational members and enabling them to act by creating a shared vision: "a realistic, attractive, credible future for your organization" (Nanus, 1992:8). Kotter suggests that leaders motivate by "the articulation of a vision that stress[es] the values of the audience being addressed ... involving people in deciding how to achieve that vision ... enlisting the enthusiastic support of their efforts at achieving that vision ... and the public recognition and rewarding of all their successes" (1990:63). Stojkovic and Farkas (2003) view correctional leadership as fundamentally linked to the creation and perpetuation of a specific set of values that underlie an organizational culture.

The impact of leadership on an organization is crucial to its long-term capability to function effectively and meet anticipated changing environmental demands. This is an area in which leadership in criminal justice is often lacking. Prison and jail overcrowding, along with the increasing numbers of geriatric, mentally ill, and other problematic inmates are issues most practicing professionals foresaw.

However, it took court intervention combined with crisis-level manifestation of such problems before they were actively addressed. The vision was apparent, but leadership to act and move the organizations to prepare for obvious future environmental demands did not exist. Conversely, law enforcement leadership did foresee a needed change in police services so that, to some extent, a move from traditional to community policing has taken place.

The criminal justice system has a well-established history of creating a cadre of managers whose experience and subsequent socialization have trained them to work heroically to protect their existing systems and culture from intrusion, outsiders, and environmental forces. Criminal justice managers have assumed and struggled to behave as if they were working in a closed system. Leadership, however, requires an explicit understanding that work be accomplished in a dynamic world within an open system that anticipates changing environments and prepares for future demands. Moreover, the criminal justice environment is becoming more complex, and other agencies and functions also are important to criminal justice organizations. In the words of Jeffrey Luke (1998), the public world, in which criminal justice managers and leaders function, is becoming increasingly interconnected and no longer can effective leadership be connected to one organization. The twenty-first-century criminal justice leader confronts issues of mental illness, school truancy, and substance abuse on a daily basis.

Being interconnected to other social service and private agencies is essential to effective leadership across the components of the criminal justice system. (See Chapter 7 for a further discussion of this issue.)

What Is Management and Leadership in the Public Sector?

Too often, discussions regarding management and leadership within criminal justice organizations miss out on the importance of the **public sector** context and how it shapes both criminal justice management and leadership. What constraints are imposed on criminal justice managers and leaders as public entities? Some would argue that management and leadership constraints are significant but not debilitating because criminal justice organizations are public agencies (Rainey, 2014). Nevertheless, the challenges are ever present and should be noted.

> **Public sector:** The context within which criminal justice administrators function.

To begin, criminal justice administrators must deal with civil service protections and obligations as well as expectations due to their public status designation. Wilson (2000) states that public bureaucracies, like criminal justice agencies, must adhere to the principles of accountability, efficiency, fiscal integrity, and equity. These principles are imposed through various legislative actions and laws. They develop expectations on how public entities are to perform their functions. In some cases, the laws are difficult to work with as criminal justice administrators. It is often said, for example, that to discipline or remove a public employee is nearly impossible or overly cumbersome and difficult. Public employees have too many protections or, at least minimally, the protections afforded public employees make it overly burdensome and time consuming to effectively manage and lead. We differ with this interpretation, as we explain in other chapters in this book. Subsequent chapters will show how effective criminal justice administration can be accomplished even within the constraints that a civil service system might impose on criminal justice administrators. Nobody said that criminal justice administration would be easy. As administrators, we have to respond to changes mandated through the legislatures and the courts. At one level, we are simply responding to the legislative inconsistencies of political leaders. There is much to be said about civil service rules that reflect the inconsistencies of the legislative process; nevertheless, as criminal justice administrators, we must deal with them on a daily basis (Wilson, 2000).

Another concern regards unions. Public employee unions are a problem for criminal justice administrators as well. Unions representing police and correctional personnel have fought hard over the years to receive good pay and benefits packages. Some contend that the pay and benefits are above private sector pay and benefits and taxpayers will be burdened for many years to come with pensions and health care insurance costs. This perception may not be totally accurate, but it is held by those who perpetuate a view that criminal justice management and leadership are hamstrung by union contracts and their concomitant protections. In fact, the governor of the state of Wisconsin has worked with the legislature to strip public employees of their collective bargaining rights. This will be a trend in the years to come as states attempt to grapple with limited resources. It will have profound implications for criminal justice administrators, but will it necessarily make criminal justice management and leadership better or worse? This is a difficult question to answer.

The question remains as to what can be reasonably accomplished by criminal justice administrators as managers and leaders as they operate through a maze of public rules and regulations and union contracts that could be perceived as inhibiting and antithetical to effective management and leadership. For criminal justice administrators, managing and leading in the public sector have always been challenging and often as cumbersome and difficult as apprehending offenders, prosecuting them, and imposing some sanction on them. At the end of the day, we still have to manage and lead criminal justice organizations.

OPEN-SYSTEM THEORY

In the past, many students of organizations have focused exclusively on what took place inside the organizations they studied. Perhaps the model of that approach is found in the work of Frederick Taylor (1919, 1947). As we will see in later chapters, one of Taylor's chief concerns was with increasing the efficiency of work through job design. Such an orientation ignored many variables outside the workplace that could influence the efficiency of labor. Taylor's orientation reflects a closed-system view, in which organizations are regarded as self-contained and unresponsive to their environments. For a closed-system organization, the factors in the environment are unchanging constants.

Such an approach to analyzing organizations has some appeal in the sense that it reassures us that relevant variables are clear, easily understood, and controllable. The model has its origins in systems theory, the view found in biology, mechanics, and other fields, and assumes that complex entities are composed of interrelated parts. Thus, as closed systems, organizations are composed of elements that are all related to one another. In this view, communication follows the lines of hierarchy, power and authority are a function of the office, and change is slow and directed by management.

Although this approach to analyzing organizations may be adequate in some circumstances, it is now seen as too simplistic. In criminal justice, for example, a closed-system analysis would suggest that the causes of a prison riot could be found only in administrative practices and procedures, types of inmates, and other such internal variables. Clearly, however, the 1971 riot in New York's Attica prison cannot be explained without reference to the political climate of the times. Likewise, the prison riots of the middle and late 1980s cannot be understood without reference to conservative criminal justice policies and the resulting overcrowding in prisons. Moreover, the country and the world are more concerned than ever before about the threat that terrorist organizations pose to free societies. The reality is that the world is much more complex and much more dangerous. Criminal justice efforts must now be understood within the context of a turbulent world that impacts criminal justice agencies directly.

Eisenstein, Flemming, and Nardulli (1988) revealed the limitations of closed-system views of criminal justice organizations in their study of trial courts. Critical of the view that the courts can be understood as simply applying the law, these authors concluded that the great differences they found in nine criminal courts could not be understood by focusing on only the legal aspects of the courts. They suggest that the metaphor for the courts as communities is productive. This view recognizes differences in the extent of prosecution–police interaction, political relationships of judges, and approaches to plea bargaining, among other factors. These differences originate in the community context and the environment of the courts, and they influence both the process and the product of the legal system.

The community analogy suggests the usefulness of an open-system view of the courts. This is also called **open-system theory** and is an approach to understanding organizations as being influenced by their environments. In this framework for analysis, organizations are viewed as constantly interacting with their environments. In business, for example, profitability fluctuates with the availability of raw materials, consumer interests, and even taxes, tariffs, and the value of the dollar relative to foreign currency. In criminal justice, isolated heinous offenses have led to major changes in legislation and policing practices. Public conservatism has led to tougher sentences, which in turn have caused prison and jail crowding and increased prisoner violence. The influence of the environment need not be so dramatic, however. State laws permitting unionization of public employees have had tremendous effects in criminal justice. Even changes in local economies have affected the number and qualifications of applicants for police and corrections jobs.

In their social–psychological analysis, Katz and Kahn (1978) describe organizations as open systems characterized by inputs from the environment, throughput (the process of changing those inputs), and outputs (the product or service of an organization). They point out that this simple model offers some advantages over closed-system analyses. First, it highlights the importance of studying organization–environment relations. Second, because the organization cannot be equally open to everything in the environment, it highlights the need to study the selection process. For example, how are job descriptions determined? What makes some constraints on decisions more important than others? How are criteria for measuring effectiveness determined? Finally, the open-system approach indicates we should also study how organizations affect their environments. It permits us to see that organizations are not necessarily passive. For example, high-profile crime-control efforts that reassure the public may lead to increased police budgets. In some states, corrections officials have used the threat of releasing prisoners to obtain support for prison construction. Community treatment programs have been closed because they have negatively affected their environments through high recidivism rates or notorious offenses by their clients.

Open-system theory: An approach to understanding organizations as being influenced by their environments.

COMPLEX GOALS

We first discussed the question of organizational goals in our effort to define the term *organization*. The point is important enough, however, to risk redundancy here. The organizations of the criminal justice system have multiple and conflicting **complex goals**. Here, we will deal with the consequences of this complexity.

Complex goals: A situation in which an organization faces many competing and conflicting purposes.

The implications of having multiple and conflicting goals were first spelled out in a classic work by Simon (1964). To be successful, organizations must endeavor to meet all their goals. For example, profit-making firms must meet production goals, quality goals, environmental protection goals, and many others. Simon pointed out, however, that the pursuit of all these goals impinges on the degree of goal attainment. Borrowing from the field of mathematics, Simon used the notion of a Pareto-optimal solution, in which everyone benefits (though not equally), to show that organizations inevitably seek satisfactory levels of attainment of several goals simultaneously rather than attempt to maximize the attainment of each goal.

Goals thus not only provide direction but also serve as constraints or limits (Wilson, 2000). For example, a manufacturing firm has both production and sales goals. For the sales force, production goals limit the quantity of items they can sell; for production workers, sales goals may set limits on the quantity of items they can produce. In criminal justice, the police may strive to control crime, but due process goals constrain their effectiveness. Likewise, prosecutors may seek justice through rigorous prosecutions, but they are limited by the goal of not having crowded dockets. Plea bargaining may represent the Pareto-optimal solution to these multiple and conflicting goals in the prosecutor's office.

Although complex and conflicting goals may thus serve as constraints, they need not be viewed in negative terms. For example, the limitations that due process requirements put on police powers are fundamental to our freedoms. Wright (1981) argues that goal conflict is in fact desirable and that a unified criminal justice system with consensus about goals would be undesirable. Goal conflict, according to Wright, limits the expression of diverse viewpoints and provides for the mediation of interests so that no single perspective dominates. Goal conflict may also promote efficiency in offender processing by enhancing the adaptability of the system.

COMPLEX ENVIRONMENT

Complex environment: A situation in which an organization faces many competing and conflicting demands from turbulent external sources.

Some researchers have attempted to specify how environments impinge on different types of organizations. A **complex environment** is a situation in which an organization faces many competing and conflicting demands from turbulent external sources. For example, Lipsky (1980) argues that the conflicting goals of human service organizations are the result of unresolved disagreements in society at large. The police, too, will always be subject to criticism as they pursue both crime control and due process because the public cannot agree on what goal or what balance of goals is appropriate.

Walmsley and Zald (1973) agree with Lipsky that public organizations absorb conflict from their environment. They also describe other effects of the environment on public organizations. They argue that because the productivity of public organizations, such as the police or prisons, is difficult to measure, the structure of those organizations is more closely tied to public beliefs about what the organizations should do than to what goes on in those organizations.

For example, the public view is that prisons should attempt to rehabilitate offenders. Prisons, therefore, maintain elaborate treatment divisions despite the fact that the staff members of those divisions are engaged primarily in security functions, such as classification and discipline. Likewise, Duffee (1986:65) points out that the modern police department continues to be organized along paramilitary lines that were instituted when police were first organized to put down labor unrest and protect the wealthy. The structure of the courts, too, more closely reflects beliefs about what they should do than what they actually do. Their rigid structure is a reflection of faith in the adversarial process, but it is widely acknowledged that the courts function in a more collegial than adversarial way.

Walmsley and Zald (1973) also point out that not only is organizational structure affected by the environment but the environment also affects the way these public organizations are evaluated. First, clients are not the legitimizers of these organizations, so service delivery may not be rewarded. For example, prisoners are not viewed as legitimate evaluators of their prisons. Second, because the marketplace does not determine the value of public organizations, they are generally evaluated on the importance of their mission rather than on the results they achieve. The enforcement of laws and the dispensing of justice are seen as important missions. Police and courts, therefore, are valued despite difficulties in measuring productivity. But the value placed on these organizations may diminish if public views change, even though the organizations' effectiveness does not change.

COMPLEX INTERNAL CONSTITUENCIES

Our discussion of basic concepts for this book must include one additional subject. One way to look at organizations is to consider them as arenas in which struggles for power occur (Hall and Tolbert, 2005). Perhaps the most obvious examples are workers' struggles for increased wages and better working conditions. Although the external environment of organizations is complex, also relevant to organizational form and function are **complex internal constituencies**, situations in which criminal justice organizations have multiple and conflicting internal personnel, each striving to achieve their own interests and objectives.

Criminal justice literature is only beginning to acknowledge the potency of these internal groups. As noted, clients often are not the legitimizers of criminal justice organizations. They cannot, however, be regarded as wholly insignificant. The prisoners' rights movement clearly illustrates the point that even inmates can dramatically influence prisons. Although these changes also have involved powerful external groups, inmates clearly exercise some power not only through their individual lawsuits but also well beyond court mandates. As a result of litigation, prisons have become more bureaucratized, prison staff have become more demoralized, and a strong movement to establish prison standards has begun (Jacobs, 1983b:86).

Internal constituencies are clearly not limited to clients. They may include groups of employees who come to pursue a distinct set of interests. Departmental legal counsel and budget managers, for example, set requirements that constrain

Complex internal constituencies: A situation in which criminal justice organizations have multiple and conflicting internal personnel, each striving to achieve their own interests and objectives.

organizations. Likewise, groups, such as court stenographers and secretaries, have special goals. In fact, the most significant internal constituency in many criminal justice organizations today may be the workforce. Through traditional grievance mechanisms and now through collective bargaining, labor is having an increasingly significant effect. The public employee unionization movement of the 1960s paved the way for organized labor in corrections and more recently in policing. Unionization has dramatically changed the role of management and has influenced everything from job and shift assignments to occupational safety. In some prisons, guards and prisoners have even united to call for better and safer institutions (Jacobs, 1978). Yet, in the beginning of the twenty-first century, we have seen a retrenchment in public unions and their influence in criminal justice organizations.

Work Perspective: BEING A PROSECUTOR IN THE TWENTY-FIRST CENTURY

In an article titled "The American Prosecutor in Historical Context," Joan Jacoby states the following:

> The American prosecutor enjoys independence and a wealth of discretionary power unmatched in the world. With few exceptions, the prosecutor is a locally elected official and the chief law enforcement official of the community. The American prosecutor represents a local jurisdiction, and his or her office is endowed with unreviewable discretionary authority. Nowhere else in the world does this combination of features define prosecution.

The unique combination of powers just described carries with it the obligation and duty to use that authority in a principled and restrained manner that serves the interest of the community and upholds the core values of the institution, which include but are not limited to public safety, fairness, respect for the rights of victims, respect for the rights of people accused of crimes, respect for the law, compassionate discretion, and appreciation for differences in responsibility across jurisdictions.

My beliefs are reflected in a national discussion centered on the role of the prosecutor. The American Bar Association Standards Committee is engaged in modifying the model ethics code and includes statements related to the prosecutor's role, such as the following: *"The prosecutor is not merely a case-processor but also a problem solver.... The prosecutor's office should seek to reform and improve the administration of criminal justice.... The prosecutor's office should be available to assist other groups in the law enforcement community and the community at large...."* These are affirmative obligations that center the role of the prosecutor in relation to the community at large.

Inherent in the discussion is the recognition that significant levels of disconnect exist between criminal justice system goals and the community they serve. I believe that the separation can be closed when prosecutors' offices become directly engaged in the community by placing prosecutors and victim advocates in the neighborhoods most impacted by crime to proactively address the numerous factors that generate crime. The concept is similar to what has been learned through hard experience in low-intensity conflicts. To achieve success requires meaningful engagement to identify the people committing crime in neighborhoods without alienating the much larger population of law-abiding citizens. By building bridges of trust, we obtain timely information that allows us to identify and isolate the negative influences, remove them from the community, and then stabilize the neighborhood.

We also must evolve the way we process people in the system with a unified vision of what we do with offenders, from first police contact to reentry from prison. I often characterize this process as moving from an "offense"-based system to an "offender/victim"-based system. The former only looks at the facts in the context of what can be proven and places the offender in a scale of priority based on prior record and then sends the person through a series of court-centered events. The second system tries to use all the information available to system actors to ask who the offender is, what is his or her risk to the community, why is he/she committing crimes, and what is the best way to

---

stop that behavior and prevent future crimes while repairing the harm to the victim and community.

I participate in the Milwaukee County Community Justice Council, which consists of the elected and appointed public safety officials in the county. We recently received a National Institute of Corrections grant to develop an Evidence-Based Decision Making (EBDM) framework for our justice system. Eric Cadora of the Justice Mapping Center recently mapped state corrections spending in Milwaukee for one year, and he estimates that we spend $200 million for correctional services that are concentrated in two aldermanic districts on the north side of the city. These are the same areas of Milwaukee with the highest density of crime, poverty, and social dysfunction. What if we developed, at the local level, through EBDM, a system that stopped the cycles of repeat incarceration, saved lives

and dollars in the process, and reinvested the savings from corrections into programs we think could prevent and effectively interrupt chronic lives of crime?

Milwaukee's public safety services are confronted with enormous fiscal constraints and undiminished demands for service. The corrections budget in the state is the fourth-largest annual expenditure of state revenue, and it has historically high rates of recidivism. We cannot survive as an effective resource of community stability if we do not do a better job preventing crime and intelligently intervening in habitual criminal behavior if we continue to rely on jail and prison as a default response. The way forward requires close collaboration between system actors informed by rigorous academic data from the social sciences.

SOURCE: John Chisholm, District Attorney

SUMMARY

Understand a definition of an organization.

- Organizations are structured along three dimensions: structure, purpose, and activity.

Comprehend the concept of management.

- Organizations are managed through a process, but management functions are not limited to a specific office within an organization.

Know the concept of leadership.

- Organizations are led through vision, motivation, and inspiration.

Comprehend the public context of both management and leadership.

- Criminal justice organizations operate within the context of a public status and are constrained and directed, in part, by civil service protections and union contracts. Criminal justice management and leadership must be aware of this public context in order to be effective.

Define and comprehend open-system theory.

- Criminal justice organizations both affect and are affected by key elements of their environments. Unlike closed-system theory, which emphasizes key operational components of an organization, open-system theory hypothesizes that criminal justice organizations are malleable and influenced differentially by elements of the environment.

Explain the importance of complex goals to criminal justice administration.

- Criminal justice organizations have many goals and many compete with one another for limited resources.

Know the complex environment of criminal justice administration.

- Criminal justice agencies have varied and complex environments that make criminal justice administration more complex. Criminal justice organizations are evaluated, in part, by the perceptions of what various environments expect of them.

Understand complex internal constituencies and criminal justice administration.

- Criminal justice organizations are influenced by many internal groups, such as line personnel, support staff, and others who perform the work. These internal groups have become more powerful over the years, but their power is now being challenged due to budgetary concerns.

Case Study: THE DEPARTMENT OF HOMELAND SECURITY

Subsequent to the terrorist attacks on September 11, 2001, the U.S. Congress created the Department of Homeland Security. The mission of this department is "to protect the American people and their homeland." As a brand-new bureaucracy on the American landscape in the twenty-first century, the Department of Homeland Security represents over 87,000 different jurisdictions at the federal, state, and local levels of government. The fiscal year 2014 budget request was $39 billion, seeking financial support for a number of key administrative and operational activities. For the first time in the country's history, an organization of government has been directed toward a national mission of protecting citizens against terrorist attacks, securing and managing the borders, enforcing and administering immigration laws, safeguarding and securing cyberspace, responding to natural disasters, and providing support to national and economic security entities. The central activity of the Department of Homeland Security is the coordination of dozens of directorates and components that involve thousands of employees with annual budgets in the billions of dollars.

Given the enormity of this structure and the diverse and varied populations and constituents that it serves, it is easy to see that the Department of Homeland Security has both complex internal and external environments. In addition, the constituencies served by such an organization represent virtually every citizen in the country and an infinite number of public and private organizational interests. It is only through efficient organization that the Department of Homeland Security can realize its mission; its mission and operations are often difficult to discern. How, for example, do the activities of the Department of Homeland Security conflict with the activities of other governmental agencies?

The Department of Homeland Security houses, for example, the U.S. Secret Service, traditionally a federal law enforcement agency administered by the U.S. Treasury. How does the mission of the Department of Homeland Security alter the historic mission of the U.S. Secret Service to investigate claims of counterfeiting and the protection of personnel designated by Congress? This is not to suggest that changing the mission is undesirable or not possible, but from a criminal justice administration perspective, how does a change in mission alter structure and constituencies such that ways of management and administration are no longer sufficient? More fundamentally, is the Department of Homeland Security really a criminal justice organization, and if so, how does it interface and interact with other criminal justice organizations whose missions are equally varied?

These questions are being directed toward the operations of police agencies, but how has the Department of Homeland Security altered the missions and operations of

---

CASE STUDY—continued

our courts and correctional agencies as well? How does the national mission of the Department of Homeland Security redirect resources otherwise used by state and local criminal justice agencies to combat crime? It is the answers to these questions that make criminal justice administration and management problematic and difficult.

The test for criminal justice administrators and managers in the twenty-first century will be how well they address the changes in their missions, purposes, and operations due to changing environments. The national mission of the Department of Homeland Security, to protect citizens against terrorist attacks, has forced new thinking about what roles, if any, criminal justice agencies have in achieving this mission. For the criminal justice administrator and manager, the twenty-first-century world is a more complex environment when compared to the twentieth century. Traditional ways of doing business will be constantly questioned as goals and environments change and outpace the

technology and resources available to criminal justice administrators. The evolving responses of criminal justice administrators and managers to these changing and varied environments will continue to define the contours of criminal justice administration into the twenty-first century.

CASE STUDY QUESTIONS

1. What do you see as central problems with the creation of the Department of Homeland Security vis-à-vis criminal justice organizations?
2. How does the creation of a Department of Homeland Security affect resources traditionally designated for local criminal justice organizations?
3. What are the due process protection questions in light of the creation of the Department of Homeland Security?

 # Think like an Administrator

As a judge, you have to consider multiple constituencies when you are deciding a criminal penalty to impose on a convicted offender. A particular case has numerous reports and facts, but beyond the facts and reports are other considerations. Take, for example, the many constituent groups that are looking to you as the person who will make justice happen. This is a tall order, one in which these groups have differing expectations of you. In addition, you must be concerned about what type of precedent you might set as you issue a decision in a particular case. How will the sentence comport with previous decisions in similar cases? How could the decision be misconstrued by both those in the community and those who work in the courtroom and the criminal justice system? Consider the courtroom work group as part of the court organization. Place yourself in the position of being the chief judge in your community court system.

As chief judge, you spend most of your time "administering" the court system. What does this involve? It may include all or some of the following: you operationalize the work rotation schedules for judges (what judge goes in what division, i.e., criminal, civil, family, probate, and so forth); you finalize the budget of the court; you address and manage personnel issues associated with employees in the court; you provide public access to the court; you represent the court at community events; and you are typically responsible for producing reports to a higher court that supervises your court. This list may be

---

THINK LIKE AN ADMINISTRATOR—continued

different for different courts. Yet, at the end of the day, you manage the court. Without you and others, the court would not function.

These activities are visible elements of the formal processing of the court, but let's get back to the courtroom work group mentioned earlier and criminal sentencing. We will see later in the book that courts as organizations are made up of defense attorneys, prosecutors, pretrial groups, such as treatment providers and witness advocates, civilian personnel such as court reporters, and sworn personnel such as deputy sheriffs who serve as bailiffs. This is known as a courtroom work group. How does a chief judge manage the expectations of a courtroom work group if a judge or a number of judges hands down sentences that are not within the accepted norm for a particular crime or crimes? This norm evolves among the many actors in the court system through a series of negotiation and deliberations over many years to define and put into place criminal sentences that meet their expectations of what justice is in any particular case. What seems obvious is that the courtroom work group has influence on how judges sentence and that on some occasions, the sentence may be seen by those who are not part of the courtroom work group to be unfair and not serving justice.

1. Should the expectations of a courtroom work group even matter in determining a criminal sentence? Are they a constituency group, just like other constituency groups that may influence the court?
2. Is the meeting of the expectations of the courtroom work group the basis for plea bargaining and repulsion by some who abhor this practice, even though it is both legal and well ensconced in the practices of courts across the land?
3. What should a chief judge think about as an administrator of a court system that has so many complex and conflicting constituencies?

FOR DISCUSSION

1. Using the concepts discussed in this chapter, describe your local probation department. What is its structure? What management functions are performed and by whom?

2. Discuss the goals of a victim–witness program. In what ways are they complex or conflicting? In what ways do some goals serve as constraints?

3. Using both a closed-system and an open-system analytical framework, describe your local jail. How might these frameworks lead to different views of the jail's effectiveness or of the causes of jail violence?

4. Discuss the potential problems in the interface between the Department of Homeland Security and a criminal justice organization. In light of the range of functions associated with the Department of Homeland Security, what internal and external constituencies are powerful?

FOR FURTHER READING

Eisenstein, J., Flemming, R., and Nardulli, P. *The Contours of Justice: Communities and Their Courts.* Boston: Little, Brown, 1988.

Fyfe, J., Greene, J., Walsh, W., Wilson, O. W., and McLaren, R. *Police Administration,* 5th ed. New York: McGraw-Hill, 1997.

Langworthy, R. *The Structure of Police Organizations.* New York: Praeger, 1986.

Luke, Jeffrey S. *Catalytic Leadership: Strategies for an Interconnected World.* San Francisco: Jossey-Bass, 1998.

National Research Council. Strengthening the National Institute of Justice. Committee on Assessing the Research Program of the National Institute of Justice. Charles E. Wellford, Betty Chemers, and Julie A. Schuck, Eds. Washington, DC: The National Academies Press, 2010.

The 9/11 Commission Report: Final Report of the National Commission on Terrorist Attacks Upon the United States. Washington, DC: General Accounting Office, 2004.

CHAPTER 2

Structure of Criminal Justice Organizations

LEARNING OBJECTIVES

After reading this chapter, the students will have achieved the following objectives:

- Define three major differences between the open system and the closed system.
- Define hierarchical and organic.
- Define the major differences between centralized and decentralized organizations.
- Define organizational mission, policy, and procedure.
- Understand the basics of agency budgeting.
- Understand the difference between a formal and an informal structure of an organization.
- Understand the administration's role in promoting agency ethics.
- Understand agencies through the four-frames perspective.

VIGNETTE

I am proposing Rule #1 of public organizations: *Large organizations will gradually increase the size and complexity of their administrative cadre at a rate faster than the ranks of their production workers and become increasingly bureaucratic and rule bound in the process.* In fact, the size of the work force may decrease, while the size of the administrative cadre increases. Students reading this vignette are most likely seniors or graduate students. During the four or five years they have spent at their respective universities, they have probably witnessed the growth of the number of vice presidents, assistant vice president, deans, associate deans, and assistant coaches as well as administrative assistants and secretaries for all of the new vice presidents, assistant vice presidents, deans, and so forth. You have witnessed, for example, the establishment of vice president or dean positions for graduate studies, and undergraduate studies, strategic planning, enrollment management, advising, student affairs, and on the list goes. It is also likely that while students witnessed their colleges' administrative ranks expand, vacant faculty positions are often left unfilled and the number of part-time faculty, who teach at a much lower pay rate and fill the void left by faculty position vacancies, increases.

The slippery slope to Rule #1 is usually a good faith commitment to accountability. Accountability simply means accounting for time spent by staff determining if the time spent by staff lead to achieving the agency's goals and objectives. However, accountability becomes a mechanism for control. A valid and reliable system of accountability is elusive and can lead to unintended consequences. Hence, agencies tend to measure items that are easy to measure and require that routine activities be recorded. Agencies impose audits to see if routine activities are taking place routinely. If one conforms and follows the script written by a rule-bound bureaucracy, he or she will have a successful career. This guarantees that Rule #1 for organizations will prevail because rules and regulations will increase and staff numbers similarly will increase to oversee conformity to rules and regulations.

Rule #1 applies to private large corporations that do not face competition as well as to public agencies. Further, the expansion of administrative ranks happens as a natural consequence of delegating work to subordinate administrators who, in turn, lobby for assistants to whom they can delegate administrative work such as recording, communicating, and linking.

The expansion of the management and administrative staff I have been complaining about is probably not really necessary. However, they will always be busy, overworked, and asking for more resources to get their job done. How does that happen? According to C. Northcote Parkinson (1955), in public bureaucracies, "Work expands so as to fill the time available for its completion." Parkinson elucidated this theory of public bureaucracies, referred to as *Parkinson's Law* in an article in 1955. Moreover, in 1957, he published a book called *Parkinson's Law*, in which he argued from his historical observation of England's civil service and military that what I call Rule #1 of Public Organizations is an empirically reality. Moreover, Anthony Downs (1967), in his classic study of bureaucracies, also discusses the rigidity cycle in which administrators, fearing loss of control, continue to add rules and regulations and reporting requirements, hence shifting increasing resources to administrative ranks and making the organization increasingly bureaucratic and rule bound.

OVERVIEW OF ORGANIZATIONAL STRUCTURE

Organizations have a formal structure and an informal structure, a phenomenon that was recognized by Chester Barnard in the 1930s: "Formal organizations arise out of and are necessary to **informal organizations**; but when they come into operation, they create and require informal organizations" (1938). Keeping Barnard's broad perspective in mind, our criminal justice administration book examines the forces that impact criminal justice organizations and develops the informal side of those organizations. It is important, therefore, to review the formal structure of organizations here to set the stage for the following chapters. This chapter examines the basic structures and dimensions of organizations and describes the logic of various structural configurations that can be implemented by agencies. In addition, the chapter reviews the basic concepts of organizational **mission, policies, procedures**, and practices and briefly introduces the informal side of organizations. The chapter also provides a brief discussion on the budgeting process for public agencies. Throughout the chapter, we apply the concepts of organizational structure to criminal justice agencies. The structure of an organization provides a framework within which its members carry out

Informal organizations: The unofficial goals, activities, communication networks, beliefs, and leadership that emerge within a formal organization.

Mission: Agencies' purpose and overriding objectives and goals. Provides agency principles and values—the prescribed basis for ethical decision making—and serves as the agencies' anchor.

Policies: Based on the mission, providing a statement of purpose for agency units. What a subunit is supposed to do.

Procedures: Step-by-step directions on how a policy is to be carried out.

Hierarchy/chain of command: The structure of authority and positions. In a police department, the chief sits at the top of the hierarchy and is highest in the chain of command. Patrol officers sit at the lowest level of the hierarchy and are at the end of the chain of command.

their prescribed activities that collectively will cause the organization to achieve its purpose. The framework is composed of the organization's mission, policies, and procedures and a **hierarchy/chain of command** of authority to direct members in the pursuit of its purpose. The formal structure creates formal roles and relationships, divides labor and allocates responsibility, and promotes rules and a hierarchy of authority to coordinate activities (Bolman and Deal, 2003).

Criminal justice organizations vary greatly in their size and structure. The vast majority of these agencies in the United States is relatively small and serves suburban and rural communities. For example, 71 percent of jails in the United States are relatively small, housing fewer than 150 inmates or less. At the other extreme, about 9 percent of the nation's jails house almost half of all jail inmates (National Institute of Justice [NIJ], 2001:3). The largest jails are New York City's Riker's Island, Chicago's Cook County Jail, Los Angeles County's multiple complexes, and Houston's Harris County Jail (NIJ, 2001). Adult correctional systems obviously vary greatly in size. The Federal Bureau of Prisons manages a prison system that extends across the country. Within systems, institutions vary dramatically in size. In Michigan, for example, the prison system comprises one prison, constructed in the 1880s, which houses more than 6,000 inmates, along with institutions with population capacities of 500 or fewer, and a number of camps that hold fewer than 100 inmates.

Law enforcement agencies across the nation also vary dramatically in the size and scope of their mission. In 2003, a number of federal agencies were placed under the jurisdiction of the Department of Homeland Security. The Department of Homeland Security now has authority over the Federal Law Enforcement Training Center, the Transportation Security Administration (TSA), U.S. Customs and Border Protection, U.S. Immigration and Customs Enforcement, and the U.S. Secret Service. Homeland Security also subsumes authority over ten other federal agencies—such as the Federal Emergency Management Agency (FEMA)—that are not specifically law enforcement agencies. The U.S. Department of Justice includes fifty-nine federal agencies, eight of which are law enforcement specific and include the Office of Attorney General, the Bureau of Alcohol, Tobacco, and Firearms, the Federal Bureau of Investigation, the Federal Bureau of Prisons, the U.S. Drug Enforcement Administration, the U.S. Marshals Service, Interpol, and the U.S. National Central Bureau. The Department of the Interior, whose mission is to protect the nation's natural resources, has authority over the Fish and Wildlife Service, the National Park Service, and the U.S. Park Police. Most law enforcement agencies, however, fall within state and local jurisdictions. "Big city" police departments are, by the nature of their jurisdictions, comparatively large. The New York City Police Department has more than 44,000 employees, with the majority, more than 36,000, sworn law enforcement officers. At the other extreme are 13,580 municipal police departments and 3,100 sheriff's departments. Many small agencies have just one full-time sworn police officer or are composed solely of part-time officers (Schmalleger, 2007). Always forgotten in criminal justice studies is the law enforcement branch of the Environmental Protection Agency (EPA). The EPA was created in 1970 by merging a number of the Federal Government's environmental protection agencies into one with the "Clean Air Act." The Mission of the EPA is to protect human health and the environment. The EPA provides research, monitoring, standard-setting, and enforcement activities to ensure environmental protection. The law enforcement branch was established in 1990 under the revised "Clean Air Act," and the scope and authority of EPA were dramatically expanded.

It is not possible to describe an organizational structure generic to all or even most organizations. A few key dimensions, however, are common to almost all organizations, regardless of size or structure. This chapter will provide a general description of those organizational dimensions and show how they operate in criminal justice agencies. The discussion will begin with a general description of two distinct models of organizations: mechanistic organizations commonly referred to as bureaucratic, formal, or hierarchical systems; and organic organizations, alternately referred to as professional or informal systems. Mechanistic organizations are typically rigid, based on strict rules and downward communication. Organic organizations have flexible networks of professional staff who may perform a variety of tasks (Kinicki and Kreitner, 2006). Henry (2007) provides a sound sketch and comparison of both of these models.

Mechanistic organizations—bureaucracies—are predicated on stable environmental conditions that create routine demands for services. In this type of organization, therefore, tasks tend to be specialized and divided among the labor force—that is, each member has a narrow range of duties that contributes to the agency's overall mission. Means or processes are emphasized over outcomes. It is assumed that if all workers perform their tasks correctly, the final product will result naturally. Every job is spelled out clearly in a formal job description that also dictates and limits the amount of authority and responsibility each individual has. Bureaucracies tend to be hierarchical, having a chain of command delegating authority and responsibility from the central authority downward (see Figure 2.1).

FIGURE 2.1 Organizational Hierarchy.

Fearless leaders (FLs)
Deputy FLs

Middle management
(majors, captains, lieutenants)

Line supervisors
Operations personnel

© Cengage Learning

Communications, power authority relationships, and loyalty are expected to flow vertically among superiors and subordinates. Bosses legitimately give orders, and subordinates obey. However, power is constrained by the organization's reliance on written rules and regulations that delimit authority and responsibility. Knowledge and expertise are assumed to exist at the top of bureaucratic organizations. Therefore, planning, conflict resolution, and decision making in general are primarily a function of top-level supervisors. Promotion of personnel to higher levels of authority and responsibility within bureaucratic organizations is based on their years of service and an assessment, usually subjective, about their capabilities. It is assumed that knowledge and expertise accumulate with longevity of career service.

Large metropolitan law enforcement agencies and state and federal correctional and law enforcement agencies are examples of criminal justice agencies structured along bureaucratic lines. It is common for large agencies, while adhering to a bureaucratic structure, to decentralize their operations by creating field offices or, in the case of large metropolitan police agencies, command districts. It is interesting that law enforcement and corrections agencies are often categorized as paramilitary organizations because a rigid chain of command exists. Subordinates are trained to "follow orders" and members are uniformed, armed, and authorized to apply coercive force in carrying out their duties.

Bureaucratic systems emphasize means rather than results. When evaluating staff, supervisors focus on conformity to rules and expectations (the means of production) rather than some level of output. For example, correctional officers are expected to make rounds on a predetermined time schedule; doing this, it is assumed, will ensure supervision and control of inmates. Some jails require corrections officers to punch cards at time clocks located at the end of each cell block to ensure they patrol the cell blocks at designated times. Similarly, law enforcement officers assigned to traffic control may be judged on the number of violation tickets they give out during a particular period. Police agencies commonly check starting and ending mileage on patrol cars to ensure that patrol officers are patrolling their assigned sections.

This emphasis on means rather than on the goals or ends explains why the criminal judicial system is often accused of delivering assembly-line justice (Paker, 1968) as prosecutors plea bargain cases so that courts can eliminate or keep up with backlogs, without considering the effects or results of these processes or practices. The need for efficiency has also resulted in simplifying sentencing decisions with legislated sentencing guidelines that judges are required to follow. The elimination of discretion and simplification of the decision-making process, with the emphasis on the means or process, has been referred to as the "McDonaldization" of the criminal justice system (Bohm, 2006). A systematic method of measuring the effects of random patrols or plea bargaining on agency goals and objectives is rarely pursued.

The hierarchical structure of a bureaucracy forces official communication to occur vertically. Commands and policy directives emanate from the top and are sent downward through the chain of command; information and reports on the activities of subordinates or problems within the organization are sent upward to appropriate levels. Because it is assumed that expertise and knowledge reside at the top of a bureaucratic agency, major policy and operational decisions tend to be made at this level. In the hierarchical structure, it follows logically that clear superior–subordinate relationships exist among personnel. The management style is, therefore, directed toward command and obedience. Loyalty toward the organization and supervisors is generally expected from subordinates. Closed-system criminal justice agencies become dysfunctional as a result of their ability to keep external forces from effecting change and innovation (Dias and Vaughn, 2006).

Professional or organic agencies are the extreme opposite of bureaucracies. Such organizations are ideally suited to function within unstable environments that demand outcomes requiring nonroutine tasks. In this type of organization, tasks are not specialized and any member of the agency may have the expertise or knowledge to take on a variety of tasks. Tasks may also be assumed by groups or teams sharing expertise. Because tasks are not specialized and responsibility is not constrained by written procedures, rules, and regulations, ends are emphasized over means. Decision making, conflict resolution, planning, policy development, and the like are mostly a result of unstructured and informal interaction among personnel rather than a prerogative reserved for executives or top managers. Decision making can emanate from groups or any individual because knowledge and expertise are assumed to be possessed by all personnel, at least within each individual's specific task area. Organic or professional agencies are best suited to lapse into or apply strategic management and match the organizational structure to environmental opportunities (Cowherd and Lucks, 1988).

In organic agencies, interactions tend to be horizontal rather than vertical, through a chain of command as prescribed for a bureaucratic agency. Leadership relationships tend to be peer-oriented rather than superior–subordinate. Advice and coaching, therefore, replace commands. Thinking about organizations as open systems leads to understanding the importance of the environmental demands and an agency's willingness and ability to be responsive to community needs. Organic agencies within the criminal judicial system include small prosecuting attorneys' offices, law enforcement departments, and jails commanding fewer than ten professional personnel. Research or planning departments within agencies will also likely organize as organic systems, taking on an informal organizational structure.

It is unlikely that any one agency is purely bureaucratic or organic; both structures are advantageous for different tasks or missions. Large bureaucratic agencies may develop organic units within their structures to perform tasks not suited to a mechanistic approach.

The traditional conflict between prison treatment and custody staff provides a common example. Generally, the conflict is viewed as a philosophical or operational conflict. What also must be considered is that custody personnel work under a bureaucratic or paramilitaristic system of management, whereas treatment staff—psychologists, social workers, and counselors—have a great deal more discretion because they work in an organic or professional subsystem of the prison. The differing degrees of autonomy and discretion among the

Task specialization: The extent to which tasks are divided into smaller units. High task specialization means employees perform a narrow range of duties. Performing a wide variety of activities describes low task specialization.

Formalization: High-to-low formalization is a function of the number of rules, regulations, and procedures personnel are expected to follow.

Span of control: The number of employees reporting to a supervisor. The span of control depends on the agency size, the tasks of personnel, and the skill level of employees.

Centralization versus decentralization: The level within a hierarchy at which decisions are made. Keeping decision making at the top of the hierarchy describes a centralized system and vice versa.

groups also create conflict, especially as it relates to enforcement of inmate rules and regulations. The conflict stems from role and work culture differences. However, the major basis of conflict is the gravitational pull that the dominant and traditional bureaucratic structure has on the professional organization of the treatment staff. The problem exists in traditional law enforcement agencies that attempt to develop community policing units with the traditional bureaucratic structure and chain of command. Failure to alter an organizational structure to fit the professionalism of community policing leads to a failure to implement a true community police operation (Geva and Shem-Tov, 2002; Williams, 2003).

Moreover, small agencies, such as small-town law enforcement agencies or jails in smaller jurisdictions, will function along the lines of an organic agency. Lines of authority tend to be weak, and decision making often evolves from consensus building. However, some degree of authoritative command exists even in small agencies. Team policing is likewise an attempt to remove a unit of law enforcement officers from the restrictions of the agency's hierarchy and structure to allow officers the freedom to work as a professional problem-solving unit (Shanahan, 1985). Small agencies or organizations structured along the lines of professional or organic agencies then must have subordinates participate in decision making. Forty years of research and prescriptions have argued that participative management and decision making strengthen subordinates' commitments to organizational goals and policies (Reeves, et al. 2012) and creates effective organizations.

Courts are generally depicted as organic systems. Defense attorneys, prosecuting attorneys, and judges work together as semiautonomous agents guided by formal procedural rules, a code of ethics, and informal rules of conduct (Neubauer, 1983). This is an easy conclusion to draw if we understand courts from the practice of the courtroom: the judge, prosecutor, and defense attorney engage in an adversarial relationship controlled by judges and serviced by lawyers. More often, proceedings take place outside the court in a negotiation process. All participants are highly paid, well-educated, trained professionals, and a bureaucratic organization is not immediately visible. However, the criminal judicial process also includes courtroom personnel, including the bailiff and court stenographer, the clerk of courts office, which is the records and information management arm of the court, the prosecutor's office, and the adult probation department. In larger jurisdictions, the clerk of courts, the prosecutor's office, and the probation department begin to develop a hierarchy, attempting to "specialize" tasks, make rules and regulations, and create other bureaucratic mechanisms in an attempt to control and regulate the flow of work. In fact, large courts will add a court administrator to their system to coordinate and regulate the flow of work across all units of the court system.

Organizations have a number of structural dimensions in common that determine the extent to which a bureaucratic or organic structure develops. These dimensions are **task specialization**, **formalization**, **span of control**, **centralization versus decentralization**, complexity, and the allocation of personnel in line versus staff positions (Baron and Greenberg, 1990).

Task specialization is the process of dividing the work into a number of smaller tasks. It can be high or nonexistent, depending on an agency's size and the divisibility of the work. High levels of task specialization suggest that each person or subunit performs a very narrow range of activities, as in an auto plant assembly line. Low task specialization implies that employees or subunits perform a wide range of tasks. Criminal justice agencies feature both high and low task specialization. Corrections officers may be given specialized assignments that include supervising intake and receiving, recreational facilities, or the infamous "yard." Each assignment requires a unique and specialized array of knowledge and expertise. Yet each assignment also requires both knowledge of the overall prison operation and a rather wide range of human relations and communications skills to carry out the task.

Police agencies also divide tasks by related function. A large law enforcement agency has units to deal with computer crimes, homicides, burglaries, drugs, gangs, traffic, and a multitude of other tasks. Currently, homeland security or counterterrorism units have been implemented in police agencies. Each officer, however, is expected to respond to a broad array of situations during the course of his or her duty. Small criminal justice agencies do not have enough personnel or a sufficiently complex workload to be concerned with high, often excessive, specialization. It is not uncommon for one or two individuals to be responsible for everything from booking prisoners to responding to service calls.

Formalization consists of the establishment of rules and regulations, usually written, that govern the work activities of an agency's personnel. Rules and regulations are often considered or identified as policies and procedures. An agency with a high degree of formalization will have rules governing almost every aspect of the work process, and the expected work behaviors of the organization's members will be spelled out in great detail. High levels of formalization reduce uncertainty and clearly define authority, responsibility, and decision-making procedures in most situations. Research suggests that formalization has a significant positive impact on correctional officers' job satisfaction and commitment to the organization (Lambert, Paoline, and Hogan, 2006).

Prisons typically have pages of written rules and regulations. Prison personnel face written regulations on issues ranging from employee parking to the amount of force that can be used on inmates. In spite of claims of professionalism, law enforcement personnel also often face a high degree of formalization. A case in point is the midsized law enforcement agency claiming to be professional and progressive that was in the habit of disciplining officers for being out of their cars without wearing their caps.

The judicial process is also governed by a number of written rules and procedures. Colleges and law schools offer classes in criminal procedures that describe in detail the rules and regulations that govern the criminal side of courts. Agencies with low levels of formalization rely on the expertise of staff rather than rules and regulations to direct work activities. Subordinates are allowed a great deal of latitude and authority in decision making. Typically, more "professional" organizations, in which tasks demand a high level of expertise from subordinates, require low levels of formalization. The prosecutor's office, while bound by legal procedures in formal court hearings, rarely has written rules on selecting cases, charging, and plea bargaining. Instead, judgments are guided by prosecutors' experience and expertise in analyzing individual cases.

The span of control—the number of subordinates reporting to a supervisor—is another significant dimension of organizational structure. (The number of individuals reporting to one supervisor is often referred to as the scalar principle.) A wide span of control implies that a large number of subordinates report to one supervisor. Conversely, a narrow span of control suggests that a small number of subordinates report to one supervisor. Deciding if the span of control should be wide or narrow depends on the size of the organization, the task at hand, and the skills of subordinates. For example, a shift sergeant may have ten to twenty street patrol officers under his or her supervision, constituting a wide span of control. This may be appropriate if patrol officers know what is expected of them, have the skills to carry out their tasks, and need little supervision or coaching. In the same law enforcement agency, the shift lieutenant may supervise only five sergeants, who in turn are supervising twenty patrol officers. This narrow span of control may exist in part as an artificial artifact of the way the agency has set up five districts, each with twenty patrol officers. If, in this example, the complement of sergeants were doubled to improve supervision over patrol officers, the span of control under the sergeants would have been narrowed, while the span of control under the lieutenant would have been widened.

Organizations described as having tall hierarchies contain a relatively high number of supervision levels. A tall hierarchy is generally found in organizations that utilize a narrow span of control, which is employed to provide intense supervision over subordinates. This suggests a work situation in which staff lacks competence to carry out the work without supervision or requires a great deal of coordination imposed from above. Organizations with flat hierarchies have few levels of command and typically exhibit wide spans of control at most levels. Figure 2.2 contrasts a tall organization having a narrow span of control with an organization having a wide span of control.

Decision making in organizations may be centralized or decentralized. Decision making is centralized to the extent that decisions on personnel actions, planning, formulation of policies and procedures, adjudication of conflict, and other significant issues are made by managers at the top of the hierarchy. Decision making is decentralized if decisions on significant issues occur with routine frequency throughout an agency or by staff at the grassroots level. The extent to which decision making is centralized or decentralized depends on the organization's basic values and management philosophy as well as on rationally constructed decision-making processes. Observers of bureaucracies view centralized decision making as a natural state resulting from a basic organizational belief that top managers have the expertise and system-wide vision to make the most effective decisions (Baron and Greenberg, 1990). A warden of a correctional institution, for example, is usually a career civil servant who has been promoted based on professional merit, skill, and time employed, all characteristics typical of top-level public administrators. The warden is viewed as having greater decision-making skills than subordinates as a consequence of coming up through the ranks and serving at a variety of posts along his or her career.

However, the warden in his or her wisdom may decentralize the decision-making process for a number of reasons. First, the warden may believe that

FIGURE 2.2 Tall and Flat Hierarchies.

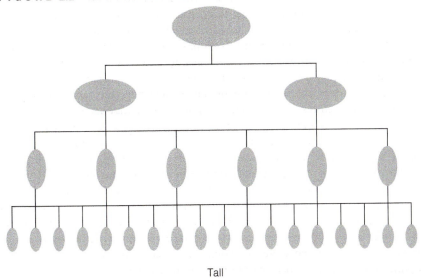

Tall

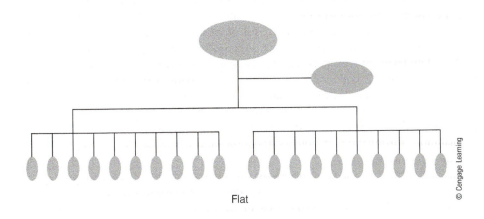

Flat

© Cengage Learning

participation in decisions creates commitment in subordinates. Also, taking into account the limited knowledge a top manager may have about all components of the agency individually or synergistically, the warden may believe that the work or goals of each component are complex and dynamic and will, therefore, institute a decentralized decision-making process. Federal law enforcement agencies, such as the Federal Bureau of Investigation, have a common set of policies and procedures and recruit, train, and assign personnel to field offices from its central office. Decision making on aspects of case management, however, is decentralized to the field offices.

Organizations are considered simple or complex depending on the number of levels in the chain of command—vertical **complexity**—or the number of existing

Organizational complexity: Vertical complexity describes agencies with a high number of levels in the chain of command. Horizontal complexity describes agencies with a high number of subunits.

divisions or subunits across the organization—horizontal complexity. Large organizations with a number of functions are both vertically and horizontally complex. A big city police department usually has a tall hierarchy with a number of layers between the chief and line staff. The department is horizontally complex if tasks are divided or specialized and task sets are assigned to individual units. A large police department, for example, has a homicide investigation unit, a burglary unit, and traffic control coupled with parking enforcement, drug enforcement, lockup, and a number of units too numerous to mention. Conversely, small police departments may have a chief and a number of officers and thus almost no hierarchy. Also, all their officers perform a wide range of tasks and perform traffic safety, drug enforcement, crime prevention, investigative, and other functions during the course of a shift. Thus, small police departments tend to be simple organizations, vertically and horizontally.

Organizations of any size have both line and staff personnel. Line personnel are those individuals directly responsible for production or the delivery of services. Staff personnel are support staff that assist and/or serve line personnel in their performance. Line personnel can be found in the chain of command of an organization's hierarchy. Staff personnel have slots in the hierarchy but do not have command authority over staff personnel. Large agencies have proportionally more staff personnel than smaller, less complex agencies. Examples of staff personnel in organizations are accountants, secretaries, mechanics, and trainers, to name a few. Moreover, large prisons may hire psychologists (staff personnel) to help correctional officers (line personnel) deal with stress-related problems. A final note: The term *staff* is used interchangeably and can cause confusion. Often, staff is used to denote agency personnel such as the jail staff. Staff personnel refer more precisely to organizational support personnel.

Work Perspective: A DAY AT WORK

A Day in the Life of Homeland Security

Below is a sampling of what the men and women of the Department do in a day.

(Not all agencies under DHS are included in this example.)

Today, U.S. Customs and Border Protection will:

- Process more than 1.1 million passengers and pedestrians
- Inspect more than 70,000 truck, rail, and sea containers
- Process more than $88M in fees, duties, and tariffs
- Make 2,402 apprehensions between ports for illegal entry
- Execute 70 arrests of criminals at ports of entry

- Seize over 7,000 pounds of narcotics
- Seize over 4,000 prohibited agricultural items
- Deploy more than 1,000 canine enforcement teams to aid inspections
- Make 5,479 pre-departure seizures of prohibited agricultural items

Today, U.S. Immigration and Customs Enforcement will:

- Make an average 153 administrative arrests and 61 criminal arrests
- Make an average of 10 currency seizures totalling $731,309
- Participate in an average 21 drug seizures each day, totalling more than 3,560 lbs. of marijuana, 11.8 lbs. of heroin, and 663 lbs. of cocaine

WORK PERSPECTIVE—continued

- ICE attorneys prepare 2,462 cases and on average obtain 450 final orders of removal, including 71 final orders of removal against criminal aliens.
- House approximately 29,786 illegal aliens in facilities nationwide
- Prevent nearly 2,082 prohibited items from entering federal facilities

Today, the United States Coast Guard will:

- Save 14 lives
- Assist 98 people in distress
- Conduct 74 search and rescue cases
- Complete 31 Port State Control safety and environmental exams on foreign vessels
- Perform 18 safety examinations on commercial fishing vessels
- Conduct 24 marine casualty investigations
- Issue 102 Certificates of Inspection to U.S. commercial vessels
- Service 135 aids-to-navigation and corrects 23 aids-to-navigation discrepancies
- Interdict 17 illegal migrants at sea
- Seize or remove over 1,000 pounds of illegal drugs ($12.9M value)
- Administer 25 International Ship and Port Facility Security (ISPS) Code vessel Exams
- Escort over 20 larger passenger vessels, military outload vessels, high interest vessels (HIVs) or vessels carrying especially hazardous cargo
- Board 193 ships and boats
- Board 17 vessels at sea to enforce domestic fisheries and marine protected species regulations
- Facilitate safe and efficient marine transportation on the Nation's 15,000 miles of inland waterways
- Inspect 53 HAZMAT containers
- Respond to 12 oil pollution/hazardous chemical material spills
- Welcome 3,200 new citizens
- Welcome 3,300 new permanent residents

- Adjudicate nearly 200 refugee applications from around the world
- Help American parents adopt nearly 125 foreign born orphans
- Grant asylum to 40 individuals already in the United States
- Naturalize 27 individuals serving in the Unites States military

Today, the DHS Office of Operation Coordination will:

- Work to secure the Homeland by coordinating the work of federal, state, territorial, tribal, local, and private sector partners and by collecting and fusing information from a variety of sources
- Create a real-time snap shot of the Nation's threat environment at any moment
- Provide real-time situational awareness and monitoring of the Homeland, through the National Operations Center

Today, the DHS Office of Intelligence and Analysis will:

- Review all-source intelligence information and produce analysis to distribute to federal, state, local, and private sector partners regarding current and developing threats and vulnerabilities, as well as providing recommendations for potential protective measures

Today, the United States Secret Service will:

- Protect dozens of high profile government officials, including the President, the Vice President, visiting heads of state, and former Presidents
- Seize more than $145,000 in counterfeit currency and suppress 2 counterfeit operations
- Open 42 new financial crimes and counterfeit investigations worldwide and conduct 17 computer forensic examinations
- Seize more than $52,000 in illegal profits and arrest 19 individuals
- Conduct 7 public education seminars on counterfeit recognition and financial fraud schemes

SOURCE: http://www.dhs.gov/xabout/gc_1212011814375.shtm (DHS Home page, 10/23/2010)

MISSION, POLICIES, AND PROCEDURES

The ideal bureaucracy has a written mission that is logically implemented by policies and procedures. The mission, policies, and procedures will be contained in a neatly bound policy and procedure manual. All personnel understand and accept the agency's mission and have a general knowledge of policies as well as a working knowledge of policies and procedures that apply to their specific duties. Ideally, all personnel will carry out their tasks in accordance with their job description and applicable policies and procedures.

A mission is a statement or description of an organization's common purpose; continuing purpose for existing responsibility to its clients or constituents; and, at least by implication, its ideology, values, and operating principles (Houston and Parsons, 2006). Walton (1986) reviews Ford Motor Company's adoption of its "Total Quality Management" philosophy. The process, which began with a reexamination of the organization's goals, evolved into a mission statement that took three years to complete. The mission statement emphasized the need to continually improve products to meet customers' needs. Only through meeting these needs, it was reasoned, could the company prosper. The mission statement was followed by a statement of organizational values proclaiming that people are the source of the company's strength, that the company would ultimately be judged by the quality of its products, and that profits would be the ultimate measure of how efficiently customers were provided with quality products. Ford's statement was strengthened by a set of guiding principles paraphrased as follows (see Walton, 1986:136):

Quality comes first.

Customers are the focus of everything we do.

Continuous improvement is essential to everything we do.

Employment/involvement is our way of life.

Dealers and suppliers are our partners. Integrity is never compromised.

Criminal justice agencies typically have written mission statements. A state department of corrections, for example, might have the following mission:

The mission of the department is to incarcerate convicted felons safely; to keep inmates secure, safe from physical and psychological harm or deterioration; and to provide inmates with opportunities for a successful crime-free reentry into society while providing a safe, secure, and stress-free work environment for staff.

Ideally, the mission can provide organizational members and constituents a clear understanding of an agency's purpose, goals, and objectives. Moreover, a declaration of the agency's values and operating philosophy within the mission statement can provide a basis for ethical decision making on the part of its members. The mission for the hypothetical corrections agency just given suggests several agency goals, including positive treatment and relationships of staff and inmates. In addition, the mission can direct or mold the activities of organizational members according to the organization's stated preference for specific guiding principles or values. Moreover, an agency's mission statement can serve as an anchor, or direction, for all organizational activities and can keep an organization from drifting away from its original purpose.

Not all organizations have written or clearly articulated missions, but all organizations have a mission. This paradox can be understood by considering the creation of an agency's mission. Private groups that form may charter their own mission by consensus of the members. For example, a group may come together with the purpose of housing street people, feeding the community's poor, or forming planned activities for local teenagers. Private enterprises may organize to earn a profit, but their mission will be to provide goods or services to consumers efficiently and effectively. In other words, the mission is based on providing a needed service or commodity. Therefore, the core of the mission—the organization's purpose—is found in meeting the needs of groups or individuals usually external to the organization. (A number of organizations, such as college fraternities or sororities, exist to meet their needs exclusively.) Political scientists posit that governmental agencies, and government itself, evolve to meet social needs that presumably cannot be met effectively by the private sector (Schattschnieder, 1969). In the ideal state, then, the purpose or mission of a public bureaucracy or a criminal justice agency is determined by the services required by society.

The mission of public bureaucracies emanates, in part, from legislation that mandates their existence and general purpose. Moreover, much of a criminal justice agency's ideology and value structure is imposed on it by external environmental forces. Constituents served want agencies to manifest a preferred ethos or to hold a particular ideology as well as to more narrowly define their purpose. Decisions rendered by both state and federal courts also have constrained and directed criminal justice agency missions, hence the statement in our example of a local jail's mission—protect the constitutional rights of inmates. A key role of top administrators in public agencies is to render the general or broad mandates their agencies have received from legislation and pressures from other external sources into narrower operational mission statements for their agencies.

Agencies, especially large bureaucracies, are not, however, helpless in the face of demands placed on them. Rourke (1976) argues that agencies have a great deal of power with legislators and the legislative process. In effect, bureaucracies have sufficient power to influence legislation and direct their legislative mandates. Agencies also are becoming more proficient in civil litigation and protecting themselves from judicial intervention. For example, the Los Angeles County Jail System successfully litigated in the U.S. Supreme Court to overturn a federal district court order to reinstate contact visitation for inmates (see *Block v. Rutherford*, 104 S.Ct. 3227, 1984). The court ruled that implementing contact visitations was a penological, not a constitutional, matter. A general concern of public administration theorists is the reluctance or inability of public bureaucracies to be responsive to the public (Denhardt, 1984; Houston and Parsons, 2006). In the less-than-ideal world, agencies may establish their missions with limited sensitivity to public needs or demands.

Most members of an organization have a view or understanding of their organization's purpose and values. However, members' understanding may not necessarily be congruent with their agency's mission statement. This is true for a number of reasons, most of which will unfold throughout this book. The pivotal point here is that the collective values, attitudes, expectations, and behaviors of an organization's members—the true culture of an organization—also impact the organization's mission. The culture may impact directly and formally on the mission and be reflected in the written presentation of the mission. Or, as suggested earlier, the culture may create a de facto mission that may differ substantially from the de jure, or official, mission of the organization. As a result, the purpose, structure, and activities of the organization may differ from those officially prescribed or planned. The extent to which the actual organizational purpose, structure, and activities differ from official purpose, structure, and activities is a function of several factors.

POLICIES AND PROCEDURES IN ORGANIZATIONS

The link between an organization's stated mission and the activities of its members lies in the promulgation and implementation of policies and procedures. Organizations tend to specialize tasks and create a number of subunits. Each unit of activity is directed by policies and procedures. A policy is a clear statement that defines what action is to be taken and why. A well-written policy provides a statement of purpose, action, and a rationale for the purpose. Here is an example of a policy about inmate visitation in a typical jail:

Inmate Visitation Policy

The Pine Mountain County Jail will provide inmates with every reasonable opportunity to visit with family members, lawyers, social workers, clergy, and other pertinent professionals.

Visitation will be limited by safety and security needs and court schedules. Inmates will not be denied visitation with legal counsel except in extreme circumstances.

Rationale

Visitation supports inmate morale and may alleviate much of the stress involved in being separated from families. Also, most of the inmates will be released back into the community. Visitation and contact with families and professionals will help prepare them for their release. Inmates with good morale and low stress will be more manageable and more likely to conform to inmate rules and regulations and behave in a civil manner while incarcerated. It is especially important to provide inmates who conform to jail rules ample opportunity for family visits at the jail.

Table 2.1 shows the number of components of a jail system that must be directed by policies.

T A B L E 2.1   JAIL OPERATIONS

1. Physical conditions—plumbing, lighting, bedding, and so on
2. Visitation—friends, relatives, attorneys, and so on
3. Correspondence—inflow and outflow; letters, packages, and so on
4. Telephone calls
5. Exercise
6. Law library
7. Street clothes for court appearance
8. Religious services—church and individual
9. Disciplinary proceedings
10. Use of incorrigible cells
11. Inmate guide—rules of behavior, lockup policies, and so on
12. Classification procedures
13. Intake screening
14. Special problems
    a. handicapped
    b. suicide threats/risks
    c. medically ill—epileptic, diabetic, and so on
    d. mentally ill/mentally impaired
    e. alcohol/drug problem
15. Medical care—dispensing medication, doctor/dental care, and so on
16. Use of force—both deadly and nondeadly
17. Application of leg and hand irons
18. Feeding—times, quantities, diet, special diets, and so on
19. Showers/cleanliness—personal and area
20. Detoxification cell and practices
21. Jail/lockup personnel standards—numbers, where essential, and so on
22. Preemployment issues—records/background checks, criteria for employment, Equal Employment Opportunity (EEO) issues, and so on
23. Preservice training
24. In-service training
25. Employee evaluation
26. Employee disciplinary matters

© Cengage Learning

Procedures are step-by-step descriptions of the activities that agency members need to follow to achieve the objective or goal put forward by policy. Agency policies should be directed by an agency's mission and procedures and directed by its policies. Policies also direct and define authority as well as subdivide the agency's work into specialized areas from which specialized tasks can be derived. The following is an example of procedures directing activities to carry out the preceding visitation policy example:

Inmate Visitation Procedures

1. Family visitation hours are Monday through Friday 8:00 a.m. to 8:00 p.m., and Saturday and Sunday 9:00 a.m. to 7:00 p.m. Inmates will have three visits per week for 20 minutes.

2. Visitation with legal counsel, probation and parole officers, registered clergy, social service workers, and medical personnel is authorized 24 hours a day, unless extreme security and safety problems will occur concurrent with the visit. The time of the visit will be determined by the visiting agent but will be reasonable in length.

3. Only minimum security inmates may have contact visits. Inmates will be pat-searched before and after contact visits. Inmates may be strip-searched after a contact visit if the supervising officer has reason to believe the inmate may be attempting to smuggle contraband into the jail.

4. Inmates with a history of violence or hostility between them, such as members of opposing gangs, may not be in the visitation area at the same time.

This list of procedures can be expanded to cover every aspect of visitation, including rotation of inmates to visits, rights of officers to deny visits, and reasons to remove visitors or otherwise conclude visits.

We can see how procedures become operational rules and regulations and further organize task specialization. The more specialized and formalized an organization becomes, the more written procedures will be promulgated to direct the activities of its personnel. In the ideal bureaucracy, the actual practices of an agency's members—the routinized activities of the agency staff—will conform to agency policies and procedures. In the ideal bureaucracy, all staff will achieve a comprehensive understanding of policies and procedures through some form of training or education. Also, the chain of command theoretically provides levels of management and supervision to direct the activities of subordinates toward conformity with agency rules and regulations.

Training, education, and supervision in the ideal organization also serve to socialize staff to conform to the official or approved organizational culture (see Chapter 9 on occupational socialization). A common state of affairs among organizations, however, is that mission, policies, and procedures evolve and accumulate in an unsystematic manner. New policies are created to deal with problems as they arise, and old policies and procedures are rarely reviewed, changed, or eliminated. Under these conditions, a legitimate or useful set of written policies and procedures may not exist. Moreover, policy and procedure manuals may gather dust, and the activities of agency members are based instead on how "it's always been done" or on well-established organizational routines.

Another consideration is the scope and detailed nature of policies and procedures. As discussed, agencies may form as bureaucracies or as professional or open systems. Large criminal justice agencies, such as big-city police departments, county sheriff systems in large counties, and state and federal correctional and law enforcement agencies, tend to take on bureaucratic structures. These agencies develop comprehensive and detailed policy and procedure manuals and provide intensive training to increase the likelihood that staff activities will conform to desired agency rules and regulations.

For criminal justice agencies in general, written policies and procedures and the expectation of staff conformity to them have taken on added significance in the last two decades. Civil suits against criminal justice agencies, especially corrections and law enforcement agencies, have become a rather common occurrence. Individuals who believe they have been harmed as a result of being involved with criminal justice agencies as suspects, offenders, inmates, victims of crime, or employees readily sue agencies to redress their perceived damages. Civil litigation almost always begins with a review of the agency's written policies and procedures. The first test is whether agency policies and procedures conform to applicable statutory and administrative law and general constitutional requirements. The second test asks if policies and procedures prescribe "sound" practice for the staff based on current standards for the field. Given the first two tests, the third general test asks to what extent staff is conforming to prescribed policies and procedures. Also, to the extent that staff does not follow policies and procedures, it asks to what extent failure to follow policies and procedures is a function of faulty training and/or supervision.

BUDGETING IN ORGANIZATIONS

Creating and managing budgets for agencies is a complex topic. A complete or comprehensive discussion of agency **budgeting** is beyond the scope of this book. However, the budget process is the backbone of any agency, as is the process by which an agency receives and allocates funds in order to operate and achieve its mission.

Every public agency goes through the budgeting cycle (Lee, Johnson, and Phillip, 2008). Each "fiscal period," usually each calendar year, an agency prepares its budget and submits it to the appropriate government body, seeks approval, executes the budget, and completes the cycle with some form of audit and evaluation. The chief executive officer—the chief of police, a sheriff, or a director of corrections, for example—has the primary responsibility for preparing and submitting the budget to their respective branches of government. In a large system, like a state department of corrections, the director of corrections may request budget submissions from lower-order components of the system, such as prisons and community corrections agencies. Each prison warden, in turn, may request budget submissions from subcomponents of his or her prison. The warden may ask the directors of custody, treatment, medical services, physical plant maintenance, training, and so forth, to submit a budget request up the chain of command to them.

It can be seen from this example that preparing a budget can follow the chain of command in the agency's hierarchy. This kind of "bottom-up" budgeting process, while logical, also can be time consuming. As a practical matter, therefore, agencies often base their annual budget request on last year's budget after making incremental categorical changes of previous expenditures. This form of budgeting is called line-item budgeting and is in reality the most common form of an agency's budget preparation. Budget requests also can be altered due to innovative

Budgeting: The process of allocating funds (dollars) within an agency to various hierarchical levels and subunits.

programming that appears to be successful or politically appealing. For example, expanding community-based policing may require more than an incremental change in a police department's budget request. It may require shifting funds from one category, such as traffic patrol to community policing, or requesting additional funding for that program when seeking budgetary approval.

The next steps in the budgeting cycle are to submit the budget to the appropriate legislative body and seek approval of the budget request. The legislative body will be Congress, a state legislature, and county or city commissioners. Each body will have subcommittees—such as a state budget committee or ways and means committee—to recommend approval of the budget request to the entire legislative body. Again, as a practical matter, the change in size of an agency budget or additions or elimination of funds for a program may begin with legislative bodies. During an economic downturn that reduces revenues to a government, agencies may be instructed to reduce their budget submission by a certain percentage. Legislative bodies may also eliminate or add funds for programs that are popular or very unpopular with the public. For example, legislative bodies may eliminate funds for recreational programs for inmates when those programs become unpopular. During the approval process, chief executives are typically asked to testify to the body on behalf of their request. This can be a straightforward process in which the executive tries to justify his or her request; or it may be a political process in which both agency supporters and detractors testify at the budget hearings.

The next step in the cycle is execution. This is the process by which funds that have been appropriated are distributed to agencies and within the agency. Typically, funds are allocated on a quarterly basis. The agency executives are responsible for managing the allocation and expenditure of allotted funds. Finally, agency executives conduct preaudits, processes that assure that funds are allocated as planned and sufficient funds are made available to meet proposed expenditures.

The final step in the budget cycle is the final audit and evaluation process. The purpose of this process is to assure that executives—police chief, director of corrections, wardens, and so forth—are in compliance with the planned allocation of funds; that is, did the executives and agencies expend funds as prescribed in the budget plan? For example, if a sum of money was allocated for community policing, the audit will check to see if that has happened and funds were not shifted from community policing to another function. Agencies can ask for exceptions to the original budget plan if unforeseen contingencies arise during the budget period. For example, if managing criminal gangs in a prison requires the use of additional personnel, a request for a shift of funds for additional corrections officers in a high-risk area can be made.

INFORMAL STRUCTURES IN ORGANIZATIONS

We have discussed the formal or official side of organizations—that is, the purpose, structure, and activities of an organization prescribed by top management. An informal side also develops in almost all organizations.

By informal structure, we are referring to goals, activities, or structures that are not officially acknowledged. An organization's informal structure differs to a greater or lesser extent from its formal structure, depending on the ability of top administrators to control the behaviors of staff and/or the extent to which staff buys into the organization's mission, policies and procedures, and desired culture, if one is articulated. As a complicating factor, the informal structure also is a product or manifestation of an organization's actual culture.

We will describe here a number of informal organizational phenomena. Almost all agencies have a formal communications system. In hierarchical systems, official communications flow upward and downward through the chain of command (blame, of course, always flows downward). Communicating through the chain of command, however, can be inefficient and ineffective, as we will see in Chapter 4. Also, the original source of messages is readily identifiable. As a result, every organization has a robust and often intractable communication network often referred to as the rumor mill or grapevine. Information, usually not verified but often credible, moves with speed vertically, laterally, and across working units. It can easily be argued that subjective evaluation of the performance or worth of a criminal justice practitioner begins and ends with information distributed through the informal communications network.

Almost all organizations develop informal work groups in which individuals work as loosely knit teams on an ad hoc or ongoing basis. The work groups may consist of members of different components of an agency and different levels of its hierarchy. Informal work groups may be productive if they are working toward organizational goals and following sanctioned organizational means. Informal groups also can be considered productive even in cases where groups circumvent the organization's sanctioned means while pursuing organizational goals. Van Zelst (1952) and Long (1984) point out that productivity can increase with the development of informal work groups. Court systems function on informal work groups rather than formally structured work systems (Neubauer, 1983). Informal work groups, however, can become completely aberrant and utilize the legitimacy and resources of the organization to pursue group goals and ignore legitimate means. An extreme example of this phenomenon is displayed in the well-known book and movie *Serpico*, which describes a group of New York City police officers who became corrupt, pocketing money from the drug trade for themselves and only minimally pursuing organizational goals.

Informal leadership also emerges in organizations. Informal leaders are organizational members who do not have formal authority vested in them by rank or supervisory status but who have developed sufficient power to routinely influence other members. Informal leaders are typically individuals who are perceived as having a great deal of knowledge and expertise about the organization and its business and typically have above-average communication skills (see Chapter 7 on leadership and Chapter 10 on power). Moreover, as informal work groups form, informal leaders evolve to provide groups with direction and structure. Even among prisoners, a group subjected to intense formal structure and discipline, informal groups and leaders emerge to meet their particular needs (see Stojkovic and Lovell, 1997).

The emergence and perpetuation of informal structures within organizations are explained to a great extent by the process of socialization within organizations. Individuals are socialized into the culture of an organization by formal, or sanctioned, and informal means (see Chapter 9 on occupational socialization). The development of a culture within an organization dictates to a great extent the values, attitudes, and behaviors of its members. Through the mechanisms of recruiting, training, and supervision provided by their formal structure, organizations attempt to impose a set of attitudes, values, and behaviors on their members. However, a degree of leakage of power exists in most organizations, especially large systems. As a result, the culture of an organization is based to some degree on the values and preferences of its members.

A potential negative consequence of any informal system is that the system may be beyond the control of the formal system, and members of the informal system may manifest unethical behaviors and activities under the guise of legitimate authority. A key role of agency executives is to prescribe and enforce ethical and professional behavior on the part of its members. Criminal justice practitioners are professional because they "have greater rights and responsibilities than nonprofessionals. The responsibilities inform and stem from public demand; the rights inform and stem from public acceptance" (Dreisbach, 2008, p. 202). Unfortunately, a function of most informal systems is to keep out of the range of control of agency supervision and to write its own rules. To the extent that members of informal systems do not fully understand and accept their responsibilities as professionals, corruption, deviance, and other unethical behaviors may occur on and off duty.

ORGANIZATIONAL FRAMES

Organizational frames:
A conceptual way of viewing organizations to identify problems and find solutions. Also, an innovative method to understand organizations.

Bolman and Deal (2003) argue that organizations can be conceptualized as being composed of four frames: the structural frame, the human resource frame, the political frame, and the symbolic frame. Thinking about organizations with the four frames allows analysis to become more discrete than does considering only formal and informal structures. The authors suggest that understanding the four frames provides paths to understanding and locating root sources of organizational problems, guides planners and change agents, and is significant to management and leadership. The frames are described with some detail in this section.

The structural frame has been discussed throughout this chapter. Structure refers to the organizational hierarchy, division of labor, job descriptions, mission, policies and procedures, and so forth. Certain key assumptions underlie the structural frame: (1) organizations exist to achieve goals and objectives, (2) productivity is enhanced through task specialization and the division of labor, (3) managerial control of staff and units is necessary to affect coordinated efforts, (4) organizational rationality prevails over personal preferences, (5) organizational structures are designed to fit the organization's needs, and (6) problems and failures to meet goals and objectives can be remedied through altering aspects of the organization's structure. In other words, problems and shortcomings can be remedied by altering the hierarchy, division of labor, job descriptions, and task assignments and by changing the level of decision making.

The human resource frame assumes that organizations exist to serve human needs rather than organizational needs. People and organizations need each other. When the fit between staff and the system is poor, both suffer. When the fit is good, individuals prosper from their experience in the organization, and the organization will be successful. Most theories of motivation are based within this frame. Organizations typically develop programs and awards to meet their members' need for recognition. Criminal justice bureaucracies that are paramilitary in structure are often criticized for lacking the ability to motivate staff and for suppressing motivation by overmanagement or practicing excessively authoritarian supervision. Recognition for successful work is often lacking, and routine feedback to staff from the hierarchy takes place through formal evaluation procedures that often become hurdles rather than sources of legitimate recognition.

Correctional and law enforcement agencies typically screen applicants to weed out individuals who will not fit into the organization. Rigorous preservice training programs also are required and serve to screen out individuals who presumably will not be able to cope with the problems prevalent in the work. The concept of job design considers changing the fit between jobs and people. Also, restructuring tasks allows staff to fulfill their need for challenges and responsibility.

Human resource issues also focus on the interpersonal dynamics that underpin staff relations: formation of cliques, networks, and subcultures. Concern for interpersonal relations always comes to light in the informal socialization process of criminal justice practitioners. Training and supervision are often weak attempts by the formal structure to socialize its members with its values. The inability of organizations to impact the interpersonal relations of their staff, however, allows staff to create their subcultures. This has been a particular problem with rapid recruitment of minorities and women into the male-dominated criminal justice world. Criminal justice agencies are almost always at a loss in dealing with the interpersonal relations between traditional staff and newly recruited personnel from different races and genders.

Rather than relying on a human resource approach to deal with this crucial issue, administrators typically fall back on tools available to them in the formal structure, and they promulgate rules, such as banning profane language and sexually oriented humor. This approach shows their inability to form partnerships with the informal structure to deal with problems.

The political frame views organizations as "arenas in which different interest groups compete for scarce resources" and problems arise because power is concentrated in the wrong places (Bolman and Deal, 1997: 14). The key assumption underpinning the political frame is that organizations are coalitions and cliques of diverse individuals and interest groups who are competing for control and resources. Significant differences of values, interests, information, and perceptions exist among coalitions. In addition, scarce resources and enduring differences make conflict central to organizational dynamics and goals, and decisions are a product of bargaining, negotiating, and competition for power among competing coalitions. Politics here consists of the application of influence and power, and it abounds in both the formal and informal structures of agencies. A clear example of the redistribution of power is the growing membership in corrections and law enforcement officer unions. The power of these groups is used primarily to extract material benefits from their employers. Unions also are concerned with working conditions and often impact policy decisions to meet that goal. They may go outside the organization, directly to the public and to political bodies to obtain legislation favorable to their membership or to impact funding or its allocation within the agency. Internally, groups and cliques form on a semipermanent or temporary basis and can influence the outcome of programs or policies. Informal leaders with no formal authority but with political clout commonly emerge among the rank and file of criminal justice agencies.

A number of studies have examined the process by which corrections officers gain political power in their institutions (Jacobs, 1977; Johnson, 2002; Welch, 1996). Law enforcement officers have reportedly resisted organizational change, and successful change has depended on the ability of the organization's leaders to directly influence the informal structure and garner sufficient power to affect the planned changes (Skolnick and Bayley, 1986). Inmates take on political power within institutions by virtue of the cliques, gangs, and social systems they form, and often corrections officers must utilize the power of the inmates to manage their institutions (Kalinich and Stojkovic, 1985). Administrators who rely solely on the tools of the formal structure to control political power will ultimately be rendered ineffective.

The symbolic frame views organizations as tribes, theater, or carnivals in which an organization's culture is driven by rituals, ceremonies, stories, heroes, and myths rather than by rules or managerial authority. Problems arise when "actors play out their parts badly, when symbols lose their meaning and rituals lose their potency" (Bolman and Deal, 1997:14). For the symbolic frame, it is assumed that the meaning attached to activity is more important than what actually happens, and events have multiple meanings. Also, when organizational members are faced with uncertainty and ambiguity, the members create symbols and metaphors to explain away ambiguity. Ultimately, symbols help individuals find meaning and certainty and bind organizational members together. One could argue that the criminal justice system is designed to put on major dramatic performances for the public. Uniforms and artifacts of authority are worn by judges, police, and corrections officers to display the role and power of the actors in the criminal justice theater. This display of righteous authority and power is intended to frighten thieves and cutthroats and reassure the citizenry that they are safe from the criminal element, protected by the system's players.

Manning (1997) suggests that drama touches every aspect of police work, and the public theater serves to give a picture of an ordered and controlled system, while the backstage drama serves to protect the clandestine nature of police work. Crank and Langworthy (1992) and Kalinich, Lorinskas, and Banas (1985) further argue that myth and symbols are instinctively invoked by criminal justice organizations to protect their agencies' boundaries from intrusion by powerful constituents. The drama paradigm would suggest that capital punishment might be favored by those who require that a high level of drama be evoked by the system.

The number and popularity of cops-and-robbers television programs is indicative of the drama expected from the criminal justice work world. This drama also is often represented by folklore, war stories that represent the players' beliefs either about their tasks/roles or the roles in which they would like to be cast. The "war" on crime and on drugs is an example of evoking symbols that cast the tasks/roles of actors as dramatic, heroic, dangerous, and important. The extent to which the public gives law enforcement officers greater status than corrections officers may lie in the visibility of police drama. Prison drama, in contrast, is hidden behind prison walls, though the prison walls alone may evoke a symbol sufficient to appease the audience.

Danger and fear are experienced by criminal justice professionals, but a great deal of their drama consists of mundane and often boring activities, for which exciting folklore and drama cannot be easily produced. And the actors often resent being reminded of the mundane and boring aspects of their work for fear that their heroic image will become tarnished. The vision of correctional reformers for a system focusing on treatment and reintegration of criminal offenders was destroyed in the early 1970s, when rehabilitation as a symbolic statement representing the role of correctional institutions lost its effectiveness. Ironically, both political liberals and conservatives opposed rehabilitation because the symbol and its accompanying rhetoric dramatized a profoundly disparate set of evils for each group (Travis, Latessa, and Vito, 1985).

The formal structure builds the stage and organizes the theater. Managers may see that the scripts are played out correctly in the informal structure. Leaders attempt to alter the script. But the question remains: Who writes the script?

SUMMARY

Define three major differences between open and closed systems.

- Closed systems are hierarchical, formal, and mechanistic. Open systems are organic in nature, rely on professionalism, and are informal.

Define hierarchical and organic.

- Hierarchy refers to an agency's chain of command. The term *organic* is used to describe the loose structure of professional organizations.

Define the major differences between centralized and decentralized organizations.

- In centralized organizations, authority and decision making are generally performed by top-level executives. In decentralized systems, authority and decision making are generally found at lower levels of an agency's hierarchy.

Define organizational mission, policy, and procedure.

- The mission is a statement of the agency's purpose. Policies explain what needs to be done to achieve the mission. Procedures are step-by-step directions on how to implement policies.

Define the basics of agency budgeting.

- Public agencies submit requests for funds to operate from the political entities they serve. Budgets need to be approved, implemented, and audited for compliance.

Define the difference between the formal and informal structure of an organization.

- Formal structure refers to purpose, goals, and activities that are sanctioned by legal mandates and organizational executives. Informal structure refers to purpose, goals, and activities that evolve in organizations and are not officially acknowledged or approved by executives.

Define the role of administration in promoting agency ethics.

- Agency administrators have the duty to operate ethically and indoctrinate agency members with organizational ethics.

Define agencies through the four-frames perspective.

- Viewing organizations through structural, human resource, political, and symbolic frames provides a unique analytical perspective for agencies.

Case Study: CENTRALIZATION VS. DECENTRALIZATION

In 1973, the National Advisory Commission (NAC) on Criminal Justice Standards and Goals set forth sweeping recommendations regarding the structure of criminal justice organizations. The NAC recommendations spanned all components of the criminal justice system—courts, police, corrections, prosecution and defense (Skoler, 1988). The NAC recommendation for correctional systems (Standard #16.4) called for the unification of all correctional services at the state level. This included bringing institutional and community correctional

services for adult and juvenile offenders and felony and misdemeanant offenders under the central authority of each state. In other words, the state government would manage and fund adult correctional institutions, jails, lockups, juvenile detention and correctional centers, and adult and juvenile community corrections under its authority. The state would be responsible for managing and funding all of the state's correctional services.

When the standards were written, approximately 80 percent of the nation's police departments were

CASE STUDY—continued

staffed by 10 sworn police officers or fewer. The standard for police (#2.5) recommended the unification of police service at the comity level. Police departments from big cities or small rural communities would be integrated into the county sheriff's department either by contracting services to small communities or merging resources from larger jurisdictions with the sheriff's department. The commission also called for a unified criminal court system under the financial and administrative jurisdiction of a state-level court administrator's office that would be supervised by the chief justice of the state supreme court.

The commission took a different approach for prosecuting attorneys and public defenders. The commission did not call for unification at the state level but recommended that the state provide financial support for both entities, Courts Standards 12.4 and 13.6.

CASE STUDY QUESTIONS:

1. What did NAC think would be achieved by the unification of criminal justice agencies? What are the political impediments to unification of control of criminal justice agencies?

2. Based on what you learned in this chapter, what are the pros and cons of implementing the commission's recommendations?

3. Why do you think the commission called for unification of police at the county or state level?

4. If police departments had been unified at the state or county levels of government, would creating community policing and other innovations in law enforcement have been more or less likely to happen?

5. Discuss the comparative effectiveness of large police departments versus police departments with 10 officers or fewer (consider the likely structure of a small police department).

6. What are the negative consequences of having the local prosecuting attorney's office funded by the state?

7. If you lived in a small community, would you prefer to have your own police department or be served by the county sheriff's department? Why?

8. Using the Four Frames analysis, critique unification of criminal justice agencies versus decentralization.

9. In what organizational structure is the formal and informal structure the most congruent? How does this help us consider the pros and cons of centralization versus decentralization?

 ## Think like an Administrator

Imagine that you are the city manager of a small residential town with a population of 15,000. The crime rate is relatively low and most of your calls are nonemergency in nature. You have a force of 15 patrol officers, one of whom is a detective, sergeants, and one lieutenant who works in the field but also has administrative duties. There are three full-time clerks in the office who word process, answer the phone, and take care of other clerical matters. Your emergency 911 calls are handled by the county system and relayed to your department as appropriate. Because your department is small, your work is done in an informal manner. Getting the job done outweighs rank and authority. Your relationships with the community members are good to favorable. Your city council members are considering shutting down the police department and contracting for police service with the county sheriff's department. Under the terms of the contract, almost all of the staff working at the department would be absorbed by the sheriff's department but could be assigned anywhere in the county as needed. The city council's motive for contracting is a 10 percent savings in the cost of policing the city, compared to the present budget for the police department. The city council has listed several questions that they want you to answer before they enter into a contract with the sheriff's department. (Many of the questions can be answered from the material in this chapter. However, you may have to stretch to answer some of the questions.)

> ### THINK LIKE AN ADMINISTRATOR—continued
>
> 1. Will the police who serve the city be more or less responsive to the needs of the community?
> 2. Will reporting channels between the police serving the community and the city government be improved or hindered post contract?
> 3. Will professionalism among officers who would work for the city after contracting be enhanced or reduced?
> 4. How would response time to emergency and nonemergency situations be affected post-contract?
> 5. What impact will the new organizational arraignment have on local citizens' ability to report crime, critical situations, and complaints?
> 6. Will crime rates and public order be affected by the change for better or for worse?
> 7. Will citizens' perceptions of safety change for better or for worse post contract?
> 8. Can you identify hidden costs that will negate the direct 10 percent savings to the city's budget?

FOR DISCUSSION

1. Identify the impediments to altering the structure of a large criminal justice agency. Take into account all of the issues involved with organizational structure.

2. What steps should an administrator take to build a partnership between the agency's formal and informal structures? In your opinion, what role, if any, do leaders of the informal structure have in building such a relationship?

FOR FURTHER READING

Baron, A., and Greenberg, J. *Behavior in Organizations: Understanding and Managing the Human Side of Work*. Boston: Allyn & Bacon, 1990.

Bohm, R. M. "'McJustice': On the McDonaldization of Criminal Justice." *Justice Quarterly*, 2006, 23, (1), 127–144.

Bolman, L. G., and Deal, T. E. *Reframing Organizations, Artistry, Choice, and Leadership*. 3rd ed. San Francisco: Jossey-Bass, 2003.

Crank, J., and Langworthy, R. " An Institutional Perspective of Policing." *Journal of Criminal Law and Criminal Justice*, 1992, 83, 338–363.

Denhardt, R. B. *Theories of Public Organizations*. Belmont, CA: Wadsworth, 1984.

Gains, L., Southerland, M., and Angell, J. *Police Administration*. New York: McGraw-Hill, 1991.

Houston, J., and Parsons, W. *Criminal Justice and the Policy Process*. Chicago: Nelson Hall, 2006.

Jacobs, J. B. *Stateville: The Penitentiary in Mass Society*. Chicago: University of Chicago Press, 1977.

Johnson, R. *Hard Time: Understanding and Reforming the Prison*, 3rd ed. Belmont, CA: Wadsworth, 2002.

Manning, P. *Police Work: The Social Organization of Policing*. Chicago: Waveland, 1997.

VIGNETTE

On September 11, 2001, the United States of America was invaded by a foreign enemy. Al-Qaeda terrorists hijacked four commercial airliners, two from Boston Logan Airport, one from Dulles Airport, and one from Newark Airport. The terrorists flew one of the planes into the Pentagon, and two were flown into the World Trade Center (Twin Towers) in downtown Manhattan. The fourth airliner was headed for the White House; its passengers took it back from the hijackers, but it eventually crashed in a field killing all aboard. Over 3,000 innocent people working in the Twin Towers and at the Pentagon were killed as a result of the attack as well as the passengers killed in the crashes of all four hijacked airliners. America had been invaded. The invasion has been stamped into our national psyche as the 9/11 terrorists' attack. Our outrage and fear resulting from the 9/11 invasion caused most Americans to be willing to take almost any steps necessary steps to prevent future terrorists' attacks.

In response to the 9/11 attack, we took a series of dramatic steps to prevent future terrorists' attacks from foreign invaders. We sent military forces into Afghanistan to destroy terrorists' camps and bases sponsored by the Taliban, an Afghanistan militant group. Shortly after invading Afghanistan, we invaded Iraq to locate and destroy weapons of mass destruction that our intelligence agencies believed had been stockpiled by the Iraqi dictator, Saddam Hussein. Saddam was our enemy and we feared that he would allow terrorists from the Mideast to obtain the weapons and then use them against us. No weapons of mass destructions were found. During the Iraq war, physical torture was used by American agents to interrogate Iraqi prisoners of war. Members of the White House staff and the United States Attorney General attempted to argue that torture was legal. The torture was euphemistically referred to as "enhanced interrogation techniques." Most Americans were not sympathetic to captured enemy soldiers subjected to torture. Nor were most Americans concerned when our government incarcerated "enemy combatants" without oversight or legal recourse on the part of the individuals imprisoned.

At home, we passed the Patriot Act that dramatically expanded the power of the federal government and the ability of federal police agencies to search homes and property and to wiretap phones and Internet communications. We also created the Department of Homeland Security to consolidate federal agencies to assure they would be more efficient at gathering and sharing intelligence at home and abroad. The National Security Agency, with the explicit support of the president and his staff, was allowed to wiretap phones of American citizens without judicial or congressional oversight. Libertarian Congressman from Texas and presidential candidate Ron Paul expressed fears that we are indeed moving to a police state (Conspiracy Planet, 2013):

In 2002, I asked my House colleagues a rhetorical question with regard to the onslaught of government growth in the post-September eleventh era:

Is America becoming a police state?

The question is no longer rhetorical. We are not yet living in a total police state, but it is fast approaching.

The seeds of future tyranny have been sown, and many of our basic protections against government have been undermined. The atmosphere since 2001 has permitted Congress to create whole new departments and agencies that purport to make us safer—always at the expense of our liberty. But security and liberty go hand in hand.

We may also soon be required to have a common form of personal identification to travel or to vote. Also, legal immigrants in many states are required by law to carry their immigration papers. Failure to provide papers to law enforcement officials in those states can result in one's arrest. Imagine that you are an American citizen with a heavy foreign accent and you are asked for your immigration papers. A German national CEO of a major corporation in Alabama spent a night in jail because he could not show his immigration papers to local law enforcement officials when asked. Interesting that it is a crime to lie to police officials and if you do not cooperate fully with police during an investigation, you can be charged with obstruction of justice.

The next time you walk through an urban area, look at the buildings and take stock of the growing number of digital cameras that are tracking your activities. It is hard to determine the frequency with which personal conversations are recorded by third parties' mobile phones. We are also reliant on cell phones, e-mail, Twitter, Facebook, and other electronic media for our personal communication. Records of our electronic activities are easily stored for long periods of time and we have had instances when the federal government obtained massive amounts of data and personal records from phone companies with just a request and bit of arm twisting, but without a court order. The phone companies complied in the name of national security. In May 2013, the Justice Department obtained phone records of editors and reporters from the Associated Press to track down intelligence leaks from a person or persons in the federal military/police bureaucracy. This intrusion may severely inhibit our nation's free press that acts as a watchdog over government. This was done in the name of national security.

Most of us succumb passively to the new powers of government and the police. After the recent terrorists' bombings during the Boston Marathon, the citizens of Boston and its suburbs were told to stay at home and lock down. The citizens of Boston did lock down as requested. Boston and federal police officials thanked people for cooperating. Few voices were heard complaining about being ordered to stay at home by the local police during the aftermath of the bombings. Almost everyone passively complied so the police could make them safe again.

Most Americans are not fearful of the increased power the government has been handed. Many people say they don't mind their loss of privacy as they have nothing to hide. This thoughtless attitude causes me to be afraid.

In the early 1980s, four of my students who were corrections officers offered a prediction about the near future of corrections. Their "environmental scanning" was based on their professional experience and watching general trends in politics and government. During a conversation that took place over coffee, they predicted that in the next decade imprisonment rates would soar, followed by problems of overcrowding, and then by a prison-building binge. They also thought that the size, number, and sophistication of youth gangs from the inner-city areas would increase; that the number of mentally ill inmates would increase at rates greater than the general inmate population, and that facilities would be constructed or dedicated to managing mentally ill inmates. They also saw a huge investment for medical treatment of inmates in the future and suggested that the AIDS virus would become rather common among prisoners and would be a psychological problem for both inmates and staff. It was obvious to the officers that the rapid expansion of prisons would result in a large group of relatively young, inexperienced officers and administrators. They all predicted the corrections system would respond to the predicted problems only after their impact became so blatant that politicians and policymakers would be forced to take action.

Although the predictions were heuristic, they were uncannily accurate. The ability of these young professionals to see the future came from their intuitive ability to "scan the environment." They understood how environmental conditions, events, forces, and circumstances would alter their department's purpose, structure, and activities as well as that the criminal justice system is an open system and ultimately governed by environmental forces (Perrow, 1986). Since the officers made their predictions, the rate of incarceration to the adult prison system has gone from approximately 200 inmates per 100,000 general population to over 500 inmates per 100,000. Moreover, the jail incarceration rates have grown from less than 100 inmates per 100,000 population to over 200 inmates per 100,000, and the total number of prisoners in state and federal prisons has soared to 1,367,865 (Stinchcomb, 2005). Although estimates of the percentage of inmates who are mentally ill vary, it is estimated that less than half of the inmates who are in need of mental health treatment receive any meaningful assistance. In addition, the rate of AIDS cases among inmates is about five times higher than the general population, placing a profound burden on medical care units in prisons (National Commission on Correctional Health Care, 2004).

In this chapter, we discuss the interdependence of the criminal justice system and its environment. Our focus is on the constraint and impact that environmental forces place on the system. The rapid development and application of information communication technology will have a profound impact on the operations of government and our personal lives. The technology also will have a similarly profound impact on individual privacy and security; it will alter the nature of the workforce in the government and further the growing tendency toward social distance (Asgarkhani, 2005). As we will see, these forces affect the mission of the system and its individual agencies as well as its objectives, policies, procedures, and day-to-day practices. Ismaili (2003), for example, argues that changes in our social, cultural, political, and economic conditions have given rise to the nation's highly punitive attitudes toward criminal offenders. In addition, we discuss how environmental forces allocate resources and personnel to the criminal justice system. Finally, we argue that environmental forces can be stable or complex and unpredictable; they often push the criminal justice system in contradictory directions. Environmental forces, however, will be the final determinants of the effectiveness and efficiency of that system. Environmental forces impose conflicting demands on members of criminal justice agencies and how those agencies attempt to survive in this complex environment.

DEFINING THE ENVIRONMENT OF THE CRIMINAL JUSTICE SYSTEM

Environment:
Conditions, forces, and circumstances external to organizations that affect the organizations' mandates and constraints.

We define an organization's environment as any external phenomenon, event, group, individual, or system. This definition can be broken down into finite dimensions to make the concept of the interdependence of an organization and its environment understandable. The **environment** of an advanced society is at least composed of technological, legal, political, economic, demographic, ecological, and cultural forces (Hall, 1987). Each of these plays a role in creating, maintaining, changing, or purging organizations. As environmental conditions change, demands for goods and services, resources, and support for and opposition to the programs of both public and private organizations also may change. Agencies, public or private, that fail to meet changing demands, expectations, or constraints may suffer severe loss of resources or public support before they catch on. Agencies that fail to catch on may become extinct. We discuss each of the environmental forces and, through the use of examples, examine the effect of each on the criminal justice system. Figure 3.1 displays the environmental conditions as forces that affect the criminal justice system.

Technology

Technology has had many direct and indirect effects on the criminal justice system. The introduction of the automobile into our society is an excellent example. The automobile allowed police agencies to increase the efficiency of patrols. Yet automobiles also became a major social control problem for the criminal justice system: The automobile expanded the range of operations for thieves. The high price of automobiles and auto parts makes them valuable items to steal and resell to "chop

FIGURE 3.1   How Environmental Conditions Affect the Criminal Justice System.

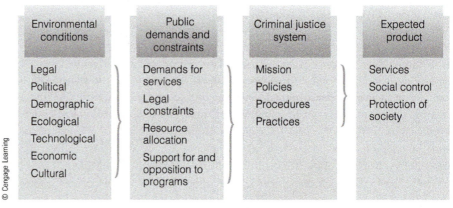

Environmental conditions	Public demands and constraints	Criminal justice system	Expected product
Legal	Demands for services	Mission	Services
Political	Legal constraints	Policies	Social control
Demographic	Resource allocation	Procedures	Protection of society
Ecological	Support for and opposition to programs	Practices	
Technological			
Economic			
Cultural			

© Cengage Learning

shops" and other outlets. Automobiles also create a public safety problem. For example, in 2005, approximately 43,000 people died in highway accidents and other traffic-related incidents. Currently, great efforts and resource expenditures are allocated to reduce highway deaths, such as zero tolerance enforcement for motorists driving under the influence of alcohol. Also, several states have banned the use of cell phones by vehicle drivers because using cell phones while driving distracts drivers and creates a potential traffic safety hazard.

The communications revolution allows instant communication of information. For example, the Law Enforcement Information Network System (LEIN) allows officers to obtain information on suspects and warrants from computers. Computer technology also has facilitated the sharing of large amounts of data for all criminal justice agencies. Particular to police, computer-aided dispatch and records management systems store data that are used to examine crime reports, arrests, and calls for service. The ability to collect and organize such data is the basis for crime analysis, a new discipline in law enforcement that analyzes crime patterns to assist police in everyday operations (Boba, 2005). Video cameras are often mounted on the dashboards of patrol cars to record arrests. Video documentation is especially useful as evidence in "driving while under the influence" arrests and for protecting police officers from false claims of brutality during arrests. It is speculated that being videotaped may change or control the behavior of the police during an arrest. The infamous Rodney King beating at the hands of Los Angeles police was taped by a citizen and received widespread television coverage that likely contributed to subsequent civil protests and riots. The tape also was used as evidence in a subsequent criminal case filed against the police officers; eventually, one of the officers received a federal criminal sentence for violating the civil rights of Mr. King.

The judicial system also has benefited from the use of computer technology. Legal research is more efficient, and judges can do a case law search from the bench while court is in session. Most of the nation had the opportunity to watch Judge Lance Ito in the O. J. Simpson criminal trial as he obtained case law on his laptop computer. Theoretically, this instant access to information should have sped up the proceedings, but it may also hold judges to higher standards, cause them to suffer an information overload, and slow the process down or create confusion. In the Simpson case, Judge Ito's chronic use of his laptop to search cases may have slowed the progress of the case, often by causing lengthy delays.

Computer technology also impacts the corrections system with the development of electronic tethers that can be strapped to offenders to bolster probation surveillance. Higher-risk offenders who would ordinarily be incarcerated can now be safely monitored under community supervision programs. Theoretically, this use of electronic monitoring can reduce prison and jail populations and increase the use of community corrections. Concurrently, agencies must create technology-based systems and train practitioners to utilize the innovations. From the standpoint of public safety, many states provide the names and addresses of criminals released from prison on the state's web site. This approach is especially popular for gaining information regarding so-called sex offenders and sexual predators.

However, the computer information age has created an opportunity for an array of innovative high-tech crimes. Grau (1999), for example, describes the ability of "computer hackers" to destroy linked systems out of malice and to penetrate online banking, finance, and investment systems to steal money without guns. Computer crimes, such as identity theft, stalking by sexual predators, cyberbullying, and industrial espionage (Hinduja, 2006), have risen to the extent that it is common for law enforcement agencies at every level to have separate units that specialize in investigating and prosecuting computer crimes. In this regard, cell phones and smartphones have dramatically increased the efficiency of our ability to communicate at great distances as well as store and transmit enormous amounts of information. Even countries with low economic bases have been able to integrate cell and smartphone technology into their daily lives. With this blessing comes an array of problems, such as the misuse of cell and smartphones in prisons. Moreover, cell phones are handy tools for drug dealers and other criminal actors who benefit from an efficient and inexpensive communication system.

New laws, policies, procedures, and practices must be created to deal with computer-based theft from electronic banking systems. Criminal investigators must have expertise in tracking crimes created on the World Wide Web or the Internet. Police patrol patterns must now consider protecting bank customers who use automated banking machines. The list of technological changes that will impact the criminal justice system could be expanded here. But the point is clear: Technology impacts the inner workings of the criminal justice system and changes the demands it must face.

The most recent technological advance that impacts the criminal justice system is the use of so-called DNA as forensics evidence:

> Among the many new tools that science has provided for the analysis of forensic evidence is the powerful and controversial analysis of deoxyribonucleic acid, or DNA, the material that makes up the genetic code of most organisms. DNA analysis, also called DNA typing or DNA profiling, examines DNA found in physical evidence such as blood, hair, and semen, and determines whether it can be matched to DNA taken from specific individuals (NIJ 1996, P1).

DNA evidence has routinely been applied to individuals convicted of usually violent crimes such as rape and murder and has led to the reversal of convictions of 1,090 offenders to date in the United States (National Registry, 2013). The use of DNA evidence also has strengthened the prosecution of criminal cases where DNA is present. Also, great doubt has been placed upon the values of "confessions" without physical evidence present, and jurors now expect to see prosecutors present more physical and scientific evidence in jury trials.

Law

Legislation and court decisions provide the basic rules and authority for the criminal justice system. The mandate for all public agencies lies in state and federal statutes. As discussed in Chapter 2, an agency's mission is directed by its legislated mandate. Criminal justice agencies are also bound by laws that direct their activities. Procedures for arrest, pretrial detention, bail bond, and adjudication procedures are often laid out, in part, by statute. In short, the criminal justice system is framed with legislation. The legal definition of crime is, of course, statutory. Criminal sentences and procedures for sentencing are directed by legislation. California recently created the "three strikes and you're out" legislation, which mandates a life sentence for conviction of a third felony within a category of crimes. Thought to prevent crime, three strikes has had a profound impact on jail and prison populations and has created a critical mass of geriatric prisoners who require extensive and expensive medical care. Offenders facing three-strikes sentencing have no incentive to plea bargain for a reduced charge and will invariably seek jury trials. This pattern has created backlogs for criminal courts, increased workloads for the prosecutor's office, and impacted the population capacity of local jails. It may be worth the cost if the three-strikes sentencing laws reduce crime. However, researchers using large data sets to analyze the impact of the three-strikes sentencing laws observed no significant impact on crime reduction in jurisdictions where it is applied (Kovandzic, Sloan, and Vieraitis, 2004). A common theme among states has been to attempt to reduce the rate of domestic violence by passing legislation that requires perpetrators of domestic violence to be arrested. Research has shown that in at least one jurisdiction, arrest rates have increased, and the incidence of domestic violence has decreased (Simpson, Bouffard, and Hickman, 2006).

Perhaps the most dramatic legislation to affect the operations of the criminal justice system is the Patriot Act. The Patriot Act was passed by Congress and signed by President George W. Bush on October 26, 2001. The Act was created as a result of the terrorist attacks on the United States on September 11, 2001. The Act allows broader authorization to tap phone messages or other electronic means of communication and includes authority to tap "roving calls," targeting individuals rather than specific phones. The Act also expanded the use of subpoenas against Internet service providers and required information sharing among law enforcement and intelligence communities. Finally, the Act also defined as a crime the facilitating of terrorist acts, whether or not the facilitator knew his or her activities were tied to a potential terrorist act. It also authorizes the attorney general to issue search warrants against terrorist suspects. In short, the power of law enforcement vis-a-vis constitutional constraints was expanded dramatically.

Case law—actual court cases that review activities of criminal justice practitioners—impacts powerfully on criminal justice agencies. Case law can be a review of criminal court cases by state and/or federal appellate or supreme courts; it also can emanate from civil litigation pled against criminal justice agencies. Typically, case laws reviewing criminal cases stemming from the U.S. Supreme Court are the most salient and have national impact. For example, *Tennessee v. Garner* (1985) restricts the ability of a police officer to shoot a fleeing felon. *Furman v. Georgia* (1972) in effect ended capital punishment in the United States for over a decade. **Civil litigation** has also had a powerful impact on the criminal justice system. Successful litigation against agencies may impose

Civil Litigation: Asking through court action to redress grievances. Many changes in the system are the result of civil litigation against criminal justice agencies.

monetary and/or injunctive relief against the agency (defendant) in favor of the individual or group bringing suit against the agency (plaintiff). In a recent U.S. Supreme Court case (*Blakeley v. Washington*), the Supreme Court invalidated a sentence imposed under the State of Washington's sentencing guidelines system. Basically, the court reasoned that giving longer sentences to offenders for "aggravating circumstances" was unconstitutional because sentencing for such exogenous circumstances without due process (a trial) violated the offenders' basic constitutional rights. This ruling caused all states and the federal system to reconsider and change their system of sentencing to conform to the *Blakeley* ruling.

Monetary relief provides the plaintiff with a sum of money, paid by the defendant agency, to rectify the harm done to the individual bringing the suit. Monetary relief can serve to compensate for the actual damages received by the plaintiff or punitive damages against the agency to punish the agency for its actions. Significant monetary awards against an agency typically cause the agency to change its practices. Injunctive relief is, in effect, a court order requiring the agency to make changes in its practices. Moreover, courts have often taken control of agencies through injunctive relief and appointed a court monitor who administers the agency de facto until the required changes have been made. Agencies also enter into a negotiated consent decree, an agreement with the court to make changes in the future, as a response to civil litigation.

Civil litigation can be filed with state or federal courts; state court litigation is based on simple common law tort action. Typically, states provide criminal justice practitioners with immunity for simple negligence because it is expected they will make mistakes—acts of negligence—in their complex environment. Thus, a plaintiff would have to show that agency members acted with gross negligence, wanton or deliberate indifference, or in a criminal manner that caused damages to the plaintiff. Cases that most dramatically impact criminal justice agencies are federal cases pled under *United States Code (USC)*, section *1983*, enacted in 1871. The essence of the *USC 1983* is to prevent governmental agencies from circumventing "under the color of law" the constitutional rights of citizens: "Every person who, under the color of any statute, ordinance, regulation … subjects … any citizen of the United States or other persons under the jurisdiction thereof … shall be liable to the party injured." Suits pled under *USC 1983* are referred to generically as federal civil rights suits and have implications for agencies in all states. The major body of law referred to as "corrections law," which provided limited constitutional rights to prisoners and dramatically changed the operations of corrections, has its base in case law emanating from civil litigation (Baro, 1988), often based on *USC 1983*, the *Civil Rights Act of 1871*.

Civil Rights Act of 1964: Federal law making it illegal to discriminate against citizens based on their race, gender, or religious preference.

The **Civil Rights Act** created by Congress in 1964 also had an impact on the criminal justice system and opened the door to civil litigation against criminal justice agencies. The requirement of equal opportunity also changed the personnel composition of criminal justice agencies so that they include more minorities. Women are now police and corrections officers, positions that were traditionally male. Policies and procedures protecting minorities from racial and sexual harassment have to be developed within criminal justice agencies. In some prison systems, preservice training now includes courses for female corrections officers to help them cope with the unique problems they face in male prisons.

Changes in the legal sector of the environment have thus created a new set of constraints to which the criminal justice system must adapt. In response to the civil litigation changes, criminal law, and increased departmental accountability on the part of police practitioners, many police departments have hired their own lawyers to provide legal guidance and assistance (Archbold, 2006).

Case law has also had an impact on the court system itself. The evolution of suits in the criminal justice system has created a snowball effect; suits ranging from gender and race discrimination by employees and potential employees to tort and civil rights actions by inmates are now common and have dramatically increased the workload of the courts. In effect, case law has changed past practices and rules of the court to allow more access to address grievances.

Economic Conditions

Clearly, the resources available to public bureaucracies limit the numbers and scope of these organizations. In a highly productive society, a great many resources are available, but many organizations are required to produce and distribute goods and services and to regulate the production and distribution systems. These organizations compete for resources, however plentiful. In our society, business cycles cause production and employment rates to fluctuate, and the resources allocated to public agencies fluctuate along with business cycles. Even though it derives its funds from government rather than the marketplace, the criminal justice system is affected by the business cycle because it competes with private and public organizations and with other regulatory agencies for existing resources. For example, during times of high unemployment, criminal justice agencies have a large labor pool from which to choose and have the opportunity to be highly selective in recruiting personnel. During periods of prosperity, criminal justice agencies have little difficulty in obtaining resources but cannot be highly selective in personnel recruiting because members of the labor force have so many career choices. The recent economic crises—the great recession of 2008—have caused major shortfalls in governmental budgets. States, for example, have been searching for ways to reduce spending in order to balance their budgets. The dramatic increase in the percentage of state budgets allocated to corrections, especially prisons, has caused legislators to reconsider earlier tough criminal sentencing. Also, the high cost of medical and mental health treatment for inmates is causing legislators to rethink prisons as a solution to crime problems. The wealth of a community also can affect the level of professionalism of public safety officers, the technological sophistication of the public safety system, and the total investment in public safety made by a community. It is suggested that per capita income of a community is a good predictor of the size of the budget for law enforcement agencies as well as the rate of officers per community (Holmes et. al., 2008).

Economic conditions may influence the criminal justice system in other ways. To the extent that unemployment rates affect crime rates and jail and prison populations, economic conditions affect the workload of criminal justice agencies. The research on unemployment rates and crime rates is conflicting (Thompson, Svirdoff, and McElroy, 1981). However, Belknap (1989) suggests that income inequality may be a better indicator of crime rate than poverty or unemployment. The differences in criminal participation among young Black and White males may reflect, in part, differences in labor market conditions. Also, the increasing rate of incarceration of African Americans may be linked to labor market conditions (Meyers and Simms, 1989). Fearn (2005) also finds that offenders in communities with extreme income inequality typically receive harsher sentences than offenders in other jurisdictions.

Research also suggests that homicide rates may be linked to economic discrimination against social groups (Meisner, 1989) and that larceny and other property crimes may be the result of a society's growth in material wealth (Shichor, 1990). Moreover, the literature indicates that prison populations and sentencing rates increase as unemployment increases, and vice versa (Yeager, 1979). In spite of the lack of certainty in this area of research, it serves as a good example of how environmental conditions beyond the control of the criminal justice system can affect it. Workhouses were built in London during the fifteenth century to incarcerate large numbers of unemployed and vagrant citizens (Barnes and Teeters, 1959). In this historical instance, a corrections system was created in response to the economic conditions.

Demographic Factors

Age, sex, race, ethnicity, and number of people in a community all have an impact on organizations. For example, the majority of criminal activity is carried out by individuals under the age of 25 (Reid, 1982). A community with a high proportion of individuals under the age of 25 will probably have a relatively high crime rate. Large cities tend to have higher per capita crime rates than smaller communities, and cities with more citizens of lower rather than higher economic status also have higher per capita crime rates (Sutherland and Cressey, 1978). It is interesting that Fearn (2005) finds that offenders receive harsher criminal sentences in communities with large proportions of evangelicals or Christian fundamentalists than in other communities.

A sudden influx or exodus of people creates a new set of demographic characteristics within the community that, in turn, can alter crime patterns. For example, an increase in the population of a state generally indicates that the state will soon be building additional prisons (Benton and Silberstein, 1983). The flight of working- and middle-class populations to the suburbs has left inner cities with the poor and minorities, creating a new clientele for urban police departments. The flight to the suburbs has also significantly eroded the tax base for major cities (Danzinger and Weinstein, 1976; Frey, 1979; Grubb, 1982) and has limited resources for their criminal justice systems at a time when they have to deal with a problematic population. In addition, Jaworsky and Park (2009) find that violent crime rates for cities of more than 250,000 were three times higher than suburban counties. They also argue that flights to the suburbs leave inner cities with concentrations of poverty where young residents view crime as normative. These factors lead to an easy adoption of criminal lifestyles for young individuals.

Migration and immigration patterns obviously impact demographics. Historically, industrial expansion in the cities created mass migration from rural farm communities and encouraged immigration from foreign nations (Faris, 1948).

Groups of individuals from different cultures, often with limited skills but a great will to work, converge in industrial cities seeking employment. A dramatic increase in the population of a city automatically increases its crime rate and presses the system for additional services; agencies are required to deal with cultures that often differ profoundly from the dominant, established culture. The unique behaviors and moral codes of merging cultures manifest in a variety of unfamiliar behaviors, some of which will be offensive and considered criminal by the dominant culture and will, in effect, create more crime (Sellin, 1934). One of the nation's current problems is 11 million illegal immigrants. Debate has been ongoing in the U.S. Congress on how to deal with this immigrant population. A significant number of the immigrants are referred to as "guest workers," and they play a significant role in our economy. However, the cities that border Mexico and port cities in Florida have to deal with the influx of illegal immigrants. In many of the border towns in California and Texas, citizens complain of the possible criminal threat posed to them by the influx of illegal immigrants. Armed vigilante groups have formed in many border cities to protect their borders. Some legislators want to construct a wall along the border to keep unwanted guests out. The implications for order and law enforcement are complicated, as is the proposed legislation to deal with the problem of illegal immigrants. The Mexican government's military battle with its drug lords often spills across the border into border towns in Texas and Arizona. Resulting anti-immigrant sentiment has driven Arizona to pass legislation giving local police more authority to arrest illegal aliens. No additional resources, however, were provided by the state to local governments to implement their new mandate.

Cultural Conditions

Culture can be defined briefly as the collective norms, values, symbols, behaviors, and expectations of a society's members. Ultimately, a society's political and economic systems reflect its culture. Thus, laws are codified social norms. Moreover, the roles attributed to a society's organizations are based in its culture. In other words, the missions, constraints, images, symbols, and validity of organizations are rooted in a society's cultural makeup. Society's dictates are imposed on bureaucracies through its political–legal system, which is linked to its cultural and social fabric. This is especially true for the criminal justice system, which is expected to carry out its duty of providing safety for the public in a manner that receives public approval.

American culture, however, is heterogeneous and dynamic, and the demands on and expectations of its institutions often conflict. During the racial riots of the 1960s and the anti-Vietnam War riots of the early 1970s, for example, many citizens were outraged by the conduct of the police, and charges of racism and brutality were common. In general, liberals viewed the social-control problems as a result of poverty, racism, and a justice system biased against the lower class. Conservatives viewed the civil disobedience, rioting, and looting simply as lawless conduct and advocated the increased use of police force to deal with it (Rosch, 1985). Moreover, even when we are incarcerating offenders at a high rate, most citizens are not supportive of allocating funds for more prison construction (Cohn, Rust, and Steen, 2006).

These conflicting views of crime and civil disorder are an excellent example of the lack of consistency in norms and values among the members of our society. Our cultural mix can create homogeneous or heterogeneous demands (Hall, 1987), depending on the issues at hand and our collective or individual perceptions of the issues. When demands are heterogeneous, government and organizations must work to appease or mitigate conflicting interests or must ignore one set of interests in favor of others. A striking historical example of our conflicting norms can be seen in the attempt to eliminate the consumption of alcohol through federal legislation. The Eighteenth Amendment (the *Volstead Act*), passed in 1919 and repealed in 1933 (the Twenty-First Amendment), created the nation's infamous period of prohibition. Basically, a coalition of politically powerful moral and religious groups created the amendment, which was intended to make the nation righteous by preventing a large number of Americans from consuming alcohol. The law forbidding the consumption of alcoholic beverages for recreational purposes was to be implemented by the criminal justice system at the federal, state, and local levels. However, alcoholic beverages were nonetheless consumed by "good citizens" from all walks of life. Beer and gin were often homemade, but bootleggers and members of organized crime supplied most of the beverages to the consuming public.

Because the values and preferences of large numbers of Americans seemingly were ignored by the prohibition lobby, the criminal justice system was, in effect, mandated to enforce a law that a great number of people would not follow. While the amendment ignored the wishes of "drinking" citizens, local criminal justice systems ignored the amendment; stories from the Roaring Twenties recount the corruption of local law enforcement officials who allowed speakeasies to market beer and liquor openly. Hence, the power the "moral minority" had over others was mitigated in favor of the "drinking minority" by the practices of local criminal justice systems.

In many respects, our present attempts to control the consumption of recreational drugs, such as marijuana, heroin, and cocaine, resemble our efforts at prohibiting the use of alcohol (Warren, 1981). Again, a large minority of American citizens forms a lucrative market that attracts suppliers of illegal recreational drugs. Traditional organized crime has its share of the illegal market, and new criminal cartels have been formed to supply illegal drugs to consumers. Despite the war on drugs, increased sentences for the sale and use of drugs, and intensified enforcement efforts, we seem unable to prevent the marketing of a product demanded by a substantial number of citizens. However, while a significant number of citizens believe that harsh sentencing for the sale or use of drugs will lead to decreased consumption, a significant number of citizens also doubt this and often rally for legalization of drugs. The outcome of the cultural conflict toward the use of coercive force to reduce drug consumption has contributed to the constantly growing rate of incarceration, the need for more prisons, and pressure for more resources for the criminal justice system.

Ecological Conditions

Ecological factors are components of the environment, such as climate, geographical location, size of a community, and its economic base—industrial, service, or agrarian. Ecological factors make a major contribution to the total environment of an organization and subsequently affect its mission and constraints. A small city in the midst of a farm area is profoundly different from a small city with an industrial base, and both are profoundly different from a large industrial community. Small agricultural communities tend to have homogeneous cultures and a history of relative stability.

The criminal justice system in small communities typically does not receive mixed signals from community members. An immediate link between criminal justice agencies and community members exists because citizens typically have access to political leaders and criminal justice officials and probably associate with them consistently on a social basis. From an operational point of view, most community members are probably well known to the local police, and many problems are handled informally based on local preference rather than on formal procedures.

As communities change from agrarian to industrial, migration patterns bring in new citizens who may have values different from those of the longtime residents, thus creating a heterogeneous environment for the criminal justice system. In addition, crime patterns may change, and an increased number of social control problems may require formal rather than informal processing. Large urban industrial communities offer an even more complex environment in which criminal justice agencies must work. Values of community members and their demands for services from governmental and criminal justice agencies may vary greatly. Social control problems are handled with formality. Criminal justice bureaucracies become large, and their members may not be easily accessible to citizens. Therefore, direct input from community members into criminal justice agencies may be limited.

Geographical conditions also have an impact on both the services demanded in a community and the resources available. In northern cities, winter climates create traffic hazards. Western areas have forest fires and droughts. Coastal areas or lakes and streams present safety hazards. Areas that attract tourists have distinctive social control problems. Las Vegas, for example, attracts more than its share of drifters and criminals as well as legitimate tourists looking for excitement. Little imagination is needed to consider how the problems the Las Vegas criminal justice system faces compare with those of stable industrial or rural communities. As discussed earlier, communities in California and Texas that border Mexico have a unique set of problems as the result of illegal immigrants traveling through their communities on their way to other communities in the country to meet their economic needs.

Political Conditions

Political conditions:
Demands and constraints imposed on organizations by government bodies, courts, public groups, or general cultural shifts.

Political conditions can affect an organization directly through pressures from constituents and clients and indirectly through governmental action. In theory, this linkage is established through representative government. However, election results rarely produce significant effects on public policy, and nonelectoral linkages are often the most powerful (Houston and Parsons, 2006). The governmental response to political conditions can be passed on to organizations and agencies in a number of ways. To focus on public agencies, governments can alter agency budgets, change mandates, alter the composition of top administrative personnel—which often happens after an election—or write legislation that changes the purpose or power base of a bureaucracy. On the other hand, legislation alone may not have a significant impact on agency operations. Research suggests that legislation requiring rehabilitation as a goal for state correctional agencies may not positively affect such an outcome (Kelly, Mueller, and Hemmens, 2004). Court decisions that affect the operations or mission of an agency are made in the existing political climate and are not exempt from political forces. As we saw earlier in the chapter, a body of case law has evolved as individual rights have become a deep political concern.

Political pressure by interest groups can be placed directly on criminal justice agencies rather than through the governmental structure (Houston and Parsons, 2006). For example, Mothers Against Drunk Driving (MADD) has been successful in causing police agencies to be concerned with the safety hazards created by drunk drivers. The MADD group has been able to focus national attention on the highway safety problem created by drunk drivers, which has, in turn, pressured courts to impose stiffer penalties and police to increase the frequency of arrests of those driving under the influence of drugs or alcohol. In another example, the national media exposure along with pressure from child protective groups have resulted in the implementation of the AMBER Alert system that provides information to law enforcement and the general public about child abductions.

The National Association for the Advancement of Colored People (NAACP) is a well-organized political force that has historically placed direct pressure on police agencies for fair treatment of African Americans and for equal opportunity employment within criminal justice agencies. In addition, the American Friends Service Committee (1971) has a history of attempting to bring humane reform to our prison system. Finally, pleas from the public at large often ask for tougher criminal sentencing.

Judges, as elected officials, are vulnerable to such pressures. Because demands placed on the political–legal system and ultimately on the criminal justice system often conflict, criminal justice agencies have difficulty establishing priorities. Justice may, therefore, be applied inconsistently within a particular criminal justice system and differently from system to system. As a result, some dissatisfaction with the performance of the criminal justice system will always be present among certain members, groups, or forces in its environment. Fearn (2005) suggests that community differences impact the severity of criminal sentencing.

Much of what has been discussed in this section on political conditions within the environment is based on cultural considerations. Cultural views and values become political when we try to operationalize them or make them part of the official domain of government. For example, Sample and Kadleck (2008) find that current sex offender laws, such as requiring sex offenders to register, is a product of legislators' personal opinions about sex offenders as informed by public opinion and media reporting of events. A society utilizes its political–legal system to perpetuate its most basic values. Hence, the political–legal system becomes a conduit between the forces of the environment and governmental agencies by rendering the conflicting demands and needs of the environment into manageable mandates for governmental agencies. Thus, criminal justice agencies are linked directly to and must be most responsive to the political environment in which they function.

Moreover, implicit up to now is the fact that environmental conditions merge and interact within the political environment and create or manifest a political climate. We have already seen how environmental conditions create demands and constraints on government, which, in turn, places demands, constraints, and expectations on public bureaucracies. Often the policies, activities, or subsequent outcomes of government or its agencies impact environmental conditions, thus creating a new set of problems and demands. For example, the fear of crime and the war on drugs, often fueled by political leaders, has led to a prison-building and incarceration binge, which in turn has expanded the number of corrections officers across the country. Public concern and support for the prison system typically emerge after a major prison riot (Stinchcomb, 2005). The fear of personal liability resulting from chronic litigation and concern for wages and working conditions have advanced collective bargaining for corrections officers. Corrections officers' unions in several states have expanded; they are well funded and sophisticated in influencing both the formal and informal political systems. In short, the unions have the political strength to lobby openly for legislation, support legislators and governors, contribute large sums of money to political candidates, and fund public relations activities to vest their interest directly and indirectly into the political process. Prison guards, who once lacked professional and often personal status, have now become politically powerful, a predictable outcome not foreseen by policymakers or political leaders, but resulting from environmental conditions funneled through the political environment.

THE POLITICAL ENVIRONMENT

The political environment of the criminal justice system can be thought of as a complex decision-making apparatus containing both formal and informal overlapping subsystems (Fairchild and Webb, 1985). The *formal political system* includes legislative bodies at the federal, state, and local levels. These bodies pass legislation that determines and limits the operation of the criminal justice system; they also allocate to criminal justice agencies resources that can have a substantial impact on operations. Legislative bodies, in theory, pass on demands from the general public to public service agencies. They also are subjected to the potential influence of pressure groups, whose goal is to influence the policies or operations of the criminal justice system (Fairchild, 1981; Stolz, 1985). Moreover, and not surprisingly, legislators' personal views, on matters such as criminal sentencing and rehabilitation, often frame legislative outcomes (Cook and Lane, 2009).

The court system, although it is a component of the criminal justice system, also is a part of the formal political system. The court system, especially the federal system, regulates the operations of criminal justice agencies. Regulation imposed by the courts is, in theory, based on statutory and case law and constitutional law, much of which is constantly being redefined by new court decisions or case law. In making sure the criminal justice system operates within the law, the courts are theoretically blind to demands of the general public or changes in cultural and other environmental factors. A significant body of research, however, suggests that judges, whether elected or appointed, make decisions congruent with the values they bring to the office. Their decision making often reflects the regional or political values they have acquired more than a strict interpretation of the law, hence creating a hybrid or a **political/legal system** (Cole, 2002; Frazier and Block, 1982; Kolonski and Mendelsohn, 1970).

Political system: Viewing legislation, government regulations, and court decisions as overlapping subsystems.

The *informal political system* comprises those pressures and demands that are placed directly on the criminal justice system. These pressures support or oppose existing programs or practices or they may demand new programs or services. In other words, individuals, groups, or organizations may bypass the formal political system and focus directly on a criminal justice agency—or attack the formal political structure and agency simultaneously—to bring about a desired effect. In the previous section on political environmental factors, examples were given of change that was imposed on the criminal justice system by direct pressure from such groups.

Informal pressure can also be placed on the criminal justice system by legislative bodies. Short of writing new laws, legislatures may voice support for, or opposition to, agency programs or practices. In short, governmental bodies may interfere with the routine operations of an agency as well as define the agency's official goal or mission (Guyot, 1985). Most state legislatures have both house and senate committees on corrections, police, or the courts. Such committees may show intense interest in a criminal justice agency program or operation and may voice an opinion on appropriate agency philosophy, policies, or procedures. Such an opinion itself may create a response from the agency without official legislation. In Michigan, for example, the state senate committee on criminal justice argued for the development of a military-style camp for young inmates. The state department of corrections, initially opposed to the boot camp, eventually established one boot camp structured to house 150 inmates in order to appease the committee. Often, antiquated prisons planned for closing have been kept open by legislators to protect the local employment opportunities and jobs for their voters.

The formal and informal political systems faced by the criminal justice agencies are not mutually exclusive. The example just given shows how members of the formal political system exert informal influence. We can also return to MADD to see other ways in which the two systems mix or overlap. MADD can consistently pressure police agencies to increase the frequency with which they arrest drunk drivers and can pressure judges to give out tough sentences while lobbying legislators to toughen legislation against drunk drivers and provide increased resources to improve anti-drunk-driving efforts.

Agencies may respond directly to pressure from the public or from a particular constituency and plan to effect an operational or programmatic change. They may first, however, approach the formal system for support by asking legislative bodies for additional funding (Cordner and Hudzik, 1983) or statutory support for their plan. In this manner, the formal political system is pressured by the agency to respond to demands from the informal political system. The move to community policing, or the foot patrol program, is a rich and interesting example of political interactions among the community, the police, and city government.

In Flint, Michigan, an industrial town that had unemployment rates of up to 23 percent in the 1980s, the crime rate rose rapidly, and community members demanded increased police service. City funds were unavailable because of the economic problems, but the Mott Foundation, a local organization created to assure the quality of life in Flint, funded the establishment of a foot patrol experiment. Funds from Mott were used to pay foot patrol police officers' salaries for a three-year period.

The program was evaluated periodically through direct interviews with residents in the foot patrol neighborhoods. Although the foot patrol program did not seem to affect crime rates, it provided residents with increased perceptions of safety, and they favored the availability of foot patrol officers (Trojanowicz, 1983). When the Mott Foundation grant ran out, the community voted overwhelmingly for a tax increase to continue the program as a permanent part of the police force.

The foot patrol program was not overly popular, however, with many police administrators or members of the city government. Although they were pleased with the tax increase, police executives and members of the city government continued to struggle to have the monies allocated lumped into the total police department budget rather than earmarked for foot patrol operations. When administrators also observed that the foot patrol officers were gaining, or had the capacity to gain, credibility and political influence among the constituents in the neighborhoods they served, they became concerned with the possible loss of bureaucratic control over the foot patrol officers (Trojanowicz, Steele, and Trojanowicz, 1986). These officers became, in effect, capable of being significant figures in the informal political system themselves through the influence and credibility they built within the community. Political forces within police departments and city governments often mitigate against the establishment of community policing. It usually takes extraordinary funding from government, such as the Federally Legislated Violent Crime and Law Enforcement Act of 1994 that provided $30 billion to fund community policing and to initiate innovative policing programs (He, Zhao, and Lovrich, 2005). The funds were used to add an additional 100,000 police officers across the country and created the office of Community Oriented Policing Services (COPS program) to distribute the funds to state and local police agencies.

Clearly, the political environment varies greatly in influence, structure, and form. In small rural communities, for example, criminal justice actors may be subjected to constant community input because they are part of the local social system. Citizens may be able to get something done by attending city council meetings, banging on the police chief's desk, or seeking out the judge at the local restaurant. In large urban communities, criminal justice agencies are shielded from such direct input from community members. Citizen complaints are handled through formal channels with much red tape. Influence is gained only through concerted interest group efforts, which usually include pressure through the formal political system and pressure on the criminal justice system itself (Olsen, 1973). State and federal agencies, especially corrections systems, are large, bureaucratic, and distant from the general public. They are, therefore, protected from the informal political system. To the extent they are vulnerable to political influence, it is most likely to be from the formal political system. Public agencies take their general mandates from the political system and are constrained by the legal and budgetary controls of the formal political system. However, they are subject to other pressures, demands, and constraints from clientele and constituencies served, competing and cooperating agencies, and other specific elements of their task environment. In the following section, we attempt to identify these groups.

TASK ENVIRONMENT ELEMENTS SPECIFIC
TO THE CRIMINAL JUSTICE SYSTEM

The task environment of an agency can be defined generally as the forces in the environment that are related directly to the goal-setting and goal-directed activities of the criminal justice system (Steers, 1977). The task environment is composed of a number of groups, agencies, and organizations that fall roughly into six categories: beneficiaries, funders, providers of nonfiscal resources, providers of complementary services, competitors, and legitimizers (Lauffer, 1984). *Funders* include governmental bodies that allocate scarce resources to public agencies. Planned activities, programs, goals, agency problems, and future challenges will be reviewed by funders before allocating budget requests.

Competitors are other public agencies competing for limited resources. With the move to privatization, firms such as Corrections Corporation of America are competing for tax dollars to provide correctional services (Mays and Gray, 1996). The public at large can be considered *beneficiaries*. However, particular groups often demand specific services from the system. Merchants want business districts to be safe and orderly for customers, and Mothers Against Drunk Driving was successful in requiring stricter enforcement and sentencing of drunk drivers.

Employees are major beneficiaries. Police and corrections officers' unions are common. In addition to bargaining for wages, they often play a role in policy development and attempt to force bureaus to alter their practices toward employees (Swanson, Territo, and Taylor, 1997). New personnel bring their own values and beliefs into an organization; to the extent their values vary from existing values, they may affect goals, practices, and decision making within the system (Eisenstein, 1973). It was hoped, for example, that upgrading the educational levels of police officers—that is, making a baccalaureate degree common—would make officers nonracist and able to relate well to members of the communities they served (National Advisory Commission on Criminal Justice Standards and Goals, 1973b).

Affirmative action also has had an impact on particular aspects of criminal justice agencies. Hiring women police and corrections officers has caused agencies to alter physical requirements for recruitment, including physical fitness testing for entry (Booth and Harwick, 1984). More important, perhaps, the mixing of genders has forced agencies to provide methods to assimilate female personnel and accord them professional status (Price, 1974). Agencies must now provide procedures to protect each gender from sexual harassment from the other, especially when one has a position of authority over the other. Criminal offenders can easily—if not ironically—be considered nonfiscal resource providers. The type and number of offenders clearly have an impact on the operations of criminal justice agencies. The emergence of street gangs causes police agencies to alter policies, procedures, and resources. Antigang units are often formed to respond to the gangs as a crime threat or in response to public fears (Center for Assessment of the Juvenile Justice System, 1982). The increased arrests of gang members affect the corrections system, especially large jails and prisons, because gangs tend to coalesce in correctional institutions and attempt to rule them (Irwin, 1980; Jacobs, 1983a). Increasing the number of arrests—as a result of increased crime, public pressure on police, luck, or skill—will affect operations throughout the criminal justice system. The populations of local jails and lockups will increase, court dockets and caseloads of prosecuting attorneys will expand, and, perhaps plea bargaining will favor defendants more than usual as a result of high caseloads. Finally, prison populations may increase.

Changes in the seriousness and type of criminal activity may affect the operational goals and procedures of agencies. In our example of street gangs, allocating additional law enforcement resources to that problem will take resources away from other activities. Response time to burglaries or accidents may increase and traffic control may be reduced as resources are taken away from these areas to deal with street gangs. Prison administrators may become more concerned with maintaining order than with treatment or rehabilitation in institutions populated by street gang members.

Historically, mentally ill citizens were confined in state mental institutions; in effect, they were controlled through incarceration. During the late 1960s and early 1970s, mental health professionals and legislators moved away from confining mentally ill people for long periods of time and instituted a program of community mental health, keeping mentally ill citizens out of institutions unless they posed a substantial danger to themselves or others. This change came about in part in response to the recognition of abuses and arbitrary decision making within mental institutions. In addition, mental health professionals reasoned, individuals suffering from mental problems could be cured only in the community, where they must ultimately live and survive. State mental hospitals were thus emptied during the 1970s, and since then, strict legal constraints have kept mental hospital admissions at a low level.

Mentally ill citizens who behave in criminal or antisocial ways now must be controlled and cared for by the criminal justice system instead of by the state mental health systems (Guy, Platt, and Zwerling, 1985). As a consequence, a growing number of jail and prison inmates across the nation are mentally ill (Steadman et al., 1984). In analyzing the data from the U.S. Bureau of Justice Statistics in the Survey of Jail Inmates, researchers found that approximately 16 percent of inmates incarcerated in our nation's jails in 1983 reported symptoms of mental illness or prior institutionalization in a mental hospital. It has been reported that nearly 70 percent of jail inmates report symptoms of mental illness (Hartwell and Orr, 2000). In addition, standards of care for inmates imposed on jails and prisons by the courts require that they be provided with adequate psychiatric and medical assistance (Embert, 1986). In effect, the role of the local jail and prison has been modified by changes within the mental health system, specifically by the closure of mental hospitals that housed the mentally ill for decades. Policies, procedures, and behaviors of jail and correctional institution employees must also be changed to perform the new tasks imposed by this aspect of the environment.

Components of the system and individual agencies become providers of complementary services, and they are all interdependent. Changes in the practices or priorities of one component or agency will have an effect on the other agencies. Moreover, human service agencies often become complementary providers of services because they often have problems and cases in common with the criminal justice system. Dealing with child abuse cases is a clear example of substantive interactions among the criminal justice and social welfare agencies.

Legitimization, finally, derives directly from legislation, preentry training, and educational requirements. Practices, performance, and personal standards can be dictated by legislation and implemented in part by mandated training and education. Most states have established standards and curricula for police training academies. The academies almost always are required to accept only applicants who meet personal, physical, mental, and emotional standards. Federal agencies and many state correctional agencies require extensive training before a trainee works in the system.

Legitimization can be derived indirectly from professional organizations as well as unions. Professional organizations, such as the American Correctional Association, American Jail Association, and state and local bar associations, attempt to set standards for their profession. It can be argued that the popularity of criminal justice programs at colleges and universities across the country has allowed higher education to provide legitimacy for the criminal justice system in much the same way law schools legitimize the legal profession.

A general analysis of the dynamics of an organization's environment provides an understanding of the general nature of environmental forces. Understanding environmental forces is pivotal to administrators in understanding the expected role of their agencies. In the next section, we add another dimension to our understanding of a system's environment by exploring the types of environments states faced by organizations.

ENVIRONMENTAL STATES

The specific environment of an organization can range from simple to complex and from static to dynamic. A **simple environment** is one in which the external forces that affect the organization, or with which the organization must interact, are few in number and are relatively homogeneous. Conversely, an organization that deals with a number of heterogeneous external factors exists within a relatively **complex environment** (Duncan, 1972). Each **environmental state** will affect the behavior of an organization differently. Police agencies that work in small communities with stable populations and little demographic change face a limited number of problems, most of which are recurring and predictable. The small-town cop probably knows many of the citizens personally, knows who the troublemakers are and where trouble spots are, can predict the behaviors and expectations of the political leaders, and is in a position to influence aspects of his or her environment. If such a "Sleepy Hollow" begins to change demographically, economically, or culturally, the environment becomes increasingly complex. If, for example, a relatively large firm moves into "Sleepy Hollow," the population will increase, additional housing will be built, individuals with different ethnic backgrounds may settle there, traffic patterns will change, and crime and interpersonal conflict may increase. The police agency may need to expand, to be concerned with the behavior of the new community members (at least initially), and to cope with altered traffic patterns, more taverns, and tavern patrons. The environment for the small-town cops thus moves from placid and simple to complex and diverse.

The police no longer will personally know all the people they will be dealing with and, as a result, will become increasingly formal in their interactions with citizens. If a new firm creates hazardous waste, think of the new expertise and enforcement obligations the officers of the town need to acquire.

There are profound differences between big-city and rural policing because of their complex versus simple task environments. The most complex environment for criminal justice agencies exists within a densely populated industrial county in which a number of cities of varying sizes have police agencies, courts with misdemeanor jurisdiction, and lockups, all of which link to the county or circuit courts of felony jurisdiction and the county sheriff (road patrol and county jail). The members of the criminal justice system must deal with a number of jurisdictions, agencies within and across jurisdictions, and heterogeneous political and cultural systems. We would expect criminal justice practitioners in such large or densely populated jurisdictions to behave in impersonal and highly bureaucratic ways. In addition, criminal justice practitioners in large jurisdictions have little opportunity for personal contact with influential community members and

Simple environment:
Environmental forces are homogenous and few in number.

Complex environment:
Environmental forces are heterogeneous and large in number.

Environmental state:
May be simple or complex, and static or dynamic.

political figures. Such contact is left to criminal justice administrators, who interact with the political–legal system, interpreting public opinions and demands into criminal justice policy.

An organization's environment may be static or dynamic as well as simple or complex. A **static environment** is one that remains constant or stable over time; it is predictable. In our "Sleepy Hollow" example, the police department worked in a static environment before the hypothetical economic and demographic changes took place. As demands on an agency become diverse and unpredictable, the environment takes on a dynamic nature. A **dynamic environment** is one that is subject to unpredictable change (Duncan, 1972; Steers, 1977). A single task environment can also have both simple and dynamic components. Much of the criminal justice practitioner's work is routine, repetitive, and predictable; yet some facets are unpredictable. In many respects, the ultimate art of the criminal justice practitioner or administrator is to predict or anticipate as many contingencies as possible, thereby simplifying some aspects of a complex, dynamic environment. For example, police agencies attempt to predict crime patterns, traffic patterns, and gang behavior. Parole boards attempt to predict the post-release behavior of inmates. Inasmuch as certain demands placed on the criminal justice system are routine and predictable, much of its agencies' environment can be considered stable. However, criminal justice agencies are often confronted with surprises and new demands from their environment. The influx of mentally ill inmates into the jails and prisons may, in retrospect, have been predictable, but it was not predicted, at least in an operational sense. The smooth flow of cases through a prosecutor's office and the court may be disrupted by a heinous crime that gains a great deal of notoriety. The prosecutor and staff may be forced to spend a great deal of time and energy on the case to satisfy public expectations for successful prosecution.

Urban police work can often be highly complex and unpredictable. An excellent example occurred in New York City in 1967, when a citywide power outage occurred because of a problem in a utility company generator. In the chaos that followed, looters broke retail store windows and stole merchandise. In mobilizing and dealing with this unexpected contingency, the police increased arrests, which, in turn, put pressure on lockups, bail and bond systems, prosecutors' staffs, courts, probation departments, and county correctional facilities. More recently, the emergence of homeless people in cities of any size has given the criminal justice system a new social control challenge. It is estimated that there are more than 600,000 homeless people in large cities across the nation and at least one-third of the homeless suffer from mental illness (Stranton, Blough, and Hawk, 2004). The point here is that the criminal justice system typically bears the responsibility for dealing with unique and unforeseen situations that impact the social infrastructure.

ORGANIZATIONAL RESPONSE TO THE ENVIRONMENT

The more dynamic and complex an organizational environment is, the greater the **environmental uncertainty** associated with it. And the more an organization perceives uncertainty in the cues and demands from its environment, the more difficulty it will have in making effective decisions.

Static Environment: Environmental factors are stable over time.

Dynamic Environment: Rapidly changing over time and unpredictable.

Environmental uncertainty: Lack of information about environmental factors important to decision making.

Environmental Uncertainty

The perception of uncertainty in the environment is the result of three conditions: a lack of information about environmental factors important to decision making, an inability to estimate how probabilities will affect a decision until it is implemented, and a lack of information about the cost associated with an incorrect decision (Duncan, 1972). What is pivotal, as we see later in this chapter, is an organization's ability to respond appropriately to its environment. A public agency that fails to maintain successful relationships with its environment will fail to be responsive to demands, will not appropriate adequate resources and support for its activities (Rourke, 1986; Sharkansky, 1972; Wildavsky, 1974), and will be unable to adapt to significant environmental change (Scott, 1987).

Decoupled Organizations

To add to the issue of uncertainty, large organizations tend to become **decoupled**—that is, they face multiple environments and interact with each environment at different organizational levels. To complicate matters further, an environment may have two *subenvironments* to which an agency may have to respond: the political–legal and service–delivery subenvironments. We can understand this concept by looking outward from organizations as they interact with the environment. Large organizations tend to break into overlapping subgroups, the dominant coalition and the work processors. The *dominant coalition* is the small group of employees who oversee the organization and dictate policy decisions; the **work processors** are the bulk of the organization's members who are directly involved with its primary clientele (Nokes, 1960). Each subgroup of the organization faces different demands and pressures from different sources. Members of the dominant coalition interact with the political–legal system, administrators of related organizations, organized support and opposition groups, and the news media; the dominant coalition typically becomes the focal point of public pressure.

These policy-level administrators must deal with political and public opinions that reflect the often conflicting views of the organization's multiple constituencies. In responding to the variety of pressures from the political environment, the dominant coalition must be concerned with their agency's myths, image, and posture. The work processors, in contrast, deal directly with agency clientele and deliver services to them (Meyer and Rowan, 1978; Nokes, 1960). In large systems, work processors become "street-level bureaucrats" who negotiate rules for the allocation of scarce agency resources with clients (Lipsky, 1980). Figure 3.2 shows a decoupled organization interacting with its subenvironments.

Decoupled organizations face a unique set of problems. To begin with, the cues, pressures, and constraints that the dominant coalition faces may be profoundly different from those faced by members of the work process group. For example, elites may demand that wife abusers be arrested more

Decoupled organization: Organization within which staff who work in the field—patrol officers, correctional officers—operate with definitions that are different from the organization's executive definitions.

Work processors (work process staff): Pertaining to agency employees, such as patrol officers or correctional officers who work in the field with street-level clients.

FIGURE 3.2 A Decoupled Organization.

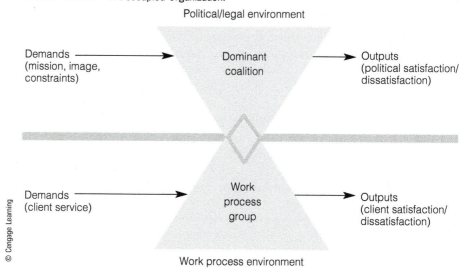

Political/legal environment

Demands ———————→ Dominant coalition ———————→ Outputs
(mission, image, constraints)   (political satisfaction/ dissatisfaction)

Demands ———————→ Work process group ———————→ Outputs
(client service)   (client satisfaction/ dissatisfaction)

Work process environment

© Cengage Learning

frequently—or policymakers may perceive that such demands will be forth-coming—and policy will be directed toward increased arrests of wife abusers. However, street police officers may be reluctant to do so because past experience with their clientele has convinced them that arresting wife abusers may not be an effective way to deal with the problem (Galliher, 1985). Or, administrators may feel they must wage wars on drugs or gambling, while law enforcement officers may understand that certain forms of drug use or gambling are approved behaviors within their community, and they may actively avoid controlling those types of crimes on their beats (Wilson, 1968).

Corrections systems provide especially fruitful examples of decoupled organizations. Corrections reform has been the concern of concerted political elites since 1870, when the National Congress of Penitentiary and Reformatory Discipline met in Cincinnati. This group called for sweeping reforms and implementation of standards for the maintenance and management of inmates. Since then, other meetings of establishment elites (Quinney, 1974) have been convened with this goal, and lasting groups, such as the American Correctional Association, have been formed and have prescribed standards for corrections. Courts have intervened and provided inmates with constitutional rights and have examined prison and jail conditions under a constitutional microscope. Even though it is reflected in the written policies and procedures of most corrections systems, this collective effort for change has functioned primarily to maintain and legitimize the corrections system by updating the language and symbols that explain the system to the public (Kalinich and Banas, 1984).

As demands from the political–legal environment are by the dominant coalition, the work processors—corrections officers and other staff—work pragmatically with the raw material—the inmates—to keep the system in some semblance of order. Day-to-day work is typically based on a series of informal rules negotiated between corrections staff and inmates (Kalinich and Stojkovic, 1985) and may have nothing to do with the prescriptions and standards promulgated by interested elites, pressure groups, or the courts.

The process of decentralizing, or federalizing, a large bureaucracy is typically done so that work processors have enough flexibility to deal with their local clientele or to respond to the demands of their local constituents. Decentralization is, in effect, recognition that local environmental dimensions may differ at various levels of the organization and that the organization may face more than one environment. Police agencies in large metropolitan areas are often broken into a number of districts that are governed by district commanders, who work with some degree of autonomy from the central bureaucracy. Parole agencies are typically governed loosely by a central office and broken into geographical districts, with each district expected to function with some degree of autonomy. However, the different environments an agency faces can create friction between central office staff and field staff even in formally decentralized bureaucracies (McCleary, 1978; also see Pfeffer, 1978 and Selznick 1949).

McCleary's (1978) interesting organizational study of a parole system describes the impact of different operational philosophies held by the dominant coalition—the central office—and the work processors—parole officers and district supervisors—on fundamentals of parole supervision in a state agency. The central office, for example, attempting to update the system, felt that it was inappropriate for a modern, professional parole system to have its officers carry guns. The central office decreed that officers would no longer be allowed to carry guns in the field. Parole officers, however, continued to carry guns, and their immediate supervisors supported them by not enforcing the central office ban on firearms. The central office attempted to alter the image of the agency to be congruent with external expectations about modern professionalism. However, the parole officers responded to their perceived environmental constraints.

It might be argued that the differing views in this situation were based primarily on the personal values of the community members. However, many of our job-related values and norms come from our immediate work group, which is affected by the environment in which it is immersed (Hall, 1987; Steers, 1977). Basically, each group responded to what it perceived to be the realities or expectations of its own environment. However, their perceptions of environmental demands were filtered by their work-group norms, past practices, and personal agendas (McCleary, 1978). But organizations are not helpless entities that ritualistically respond to environmental forces. In the following section, we discuss the common methods agencies use to manage environmental forces.

Work Perspective: CALIFORNIA OFFICE OF THE INSPECTOR GENERAL

When California Governor Arnold Schwarzenegger appointed me to the position of Inspector General in March, 2004, I found a state prison system in desperate need of oversight. The prisons were terribly overcrowded, health care for inmates was abysmal, and the organization was unable to effectively investigate and discipline officers who committed misconduct. These problems were exacerbated by the sheer size of the California prison system, with a current annual budget exceeding $8 billion, more than 55,000 employees, over 170,000 inmates in 33 adult prisons, and 115,000 parolees. Needless to say, the job of leading an oversight agency in this environment was daunting. To make matters worse, between 2002 and 2003, the California legislature had cut the budget of the Office of the Inspector General (OIG) by 80 percent, which resulted in a reduction in staffing levels for the agency from 115 to 20. Fortunately, in early 2004, the governor and the legislature agreed to commit the state to a vigorous oversight model. The governor's budget provided the funding and statutory changes necessary to get the OIG back on its feet and on the road to making the California prison system more transparent and accountable to the public.

Almost three years later, it is apparent that, although some progress has been made, California prisons are still struggling with several core issues. For example, the U.S. District Court, Northern District, has praised the department and the OIG for important improvements made to internal affairs investigations and the officer discipline process. In addition, I am particularly proud of the work accomplished by my staff in re-establishing the OIG as a fully staffed, independent oversight agency. However, some problems are proving to be quite intractable. Prison overcrowding is worse than ever, prompting the governor to declare a state of emergency, permitting the state to send inmates to prisons in other states. Similarly, the availability and quality of medical care has been so poor that the federal court has decided to appoint a receiver to take complete control of this $1 billion operation.

In these challenging circumstances, the OIG has established four goals or guiding principles: (1) to rigorously investigate and audit the California prison system, (2) to infuse maximum public transparency into the operation of California prisons, (3) to collaborate with state correctional leaders and outside stakeholders to facilitate finding the best solution to each identified problem, and (4) to hold the prison system administrators publicly accountable for implementing necessary reforms.

Experience has taught me that to accomplish these goals, one must acquire a keen understanding of the politi-

cal, legal, and bureaucratic landscape in California, as well as the ability to work effectively with the myriad of power brokers, both inside and outside of state government, who have the ability to effectuate change.

Of course, the most powerful person in California government is the head of state, Governor Arnold Schwarzenegger. The governor not only decides which bills will become law and which agencies will receive the lion's share of state funding, but he also appoints all of the executives in the correctional system, who in turn make correctional policy. Accordingly, I make a point to meet with the governor's staff on a regular basis to discuss the state of California's prisons and suggest ways in which they can be improved. Moreover, even with his incredibly busy schedule, the governor has personally met with me on several occasions to discuss the most serious of California's prison-related problems.

On the other end of the political spectrum is the California Correctional Peace Officers Association (CCPOA), a labor union that has frequently criticized the governor's approach to correctional reform and, most recently, has placed both its endorsement and its multimillion-dollar war chest behind the governor's Democratic rival for the position of governor in the 2006 election. Through a series of meetings and correspondence, the CCPOA has brought forward its views concerning what it sees as wrong with the prison system and how the system should be fixed. The union has been very public with its views in this regard and has focused the majority of its criticism on the alleged missteps of the administrators the governor has appointed. As with every member of the public, the union has the ability to make complaints to the OIG and request audits of systemic problems or investigations of employee misconduct. Depending on the merits of the request, some are accepted by the OIG intake committee while others are rejected. The governor's office is not consulted in this process.

The California legislature is also a key player in the field of prison reform. Legislators not only write the laws, but they also hold the government purse strings through their power over appropriations. Further, individual legislators or committees have the authority to call for public hearings on issues before them, including misconduct of prison employees or, more commonly, mismanagement of aspects of the prison system. As such, the legislature has both the authority to uncover misconduct and the ability to address it by changing applicable laws. Often the OIG and legislators will work together to address issues. For example, the OIG currently is investigating misconduct by a correctional administrator at the request of a special legislative committee. In addition, at the request of a state senator, the OIG has just completed an audit of several

---

WORK PERSPECTIVE—continued

substance abuse treatment providers whom the audit discovered had overcharged the state for their services by almost $5,000,000. In turn, the senator has announced that she will now hold a hearing on the matter to determine whether a legislative solution is possible.

Due to the powerful political players involved in the management and reform of the correctional system, it is absolutely necessary for an oversight agency to have complete independence. Fortunately, this is now built into the OIG statutory framework. For example, although the inspector general is appointed by the governor, he or she must be confirmed by the majority of the state Senate based on the candidate's skills and experience. In addition, once confirmed the inspector general serves a six-year term and cannot be removed, except for misconduct. Further independence has been achieved through a recent legislative change requiring that the OIG's budget be based on the office's workload from the previous year, thereby preventing a future administration from starving the OIG through budget cuts. As a result, the inspector general is able to accept the most meritorious audit and investigative projects, regardless of how the political winds may blow.

There are, however, stakeholders in the prison reform process who are outside of the political process altogether. The most important of these by far is the federal court. In California, inmate lawsuits have resulted in the court's total control of medical care and close oversight of mental health care, dental care, juvenile custody and treatment, parole practices, care

of disabled inmates, and the officer discipline process. Although the OIG is not a party to any of these suits, it has been called on in several of these cases to provide part of the solution. The best example is in the field of officer discipline. Through an agreement between the federal court and the governor, the OIG was asked to create a new bureau that would be tasked with providing "real-time" oversight of the department's internal affairs cases and to publicly report on the quality of the investigations, the appropriateness of the punishment meted out, and any systemic changes that should be made to improve the officer discipline process. This agreement has resulted in the creation of the Bureau of Independent Review within the OIG. The new bureau has now hired lawyers and investigators with experience in this field, opened offices, and started to publicly report on the progress made by the department in reforming the officer discipline process. In creating this bureau, the OIG has met regularly with the federal court to report on its progress, the prisoner's attorneys to discuss their concerns with the system, department administrators to hold them accountable for reform, and the governor's office to discuss our vision for the future. The development of the Bureau of Independent Review is a very good example of how, in a complex environment with multiple interested parties, it is necessary to work closely with all factions in order to reach the best solutions for the people of the state.

SOURCE: Matthew L. Cate, Inspector General, 2012.

MANAGING ENVIRONMENTAL FORCES

Almost all organizations are vulnerable to environmental forces, although to varying degrees (Jacobs, 1974). Organizations are open systems dependent on, and constrained by, environmental systems for mandates, authority, and resources, and they must produce goods or services for their clients. In effect, organizations must enter into exchange relations across their boundaries with other systems (Scott, 1987). Moreover, organizations constantly adapt to environmental pressures by altering their mission, goals, and means of doing business and evaluating their success or failure (Schein, 2004).

This is an important consideration because the ability of an organization to develop favorable exchange relations with its environment is ultimately related to its effectiveness (Osborn and Hunt, 1974). Organizations, however, often do not maintain such relations and instead attempt to behave as rational, or closed, systems. They expend efforts at setting and policing their boundaries in an effort to protect their core from external environmental influences (Thompson, 1967). For example, police agencies moving to community policing must deal with external challenges as well as internal threats if implementation is to be successful (Giacomazzi, Riley, and Merz, 2004). Organizations are, therefore, subjected to the task of managing and coping with their environments. Managing environments requires exerting control over environmental forces or creating mechanisms to buffer the agency from inputs. Production organizations stockpile raw materials, accumulate cash reserves, and control their markets with advertising and other strategies, all in an attempt to make them less dependent on their environments (Blau, 1955). As public bureaucracies, criminal justice agencies get their inputs (mandates, resources, support and opposition for programs) from the political–legal and cultural systems. Like other public agencies, they can protect their boundaries by invoking their bureaucratic power in both the formal and informal political systems or by conforming or appearing to conform to environmental demands or expectations through symbols and rhetoric.

Influencing Input

It is tempting to think of public bureaucracies, especially criminal justice agencies, as apolitical or above politics in the performance of their duties. An earlier version of this rationalistic view of public organizations posited that the political structure created policy and that public administrators carried out policy (Henry, 2007). However, bureaus have the power to influence policy inputs from the political system (Long, 1949). Legislators who control budgets and create social policy depend on agencies to carry out their programs. In addition, agencies have expertise on which lawmakers depend when creating policy changes (Rourke, 1976). Agency administrators are typically called on to provide information and to advise or state their position to legislative bodies that are proposing legislation that would restrict or broaden the scope of an agency's duties or powers. Legislative committees routinely call on directors of corrections, chiefs of police, and jail administrators to define problems and solutions or to respond to questions and issues put to them by the public. Police, courts, and correctional agencies also forward budgets and programs annually to their governing political bodies and argue their positions based on their unique understanding and expertise. The budgeting process is an opportunity for criminal justice administrators to propose programs and legislation that would alter the scope of their organization's duties as well as expand their resources (Cordner and Hudzik, 1983).

Criminal justice administrators who understand the political process and are capable of acting as "statespersons" (Downs, 1967; Rourke, 1976) for their agencies can have extraordinary influence and power over political inputs. The Federal Bureau of Investigation under the directorship of J. Edgar Hoover is a testimony to the ability of a criminal justice agency to protect its boundaries through its influence over the formal political process (Powers, 1987). Chiefs of police or corrections administrators who either reject the political aspects of their role or are simply inept at functioning within the political process typically fail to protect their agencies from political inputs.

Bureaus may also influence the open political system by gathering support from public groups. Allen (2008) suggests that efforts to increase public confidence for community service sentences can be effective. He proposes strategies to publicize the good work done for the public by community-service sentenced offenders to impact public attitudes toward community service sentences. A number of groups exist outside the criminal justice system that attempt to constrain, support, or direct organizational policy. Such groups include the American Correctional Association, National Sheriffs' Association, American Friends Service Committee, Fraternal Order of Police, American Bar Association, American Civil Liberties Union, and to some extent for corrections, the American Medical Association (Fairchild, 1981; Stolz, 1985). Although their means may differ—the American Civil Liberties Union brings issues to the public through lawsuits and public decrees, and the American Correctional Association promulgates standards for corrections operations—the views of such groups can have an effect on the formal political and legal systems (Melone, 1985; Stolz, 1985). However, criminal justice administrators may use these groups for support in the open political system because the membership of many of these organizations is made up primarily of criminal justice practitioners and administrators.

The news media act as a conduit between agencies and the environment. A media message can create support for or opposition to an agency or its programs and can also be a vehicle for a bureau to influence key sources in its environment. It is common for agencies at the federal level to exploit the news media to influence their immediate environment as well as the public. Information can be leaked, for example, to test for responses or to bring pressure to bear on other subcomponents or the hierarchical levels of a bureau (Halperin, 1978). Using the media's influence to protect agency boundaries is a robust technique that criminal justice agencies do not exploit, even though the opportunity seems eminently available; public interest in "cops and robbers" appears insatiable. Criminal justice agencies have made clumsy ventures at public relations and public influence by using the media, especially with police community relations advertising campaigns encouraging citizens to take steps to prevent crime (Radelet, 1986). The exception to this rule is again the Federal Bureau of Investigation, which has done an outstanding job of developing contacts with the media and presenting an impeccable image of itself. Also, most elected sheriffs, being political by nature, typically have a good sense of how to deal with the media.

However, police and corrections agencies have typically received negative press coverage, both because of the sensationalism of the enterprise and, perhaps in part, because the lack of motivation of local or state civil servants may be compared with a politically oriented administrator, such as an elected sheriff or a federal bureaucrat. Our heuristic view is that media information about the criminal justice system has been generally negative and has brought occasional hostile pressures to bear on criminal justice agencies rather than presenting their practices in a favorable light to the public and the political–legal system (Radelet, 1986).

Using Symbols

Symbolic (symbolism and theater): Creating policies or programs primarily to create public satisfaction and quiescence.

An organization can also protect its boundaries by using **symbolic** expressions that represent an organization's portion, belief, or values. For example, the uniform a police officer wears acts as a symbol of his or her authority and helps set the boundaries between citizens and the police. Symbolic statements are often published as slogans, and pithy rhetoric is used to express philosophy, policies, and means of operations in abbreviated form. The limited understanding of bureaus by most outside their boundaries, along with the sloppiness of human thinking, causes excessive reliance on symbolism, making it a powerful communication tool. The symbols, slogans, or rhetoric evoked by an organization become codes, representing agency philosophy and lending meaning to entrenched policy (Kalinich, Lorinskas, and Banas, 1985).

The process of evoking symbols is a significant aspect of the criminal justice system because the system is shaped by innumerable symbols and myths (Atkins and Pogrebin, 1981). Organizations consequently spend a significant part of their resources on such window dressing (Wilensky, 1967). Symbols can be seen, for example, in sweeping goal statements that are non-operational and encompass the needs or demands of a broad constituency. Agencies use these general symbolic statements to give them the appearance of conforming to the demands of clients, constituents, and other forces in the environment. When environmental pressures demand changes in an agency's philosophies, scope of duties, activities, and the like, the agency will search for the least profound change (Downs, 1967) and do so by first manipulating its symbols (Kalinich, Lorinskas, and Banas, 1985). In other words, bureaus manipulate their symbols to ward off pressures for substantive change. The art of manipulating symbols thus becomes a technique to protect the bureau's boundaries.

Examples of the use of symbols in the face of environmental pressures are abundant (Lovell and Stojkovic, 1987). As times changed, the posture of penology moved from a philosophy of discipline to corrections and rehabilitation. Guards became corrections officers; convicts turned into prisoners, then inmates, and finally clients. In many places, corrections officers wear blazers rather than uniforms and badges. Police no longer fight crime; they "serve and protect" or act as agents for crime prevention.

Reform bodies, such as the National Advisory Commission on Criminal Justice Standards and Goals (1973a) may have actually inhibited change because they gave the system the appearance of having changed simply by revising and updating the language through which the system is conceptualized (Kalinich and Banas, 1984).

It can similarly be argued that police–community programs were symbolic responses to protect police agencies from political inputs. Traditionally, police projected the image of crime fighters. When the racial riots of the late 1960s brought hostile pressure on police agencies from minority and liberal groups, the police responded with the temporary measure of creating, with limited resources, police–community units aimed at promoting shallow public relations. Police agencies avoided expending substantial resources on these programs to avoid structural changes (Kalinich, Lorinskas, and Banas, 1985).

A current example of symbolism at work can be found with the American Missing Broadcast Emergency Response or the AMBER Alert. The AMBER Alert is a broadcast system that announces through broadcast media the event of a missing or abducted child and seeks tips from the citizenry. The alert can also provide details of likely suspects and particulars of any vehicle that is suspected to be involved. The program was developed after the public demanded that something needed to be done to protect our children. Griffin and Miller (2008) refer to programs like AMBER Alert and Three Strikes You're Out as crime control theater created out of moral panic and fear. Further, they suggest that little empirical evidence exists to support the effectiveness of such programs. However, the public perceives that a dramatic step has been taken to protect children and reduce crime as a result of the programs.

Responding to Client Demand

Agency boundaries, especially those of decoupled agencies, are also permeable at the operational level (Houston and Parsons, 2006). A very good example of this effect is found within prisons. The administrators of corrections systems—the director of corrections, wardens, and deputy wardens—promulgate policies, procedures, and rules for corrections officers and inmates to follow in the institution's day-to-day operations. However, bureaucracies experience a great deal of leakage of authority between the hierarchy and the line staff (Downs, 1967)—in this case, the corrections officers. In an effort to keep order in the cell blocks, corrections officers conform to many of the demands of the inmates—their clients—rather than to the formal organizational rules. In effect, an informal system of governance that circumvents many of the formal policies, procedures, and institutional rules is created based to a great extent on inmates' values, needs, and norms (Kalinich and Stojkovic, 1985). In the police world, line police officers are granted a great deal of discretion to deal with the day-to-day problems they face within the communities they serve.

Officers have choices in how and on whom they will enforce the law or implement policy and procedures. In the "watchman" style of policing (Wilson, 1968), the officer is extremely sensitive to community norms and ignores law and agency policy in favor of local norms and behaviors. For example, if gambling is an accepted form of behavior in the community, the officer will not enforce antigambling statutes, in deference to community members. In this instance, the norms of the client influence and alter the formal rules of the agency. In the jargon of organizational theory, the agency's boundaries have been penetrated by the norms of the clientele, and the agency has become de-bureaucratized (Kaufman, 1969; Scott, 1987).

We have already seen several examples of boundaries permeated by nonorganizational norms in this chapter; the politicization of foot patrol programs are dramatic examples. It can be argued that eliminating the foot patrol officer in Chicago in favor of putting police in patrol cars was Taylorism, treating workers as machines, in action (Fischer and Sirianni, 1984); separating police officers from their community constituents was an effective way to seal off the police organization from its immediate environment and to exert control over the rank and file. Organizations can attempt to protect their boundaries from infringement at the operational level by attempting to control the norms and behaviors of their members. This control can be accomplished by indoctrinating its members in organizational norms, clarifying organizational behavioral expectations through declarations of clear and narrow policies, and enforcing organizational rules and regulations.

Control over agency members limits their responsiveness to demands from external sources and keeps the organization from becoming de-bureaucratized. Organizations, however, have less than complete control over their members. In fact, criminal justice practitioners exercise a great deal of discretion and power and routinely make ad hoc decisions in the course of their work (Atkins and Pogrebin, 1981). Making judgment calls on a case-by-case basis—the application of discretion—defines criminal justice practitioners as professionals. In addition, it is difficult for agencies to control subordinates' behavior, especially where (as is the case with most criminal justice agencies) the structure of the agency requires that line staff perform their duties without continuous observation by supervisory personnel. Hence, the operational boundaries of criminal justice agencies, especially decoupled ones, are highly permeable.

Decreasing Vulnerability to Pressure

Organizations vary in their vulnerability to environmental pressures (Jacobs, 1974). Large, well-established organizations with sufficient resources to police their boundaries, influence their environments, and function within predictable work environments are the most impermeable agencies. Conversely, those that are dependent on their environments have limited resources, function within turbulent environments, and are forced to adapt to environmental conditions and demands or fail (Hall, 1987; Scott, 1987). Organizations that do not modify their structures will also fail to manage environmental demands (Hannan and Freeman, 1984), whereas agencies that have inherent flexibility can readily adapt to changes in the environment (Duffee, 1985). Criminal justice agencies are, for the most part, well established and can be thought of as rather large systems within the immediate community each serves.

Goffman (1961) described prisons and mental institutions as "total institutions," suggesting that they were almost closed systems. Historically, these institutions were highly protected from intrusion by environmental forces. Prisons were protected from the legal system by federal courts, the legal system itself, and the hands-off doctrine that kept prisons exempt from civil litigation. Because the hands-off doctrine eroded, prisons are now vulnerable to civil litigation. In urban settings and at the state and federal levels, the boundary between the criminal justice system and the general community at the policy level may be difficult to penetrate, but the boundary between the system and the community may be porous at the operational level, suggesting that large criminal justice systems tend to be decoupled. They face heterogeneous constituencies and a wide range of problems and function within a turbulent and somewhat unpredictable environment. In small communities, the social exchange between community members and members of the criminal justice system may effectively minimize boundaries except in symbolic ways, and policies and practices may be heavily based on local values and demands. Criminal justice agencies in these communities usually have homogeneous constituencies, a relatively narrow scope of problems, and they function within a stable and predictable environment. Administrators need not expend great efforts protecting the agency's boundary.

SUMMARY AND IMPLICATIONS FOR ADMINISTRATORS

We have described environmental pressures at length and have discussed the notion of organizational boundaries that protect organizations from unwanted pressures. We also have provided a general description of the methods that bureaus typically use to control environmental pressures and avoid becoming de-bureaucratized. In this regard, we have discussed the administrator's role as defending the agency against environmental intrusions. We have not explicitly discussed the related, yet opposing, role of an administrator: to make the agency responsive to the community or its constituencies.

Parsons (1960) argued that organizations can be viewed as having three distinct parts: technical, managerial, and institutional. Organizations possess a core technology that is accommodated by management. Organizations exist, however, by virtue of their contribution to the greater social system. The need for the organization's contribution legitimizes the organization's right to exist and command resources.

The role of management, therefore, is to mitigate the uncertainty imposed by the agency's institutional role and increase the certainty needed by the agency's technical core. In other words, management attempts to keep the internal workings of an agency "rational" by buffering the agency from environmental forces, smoothing input–output relations between the agency and its clients, and/or adapting to anticipated changes in environmental demands (Houston and Parsons, 2006; Thompson, 1967).

An organization must, on one hand, survive and maintain some sense of internal stability and protect its established routines in order to deliver services successfully (Nelson and Winter, 1982). On the other hand, it must provide services by means that are congruent with community preferences. Although organizational members may make decisions about what constitutes appropriate services, environmental constituents ultimately judge the value of an organization's outputs. In other words, an agency that develops favorable relations with its environment will likely be perceived as a responsive, productive, and contributing organization.

The presentation of an organization as possessing crucial expertise, dedicated members, and dynamic leadership will be held in high esteem by community members. Agencies that present themselves as "rational" and goal-directed will typically enjoy higher status with legislative bodies and be able to compete favorably for resources (Greene, Bynum, and Cordner, 1986). To the extent that demands and pressures from the environment vary, administrators may need to make structural, functional, or symbolic changes within the agency. Administrators who resist change may find themselves out of work or find the formal political–legal system bringing change to the agency.

A reactive posture can be taken; administrators may respond to altered demands and constraints as they fall on their desks. However, administrators cannot respond to all inputs if environmental demands are contradictory or capricious: They must consider the agency's resources, expertise, and scope of authority, as well as turf issues and relationships with cooperating and competing agencies and clientele, before meeting new demands. They must also identify and activate constituent groups to support their programs. Responding in a knee-jerk fashion to all demands may create chaos within an agency rather than responsiveness.

Ideally, administrators should continually scan their environments to predict environmental changes and enter into planned change, prepare for future demands, and prepare the members of the organization to be responsive to changes in environmental demands (Weiner and Johnson, 1981). **Environmental scanning** is a process common to the private sector but historically uncommon to criminal justice executives. Scanning is a process by which planners and managers look out at the environment to identify changes in environmental forces that will constrain agency goals, objectives, operations, and practices. In the private sector, planners and executives are interested in market changes that will affect demand for their products or prices and availability for products they use to produce their goods and services. Private sector scanners also will be interested in changes in government that will affect them. The purpose of the scanning is to allow firms to plan and adapt to future changes (Choo, 2001). Private sector firms that are accustomed to

Environmental scanning: A process by which planners and managers look out at the environment to identify changes in environmental forces that will constrain agency goals, objectives, operations, and practices.

working in volatile markets scan their environments as a matter of routine. Public sector executives have been accustomed to functioning in stable environments and do not have a history of systematic environmental scanning (Babalhavaeji and Farhadpoor, 2013). Hence criminal justice administrators have been left to react to changes that—as we have seen—are sometimes obvious.

Our previous discussion of the impact that emptying mental institutions has had on the corrections system is an example of a change that could have been predicted and planned for. However, planned change is easier to write about than to implement. Although an organization may be able to readily predict future demands on the system, support from the organization's members or the formal or informal political systems may not be sufficient to provide it with enough momentum to reallocate resources, change philosophies or policies, or remove the impediments to change.

During the late 1970s and early 1980s, for example, many public and political figures predicted that the prisons would become overcrowded and argued for facility construction. In fact, a bond issue to build more prisons was put on the ballot in Michigan in 1981. Despite support from the state attorney general, the bond issue failed. Seven years later, overcrowding was a reality rather than a predicted possibility, and prisons were being built at a rapid rate. The uncontrolled influx of offenders from the environment overpowered the environmental forces that resisted the construction of new facilities. Change in this case was reactive rather than managed through planning and was created by environmental conditions beyond the control of the corrections system.

We will not provide a set of ready-made procedures that a criminal justice agency administrator can apply in dealing with environmental pressures. (These issues will be examined in some detail in Chapter 14, which discusses change and planned change.) However, we can offer some general prescriptions. Most important, administrators of criminal justice agencies should avoid believing they work in a closed, or rational, system. Enforcing laws, being encumbered by written policies and procedures, working within a classic chain of command, and wearing uniforms and badges can contribute to the myth that criminal justice stands aloof from environmental pressures and its boundaries are sacred. But administrators must interact with agency environments whether or not they accept that reality, and they must be prepared to protect the agency from capricious or disabling inputs while staying responsive to legitimate demands. They must be able to interpret legitimate environmental demands to their organization's members and attempt to adapt to these demands in a systematic way. Ultimately, criminal justice organizations receive their mandates, authority, and resources as inputs from the environment. Judgments on the performance and effectiveness of criminal justice agencies and practitioners will ultimately be made by the broad and conflicting range of the constituencies they serve.

Case Study: CLIMATE CHANGE

You are the police chief of a city with about a million inhabitants on the east coast of Florida. The changing climate and the resulting rise of the sea level, as well as recent weather events, have caused the local leaders and governmental officials to consider building dikes and sea walls along particular sections of the beach to prevent beach erosion and destruction of oceanfront property. Along with the sea wall and dikes, officials have considered plans to dredge an inlet presently used for recreational boating and fishing to build a major seaport for cruise ships and ocean-going freighters. Private investment will be sought to build hotels and other commercial properties within the new seaport. Sand from the dredging would be used to replenish the eroding beaches. The rising sea levels and building the sea wall, dikes, and commercial port would eliminate many current roads and require building new roads to accommodate the structural changes. To obtain property for the projects, the city will have to use the process of eminent domain. According to the plan, around 1,000 low-income homes will have to be razed to allow the building of the seaport. The residents of those homes will have to be relocated. To finance the major changes, property and sales taxes for city residents also would have to be raised.

In addition to eroding beaches and oceanfront property, rising sea levels also will contaminate local water tables. Hence, the supply of water for household and commercial use may be reduced. Water use for farms that surround the city also may become scarce. Also, the changing climate will cause the winter dry season to be longer and more severe. The rainy season is predicted to be shorter, but it will have a higher number of severe rainstorms with high winds causing damage and possibly more severe local flooding.

The land contiguous to the city is owned by the local Seminole tribe and is part of their reservation. The tribe stated that they would build a casino if the city followed through with its plans to build the oceanport. But the tribe would only do this if the city promised to build a four-lane highway from the downtown area to the casino.

CASE STUDY QUESTIONS

1. Make two lists and identify the issues in the scenario that will affect the criminal justice system and the police directly and indirectly. Exhaust all possibilities.
2. Cross-check your answer to question one by making two more lists: How will the criminal justice system be affected by climate change and the planned changes?
3. What are the major threats and opportunities for the police department that will result from the changing climate and planned changes?
4. Given the effect the changes will have on the criminal justice system, what steps must your police department take to deal with the changes?

Think like an Administrator

For this exercise, take the role of the planner for the city police department of a large Midwestern city with a diminishing industrial base. Crime rates have remained stable for the last several years but the unemployment rate keeps creeping up. You recently read a report by a local prominent economist. The economist claims that the structure of the regional economy has changed and predicts that the national unemployment rate will fall to 6.5 percent in the near future, but the unemployment rate in the region for individuals under 30 will rise to 15 percent. Furthermore, the economist says the unemployment rate for young urban minorities will increase from the present 18 percent to as high as 30 percent by 2020. As the city planner, you need to predict within reasonable limits how your police department will be affected by the increase in unemployment rates

---

THINK LIKE AN ADMINISTRATOR—continued

among individuals under 30 and how the department should respond to the social and political effects of this economic shift. (Have fun speculating about the questions.)

1. How will you verify the prominent economist's predictions?
2. To what extent will the predicted increases in the unemployment rate for people under 30 affect crime rates?
3. Will the increase in unemployment rates for young people impact local incarceration rates?
4. Will the quality or crime types change, for example, will drug sales, food stamp fraud, and interpersonal violence increase?
5. How will the increase in the unemployment rates affect private capital investments in the region? How, in turn, will a change in capital investments affect unemployment rates and crime?
6. Consider how the high unemployment rates will affect local and state government policy decisions.
7. To what extent will the regional political climate change?
8. To what extent will social and political activities change in your community? For example, will protests similar to the occupy marches on Wall Street occur?
9. Identify other forces in the city's environment that will be affected by the increase in unemployment rates.
10. Put it all together: How will the changing forces in the environment affect your police department, and what plans will you propose for the new challenges?

FOR DISCUSSION

1. Identify the changes that have been imposed on law enforcement agencies as a result of the "war on terror." Go to the Department of Homeland Security's web site home page and see if you can find recommendations for local law enforcement on antiterrorism strategies.

2. In your opinion, to what extent has the "war on terror" impacted local law enforcement practices? What is your reasoning?

3. Identify the economic/political forces that limit the ability of federal agencies to enforce immigration laws.

4. Identify future environmental changes that will affect the criminal justice system.

FOR FURTHER READING

Grau, J. "Technology and Criminal Justice." In *Vision for Change*, edited by R. Muraskint and A. Brooks, pp. 231-247. New York: Prentice Hall, 1999.

Mays, G. L., and Gray, T. (Eds.). *Privatization and the Provision of Correctional Services*. Cincinnati, OH: Anderson Publishing, 1996.

Olsen, M. *The Logic of Collective Action: Public Goods and the Theory of Groups*. Cambridge, MA: Harvard University Press, 1973.

Rourke, F. *Bureaucracy, Politics, and Public Policy*. Boston: Little, Brown, 1976.

Thompson, J. *Organizations in Action*. New York: McGraw-Hill, 1967.

White, J. *Terrorism and Homeland Security*. Belmont, CA: Thomson Learning, 2006.

Part II

Individuals in Criminal Justice Organizations

C riminal justice administrators lead and manage people. Organizations are collections of individuals. It is difficult to get diverse individuals to agree on organizational purposes and the methods to achieve them. This part of the book examines individuals in criminal justice organizations.

Communications are at the root of all interaction in criminal justice organizations. Chapter 4 offers a fundamental way to understand the communications process within and across criminal justice organizations. Communications is a subtle process, oftentimes nuanced and difficult to understand, yet effective communication is essential within criminal justice organizations.

Chapter 5 examines an equally elusive concept: motivation. Motivation is hard to define and even more difficult to accomplish due to the diversity of employees and the differing levels of individual expectations found among them. Anyone who says they know how to motivate people should be viewed with some circumspection. Motivation, as both an outcome and a process, is an ongoing effort for criminal justice administrators.

Job design is the responsibility of criminal justice administrators. How do we design criminal justice positions to achieve our diverse purposes? Chapter 6 addresses this difficult question. This chapter suggests that we can never lose sight of our purposes when designing positions within criminal justice agencies.

Chapter 7 tackles the thorny issue of leadership in criminal justice organizations. The complexity of leadership must be examined within the intricacies of employees and their interests. Some have suggested effective leadership is almost impossible to define, yet solid leadership prescriptions do exist, and we can distinguish good leaders from bad leaders.

Personnel evaluation and supervision are examined in Chapter 8. The chapter offers ways to examine personnel evaluation and supervision within criminal justice organizations. Models of employee evaluation must be understood within the context of goals and objectives being pursued. Chapter 8 is not a "how-to-evaluate-employees" chapter. It is more about placing employee evaluation and supervision within the context of larger organizational purposes and goals.

CHAPTER 4

Problems of Communication

Basic Theory of Communication
Communication Process
Nine Barriers to Communication

Communication in Organizations
Chain of Command
Informal Communication
Organizational Rules for Communication
Informal Communication
Networks
Nonverbal Communication
Information and Communication

Communication Roles for Criminal Justice Practitioners
Communication Barriers

Developing Informal Communication Networks
Exchange Theory

Work Perspective: Interorganizational Communication Goes Lacking
The Linking Pin and Communication

Implications for Criminal Justice Managers
Communication with the Environment

LEARNING OBJECTIVES

After reading this chapter, the students will have achieved the following objectives:

- Know the five steps of the communication process.

- Be familiar with the nine barriers to communications.

- Understand how communication and information flow through an agency's chain of command.

- Understand informal communication networks in the workplace.

- Understand nonverbal communication.

- Understand the difference between communication and information.

- Understand exchange theory and exchange networks.

- Define linking pin theory.

VIGNETTE

My undergraduate economics professor wrote a book recently on his academic and personal experiences. He made mention of two of his more interesting students who happened to be me and a close friend of mine. His comments speak to the issue of diversity and communication:

"Both were kids from Cleveland and had Polish thick in their blood. If one listened to one of these students carelessly and heard only his accent and not his word choice and what he said, he sounded as if he had been admitted by mistake. He won the freshman writing prize; hence, he was a good writer. The other went on to earn a PhD in economics and surprised me by sending me a copy of a book he had written" (Landreth, 2012, p. 39).

My friend and I were students at Miami University of Ohio in the late 1950s and early 1960s. Dr. Harry Landreth, our Harvard-trained economics professor, had the ability to listen beyond our guttural Slavic, Cleveland, Ohio, accents and hear what we were saying. Not all listeners can get past the barrier of a regional or ethnic-based speaking accent. Conventional wisdom during that time period held that our country was a "melting pot" that would continuously homogenize all citizens into common values and a common spoken language. Civil rights for African-Americans were being discussed then, but the current notion of diversity—a nation of multiple cultures and languages—was not on anyone's radar.

Things have changed dramatically over the last few decades. We recognize diversity and systematically try not to discriminate against anyone because of their ethnicity or gender. Decades of immigration and relative differences in birthrates between ethnic groups have changed the demographic makeup of our Nation. Some demographers believe that by 2050, most Americans will be from Hispanic backgrounds and African Americans will represent about 20 percent of the population. Some areas like the Midwest remain predominantly white, but a number of communities throughout the country are profoundly diverse. In my community, Delray Beach, Florida, for example, we have Caucasians, Hispanics, a large Haitian community, and a growing number of Asians. Moreover, English is a second language for most of our community's Haitian, Hispanic, and Asian citizens. This mixed demographic with English as a second language is the rule for most southeastern, southern, and southwestern states as well as New York City, perhaps the most ethnically diverse city in the country.

The diversity we are experiencing and growing number of American citizens for whom English is their second language creates a communication problem. Hence, when we call most businesses of any size or governmental offices, the phone system directs us to press 1 for English and 2 for Spanish—and in some places, 3 for Haitians, and 4 for Asians. Some people find this annoying. But businesses that don't accommodate non-English-speaking customers are not competitive. Many cities in South Florida attempt to hire police officers who are from multiple ethnic groups in the community. It is reasoned, for example, that Haitian American police officers will better understand and communicate with the city's Haitian population. While it probably it is wise to have a police force that is representative of a city's ethnic makeup, unintended issues with communication within diverse departments will exist.

Yong (2013) discusses stereotype traps individuals fall into based on their own negative feelings about their primary reference group—ethnicity/gender, and so forth—and feelings of others. "I am a woman, women are not good at math, and therefore I will do poorly on a math test" is one example. The anxiety that comes from being caught in the stereotype trap tends to limit academic success. Dr. Landreth, my economics professor, was able to avoid the stereotype trap and listened to my friend and me and heard what we were saying. English is our dominant language, all reports in criminal justice agencies are written in English, and good grammar and spelling are required. But during formal and informal verbal exchanges among staff, listeners may not be able to hear past the ethnic or regional dialect of minority organizational member; hence, communication will be hampered.

Communication is the exchange of information between a sender and receiver that delivers meaning between the parties involved (Bowditch and Buono, 1997). From an organizational perspective, communication is the glue that holds a system together. Karl Weick (1979) describes the organizational process as a method to resolve ambiguities through the collective processing of information. The typical organization—private firm, federal regulatory agency, police, court system, or corrections agency—is structured in some logical way. To function effectively and meet its goals, the individuals in an organization must establish a system of communication along with a language that permits an understanding of the system's processes and logic (Schein, 2004). Consider also the extent of communication that goes on in the workplace. Throughout the day, memoranda and e-mail messages abound as well as constant face-to-face conversations. In addition, staff attends formal meetings and they meet informally at the "water cooler." Staff can communicate with text messages or through personal or business phones. Communication is an endless stream of messages, and all the information is difficult to harness and manage.

But whether or not the organization functions logically, in a coordinated manner, and achieves its goals depends greatly on the quality of its communication—its ability to process information. Hence, all members of an organization are directed to communicate along certain pathways and, within certain limits, to facilitate coordination among members and among components of the organization. Most, if not all, organizational members understand the importance of communication.

Poor communication, however, is often blamed for problems that occur within an organization. For example, when subordinates disobey directives and are difficult to control, managers often assume that communication is faulty rather than examining more fundamental issues, such as the applicability of directives or the willingness of subordinates to follow orders. The pivotal question here is what we mean by poor communication or, for that matter, communication itself. Communication impacts and is scripted by an organization's environmental forces, formal structure, human interactions between its members and clients, and organizational politics, as well as by the theater, rich with symbols and self-expression, in which organizational members play out their roles (Bolman and Deal, 2003). In complex organizations, poor communication in the theater of human dialogue carries implications far beyond a poorly worded memo or a broken fax machine—although all three contribute to poor communications. Identifying an organizational breakdown as a function of faulty communication is often a convenient solution for problems but is typically only the tip of the proverbial iceberg.

The basic element of communication is a *dyad*: two individuals **transmitting** symbols back and forth or, more simply, two people communicating. Dyads may range from intimate to professional to ad hoc (Kinicki and Kreitner, 2006; Trenholm and Jensen, 1992). To understand the complexity of communication within organizations, we can think of an infinite number of interchangeable dyads attempting to process information using an infinite number of symbols through a number of charted and uncharted pathways and over a number of identifiable and invisible hurdles.

This chapter is an attempt to identify and discuss briefly the complex strands of communication in the criminal justice system. We begin with a description of the basic dyad and discuss briefly the hurdles and pathways faced by actors playing a role in the criminal justice system. We also apply the basic theories of communication to individual practitioners in the criminal justice system, considering the unique and varied interactions they routinely perform. We conclude with prescriptions for criminal justice administrators, advising our readers not to view communication as a phenomenon separable from an organization's formal and informal structures and its culture. Communication dyads dance in a complex and changing community.

Transmitting: Sender conveys his or her message through a medium, for example, the sender makes a phone call.

BASIC THEORY OF COMMUNICATION

Interpersonal communication begins with a basic dyad—one individual sending a message to another. Communication between two people can be thought of as a sequential process, with Person A encoding a message and then transmitting it through some medium, after which the message is received by Person B and decoded. If a message sent from Person A fails to get to Person B, no communication has taken place.

Communication Process

Encoding is the first step in the communication process. The sender feels the need to convey a message to another individual or individuals and encodes the meaning of the message into symbols. Words are the most familiar symbolic form to us, although communication with nonverbal symbols—Morse code flag signals, codes used by police dispatchers to briefly describe situations or orders—is also common.

The sender's thoughts and meaning must be encoded into some verbal or nonverbal symbolic form before the message can be transmitted. The next step in the process is to transmit the message through a medium the sender selects. The intended receiver of the message must then receive the message and **decode** it—the receiver interprets the symbols conveyed in the message and gives them meaning. If the communication flows both ways, the receiver responds to the message with communication back to the sender, who now becomes the receiver. The completion of the dyad requires observation by the receiver, intention to communicate by the sender, and normative

Encoding: A sent message using appropriate symbols.

Decode: The receiver of a message interprets and determines its meaning.

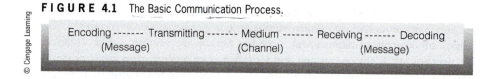

FIGURE 4.1   The Basic Communication Process.

Encoding ------- Transmitting ------- Medium ------- Receiving ------- Decoding
(Message)   (Channel)   (Message)

judgment on the part of the sender and receiver (Littlejohn and Foss, 2005). Figure 4.1 shows the basic dyad interaction.

Nine Barriers to Communication

Although this process seems straightforward and reliable, we all know from personal experience that simple messages between two individuals are often not communicated effectively. The communication process is frequently unreliable for a number of reasons. Senders may not formulate their meaning properly in symbols that can be transmitted to the receiver. Stated simply, one must say what one intends to say. Assuming the sender has encoded and transmitted the message to the receiver with some accuracy, a series of communication barriers may intervene to block the communication or alter the meaning of the message. These include the following:

1. Preconceived ideas
2. Denial of contrary information
3. Use of personalized meanings
4. Lack of motivation or interest
5. Noncredibility of the source
6. Lack of communication skills
7. Poor organizational climate
8. Use of complex channels
9. Communication gap

Preconceived ideas:
Receiver hears what he or she wants to hear.

Preconceived Ideas   "People hear what they want to hear" best describes the phenomenon of **preconceived ideas**. If we have a preconceived idea about the information transmitted to us, we tend to receive and understand the message as that idea. Because conflict and mistrust between inmates and corrections officers are often based upon the stereotypical views each group holds toward the other (Kagehiro and Werner, 1981), it is not uncommon for corrections officers to encode their views inaccurately. A similar impediment to communication may exist between community police officers and residents of low-income communities (Carlson, 2005; Schneider, 1999).

Denial of Contrary Information   Messages that conflict with information we have already accepted as valid are often denied or rejected. After assessing the message, we may reject information about the stock market based on prior information. This is a prudent or rational communication decision. However, the message may conflict with our personal beliefs or values, in which case we reject it or deny its validity without any deliberation or thought. This **denial of contrary information** process, known as cognitive dissonance in the psychology literature, is the kind of denial of information that creates a communication barrier. Denial is also a common problem faced in rehabilitating offenders. Social-skills training, of which communication is a significant part, is considered therapeutic for young adult and juvenile offenders. Henderson and Hollin (1983) suggest improvement of such skills, including communication skills, will improve offenders' ability to overcome denial and adjust to their environments. Moreover, the denial of contrary information is a major impediment to interpersonal communication and communication competence (Sypher and Zorn 1986).

Use of Personalized Meanings The words chosen by the sender and his or her **use of personalized meanings** may have a different meaning for the message receiver. Professional jargon or legal terminology may have little, no, or a different meaning to those outside the profession or legal system. Words and sentences that convey images of pleasure for one party may convey contrary images for another. A young person may refer to an experience with enthusiasm and say it was "really bad," meaning it was very good. Guilt is based on fact in the criminal justice system, but in psychiatry it depends on the state of one's conscience. Cultural differences between ethnic and gender groups may also affect personalized meanings (Madera 2011).

Lack of Motivation or Interest Motivation in communicating and interest in the message must exist for both the sender and receiver, at least to some reasonable extent, if a message is to be communicated effectively and to avoid **lack of motivation or interest**. Memo writing in organizations is a standard method of communication. However, if memoranda become excessive, personnel may lose interest in spending time reading them. If such a situation exists, a motivated communicator may supplement memos with a fresh or unique medium to get the attention of receivers.

Noncredibility of the Source The sender of a message may not be believable for a number of reasons. **Noncredibility of the source** is present when individuals have given out inaccurate information in the past. Individuals who have a history of providing reliable information are considered highly credible senders of messages and get the attention of prospective receivers. Individuals with relatively greater status in an organization have more credibility than those with little or no status.

Lack of Communication Skills Poor or a **lack of communication skills** can be attributed to an individual's lack of proper training, educational level, experience, and cognitive capacity, as well as personality traits. Practitioners in the field of criminal justice must master the art of receiving, collecting, recording, and disseminating information. This can be accomplished

Denial of contrary information: Rejecting a message that conflicts with our personal beliefs.

Use of personalized meanings: The words chosen by the sender may have a different meaning for the message receiver.

Lack of motivation or interest: Interest in the message or motivation to receive the message must be present to create a successful communication process.

Noncredibility of the source: A sender who is not believable.

Lack of communication skills: Lacking the ability to encode or decode messages, such as poor speaking, listening, or writing skills.

through formal education, academy training, and experience throughout the practitioner's career. A "streetwise" education also is important for developing a full range of communication skills. It is necessary to understand street language and even be fluent in it to achieve maximum delivery of services to clients and the public.

In our changing society, with its influx of legal and illegal immigrants, language barriers often exist between members of a community and governmental agencies. South Florida, Arizona, and California are examples of areas where English is not the first language for many members of society and is not spoken well by many. Also, the rise of diversity in our nation has dramatically increased the numbers of women and minority members of criminal justice agencies. The slight differences in language presentation and levels of sensitivity between ethnic and gender groups can also affect communication skills and become communication barriers on their own (Madera, 2011).

Poor organizational climate: An organization or social system that discourages or impedes communication.

Poor Organizational Climate   An organization that promotes openness and trust among its members encourages active communication. Typically, organizations that decentralize decision making include subordinates in higher-order policy decisions and foster risk taking in their members. These strategies will foster a favorable communication climate. Highly formal organizations may discourage all but formal and approved communications among their members, which can result in a **poor organizational climate**. An insistence on formality often promotes an active, informal grapevine that often creates a suitable climate for gossip. Here again, the complexity of verbal and nonverbal communication across ethnic and gender lines can affect the receptiveness of communications and hence the climate.

Use of complex channels: The more gates a message passes through, the more complex the channels.

Use of Complex Channels   The more gates through which communication must pass—the **use of complex channels**—makes it more likely that the message will pass slowly and be altered. The highly complex channels of communication characteristic of large, complex organizations make communicating inefficient and ineffective. Such organizations tend to create red tape and usually become rigid because important information cannot be transmitted readily from clients or to policymakers.

Communication gap: The difference between the message the sender intended to communicate and what the receiver understands the message to be.

Communication Gap   These barriers to communication can create a **communication gap**: the difference between the message the sender intended to communicate and what the receiver understands the message to be. The existence of a communication gap between individuals in an organization becomes an organizational problem that impedes effective management and operations.

COMMUNICATION IN ORGANIZATIONS

As the discussion of barriers to communication illustrates, simple messages between individuals can be inadvertently filtered or even lost. Moreover, when the individual is a sender or receiver within an organization, additional factors—

organizational climate and complexity of communication channels—can make the communication process even more difficult. Both the formal organizational structure—the chain of command and hierarchy—and the informal social system within the organization affect the organizational climate and the complexity of communication channels.

Chain of Command

Scholars concerned with organizational behavior have pointed out that the innate weakness of the communication process in a large bureaucracy can lead to a weakening of administrative power or to leakage of authority. Downs (1967) describes this phenomenon in depth. Almost all current public administration and management books, especially those written by so-called postmodernists (Miller and Fox, 2006), also raise this issue when discussing communication in organizations. This conclusion is somewhat ironic because the traditional chain of command provides a clear set of communication paths for its members. An agency's policies and procedures, as well as traditionally accepted practices, direct members' official communications rather explicitly. Directives from top management are usually sent down through the chain of command, and subordinates are routinely required to report to superiors. However, each level of a chain of command through which messages must pass can filter and alter information. Each level in a typical agency's hierarchy thus becomes a gate that imposes control over the communication flow.

Messages can be filtered intentionally or unintentionally. Subordinates can intentionally avoid putting forward information that will make them look inept; similarly, supervisors can avoid communicating directives to subordinates that they feel will create problems in productivity or lower their status. Messages may be filtered unintentionally as they pass through the chain of command because of common communication barriers. Memos sent upward or downward through the chain of command may stack up on the desk of a middle manager. Thus, individual efforts at affecting official communication through formal channels can be a challenge rather than a matter of routine.

Kreps (1990) summarizes the process, advantages, and problems of the hierarchical flow of information. *Downward communication* allows executives a clear path to send information downward. It gives organizational members job-related information, job performance review, and indoctrination in recognizing and implementing organizational goals. *Upward communication* provides managers with their primary source of feedback, allows lower-level staff to share information with managers, and can encourage employee participation. Both types of communication, however, have their drawbacks. Downward communication tends to be overused; it is often unclear and can communicate superiors' lack of regard for subordinates. Superiors also tend to distribute contrary and conflicting messages to line personnel. Upward communication by subordinates can also be problematic. It may be risky for subordinates to be truthful with superiors because bosses may not be receptive to criticism. Upward channels of communication are also typically not sufficient to carry messages from all subordinates up the funnel of the hierarchy. We can see how easily the chain of command can break down in terms of communication. For organizations that depend on the chain of command as the backbone of their structure, a breakdown in that chain of command will weaken the effectiveness of management (Dias and Vaughn, 2006).

Horizontal communication among organizational members at the same level can facilitate task coordination, provide a means of sharing information, provide a formal channel of communication for problem solving, and facilitate mutual support for staff involved. Excessive reliance on horizontal communication can also isolate groups from the hierarchy.

Informal Communication

Because it is cumbersome, the flow of information through formal channels gives rise to the grapevine, or *informal communication*, because formal channels fail to provide an agency's members with sufficient information to satisfy their curiosity or needs. Moreover, literature on community policing shows the difficulty of maintaining hierarchal communication with the more organic structure of a community police division (Clarke, 2006), which gives rise to greater channels of informal communication. Formal organizational rules and hurdles do not encumber informal channels, but information is typically altered as it passes through the gatekeepers of the informal system. Organizational members who are privy to accurate information can derive power and informal leadership status. They can use the information for barter and to influence other organizational members. McCleary (1968), in his classic study, showed that the Hawaiian prison system lost control to younger inmates when older inmates who ran the institution lost their power after being denied access to information from the warden's office. The following sections in this chapter discuss networking, information exchange, and Likert's **linking pin** theory of organizational effectiveness (1967), all of which rely on informal channels of communication.

Linking pin: Individual who is a member of two or more work networks and who coordinates efforts among the work groups.

Organizational Rules for Communication

Every organization has a set of rules for communication that may be spelled out clearly in written policies and procedures. *Exclusionary rules* in criminal trials dictate the admission of evidence into court proceedings and prohibit the communication of evidence that has been obtained in ways that are considered illegal. In effect, this purposeful communication barrier sometimes creates a difference between "real" facts and "legal" facts—facts that can be presented in a court. Chapper (1983) suggests the efficiency of the civil appeals process could be increased by changing the rules and requiring oral rather than written arguments in specific cases. Because the present format of instructions inadvertently restricts most juries by limiting their decision alternatives, Craig (1983) argues that juries can be more flexible in their findings if the instructions from the judge are altered so that juries have more discretion. Katzev and Wishart (1985) discuss methods of judicial instruction to jurors to avoid false testimony of eyewitnesses. The 9/11 Commission (2003) confronted well-vested organizational rules of intelligence agencies that prevented agencies from sharing information. Their recommendation strongly urged intelligence agencies to, in effect, change that traditional rule and share information to work together to confront the current terrorist threat.

In hierarchical organizations, subordinates are typically required to give particular information to their supervisors, and supervisors are expected to provide direct instruction and guidance to their subordinates. Routine reports that discuss production status, arrest rates, and violation of the rules by inmates are often required. Traditional practices can pass on unwritten rules. It is usually unacceptable for a supervisor to chastise a subordinate who is not directly under that supervisor. Standard courtesies, such as calling a superior by title, also fall into this category (Cushman and Whiting, 1972). In addition to well-established and explicit communication procedures and protocols, rules may be subtle and based on the organization's social system. "Informal rules that exist within the organization, e.g., rules governing when to meet face-to-face rather than send a memo, or which topics are appropriate and which are not" are far more common than formal rules (Farace, Monge, and Russell, 1977:134). Communication rules can be *content rules* that govern standard word usage or consensus on the name of a concept, or *procedural rules* that deal with the actual ways that interactions take place. New members of an organization typically learn communication rules through trial and error or informal training (Farace, Monge, and Russell, 1977). Failure to understand or conform to these rules impedes successful communication. In a complex system, such as the criminal justice system that comprises many interacting agencies and diverse work environments, members face a complicated and diverse set of communication rules (Littlejohn and Foss, 2005).

Informal Communication Networks

Networks are social structures that evolve by repeated communication among individuals and groups within organizations. Since organizational members communicate in patterns, clusters—or networks—of individuals begin to communicate with continued frequency (Littlejohn and Foss, 2005). Burt (2012) argues that information in organizations gets stuck or trapped within groups or silos, and individuals whose networks span the silos become network brokers and are rewarded socially and materially for brokering information. Every organization has its formal or official structure as well as its informal work groups. Each has its channels of communication, which overlap to some extent. The communication among individuals within and between the official and informal subsystems can be viewed as a communication network. A simple communication network is a social system created by communication between individuals interconnected by continuous patterns of communication (Hellriegel, Slocum, and Woodman, 1995; Stohl, 1995). Networks can be transitional or developed purposefully by organizations (Bolman and Deal, 2003) and are considered formal networks. Whether formal or informal, a communication network can be a production network, an innovation network, or a maintenance network through which members learn about social roles and power relationships and links between work groups (Book et al., 1980). Networks can also be formed and can function through computer communication (Brodeur and Dupont, 2006). Likert (1967), in his classic study of medical organizations, found that organizations with individuals who communicated across subgroups and thereby linked them together were highly productive.

Individuals may also be part of *kinship networks* within organizations. These social groups are formed more for personal than for professional motives and may not have much to do with the goals of their agency. Such networks, called "old-boy" groups, may be made up of old college friends or people with the same political views or other significant personal similarities (Book et al., 1980). Police and corrections officers often meet socially at a local tavern after their shifts. At these meetings, a great deal of discussion about work-related problems goes on and strengthens the bonds of the group. Entry into a kinship network is typically restricted, and it is difficult for an outsider to be a communicator within this type of network.

In a connected group of organizations like the criminal justice system, the basis for a kinship network can be the uniqueness of one's task role or the prescribed role of the agency itself. Each component of the criminal justice system has different roles: police fight crime; courts protect the rights of the accused and distribute justice; and corrections controls and treats offenders. These differing roles create commonalities for members of each agency. But within each agency, the role is further subdivided. Police do road patrol, walk beats, investigate crimes, and administer the agency. Officers who work on the streets have a great deal in common with each other and much less in common with administrators. Thus, kinship networks form within the criminal justice system as a natural consequence of its differing structures and functions in addition to those factors that typically help develop networks in the workplace. In response to the ongoing terrorist threat, Gil (2006) argues that security networks across agency boundaries should be actively constructed. Moreover, Lippert and O'Connor (2006) point out that private security agencies collect a vast amount of information, and networks between governmental and private intelligence agencies should be constructed. This is in effect what the 9/11 Commission (2003) has recommended.

Nonverbal Communication

Communication theorists consider nonverbal communication an extremely powerful part of the communication process for an organization and its individuals. Nonverbal codes are older, more trusted forms of communication; they are more emotionally powerful, express more universal meaning, and are continuous and natural. They express meaning in and of themselves, modify verbal messages, and regulate the flow of interaction (Trenholm and Jensen, 1992). Police investigators commonly interpret nonverbal communications when they interview and interrogate suspects (Waltman, 1983). However, verbal communication has been studied by scholars at far greater length than nonverbal communication and, as a result, our discussion of nonverbal communication will be brief.

Organizations do not evoke these types of nonverbal communications but, as a matter of course, evoke symbols that are meant to communicate meaning to the public. It is argued the public organizations are especially weak at designing and presenting visual communications such as photos that could capitalize on individuals' abilities to process visual information (Agrawala, Li, and Berthouzoz,

2012). Organizations may intentionally use nonverbal symbols to represent them. Capital punishment is a strikingly clear example of a stand-alone, nonverbal message sent to would-be perpetrators of certain crimes about the potential consequences; in effect, criminal deterrence is premised on the symbolic message evoked through punishment of the criminal offender. On a lower level, police officers wear distinct uniforms and carry guns to make an authoritative statement. Judges wear black robes and sit at an elevated bench to set them apart from and above everyone else involved in the process.

Nonverbal symbols evoked by individuals may stand on their own but are usually integrated with verbal messages. For individuals, nonverbal communication includes facial expressions, such as one's body posture during a conversation or interview, and touching techniques such as shaking hands and patting another on the back. Facial expressions may convey fear, friendship, or deceit. Eye contact is another nonverbal form of communication, the appropriateness of which is culturally based (Kinicki and Kreitner, 2006). Messages may also be conveyed through dress, hairstyle, tone of voice, or actions (Book et al., 1980). Reading nonverbal messages is an important part of interviews, interrogations, and even polygraph exams (Inbau, Reid, and Buckley, 1986). Again, using nonverbal messages that are congruent with verbal messages or the substance of the intended message is important for clear communication.

Nonverbal messages can be sent by one's actions or failure to act. Nonverbal behaviors of administrators may send messages that describe the agency, messages that may be congruent or incongruent with the organization's written or stated purposes or philosophy. Criminal justice administrators who give the appearance of being corrupt or inept may reduce the credibility of their agency's stated purposes. Internally, bosses who advocate participative management but pay no attention to feedback from subordinates send a nonverbal message that is incongruent with their stated message. Conversely, the recipient of nonverbal symbols needs to understand the sender's nonverbal repertoire to decode a message accurately. Limited understanding of nonverbal codes can thus pose an additional communication barrier. It is important to understand nonverbal communication for one to be an effective listener.

The use of memoranda, e-mail, phone contacts, texting, and so forth eliminates face-to-face communication and the visibility of nonverbal cues. Face-to-face conversation has likely dropped dramatically with the increased availability of such technology. But direct interpersonal communication remains the mainstream of human and organizational communication. Person-to-person discussions take place in structured settings, such as training sessions, staff meetings, roll call meetings, and so forth. However, most face-to-face communication takes place through continuous discussions throughout the workday between peers and immediate subordinates and superiors. Mengas and Martin (2008) suggest that face-to-face communication is central for passing and sharing organizational knowledge; however, most communication rules for face-to-face communication are implicit, making conversations highly flexible and creating a degree of chaos. To the extent this is true, understanding nonverbal cues becomes more crucial in promoting effective communication.

Information and Communication

The terms *communication* and *information* are often interchangeable. However, they are distinguishable concepts if we think of communication as the process of passing on information. In other words, information is the substance that we attempt to share through symbols in communication. Intelligence in policing and security is a form of information that is collected and communicated for law enforcement purposes (*Policing and Society*, 2006). Communication becomes, then, the exchange of symbols that represent the information. Borrowing freely from Farace, Monge, and Russell (1977), we will look briefly at the relationship between information and communication, considering such factors as communication load; absolute versus **distributed information**; and environmental, motivational, and instructional information.

Communication Load   **Communication load** is the rate and complexity of communication inputs to an individual. Rate is the number of pieces of information that are received and resolved per time period. Complexity is the number of judgments that must be made or factors that must be taken into account while communicating. *Overload* occurs when the flow of messages exceeds an individual's or system's capacity to process them. Brodeur and Dupont (2006) suggest that the amount of data police deal with may be overwhelming. Further, the intake of information will increase exponentially in the future and cause a classic information overload. In addition, the efficiency and speed of communication have improved exponentially with computerized information systems, and the distance we can now communicate has become almost unlimited. However, the amount and speed of information we can transmit can cause serious information-overload problems.

There are three major determinants of load for an individual or system. First is the environment. A stable and predictable environment provides a less complex set of messages than does an unstable environment. In addition, the extent to which a person or system depends on elements in the environment affects the input of messages. In intelligence work, information flows from a number of sources, including informants who may not be reliable (Brodeur and Dupont, 2006). Second, the capacity of the individual or system to assimilate messages plays a key role in determining overload. Third, the individual's or system's desire for information affects information load. Computer technology can greatly increase the criminal justice system's capability to collect and store information, thereby expanding the communication load at the input end (Hinduja, 2006). However, because the ability to process and utilize the information is a function of organizational intellect, not of computer technology, an information overload may be created.

These three determinants of communication load affect the management of information and communication within an organization. Criminal justice agencies, structured along traditional bureaucratic lines, provide stable working environments even though a great deal of uncertainty exists within those environments. At the same time, limited resources and old habits help keep criminal justice agencies from being able to process information efficiently.

Distributed information: An idea, data, or information that is distributed throughout a system.

Communication load: Rate and complexity of communication inputs.

Absolute vs. Distributed Information   Absolute information is an idea or piece of knowledge expressed in recognized symbolic terms. *Distributed information* is an idea or piece of knowledge that is dispersed throughout a system: "What is known in an organization and who knows it are obviously very important in determining the overall function of an organization" (Farace, Monge, and Russell, 1977:27). In criminal justice organizations, information is often tucked nicely into a policy and procedures manual that no one reads. As we have seen from the 9/11 Commission Report (2003), information is often kept within the boundaries of an intelligence agency and not distributed. The rationale for training is, in part, to assure the distribution of absolute information.

Absolute information: An idea, data, or information expressed in a recognizable symbol.

Forms of Information   Information takes on three forms that are important for the well-being of an organization or its members. First, information can be environmental—that is, it describes the environment that surrounds the organization or its members; recipients of the communication are getting information that describes actions, events, constraints, or processes in the world in which the individuals exist. Corrections officers are instructed that inmates must be given due process before being punished for an infraction of a prison rule. Lawyers, judges, and prosecuting attorneys often learn the rules of their environment from information they get as a result of practice and experience.

Second, motivational communications provide information about organizational or personal goals or values. Corrections officers may dislike the fact that inmates must have a hearing before they can be punished for violating a prison rule. Therefore, officers must be told that they will be held accountable for punishing inmates without giving them the benefit of a hearing. Or they may be sold the idea that giving inmates a hearing will increase the system's credibility with inmates and make their job easier. Community police officers may get information about the social good and intrinsic rewards that will result from their efforts. Motivating listeners in education and training is important because interest in materials presented and retaining the information are related (Mazer, 2013).

Third, instructional information, or communication, tells individuals how to proceed or what course of action to take to reach a goal. Continuing with our example, corrections officers must receive instructions about how a hearing will proceed and what their role is in it. Police must learn about procedural law in order to bring a case to trial. Judges learn—and relearn—the rules that apply to court proceedings. Simply stated, individuals in an organization must be provided with information about the environment, expectations, and how to perform their roles in it. Cogent communication on these three topics is, therefore, the most basic step of policy and program implementation and the basis of training in organizations.

COMMUNICATION ROLES FOR CRIMINAL JUSTICE PRACTITIONERS

In this section, we briefly discuss communication networks in the criminal justice system. A network is a group of individuals who are connected over some time period by purposeful communication that is common to all members. A network is dynamic rather than static because members may enter or leave the network system.

Corrections officers in a large prison may be part of four or five networks simultaneously. They are part of the formal network—the chain of command—by decree. Also, as the literature has established, experienced officers build working relationships with older stable inmate leaders (Stinchcomb, 2005). Because of the high turnover rate, corrections officers who remain for any length of time probably have formed an old-boy network that includes both officers and inmate leaders. Officers may also be active union members, thus making up a part of that network. An officer respected by the administrative staff may further be a member of the organization's dominant coalition. These networks are not mutually exclusive but they overlap. Where these subsets of networks merge, another network is created with membership from all subsets.

We do not wish to imply that corrections officers are the only focal point of networking in a corrections system. Middle managers may network with those above and below them in the agency's hierarchy. Top managers may network with community members or political figures. Figure 4.2 diagrams the interlocking of the networks just described. Current proposals argue that networks need to be built among intelligence agencies (Brodeur and Dupont, 2006) and between private security firms and public intelligence agencies (Gil, 2006). The street police officer may be the focal point of an even more diverse subset of networks (Gaines et al., 2003); Figure 4.3 explores the possible links. Prosecuting attorneys may be the focus of the network shown in Figure 4.4. To meet the

FIGURE 4.2   Multiple Networks for Prison Corrections Officers.

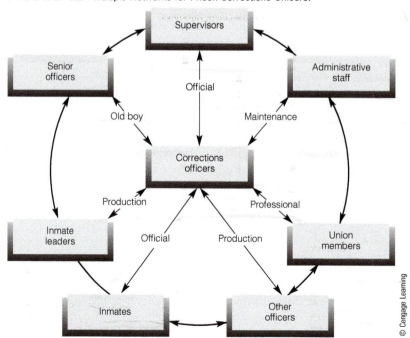

© Cengage Learning

FIGURE 4.3 Multiple Networks for Line Police Officers.

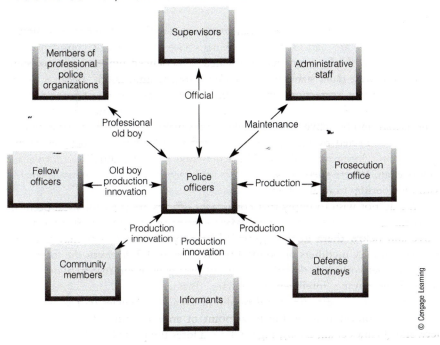

FIGURE 4.4 Multiple Networks for Prosecuting Attorneys.

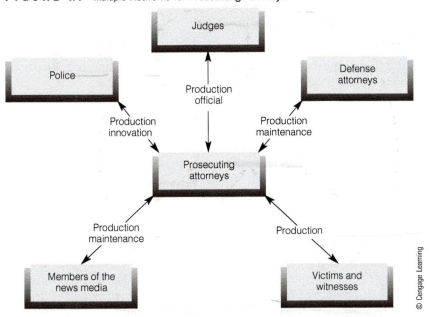

FIGURE 4.5   Multiple Networks for Local and County Jail Administrators.

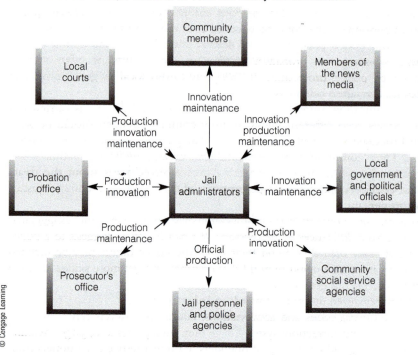

© Cengage Learning

demands of managing a modern jail, administrators may attempt to build a network that includes jail personnel, local courts, probation departments, police agencies, and community social service agencies, as well as key members of the community. Figure 4.5 depicts such a network. We could continue to design hypothetical networks within and across criminal justice agencies, as well as networks that link members of criminal justice systems to exogenous political forces, community members, and public and private agencies.

Both formal and informal communication networks must focus ultimately on results and productivity for efficient operations. However, rather than nurturing productive informal networks, bureaucracies expend resources to thwart their development in an effort to protect hierarchical authority. Such quasi-military efforts are naive and counterproductive. Concepts such as team policing are implicitly based on networking, but agencies put little effort into the development of informal networks with such a focus.

Barriers to communication:

Personal, psychological, or emotional conditions of a receiver of communication that prevent him or her from decoding the message accurately.

Communication Barriers

More pronounced **communication barriers** exist in the criminal justice system than in other systems because criminal justice historically has been organized so that its agencies check and balance each other. In theory, police arrest offenders whom they view as probably guilty, whereas the court system assumes the offender innocent until proven guilty. Although plea bargaining makes this proposition questionable, conflicts in roles and priorities do exist between police and court personnel. The conflicts become even more pronounced in the interactions among police, prosecutors, and defense attorneys. The murky role of corrections, including the probation systems of local courts, is often viewed negatively by police, prosecuting attorneys, and even local judges as providing services for convicted offenders.

Communication among criminal justice agencies, in short, is carried out by individuals with different views on how criminal offenders should be treated and processed, as well as on the role and purpose of the criminal justice system. Thus, communication networks that include individuals from different agencies must begin by overcoming preconceived ideas about the treatment of offenders and different perceptions of the role of the criminal justice system in general.

We can see how other communication barriers can become exaggerated because of basic differences in perceptions. If a parole officer suggests to a police officer that many offenders mend their ways, the police officer may be inclined to deny this information and respond that criminals just get more skilled at crime and therefore do not get caught.

The personalized meaning of words and phrases varies from agency to agency. Police have official codes and abbreviations; courts and lawyers rely heavily on legal language; and corrections systems have their own professional jargon relating to the sentencing and processing of offenders. Criminal justice practitioners from any agency should learn the unique languages of other agencies and know how to use them in the proper context for good communication to take place.

At the official level, the motivation for and interest in communicating certain information from one criminal justice agency to another may vary greatly. Police provide evidence on a case to the prosecutor, and after conviction both agencies pass that information on to the corrections system. But they are often reluctant to pass information on to other criminal justice agencies. The police are not open with defense attorneys about a case; defense attorneys by oath do not provide information about a criminal defendant that will harm the defendant; corrections agencies are often reluctant to open their files to police agencies, fearing police will use the information to the detriment of a corrections client. In addition, police agencies with similar functions in the same jurisdiction may not be willing to share information because they view themselves as competitors. Thus, agencies are motivated to conceal information because of their conflicting perceptions of the functions of the criminal justice system. As we see later, however, information is often readily exchanged among agencies and individual practitioners if they are members of networks based on an exchange model. This model provides incentives to trade information that ordinarily might be withheld.

It is easy to understand how the conflicting roles of criminal justice agencies and the differing perceptions of their practitioners can create an organizational climate that is not conducive to ongoing and open communication. Clearly, the credibility of a communicator from another agency or even within one's own agency can be suspect, and therefore trust and some degree of confidentiality are required for an organization to function (Brodeur and Dupont, 2006). Another mitigating factor is the complexity of formal communication channels in the criminal justice system. Large criminal justice organizations and their component agencies have many hierarchical levels, many specialized subunits, and much isolation of members from one another. Channels of communication in such an organization will be much more complex than those in a smaller criminal justice organization.

Besides communicating with others in the criminal justice system, practitioners may come into contact with victims, suspected or convicted offenders, witnesses, members of public interest groups, news media representatives, employees of public social service agencies and private security companies, and even elected officials. These individuals have differing values, nonverbal codes, subgroup languages with personalized meanings, motivations for and degrees of interest in entering into communication, and communication rules and styles. Barriers to communication will be different for each set of individuals the criminal justice practitioner must deal with, and these barriers can confound the communication process with harsh regularity.

DEVELOPING INFORMAL COMMUNICATION NETWORKS

We have suggested that communication networks are important for efficient and effective operations in criminal justice agencies. Informal networks within and among agencies evolve in the search for efficient methods to achieve the goals of the system. These networks are often based on one of two principles: exchange theory or linking pins.

Exchange Theory

The basis of *exchange theory* is relatively simple: Worker A assists Worker B, and B pays for the assistance by helping A in some way. This shared assistance may be in the form of effort or labor, but typically it is information or help in cutting bureaucratic red tape. The exchange is based on bargaining among practitioners in the criminal justice system over time and is a product of the social system in which it functions (Marsden, 1981). Exchanges may be random or *ad hoc*. It is common, however, for exchange systems to be somewhat stable and to include a cadre of participants who link up with peripheral members when appropriate.

Exchange networks exist for several reasons. First, large bureaucratic systems tend to pass on work and information slowly, requiring a relatively high number of transactions. By forming exchange networks that circumvent the formal structure, workers can economize on effort, time, and resources by cutting down the number of transactions (Williamson, 1981). In effect, through exchange systems, the work of the organization can be done with relative efficiency.

Second, the rules that govern practitioners' work efforts and territories are not rigid, and an individual worker may shift resources, efforts, and priorities for some external motivation or reward. In an exchange network, the reward may be an implied promise of extra effort from the recipient in the near future. Police officers may forward information to parole officers on the conduct of parolees if the parole officers will reciprocate. The information may be exchanged by phone or over lunch rather than through formal communication links.

Work Perspective: INTERORGANIZATIONAL COMMUNICATION GOES LACKING

In the post-9/11 world, communication between agencies has been dramatically overhauled, yet as local, county, state, and federal agencies become more reliant on each other to accomplish their part in what is billed as *Homeland Security*, it is important to understand the intended *need* for communication as much as the transmitted *words* for the communication.

In the not-too-distant past, federal agencies were often perceived to be one-way streets of information; we received it, but rarely shared it with our local, county, or state counterparts. The perception was not that different from the reality. We might have *appeared* to be open in our communication, and we might often have publicly touted the high level of cooperation with the local agency, but nothing was released to an outside agency before it was discussed in depth with our headquarters staff. That practice was especially true of other federal agencies that were perceived to be encroaching on local jurisdictions. There is no question that this organizational value to "filter" information actually slowed things down. In short, every agency has a mission, vision, and an untold number of values that they embed in the directives, policies, and guidelines issued to the field personnel. The mission and vision are often clearly stated, succinct pieces of verbiage that can be found in almost every corner of the agency and can often be found neatly framed in the entryway to an office. On the other hand, the values of an organization are often not as clear or succinct and individual members are free to bring their values to the workplace.

The drug war is a perfect example. Agencies at every level have a stake in stemming the flow of illegal drugs before they hit the streets. Since the advent of asset sharing, the stakes are high. An agency that intercepts a significant load of narcotics, or cash proceeds from narcotics, stands to benefit financially and therefore be better able to equip their personnel with equipment, overtime compensation, or even additional troops that could otherwise not be afforded. Additionally, the media attention drawn to such cases is also worth noting because it produces in the public view the perception that the agency is at the forefront of the battle and thus deserving of more tax dollars.

Two federal agencies that share narcotics jurisdiction are the Drug Enforcement Administration (DEA) and the former U.S. Customs Office of Enforcement, now known as the Bureau of Immigration and Customs Enforcement (ICE). One example of interagency lack of communication occurred when both agencies were mandated to share their strategic tactical information and operational plans. If the DEA was using undercover personnel to bring a shipment of drugs into the country, that information was to be carefully transmitted to the Customs Office to ensure safe passage of the drugs and agents so that the trail could be established from importation to the street distributors. They were called controlled deliveries. Unfortunately, controlled deliveries often involved large quantities of drugs, money, or even transportation assets that the agents knew might convert eventually to assets that they could later use. So when the time came for information to be shared with Customs or DEA, it was not uncommon that someone might "forget" to make the call to the other agency. After all, a plane could either be converted to government use or to cash that might buy a significant amount of surveillance equipment or similar tactical assets and, in the era of shrinking budgets, the agents in the field grew to learn the fact that "sharing" information equated to less publicity, less equipment, and less money to do the job. What resulted instead from these lapses of mandated protocol were wasted time, seized assets and personnel, and bad relationships at the higher ends of each organization. A typical result occurred one night when the U.S. Customs Office learned of an inbound controlled delivery that had not been communicated from one agency to another. Not wanting to take chances on what could be a rogue operation, customs officials seized a shipment of cocaine, a single-engine aircraft, and arrested DEA undercover personnel, thus effectively terminating the progressive criminal investigation in place by the DEA. Was the outcome preventable? Certainly. Was the seizure justifiable? Certainly, given the lack of transmitted information. Was there much more to be gained if the agencies had worked together more closely? Without question, yes.

SOURCE: Dr. John J. Sullivan, Executive Director, International Center for Leadership and Development (Resident Agent in Charge, Bureau of Customs and Immigration, Ret.).

Third, the exchange of information helps both parties perform their legitimate functions and contributes to the attainment of the overriding goals of the criminal justice system. The system exists for the mutual good of its participants. If participants are seeking legitimate agency goals, it will serve the goals of the criminal justice system (Gaines et al., 2003). "Continued exchange relationships generate a sense of trust between the system's participants, which in turn promote a cooperative attitude that is strengthened by the organization's reward structure" (Cole, 1983:112). The glue that links exchange systems together is communication. Thus, exchange systems become communication networks that enhance the productivity of their members. Because the members' motivation for and interest in communicating are based on self-interest, they are able to overcome the usual communication barriers.

However, exchange networks and informal communication systems are not always created to enhance an organization's efficiency. The traditional agency grapevine may carry false or inaccurate information. Networks may be created to facilitate personal rather than organizational goals. In addition, well-intentioned workers may pursue their own interpretations of their agency's goals in their exchange networks, interpretations that may often be different from those of the system's policymakers, who presumably are attuned to public demands through the political system. And although information may flow freely within a network, members may intentionally or unintentionally withhold crucial information.

The Linking Pin and Communication

Likert (1961) found that productivity in industry was highest in companies that were coordinated by a hierarchy of interlocking groups rather than by a traditional chain of command and its directed policies and procedures. The interlocking groups are bound together by *linking pins*, persons who serve as members of two or more groups or are part of the social system of two or more groups. Linking pins are individuals who make a concerted effort to have credibility and influence in their own units as well as in other units that affect the efficient operation of their units. The linking pin acts as an informal coordinator and communicator, making ad hoc efforts to smooth the workflow between units. We can surmise that the person acting as the linking pin could overcome the barriers of communication between units and probably establish an exchange system between units.

In the prison system, there is always a degree of conflict or mistrust between custody and treatment personnel. Both groups are concerned that their authority over inmates and their ability to perform their assigned tasks will be eroded as a result of the overlap between the groups. This conflict has been resolved to a great extent when a member of one group links the groups into a working relationship. A medical doctor in a large state prison met with an informal leader among custody personnel, and the two individuals set out informal rules and compromises on how the two groups will work together. Likert was a champion of participative management as a means to open communication in organizations. He reasoned that communication across groups was not possible in hierarchical organizations managed from the top down. However, his study showed that even in hierarchical organizations, individuals can become linking pins and foster communication across groups. It has been common for federal agents to cross agency borders to build working relationships with agents in other agencies in an effort to meet their agency goals. In the past, this linking pin effort has been done informally because it was contrary to their agency's culture and, in some instances, a violation of agency policy. With the current need for intelligence agencies to share information, agency policy should encourage agents to act as linking pins and build working relationships with agents of sister agencies to communicate their operations across agency boundaries.

Productivity and innovation require broad-based networks that can be created by skilled networkers in exchange and linking-pin structures. Granovetter (1983) makes a good argument that having a number of loose ties extends one's information network and the ability to gather information and ideas outside his or her immediate social system. Granovetter's argument is directed at groups that live in chronic poverty and are underemployed. His thesis is that members of poverty cultures have strong ties with their immediate groups at the expense of having a number of weak ties outside the group, where they can learn about economic opportunities. In application to organizations, weak ties need to develop in agencies where tasks are specialized in order to ensure fluid flow of horizontal information.

IMPLICATIONS FOR CRIMINAL JUSTICE MANAGERS

It is clear that effective and efficient communication is crucial for an organization to function. However, communication in all organizations is less than perfect. This is especially true of criminal justice organizations that face multiple and conflicting constituents and a complex and changing environment. Several general areas that criminal justice administrators need to emphasize to improve communications for their organizations are discussed here.

Communication with the Environment

Understanding the importance of **communicating with the external environment** requires a unique perspective. The criminal justice system has inherited the perceived responsibility of providing society with a sense of personal and psychological safety. Society expects crimes to be solved and criminal offenders to be successfully prosecuted and justly punished. Theoretically, prosecuting and punishing offenders will, by example, deter others from criminal activity. This assumption is premised on the notion that the punishment of criminal offenders is communicated to the public (Kohfeld, 1983).

However, no systematic efforts exist to communicate clearly to citizens the factual relationship between an offender's crime and his or her punishment. This situation is made more problematic because the punishment of juvenile offenders

Communicating with the environment: The criminal justice system sends messages to society to create a perception of safety.

is generally kept from public knowledge by the expunging of juvenile records (SEARCH Group, Inc., 1982). Communicating the outcomes of the criminal justice system is left to the media and politicians, who communicate and reinterpret the system's activities to the public, often in a pejorative light, to enhance their own popularity. Administrators need to develop routinized methods of providing useful information to the public and the political system; they must learn to cultivate, not shun, media relations.

Dealing with the public through the news media to produce favorable police–community relations may be fraught with deep and fundamental problems. Selke and Bartoszek (1984) found through surveying criminal justice and journalism students that a great deal of suspicion and distrust exists between the two groups even before they enter the field. Hence, both sender and receiver in the police–media dyad have preconceived notions about the information communicated, and the communicator typically lacks credibility. Building a relationship with the media is a formidable challenge fraught with potential problems, but it must be a major goal of an agency administrator.

In the last decade, forms of systematic communication to the public have been attempted. A major attempt to communicate the problem of crime and encourage citizens to take personal action to protect themselves was a Sears-sponsored public relations program titled "Take a Bite Out of Crime." The campaign utilized the media and provided public service ads that encouraged citizens to take standard precautions to protect themselves from crime. Follow-up studies by the Center for the Study of Mass Communications Research (1982) and by O'Keefe and Mendelsohn (1984) showed that community members had seen or heard the crime prevention ads and were motivated to take some anticrime steps in their communities.

Efforts at developing team and foot patrol policing rely heavily on the interaction and exchange of information between police and community members (Gaines et al., 2003; Trojanowicz and Banas, 1985). Attempts have been made to improve the contacts between police and community members by improving procedures for citizens' complaints against police (Brown, 1983). Scott (1981) suggests that police services and community relations were dramatically improved for a metropolitan police department as a result of a referral system developed by the department to refer citizens who contact police for social service assistance to appropriate agencies. Improved referral systems among metropolitan police departments, the community members who contact the police, and other public service agencies can improve police services and community relations (Scott, 1981). Tullar and Glauser (1985) and Missonellie and D'Angelo (1984) also recommend improved use of technology to strengthen police communications with the public. Over the last decade, law enforcement and correctional agencies have created public information or public relations officers in an attempt to improve media relations and exposure (Motschall and Cao, 2002). Carlson (2005) suggests that police departments form and utilize "citizens academies" to connect with key members of the community by offering them an abbreviated academy experience.

Although technology, referral methods, and so on can be added to systems to improve communication, often a fundamental practice or structure of a police agency can hamper police–community interactions. Capowich (1998) tracked the communication between community members and local police in a community policing program. He discovered that many of the special police programs aimed at solving community problems were flawed because they were formulated by top administrators based on information received via traditional communication channels, such as dispatch reports and reports through the chain of command. Both traditional organizational procedures tended to reframe the information to fit the traditional organizational paradigm, hence limiting the chance for community members and community police officers to identify and solve local problems.

Relations between corrections and the public can sometimes lead to conflict. In an effort to improve the information flow between corrections and the media, the National Jail Coalition (1984) produced a short manual of briefing reports on complex jail issues. Tully et al. (1982) present recommendations to assist corrections departments with community relations. In the case of a corrections department that is attempting to build a facility in a resistant community, they recommended that speakers from corrections trying to sell these programs know how to communicate with the public and have credibility with them. They should not simply be administrators or public relations people drafted for this purpose (Stinchcomb, 2005).

Victims are often left out of the criminal process, yet they are immediate stakeholders who will evaluate the process and the system. Hagan (1983) suggests that victims need to be made active participants in their cases by being kept abreast of progress and having procedures explained to them. After extensive interviews with 600 victims, Hagan found that those who were kept advised of the progress of their cases and who understood the criminal justice process as it applied to their cases were typically satisfied with the outcome. Conversely, those who were not given information were typically unhappy about the outcome of their cases.

Intraorganizational Communication

The components of the criminal justice system are designed to oppose each other to assure the rights of the criminal defendant. Members of different criminal justice components have differing roles, duties, and perceptions about the purpose and mission of the system. The conflicting roles of criminal justice agencies often cause the day-to-day interaction and communication between practitioners to be adversarial rather than cooperative in nature and intent. Hence, practitioners are not encouraged to communicate cooperatively with professional colleagues not in their agencies.

Nonetheless, administrators and individual practitioners can develop programs and initiatives to improve communication across agencies. When Ryan (1981) examined conflict levels between police and probation officers, he showed that the quality and quantity of contacts between police and probation officers had an impact on their level of conflict. For officers with a great deal of work-related and personal contact, conflict was extremely low. Such contacts may minimize inaccurate stereotypes and communication barriers between the two groups. Finally, Pindur and Lipiec (1982) found that a system that required continual and immediate contact between arresting police officers and members of the prosecuting attorney's staff improved the relationship between the two agencies.

Communication can be improved within each agency by improving the climate. Nuchia (1983) suggests that law enforcement officers should exercise their own "First Amendment right" to be critical of their departments. Archambeault and Wierman (1983) recommend that police bureaucracies move away from the traditional chain of command to the so-called *theory Z approach*, which encourages teamwork rather than adversarial and competitive relationships among agency staff. Similarly, Melancon (1984) argues that police agencies should institute quality circles, which are similar in concept to theory Z and facilitate the participation of line staff in management. Lippert and O'Conner (2006) suggest that public and private security agencies should share information across boundaries more readily. Dickinson (1984) argues that prisons should radically change communication policies toward inmates and allow them much more contact with the outside world than they now have. Concerning inmate rehabilitation, Jacks (1984) recommends an eclectic approach for interacting with inmates called *positive therapeutic intervention*. The approach simply requires that corrections staff be trained to be good listeners and pay constant attention to inmates when they discuss their problems. In a similar vein, Cole, Hanson, and Silbert (1982) suggest that the implementation of inmate mediation within a prison system precludes full-blown formal litigation, saves time and resources, and achieves amicable solutions.

Interorganizational Communication

The need for broad-based communication among law enforcement and security agencies at every level of government is imperative for successful counterterrorist strategies to be successful (9/11 Commission, 2003). Interagency communication has taken on a new importance, and agencies will have to alter past practices and policies in order to deal with our current international threat. It is imperative, therefore, that criminal justice agency executives improve communication with sister agencies that function at least within their region in order to share significant intelligence that would serve to prevent terrorism as well as criminal activity.

The 9/11 Commission, arguing for more effective interagency communication and information sharing, proposed the following:

> The application of newly developed scientific technology to the mission of U.S. war fighters and national security decision makers is one of the great success stories of the twentieth century.... But technology produces its best results when an organization has the doctrine, structure, and incentives to exploit it (2003: 127).

The need for better interagency communication became strikingly apparent after the terrorists' attack on the World Trade Center. The Commission has suggested that the lack of intelligence sharing between the Federal Bureau of Investigation (FBI) and the Central Intelligence Agency (CIA) may have led to the success of that attack. The initial response to the Commission's report was to create the Department of Homeland Security, whose initial mission was to find ways to improve communication and intelligence sharing across intelligence-gathering agencies. A product of this effort is the development of Fusion Centers. A Fusion Center is a mechanism for exchanging information and intelligence. The Center's goal is to provide a mechanism for law enforcement and intelligence-gathering agencies to place and retrieve intelligence.

The Centers gather information not only from law enforcement agencies but also from the private sector. The Fusion Center managed by the Palm Beach County Sheriff's Department has developed a partnership with private sector entities referred to as Business Partners against Terrorism (BPAT). As this partnership develops, business agencies are given guidelines, training, and a venue to submit critical information for the Centers. The initial purpose was to prevent terrorists' plots from developing into attacks. However, as the Centers have evolved, intelligence on criminal activity, especially in organized crime and gang activities, is becoming a greater part of the system. To the extent that quality and quantity information on criminal or terrorist threats is now being shared across U.S. law enforcement agency boundaries, traditional barriers to interorganizational communication are being bridged. The European Union (EU) is also a target for terrorism and suffers its share of crime. Hence, the EU is attempting to manage and share critical information through better data collection and analysis. Europol's annual Organized Crime Threat Assessment (OCTA) is completing the collection and analysis. The main thrust is against organized crime, but similar to Fusion Centers, OCTA also attempts to include private sector and academic sources (Harfield, 2008).

COMMUNICATION AND TECHNOLOGY

The efficiency of communication has dramatically increased with the development of information technology. The Internet is a global interconnection of computers operating independently (Kinicki and Kreitner, 2006). The Internet connects business, governmental and private agencies, and individuals across the globe through personal computers, mainframes, and supercomputers. One individual can communicate with a host of individuals or firms with the click of a button. Also, individuals can receive an interminable number of messages without being at their computers and retrieve them when convenient. It is also possible to search the Internet for information from an almost infinite number of sources on almost any topic. Police officers can search for warrants and other important information with laptop computers in their cars. Reports can be written on computers, checked for spelling and proper grammar, and sent out instantly to a number of recipients upon completion. The main method of Internet communication is, of course, e-mail. E-mail can save agencies time and money when used properly. It can also facilitate group work and teamwork by allowing individuals to communicate across great distances in real time.

Computers allow individuals to work from home by being linked to their clients or business through personal computers rather than requiring an office—or even a classroom. This can create a significant savings for agencies because they can meet their objectives in part by allowing individuals to work from their homes.

Computers are great storage bins for reports, files, data, and other information that typically is stored in cumbersome filing cabinets, notebooks, or other traditional means of record storage. In addition to eliminating the need for space to file information, filing can be done with the click of a mouse rather than through the efforts of clerical staff. In spite of all these benefits, however, a disadvantage is that a skilled hacker can break into computer systems and steal information, making security difficult. Most agencies that are concerned with security develop an *intranet* system that can function only within agency parameters. To prevent intruders from breaking the agency's computer communication boundaries, a firewall can be installed. The firewall keeps the agency computers from being accessed by non-agency individuals. However, firewalls can be breached and information stolen. Moreover, we are all familiar with computer viruses created by computer hackers that intrude into a system to destroy programs and records.

Teleconferencing, or videoconferencing, is also a technological advancement that improves the efficiency of communication. Teleconferencing brings individuals in distant cities together with audio and video connections. This allows individuals to hold conferences and staff meetings and conduct interviews at a distance, eliminating the time and cost that would be expended to bring people together on a face-to-face basis. In some jurisdictions, arraignments for criminal defendants are held via teleconferencing between the court and the local jail. This eliminates the cost and time needed to transport inmates from jails to local courts for their arraignments, but it provides the defendant with his or her appearance in court and proper judicial procedures.

There is no guarantee that communicating with computer technology or videoconferencing will improve the effectiveness of communication. We still need to be sharp and thoughtful to effectively use these modern tools. The ease with which e-mails can be sent or data and other records stored may cause information overload. Mid-level administrators in a state correctional agency reported that administrators were calling staff meetings several times a week with teleconferencing rather than monthly as had been the practice in the past because of the ease with which such meetings could be set up. The meetings tended to be poorly planned, and the information provided often contradicted information from the previous meeting, depending on who called the meeting.

It is easy to conclude that productivity in organizations is linked to good communications. If individuals within and among organizations communicate poorly, they will find it difficult to coordinate their work and link their tasks. If directives and orders are communicated ineffectively, programs, plans, and changes in routine tasks are hard to implement. Managers and practitioners would agree on this conclusion, at least in principle, and so does current research (Hinduja, 2006). Therefore, managers and practitioners in criminal justice agencies should actively seek to improve communication channels and individual communication skills. Typically, the task of improving communication is ignored or is relegated to occasional training seminars that do not teach communication skills in the context of the organization.

To the extent that formal training in communication is provided, it focuses on law, agency rules and protocol, chain of command, and other formal aspects of communication. Report writing may be offered to new recruits, but comprehensive training in interpersonal communications is not a common part of training agendas. Some criminal justice agencies, however, do offer training in communication for their professionals. The Michigan Department of Corrections provides extensive human relations training for its corrections officers, who are taught how to recognize and deal with communication barriers between staff and inmates and about the psychological games some inmates play. They then learn effective communication skills to overcome these barriers and problems.

Communication among members of different components of the system is often limited because of conflicting goals. To the extent that members perceive interagency relationships as more conflicting than negotiative, interagency communication will be limited, formal, and closed rather than informal and open. Agencies can improve interagency communication simply by making clear to their members the situations that involve legitimate goal conflict and those that allow for negotiation and cooperation.

The development of new technology using computers to store and process communication has increased markedly during the last decade (Hinduja, 2006; Kinicki and Kreitner, 2006). A great deal of emphasis is being placed on training computer skills to criminal justice practitioners (James, 1996; Leiberg, 1996; Ricker, 1996; Van Buren, 1996), such as developing the communication skills of police dispatch and emergency services, areas that are in obvious need of technical upgrading. As communication systems become more efficient and can connect individuals and agencies to information from across the globe, information management will become extremely important. The ease of access to information will also make the technical side of confidentiality a new task for managers. The recent exposure of governmental classified documents by Wikileaks shows how vulnerable an agency can be.

Administrators will be forced to deal internally with many of these problems by restructuring or streamlining communication channels and providing training to agency members. Most significant in this regard is the crucial need for intelligence agencies to communicate and share information among agencies rather than hoard intelligence, as has been the past practice. It is just such sharing of information that the 9/11 Commission (2003) concluded is imperative for the nation's defense against terror.

ETHICAL PROBLEMS IN THE COMMUNICATION PROCESS

Ethics in organizational communication means that the flow of information from management and between members is valid, reliable, and accessible. In other words, formal transmittals of information need to be considered truthful and consistent rather than manipulative, self-serving, and opaque. A key function of an executive is to take the lead role in managing communication in his or her agency. To function well in this role, executives need to be perceived as having integrity and must send consistent information that has a clear message. First, to succeed in that role takes an understanding of the importance of communication and the agency's communication process—which is commonly taken for granted. Second, this role requires a commitment on the part of executives to create, promote, and protect ethical boundaries for conversation and information sharing in their agencies. Third, executives need to avoid misusing information themselves as a method of control. The temptation to use communication to manipulate perceptions is a constant threat to ethical discourse. This temptation is, unfortunately, an organizational constant. This is true because management and subordinates have different agendas that result in tension between superiors and subordinates. Management seeks high levels of productivity while attempting to control cost and resources expended. Subordinates also want to control their expenditures of time and effort while maximizing their benefits—whether material or symbolic (Reinsch, 1996). The ability of one group to dominate another creates the tension that lies in the power relationship between groups. The temptation for each group is to control communication and information in order to skew perceptions of reality that favor their group's needs.

Control over communication systems and access to information is a major tool of power. A temptation exists on the part of organizational members and executives to use power that feeds their self-interests over the interests of the organization. Previously, we have seen the weakness of hierarchical communication, especially how information leaks as it flows upward and downward through the chain of command. Subordinates try to pass information up the hierarchy that will lead to a favorable evaluation. Managers tend to screen out or reinterpret directives sent to them to protect their self-interests; they can then pass the reinterpreted directives to the next hierarchical level. Directives and reports can also be placed perpetually at the bottom of the "in basket" to keep them out of circulation rather than dealing directly and honestly with issues. Moreover, in this chapter, we have discussed how individuals, and even agencies, treat information as a valuable commodity, an effective bargaining tool. Also, criminal justice agencies and intelligence-gathering agencies may control or hide information from other agencies in order to gain success in critical investigations or major arrests without sharing credit. Solving major crimes, breaking up criminal gangs, and so forth can add to the status of individuals and agencies, which, in turn, can assist the agency with next year's budget requests. In this case, the self-interest of agencies is higher than the interests of the community members they serve.

The nature and content of communication are to some extent framed by the organization's culture. Simply put, what is rewarded gets reported. In that regard, organizational members may be viewed negatively by supervisors for sharing critical information. In the criminal justice system, staff will be loath to repost information that will put them in a critical light with managers. Conversely, practitioners will be anxious to report information that will make them look good. As we will see in the chapter on effectiveness (Chapter 13), information is often falsified in an attempt to make the agency, as well as agency members, "look good."

Up to this point, we have discussed intentional deceit and manipulation of communication. However, part of the executive's role is to create and maintain an effective communication structure within his or her agency. Management by indifference, carelessness, or insensitivity can lead to unethical communication within an organization. The creation of an old-boys' network, or in-group and out-group cliques, can be as much a matter of careless management as that of ill will. The old-boys' clique is often run by the head good old boy—that is, managers who seek informal input from subordinates may continue to fall back on the same people over time, forming, in effect, the "in group." Relying on the same subgroup of people for input may be due to a willingness to participate or the boss's perception about their veracity, skills, or expertise or because the in-group members usually affirm the ideas of the managers. Whatever the basis for the decision to communicate with a subgroup of staff, the results typically lead to resentment and contention by members left out of the process as well as a mistrust of information put forward by the manager. To maintain ethical formal discourse, managers need to make extraordinary attempts to include everyone. For example, a new warden called a roundtable meeting with his immediate subordinates. Agenda items were laid out. The warden asked each member of the group—one at a time—for input. He took careful notes, summarized them, and passed them back to the subordinates. He then advised his roundtable of subordinates to bring in their immediate subordinates and structure their meeting in the same way. This is not necessarily an extraordinary measure, but it is an unusual and effective measure to avoid the inadvertent creation of the old-boys' communication network.

Finally, it is management's duty to set boundaries and rules for communication. Speech and expression within or among criminal justice agencies is limited. Information on clients, inmates, or evidence may at times be legally confidential. At other times, prudence may require that information be kept confidential, therefore ethically restricting communication. While particular words or terms are a part of any profession, language and terminology that may be offensive or threatening to particular groups need to be avoided in formal and informal discourse and written communication. It is management's obligation to make the contingencies to communicating well known to staff.

SUMMARY

Know the five steps of the communication process.

- The five steps of the communication process include encoding, transmitting, selecting a medium or channel, receiving, and decoding.

Be familiar with the nine barriers to communication.

- The nine barriers to communication include preconceived ideas, denial of contrary information, use of personalized meanings, lack of motivation or interest, noncredibility of source, lack of communication skills, poor organizational climate, use of complex channels, and any communication gap.

Understand how communication and information flow through the agency's chain of command.

- In a hierarchical organization, communication and information flow downward from superior to subordinate and upward from subordinate to superior. In the case of a multileveled chain of command, top managers do not communicate directly with field workers and vice versa. Reports flow upward and directives flow downward. Horizontal communication facilitates coordination.

Understand informal communication networks in the workplace.

- Informal communication networks in the workplace form on their own and for some purpose. Individuals who are part of that network share information with each other and not with workers who are not part of the network.

Understand nonverbal communication.

- Nonverbal communication is part of the message when individuals communicate face to face. Gestures and facial features can reveal honesty or deceit, enthusiasm or boredom, or the extent to which a communication recipient understands the message.

Understand the difference between communication and information.

- Communication and information are often used interchangeably. However, communication is a process that sends a message, and information is the message.

Understand exchange theory and exchange networks.

- When we make a purchase, we exchange money for a product. In an exchange network, members communicate regularly and exchange information for information. Information becomes a commodity similar to a product purchased in exchange for money.

Be able to define linking pin theory.

- Productivity in industry is highest in agencies that are coordinated by interlocking work groups rather than by a chain of command. The groups are bound together by individuals who are members of two or more groups. Linking pin individuals make an effort to be part of more than one group.

Case Study: FICTION AND ETHICS

This case study is about creating a fictional story that communicates an image that met a city manager's political needs. The city manager of a medium-sized town had been feuding with particular members of the police department (PD) for some time. Ironically, the senior members of the department with which he was at odds had been his personal friends and drinking buddies who kept him abreast of activity and gossip in the department. The senior members of the PD that the city manager favored felt empowered by having his friendship and his ear.

Over time, the favored senior officers felt entitled to take public positions on public safety and budget issues that did not fit the city manager's agenda. The city manager felt betrayed by their actions and generalized his hostile feelings to the entire department. He convinced the city council that the PD was becoming political and they needed to fire the chief and hire a new one who would change the present political culture of the PD to a more professional culture. He fired the police chief and appointed a younger, less experienced police lieutenant. The appointment of the acting chief was done in a public ceremony in which the city manager announced that the acting chief was expected to change the culture of the department and return the PD to a professional organization. He also knew that appointing this particular person would anger many members of the PD. He made the change and in the process was publically critical of the PD and the former chief. Now, he had to prove to the city council and media that his assessment as well as his appointment of the acting police chief were correct. To do this, he had to create a fictional account of the PD before and after his actions. He also had to communicate his story to the city council, media, and general public in a convincing manner. He felt he could pull this off in spite of the performance measures that the former police chief had implemented within the department. In fact, the city manager had a scheme to use the performance measures to create his story.

The city manager called a press conference. He announced that all PD staff would be immediately subjected to performance evaluations by the acting chief. He added that he had reason to believe the former chief gave favorable evaluations to officers in his political clique and poor evaluations to any officers who did not back him. Also, recent promotions would be reconsidered. The city manager had earlier met in private with the acting chief and directed him to give lower scores to the former chief's supporters and deny particular promotions to manifest his power. In addition, the acting chief was told to take make an array of changes within the department to give the appearance of changing the PD from a political organization to a professional organization. With all of the changes being made, the city manager had the basis of a script for his story of a new and improved PD. Patting the acting chief's back often and in public for doing a great job and attributing the department's "improving" morale became a staple for the city manager.

CASE STUDY QUESTIONS

1. List and discuss all of the ethical issues involved in this case study.
2. Discuss stories you have produced to evoke a good image of your group of friends.
3. What role will redoing all of the PD staff's performance evaluations play in creating the city manager's fiction?
4. What other changes can the acting chief make to add to the story (remember, the acting chief can make symbolic as well as substantive changes—like putting up a new American flag in front of the PD).
5. Think about a fictional story the former chief or the former cronies of the city manager can create.
6. How can the city manager manipulate the local news media to communicate his fictional story?
7. If you are a local reporter and you have 24 hours to put together a report for your newspaper, who would you talk to first and why?

Think like an Administrator

Dave Binninger rose quickly to the rank of Captain in Charge of Operations at the Oshkosh, Wisconsin, Police Department. Dave was born and raised in Oshkosh, married his high school sweetheart, and had four children. On a lark, he applied for the chief of police job in a small town in Southeast Florida. Much to his surprise, he was offered

THINK LIKE AN ADMINISTRATOR—continued

the position. Oshkosh is a bit like the ideal trouble-free friendly town that hasn't changed much in decades. The Oshkosh Police Department had very few minority or female police officers. Accepting the chief's job in South Florida would be a challenge to Dave. He noticed during the interview process that most of the command staff was made up of older white men, many of whom were transplants from northern states. However, the city was composed of a diverse population of Hispanics, Haitians, Asians, and African Americans. Also, the rank and file of the police department seemed to be a diverse mix of individuals similar to the city's population. He didn't think much of it until his first day at work. Dave arrived at 6 a.m. Walking from his car, he observed three black officers laughing together and talking loudly in a language he was not familiar with. He later learned they were speaking Creole, the language of Haiti. He also observed African American officers together and white officers in their own groups. In addition, he observed that the female officers tended to hang out together regardless of their particular ethnic backgrounds or rank.

1. Describe and discuss the communication networks that Chief Binninger might have been observing.
2. Is it possible that the communication networks based on ethnicity and gender have created social cliques that do not interact?
3. Discuss in detail the communication barriers the new chief will face when he communicates with the staff as a whole and as individuals.
4. How will the chief's background make communication with his staff a challenge?
5. Do you think there might be a communication breakdown between the new chief and the command staff? Why should that be the case, particularly because they are all white males? How will anyone know if communication barriers exist between the new chief and the command staff?
6. Discus how the set of communication barriers possible here may worsen the already poor communication that affects a typical chain of command.
7. If you are in Chief Binninger's uncomfortable shoes, what steps do you have to take to make sure you communicate well with your diverse staff?
8. No doubt the new chief suspects that the cliques formed and communication networks are based primarily on ethnicity and gender. How should the new chief verify his suspicions?
9. What steps should the new chief take to make sure the diversity within his department does not impede communication among staff?
10. Discuss how this blend of police officers can improve communication with the local citizens.
11. Given your answer to the last question, would you recommend that officers be assigned to local communities that match their ethnicity—for example, Hispanics work in Hispanic neighborhoods and so forth? How would this approach impact communication in the department across ethnic lines? Discuss other options for assignments.

FOR DISCUSSION

1. As we have seen throughout this chapter, law enforcement agencies, especially intelligence-gathering agencies, keep information to themselves rather than share information. Discuss why agencies hoard information. If you were giving advice to the director of Homeland Security, what steps would you recommend to promote the flow of vital information among intelligence agencies?

2. Think about the college class you liked the most and contrast it with the class you liked the least. Compare the quality of communication between the two classes. What are some of the barriers to communication that typically emerge in a college course? If you were a professor, what steps would you take to maximize the effectiveness of communication in your class?

3. How can communication be improved in an organization that is structured in a traditional bureaucratic form? How might computerized communication be utilized to improve the effectiveness of communication in a bureaucratic organization?

4. What are the drawbacks of computerized information systems? From a management perspective, what policies and procedures could be implemented to assure the effectiveness of computerized information systems?

FOR FURTHER READING

Carlson, D. P. *When Cultures Clash*. Upper Saddle River, NJ: Prentice Hall, 2005.

Likert, R. *New Patterns of Management*. New York: McGraw-Hill, 1961.

Littlejohn, S. W., and Foss, K. A. *Theories of Human Communication*. Belmont, CA: Wadsworth, 2005.

CHAPTER 5

Motivation of Personnel

LEARNING OBJECTIVES

After reading this chapter, the students will have achieved the following objectives:

- Understand a definition of motivation.
- Comprehend organizational theory and motivation from a historical perspective.
- Know the major theories of motivation.
- Explain some prescriptions for criminal justice management regarding motivation.
- Describe public service motivation.
- Understand an integrated model of motivation.

VIGNETTE

As public agencies, criminal justice organizations are forever striving to meet infinite demands with finite resources. How does an effective criminal justice administrator foster a climate of employee motivation in lean times? The answer lies in a range of activities and behaviors that appreciate the difficulties employees are facing and how they are the best people to tackle these difficulties. Good administration comprehends and recognizes that, as public servants, employees are called on to perform a host of duties, many of which are underappreciated. Yet, at the end of the day, the criminal justice employee is called on to protect society, prevent crime, manage offenders, and even change individuals while they are under our charge. Effective criminal justice administration recognizes that many employees go into criminal justice work to assist others. Yes, the pay and benefits may be less than in the private sector, but people who perform our front-end duties are generally interested in more than pay and benefits, such as reducing crime, assisting victims of crime, and working with offenders so they get out of a life of crime. These are daunting and challenging tasks, but they are doable and can be effectively addressed with motivated employees.

Experienced criminal justice administrators have generally come up through the rank and file of their organizations. They understand the pressures and limitations of the job regarding the availability of extrinsic motivation factors, for example, pay and benefits, but in addition, they recognize that most activity within criminal justice organizations is about people. Criminal justice work is people work. The relationships created and nurtured define the nature of the work and how and why people are motivated to stay in their positions. Criminal justice administrators understand that engendering positive work environments will go a long way toward creating a climate of motivation, even during very tight budgetary times. Intrinsic factors regarding the work are especially important for maintaining a motivating environment. These intrinsic factors of motivation highlight that human service work is always challenging but also rewarding, especially if employees perceive themselves as valued members of a team, are directed toward a mission, and are sustained by a vision that things will get better.

The purpose of this chapter is to examine the subject of motivation and how it applies to the criminal justice process and its personnel. We review the major theories of motivation developed in the field of organizational behavior and, more importantly, apply these theories to the various components of the criminal justice system. Because of the dearth of material in the area focused on criminal justice personnel, it is necessary to review major findings from other fields and attempt to apply these results to criminal justice.

MOTIVATION DEFINED

Motivation can be looked at in two ways. First, we can view motivation as a psychological concept, examining the state of mind of the individual and why he or she exhibits a certain type of behavior. American culture values the work ethic, and much of this attitude can be traced to personal values transmitted to children in their formative years. Learned values, therefore, play a critical role in whether a person is motivated to perform various tasks. (Later in this chapter, we discuss, from both human and organizational points of view, those factors that lead or cause a person to act in a certain fashion.) The psychological definition of motivation depends on how the individual perceives the world and on the "psychological contract" between the individual and the work environment (Schein, 1970). In terms of criminal justice, we could ask, for example, the following questions: What factors motivate people to become police officers, or, more important, what factors in the police environment motivate individuals to do their jobs? Even more telling would be an examination of structures in the police organization that simultaneously promote the fulfillment of individual needs and motivate people to do their jobs.

Second, we can view motivation from an organizational point of view, exploring the kinds of managerial behaviors that induce employees to act in a way consistent with the expectations and demands of the organization. This organizational way of examining motivation enables us to explore motivational strategies that promote the best interests of both the individual and the organization. In seeking a sense of congruence between the employee and the organization, management has the responsibility of providing mechanisms that enable employees to be highly motivated to do the work expected of them. In criminal justice agencies, we could ask, for example, how the administrator of a police organization or a correctional institution motivates employees or what the best strategies are for motivating rank-and-file police officers or corrections officers. In the remainder of this chapter, we attempt to provide answers to these questions.

Because not much research has been done on motivation in the criminal justice system, we focus on the theories of motivation that address issues fundamental to criminal justice. It is not our intention to cover all the theories of motivation (for a comprehensive review of the theories of motivation, see Robbins and Judge, 2007:184–257). Instead, we attempt to provide the theories of motivation that provide the greatest insight into the motivations of criminal justice personnel. In addition, we provide some prescriptions for criminal justice systems based on our understanding of motivation.

UNDERSTANDING ORGANIZATIONAL THEORY AND MOTIVATION FROM A HISTORICAL POINT OF VIEW

Classical writers: Individuals, such as Frederick Taylor, Henry Fayol, and Mary Parker Follett, who stressed that a motivating environment was as important as the self-motivation of workers.

Theories of motivation evolved over the last century concurrent with the industrial revolution, the expanded role of government, and the growth of large institutions. If we examine the influence of **classical writers** within organizational theory in the early part of the twentieth century, such as Frederick Taylor, Henri Fayol, and Mary Parker Follett, to mention a few, we see that their ideas on management have significance for understanding motivation and *how* employees are motivated in the work setting. These classical writers believed in the importance of a centralized system of management and the coordination of management activity directed toward the most efficient ways of performing work. In addition, they viewed the proper role of management and administration as the creation of clear lines of authority, a well-defined chain of command, and rules and regulations to guide and assist workers in the performance of their duties.

For classically oriented writers, motivation was first and foremost a product of the efforts of managers to create clearly defined work rules and supervision strategies that reinforced what the job entailed and how the work was to be best accomplished. From the workers' perspective, they were to be self-motivated but, more important, the responsibility for developing and maintaining a motivating environment among workers was in the hands of supervisors who directed, led, and watched over employees to ensure that maximum performance was enhanced and work was accomplished in a timely and efficient manner. The ideas of the classical writers have had a profound influence on the structures and views on motivation for many criminal justice organizations.

Human relations school: A school of thought that emphasized the importance of employee needs and the role of supervisors in motivating employees.

In contrast, later writers on organizational theory, known as proponents of the **human relations school**, were concerned about how employees fit into organizations beyond simply being workers. Writers such as Chester Barnard (1930s) and Peter Drucker (1950s) and even more contemporary writers, such as Demming (1986), Schein (1997), and Meyer, Becker, and Vandenberghe (2004), viewed motivation as an interactive process between workers and supervisors. For supporters of the human relations school, motivation was tied to *how* their supervisors treated employees and how organizational relations between managers and employees were cultivated to achieve organizational goals. In the words of Barnard (1938), all organizations must be viewed as "moral entities" that require the give-and-take of concerns expressed by both administrators and employees. Under a human relations model, motivation is best understood as a *process* where both managers and employees work together to create a motivating environment. The motivation of employees rests with both the employer and the employee. Research conducted in the 1950s and 1960s sought to understand the relationship between the *behavior* of managers and leaders and subordinates that produces a motivating environment. It also has relevance to understanding leadership and job design in organizations.

The **behavioral school of management** emphasizes the importance of manager and leader behavior to motivate and other critical administrative actions. By focusing on the behaviors of leaders and managers, it is hoped that proper ways of interacting and supervising employees will lead to more motivated employees. In fact, the entire field of *organizational development* has its roots in the human relations school and the behavioral research findings of the 1950s and 1960s. **Organizational development** in the twenty-first century is more focused on the integration of ideas on motivation, leadership, and job design into one area that centers on developing motivating environments, building organizational leaders, and designing the best possible ways to organize large numbers of people to accomplish specific organizational goals. It is impossible to think about motivation without thinking about other important concerns among administrators, for example, leadership and job design.

As you examine the theories of motivation defined in the following section, do not lose sight of the importance of the history of ideas on motivation and how they are linked to broader theories of organization that evolved during the twentieth century and still influence our comprehension of how people are motivated in organizations.

THEORIES OF MOTIVATION

A number of theories have been developed to explain motivation. We highlight here those approaches most relevant to the criminal justice system and grounded in empirical literature. You will see that discussions of motivation impact other areas of criminal justice administration and management, such as job design, leadership, and supervision. For purposes of this chapter, we discuss motivation in the context of current theories of motivation, recognizing that the issues discussed and ideas presented have relevance for many other issues affecting criminal justice administration and management. Six such theories can be identified:

1. Need theory
2. Theory X and theory Y
3. Achievement–power–affiliation theory
4. Expectancy theory
5. Equity theory
6. Theory Z

Need Theory

The most recognized theory of motivation comes from the work of Abraham Maslow (1943), who argued that we can examine motivation as one result of various physical and psychological needs. The central theme of **need theory** is

---

Behavioral school of management: This school stressed the importance of manager and leader behavior in the creation of a motivating environment for employees.

Organizational development: The integration of motivation, leadership, and job design in the creation of a positive environment for employees. It is also concerned with building organizational leaders and designing the best possible way to organize large numbers of people to accomplish organizational goals.

Need theory: The relationship between human physical and psychological needs and the work environment. This theory stressed that if human needs are not met in organizations, employees will not be motivated to work.

that all people have needs, both physical and psychological, that affect their behavioral patterns. Maslow argued that human beings have five basic needs.

Physiological needs, such as food and water, assure the basic survival of the individual and must be assured before any other needs can be fulfilled. After physical needs comes the need for safety and security. Human beings must feel safe in their environments and free from any threat of attack by aggressors; they also need to live in a secure and certain environment in which they can act as social beings. Belonging needs are reflected in the desire to be loved and to belong to a group. In addition, people need to have and show affection toward other human beings. Both needs may be expressed either in joining groups or by receiving support from one's family, friends, and relatives. Besides being loved, other needs of individuals center on self-esteem, self-image, and how one is viewed by peers. Individuals seek prestige and recognition from their loved ones and their fellow workers. Self-confidence is intricately tied to this perception of self-worth. Self-actualization needs, finally, center on one's potential to grow and do one's best in endeavors. According to Maslow, these needs are different for every individual, which is why it is difficult to develop a motivational strategy that is able to meet the self-actualization needs of all employees. Figure 5.1 displays Maslow's hierarchy, divided into higher-order needs and primary needs. Higher-order needs are belonging, esteem, and self-actualization; primary needs are physiological as well as safety and security.

What does the research evidence show about a needs theory? Tosi, Rizzo, and Carroll (1986:221) conclude that there is empirical support for a needs theory and, in particular, Maslow's conceptualization of needs theory. They believe research has demonstrated that when lower-level needs are not met, concern for higher-level needs decreases; that when an individual need is satisfied, it becomes less important, except in the case of self-actualization; and, finally, that there is a difference in needs orientation among occupational groups. Rank-and-file

FIGURE 5.1   The Needs Hierarchy.

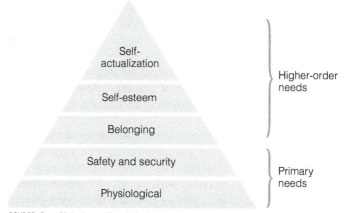

SOURCE: From *Motivation and Personality* by Abraham H. Maslow. Copyright 1954, 1987 by Harper & Row, Publishers, Inc. Reprinted by permission of the publisher.

workers, for example, consider lower-level needs to be more important in work situations than do managers. Managers perceive higher-level needs to be more important than lower-level needs.

In addition, some research indicates that age is a critical factor in needs orientation. Criminal justice research in particular suggests that older police officers and those with higher levels of education perceive control of their environments and some autonomy as critical to job satisfaction. Moreover, older police officers seek self-actualization through the completion of tasks (Griffin, Dunbar, and McGill, 1978:77–85). Providing these officers with control of their jobs through structural changes in the police department may be a way to retain and satisfy them. In addition, research on recruitment and hiring of police officers requires that more attention be paid to officer needs and community needs in the new era of community policing (Scrivner, 2001).

Support for needs theory has also been documented in the field of corrections. For example, research suggests that many corrections officers leave their positions because of the organization's inability to meet their needs for improved working conditions. Intrinsic working conditions, such as the degree of autonomy, the perceived variety of tasks, the amount of authority, and learning opportunities, are all critical to turnover (Jurik and Winn, 1987:19–21). Research also has shown that stress may be a product of the inability of correctional organizations to meet the needs of their employees. Lambert, Hogan, and Tucker (2009) found that increased input into decision making, supervision, formalization, integration, and instrumental communication are critical in the reduction of stress among correctional workers. More important, the issue of better communication overshadows both stress and motivation among correctional employees. Managerial behavior, therefore, requires attention to multiple issues and the various levels or stages of development of workers and how to motivate them to meet higher-level needs as they travel up the needs hierarchy. This seems to be a dilemma for current managers of organizations, including criminal justice, because how these needs are not only identified but also met within an organization becomes somewhat problematic (Witham, 1980). Police organizations, for example, are composed of such a wide variety of personalities that it would be difficult to identify motivational strategies for all of them. Ideus (1978) addresses this issue in institutional corrections, suggesting that the importance of motivational theory lies in its ability not only to identify these needs but, more important, to match employees' individual needs with the demands of the job. Ideally, efficiency and effectiveness would be enhanced if corrections organizations were able to match individuals to clearly identifiable tasks.

Bennett (1981) goes further by suggesting that the structuring of the police role makes it difficult for some needs to be met. Specifically, he suggests that many lower-order needs, such as physiological ones, cannot be adequately met because of the long hours and waiting associated with the job. Of greater significance, however, is the police organization's inability to deal with the self-esteem needs of officers. Bennett argues that within many police departments, leaders do not promote a sense of belonging among officers. This lack of belonging usually manifests itself in conformist behavior, which inhibits an open atmosphere of trust and recognition. Because recognition is infrequent, many officers become cynical. Although Roberg (1979) has identified this problem in relation to police management, little has been done to prescribe for police managers, or for that matter other criminal justice managers, how they are to function given the needs of their employees. Lumb and Breazeale (2002) suggest that the structuring of the police workplace to implement community policing strategies requires attention to police officer attitudes and needs for durable organizational change to occur.

Obviously, the motivational process is complex, and it is often difficult to discern which of the many variables are the most critical. Yet it does become apparent from research conducted in criminal justice organizations that the fulfillment of needs is crucial to motivating employees. Cordner (1978) suggests that many public service employees, particularly police officers, generally have their lower-level needs met by the organization. It follows, as a result, that the organization must focus on higher-order needs, in particular, the needs to be recognized, to participate in decision making, and to be given responsibility. Owen (2006) reaffirms this view regarding correctional supervisors as well. At present, fulfilling these needs is problematic, yet not impossible, in many public service organizations; criminal justice agencies are no different. What criminal justice managers can do is recognize those needs that require attention so that job tasks can be completed. For a police officer, for example, patrolling the same area day after day may not be the most self-actualizing activity, yet it is a job that must be done. Providing attention to basic needs, such as ensuring the officer's safety, may be enough for this task. In similar ways, higher needs of police officers must be understood in light of organizational tasks. It may also be that many tasks associated with the police, at least at the line level, cannot fulfill the higher needs of the rank-and-file police officer. For middle managers, finally, the issue of higher needs is more critical than for line officers. Presently, administrators in criminal justice organizations have not addressed this type of issue, and it is difficult for legitimate transformation, for example, movement from a traditional police model to one emphasizing community policing, to occur if attention is not paid to employee higher needs.

Theory X and Theory Y

Theory X: The belief that in order to motivate employees, they must be rewarded, punished, persuaded, controlled, and directed toward activities and tasks specified by management.

The second theory of motivation consists of two parts, theory X and theory Y, and is based on the work of Douglas McGregor. In his seminal piece, *The Human Side of Enterprise* (1978), McGregor describes these two approaches to human behavior and management that are based on a number of assumptions about human behavior. **Theory X** is derived from three fundamental beliefs that McGregor considers collectively as the conventional views of management:

1. Management is responsible for organizing the elements of productive enterprise—money, materials, equipment, people—for economic ends.

2.   Management directs the efforts of personnel, motivates them, controls their actions, and modifies their behavior to fit the needs of the organization.

3.   Without active intervention by management, people would ignore—even resist—organizational needs. They must, therefore, be persuaded, rewarded, punished, controlled; their activities must be directed. This is management's task.

Theory X is also based on a number of ancillary beliefs about individuals in organizations: they are lazy, lack ambition, are predominantly self-centered, are resistant to change, and on the whole are not too bright. This approach to management works to the detriment of meeting the higher needs of employees, as McGregor (1978:16) states:

> The carrot-and-stick theory does not work well at all once man has reached an adequate subsistence level and is motivated primarily by higher needs. Management cannot provide a man with self-respect or with the respect of his fellows or with the satisfaction of needs for self-fulfillment. It can create such conditions that he is encouraged and enabled to seek such satisfactions for himself, or it can thwart him by failing to create those conditions.

As a result of the inadequacy of this approach for meeting higher human needs, of which McGregor believes ego needs, social needs, and self-fulfillment needs to be the most important, he proposes an alternative view of management—**theory Y**, which views the human condition in an optimistic way. Theory Y is based on the following assumptions:

1.   Management is responsible for organizing the elements of productive enterprise—money, materials, equipment, people—for economic ends.

2.   People are not ignorant of or resistant to organizational needs. They have become so as a result of their experience in organizations.

3.   Motivation, potential for development, capacity for assuming responsibility, and readiness to direct behavior toward organizational goals are present in people. Management does not put them there. It is a responsibility of management to make it possible for people to recognize and develop these attributes themselves.

4.   The essential task of management is to arrange organizational conditions and methods of operation so that people can achieve their own goals by directing their own efforts toward organizational objectives.

Theory Y: The belief that higher-order needs—ego needs, social needs, and self-fulfillment needs—must be addressed by management in order to achieve organizational objectives and goals. Management is central to addressing these needs in the work setting.

Theory Y suggests, fundamentally, that management has a crucial role to play in motivating employees. More important, this approach to motivation suggests that there is a definite relationship between job satisfaction among employees and management style. This management approach has been supported by many in the police field, such as Roberg (1979), who argues that theory Y is more conducive than theory X to help police deal with the demands of competing groups in today's society. Furthermore, they argue that a system of supportive management is the most effective because it provides a satisfying work environment for the individual officer (Cordner, 1978). This conclusion seems to be equally applicable to prosecution, courts, and criminal corrections. But additional research on motivation and criminal justice operations needs to be conducted.

Although theory X has been the norm in traditional criminal justice organizations, theory Y deserves increased attention both by those interested in explaining motivation in these systems and by those who seek advice on how to motivate criminal justice employees. Owen (2006:179) does provide some insight on the importance of social support systems, job satisfaction, and locus of control to correctional supervisor stress levels. For correctional supervisors who have greater levels of social support, higher levels of job satisfaction, and more input or control over their workplaces, there is a likelihood of decreased levels of stress and possible increase in commitment to the workplace (Lambert, Hogan, and Tucker, 2009).

Moreover, we do have some insight into the motivation process among higher-level public administrators. For example, Downs (1967) suggests that the motives of employees are not always consistent with those of administrators. His model of motivation in public organizations is tied to aspects of both theory X and theory Y. According to Downs (1967:84–85), public administrators, such as those in the criminal justice system, have two types of motivations that are manifested in a number of goals. First, power, money, income, prestige, convenience, and security are all manifestations of self-interest (theory X), the motivating factor for many public administrators. Second, public administrators may, however, be motivated by altruism (theory Y), where the goals of loyalty, pride, desire to serve the public interest, and commitment to a specific program of action take precedence over self-interest goals (Rainey, 2014).

Achievement–Power–Affiliation Theory

Achievement–power–affiliation theory:

Motivation is predicated on high achievement, and people achieve success through their own efforts, through work on projects that are challenging but not impossible, through receiving feedback on their work, and through avoiding situations where their level of achievement is in question.

The **achievement–power–affiliation theory** of motivation was originally developed by David McClelland (1965). McClelland (1965:322) suggests that people with high achievement (nAch) values do the following:

1. Seek to achieve success through their own efforts and not have their success attributed to other factors.

2. Work on projects that are challenging but not impossible.

3. Receive identifiable and recurring feedback about their work and avoid situations where their level of achievement is in question.

This last proposition was tested by Stoller (1977) in his analysis of the effect of feedback on police performance. He examined the relationship between feedback and increased police productivity as measured by issued citations. Increased performance was achieved by forty-eight of the fifty-four officers who received the feedback. This seems to be a recurring theme in much police research: consistent feedback from upper-level managers can promote increased productivity among line officers (Roberg, 1979:114). Other research done on police has indicated that many officers need to increase their level of responsibility and participation in decision making. Hernandez (1982) found in the Mesa, Arizona, police department that a "professional model" of policing, which involved participation in problem solving and decision making, increased the officers' level of commitment to the department and their level of motivation.

The second motive associated with this theoretical position is the power motive (nPow). A growing body of literature attempts to document the role that power plays in organizations, particularly in decision-making processes (Pfeffer, 1981; Porter, Allen, and Angle, 1981; Salancik and Pfeffer, 1977). The power motive can be defined as a person's need to have some type of influence over another's behavior, and this can be expressed in two ways. First, it may be in the form of personalized power, as manifested through an adversarial relationship. Person-to-person competition is emphasized, and domination is a by-product. People are viewed simplistically as winners and losers, with the main goal being the achievement of power over others. Second, socialized power is impersonal and is expressed through a concern for others; it is employed by individuals who are sensitive to the fact that one person's gain means another person's loss. This type of power orientation is humanistic and is employed by those in leadership roles in social organizations (Tosi, Rizzo, and Carroll, 1986:228).

The high affiliation need (nAff) is one in which persons are motivated by friendships, cooperative working relationships at work, and the development of a high degree of mutual understanding. Persons with high affiliation needs have been traditionally associated with managerial success (Robbins and Judge, 2007:194). We see this evidenced in many police organizations and correctional organizations. In many police agencies, for example, the power of affiliation is expressed in how tasks are performed and goals achieved, yet it is not clear *how* high affiliation translates into higher levels of motivation among police officers. Organizational behavior research has examined the dynamic tension that exists among employees who have differential levels of achievement (nAch), power (nPow), and affiliation (nAff).

This presentation of the achievement–power–affiliation theory of motivation enables us to see how the factors of achievement, power, and affiliation are instrumental in the motivation of individuals. Surely we can say that individuals are motivated by the quest for achievement, power, affiliation, or all three. Little research supports either of these positions completely, but we do know, for example, that achievement, as defined by promotion, is important in the police field. Gaines, Tubergen, and Paiva (1984) concluded that promotions are extremely important in meeting the needs of police officers. In particular, they found that for some officers, higher needs were more important than lower needs and that promotion was, in part, related to the satisfaction of those needs. In effect, the officers' desire to achieve, in this case through promotion, was crucial to their levels of motivation.

With respect to the power motive and criminal justice personnel, research has been done primarily within correctional institutions. Stojkovic (1984) documents the types of socialized power within inmate social systems and how they affect the operation of a prison. Socialized power among corrections officers was also explored by Hepburn (1985) and by Stojkovic (1987). Specific bases of socialized power were employed by both inmates and officers to complete their respective job assignments and tasks. For example, corrections officers considered the use of legitimate power—reasonable instructions and rules—a useful tool in motivating prisoners to do what is expected of them. In addition, the use of coercive power or force was not rated highly by corrections staff as a way of gaining compliance among prisoners. Power as a motivational tool has also been documented by research on corrections administrators (Stojkovic, 1986).

Expectancy Theory

Expectancy theory:
A rational theory of motivation that posits that a certain amount of work will result in a calculated outcome.

Expectancy theory, based on the belief that if a certain amount of effort is put forth, a calculated outcome will result, is a rational approach to motivation. This theory posits that police work, for example, relies on an expectation among police officers that their efforts will produce a reduction in crime. The individual officer's motivation to perform depends, in part, on reduced crime rates. From an idealistic perspective, rational activity on the part of the police officer should reduce crime and increase the officer's satisfaction.

We summarize the concepts of expectancy theory here (Tosi, Rizzo, and Carroll, 1986:240). A basic concept is that performance equals motivation times ability. Performance is a function of the individual's ability to complete the task along with the motivation to do the task. More important, if neither motivation nor ability is present, then there will be no performance. Motivation and ability are related in a multiplicative fashion.

An *expectancy* is the likelihood that an event or outcome will occur. Expectancies take two forms. The first form is *effort–performance expectancies*, in which the person believes that a specific level of effort will result in a particular performance. The police officer, for example, may believe that a connection exists between the level of patrol activity and the crime rate in the precinct. In short, there is a correlation between the amount of work done and the end result, which in this example is the amount of crime in a specific area. The second form is *performance–outcome expectancies*, in which the person has an "expectation about the relationship between a particular level of performance and attaining certain outcomes" (Tosi, Rizzo, and Carroll, 1986:243). In this form of expectancy, the police officer may believe that a relationship exists between activity and a positive evaluation from superiors that is ultimately expressed in some type of reward, such as a promotion. However, the relationship between police activity and crime rates is somewhat problematic. If, for example, there is a low probability that police activity will lead to an actual reduction in crime, then it is difficult to see how one can reward individual police officers to produce the desired performance—that is, reduced crime. In addition, if it is unlikely that the officer will gain any reward from the activity, he or she will not be motivated to do the activity. As a result, we would expect that the motivational levels of individual officers would be low because there is a low probability that their work activity produces the desired performance. Therefore, the individual officer may not choose crime reduction as an outcome. More important, the officer may have a stronger desire for other outcomes, typically those that are attainable and rewarded consistently by the police organization.

Valences are the level of satisfaction or dissatisfaction produced by various outcomes. In brief, they are the individual's estimate of the advantages or disadvantages of a particular outcome. In the police example, if the effort required to produce a reduction in crime does not lead to a satisfactory level of reward from the organization, this activity has a low positive valence; it is not worth the effort to pursue the activity knowing the low level of reward attached to the effort.

Tosi, Rizzo, and Carroll (1986:243–244) discuss how expectancy theory can be expanded to include other factors that affect the motivational level of employees. They argue that motivation is a function of expectancies and valences. Ability is a function of performance potential and organizational factors. Performance results from motivation and ability and leads to intrinsic and extrinsic rewards. The level of performance affects the effort–performance expectancies. The rewards received for performance affect performance–outcome expectancies in later periods, and rewards also affect satisfaction.

Interpreting and applying this model to police officer motivation, we can say that first, the individual motivational levels of police officers are a function of what they expect and what valence they assign to their various activities. Second, the ability of an officer to do the job is a function of the officer's performance potential or the range of skills used in the achievement of objectives (Tosi, Rizzo, and Carroll, 1986:244). These skills may be limited by structural factors, such as job descriptions, policies, and technology. Arresting all known criminals, for example, would be impossible because of the limited resources of police organizations and the policies of the organization toward full enforcement of the law (Goldstein, 1990).

Third, when police activity leads toward some performance and that performance is a function of motivation and ability, then we would expect that a reward would follow. If an increase in arrest activity leads to an increase in pay or a promotion, then the officer receives an extrinsic reward for the performance. In addition, if arresting individuals provide the community with a safe environment and give the officer a good feeling about doing the job, the officer receives an intrinsic reward; this reward is typically self-administered by the individual. Many have suggested that a clearly identified reward structure within police departments is what is needed to properly motivate officers (Gaines, Tubergen, and Paiva, 1984:265–275). However, others have argued quite persuasively that these rewards are few and far between and are limited by the structure of many police departments. Conser (1979:286) contends that motivation is difficult in police organizations because the opportunities for advancement and promotion are limited. He recommends a number of mechanisms that would raise the motivational levels of officers, including merit pay packages, extra vacation leaves, and extra pay for education. Nevertheless, some research suggests that extrinsic rewards, such as increased pay and promotion, are only a small part of the motivation of police officers. Intrinsic rewards, such as achievement (Baker, 1976), are just as valuable. More important, it seems clear that proper motivation of specific officers requires a multitude of management strategies.

Fourth, when an officer perceives that a level of performance will consistently produce a similar positive outcome from the organization, such as a reward, this perception will affect future expectancies; this process is nothing but learning by the officer and reinforcement by the organization through the reward structure. As the police officer learns that ticket writing, for example, is positively rewarded by the organization, the officer will continue to perform the activity until rewards are discontinued by the organization. In effect, the performance expectancy is a function of reinforcement and feedback by the organization (Stoller, 1977:57).

Finally, if the police officer is consistently rewarded, both extrinsically and intrinsically, then we can say that he or she has a high level of satisfaction with the organization. Conversely, if the police officer is not receiving rewards, then we can expect that dissatisfaction is high and will continue to stay at this level until modifications are made. Criminal justice managers need to be aware of and sensitive to the level of dissatisfaction if organizational objectives are to be met (Witham, 1980:10–11).

In an attempt to apply expectancy theory to policing, DeJong, Mastrofski, and Parks (2001) tested it as an explanation for variation in police office problem solving. The researchers found that the theory did well in explaining what types of officers engaged in more problem solving. In particular, this research noted that there was a clear difference between officers who were more "traditional" in their orientation when compared to officers who were community policing oriented on the dimension of problem solving. The latter type of officer was motivated by recognition that the work performed (problem solving) was valued by the police organization. By granting a community policing assignment to an officer, the department was providing great recognition, and this, in turn, allowed the officer to creatively address problems on the beat. The key determinant is the degree to which officers are granted autonomy to make decisions regarding problem selection and solution. For traditionally structured criminal justice organizations, such autonomy is problematic.

How does increased autonomy impact employee behavior such that levels of commitment and motivation stay high and are in concordance with organizational goals? The answer to this question raises not only a concern regarding employee motivation but also issues of job design, supervision, and leadership. For now, we can say that there is support for expectancy theory in the criminal justice literature, but as noted by DeJong, Mastrofski, and Parks (2001:60), more research is needed before a definitive position on expectancy theory and its application to criminal justice employee motivation can be made.

Equity Theory

Equity theory: A theory of motivation that is based on perceived fairness among employees regarding treatment in the workplace.

Equity theory holds that an individual's motivation level is affected by her or his perception of fairness in the workplace and that individual motivation must be understood in relation to how other employees are treated by management and the organization. Equity theory stresses the importance of fairness in the organization and how employees perceive its application in the workforce. In addition, equity theory rests on two fundamental assumptions: Individuals evaluate their interpersonal relationships as they would any other commodity; and individuals develop expectations about their evaluation in the organization equivalent to the amount of individual contributions they make. As such, an examination of both inputs and outputs is critical to understanding and applying equity theory.

Inputs are those items brought into the organization by the individual. Common examples of input include age, seniority, training, and education, to mention a few. *Outputs* are the visible products of individual effort. Examples of outputs are promotion, salary or pay, recognition, and benefits. All inputs and outputs are not weighted the same. For some police officers, for example, the value of experience "on the street" is weighted much more heavily than educational attainment. As an organizational input, these same officers would view the outcome of pay to be determined more by experiential level than by educational level. For them, the weighting of work experience would be higher and deserving of greater reward. For other officers, the reverse may be true. It is the differential level of attachment to various inputs and outputs that makes equity theory problematic.

Every individual in the organization determines the relative weights of inputs and outputs. It is the ratio of a person's outcomes to inputs relative to the ratio of outputs to inputs of others that determines the level of perceived equity. Inequity occurs when the individual perceives the ratio of outcomes to inputs to be unequal. The potential negative consequences of this perceived inequity concern both managers and administrators of organizations. For criminal justice organizations, the perception of inequity is fostered by a number of factors beyond the control of administrators. The rigid structure of public contracts, for example, limits the ability of criminal justice organizations to deal effectively with perceived inequities. In addition, it is difficult for employees to feel motivated if they perceive a disjuncture between their work performance and their pay in relation to the work performance and pay of similarly situated employees. As such, it is reasonable that some research has identified this perception of inequity as causing a loss of morale and motivation among public sector employees (Schay, 1988).

For criminal justice managers, this perception of inequity can have negative effects on the motivation of employees. What can be done? Research has suggested two strategies. First, criminal justice administrators can do everything in their power to see that employees are treated equitably. One of the advantages of a union contract is that it equalizes, for the most part, everyone in the organization, yet it still can produce inequity among those who feel they are performing better than most other employees but receive no greater financial payoff for their efforts. Despite this situation, criminal justice administrators can do a great deal to ensure equitable treatment of employees, including having clearly articulated policies and procedures and applying them to all employees in a fair and consistent manner. Criminal justice administrators can best reduce perceptions of inequity if employees perceive equal application of the rules and regulations, even in organizations where remuneration is perceived to be low for work performed.

Second, emphases on aspects of the job other than pay can be brought to employees' attention. Within criminal justice organizations, employees perform a number of duties that go beyond pay considerations. Pay scales as a primary motivation device for police officers, for example, are a poor incentive. Pay incentives typically do not exist in most criminal justice organizations. Instead, we can stress to subordinates that the problem-oriented focus of their work provides them with much autonomy, which can be motivating.

Such freedom allows greater individual expression and input on how tasks can be performed. Similar observations can be made about the work of probation and parole agents, as well as those who work in correctional institutions. Such considerations can be expressed to employees by administrators and managers through job design efforts, training, and employee evaluation and supervision approaches. Such efforts can mitigate the adverse effects of perceived pay inequities among employees within criminal justice organizations.

A growing body of research in organizational behavior also suggests that questions of equity must be placed in the context of larger issues of justice within organizations. Two concepts within this evolving discussion are *procedural justice* and *interactional justice* (Robbins and Judge, 2007:206–207). The former stresses the importance of process and explanation as to why certain outcomes occurred in an organization. When, for example, a correctional officer feels that an outcome concerning pay or promotion is unfair, the appropriate response on the part of management is to explain the reasons for that outcome. Employees have to feel that the outcome is explainable and thus equitable. Such a concern puts a very heavy emphasis on management to explain its decisions through a structure that is accessible to employees.

The second concept, interactional justice, regards how employees are treated and the degree to which dignity, concern, and respect are afforded them. For criminal justice employees, these issues become more relevant to their individual levels of motivation when financial remuneration and promotion are limited. Being treated fairly and with respect goes a long way in positions where the primary motivation to perform is limited and it appeals to more intrinsic rewards that are crucial to effective employee performance.

Henderson, Wells, Maguire, and Gray (2010) suggest that the issue of equity and fairness in criminal justice organizations goes a long way to increase both legitimacy and compliance among subordinates. Defined as "procedural justice," the emphasis is on fair procedures and equal treatment of members in the community and those for whom we invoke the criminal justice process. While these authors note the methodological and measurement properties of capturing procedural justice within criminal justice organizations, they firmly support procedural justice outcomes as having benefit to managing subordinates and offenders within correctional settings.

Theory Z

Earlier in the chapter, we discussed the differences between theory X and theory Y. Here, we present an extension of theory Y known as **theory Z**, which suggests

Theory Z: A holistic theory of motivation that looks beyond the organization. By focusing, for example, on family needs and school needs, the organization attempts to address major concerns of the employee such that attention can be focused on the work environment.

that management must come to grips with the fact that organizations, either private or public, no longer can exist in a social vacuum. They not only function within a larger context but also are expected to deal effectively with the needs, desires, and problems of their employees in creative and diverse ways. Proper management and administration of contemporary organizations must consider the needs of the employee and, more important, how those needs can be met within the context of both the organization and society as a whole.

Before we discuss these changes and how they would affect criminal justice administrations, we need to examine the basic tenets of theory Z. Of its many proponents, Ouchi (1981) is probably the most notable. He suggests, along with others, that theory Z is based on three beliefs:

1. Management is concerned with production, a position expressed in theory X.

2. Management is concerned with the well-being of workers as productive employees. This position is similar to a basic assumption of theory Y.

3. Finally—and this belief distinguishes theory Z from theories X and Y—the organization cannot be viewed independently of the larger social, economic, and political conditions in society. More important, the work setting must be understood in conjunction with other institutions in society, such as family and school.

What distinguishes theory Z from both theory X and theory Y is that it attempts to integrate the concerns of both of these theories while simultaneously reaching beyond the organizational structure into the very fabric of society. Because it holds that organizations cannot be isolated from other social forces, theory Z offers a synthesis of the previous theories and a macro-orientation on employee motivation. It suggests that motivation is not only organizationally determined but also influenced by broad and powerful entities in society.

A number of benefits accrue from applying theory Z to the administration of criminal justice agencies. Though theory Z has had limited application in public organizations, including criminal justice, there nevertheless has been support for such an application. Archambeault and Wierman (1983), for example, argue for the application of theory Z to policing, suggesting several changes that have to occur in the management of police organizations for police administrators to become more responsive than they now are to their employees and their communities.

First, there must be shared decision making in police organizations, with individual officers having increased input on matters that affect them, although management would still be the final authority on key administrative issues. The traditional structure of police organizations would have to be drastically changed for theory Z to succeed. As Archambeault and Wierman (1983:427) suggest, top administrative officials in police organizations would have to make a serious commitment to such a radical approach before it could be implemented. Without such a commitment, theory Z would have a low probability of succeeding.

Second, supporters of theory Z propose a team approach to policing, with emphasis on the collective responsibility of officers. The idea here would be to get police away from the traditional notion of individual responsibility and individual work. Theory Z envisions officers working together toward the attainment of collectively defined goals, even though final responsibility would still lie with police administrators. This is consistent with modern trends to integrate community policing ideas into the operations of law enforcement agencies. The efforts of the Community Oriented Policing Service (COPS), within the U.S. Department of Justice, for example, have provided much technical assistance to police agencies attempting to integrate the ideas of community policing into their organizations. These efforts have posed many significant challenges to police departments, particularly in trying to balance the need for increased discretion among community policing officers and the need for accountability and supervision by police supervisors. Theory Z, similar to other theories of motivation discussed in this chapter, offers many benefits to criminal justice organizations. The concern, however, is how this is achieved in organizations that have been traditionally paramilitary in structure and directed toward limited aims of law enforcement, offender supervision, and/or case management. The issue of discretion and decision making is addressed more thoroughly in Chapter 12.

Third, police officers would have a clearly identified career path, with attendant rewards and promotional opportunities laid out in advance. This idea has some disadvantages because it seems to assume infinite reward opportunities and promotional paths. Although this may sometimes be the case, on the whole, promotional opportunities are often few and far between in many criminal justice organizations. What if the rewards and career opportunities are just not available? What is to be done with the police officer, for example, who has become "cross-trained" in a number of specializations yet is never able to get a promotion? As fiscal constraints increase, it is not clear how theory Z would resolve these thorny issues. This is not to suggest that nothing can be done, but at a minimum, proponents of theory Z will have to offer concrete answers to some of these practical concerns.

Fourth, Archambeault and Wierman (1983:427) suggest that the police organization must be more "holistic" in its dealings with police officers by appreciating that officers exist with ordinary demands of all workers in society. They have needs beyond the work setting that include but are not limited to, for example, educational, personal, and family needs. Although it would be unrealistic to expect criminal justice organizations in this country to provide for all of the needs of their employees, as is done in Japan, it is reasonable for administrators in criminal justice to be sensitive to the needs of workers and, in return, for employees to make a personal and professional commitment to the organization. The result of this arrangement is loyalty to the goals of the organization by subordinates and a smoothly run organization.

Similar ideas were put forward by Houston (1999) in his examination of the relevance of theory Z to the field of corrections. Quoting management expert Tom Peters (1987), Houston suggests that theory Z has application to corrections in two specific areas. It is important to (1) involve everyone in everything and (2) use self-managing teams in task completion. Integrating these ideas into a motivation plan will enhance employees' sense of commitment to the organization and increase their performance. Although such an approach is desirable in criminal justice, we must again question its feasibility. It is not clear how administrators would be able to provide a structure that deals with the many needs of subordinates. Clearly, criminal justice managers and administrators need to be attuned to their workers, but what are the most effective approaches for attaining that objective? It is likely that theory Z may require more than can be realistically expected from those who administer our criminal justice systems. This is not to suggest, however, that there is no room for the application of theory Z to criminal justice management. Its most positive aspect is the belief that there is a relationship between organizational structure and the motivation of employees.

In this chapter, we have contended that employee motivation cannot be understood independently of organizational structure. Theory Z posits that management has a responsibility to structure a work environment that promotes the highest level of employee motivation. If theory Z enables managers and administrators to rethink their roles in shaping and influencing their subordinates, then it has begun a movement of real value to the administration of criminal justice systems. Presently, it needs to be critically examined. No theory is flawless; only through future critical evaluations will we see the benefits of the application of theory Z to criminal justice organizations.

Work Perspectives: PRISONER MOTIVATION

Why should someone in jail participate in programming or follow the rules? Some people possess internal motivation. But by nature, these are not the same individuals who end up incarcerated. If they had internal motivation to begin with, what led them to jail? There are probably a host of reasons why they became incarcerated: joblessness, poverty, and lack of education. If they had had these issues addressed in their lives, they probably would not have ended up under correctional supervision.

So it is a given that in prison settings we have unmotivated individuals who carry much baggage with them once incarcerated. How do we motivate the unmotivated? External motivation is the only thing left. We all do things due to external motivation. We take a job for the money, we work overtime to be able to go on a trip, we follow the rules because if we don't, we have family, possessions, homes to lose.

Many people in jail have nothing to lose. They don't have a home, a car, a family, a job ... nothing. So if they get into a fight while in custody and have to stay in custody longer, ... so what? Many people in jail have been to jail many times before and they don't count on the current stint to be their last. They have sat through AODA and anger management classes and most prisoners are of the same opinion: "They didn't do nothing." So what can be accomplished with these types of people? What motivates offenders?

Most prisoner behavior and subsequent motivation is tied to some type of benefit for him or her. If a class will count toward requirements for an inmate's probation, they are motivated to take the class. If a class will shave some time off their sentences, they are motivated to take the class. If behaving and following the rules will earn them a movie or extra canteen, they are motivated to behave. Simple motivations affect how prisoners behave. Positive reinforcement, rewards ... that's what motivates most jail inmates.

The difference between prisons and jails should be noted, however. Prison inmates often have much more time to put toward programming and school; therefore, these programs can have a bigger impact on their lives as a whole. And oftentimes, by the time someone ends up in prison, they are tired of being incarcerated, and they have figured out that internal motivation may be all they have going for them.

WORK PERSPECTIVES—continued

At the end of the day, most prisoners live in a real world that has few benefits and many sanctions. A true correctional professional recognizes that motivating prisoners to change behavior is a daily task that can be onerous and yield limited results; yet as professionals, we are committed to making the experience as positive for inmates as is reasonably possible. To do otherwise condemns us all to failure. Without the possibility of positive rewards as a result of following a program, the incentive to change for prisoners will be weak, and, as a result, we will continue to have alarming rates of recidivism and return to correctional facilities. We owe it to ourselves, the corrections profession, the prisoner, and society to make sure we have a motivating environment for prisoners within our correctional facilities. Anything less is unacceptable.

SOURCE: Rachele Klassy, Social Worker, Milwaukee County, Correctional Facility South.

PRESCRIPTIONS FOR CRIMINAL JUSTICE MANAGEMENT

Clearly, the motivation process is complex. Moreover, the application of existing theoretical models to the various criminal justice systems is problematic because no single theory of motivation can explain the many factors that affect the motivation of criminal justice personnel. Nevertheless, we can provide some suggestions to criminal justice managers about the approaches and programs most suited to their employees. One key element links all the differing theoretical positions on employee motivation: The needs, perspectives, and viewpoints of employees are instrumental not only to their individual growth but also to organizational effectiveness. More directly, it would be accurate to conclude that effective criminal justice management recognizes that the motivation of employees requires the growth and maturity of those employees through proactive and flexible management strategies. Without such flexible approaches to motivation, employee development is stymied and organizational effectiveness is reduced, according to Lynch (1986:53):

> The present challenge to police managers is to provide a work climate in which every employee has the opportunity to mature, both as an individual and as a member of the department. However, the police manager must believe that individuals can be essentially self-directed and creative in their work environments if they are motivated by the management.

Although we recognize that the management of criminal justice systems is different from the management of private companies or other public institutions, we still believe that a number of programs can be taken from these other sectors and applied effectively to criminal justice processes. We review and interpret two of these programs here: quality circles and management by objectives. An examination of other useful programs related to job design is provided in Chapter 6. Students are encouraged to review these programs here because they are equally applicable to the motivation process. We conclude the chapter by exploring public service motivation and a basic model of motivation derived from a review of the research.

Quality Circle Programs

Quality circle programs are based on two fundamental assumptions. First, interactions among employees should provide maximum growth of the individual. Quality circles are meant to enhance workers' abilities to improve themselves, both personally and professionally. Second, by providing conditions for the growth of employees, the organization will become increasingly effective. In short, it is in the organization's best interests to promote the well-being of workers. Operating on these two assumptions, **quality circles** are defined as small groups of employees, typically nonmanagement personnel from the same work unit, who meet regularly to identify, analyze, and recommend solutions to problems relating to the work unit (Hatry and Greiner, 1984:1). In addition, management must support these groups of subordinates.

Quality circles: Small groups of employees, usually not management employees, who meet regularly to identify, analyze, and recommend solutions to organizational problems.

Within the police subsystem of the criminal justice process, researchers have strongly recommended this approach. After conducting probably the most exhaustive study to date of the implementation of quality circles and other participatory management programs in policing, Hatry and Greiner (1984) conclude that the use of quality circle programs greatly enhances the potential for producing small-scale service improvements and improves work unit morale among officers. These improvements are crucial, in our opinion, to the motivation of police officers. Moreover, this approach to improving the motivational levels of police officers is also applicable to other workers in the criminal justice process, such as corrections officers, counselors, and court personnel. Although many of the prescriptions currently being made concern the improvement of police, the application of these quality circle programs to the other components of the criminal justice system is sorely needed. Brief, Munro, and Aldag (1976) describe the applicability of such approaches, particularly job enlargement programs, to correctional institutions. And although Saari (1982) is cautious about accepting management practices that he defines as fads, he does see the value of providing more information about management programs to those who run and manage our court systems. Also, research conducted in probation departments has found that the integration of the employee into the management of the organization is essential, given the "people" work that is performed. Matthews (2009) argues that, more often than not, effective probation officers are determined by supervisors to be those employees who follow the bureaucratic rules of the position, for example, getting the paperwork done, but the truly effective officers are those who develop relationships with their colleagues, supervisors, and offenders. Probation work is people work and the greatest satisfaction from the work is successfully maintaining relationships that improve the quality of supervision and enhance the chances for success of former offenders in the community. Management approaches that recognize this reality will go a long way to motivate employees.

Although the research literature has been generally supportive of quality circle programs, it would be naive to suggest that they can be applied to all situations in criminal justice. Understanding the motivational process requires an analysis of organizational tasks. It may be inappropriate to suggest, for example, that quality circle programs be adopted by corrections administrators faced with increased militancy among both prisoners and staff. Even though it may not be a panacea for all motivation problems, we do suggest, however, that the quality circle be considered as a possible option to increase the motivation levels of criminal justice employees. Having said this, however, some research has questioned the efficacy of quality circle programs on the grounds that they don't really change a great deal in how business is accomplished in organizations. For most organizations in the private sector who adopted quality circles, the evidence is mixed, and critics argue that it is unclear how benefits could accrue under such a program when, for most organizations, the quality circle program only meets minimally during a workweek (Robbins and Judge, 2011:236–237). Within public organizations, such as criminal justice, there simply is not much evidence to show how quality circles would improve the motivation of employees. Nevertheless, there is something to be said about quality circles offering useful information on how to motivate public employees who function in more complex organizations than their counterparts in private organizations.

Management by Objectives (MBO)

Management by objectives (MBO):
A process whereby management and employees identify goals and work toward their completion and receive evaluation in a specified period of time.

Probably no other innovation within management circles since the 1950s has had as much influence on organizations as management by objectives (MBO). **Management by objectives** can be defined as a process whereby individual managers and employees identify goals, work toward their completion, and provide evaluation within a specific time period. Much research evaluates the effectiveness of MBO programs within organizations (Carroll and Tosi, 1973). In addition, this program has been widely adopted in the various components of the criminal justice system (Angell, 1971; Archambeault and Archambeault, 1982; More, 1977; Sherman, 1975). However, the efficacy of the model for the various components of the criminal justice system remains unproven.

Some believe its application to criminal justice can make the system effective and can help improve the level of motivation among criminal justice employees. Others, however, do not consider MBO to be universally applicable in criminal justice. A review of some of the research on this topic is required.

Beginning with research that supports the application of MBO to criminal justice operations, the police field has the greatest number of advocates for this view. Angell (1971) was the first to suggest that the implementation of MBO in policing would be of great benefit. In particular, Angell sees the democratization of police organizations as a step toward improving the delivery of services. Opponents, such as Sherman (1975), suggest that this democratic model, as conceived by Angell, would be deleterious to police organizations because it grants decision-making authority to teams of police and diminishes the power of middle managers in the traditional police hierarchy.

In fact, Sherman argues persuasively that his own research on team policing indicates that middle management will resist the efforts of higher-echelon personnel to democratize police organizations. Essentially, he believes that any planned change within police departments must include all members of the department. Anything short of total involvement will be viewed by the rank and file as just another one of the "boss's pet projects" (Sherman, 1975:377). Others, however, support the application of MBO to police departments and suggest that it is critical to effective management. Hatry and Greiner (1984) employed multiple research methods to assess the effectiveness of MBO programs in a number of police departments. In addition, they evaluated motivational programs in more than seventeen police departments and reviewed materials provided by an additional thirty police departments. From this evaluation, they concluded that "MBO systems have considerable potential for motivating management employees to improve service outcomes and service delivery efficiency" (1984:130). More important, they suggest that much can be done to improve the operation of MBO systems in police departments if administrators give them proper attention.

Archambeault and Archambeault (1982:92–93) suggest that for MBO to work in correctional institutions, a number of conditions have to exist. First, as others have stated, administrative personnel have to be committed to the MBO program. A lack of commitment only breeds contempt for and disapproval of the program in lower-level employees. Second, administrative staff must be able to receive criticism and suggestions from employees; otherwise, management will not be attuned to the workings of the organization. Third, any MBO program must take into consideration the organization's power structure. It is often difficult for managers to share power with subordinates; it has been a recurring problem in many MBO programs that administrators deny that power to make decisions must be shared with all workers. But the empowerment of employees and the subsequent enrichment of their jobs are implicit in the MBO approach. Fourth, workers as well as management must believe that the MBO process is worth pursuing. In many organizations, lack of commitment has led to the demise of MBO programs.

It may be time to end the search for the perfect model of MBO practices within criminal justice organizations. Recent research has suggested that many programs that emphasize general MBO principles such as those described earlier do not lead toward any increase in motivation among workers (Robbins and Judge, 2011: 239). This assertion might not be the case in criminal justice organizations, but we do not have any definitive evidence that MBO practices as espoused over the past 40 years in criminal justice organizations do anything to further motivate employees to perform better within their agencies. In addition, motivation research has moved past MBO to questioning the motivations of employees who work in the public sector.

Public Service Motivation

In the twenty-first century, there is now an interest in determining why so many people are interested in public service work. Rainey (2011) explores the concept of **public service motivation (PSM)** as a way to understand why people pursue public service work in the first place. PSM examines the basis for public service motivation and may become a relevant field of study when applied to

Public service motivation (PSM): The motivating factors found among workers in public service.

criminal justice organizations. Researchers have identified the dimensions of PSM to be the following: attraction to public service, commitment to the public interest, compassion, and self-sacrifice (Perry, 1996). Many of these attributes could be applied to those who pursue criminal justice careers. It is common for persons pursuing a criminal justice profession to express the commitment they have to a sense of duty or concern for society. Yet, it is difficult to discern the degree to which criminal justice employees are actually motivated out of a public service commitment.

As a motivator, we do not have good research to guide us in determining how influential the dimensions of PSM might be among those pursing criminal justice professions and those who are currently employed in such positions. It might be interesting to find out how PSM might change over a career. Do police officers, for example, wane on the dimensions of PSM as their careers evolve? If so, how does a change in the dimensions of PSM affect their motivation, and what can be done from an administrative point of view to address changing motivation levels among employees? More important, does a high score on PSM necessarily translate into higher levels of productivity among criminal justice employees? These and other important questions must be addressed if PSM has any real application and relevance within criminal justice organizations.

The inherent problems of motivating employees in criminal justice organizations within the constraints of a labor agreement also must be recognized. How is the motivation process understood within the context of a labor agreement? Oftentimes, the labor agreement, for example, defines the contours of the disciplinary process for administrators in criminal justice organizations. How does the labor agreement enhance or inhibit the motivation process? In many states across the country, a strong movement has taken place (post-2010) to limit the power of public unions, including those in criminal justice organizations. Much of this is in reaction to dwindling state budgets. What effect will the loss of union representation, or at least a narrowing of union power, have on the motivation process in criminal justice organizations, especially in police agencies and correctional institutions where unions are much more likely to exist in comparison to prosecutor offices and court systems? These questions have no easy answers because research has not caught up with these real-world problems and issues in criminal justice organizations.

An Integrated Model of Motivation

In spite of the questions in the previous section, it is possible to generate some conclusions on an **integrated model of motivation** that may be useful to criminal justice administrators and employees (California Department of Corrections, 1994b). This model is based on key elements of the theories and literature discussed earlier. The model has six basic elements:

1. Emphasis on personal motives and values. An effective motivation plan must take into consideration the motives and values of employees. Criminal

Integrated model of motivation: A model of motivation that incorporates various theoretical and practical ideas directed toward the completion of organizational objectives and goals. It is composed of six ideas: personal motives and values, use of incentives and rewards, reinforcement, specific and clear goals, sufficient personnel and material resources, and interpersonal and group processes that support members' goals.

justice workers have motives and values that stress public service as well as personal interests; they want to be in a profession that is both appreciated and remunerated fairly and appropriately. Often, criminal justice administrators are indifferent to or unaware of the importance of the motives and values of employees. Those in leadership positions must offer a set of motives and values as guidance for subordinates. By having an articulated mission statement, for example, the important motives and values of the organization become known, and employees are able to see how they fit into the larger picture of the organization.

2. Use of incentives and rewards. Employees need incentives to meet expectations and appropriate rewards for jobs well done. A major challenge for criminal justice administrators is the creation of formal and informal approaches to recognize and reward employees. The types of rewards can be varied. Monetary rewards are often difficult to provide, but other types of rewards, such as informal praise when a job is handled well and employee recognition programs, can be given.

3. Reinforcement. Administrators must develop feedback mechanisms so that workers understand that their performance is appropriate on assigned tasks. More often than not, the immediate supervisor provides little or no feedback to subordinates. This creates much anxiety and uncertainty among employees, causing their motivation to wane.

4. Specific and clear goals. All theories of motivation highlight the importance of goals or expected outcomes to the motivation process. This is probably the most difficult and problematic area in motivating criminal justice employees. As public agencies, criminal justice organizations are expected to address multiple, and sometimes conflicting, goals; consequently, specifying goals and prioritizing them can be very difficult. This difficulty, more than any other, poses problems for administrators. Goal clarity and goal consensus may not be possible in criminal justice organizations and, as a consequence, developing effective motivation plans will be difficult.

5. Sufficient personal and material resources. The organization must have a sufficient number of resources, both human and financial, to create a proper motivating environment for employees. Examples of such resources include support and training programs for employees, outlets for employees that allow socialization and the development of informal groups, and material support, such as adequate supplies and equipment, for tasks to be accomplished and goals attained.

6. Interpersonal and group processes that support members' goals. In criminal justice organizations, this means the development of work groups that identify with employees' individual interests as well as group concerns. Criminal justice organizations can create work environments in which individuals work together toward accomplishing group goals, exercising greater flexibility in work assignments and job responsibilities, and selecting group leaders. Group processes would work toward the accomplishment of tasks yet be sensitive to members' needs. Individual employee needs are considered as part of the process of an effective group.

FIGURE 5.2   The Basic Motivation Process.

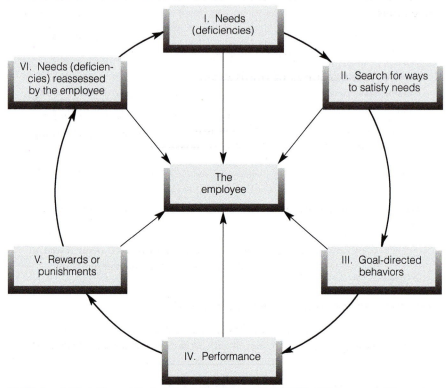

SOURCE: From Hellriegel / Slocum / Woodman. Organizational Behavior, 5E. © 1989 South-Western, a part of Cengage Learning, Inc. Reproduced by permission. www.cengage.com/permissions

Taken together, these ideas can make criminal justice organizations more aware of the motivation needs of employees. The model of the motivational process in Figure 5.2 highlights these ideas. The diagram shows the importance of employee needs, goal-directed behavior, performance, rewards and punishments, and reassessment of needs within the motivational process. Criminal justice administrators need to devote particular attention to these issues in developing and maintaining a motivational environment for employees. The goal is to create a motivational environment in which employees can exhibit maximum effort. Further research will have to test these ideas to demonstrate their relevance to employee motivation in specific situations as well as to criminal justice administration in general.

SUMMARY

Understand a definition of motivation.

- Motivation is both a psychological construct and an organizational construct.

Comprehend organizational theory and motivation from a historical perspective.

- The motivation process can be defined and must be understood as evolving over a long period of time.

Know the major theories of motivation.

- There are a number of theories of motivation (need theory, theory X and theory Y, achievement–power–affiliation theory, expectancy theory, equity theory, and theory Z), each having benefit to comprehending motivation within criminal justice organizations.
- The motivation of criminal justice employees requires recognition that employee needs, abilities, and opinions are critical.

Explain some prescriptions for criminal justice management regarding motivation.

- Two prescriptive models of employee motivation have been tested in criminal justice organizations: quality circles and management by objectives.

Understand an integrated model of motivation.

- An integrated model of motivation that incorporates many different theories may be the most beneficial to criminal justice administrators.

Case Study: "BUT HOW CAN YOU SLEEP NIGHTS?"

Unlike the portrayals that are commonly seen on television, criminal defense attorneys, for the most part, make very little money in comparison to other areas of legal specialization, and they work long and hard hours. It is estimated that there are around 20,000 criminal defense attorneys in the United States, representing less than two-tenths of 1 percent of all attorneys in the country. So, why does a person become a criminal defense attorney and, more important, what motivates them initially to pursue such a profession. Also, why do they stay in a line of work when they lose an overwhelming majority of their cases?

McIntyre's (1987) research revealed that for many criminal defense attorneys, the answers to these questions lie in their education, a belief in the presumption of innocence until proven guilty, and, in some cases, a zeal for making sure that the government proves its case against a defendant in a fair manner, a belief rooted in a legal logic and history that the adversarial system works best when the state is compelled to prove its case and not merely rely on allegation or innuendo. Remember, for the criminal defense attorney, it is not enough for the state to *believe* someone is guilty; they must *prove* that person is guilty.

McIntyre cites the fact that criminal defense attorneys are inculcated in law school that the legal system is predicated on the presumption of innocent until proven guilty. The criminal defense attorney learns in his or her legal training that the burden of proof in a criminal trial is on the state. It is the prosecutor's responsibility to prove his or her case; the defense attorney has to prove nothing. Holding the state to this standard is a belief that is drilled into the defense attorney in law school. What motivates the criminal defense attorney is the belief that when it comes to potentially depriving people of their liberty, it is paramount that the state produces evidence to meet the presumption-of-innocence threshold. Again, believing guilt is not the same as proving guilt.

This belief, as a guiding principle that motivates people to enter into criminal defense work and sustains

CASE STUDY—continued

them, is important to understand. How does a manager of criminal defense attorneys maintain enthusiasm for this belief among criminal defense lawyers? From a motivation theory perspective, much of this discussion is based on an *intrinsic* source for motivation, but as indicated in this chapter, this belief may become jaded and warped by the lack of *extrinsic* rewards for the work. It is commonly known that for many persons coming out of law school, criminal defense work is not the most desirable profession due, in large part, to the wages offered. Criminal defense attorneys make significantly less money in their careers, on the whole, and often cite their beliefs in fairness and the right to a criminal trial, as well as the presumption of innocence until proven guilty, as the reasons they continue to work. This is laudable. However, the strains of the profession and the lack of extrinsic rewards make motivation a critical issue for those who administer public defender offices.

In addition, the criminal trial can be a dirty process. Idealistic defense attorneys soon learn that the state is not always forthcoming and honest in its dealings with the defense. The harsh reality of the criminal court forces criminal attorneys to dissect and analyze the state's case. Too many experiences and conversations with other defense attorneys reinforce the belief that the state is not to be trusted, nor should they be trusted. Whether it is poor evidence touted as solid evidence or even downright fraud and misrepresentation, the savvy criminal defense attorney has learned that you can't trust the state, and it is the defense attorneys' job to force the state to play the game fairly. For many defense attorneys, this is an important belief and keeps integrity in the criminal court process. But again, reality is a harsh teacher, and this intrinsic motivation is difficult to sustain. Given the limited extrinsic rewards available to many criminal defense attorneys, how is this intrinsic belief sustained?

CASE STUDY QUESTIONS

 outside

1. How does the lack of any meaningful extrinsic reward affect the quality of work among defense attorneys?
2. What are the possible consequences of having high turnover among defense attorneys? Does the quality of justice decline as a result?
3. How far would the belief in the legal standard of innocent until proven guilty take you in being motivated as a criminal defense attorney?

 ## Think like an Administrator

Every police supervisor can tell a story about an unmotivated patrol officer. Most of these accounts highlight the details of how the employee has performed poorly (does not show up for work, late for work, poor relations with other officers), and in some cases, the documentation boils down to the fact that the employee just does not want to work. Everyone has a theory on how best to handle this type of employee, but most police administrators will also tell you that addressing this type of employee is enormously difficult.

Given what has been presented in the chapter regarding theories of motivation and what we know about how to motivate employees, how should an administrator address an unmotivated employee? In addition, does motivation filter itself out in different ways within police organizations? In other words, how a chief might motivate an employee and how a sergeant might motivate an employee in the same agency could be two different things. Correct? Do expectations and processes to deal with employees differ depending on the levels of the agency? How is this dictated by a labor agreement and possible union involvement? Yes, both the chief and the immediate supervisor have policies and procedures that spell out how employees are to be handled when they do not meet job expectations, yet is not the situation even more complicated than it might seem to appear? How do we know the lack of motivation in question is really a function of being a poorly

---

THINK LIKE AN ADMINISTRATOR—continued

motivated employee? These are important questions to consider regarding employee motivation. Consider the questions below as well as we consider the complexity of the motivation process within criminal justice organizations.

1. How does your decision as an administrator affect the departmental perception on how unmotivated officers are managed and handled?
2. Is there a possible ripple effect of a decision on how to address an unmotivated employee that will have consequences for how other officers perceive the department and their own levels of motivation?
3. How is the disciplinary process either a good or bad way to address an unmotivated employee?
4. Does the disciplinary process work against employee motivation? If so how?

FOR DISCUSSION

1. It is often said that criminal justice employees are unmotivated. Comment on this assertion and discuss possible ways the motivational levels of criminal justice workers can be raised.

2. Discuss a particular theory of motivation and apply it to one of the components of the criminal justice system.

3. Invite a police chief to class to discuss specific strategies he or she employs to motivate officers. Examine these strategies and identify their positive and negative aspects.

4. Examine quality circle programs and MBO models in criminal justice organizations. What are both the prospects for and problems with these types of programs in criminal justice?

FOR FURTHER READING

Herzberg, F., Mausner, B., and Snyderman, B. B. *The Motivation to Work*. New York: Wiley, 1959.

Hiam, A. *Motivating and Rewarding Employees: New and Better Ways to Inspire Your People*. Holbrook: Adams Media Corp., 1999.

Likert, R. *New Patterns of Management*. New York: McGraw-Hill, 1961.

Maslow, A. *Motivation and Personality*. 2nd ed. New York: Praeger, 1986.

CHAPTER 6

Job Design

159

LEARNING OBJECTIVES

After reading this chapter, the students will have achieved the following objectives:

- Understand a definition of job design.

- Explain the early importance of engineering and efficiency to job design.

- Define and explain Taylorism.

- Understand the application of Taylorism to criminal justice.

- Know how job satisfaction, job stress, and job burnout relate to job design.

- Define and explain job design theory.

- Comprehend job redesign programs and their application to criminal justice organizations.

- Explain the relationship between job design and the community.

- Define the "new criminal justice" and its relationship to job design.

VIGNETTE

An interesting revolution is taking place within criminal justice organizations. Criminal justice agencies are being challenged to be more precise and accountable in what they do. As part of a larger trend occurring in the human services, there has been an evolving and nascent movement to improve criminal justice services through better design efforts and increasing application of modern techniques of information gathering to crime-related problems. We briefly mentioned this change in Chapter 1, but in this chapter, we expand on what this change really means when it comes to designing jobs for criminal justice organizations.

Traditional questions regarding job design no longer are as relevant as they were only ten years ago. Today, we expect criminal justice employees to be smarter and more analytical in what they do. Relying primarily on past practices and legend and lore no longer can meet the needs of a modern criminal justice organization. Take, for example, the issue of intelligence-based or intelligence-led policing. The premise of this model of policing is that better information leads to better results when it comes to addressing crime. But what does this actually mean when it comes to employee job design? For many police departments, movement toward information-driven policing means recruiting a different type of employee and engendering a different type of organizational structure. The police professional of the twenty-first century must be an intelligence analyst—a person who can analyze large amounts of information in a systematic and analytical way to produce a more efficient and effective response to crime. In addition, the type of job design we create for criminal justice professionals must be predicated on differing ideas of how we recruit, train, and develop them to meet the needs of their communities.

As we analyze criminal justice job design, we'll think through the changes that have occurred within criminal justice organizations and how administrative tactics have changed to effectively implement a new way of understanding job design. Many of the ideas regarding a "new criminal justice" are based on significant changes in the organizational structures of criminal justice organizations. Questions of job design may be some of the most interesting and challenging to face criminal justice administrators as we move through the twenty-first century.

We are at work for much of our lives. This is true whether the duration of our careers or the amount of time we spend on the job every day is measured. For many of us, work is not only a place where tasks are accomplished but also is an experience that adds to the value and meaning of our lives. Although we have many work-related personal goals, our jobs also fulfill organizational goals. Our efforts may contribute to the control of crime, the processing of offenders, or the treatment of those convicted.

In this chapter, we examine the interplay of these personal and organizational goals. We focus on how the structure of work can satisfy or fail to satisfy these goals. After reviewing some of the criteria for a good job, we consider the technological aspects of job design and the influence of Frederick Taylor in industry and in human services. We also examine some of the undesirable consequences of poorly designed work. The chapter then turns to advancements made in theoretical approaches to job design and finally to examples of job design and redesign in criminal justice.

WHAT IS JOB DESIGN?

In criminal justice, the design of jobs is often taken for granted: police officers police, corrections officers guard, probation officers manage their caseloads, and judges deliberate. It is often assumed that these tasks govern the design of work. Both theory and research in industrial settings, however, question such assumptions. The term **job design** has been used to describe the "deliberate, purposeful planning of the job, including all of its structural and social aspects and their effects on the employee" (Hellriegel, Slocum, and Woodman, 1995).

There are many approaches to job design and many lists of criteria for a good job. Although efficiency was once the chief concern, a wide variety of other goals has been recognized. One popular list of "psychological job requirements" includes the following factors (Emmery and Emmery, 1974:147):

1. *Adequate elbow room.* Workers need a sense that they are their own bosses and that (except in unusual circumstances) they will not have a boss breathing down their necks. But they don't want so much elbow room that they don't know what to do next.

2. *Chances to learn on the job and go on learning.* Such learning is possible only when people are able to set goals that are reasonable challenges for them and to know results in time for them to correct their behavior.

Job design: The deliberate, purposeful planning of the job, including all of its structural and social aspects and their effects on the employee.

3. *An optimal level of variety.* Workers need to be able to vary the work—so as to avoid boredom and fatigue and to gain the best advantage from settling into a satisfying rhythm of work.

4. *Help and respect from workmates.* We need to avoid conditions in which it is in no one's interest to lift a finger to help another, in which people are pitted against each other so that one person's gain is another's loss, and in which the individual's capabilities or inabilities are denied.

5. *A sense that one's work meaningfully contributes to social welfare.* Workers do not want a job that could be done as well by a trained monkey or an industrial robot machine. They also do not want to feel that society would probably be better served by not having the job done or at least not having it done so shoddily.

6. *A desirable future.* Workers do not want dead-end jobs; they want jobs that continue to allow personal growth.

These qualities of a good job reflect a common concern in the literature and can be traced to the warnings of Karl Marx:

> What do we mean by the alienation of labor? First, that the work he performs is extraneous to the worker—that is, it is not personal to him, is not part of his nature; therefore, he does not fulfill himself in work but actually denies himself; feels miserable rather than content, cannot freely develop his physical and mental power but instead becomes physically exhausted and mentally debased. (Cited in Josephson and Josephson, 1975:871.)

These concerns were echoed in a 1973 federal government task force report entitled *Work in America.* The conclusion of the report begins with the words of the existentialist philosopher Albert Camus: "Without work all life goes rotten. But when work is soulless, life stifles and dies" (Special Task Force to the Secretary of Health, Education and Welfare, 1973:186).

ENGINEERING AND EFFICIENCY IN JOB DESIGN

The task force report was most critical of jobs characterized by "dull, repetitive, seemingly meaningless tasks" and traced these impoverished jobs to the "anachronism of Taylorism" (1973:xv). Throughout most of the last century, technological criteria or concern with the efficient completion of tasks dictated the design of most industrial jobs. Frederick Winslow Taylor and his associates are properly credited as the major influence behind this trend. Increasing the efficiency of labor through the fragmentation of work, the use of time and motion studies, and the motivation of workers with pay incentives was the main component of Taylor's *Scientific Management* (1947). From the marriage of task and technology emerged such innovations as the "science of bricklaying," worked out in detail by Frank Gilbreth:

He developed the exact position which each of the feet of the bricklayer should occupy in relation to the wall, the mortar box, and the pile of bricks, and so made it unnecessary for him to take a step or two toward the pile of bricks and back again each time a brick is laid.... Through all of this minute study of the motions of the bricklayer in laying bricks under standard conditions, Mr. Gilbreth has reduced his movements from eighteen motions per brick to five, and even in one case to as low as two motions per brick.... With union bricklayers in laying a factory wall ... he averaged, after his selected workmen had become skillful in his new methods, 350 bricks per man-hour; whereas the average speed of doing this work with the old methods, in this part of the country, was 120 bricks per man-hour (Taylor, 1947:81).

Taylorism was named after Frederick Taylor, who emphasized the application of scientific principles to job design, most notably the division of labor, time-motion studies, and pay as a primary incentive for workers. Taylor's influence on the design of jobs cannot be fully appreciated without examining his underlying assumptions. Throughout his works, Taylor presents unflattering views of human nature. In his often-cited description of a highly trained pig iron handler, Taylor refers to him as being "as stupid and phlegmatic as an ox" (1947:62). In Taylor's view, most people are unmotivated by work itself and instead are motivated by leisure and increases in pay. His belief was that close supervision by college-educated, highly trained managers and financial incentives in the form of increased wages for increased production counteracts the natural tendency toward laziness.

> **Taylorism:** Named after Frederick Taylor, who emphasized the application of scientific principles to job design, most notably the division of labor, time-motion studies, and pay as a primary incentive for workers.

TAYLORISM IN THE HUMAN SERVICES

Scientific management formed the foundation of industrial engineering and technology and has remained a principal influence in the engineer's design of job content in industrial settings. Taylor, however, was careful to distinguish the "mechanisms" of scientific management, which may have limited applicability outside the machine shop, from the "essence" of scientific management, which would have much wider utility:

> Scientific Management is not an efficiency device ... not a new system of figuring costs; it is not a new scheme for paying men; it is not a time study; it is not a motion study.... These devices are useful adjuncts to Scientific Management.... In its essence, Scientific Management involves a complete mental revolution on the part of working man (Taylor, 1919:68–69).

In the human services, the essence of Taylorism has been a potent influence, but the mechanisms have not been ignored. Time and motion study has been used to determine the best location of instruments for dentistry, the need for mechanized hospital beds, and even the advantages of rhythmic movements for surgeons. Beyond these studies, however, Taylor's concern with increasing efficiency through the fragmentation of work and close supervision has found wide application in the "people work" industries. Unlike managers in production industries, however, managers in the human services can rarely define their workers' roles in terms of the requirements of an assembly line or machine (Phillips and McConnell, 1996). In a review of policing, public welfare, and other street-level bureaucracies, Lipsky (1980:14) notes that most human services work is characterized by considerably more discretion and variety than jobs in a factory. These differences, however, have not insulated human services work from tight bureaucratic control. For example, Karger (1981:275) notes the similarities between the alienating features of industrial and human services work:

> The routinization of public welfare is complemented by increased specialization and the creation of continually narrower job descriptions.... Accountability is achieved through daily logs, regular breaks, and performance objectives. The assumption is that workers are selling their labors rather than their skills.... Even in private welfare we see "numbered contact hours"—a designation referring to quantity rather than quality.... The workplace in a large public bureaucracy—with its large rooms filled with long rows of cubicles—appears more like a bureaucratic assembly line than a private environment in which to discuss personal matters. The client is objectified as a problem that must be processed as the line grows longer. (See Hagedorn [1995] for further discussion of these issues.)

TAYLORISM IN CRIMINAL JUSTICE

In the field of criminal justice, policing has been described as a "Taylorized occupation" (Fyfe et al., 1997; Harring, 1982). Concern with productivity has led administrators to fragment the role of the police officer. Automobile-based patrolling and the use of non-sworn personnel for traffic control, bus monitoring, and other tasks have taken away from regular line officers the Florence Nightingale duties that Harring argues provided a broad, humane role for the police. He concludes that the Taylorization of police institutions is important to study because it can undermine the notion that the police are immune from the dehumanizing experiences of other workers.

This trend toward decreased discretion and increased control has been referred to as the deprofessionalization syndrome (Sharp, 1982; Stone and Stoker, 1979). The irony behind the syndrome is that as management has increased its professionalization through increased accountability and bureaucratization of work life, the status of frontline personnel has diminished. As Hahn notes: "The professionalization of police departments, therefore, acts to undermine the professional stature of individual police officers by limiting their personal discretion in handling the problems of 'clients' in the community" (1974:23). The deprofessionalization of police has also been questioned by proponents of "community policing," whereby increased discretion and involvement of officers to solve community problems is critical. Job design, under this model of policing, argues for recognition that only when police and citizens work together can crime be addressed effectively (Kelling and Coles, 1996; Wilson and Kelling, 1982). Deprofessionalization, therefore, may be counter to what police need to effectively address crime and disorder in their communities.

Similar concerns about deprofessionalization are seen in the areas of probation and parole. Because probation officers generally come under the jurisdiction of the courts, Lawrence (1984) argues that they have traditionally been uncertain of their professional status. He reports that many probation officers see themselves more as judicial servants caught in the civil service malaise than as professionals. The revolution in technology in the field of community supervision may further erode the autonomy and discretion of frontline workers (Rosecrance, 1999a). The introduction of standardized classification instruments is an example. The instruments frequently use information about an offender's criminal history and other background variables to establish a numerical score reflecting the appropriate security level. These devices not only restrict the judgment of probation and parole officers in assessing their cases but they also dictate the amount of time they can spend on cases requiring maximum, medium, or minimum supervision.

The development of electronic monitoring systems for offenders also appears to be altering the jobs of probation and parole agents. Such devices track the offender's location through an electronic device generally strapped to the ankle. A review of these and other changes in the processing of information in probation and parole offices suggests that they are likely to have a major impact on the nature of probation and parole jobs. The devices will accentuate the clearly defined law enforcement role of probation and parole officers and diminish the discretionary aspects of their work that are generally associated with their treatment function (Clear, 1995; Moran and Lindner, 1985).

In corrections, jobs have frequently been described by highly circumscribed responsibilities. Civil service job descriptions in New York state list the corrections officer's duties as follows:

Correctional officers supervise the movement and activities of inmates; make periodic rounds of assigned areas; conduct searches for contraband; and maintain order within the facility. They advise inmates on the rules and regulations governing the operation of the facility and assist in solving problems (New York Department of Corrections, 2007).

The President's Commission on Law Enforcement and the Administration of Justice (1967b) described corrections officers as the "employees who man the walls, supervise living units, escort inmates to and from work, and supervise all group movement around an institution." These responsibilities were clearly distinguished from the professional role of other corrections staff. Such descriptions reify the corrections officer's job by ignoring the discretionary human relations aspects of the role.

Parallels between criminal justice and industrial work can be overemphasized, however. As Toch and Grant suggest, "no matter how badly off human service workers are, their fate is less circumscribed than that of the men and women who serve machines and are constrained by their technology"

(1982:85). Lipsky (1980) makes a similar point when he remarks that police, judges, and probation officers continue to exercise considerable discretion because of the way their jobs are designed.

Work Perspective: TWENTY-FIRST-CENTURY JAILS TODAY AND TOMORROW

Why Jails Have Become De Facto Mental Health Hospitals in the United States

Many people who administer jails are aware of the fact the urban jails today are now the biggest mental health centers in the community. The continued closure of mental hospitals across the United States into the twenty-first century began in 1955. Thousands of people were released from mental hospitals (without much in the way of treatment) to return to the community. Then, President Kennedy persuaded Congress to enact the Community Mental Health Act of 1963. Community mental health centers would enable people to live at home and take advantage of the opportunity for treatment on an outpatient basis, but the money wasn't available to do this, so jails became the twenty-first century mental health centers by default, not by choice.

Political Action

The bright new era for the mentally ill vanished (1960s and 1970s) because it proved to be a mirage and the mentally ill were left as homeless persons with no option but the streets. Before long, citizens were upset by the mentally ill on the streets, and the public demanded action; local governments responded by pursuing a criminal justice solution. Law enforcement would arrest the mentally disturbed on the streets for primarily minor offenses and bring them to the local jails to be incarcerated. Many jails lacked sufficient staff, and frequently the staff that was available had no training in the management and care of mentally disturbed individuals.

Direct Supervision Jails and How They Operate

Significant jail changes also occurred during the final quarter of the twentieth century. Direct supervision jails tested first by the Federal Bureau of Prisons received the endorsement of the National Institute of Corrections Jail Center as a new, improved management approach for local jails. A different style of jail architecture emphasizing a more normal environment and a new management encompassing the principles of direct supervision were developed to guide jail leadership in the direction of making the management of inmates the sine qua non at the line officer level. By 2006, according to the *2006 Sourcebook on Direct Supervision Jails*, published by the National Institute of Corrections Jail Center, 349 jails in 47 states were listed as direct supervision, a substantial jump from the 199 direct supervision jails listed in 1995. The total of direct supervision beds had climbed to 183,538 in these facilities.

The basic idea underlying direct supervision was to make the jail environment resemble a more normal living environment in the outside world with carpets in the pods to cover the concrete floors and normal furniture instead of stainless steel stools and tables. A pod officer in charge of the inmates took on the responsibility of enforcing the rules and assisting prisoners with their numerous problems. The pod officer, empowered by direct supervision management principles, exercised total authority in the pod, a departure from the paramilitary model frequently found in jails when higher-ranking officers would overrule line staff for whatever reason. If the direct supervision model was to function properly, the pod officers had to be better educated and better trained to thoroughly understand the underpinnings of this model. Empowering the line officers who worked the direct supervision pods took time, but if it were done right, it worked well.

Birth of CIT (Crisis Intervention Training) and Direct Supervision

Crisis intervention training was born in Memphis, Tennessee, in the 1980s when Memphis police killed a mentally disturbed citizen. In response to citizens' outcries, crisis intervention training for police officers started. The training emphasized diverting people suspected of having mental health problems to a diagnostic center for an evaluation as opposed to booking them into the local jails. This new approach grew rapidly, and today hundreds of criminal justice agencies across the country (police, corrections, parole/probation, judges, district/defense attorneys) are now involved in training staff in CIT. Many jail officers now undergo CIT training based on the idea that if some mentally ill continue to be institutionalized, correctional staff require instruction on how to manage them. This placed a renewed emphasis on suicide-prevention training.

WORK PERSPECTIVE—continued

Making the Criminal Justice System Work for the Community

An equally important dynamic is reentry into the community upon release. Many inmates in jails exhibit co-occurring disorders (mental health and alcohol and drug problems), which are treated during incarceration. Programs and treatment centers need to be in place for inmates released into the communities; if not, it is doubtful that many of these released inmates can function successfully without this outside help. Group homes or halfway houses, where staff can check to determine whether the clients take their meds on a daily basis or go to their alcohol/drug counseling, have become a vital part of the solution. Many inmates released from institutions need assistance to avoid recidivism. A lot depends on collaboration among community groups if progress is to be successfully monitored. A feasible approach requires the use of criminal justice personnel, including jail staff, to cooperate with other non-criminal justice staff to assure a positive outcome and reduce the possibility of re-arrest.

Ironically, the dumping of the mentally ill into the local jails has produced a compelling reason for communities to do something productive for those arrested with co-occurring disorders. More and more, staff employed in jails and in other criminal justice agencies need exposure to social work training on the management and care of these populations. This is not yet well understood by the general public, but success in reducing jail populations today requires a total approach starting with diversion from the criminal justice system, treatment in the institutions of incarceration, and a solid reentry program upon release.

One of the principles of direct supervision is "Justice and Fairness," which directs the officers who work the direct supervision pods to treat each inmate in a fair and just manner. This approach will prove to benefit both the public and those incarcerated. Requiring the officers to be CIT trained only increases the chance that this management philosophy will continue to blossom.

SOURCE: Ken Kerle Board Member, CIT, Shawnee County, Topeka, Kansas 66611.

RESPONSES TO JOB CHARACTERISTICS

Much of the recent interest in job design has grown out of concerns raised in studies of worker satisfaction. Although more than 85 percent of American workers report general satisfaction with their jobs, detailed inquiry has revealed sharply declining levels of satisfaction with specific aspects of the work environment (see Hackman and Oldham, 1980). Those aspects are the **job characteristics**, and include items such as job satisfaction, job burnout, and job stress that are directly affected by job design. Discontent among hourly and clerical workers has risen to the highest level since those measurements began to be made in the 1950s. Other research has identified young workers as the most dissatisfied and the most likely to be concerned with job design issues (Sheppard and Herrick, 1972). The discontent of workers was dramatically illustrated in the early 1970s at a strike in a Lordstown, Ohio, automobile plant. Workers there did not protest low wages but instead voiced opposition to routine and boring labor. A Lordstown employee described the frustration workers felt: "You have to … break the boredom to get immediate feedback from the job because the only gratification you get is a paycheck once a week, and that's too long without any kind of gratification from the job" (quoted in Kreman, 1973:17).

Criminal justice research lacks the longitudinal data necessary to indicate changes in levels of job satisfaction. Still, the literature is suggestive about employees' expectations of their work. A study of police officer satisfaction, for

Job characteristics:
Items such as job satisfaction, job burnout, and job stress that are directly affected by job design.

example, paralleled findings in industrial settings when it revealed that many officers described themselves as generally satisfied with the tangible benefits of their jobs but were concerned about such issues as opportunities for advancement and opportunities to improve their skills. Only about half the officers reported that they would recommend police work to a friend, and many reported that their enthusiasm for the job had diminished over time (Alpert, Dunham, and Stroshine, 2005; Bayley, 1994; Buzawa, 1984).

Patterns of job satisfaction appear to be similar for police and corrections officers. Attitudinal changes appear to occur following training. During the initial years on the job, satisfaction decreases and cynicism increases (Niederhoffer, 1969; Van Maanen, 1973). Researchers have also described an inverted U-shaped curve in which negative attitudes are highest in the middle of careers and lowest among officers with the least as well as the most seniority (Poole and Regoli, 1980; Toch and Klofas, 1982). Education levels have also been found to be negatively correlated with job satisfaction among police officers. Evidence indicates that a disproportionate number of the more educated police officers voluntarily leave their jobs before retirement (Buzawa, 1984; Carter, Sapp, and Stephens, 1989). It has been suggested that this turnover results from the frustration of working in a rigid setting. One study, however, suggests that this turnover may be the result of increased job opportunities (Buzawa, 1984).

In human services occupations, reactions to work also include stress and burnout. Both of these concepts refer to physical and psychological reactions to the work environment. After reviewing the available literature, Whitehead and Lindquist (1986) argue that chronic, intense stress may lead to burnout, which has been defined as "a syndrome of emotional exhaustion and cynicism" (Maslach and Jackson, 1981).

Although much of the literature on burnout in the human services has focused on issues surrounding client contact (see Maslach, 1976), some researchers have examined organizational causes. Cherniss (1980) suggests that burnout may arise from boredom, excessive demands, and job design problems such as role conflict, role ambiguity, and lack of participation in decision making. In criminal justice research, organizational factors have been identified as the major causes of stress and burnout. In studies of corrections officers in New Jersey, Pennsylvania, Illinois, and Washington, Cheek and Miller (1982, 1983) found that "administrative sources" were the primary reasons for stress on the job. Administrative sources included lack of communication from management, lack of clear guidelines, and lax or inconsistent administrative practices (Stojkovic, 1997). The researchers argue in favor of a redesign of the corrections officer's job.

Whitehead and Lindquist (1986) came to similar conclusions from their multivariate analysis of burnout among corrections officers. Using a standardized instrument developed by Maslach and Jackson (1981), these authors found that inmate contact was not only a cause of burnout but also that such contact was positively associated with feelings of accomplishment. However, administrative policies and procedures were identified as sources of stress. This finding was also replicated with a sample of federal corrections officers (Lasky, Gordon, and Srebalus, 1986). Whitehead and Lindquist suggest that these findings may support the view that managerial control efforts conflict with officers' desires for autonomy and discretion. In another study by Stohr et al. (1994), the authors found that correctional officers in jail settings were much more satisfied in work environments that stressed employee concerns and more involvement in the day-to-day operations of their facilities rather than simply bald, custodial control of prisoners. Moreover, Britton (1997) suggests that there are differences among correctional officers concerning their perceptions of their work environment along racial and gender lines and that the work environment does affect, in part, the perceptions of correctional officers.

Whitehead (1985) also studied burnout among probation and parole officers. Using the Maslach Inventory (Maslach and Jackson, 1981) with a sample of nearly 1,500 probation and parole officers in four states, he found that respondents scored higher than other human services workers on most of the burnout dimensions. In considering causes, Whitehead argues that his data do not support theories that link burnout to emotionally charged contact with clients. Instead, burnout among probation and parole agents was tied to the officers' need for efficacy and a sense of providing competent service to clients. These findings support theoretical perspectives that view job design factors as important sources of burnout. (See Alpert, Dunham, and Stroshine, 2005, as well as Fyfe et al., 1997, for a discussion of these issues in relation to police organizations.)

It is interesting that research has also identified the importance of job satisfaction to overall innovation and creativity in manufacturing settings. Shipton et al. (2006) report that job satisfaction is related to increased innovation and creativity when taking into account job variety and a commitment to a "single status" reward distribution system. Single status refers to a reward structure that is based on relevant job criteria (such as task performance) rather than on arbitrary factors, such as status differentials (e.g., whether individuals are blue-collar or white-collar workers). Within criminal justice organizations, consistent with equity theory examined in Chapter 5, designing work so that there is a perception of fairness among employees is critical to motivating them and avoiding the negative consequences of work, such as absenteeism and burnout. Although the research identified by Shipton and coworkers is based on manufacturing settings, the relevance to criminal justice organizations is equally important. For criminal justice administrators, the issue centers on their ability to design work in such a way that personnel are satisfied and innovation is possible. The whole concept of problem-oriented policing, for example, is predicated on police officers working with citizens in innovative ways to address crime. The Office of Community Oriented Policing Services (COPS) works toward the development of innovative community policing programs that are supported by the federal government (Uchida, 2005).

Similarly, Lambert and Hogan (2010) document the impact of innovation on job stress, job satisfaction, and organizational commitment among correctional employees. It is interesting that they found that *perceptions* of innovation can lead toward reduced job stress, increased job satisfaction, and more organizational commitment among employees. It must be noted that they were dealing with perceptions, and, as such, the impact of actual innovation on these key dimensions of the work environment is unknown. It is easy to say that one favors innovation, but at the end of the day, innovation must be understood as highly episodic and dynamic, leading toward probable differential impacts on persons within organizations. Nevertheless, innovation as an ongoing process within criminal justice organizations may be very valuable to administrators. It may be part of a new approach to criminal justice, something we discuss later in the chapter.

JOB DESIGN THEORY

Job design theory: Explanations that move beyond Taylorism to include job enrichment and job enlargement.

Hawthorne effect: The increase in productivity of workers due to the attention given them by management.

Motivation–hygiene theory: Employees are motivated by two sets of factors. The first are hygiene factors that are external to the work, such as pay, supervision, physical conditions, and interpersonal relations. The second are motivator factors, such as responsibility, recognition, and opportunities for achievement and growth. The former factors affect satisfaction levels among employees, while the latter factors affect motivation.

Ten years after Taylor first published a description of scientific management in 1911, the Hawthorne studies at the Western Electric Company in Chicago began to demonstrate the importance of nontechnical considerations in job design. In these studies, researchers under the direction of Elton Mayo tested the effects of experimentally induced conditions on worker fatigue and monotony. Set up as standard engineering experiments, the research focused on independent variables that were physical or technical in nature. Researchers found, however, that productivity increased regardless of increased or decreased illumination and regardless of the timing of work breaks or the length of the workday. The researchers soon abandoned concern with the technical variables and focused on social and psychological explanations (Roethlisberger and Dickson, 1939) such as **job design theory**, which is an explanation that moves beyond Taylorism to include job enrichment and job enlargement.

Although workers performed dull, repetitive tasks that required little skill and afforded little status, productivity and job satisfaction increased under the attention of the investigators. One explanation for the increases became known as the **Hawthorne effect**, which suggested that the novelty of having research conducted and the increased attention from management could lead to temporary increases in productivity. To explain persistent increases, the researchers focused on the informal interpersonal relationships of the workers. From these findings developed the human relations school of management, which became associated with the work of Mayo (1946) and Roethlisberger and Dickson (1939).

The human relations school replaced Taylor's portrait of the workers as motivated by money and leisure with a view of workers as motivated also by social attachments (for a critical examination of the human relations school, see Perrow, 1986). Contemporary job redesign theories have built on these models and have also incorporated increasingly complex theories of motivation. Much of modern job design theory can be traced to the motivational sequence proposed by Maslow (1943) and applied to management by McGregor (1978) (see Chapter 5) and to the empirically based theories of Herzberg (1966). Although some have argued for the redesign of jobs as a response to changes in society, most contemporary theories have been described as "classical theories of job redesign" with a foundation in the works of Maslow and Herzberg (Kelly, 1982:37).

Job enrichment can be traced to the work of Herzberg, beginning in the 1950s. **Motivation–hygiene theory** was developed by Herzberg from critical incident research in which he asked workers to describe the high and low points in their work lives. The research uncovered two sets of factors involved in motivation at the workplace (Herzberg, 1966; Herzberg, Mausner, and Snyderman, 1959). *Hygiene factors* are external to the work being performed. These include pay, supervision, physical conditions at the work site, and interpersonal relations. Contentment with these factors, however, does not motivate workers; it simply prevents dissatisfaction. Herzberg labeled a second set of factors *motivators*. These factors, intrinsic to the work itself, include responsibility, recognition, and opportunities for achievement and growth (one study replicated Herzberg's finding regarding hygiene factors and motivators with a sample of corrections officers [Hayslip, 1982]). Job enrichment models, which Herzberg calls "orthodox job enrichment," build on motivation–hygiene theory by assuming that workers will be motivated only after hygiene needs are met and sources of intrinsic satisfaction are built into jobs. Job design, according to this theory, is concerned not simply with improved efficiency but also with motivating employees by meeting their higher-order needs.

Some research (Hackman and Oldham, 1980), however, has not supported the original dichotomy between hygiene factors and motivators and suggests that the findings may be an artifact of the particular interview techniques used by Herzberg. The substantive issue flowing from this criticism concerns the relationship between satisfaction with extrinsic factors and motivation. For instance, some theories argue that motivated employees need not be satisfied with the contexts of work (Morse, 1973). A related criticism of motivation–hygiene theory is that it pays too little attention to differences in workers' responses to jobs. Workers may attach different interpretations to job situations, and they may respond differently to jobs with varying levels of enrichment (Hackman and Oldham, 1980:57). Some workers may thrive in enriched jobs, while others may respond with confusion, resentment, and inability to cope with the new demands.

Enrichment theory and research have expanded to accommodate criticisms of the motivation–hygiene theory, and other theoretical orientations have been incorporated into job design efforts. One popular approach to job enrichment has been developed by Hackman and Oldham (1980). This model has the virtues of being empirically based and attentive to individual differences. For Hackman and Oldham, job redesign involves increasing certain core job dimensions that influence the psychological states of workers, which in turn affect personal and work outcomes. This sequence can be moderated, however, by certain variables: an individual's level of knowledge and skill, need for accomplishment and growth, and satisfaction with pay and working conditions (Robbins and Judge, 2007:235). This theoretical perspective recognizes the importance of matching individual workers with their jobs. Under the model, job enrichment is inappropriate and is likely to have negative consequences if workers have a low need for growth and jobs are relatively high on the core dimensions. However, when jobs are low on the core dimensions and workers are satisfied, have appropriate knowledge, and possess high needs for accomplishment and development, the potential for job enrichment is great.

As part of their theory, Hackman and Oldham (1980) describe the job characteristics they regard as most significant for employee motivation. These characteristics can also be combined into a single measure of the motivating potential of a particular job. These are the core job dimensions:

1. *Skill variety*—the degree to which jobs require a variety of different activities, skills, and talents

2. *Task identity*—the degree to which a job requires the completion of a whole task rather than bits or pieces of a project

3. *Task significance*—the extent to which a job has a meaningful impact on others; the importance of the job

4. *Autonomy*—the degree of freedom, independence, and discretion provided by a job

5. *Feedback*—the extent to which workers get direct and clear information about the effectiveness of their performance

Job design efforts have frequently incorporated a process known as job analysis, or the study of work assignments with the goal of specifying the precise skills and training needed for the work. Most often, job analysis is limited to the technical dimensions of jobs and is used to produce job descriptions (Ghorpade and Atchison, 1980) or to identify appropriate levels of compensation.

Hackman and Oldham's model takes a broader view than job analysis of the kinds of information needed in job redesign efforts. The authors have developed an instrument, called the Job Diagnostic Survey, that allows managers to measure all the variables in the theory and to assess both jobs and workers with regard to the need as well as the potential for job enrichment. The Job Diagnostic Survey provides measures of the core job dimensions as well as measures of the worker-related variables. Considerable research has been done with the instrument, and Hackman and Oldham have published averages for all the variables for nine separate job families. The Job Diagnostic Survey has also been used to study criminal justice occupations. Brief, Munro, and Aldag (1976) used the instrument as the foundation of a data-based argument for redesign of some corrections officer tasks. The researchers found that the most satisfied corrections officers were those whose jobs had the highest variety, task identity, feedback, and autonomy. They also found, as the theory predicts, that these relationships tended to be moderated by individual needs for growth.

Similar ideas are expressed by Houston (1999) and Wright (1994). Houston suggests that effective correctional employees require opportunities to grow and develop in their jobs. Increasing the variety of work, as well as the employee's scope of influence in decision making, provides correctional employees avenues to experiment in their jobs. Through such experimentation, employees learn to adapt to their problems, and the organization learns new ways of approaching challenging situations. Wright reinforces this view by stating that correctional employees are the essence of prison organizations. Greater recognition of their experiences and ideas can only work toward the attainment of organizational objectives and the creation of a positive prison culture (Stojkovic and Farkas, 2003). Moreover, the correctional employee views himself or herself as an integral part of the organization. Goldstein (1990) offers similar views in his examination of the influence of traditional police organizations and their stifling structures on police officers' development and growth. In his view, police organizations require more decentralization and greater autonomy for police officers to enable them to respond to the varied needs of the community. This would require an examination of the tasks that are central to the police role and the method(s) of structuring that would be the most appropriate to respond to them. Job redesign issues are, therefore, critical for effective criminal justice administration.

JOB REDESIGN PROGRAMS

Since IBM first began to experiment with job redesign in 1943, programs have been implemented in numerous work settings. In reviewing much of the literature on these programs, Kelly (1982) suggests that three approaches to work redesign have emerged. In mass-production industries, often characterized by fragmented jobs on assembly lines, job redesign efforts have sought to reduce or eliminate assembly lines. In continuous-process industries, such as chemical production, jobs have been enriched through the creation of autonomous work groups. In service industries, Kelly argues that enrichment has occurred principally through the combination of work roles from different parts of the job hierarchy. Other authors have distinguished job enlargement that involves the addition of tasks to job descriptions from job enrichment. The latter is more concerned with instilling greater responsibilities within positions. Still others have characterized programs as involving additions along the horizontal dimension, as in job enlargement, and strengthening the vertical dimension, as in job enrichment.

Many redesign programs have included combinations of strategies. In a well-known redesign of assembly-line tasks, AB Volvo of Sweden incorporated a variety of approaches (Gyllenhammer, 1975). In one auto assembly plant, managers turned to job enlargement by adding variety to workers' tasks. Some 1,600 workers rotated their jobs, often making several changes a day. In another plant, Volvo rotated assembly-line jobs within teams of twelve to fifteen members. Workers themselves decided how to rotate jobs within the groups and also met regularly with management to discuss how the work could be improved. In the production of trucks and buses, which was considered slower and more complex than the auto assembly line, Volvo formed smaller work groups with increased autonomy. Within these groups, some workers performed specialized assignments, while others opted to take alternate tasks. In their new plants, Volvo eliminated assembly lines and replaced them with work teams, each operating out of separate sections of the shop floor and responsible for completed parts of the final product.

In another well-known redesign project, managers at Texas Instruments sought to enrich the jobs of building janitors and matrons. The program began with training in managerial techniques, including those derived from McGregor's (1978) theory X and theory Y (see Chapter 5). Early program recruits later hired additional staff and chaired regular meetings that included training in management concepts as well as discussions of work-related problems. Teams of workers became responsible for redesigning the maintenance tasks as well as for quality control. The results of the program included improved cleanliness at reduced costs, reductions in worker turnover, and other improvements, including the following worker-originated innovations (Toch and Grant, 1982:78):

1. Teams eliminated cleaning carts, installed supply cabinets, and took responsibility for their own inventories.

2. Work groups divided and controlled their own work, including scheduling the closing down of washrooms to minimize unpredictability for other employees.

3. Matrons, unhappy with a disinfectant that had corrosive effects and caused dermatitis, negotiated with a vendor who developed a new chemical to their specifications. Cleaning time was cut in half when the new chemical was packaged in spray form.

4. Janitors and matrons took responsibility for inspections of facilities.

5. The workers also became concerned with preventive maintenance.

Texas Instruments also embarked on an ingenious campaign to educate and involve the users. For example, matrons spoke to new hires as part of the company's employee-orientation sessions to explain their cleanliness goals and to solicit cooperation. In another approach, matrons and janitors photographed areas that were particularly untidy or dirty. These photos were circulated on production lines in an attempt to elicit cooperation from factory, laboratory, and office employees.

The Texas Instruments program is cited for disconfirming the assumption that the higher reaches of the Maslow hierarchy have been reserved for skilled workers. As Toch and Grant (1982:79) point out, "If toilet bowls can acquire motivating potential, any job is more enrichable than we first suspect." Other redesign efforts have been accomplished and documented by researchers in a number of different occupational settings (Kopelman, 1985; Lawler, 1986).

Robbins and Judge (2007:232–234) offer three alternative work arrangements that may enrich the work setting. They are flextime, job sharing, and telecommuting. *Flextime* provides the opportunity for workers to schedule their own hours, *job sharing* involves persons sharing job responsibilities and performing them on an agreed-upon schedule, and *telecommuting* enables persons to work at home through a computer for a specified number of days. The application of these newer ideas is even questionable in ordinary business settings (Robbins and Judge, 2007:234) and may have added difficulties being applied to traditional criminal justice settings; nevertheless, these more contemporary work arrangements deserve consideration by criminal justice administrators.

JOB REDESIGN IN CRIMINAL JUSTICE AND OTHER HUMAN SERVICES

Although few job redesign efforts in human services have incorporated the specific types of data Hackman and Oldham called for, considerable research supports the efficacy of such efforts. Sarrata and Jeppensen (1977), for example, found that the job design features that Hackman and Oldham identified as producing satisfaction in blue-collar workers functioned the same way for child-care workers.

Research has also shown that human services workers often value the most enriched aspects of their work or even take steps to enrich their own jobs. In a classic job design study of psychiatric aides, Simpson and Simpson (1959) found that the attendants reported intrinsically rewarding tasks involving patient care as their main reasons for staying on the job. The same aides reported originally being attracted to the job for extrinsic reasons, including job security and pay. In a study of corrections officers, Toch (1978:19) found that 20 percent of officers were independently experimenting with nontraditional enriched roles, which included "the officer as dispenser of mental health services, as a person who resonates to adjustment problems of inmates in crisis." Lombardo (1981) and Johnson (2002) also identified diversity in the way corrections officers perform their tasks.

Apart from the efforts of individual innovators, numerous formal programs have also involved the redesign of work in the human services. In mental health settings, aides' jobs have been enriched through the addition of treatment responsibilities (Ellsworth and Ellsworth, 1970). In criminal justice, the jobs of frontline workers have been redesigned through a variety of approaches, including job enlargement, vertical loading (job enrichment), and the creation of autonomous work groups.

One of the earliest documented job redesign efforts in corrections occurred under Howard Gill, superintendent of the Norfolk Prison Colony in Norfolk, Massachusetts, between 1931 and 1934 (Doering, 1940). Under Gill's grand scheme for creating as normal a community setting as possible, a new kind of prison guard was required. Officers who patrolled the perimeter and stood watch in the towers played the traditional role, but inside the colony, house officers performed additional tasks that included casework and counseling as well as facilitating inmate self-government within the housing units.

Lindquist and Whitehead (1986) report on a more recent experiment in job enlargement involving corrections officers. In the Alabama Supervised Intensive Restitution (SIR) program, corrections officers supervised inmates in the community as a solution to the problem of prison overcrowding. The officers managed caseloads of approximately thirty-five and acted much the same as probation and parole officers. The SIR officers experienced a greater sense of personal accomplishment and higher levels of job satisfaction than a sample of regular corrections officers and a sample of probation and parole officers.

Several efforts have also been made to enrich criminal justice jobs. Rather than add tasks to the job description, these programs generally increase responsibilities of frontline staff, a process known as *vertical loading*. One example is Carter and Wilkins's (1976:211) caseload distribution program in probation and parole. In the Work Unit Parole Program begun in California in 1965 and later introduced in Wisconsin, cases are assigned a weight based on the amount and type of supervision needed, and caseloads are determined by equal distribution of weighted cases. This program has allowed staff to spend time in the treatment and custodial supervision of cases, where the need is greatest (Dickey, 1988, 1996).

A different approach to the vertical loading of jobs is seen in the work of Toch and Grant (1982). They added responsibilities often reserved for management to the tasks of both police and corrections officers by involving frontline staff in examining and resolving significant work-related problems. Although Herzberg (1978:40) argues that such participation is not part of the work itself and is, therefore, a hygiene factor rather than a motivator, Toch and Grant argue that participation is a necessary part of job enrichment in the human services because of the wide discretion human services workers have. As they point out, "enriching a guard's or police officer's job means expanding the prison's or police department's human services involvement, a task that cannot be accomplished by edict" (1982:133). Similarly, Skolnick and Fyfe (1993) argue that police violence against citizens can be tied to the military structure of police organizations, where officers are discouraged, not encouraged, from providing input on how to perform their jobs. Skolnick and Fyfe suggest that greater police officer and citizen involvement in the definition of what the police role entails may reduce the likelihood of future violent confrontations between police and citizens. Furthermore, Fyfe (2004a: 163) argues that good police officers can be recruited to identify the characteristics of good policing. This valuable information can be used in the selection, training, and evaluation of police performance.

In a program with the Oakland, California, police department, Toch, Grant, and Galvin (1975) used groups of officers with records of violent confrontations with citizens to study and resolve problems of police violence. The groups collected and analyzed data (tape recordings of confrontations) and devised innovations, including peer review panels, specialized training, and mediation units to deal with family crises and landlord–tenant disputes. In a project with New York State corrections officers, group participants were selected on the basis of their interest in job enrichment as determined by a questionnaire. The groups at four separate prisons analyzed the corrections officer's job and suggested alterations. The project resulted in blueprints for training, increased involvement of officers in treatment and classification, and mechanisms for increasing communication with management.

In a replication of the Toch and Grant method, Klofas, Smith, and Meister (1986) used groups of jail officers to plan the operation of a new jail in Peoria, Illinois. In a program lasting two years, frontline officers wrote policies and procedures for the facility. Included in the products of their planning were innovations in classification and programming and a revision of the shift pattern and job assignments. Job satisfaction increased over the course of the program, particularly in perceived support from supervisors and opportunities to contribute new ideas.

Perhaps the best-known restructuring of the traditional police role is offered in Angell's (1971) model of team policing, which parallels autonomous work groups in industry. Linking police morale problems to the practices of classical management, Angell provides an alternative to the traditional police hierarchy. The core of his democratic model of policing involves teams of police generalists who provide services to designated neighborhoods. Teams are composed of officers of equal rank who are assigned to relatively small geographical areas for extended periods, which gives them a chance to become familiar with the culturally homogeneous neighborhoods and to work closely with residents (Trojanowicz and Bucqueroux, 1990). The team initiates all investigations and may call in specialists if they are needed. Evaluations of team policing have highlighted its potential but have also called attention to forces within the organization that are resistant to change (Mastrofski, 1991; Sherman, Milton, and Kelly, 1973). In a review of innovations in policing in six American cities, Skolnick and Bayley (1986) also elaborate the benefits of team policing. They argue that, whereas the old professionalism leaned toward "legalistic" styles of policing, the new professionalism is marked by a service-oriented style. They illustrate their arguments with a review of changes in several cities: "Detroit's mini-stations exclusively organize community crime prevention; and Santa Ana's substations function as community ... meeting areas as well as locales for disseminating crime prevention information" (1986:214). The programs thus benefit the community as well as the participating officers.

In their discussion of a Houston program that integrates patrol, investigation, and intelligence collection, Skolnick and Bayley (1986:95) highlight another advantage of decentralization:

> To be successful, this kind of teamwork among patrol officers and spe-
> cialists requires a radical change in the traditional management style.
> Decisions must be made from the bottom up rather than the top down.
> The supervisor's job is not to produce conformity with a preordained
> plan but to help develop a plan out of the insights of the many people
> doing the work on the street.... Not only will policing become more
> purposeful this way, but, it is hoped, officers will develop greater
> enthusiasm for their work. No longer are they spear carriers in someone
> else's drama, they become responsible directors in their own right.

Revitalization of community policing is also being advocated by members of the Executive Session on Policing, which is associated with Harvard University's Kennedy School of Government (Kelling, 1988). Sometimes referred to as "problem-oriented" policing, the approach calls for police to work closely with citizens in identifying and solving problems before crimes occur. Officers and citizens resolve problems such as broken windows, local bullies, and other disruptions that make neighborhoods look and feel unsafe (Bayley, 1994; Iannone, 1994). As its supporters note, "The resourcefulness of police officers ... can at last be put to the service of the department" (Sparrow, 1999:494).

In addition, an evaluation of the Community Oriented Policing (COPS) program mentioned earlier describes the many organizational changes that must occur for police departments to fully implement the community policing idea, including revised mission, vision, and value statements, a strategic plan, changing policies and procedures, provision of training on community policing practices, and changing performance criteria to reflect community policing principles (U.S. Department of Justice, 2000b). The evidence is not in regarding the actual implementation of community policing efforts in police organizations, and, in fact, some critics have posited that actual job design changes in police organizations have been minimal even though the federal government has invested billions of dollars in the COPS program (Cole and Smith, 2007). Nevertheless, community policing principles do reflect a commitment to organizational change consistent with some of the job design efforts mentioned in this chapter.

Programs creating autonomous work groups and other job design efforts have also been initiated in correctional institutions. Under the Unit Management system, pioneered in the Federal Bureau of Prisons, an alternative to the traditional prison hierarchy is established (Levinson and Gerard, 1973). Large institutions are divided into architecturally distinct housing units that typically have from fifty to one hundred inmates. Inmates can be assigned to the units based on similar treatment or security needs. A group of corrections officers and counseling staff has ongoing contact with a small group of inmates in their unit. Frequently headed by a corrections officer, the teams are responsible for all decision making in the unit. Although the distinction between custodial and treatment staff remains, officers and counselors share some duties. The roles of the team members are thus changed in both the horizontal and vertical dimensions.

Both Houston (1999) and Wright (1994) argue that unit management is the wave of the future in corrections. Through decentralization and more employee autonomy, correctional personnel are given the opportunity to "own" their work environments. Wright (1994) shows that through a process of sharing power, the functional capabilities of the unit and the prison are enhanced. Similar ideas are forwarded by those interested in the "direct supervision" model of jail management (Zupan, 1991). Research has shown how a management philosophy and job redesign effort have revolutionized how correctional workers view their work and the organization. Stohr et al. (1994) report how workers in direct supervision jails are much more satisfied in their work, compared to the attitudes of correctional workers in more traditional jail settings. The authors attribute these positive attitude changes to the new philosophy of employee empowerment exhibited in a jail managed under the direct supervision philosophy. In addition, Stojkovic and Farkas (2003) argue the importance of leadership in redesign efforts within prisons and how they can be used to alter the culture of a prison. Finally, we see a move toward more education and training requirements for correctional personnel that will demand a serious look at how employees are recruited, trained, and supervised. Camp and Camp (2000) report that correctional officers in the year 2000 had to complete, on average, a 9.9-month probationary period, 250 hours of introductory training, and 38 hours of in-service training before becoming full-time correctional officers. These increases in training and probationary periods make the twenty-first-century correctional officer better trained and equipped to handle the tasks of the job than her or his predecessors. Moreover, correctional officers will be demanding more of their managers and administrators regarding how they will be organized and supervised to address the tasks they will face, so job redesign issues will continue to be an important issue for prison administrators.

In probation and parole, the Community Resource Management Team (CRMT) has been developed as an alternative to the traditional caseload model (Clear and O'Leary, 1983:126). Based on the assumption that "no one person can possess all the skills to deal with the variety of human problems presented by probationers" (Dell' Appa et al., cited in Clear and O'Leary, 1983:126), the model creates specialists in skill areas. Probation officers act as advocates concerned with the purchase of services or referrals in specific areas, such as employment, counseling, legal assistance, and drug abuse. CRMT staff have "duty areas" or functional responsibilities rather than caseloads. Clear and O'Leary (1983) describe a project that gave probation officers functional rather than caseload responsibilities. The project directors discovered that some officers naturally adopted functional approaches:

> One officer, regarded as especially skilled in intensive counseling activities, had in fact stopped seeing some of her caseload so that she could see a minority of cases more intensively. Other areas of officer interest and knowledge included drugs, the military, and language problems. One officer had developed a system of mail reporting for a large non-contact caseload. The problem facing the supervisor was to make the best use of these existing officer skills and interests in the supervision of clients (Clear and O'Leary, 1983:127).

Probation officers in the large urban department involved in the change project altered the organizational structure to accommodate officer interests as well as the existing classification scheme. A two-person team became responsible for intake and initial case analysis. One of the intake officers also handled low-risk cases on a low reporting basis. Medium-level cases were handled by a team divided by functional interests, and high-risk cases were handled in small caseloads by single officers with counseling interests. Clear and O'Leary, however, make the important observation that this model may not be appropriate for other agencies or even for some other big-city agencies. They call for the direct involvement of staff and for flexibility in the redesign of probation officer tasks so that each organization can take advantage of its own resources. Dickey (1996) reports that in the state of Wisconsin, attempts were being made to restructure the probation officer role so that greater attention could be given to the law enforcement and supervision requirements of the job. Wisconsin, like other states, is interested in improving its supervision of offenders while in the community. Part of this focus includes concern over offender/staff ratios as well as the appropriate usage of finite resources. Utilizing employees as scarce resources is a theme consistent with a belief that community protection can be enhanced through more effective ways of designing job tasks among probation officers. Job redesign efforts, as part of a larger refocusing strategy in corrections, provide a rationale for more investment in community corrections (Petersilia, 1995).

The idea of job redesign, however, is not limited to corrections. Police organizations have gone through some revolutionary changes over the last twenty years, and the issue of police organization has raised some serious questions concerning the ways departments are organized and personnel supervised (Whisenand and Ferguson, 1996). Police organizations of the twenty-first century are much larger and more diverse with respect to the number of minority personnel, the degree to which line officers have a college education, and a commitment to a community policing philosophy. According to the Bureau of Justice Statistics

(2005b), there are close to 900,000 law enforcement officers across almost 16,000 agencies. A vast majority of officers are within the following structures: local police departments (56 percent), county police (21 percent), state police (7 percent), special police (5 percent), and federal law enforcement (11 percent). According to the Law Enforcement Management and Administrative Statistics (LEMAS) survey (2003), 14 percent of local police departments and 11 percent of sheriffs' departments had some type of college education requirement. One percent of agencies require a four-year degree. The increase in educational achievements now required for entry-level police officers makes job design questions of extreme importance to police administrators. More educated officers demand different ways of organizing and administering police organizations.

Nothing, however, has had more of an impact on police organization than the move toward community policing. The LEMAS survey reveals that nine in ten local police departments serving a population of 25,000 or more had full-time sworn personnel regularly engaged in community policing activities. Among municipal police departments, 62 percent had a formally written community policing plan, 76 percent operated one or more community substations, 73 percent had full-time school resource officers, and an overwhelming majority of these police departments invested dollars and other resources into community policing training for both officers and citizens alike.

Fyfe et al. (1997) suggest that many issues of both philosophy and practice must be considered when moving a police department from a traditional police organization structure with its top-down management philosophy to a community policing structure that emphasizes more decentralization and involvement by line police officers in the structuring of police duties and activities. Issues of job design become very important to police managers and administrators. Recruitment, selection, evaluation, and the retention of employees are significantly altered under a community policing approach. Fundamentally, line officers, supervisors, and administrators require more group cohesion to effectively operationalize the community policing philosophy. Most important, line officers require the support of frontline supervisors to make community policing strategies viable. Communication must be improved and increased across groups in the police organization. Officers have to feel their ideas have merit and will not be routinely dismissed. In the words of Fyfe and colleagues: "But line officers will not do so [increase communication] unless their cooperation is sought out and encouraged" (1997:272). Moreover, there must be a strong commitment to community policing principles for any effective job design effort to be successful (U.S. Department of Justice, 2000b).

JOB DESIGN AND THE COMMUNITY

Job design issues within criminal justice organizations cannot be adequately addressed without the inclusion of broader issues of the community and how they affect job design efforts. One of the most recent revolutionary social changes was the passage of the Americans with Disabilities Act (ADA) in

1990 that changed how the law views people with disabilities. As in other human service organizations, provisions of ADA have direct relevance for criminal justice organizations. Job design efforts in criminal justice have to consider the importance of ADA on how we alter or modify criminal justice organizations.

The U.S. Department of Justice (2000a), in the document *Enforcing ADA: Looking Back on a Decade of Progress*, notes the significant gains made within criminal justice organizations to be in compliance with ADA mandates. The monograph notes the advances but also points out the central concerns ADA places on criminal justice administrators. Most notable are the issues of access to the courts, the fair treatment of persons with disabilities in law enforcement, employment opportunities for persons with disabilities within criminal justice organizations, architectural issues and accessibility to criminal justice buildings, and access to health care and emergency services for those with disabilities.

With regard to design efforts in criminal justice organizations, the ADA has had a major role in directing criminal justice administrators. People with disabilities have the full force of the law in how these job design efforts are created and enforced by criminal justice organizations. The Department of Justice's study makes clear that criminal justice organizations can work with those with disabilities to make the work settings aware of the concerns they have and include the use of mediation to resolve issues and address ADA requirements.

Similarly, job design efforts must be cognizant of the demographic changes occurring within criminal justice organizations. With the increased diversity of criminal justice personnel, they need to be aware of how this diversity will challenge traditional ways of designing criminal justice organizations. The most notable demographic change is the greater involvement of women within criminal justice agencies. More women within criminal justice organizations pose serious challenges for criminal justice administrators. Research literature has documented the difficulties women have faced in both police and correctional organizations (Pogrebin and Poole, 1997). The Bureau of Justice Assistance (2001) offers a self-assessment guide for recruiting and retaining women in law enforcement. Job design efforts within criminal justice organizations will have to be sensitive to the contributions that increased diversity brings to the workforce and diligently work toward incorporating changes that recognize diversity as a value to the overall functioning of the organization.

The New Criminal Justice and Job Design

From Taylor and scientific management to human relations and human service, there have been many ideas on how to design criminal justice work. We have seen some profound changes over the past one hundred years, yet nothing as revolutionary as what we will see in criminal justice organizations in the twenty-first century. In the opening vignette of the chapter, we mentioned the "new criminal justice." What is the new criminal justice and how will it impact job design efforts of criminal justice employees? Moreover, how will this new criminal justice alter criminal justice administration?

New criminal justice: An approach to increase the effectiveness of criminal justice organizations through the reliance on systematic data collection and collaboration with other agencies and community groups.

The term **new criminal justice** can be attributed to the work of Klofas, Hipple, and McGarrell (2010). The basic premise of the new criminal justice is that responding to crime is no longer possible in an organizational vacuum. Crime is a social and political phenomenon, but most important, it exists within varied communities with unique problems and issues. To simply view crime as primarily a criminal justice concern is erroneous and ineffective. Under the new criminal justice, criminal justice organizations would actively seek partnerships and collaborations with community organizations, both public and private, to address their crime issues. What is needed in one community may make no sense in another community. What follows is an example of such a collaboration.

Klofas and colleagues (2010) identify the efforts of Project Safe Neighborhoods (PSN) as an example of a community strategy to enlist the assistance and support of many public and private agencies to address serious gun-related crime. Funded through U.S. attorneys' offices across the country, PSN works with many community agencies and groups to address serious violent crime, employing a direct and confrontational approach with offenders. By confronting offenders regarding the potential consequences of their behaviors, the PSN initiative offers a differing set of strategies to address serious crime. By building bridges and coordinating functions across many disparate agencies, criminal justice organizations under the PSN strategy were able to address the issue of guns and violence in innovative ways. The evidence on these efforts is somewhat limited to date, but early research suggests encouraging signs for the future (see Kroovand-Hipple, 2010 for a review of the effectiveness of PSN initiatives in the state of Alabama).

What do these new efforts mean for job design within criminal justice organizations? As noted in other chapters in this book, criminal justice organizations are open systems. They are both impacted by the environment and influence the environment. Under the new criminal justice, criminal justice agencies must open up further to their communities. The new criminal justice organization is a more permeable organization, allowing the differing elements of the community to access it and to become more intricately involved in addressing crime problems. The cornerstone of the new criminal justice centers on collaboration, information sharing, dissemination, and innovation and is supported by research and practice. Known in some circles as "action-oriented" research, this strategy incorporates the best practices of academicians and practitioners to come to solutions regarding crime in the community.

Mock (2010) examines the history of the National Institute of Justice in attempting to integrate the work of both practitioners and researchers to address crime. She argues that such collaborations prove to be fruitful to both academic researchers and practitioners; the former group understands the complexity and difficulty of doing research within criminal justice organizations, while the latter becomes more informed through the use of social science techniques to manage specific crime problems. The union of the practitioner with the academic is the future of the new criminal justice. What types of changes would we see in the new criminal justice? These changes would be in a number of areas, but are probably most notable in recruitment, training, and ongoing employee development.

We need a different type of employee under the new criminal justice. This person requires some basic analytical skills and certain educational competencies. Klofas (2010) describes the development of the new criminal justice employee as being educated on the power of analytics and information collection. This knowledge would be gained through classroom preparation but most important also through on-the-job collaborations with criminal justice organizations. Students regularly take field placements while in college. Under this model, the field placement would be more structured and more realistic in relation to the problems of crime in the community. This approach is somewhat similar to that already taken by other professionals, like nurses, teachers, and social workers. The curriculum for students is integrated into the work setting. Students could be placed, for example, at a police organization or a prison with the role of addressing a specific problem faced by that agency. They would learn the basics of understanding crime methodologies through a university setting, but the practical application would be in the field of criminal justice.

Right now, some of the High Intensity Drug Traffic Areas (HIDTAS) use student interns in this capacity, learning data analysis on the job. This enables them to engage firsthand with law enforcement professionals within an agency setting to prepare themselves for a career in law enforcement. Upon graduation, this type of student is ready to assume a law enforcement position, armed with strategies to approach crime that challenge conventional wisdom and use information in a comprehensive way (Polachek, 2011). In addition, some colleges, like the University of Wisconsin–Milwaukee, have instituted new "crime analysis" certificates and emphases that educate people on the new criminal justice analytics, with a focus on addressing specific crime-related problems (Stojkovic, 2013).

Training modules also would have to change within criminal justice organizations under the new criminal justice. To stay on top of crime, new training would be an ongoing process for current employees. While new recruits may be more familiar with the analytical techniques of the new criminal justice, established employees would require incentives to change how they perform tasks. A change in job design would alter performance expectations. Any kind of change will always be problematical (see Chapter 14), yet changes in the ways of doing business provide the opportunity to change culture, and this is where leadership will be critical (see Chapter 7). In addition, we will be using training to alter jobs, as employees, citizens, and the community develop innovative and effective ways to deal with crime. We are already seeing how prosecutors across the country, for example, are working toward restructuring their offices to be more receptive to citizen demands through the creation of "community prosecution" initiatives, employing prosecutorial, police, and correctional resources and public groups to deal with crime (Chisholm, 2010).

The new criminal justice will have implications for the structural components of criminal justice organizations as well. What type of employee will we need to sustain the new criminal justice? We have already stated the importance of analytics and other educational requirements, such as information-gathering techniques, but the issues are even more complex for criminal justice administrators. They involve how we manage and supervise the new generation of criminal justice employees and provide for their continued development. Similar to the arguments presented earlier in the chapter regarding job enrichment, the new criminal justice employee may seek continued development and new ideas as ways to enrich the job experience. Moreover, the larger context of employee expectations must be addressed because younger employees have differing expectations of employers when compared to past employee expectations of employers. For the "new" criminal justice employee, questions of commitment, dedication, and a career orientation to any one organization over a lifetime no longer seem realistic (Rainey, 2014). How criminal justice administrators respond to this challenge is a very important issue as we continue into the twenty-first century.

Also, will these new employees require more flexibility consistent with the human service ideas of job design discussed earlier in the chapter? It is quite possible that the new criminal justice will be the beginning of the end of appeals to traditional hierarchy as the primary method of structuring criminal justice organizations. With increased training and knowledge as a prerequisite for employment in new criminal justice organizations, there will have to be a concomitant alteration of rules for organizations, divisions of labor, employee supervision, and a host of other issues germane to organizational structure. The new criminal justice will seriously call into question traditional Tayloristic notions of job design as discussed earlier in the chapter. The future of criminal justice organizations will be truly exciting yet challenging for those who administer. On the one hand, the administrators will always be drawn to the traditional approaches of designing criminal justice jobs, but on the other hand, antiquated notions of criminal justice job design may have outlived their usefulness and may be better off left in the dustbins of history.

SUMMARY

Understand a definition of job design.

- The deliberate and purposeful planning of the job, including all of its structural and social aspects and their effects on the employee.

Explain the early importance of engineering and efficiency to job design.

- Application of basic scientific principles to job design.

Define and explain Taylorism.

- Attributed to the work of Frederick Taylor, who believed in the division of labor, the use of time–motion studies, and pay as the primary motivator of employees.

Comprehend the application of Taylorism to criminal justice.

- Utilizing Taylor's principles, criminal justice work is designed to maximize the control of employees and enhance efficiency.

Know how job satisfaction, job stress, and job burnout relate to job design.

- Job design is critical to reducing burnout, relieving work stress, and elevating job satisfaction among employees.

Define and explain job design theory.

- Job design theory has moved past Taylorism to include an examination of job enlargement and job enrichment.
- How jobs are structured does matter regarding organizational performance.

Comprehend job redesign programs and application to criminal justice organizations.

- An attempt to alter jobs so employees have more of a say in how jobs are accomplished.
- There have been numerous examples of redesign efforts within criminal justice organizations.

Explain the relationship between job design and the community.

- Job design efforts are no longer limited to organizational settings and must include community concerns.

Define the "new criminal justice" and its relationship to job design.

- The new criminal justice focuses on the systematic collection of information and collaboration with other agencies and community groups.
- The new criminal justice will force administrators to consider changes in a number of ways they do business, in particular, in the following areas: recruitment, training, and ongoing development activities for employees.

 Case Study: "SO, YOU WANT TO BE A FORENSIC SCIENTIST"

No more glamorous position exists in the criminal justice system than being a forensic scientist, at least as portrayed by contemporary television shows such as *CSI* and *CSI: Miami*. For many students interested in a career in forensic science, the weekly portrayals conjure up images of excitement and fulfillment tracking down suspects and ultimately catching the bad guy through the use of fancy technology and techniques of forensic investigation. Too bad television portrayals of forensics work are not consistent with the reality of the work. Here is the reality.

A vast majority of forensics work is structured through a laboratory and involves techniques that have nowhere near the degree of sophistication presented by weekly tele-

vision shows. To begin, to become a forensic scientist means knowing the basics of biology, chemistry, and life sciences. Forensic scientists are just that—scientists! All of them come from backgrounds that require a heavy dose of biology, molecular biology, organic chemistry, inorganic chemistry, analytical chemistry, and, to some degree, depending on specialty, training in human anatomy, blood serology, and the modern techniques of DNA analysis. Forensic science is about science, and preparation through the hard sciences is extensive and necessary.

In addition, a career in forensic science very rarely leads you out of the laboratory. Most physical evidence forensic scientists use in criminal cases is brought to

CASE STUDY—continued

them by police and other investigative agencies. Analyses of blood samples, hair fibers, and other trace evidence, for example, are conducted in laboratories under restrictions to which forensics laboratories must comply, given their accreditation standards and governmental rules and regulations. In recent years, these laboratories have come under much scrutiny for poor handling of evidence, the contamination of evidence, and, in some rare cases, the fabrication of evidence. Forensic laboratories must hire people who have a heavy science background, usually college degrees in biology and chemistry, and provide a work environment that is fairly routine and predictable, akin to the Tayloristic strategies outlined in the chapter. This allows them to defend their practices when allegations of wrongdoing are made.

Moreover, careers in forensics work are fairly limited, and, for most starting their careers in crime labs, the vast majority of the work involves drug screening. Unless you have highly specialized knowledge, forensic entomology, for example, you will probably be stuck in the lab doing rather routine work. Can the work be structured any differently? This question is difficult to answer. Unlike many other jobs in criminal justice that have wider autonomy and greater discretion, most forensics work is routine and structured best under a traditional design strategy.

This is not to suggest that exciting developments are not happening in the forensics field, such as advances in DNA training and the promulgation of death investigation standards for medical examiners, police, and coroners, which may require alternative work arrangements. Yet, for most crime lab work, the future is the same as the past: We uncover relevant evidence in the laboratory, and the work is very routine and mundane.

So, do you still want to be a forensic scientist? Given the structure and design of most state crime laboratories, it is not clear that many alternatives exist to the traditional ways of doing forensics work. Forensic scientists will always be needed to employ scientific techniques to aid in the prosecution of criminal suspects, but from a job design perspective, given the nature of most of the work, the reality is that you will more likely be chasing the bad guy through your microscope rather than a red Ferrari.

CASE STUDY QUESTIONS

1. Is it possible to enrich forensics work in any way, given the description in the case study?
2. What about job growth and development opportunities in forensics work, such as career training in modern techniques of DNA analysis? Could such opportunities provide incentives to becoming a forensic scientist?
3. Do modern approaches to altering work (flextime, job sharing, and telecommuting) have relevance to structuring forensics work? What are the strengths and limitations of these approaches to forensics work?

 Think like an Administrator

There has been a movement in corrections to employ the strategies and findings of recent advances in cognitive-behavioral (CB) approaches to treating prisoners. These approaches were based on addressing the cognitive and behavioral strengths found among prisoners based on the notion that they are driven toward behaviors that have clearly defined incentives and will avoid behaviors where there are limited or no incentives and/or bad outcomes. In the 1990s, academic researchers identified the importance of CB to changing attitudes and behaviors of prisoners, but what was not realized was the benefit of such approaches to correctional administrators and correctional officers. CB offered more tools to correctional officers and empowered them in their interactions with prisoners. Under CB, correctional officers have incentives that they can use to direct

---

THINK LIKE AN ADMINISTRATOR—continued

prisoner behavior. In a strange twist to what was expected, CB offered correctional officers a wider array of strategies to address prisoner concerns.

Correctional officers could employ CB techniques as a way to control the inmate population. Armed with incentives they could provide prisoners, correctional officers are empowered. Traditionally, correctional officers could only provide punishments for bad behavior. By utilizing CB approaches, correctional officers could use positive outcomes and rewards to change prisoner behavior, for example, providing inmates with increased access to canteen materials. Under CB, the correctional officer could provide *more* access to canteen goods, not just simply deny access to canteen items as part of a strategy to gain compliance among prisoners. The prisoner then had more reasons to act correctly, and the correctional officers had more options to assist them in the performance of their duties.

1. How do you think correctional officers will receive CB?
2. Will correctional officers view CB as an advancement of or an encroachment on their authority?
3. How does treatment staff fit into this new initiative for correctional officers?
4. Are there any other personnel issues that would have to be addressed through the introduction of CB for correctional officers, for example, union or labor agreement issues?
5. What type of training routine would have to be created for CB to be effective among correctional officers?
6. How would you deal with an unmotivated officer when introducing CB?
7. How would the introduction of CB affect turnover rate among correctional officers?
8. Is this new job design cost effective?

FOR DISCUSSION

1. The argument has been made that scientific management has been influential in criminal justice and that, as managers have become more advanced professionally, frontline criminal justice jobs have become more impoverished. Is the de-professionalization syndrome an inevitable consequence of improvements in the technology of criminal justice?

2. Consider a specific job within the criminal justice system. What characteristics of that job are sources of motivation and what characteristics may lead to dissatisfaction or burnout?

3. Examine the job characteristics model of Hackman and Oldham. How well does that model account for motivation in criminal justice workers? Describe the core job characteristics of a particular job. How do they relate to important psychological states?

4. Explore the "new criminal justice." Does it make sense? How would collection of systematic information and collaboration occur within criminal justice organizations?

FOR FURTHER READING

Bayley, D. *Police for the Future.* New York: Free Press, 1994.

Fyfe, J., Greene, J., Walsh, W., Wilson, O., and McLaren, R. *Police Administration.* 5th ed. New York: McGraw-Hill, 1997.

Hackman, J. R., and Oldham, G. R. *Work Redesign.* Reading, MA: Addison-Wesley, 1987.

Houston, J. *Correctional Management: Functions, Skills, and Systems.* 2nd ed. Chicago: Nelson Hall, 1999.

Klofas, J., Hipple, N. K., and McGarrell, E. F. *The New Criminal Justice: American Communities and the Changing World of Criminal Justice.* New York: Taylor-Francis, 2010.

Skolnick, J. H., and Bayley, D. H. *The New Blue Line: Police Innovation in Six American Cities.* New York: Free Press, 1986.

U.S. Department of Justice. *National Evaluation of the COPS Program.* Washington, DC: National Institute of Justice, 2000.

Wright, K. *Effective Prison Leadership.* Binghamton, NY: William Neil, 1994.

CHAPTER 7

Leadership

LEARNING OBJECTIVES

After reading this chapter, the students will have achieved the following objectives:

- Comprehend the complexities of leadership within criminal justice organizations.

- Understand the many theories of leadership.

- Know the limitations of leadership research in criminal justice organizations.

- Explain the importance of leadership development in criminal justice organizations.

VIGNETTE

One of the major difficulties facing criminal justice organizations is the dearth of quality leaders found among the rank and file. Current research has underscored the importance of leadership to criminal justice agencies, yet when we investigate the number and quality of leadership-development programs in criminal justice organizations, we find very few agencies actually investing in leadership development.

The costs of leadership programs are miniscule by comparison to other entities and programs on which we spend monies in our efforts as criminal justice administrators. Take, for example, the Drug Abuse Resistance Education (DARE) program. Communities and police departments spend millions of dollars on this initiative to reduce drug use among youth, yet the evidence is clear that the program has no appreciable impact on drug usage among young people. What does the efficacy of a drug program for young people have to do with leadership development in criminal justice organizations? A lot. When you fail to invest in good leadership education programs (not training programs), you get the quality of leader who will make decisions that do not reflect the best possible practices; communities will ultimately suffer and waste an enormous number of resources.

Similarly, as an investment strategy, endorsing leadership development is critical to maintaining quality personnel up and down the hierarchies of criminal justice organizations. Research has shown that many of our executive leaders within criminal justice organizations do not last long. Their tenure, in many cases, is limited. Police chiefs, especially police chiefs in large urban communities, do not have long tenure. There are many reasons for this outcome. One primary reason is that police executives do not know how to lead their agencies; they confuse leadership with management, the former being more visionary and the latter more bureaucratic. The lack of leadership development has consequences for all criminal justice organizations.

The contemporary criminal justice administrator is expected to be an effective leader, an expectation that fits with the general demand for competent leaders in all organizations, both public and private. Although a great deal of prescriptive material tells the criminal justice administrator how to lead an organization effectively, there is little empirical evidence on what effective leadership actually involves. In this chapter, we review the relevant aspects of these models and apply our understanding of the leadership process to the requirements of the criminal justice system.

Our review, however, will not be prescriptive. Instead, we will offer an analytical framework rooted in empirical research and theoretical models of leadership. In this way, we hope not only to provide an increased understanding of how the process of leadership works in criminal justice organizations but also to suggest what our expectations of criminal justice leaders should and should not be.

To accomplish these objectives, we explore several areas. First, we define leadership and argue that, because criminal justice administration is fundamentally politically driven, it is useful to understand leadership within the political arena. Second, the chapter reviews the major theories of leadership that have been developed in research on organizational behavior. Our discussion in this section integrates what we know about leadership research done in other organizations and applies these findings to the criminal justice system. Our review in this section includes an analysis of behavioral and contingency theories of leadership and more twenty-first-century ideas on leadership—theories that hold promise for explaining the leadership process in criminal justice organizations.

Finally, the chapter explores criminal justice research that addresses the issue of leadership. Although much of this literature is overly prescriptive, we provide an overview of those few pieces of research that empirically test theoretical models of leadership and make some recommendations for future research. In addition, we present a model of leadership education that was in operation in a department of corrections. This model suggests future concerns that criminal justice administrators need to consider to be effective leaders.

LEADERSHIP DEFINED

Four distinct but not separate ideas about administration guide our definitions of leadership. First, leadership is a process that effectively accomplishes organizational goals. Leadership cannot be conceptually separated from organizational effectiveness (Tosi, Rizzo, and Carroll, 1986) and the accomplishment of objectives. Second, administrators can learn leadership skills. Even though the process of leadership is complex, we believe it can be learned and applied to the effective administration of criminal justice organizations. Much of criminal justice management literature assumes that effective leadership can be taught, and millions of dollars have been spent since the 1960s by criminal justice organizations, especially police, to develop training modules that help administrators accomplish organizational goals. Although there may be little or no value in knowing the "correct" style of leadership, the characteristics of good leaders as identified by empirical research can serve as the basis of suggestions and recommendations to criminal justice administrators. These leadership characteristics, however, are always subject to the tasks, functions, and objectives the organization expects to accomplish. In addition, criminal justice research has examined the many variables affecting leadership and ultimately subordinate outcomes. Take, for example, the issue of emotional intelligence and its relationship to leadership. The research literature of the 1990s and the early part of the twenty-first century had focused directly on the power of emotional components to leadership. The relationship, however, between emotional intelligence and leadership is thorny and problematical (Weinberger, 2009).

Third, leadership is a group process. To accomplish organizational objectives, leaders must influence a number of people, or, to put it simply: no group, no leader. The process of leadership must thus be examined in light of the strategies leaders use to get people to achieve the tasks necessary for organizational existence and survival. Ostensibly, we may be talking about methods of compliance and power in organizations. Chapter 10 will examine these topics in criminal justice organizations. For now, however, we want to know the kinds of techniques that are used in the relationship between a leader and subordinates. Yukl (1981:12–17) suggests eleven **techniques of influence**, used singly or in combination, that affect the leadership process:

Techniques of influence: Strategies that gain the compliance of subordinates and are essential to the leadership process.

1. *Legitimate request.* A person complies with an agent's request because the person recognizes the agent's "right" as a leader to make such a request.

2. *Instrumental compliance.* A person is induced to alter his or her behavior by an agent's implicit or explicit promise to ensure some tangible outcome desired by the person.

3. *Coercion.* A person is induced to comply by an agent's explicit or implicit threat to ensure adverse outcomes if the person fails to do so.

4. *Rational persuasion.* An agent convinces a person that the suggested behavior is the best way for the person to satisfy his or her needs or to attain his or her objectives.

5. *Rational faith.* An agent's suggestion is sufficient to evoke compliance by a person without the necessity for any explanation.

6. *Inspirational appeal.* An agent persuades a person that there is a necessary link between the requested behavior and some value important enough to justify the behavior.

7. *Indoctrination.* A person acts because of induced internalization of strong values relevant to the desired behavior.

8. *Information distortion.* A person is unconsciously influenced by an agent's limiting, falsifying, or interpreting information in a way conducive to compliance.

9. *Situational engineering.* A person's attitudes and behavior are indirectly influenced by an agent's manipulation of relevant aspects of the physical and social situation.

10. *Personal identification.* A person imitates an agent's attitudes and behavior because the person admires or worships the agent.

11. *Decision identification.* An agent allows a person to participate in and have substantial influence over the making of a decision, thereby gaining the person's identification with the final choice.

Think of how administrators in criminal justice use any one or a combination of these techniques to influence their subordinates and lead their agencies. For example, the prison warden who rules his institution with an iron fist employs coercion as a method of leadership, while the police sergeant who suggests to the beat officer that cordial interactions with citizens are essential to effective police work is using persuasion. Effective leaders, however, are able to get subordinates to work toward the stated objectives of the organization regardless of the method.

Techniques of leadership are not the same as styles of leadership. A style of leadership consists of all the techniques a leader uses to achieve organizational goals. The prison warden who employs coercion, information distortion, and indoctrination as techniques of influence with inmates and corrections officers is exhibiting an autocratic style of leadership. Later in the chapter, we explore other styles of leadership, some of which are more effective than others in criminal justice administration.

Fourth, leadership in public bureaucracies, such as criminal justice agencies, is inherently political and must be examined within the political arena. Leadership in organizations is often discussed with an internal focus. Little is said about the external nature of leadership, even though an external view is critical to a complete understanding of how public agencies are run. A common criticism of applying research findings on leadership in private or public organizations has been its limited value given the political contexts within which public organizations operate. In fact, some would say that the lack of research attention to the external and political nature of leadership makes many existing theories on leadership of little or no value to those who operate public bureaucracies (Rainey, 2014).

Some have suggested that criminal justice organizations are unique entities with well-defined histories and legal contexts. To understand leadership within these organizations requires a comprehension of how these elements further constrain criminal justice leadership. Correctional leadership, especially within the context of prisons and the role of the courts in the management and leadership of prisons, is now experiencing a crisis. In some cases, prison leadership has been, once again, directed by the courts. This type of direction has not been so evident since the 1960s. The California Department of Corrections and Rehabilitation, for example, has been placed under the authority of the U.S. Supreme Court due to massive overcrowding since 2011. The state of California had been directed to reduce its prison population to 137.5 percent of its capacity by May 2013 to meet the expectations of the court. It came close to meeting this goal but fell short and requested assistance and guidance to meet constitutional standards as stipulated by the court. It is interesting that this comes at a time when there are questions regarding the effectiveness of the measures put in place to supervise and monitor released offenders in the community (Petersilia and Snyder, 2013).

There is no doubt this example suggests the unique position that correctional systems are in and the importance of leadership to them, yet it is not totally clear nor evident that as public entities they are that different from other publicly funded agencies, such as school systems and transportation agencies. A growing body of literature both supports the uniqueness of public agencies on the one hand and their similarity to private organizations on the other hand and the relevance of leadership (Daft, 2010). The student will have to review the existing theories and models presented in this chapter to see if criminal justice organizations are truly unique and therefore require specific prescriptions regarding leadership or are so similar to private businesses that no special circumstances or prescriptions are required. Is good leadership just good leadership, whether it is a police department or a fast food restaurant?

Existing theories of leadership are relevant to understanding the leadership process within the criminal justice system, but some consideration must be given as to how criminal justice administrators, as public bureaucrats, lead their agencies. In other words, we need an examination of the leadership phenomenon as it operates within the political arena. For example, take the career of former FBI Director J. Edgar Hoover, who was said to have employed charismatic and legitimate forms of authority (techniques of influence) to lead the FBI. This characterization, however, does not describe the political relationships that made him an effective leader of a large public bureaucracy over a fifty-year period, even though many questioned the legality and morality of how he lead the FBI (Powers, 1987). Leadership must thus be understood as a process that reaches well beyond the formal boundaries of the organization. Leadership in criminal justice agencies involves convincing both subordinates and those outside the agencies in the political arena that a particular method (usually the leader's) is the best one for accomplishing organizational objectives.

Many leaders of criminal justice bureaucracies understand the political nature of their positions, but they must equally be aware of the vacillations in public interest in and concern about their agencies. Thus, leadership of a criminal justice agency requires flexibility, but, as Selznick (1957) reminds us, public agencies must also clearly define their mission, structure this mission into their hierarchy, maintain the values of the organization that give it its identity, and control conflicts among competing interests within the organization (see also Wilson, 2000 for a similar discussion). In short, criminal justice administrators must operate their organizations in tune with the political realities of the external environment while simultaneously maintaining their own role identities. Because of the tension between changes in the external political environment and administrators' desires to keep control of the organization, leadership becomes a crucial and critical process. Dealing with this tension makes criminal justice administration difficult today, especially because many observers have noted the increased politicization of criminal justice policy and practice. Although the political process is integral to the development of criminal justice policies and external influences direct what policies will be developed, the degree to which politics plays a role in leader decision making has become more pronounced and, in some people's minds, detrimental to rational policy making at the executive level of criminal justice organizations (Gomez, 1995; Hickman, 2005; Woodford, 2006).

In sum, we can define leadership as invariably tied to the effectiveness of an organization; as learnable, contingent on the tasks, functions, and objectives of the organization; as carried out in a group setting; and, probably most important of all for criminal justice agencies, as focused on political and public concerns.

THEORIES OF LEADERSHIP

Much of what we know about leadership comes from research that takes one of three approaches. The first, and probably the oldest, assumes that a leader is born, not made. This approach, which tends to emphasize inherent personality traits, also assumes that leadership can be evaluated on the basis of these traits. Much research, however, questions whether personal characteristics of "leadership" actually exist or, more important, can be viewed separately from the situational context (Bass, 1981; Tosi, Rizzo, and Carroll, 1986:553). Thus, it is difficult to know whether the leader's overall personality or particular traits are critical to the leadership process. An authoritarian police sergeant may be successful in a situation that requires a clear, concise, and immediate response, such as a hostage situation, yet this style of leadership may be totally ineffective in a situation that requires deliberation and patience, such as police officer training. Because a number of difficulties are associated with this approach, those studying the leadership process have largely abandoned it. Yet, some have suggested that an important element of effective leadership is "emotional intelligence." This concept suggests that leaders are most effective when they understand people in organizations and have a passion about doing what is right in an organization such that people perform for them. Research, however, on emotional intelligence and leadership is lacking; nevertheless, it does signal that trait approaches to leadership are not totally dismissed by leadership proponents (Robbins and Judge, 2007:404; Weinberger, 2009).

Much contemporary research done on leadership now takes one of two other approaches. The behavioral approach, which emphasizes the behaviors of individual leaders, is the focus of much of the criminal justice research on leadership. As suggested by Tosi, Rizzo, and Carroll (1986:554–557), behavioral approaches fall into two distinct areas: the distribution of influence and the tasks and social behaviors of leaders. The contingency approach, finally, is a product of the 1970s and tends to emphasize multiple variables, particularly situational variables that constrain leadership. These situational variables include characteristics of subordinates, organizational context, and style of leadership.

Our review of behavioral and contingency models in this chapter provides us with insight into theories of leadership from the perspective of organizational behavior. Our next goal is to see how and whether these theories fit the actual leadership process in criminal justice organizations. We begin our review with an examination of the behavioral approaches.

Behavioral Models

Because of the many problems associated with the character trait approach to understanding leadership, researchers have increasingly focused on behaviors instead. This approach suggests that effective leadership depends on how leaders interact with their subordinates. Part of this approach is using **behavioral models**, a set of leadership theories that focus on the interaction of leaders and subordinates. More important, the behavioral approach accentuates how leaders get subordinates to accomplish organizational tasks, a process known as initiating structures. Using a behavioral approach, for example, we would be interested in knowing the ways in which the warden of a prison interacts with administrative staff, treatment specialists, and corrections officers so that the tasks essential to the prison's mission are completed.

The behavioral approach is also concerned with how employees are able to achieve personal goals within the organization at the same time that they accomplish its central tasks. In our example, we would be interested in what the prison warden does to accommodate or consider staff opinions, ideas, and feelings about the day-to-day workings of the prison. Do the corrections officers feel supported? Do treatment personnel feel they have a central role? Is there room for advancement in the prison's hierarchy?

These two concepts, consideration for subordinates and initiating structures, guide the behavioral approach to leadership. They evolved from two sets of leadership studies done in the 1940s, 1950s, and early 1960s: the Ohio State studies and the Michigan studies. In addition, a popular model of supervision was created at this time; it is known as the managerial grid. Originally devised by Blake and Mouton (1964), this grid was based on two dimensions of behavior —concern for people and concern for production—that are analogous to the concepts of consideration and initiating structure. Fundamentally, according to Blake and Mouton, the most effective manager is equally concerned with high levels of production among employees and their needs. The managerial grid has been extensively applied to criminal justice (see Duffee, 1986). Here, however, we will not focus on the grid itself but instead present the original research from which it was derived.

The **Ohio State studies**, which began in the late 1940s, concluded that leadership could be examined on the two dimensions of consideration and initiating structure. Consideration is the leader's expression of concern for subordinates' feelings, ideas, and opinions about job-related matters. Considerate leaders are concerned about employees, develop trust between leaders and subordinates, and more often than not develop good communication. Initiating structure is the leader's direction of subordinates toward specific goals. The role of the leader is to make sure that an adequate structure is available for employees so that organizational objectives are accomplished. The Ohio State studies concluded that effective leadership is present in an organization when the levels of consideration and initiating structure are high among leaders.

As suggested by Hellriegel, Slocum, and Woodman (1995), however, the central limitation of the Ohio State studies was a failure to recognize the

Behavioral models: A set of leadership theories that focus on the interaction of leaders and subordinates.

Ohio State studies: A behavioral-based set of studies that examined leadership on two dimensions of organization: consideration and initiating structure.

importance of specific situations in the leadership process. The police sergeant who heads a tactical unit, for example, does not need to be considerate of employees when faced with an emergency situation; rather, the sergeant needs to delineate roles and duties to patrol officers in the unit as quickly as possible. A high degree of initiating structure, in other words, is critical. The Ohio State studies thus seem applicable only to specific situations where both consideration and initiating structure are appropriate.

The **Michigan studies**, in contrast, sought to dichotomize the leadership process into two dimensions of supervisory behavior: production-centered and employee-centered. We know that not all supervisors have the same outlook toward their jobs, employees, and tasks required to meet the organization's objectives and goals. Some police sergeants, as immediate supervisors, are interested in high activity by their subordinates, whether that be ticket writing, arrests, or some other police performance measure. Other police sergeants are concerned with the perceptions of rank-and-file officers about their roles in the organization. These supervisors care about how officers fit into the organizational hierarchy and about their level of satisfaction with their work. According to the Michigan studies, the effective leader attempts to be employee-centered, a behavior that in turn engenders productive subordinates. It is questionable, however, whether the phenomenon of leadership can be understood as either employee-centered or production-centered.

Michigan studies: A behavioral-based set of studies that examined leadership on two dimensions of supervisory behavior: production-centered and employee-centered.

The findings of both studies, in fact, have serious problems that limit their application to criminal justice organizations. First, it is not clear that either the Ohio State studies or the Michigan studies adequately assessed the concept of leadership. We are concerned here with the methodological problem of construct validity. Do these studies actually measure the notion of leadership? Distinctions must be made, for example, between leadership and power. Does the prison guard who befriends an inmate and is respected by the inmate exhibit some type of leadership or what is known as referent power? How do we know what factor is operating in this relationship? How can we separate the two processes both conceptually and practically? Because much of the behavioral research has not made distinctions between these concepts, it is not evident that leadership itself is being studied. The same point can be made about distinctions between leadership and authority. (For further discussion of the concepts of power and authority, see Chapter 9.)

A second concern is that much of the leadership research within the behavioral framework is based on convenient but limited conceptualizations of the leadership process. By viewing leadership in a dichotomous fashion, we are creating for ourselves, as researchers, an easy method for exploring the process while limiting our overall understanding of it. Dichotomies are convenient, yet they do not always provide us with an explanation that is both testable and comprehensive. Take, for example, police sergeants. Can we understand their leadership behavior simply by stating that they are either employee-centered or production-oriented supervisors? Isn't it realistic to say that any sergeant could be both? For that matter, couldn't a sergeant exhibit other leadership behaviors besides merely these two?

More important, isn't a sergeant's leadership approach highly influenced by the tasks to be accomplished, along with the technology available? A task may require subordinates to follow a predetermined set of policies and procedures as the only acceptable or the only tested way of accomplishing that task. The sergeant of a tactical unit, for example, may need a production-oriented style of leadership because of the nature of the work—many dangerous tasks and highly uncertain situations. Thus, to suggest that in criminal justice organizations one approach to leadership is more applicable than another approach to leadership is simplistic and not sufficient to explain the intricacies of the leadership process in those organizations.

Third, our concern with external validity requires us to question the application of research findings done largely in private organizations or public organizations, such as criminal justice. Is it possible for the police sergeant or the corrections manager to be employee-centered in the same way as a bank manager? In addition, what does "employee-centered" mean in the context of the expected roles of both supervisor and subordinate in criminal justice organizations? How are the dimensions of leadership identified by this body of research affected by the tasks of the organization? In attempting to be employee-centered, is the police sergeant constrained by the tasks required? In short, is leadership affected by the situation and the tasks of the supervisor and the subordinate?

With these three criticisms in mind, we must be cautious in applying the findings from either the Ohio State studies or the Michigan studies to the workings of middle-level managers or administrators in the criminal justice system. Instead, we can say that these behavioral studies were the first to address the concept of leadership in an accessible way, and much of the research in criminal justice leadership has been rooted in these studies. Although we are somewhat critical of this research, we believe that the application and testing of these theoretical models in criminal justice organizations have provided the incentive to view the leadership process in a comprehensive fashion. Recent leadership research has been directed toward understanding the situation in criminal justice organizations. This research is rooted in contingency theories of leadership, which we discuss next.

Contingency Theories

Contingency theories: A group of leadership theories that stress the importance of the situation to leadership effectiveness in the accomplishment of organizational goals and objectives.

Contingency theories of leadership differ from both trait and behavioral theories in emphasizing the situation or context. Examining various situational variables is central to understanding leadership in organizations, according to contingency theorists. We can see how this approach is useful for studying leadership in criminal justice organizations. The lieutenant in a prison, for example, is constrained by situational factors in dealing with both corrections officers and prisoners. Prison officials cannot exercise total power; depending on the organizational structure of the prison, there are limits to what can be done to lead groups toward organizational objectives. The leadership style employed is therefore contingent on the situational aspects of the prison and the nature of the relationship between keeper and kept.

The two contingency theories we examine in this chapter, Fiedler's contingency model and the path–goal theory, both have distinctive elements that contribute to our understanding of leadership in criminal justice organizations. In addition, we can draw different implications from each model for the management and administration of criminal justice systems.

Fiedler's Contingency Model   **Fiedler's contingency model** is a contingency theory of leadership that emphasizes leader–member relations, the task structure of the organization, and the position power of leaders. According to Fiedler (1967), the leadership process is constrained by these three major situational dimensions. First, leader–member relations are the level of trust and the degree of likeability the leader enjoys with subordinate groups. According to Fiedler, how well a leader is able to guide immediate subordinates is contingent on the relationship he or she has with them. It is easy to see in police organizations, for example, that some supervisors are better liked by rank-and-file officers than other supervisors. The leader who is not liked or well received by subordinates is constrained by this situation and can be ineffective in guiding and influencing workers to accomplish organizational tasks.

Second, the task structure of the organization is, in Fiedler's (1967:53) words, "the degree to which the task is spelled out or must be left nebulous and undefined." Routinized task structure has clearly defined procedures for accomplishing organizational objectives. The machine-based factory has clear directions for running the machine. It is easier to lead when the task structure is clearly defined and open to direct monitoring by the supervisor. The organization with an undefined task structure or uncertainty about achieving its objective presents problems. Most of the activities of criminal justice organizations have uncertain task structures even though these agencies have relatively stable policies and procedures, simply because it is not all that certain that the tasks accomplish the goals professed. It is one thing to say, for example, that officers patrol the streets of the city (a task) and another to say that this task accomplishes the goals of crime prevention and societal protection. This uncertainty about the relationship between task performance and goal accomplishment produces agencies that, more often than not, are unstructured and loosely coupled. As a result, effective leadership becomes problematic for both administrators and immediate supervisors.

Third, position power is the leader's ability to exercise power in the organization. Fiedler's test of position power is the ability to hire and fire subordinates. A leader with high position power is able to hire or fire at will. A leader with low position power has limited authority in this area. Here again, we can see how criminal justice administrators are constrained because of their limited authority to hire or dismiss someone. Because they are public agencies, many organizations of criminal justice are governed by civil service or independent commissions that regulate, monitor, and control all personnel decisions. Administrators cannot dismiss someone without going through an elaborate process of review, typically by an external group or agency. Moreover, immediate supervisors—for example, police sergeants—have no power to make such critical

Fiedler's contingency model: A contingency theory of leadership that emphasizes leader–member relations, the task structure of the organization, and the position power of leaders.

decisions. In fact, much of the position power in the immediate supervisory positions of criminal justice has been limited by legal decisions, an environmental constraint over which administrators have little control. Although it would be inaccurate to state that administrators and frontline supervisors have no position power at all, that power is limited and is relatively weak when compared with the position power of comparable groups in the private sector.

Given these situational dimensions—leader–member relations, task structure, and position power—we can match the proper leadership styles with the right situations to produce the most effective form of leadership. Leadership style can be determined by asking leaders to describe, either favorably or unfavorably, their least preferred coworker. This is known as an LPC score. According to Fiedler, the leader who describes a least preferred coworker in a favorable manner tends to be permissive and human-relations-oriented; the leader who describes a least preferred coworker in unfavorable terms is concerned with task production and getting the job done. Moreover, Fiedler suggests that, for the most part, task-production leaders tend to be more effective in structured situations, whereas human-relations-oriented leaders are more effective in situations that require a creative response from supervisors and subordinates.

In addition, a leader has high situational control when he or she has good leader–member relations, a high task structure, and high position power. Low situational control exists when the opposite conditions are present: poor leader–member relations, low task structure, and little or no position power. Finally, moderate situation control means the situational characteristics are mixed; some characteristics work to the advantage of the leader (e.g., high leader–member relations), while others do not (poor position power) (Tosi, Rizzo, and Carroll, 1986:503–504).

By matching the degree of situational control with differing LPC orientations, says Fiedler, we can determine the most appropriate leadership approach. The low-LPC leader would be the most effective in situations where there is low situational control (poor leader–member relations, low task structure, and little or no position power). In this example, the low-LPC leader would be most effective in situations that required situational control and specific directions to employees; workers might believe that their own success in accomplishing the tasks of the organization was related to the guidance of the leader. The human-relations-oriented leader (high LPC) will be the most successful where the group has structured tasks and a dislike of the leader. The human-relations-oriented leader is effective in a situation where the group likes the leader and has an unstructured task to perform.

Within criminal justice organizations, we can see how leadership style can be effective, depending on situational factors. The sergeant who directs a tactical unit in a police organization may be more effective by employing a task-oriented rather than a human-relations-oriented leadership style because many tactical unit tasks are structured, leader position power is relatively high (the sergeant often has direct input into who is in the unit and how they function), and strong identification with the leader is critical because of the nature of the tasks being performed. We would not expect the sergeant in this unit to ask for input from subordinates on how to run the unit because the sergeant has to issue orders and directives to achieve the goals of the unit.

The situational factors faced by a supervisor of corrections officers, however, may require a different type of leadership style. If the supervisor is well liked by officers, if tasks are only vaguely related to the goals of the organization, and if the supervisor has weak position power, it may be advantageous to be human-relations oriented. In fact, in institutional corrections today, it has been said that the uncertainty about the relationship between tasks and organizational objectives, on one hand, and the weak position power of both supervisors and administrators, on the other, requires leaders to be more oriented toward human relations. In effect, corrections supervisors need to be open and flexible with subordinates if their organizational goals are to be accomplished. Yet, task-oriented leaders can argue equally that if leader–member relations in correctional institutions are poor, tasks unstructured, and leader position power weak, an autocratic management style would be more effective.

Two basic criticisms can be leveled against the contingency model of leader-ship. First, Fiedler seems to treat LPC as a dichotomous and unidimensional vari-able, implying that leaders are either totally task oriented or totally human relations oriented; the theory does not admit the possibility that leaders could be equally high on both dimensions. Our understanding of administrative behavior intuitively suggests that this kind of polarization is not the case and that managers do exhibit both styles of leadership, depending on the situation. Moreover, we have seen an explosion in research examining the relationship between leaders and subordinates being affected by other situational variables outside of those developed by Fiedler. Elias (2009) examines the complex relationship that exists between leaders and subordinates and suggests that the type of managerial control and internal locus of control that an employee exhibits influences specific work outcomes.

Police officers, for example, who have a locus of control that assumes they are responsible for what happens to them and are influenced by a form of control that is reactive (rooted in the authority structures of the police department) might respond well and have increased levels of satisfaction, lower rates of turnover, and more commitment to the department when compared to a proac-tive form of management. The latter style of management may not sit well with people who feel they are ultimately responsible for their behaviors within the context of the police agency. They require direction, and reactive management strategies may be the best in this type of situation. On the other hand, reactive strategies might backfire if the officer has a locus of control that is more external (things happen beyond an officer's control) and require greater input and proac-tive management to perform the duties of the job. As stated by Elias (2009:387), "the reliance on the organization's power structure to influence a subordinate may result in contradictory employee outcomes based on the employee's locus of control." As such, we may have many "contingent" situations and factors that have not been adequately defined nor sufficiently investigated to truly under-stand the factors that influence employees and under what conditions. We dis-cuss the issue of locus of control when we examine another contingency theory —the path–goal theory of leadership.

Second, this theory implicitly assumes that task structure and leader–member relations cannot be modified or changed by the leader's style. Fiedler argues that it is easier to alter situations within the organization rather than the style of leadership exhibited by the leader. If leader–member relations are not good, for example, it may be more appropriate to spend time rearranging this situation than trying to change the leader's style. There may be much truth in this statement, yet there is no reason to believe that style of leadership cannot be modified as easily as situational dimensions. In fact, it can be reasonably argued that leadership style can affect some situational dimensions and change them for the good of the organization. Is it not possible, for example, for a leader to modify his or her style so that an unstructured task becomes more structured? Two implications of this theory for criminal justice management can be drawn. First, if effective leadership is the goal in criminal justice organizations, then matching the right leader with specific tasks becomes critical; yet this luxury may not be possible. Given that many administrators and supervisors in criminal justice organizations are not chosen because of their ability to lead but rather because of their years of service, scores on tests, and loyalty to the organization (to mention only a few criteria), it is not clear how leaders can be matched to specific situations. Although private organizations may have the luxury of removing and replacing ineffective leaders, such is typically not the case in criminal justice organizations. Second, if Fiedler's ideas on leadership are to be applied to criminal justice agencies, then administrative officials and those in supervisory positions need training to become aware of their personality orientations and the organizational consequences of expressing these orientations. Although officials have been requesting it for many years, such training is still severely lacking (Geller, 1985). Moreover, Fiedler and Garcia (1987, cited in Robbins and Judge, 2007:412) have introduced another factor to consider in assessing effective leadership. This factor is stress and how leaders cope with it. Under the title of "cognitive resource theory," Fiedler and Garcia suggest that how leaders cope with stress, employing their intelligence and experience, will have differential levels of success. In situations of high stress, acting rationally is difficult. Fiedler and Garcia found that intelligence and experience impact leadership effectiveness, with high intelligence working in situations of low stress and experience working in situations of high stress.

Fiedler and Garcia's new conceptualization of contingency theory has much relevance for understanding criminal justice leadership. Owen (2006) has shown that stress is an important consideration for correctional supervisors. Similar research in police organizations has also suggested that stress among police supervisors is high (Alpert, Dunham, and Stroshine, 2005). What is not known, however, is how leadership is mediated by the multitude of stressful situations that criminal justice workers face on a daily basis. It is one thing to state criminal justice personnel are under a tremendous amount of stress, yet it is something different to show how stress affects the quality of leadership within criminal justice organizations. Future research will have to address this issue.

We return to a discussion of contingency theory later in this chapter when we apply some of its ideas to a broader notion of leadership and how contingent external factors affect criminal justice organizations.

Path–goal Theory   Whereas Fiedler's theory of leadership attempts to isolate situational characteristics and leader orientation to understand the leadership process, **path–goal theory** suggests that the interaction between leader behavior and the situational aspects of the organization is important (House and Mitchell, 1985). In addition, this theory argues that leadership is linked to an expectancy theory of motivation (see Chapter 4), which posits that the leader's behavior directly influences the actions of employees if it is a source of satisfaction for them. Effective leadership, according to path–goal theory, is situational and does not depend on a single style or theory. Moreover, effective leadership is tied to the degree of direction and guidance the leader provides in the work situation.

This guidance and direction can be tied to four styles of leadership that are independent. A leader can exhibit any one of the four styles of leadership when faced with different conditions and situations. *Directive leadership* emphasizes the leader's expectations and the tasks that subordinates perform. The leader instills into subordinates the importance of the organization's rules and regulations and their relationship to task performance. Under this style of leadership, the leader provides the necessary guidance to subordinates to motivate them to accomplish the tasks required by the organization. *Supportive leadership* stresses a concern for employees. This type of leader is friendly with employees and desires to be approachable. The leader's primary concern is both to accomplish the organizational tasks and meet workers' needs. *Participative leadership* emphasizes collaboration of the leader and subordinates. The leader employing this style attempts to involve subordinates in the organization's decision-making process and assure them of their importance in the organization. *Achievement-oriented leadership* is concerned with having subordinates produce results. Such a leader expects that workers will attempt to do their best and that if goals are set high enough and subordinates are properly motivated, they will achieve those goals. The leader confidently expects that employees will achieve the stated goals and tasks.

Two contingency factors shape subordinates' performance and level of satisfaction in this theory. According to House and Mitchell (1985:494), three subordinate characteristics—aspects of the worker, most of which are rooted in personality—determine which leadership style will be most effective. These are locus of control, in which internally focused individuals are receptive to a participative leadership style and externally controlled individuals are comfortable with a directive form of leadership; authoritarianism, in which individuals high in authoritarianism react positively to directive leadership and those low in authoritarianism are receptive to participative leadership; and ability, in which employees who are highly competent in their jobs do not need to be led or directed and may benefit from a participative style of leadership, whereas those who are not so competent need directive leadership.

Path-goal theory: A contingency theory of leadership that highlights the relationship between leader behavior and situational aspects of the organization. Styles of leadership are important to this theory of leadership.

Environmental factors are characteristics of the work situation. According to path–goal theory, three environmental factors affect a subordinate's ability to perform the tasks required; these factors intervene between the subordinate and the leader. Task is the structure or level of uncertainty that enables the employee to accomplish the task or prevents the employee from accomplishing the task. The directive style of leadership may be appropriate when the subordinate does not understand how to do the task. Without proper leadership, the subordinate will never be able to clear the path necessary to accomplish the task; proper leadership style is critical here.

The formal authority system of the organization is a second critical factor in the environment. If, for example, the worker perceives the formal structure of the organization as a barrier to the accomplishment of goals and thereby to the rewards associated with the accomplishment of those goals, the leader must remove the barriers so that the worker can effectively meet the organization's stated objectives.

Finally, the primary work group is the third environmental factor that may prevent the worker from achieving organizational tasks and objectives, which in turn affects the number of rewards the worker will receive from the organization. The leader, therefore, makes sure that the task expected of the worker is clearly stated and defined, that goals of the organization are attainable and have rewards, and that there are no barriers to performance. Under optimal conditions, the leader provides the atmosphere where uncertainty about the relationship between task performance and organizational rewards is low. The leader thus clears a path through these environmental factors primarily by increasing the value of tasks and rewards, removing barriers to the accomplishment of organizational goals, and reducing uncertainty so that tasks can be achieved by subordinates.

Directive leadership is clearly the most effective (effectiveness being defined by the degree of satisfaction expressed by workers) in situations when the task is ambiguous and uncertain, but this leadership style produces lower levels of satisfaction among workers when the task is relatively clear and the workers are easily able to complete the task. Supportive leadership is best employed when the tasks being performed by subordinates are stressful, dissatisfying, and frustrating. Finally, participative leadership may be the most effective when the individual is highly involved in the task or when the task is relatively nonroutine and somewhat ambiguous. In this situation, the leader provides the necessary platform for the subordinate to express concerns about how the task can be accomplished and rewards maximized. Once again, path–goal theory suggests that the primary role of the leader is to provide the paths by which subordinates' rewards can be maximized while simultaneously meeting the objectives of the organization.

Path–goal theory can make three contributions to criminal justice administration. First, criminal justice administrators need to spell out clearly the types of rewards that subordinates can receive if and when they follow specific paths designed and structured by the organization. If, for example, Officer Jones is told that she will receive a promotion or a positive evaluation from her supervisor if she accomplishes the tasks assigned, a reward system must be in place that promotes and reinforces that behavior. All that path–goal theory suggests is that subordinates will follow and accomplish tasks defined and assigned by the organization if rewards are attached to the accomplishment of those tasks. If leadership cannot develop and promote such a structure, then leadership is at fault.

Such, in fact, may be the case in many criminal justice organizations. Take police organizations as an example: If the principles of path–goal theory were followed, administrators would have as a primary goal the removal of obstacles to officers so that they would follow the rules and regulations of the organization with the hope of being promoted someday. Often, police rules are written when full enforcement of the law is not possible. Limited resources, for example, make full enforcement problematic. On one hand, officers are told to enforce the rules for evaluation and promotion purposes; yet, on the other hand, they are not given adequate resources and support to complete their jobs. By applying various styles of leadership, contingent on the personal characteristics of subordinates and the environmental characteristics of the work situation, leaders would clear the path for subordinates to accomplish the goals of the organization while simultaneously meeting their own expectations and enhancing their rewards, such as a promotion.

Yet police organizations often cannot provide the rewards sought by police officers. Because supervisors have little control over reward distribution, the style of leadership they exhibit is somewhat meaningless. If, for example, a court orders a police department to hire and promote minority candidates over majority candidates because of past practices of discrimination in the department, the police supervisor may have limited control over who gets promoted and, more important, may have a difficult time convincing subordinates that there actually is a clear path to promotion or mobility in the organization.

Second, path–goal theory suggests, correctly, that no one style of leadership is sufficient for all the situations faced by criminal justice administrators and supervisors. This point cannot be stated too often. In many instances, good administrators in criminal justice organizations have recognized that proper leadership requires a correct assessment of the situation. In addition, it becomes clear that leadership is an ongoing and proactive process that demands constant evaluations of multiple situations. More important, leaders must constantly reevaluate the situations faced by subordinates and how paths can be cleared for the attainment of both organizational objectives and employee goals.

Third, path–goal theory requires that criminal justice administrators design paths and goals for employees that are reasonable and attainable. Path–goal theory assumes active leadership on the part of supervisors. Criminal justice administrators who do not clarify paths for subordinates only create confusion for themselves and much alienation and disillusionment among employees. Such ineffective leadership places obstacles between supervisors and subordinates that may be difficult to overcome. The issue of path specificity is significant in criminal justice organizations, especially as it relates to the structural components of how we do our work. This suggests that an incongruence between our work structure and our environment must be addressed by criminal justice administrators, or otherwise no clear path can be established and leadership effectiveness is minimized.

Zhao, Ren, and Lovrich (2010) address this issue in their examination of police organizational structural change during the 1990s. By exploring 280 municipal police departments on the dimension of structural change, they found most departments remained relatively stable, even though their environments were drastically changing in response to police reform efforts at both the state level and federal levels. These proposed changes recommended that police adopt more community-oriented policing structures that fostered increased decentralization, flattening of organizational hierarchies, more civilian hires, and a reduction in administrative staff. Such changes would require a drastic structural alteration in how we deliver police services and lead officers. If police administrators are receiving pressures from the environment to change structures so departments are more responsive to their communities, yet no change occurs, police officers are given mixed messages and the path to effective organizational outcomes becomes cluttered with ambiguity and conflict. The question becomes: How can you lead at all?

Transformational Leadership

Twenty-first-century leadership research has focused on one leadership approach that has changed the way we understand leadership. Up until the early 1990s, leadership was viewed and understood largely as a process that was trait based, behaviorally based, or highly contingent on a number of factors that were either within the control of the leader or not. The theories on leadership were focused on how leaders can alter their leadership styles or their work situations to improve leadership and ultimately organizational outcomes.

Transformational leadership: A leadership approach that stresses the importance of leadership behaviors in transforming organizations to produce optimal results.

Dissatisfaction over these theories of leadership led others to suggest that leadership can best be understood not as a series of transactions per se, but instead, as how leaders transform organizations to yield optimal results. This approach to leadership is labeled **transformational leadership**. Central to transformational leadership are three related concepts: mission and vision statement, goal setting, and cultivation of creativity and imagination to address organizational concerns and problems.

The creation of a mission cuts to the question of what the central purposes are of an organization. We have already discussed how this is particularly problematic within criminal justice organizations (see Chapter 1). Our environments are layered, complex, and interest based, yet effective criminal justice organizations do define clear missions and visions. For example, although we expect prisons to perform multiple goals, for many correctional workers, knowing that the prison is safe and secure is central to its success. Effective leadership within the context of prisons is making sure the safety and security of staff and prisoners are achieved. In the world of corrections, however, expectations are changing and communities are demanding departments do something such that criminal behavior is changed (King, 2006). Recognizing these changing expectations, many departments of corrections are embarking on a vision to make prisons places in which productive change can occur among prisoners. The California Department of Corrections and Rehabilitation, for example, changed its name to include the rehabilitation component, a new vision for the department that moves well beyond simple custody and control in prisons (Hickman, 2005).

To make organizations accountable, many have instituted elaborate goal statements. It is not enough to have a mission and vision. In addition, organizations need to see how goals transform the mission and vision into action. In criminal justice organizations, we see similar attempts by police chiefs, chief judges, and probation and parole officials to become more strategic in their missions and visions. One organization that is assisting police organizations in this quest is the International Association of Chiefs of Police (IACP). In its Developing Leaders in Police Organizations (LPO) program, IACP is committed to working with police organizations to develop and inculcate leadership throughout the police hierarchy. Called "dispersed leadership," the LPO program has five component parts: shared understanding of what leadership means, commitment to shared goals and values by leaders at all levels of the organization, a recognition of different styles of leadership, and dispersed leadership focusing both on the individual and the organization (International Association of Chiefs of Police [IACP], 2006).

The LPO program is designed to promote leadership throughout the police organization and seeks leadership behavior that promotes the best practices in police work, reflecting the values of "duty, honor, service, dignity, respect for others, integrity, courage, and loyalty" (IACP, 2006:1). Through such a commitment, the hope is that police organizations will be able to transform traditional police cultures into new ways of thinking about police service delivery so that organizational goals are attained. In addition, such a transformation requires more imagination and creativity on how the police of the twenty-first century will respond to the new challenges of crime, the third element of transformational leadership.

Creativity and new ways of doing business within criminal justice organizations are required given the evolving threats that new crimes pose for criminal justice organizations. Identity theft, Internet sex predators, and terrorist threats all pose significant challenges to criminal justice administration. As suggested in Chapter 1, these new challenges require new ways of responding to these nascent crimes. One of the most pressing demands for criminal justice administrators will be how they are able to transform their work organizations to be more flexible and creative in responding to crime. As noted by the 9/11 Commission (2003), the most serious threat we face in dealing with potential terrorist attacks is our lack of imagination.

The power of transformational leadership will lie in how it is able to change traditional criminal justice operations to achieve organizational results. What does the research indicate on the effectiveness of transformational leadership? In the business literature, the evidence is quite impressive on the impact that transformational leadership has had on a number of organizational outcomes, including productivity, turnover, and satisfaction levels among employees (Robbins and Judge, 2007:440); yet these same findings cannot be stated regarding criminal justice organizations. The simple fact is that we do not know much about whether transformational leadership within the context of criminal justice organizations actually exists and if it really matters. More important, some research on transformational leadership suggests that the "social distance" between leaders and followers moderates the potential positive effects of transformational leadership, yet it may have some impact on the perceptions of workers, their emotional climate at work, and their collective efficacy (Cole, Bruch, and Shamir, 2010). By social distance, we are referring to both levels of intimacy that characterize social relations in criminal justice organizations. Is it really that important in criminal justice organizations to understand the nature and quality of social relations, especially for criminal justice administrators (see Chapters 6 and 9)? It might be important, but we need more research to answer this question definitively. We have much prescription when it comes to transformational leadership and criminal justice administration but very little substance when it comes to showing how such a leadership approach actually improves the operations of criminal justice organizations. We now turn to the issue of research in criminal justice leadership.

Work Perspective: SIGNIFICANT CHALLENGES FACING POLICE LEADERS

At the end of the twentieth century, we were consumed with worry about the mass failure of technological systems and spent considerable energy preparing for Y2K. The (first) Gulf War had ended; we were experiencing an era of relative prosperity, and we were more than a year away from the onslaught of generous pension plan approvals that started in 2001. Since then, we have seen a general move toward militarization of the police, entry into a two-front war (Iraq and Afghanistan), and the collapse of the housing market. Those drivers, in tandem with the devaluation of the dollar, the bankruptcy of some members of the European Union, and the inevitable decline in confidence in government systems, led both to great duress as well as significant opportunity for leaders in the coming decade.

While it might seem that responding to calls for service is at the core, it may be the time to radically reconceive what it means to "police" a community. The prevalent mind-set of contemporary policing focuses largely on apprehension and prosecution of criminals. Even community policing programs largely focus on mitigating incidents to minimize the recurrence of deviant acts. A change to three differing areas of priority might be in order. The first is to seek ways to prevent crime and disorder by addressing root causes. This could entail working with schools, social services, and similar agencies to engage families in the prevention of child abuse,

to strengthen parenting, and to help curtail intimate partner assaults. Peace in the home is the bedrock of peace in a community and it should be one of the primary areas of emphasis in a law enforcement agency. That does not mean "cops as social workers." Rather, the police should work with professionals in related disciplines to create programs and services to meet the latent need of many families and children in ways that might seem foreign to the experienced police practitioner.

The second area of focus would be to move priorities to predictive policing: strong analysis of crime trends and data and placing scarce police resources where they are actually needed in lieu of the "organized wandering" of patrol work. Emerging capabilities of analytic systems should afford us a chance to get ahead of crime and to align our work and suppress incidents by virtue of an intelligent, data-driven police force. This is not to encourage mindless adherence to the data but to incorporate analytics into the fabric of what we do.

The last area to consider is the level of innovation in your organization. This goes beyond brainstorming sessions or occasional strategic planning efforts. It also does not mean that the agency waits for the right idea to emerge. The successful law enforcement organization of the future will place value on new ways to address old problems and will create ways to foster that throughout the organization. In larger agencies, that could mean the development of R&D units or similar pockets of trial balloons and pilot programs. In smaller agencies, that could mean learning concepts of systems, design thinking, and then utilizing them in the agency's planning and execution of effort.

As a leader, it is your job to provide structure and to paint the broad brushstrokes from which others create an identity. Most important, though, your job is to give others hope. Help them see a future that is different from today, that is better, and that includes them, and you can lead them there. Absent that, you will not lead them anywhere.

SOURCE: Bob Harrison, Retired Police Chief, Course Manager, California POST Command College.

LEADERSHIP RESEARCH IN CRIMINAL JUSTICE

As we have seen, little empirical testing of the theoretical models of leadership in criminal justice organizations has been attempted. What has been done, moreover, is still rooted in 1950s research of the Ohio State studies and the Michigan studies. This situation may be caused either by the slow testing of current theories of leadership within criminal justice organizations or the limited number of reliable instruments to test the new theoretical positions. However, some new research, particularly in the police field, does tell us about leadership in criminal justice agencies; from it, we can draw implications for management.

Research by Kuykendall and Unsinger (1982) suggests that police managers have a preferred leadership orientation. Employing an instrument created by Hershey and Blanchard (1977), the researchers found that police managers are likely to use styles of leadership known as selling (high task and high relationship emphasis), telling (high task and low relationship emphasis), and participating (high relationship and low task emphasis), with very little concern for delegating (low relationship and low task emphasis). Of these styles of leadership, which are similar to those discussed previously, the most preferred style is selling. The researchers suggest that police managers are no less effective than managers in other organizational settings and that the selling, telling, and participating styles lead to organizational effectiveness.

Similar findings were generated by Swanson and Territo (1982) in their research involving 104 police supervisors in the Southeast in the late 1970s. Using the managerial grid, the researchers found that their sample of police supervisors showed high concern for both production and people and emphasized team management in their organizations. Employing other measures, the researchers also found that police supervisors used a style of communication that emphasized the open and candid expression of their feelings and knowledge to subordinates rather than a style of communication that emphasized feedback from subordinates to managers about their supervisory capabilities. This research suggested that police managers had an open communication style with subordinates and supported the idea that police managers were indeed democratic in their leadership styles. (At least, they professed to be.) More recently, Madlock (2008) suggests that the leader's "communication competency" is a critical factor when assessing leadership effectiveness in organizations. In fact, he found that effective communicators not only were rated high by their subordinates regarding their communication abilities, but, more important, a high level of communication competence was strongly correlated to job satisfaction by workers. We may have to improve the communication skills of criminal justice supervisors to improve their leadership capabilities. Whether or not improved communication skills are associated with participative styles of leadership is still unknown.

Research suggests that such a participative and democratic leadership style is not as ubiquitous in police organizations as previously indicated. Auten (1985), for example, found in his sample of police supervisors and operations personnel in state police agencies in Illinois that the dominant managerial model was the traditional paramilitary type with one-way communication. In addition, these police supervisors and operations personnel strongly believed that they had no meaningful role in organizational decision making. The researchers suggest that there were communication breakdowns between the supervisory and operations personnel and the administrative heads of the agencies.

Not only is there limited consensus on what type of leadership styles predominate among police managers and administrators, but when police supervisors are asked to think about a leadership style as opposed to acting out a style in a specific situation, they also tend to change their approach to leadership (Kuykendall, 1985). Clearly, what a supervisor regards as an appropriate style of leadership may not be in agreement with what he or she actually does in a given situation. Current research, for example, on occupational stress, high turnover, absenteeism, and substance abuse in the police field suggests that the traditional paramilitary structure of police organizations, with its emphasis on an autocratic style of leadership, creates and perpetuates these problems. These problems may be traced to other factors in the police role, such as the danger associated with the job, yet it is important to examine how specific leadership styles contribute to many of these problems. Much leadership research in policing needs to be done.

In the field of corrections, much of what we know about leadership is rooted in highly prescriptive material, which limits our understanding of the process. However, many of the problems experienced in police organizations are experienced equally in correctional organizations; hierarchical structure, limited and often rigid communications systems, and centralized decision-making authority in correctional organizations produce many of these problems (Archambeault and Archambeault, 1982). As with police research, leadership research in corrections is not only limited but also offers little information that is useful to corrections administrators.

Given the current state of leadership research in both police organizations and correctional organizations, we recommend that future researchers address the following issues. First, we need additional research on how criminal justice administrators actually lead their organizations; from this data, prescriptions for policy can be made useful to the criminal justice manager. Much existing research is out of date and tells us little about the increasing complexities of the leadership process. Some current research, however, in the field of corrections lends credence to the idea that leadership does matter and does affect the quality of practice exhibited by employees. Dale and Trlin (2010) investigated the impact of a new public management scheme in New Zealand on the performance of probation officers. The research highlighted the initial tension that existed between management and workers as the former sought greater managerial efficiencies in exchange for less professionalism based on traditional practices. The authors contend that if new systems of efficiencies were to be created within the probation practice, more "supportive" relationships needed to be built by managers and leaders, buttressed by a clear articulation of professional values, expertise, and knowledge and a recognition that practice should be a defining element in assessing the effectiveness of both employees and leaders.

Second, the contemporary models of leadership offered by organizational behavior theory need to be examined. Contingency approaches should be examined in relation to criminal justice organizations, along with refinement of instruments to test these theories in the criminal justice environment. The situational factors influencing the leadership process must be examined in the operations of criminal justice systems. Too often, research in criminal justice organizations has been set up to ascertain whether administrators are participative or autocratic in relation to their subordinates. It is possibly time to stop searching for the perfect criminal justice manager and to begin examining situational aspects of the work environment that constrain administrators in their leadership functions.

Third, to fully understand the leadership phenomenon in criminal justice organizations, we must use the new methodologies to look at the intricacies associated with the leadership process. Traditional survey methods in criminal justice organizations have yielded some valuable information, yet field methods would provide information about the actual leadership mechanisms used by criminal justice administrators. To understand the leadership process, it is helpful to watch and document what criminal justice leaders actually do and, more important, be able to distinguish effective criminal justice leaders from ineffective ones. In this way, prescriptions for administrators would be informed by data and useful in their day-to-day interactions with subordinates.

Finally, we need to discuss how much we can expect of our criminal justice managers in leadership. It is common to blame the poor performance of subordinates on ineffective management or leadership; we often hear this complaint in criminal justice organizations. Yet it is shortsighted to suggest that all problems in criminal justice can be attributed to faulty leadership. Criminal justice administrators have limited or no control over some aspects of the work of their organizations. As a result, requesting a new leader "to set the organization back on path" is probably, in the words of Hall and Tolbert (2005:160), "little more than a cosmetic treatment." An uncertain and unstable political environment, for example, makes multiple demands on a police chief. Not being able to appease all groups all the time, the chief is constrained in decision making. On many occasions, because the chief has limited resources and multiple demands, all community expectations for police services cannot be met. Too often, the chief is viewed as an ineffective leader when leadership has little to do with the problem.

To be effective, a leader must provide some degree of control over the external environment. But we need to be realistic about how much a police administrator can control. Perhaps for this reason, many experts recommend that incoming police chiefs develop clear and stable relations with local political groups so that expectations can be spelled out on both sides (Murphy, 1985).

Similar concerns can be raised about leadership in the courts, prisons, and probation and parole organizations. Leaders of these departments have problems of trying to understand the political process and how it affects their organizations. Many have concerns about how much of their organizations they really control, particularly in tight fiscal times when resources are stretched and competition among social service agencies for finite dollars is fierce. Similar to police administrators, court officials and correctional administrators are expected to achieve aims that they neither agree with nor have resources to successfully complete. A prime example of this difficulty is the "three strikes" initiatives that swept the country during the early 1990s. For many departments of corrections' leaders and prison administrators, such a law was impossible to live with and had dire practical consequences for prison management, yet its political appeal was so great that political leaders jumped on the bandwagon to pass laws that were not only difficult to implement but in some cases also were draconian in their effects (Irwin and Austin, 2002). Under such difficult circumstances, how are criminal justice administrators to respond? An answer to this question may lie in a model of leadership education, to which we now turn.

LEADERSHIP EDUCATION: THE CALIFORNIA DEPARTMENT OF CORRECTIONS EXPERIENCE

In response to unprecedented growth in the California Department of Corrections (DOC) in both employee and offender populations, the director responded by developing a Leadership Institute in joint collaboration with the California State University at Chico Center for Regional and Continuing Education. This initiative, designed to prepare future leaders within the department, viewed leadership as an educational process that could be taught to administrators. The primary emphasis was on education rather than training. Participants were asked to move beyond their formal structures, policies and procedures, and ways of doing business to critically question the direction and methods of operation within the department. Participants were selected based on their years of experience, commitment to productive change, and potential for promotion within the department. All participants were screened by the DOC director and charged with addressing a significant issue facing the DOC today and into the twenty-first century.

In the fall of 1994, the Leadership Institute convened for the first time. This program initiative ran for ten years until the fall of 2004. Over 350 participants took part in the institute. Unlike other leadership training programs, this effort was much more intensive and project-oriented. Participants were required to attend week-long sessions over a six-month period, totaling six weeks of intensive study on leadership development and application within the DOC. Within each cohort, approximately twenty-five persons were assembled from varying management and administrative positions within the DOC. Attendees came from prisons, medical services, procurement services, training and evaluation, and parole agencies, to mention a few. They were split up into four groups of six individuals, and they jointly developed an issue facing the department through a series of exercises given to them in the first two weeks. Upon completing the program, the groups would present their issues, solutions, and findings to the director and top administrative staff at a graduation ceremony.

Through such an intensive process, the institute's organizers hoped that the key elements of leadership could be transmitted to individuals through a number of complex exercises and tasks. Many of the exercises required the use of computer-assisted technologies as well as library and external resources. Instructors were all university professors who had experience working within the field of corrections and were serving as consultants to the DOC. The institute recognized specific elements as essential for effective leadership for any criminal justice administrator. The experiences of the participants through the various exercises indicated that effective criminal justice leaders must possess the following attributes:

1. Traits indicative of a proactive approach to leadership. These traits include, but are not limited to, good communication skills, an honest and trustworthy approach to dealing with staff, an attitude of excellence, and a firm knowledge of the organization and the problems and issues it faces.

2. Awareness of the importance of building professional relationships with employees. Effective leaders recognize that listening to employee concerns is relevant to achieving organizational goals. Showing concern for employees as persons, rewarding excellence in performance, and conveying a friendly and approachable manner or presence are critical for effective leadership. Such behaviors show a concern for employees as members of a team working toward the attainment of specific organizational objectives.

3. Ability to balance the needs of employees with concern for production. Effective leaders encourage cooperative decision making through shared ideas and shared power; they also encourage participation in decision making as well as allow freedom for employees to grow and experiment with new methods to accomplish tasks. They recognize that failure is a part of a learning process for employees.

4. Ability to incorporate a sense of vision within the organization and serve as a transformer of culture when necessary. The purpose behind the identification of vision is to direct employees and their behaviors specifically toward the central purpose(s) of the organization. Good leaders are able to identify challenges that the organization faces as well as specify

appropriate alternatives when addressing current problems and those well into the future. Effective leaders understand that employee acceptance of the organization's vision means that there may need to be cultural change within the organization. A good leader is able to identify new symbols and values for the organization that employees will accept. These symbols and values may be new to the organization, and the leader recognizes that cultural change is a prerequisite for long-term change. The leader solicits support among employees and shows the value of transformation toward the accomplishment of organizational objectives and goals.

5. Recognition that an array of contingent strategies is required for effective leadership. Recognizing the right tool for the job is a central task. Leaders understand that changes in the political environment, for example, may require changes in how the organization functions and completes its tasks. Leaders must identify effective mechanisms to predict these changes and make appropriate adjustments either to deflect them or to alter ways of doing business so that the changes are no longer problematic for the organization. Having a diverse set of strategies improves the chances that changes will not have an adverse impact on the organization. For example, effective and contingent strategies for dealing with the political environment may be invaluable to protecting the organization from a budget cut or a reduction in personnel.

These elements make up the core of effective leadership as identified by participants in the leadership institute. The list is by no means exhaustive, yet it does oblige us to think about what criminal justice leadership actually is and the importance of some issues—such as leadership traits, employee development, balancing the needs of employees with production concerns, incorporating a sense of vision to the organization, and using multiple and contingent strategies—for effective leadership. A review of Chapters 5 and 6 shows how these issues are also relevant to employee motivation and job design.

CRIMINAL JUSTICE LEADERSHIP: A BRIEF WORD ON ORGANIZATIONAL CULTURE

Individuals are either elected or appointed to lead criminal justice organizations. These leaders usually have come up through the ranks of the organization. They understand the importance of creating and setting the "tone" in the organization and, in the words of Schein (1997), influencing the culture of the organization. Criminal justice literature is replete with accounts of both the good and the bad in the cultures of criminal justice organizations.

Whether these accounts reflect corruption in police organizations (Skolnick and Fyfe, 1993) or the alleged violence and brutality of correctional work (Conover,

2000), concerns have been raised about how such cultures are created, sustained, and perpetuated in criminal justice organizations. For many, the issue hinges on the role of leadership in influencing organizational culture. Many writers on criminal justice administration have noted the importance of leadership to organizational culture (Crank, 1998; Stojkovic and Farkas, 2003). This research suggests that effective leadership within criminal justice organizations must pay attention to how cultures are created, the mechanisms through which culture is transmitted to new employees, the role of leaders in the transmission of culture, and how culture can be influenced by administrators. Future research in criminal justice leadership will have to address the importance of organizational culture and offer suggestions on how it can be created and nurtured to fulfill organizational goals.

SUMMARY

Comprehend the complexities of leadership within criminal justice organizations.

- Leadership in criminal justice organizations must be understood within a political context. What is sometimes viewed as poor leadership may actually reflect a lack of understanding regarding the political realities and complexities of criminal justice leadership.

Understand the many theories of leadership.

- There are many leadership theories. The chapter highlighted these major theories of leadership and noted their application to criminal justice organizations.

Know the limitations of leadership research in criminal justice organizations.

- There are many benefits to applying various theoretical models of leadership to criminal justice organizations, yet very little application and testing of these models of leadership within criminal justice organizations has occurred. Much of what we know from the leadership literature in criminal justice is highly prescriptive.

Explain the importance of leadership development in criminal justice organizations.

- One model of leadership development was offered from the California Department of Corrections. While the program has value, there has been very little evaluation of such efforts to see if the quality of leadership matters when it comes to achieving the goals of correctional organizations.

Case Study: MANDATORY MINIMUM SENTENCES AND DRUG OFFENDERS

In *Alleyene v. United States* (2013), the Supreme Court ruled that before any mandatory minimum sentence can be handed down, it must be shown that the defendant did in fact exhibit behavior that would trigger a mandatory minimum sentence. This has, in part, changed the prosecution process at the federal level and requires that all relevant information concerning a criminal defendant be included in a charging document. Juries or judges must be shown that a defendant's actions are culpable before any mandatory minimum penalty can be imposed. For prosecutors, this means further deliberations on what cases are warranted for mandatory minimum sentence recommendations to judges and juries.

Where mandatory minimum cases have been especially problematic is in criminal drug cases, especially at the federal level of government where criminal prosecutions for drug offenses began in earnest in the late 1980s and went somewhat unabated until the Alleyene decision. Subsequent to the decision, Attorney General Eric Holder issued an opinion that directed U.S. Attorneys to reevaluate how mandatory minimum sentence recommendations are pursued in the federal courts. For many, the Alleyene decision is the beginning of reexamining the role of federal prosecutors in addressing the thorny problem of drug usage in America. Attorney General Holder in his opinion suggested specific criteria for prosecutors as they assess whether or not a particular case deserves a mandatory minimum sentence recommendation. The new policy directs U.S. Attorneys to reexamine carefully their existing charging policies and the importance of drug quality and quantity in a charging decision, as well as timing and plea agreements, advocacy at sentencing, and recidivist enhancements. Attorney General Holder is asking federal prosecutors to think differently about drug prosecution and to produce other practices and outcomes from what has been done the past 25 years, which was aggressive prosecution of both users and dealers of illegal drugs and handing down long prison sentences.

Attorney General Holder was not only guided by the Alleyene decision but also possibly by a changing climate in America regarding drug enforcement and the role of the criminal justice system in addressing drug use, abuse, and addiction. Placed in the context of legislative changes occurring around medical marijuana and even the legalization of the possession of small amounts of marijuana in some states (Colorado and Washington in 2012) through public referendum, Attorney General Holder and his boss, the president of the United States, were facing stiff pressure from an American public that saw drug enforcement and prosecution as not being the answer to the drug problem. In some cases, the American public viewed drug enforcement and prosecution as the problem, costing the federal government and the states billions of dollars.

In addition, in 2008, the economy tanked. The federal government and the states were strapped for cash. Pursuing a drug war through the criminal justice system was costly and inefficient. Both conservatives and liberals were calling for a scaling back on criminal justice efforts to address illegal drug use. With this changing political landscape came also the realization that since 2008 the federal government had become parsimonious in its arrest and prosecution of persons consuming marijuana for medical reasons. While the federal government still had the authority to prosecute marijuana users under federal law, states were making marijuana available to persons by a doctor's prescription through state law, the grandest adventure in the state of California. For some, the writing was on the wall: The drug war was over.

In such a changing political environment, Attorney General Holder's view on criminal prosecution of drug offenders and those deserving mandatory minimum sentences has changed significantly and may represent a new and bold form of leadership.

CASE STUDY QUESTIONS

1. What do you think about the prominent role of the criminal justice system in drug enforcement? Is it time to rethink the role the criminal justice system has played in dealing with society's drug problem? Why is leadership so important in this discussion?
2. What difficulties do criminal justice administrators face when societal expectations change so dramatically in such a short period of time? How and why does criminal justice leadership matter in such a situation?
3. Is Attorney General Holder's change in prosecution policies for federal prosecutors simply a reactive strategy, or is it a proactive attempt to improve federal criminal prosecution policies and practices?

Think like an Administrator

Criminal justice administrators have many opportunities to attend leadership development programs. More often than not, they are programs that have been in existence for many years. Many criminal justice professional organizations, such as the American Correctional Association or the International Association of Chiefs of Police, offer leadership development programs and workshops, yet for the criminal justice administrator, it is difficult to determine how such programs would be transferred into their organizations. It is one thing to talk about the elements of effective leadership, but how do you actually make effective leadership a part of your agency?

Take, for example, the issue of organizational culture. It is common to hear the phrase "the culture of the police agency" needs to be changed. For the police administrator, this is a simplistic statement on its face. As a police administrator, you may or may not know the drivers of the police culture of your agency. In fact, it might seem odd that you would not know your police culture. This may be reflective of poor leadership. The chances are that police administrators do have a good understanding of the police culture in their own agency because many rise from the agency's rank and file into their current positions. Yet, it is another matter to say how would you influence this culture.

1. Define organizational culture.
2. Is organizational culture dynamic or static?
3. What immediate barriers exist in the agency to inhibit the change of organizational culture?
4. To what extent would a change in organizational "vision" change organizational culture?
5. How does the existing labor agreement affect any attempt to change organizational culture?
6. What costs are inherent to attempts to change organizational culture?
7. What impact does a rigid chain of command have on organizational culture?

FOR DISCUSSION

1. Discuss the limitations of leadership in criminal justice organizations. Do the best individuals become criminal justice administrators or managers? If not, why not? In addition, are many of the problems associated with or attributed to criminal justice leadership really leadership problems?

2. Explore the findings of the Ohio State studies and the Michigan studies as they apply to the agencies of criminal justice. Are their findings applicable or not?

3. Suggest a specific path–goal model a criminal justice manager could employ. Discuss the implications of your path–goal model for effective leadership in that organization of criminal justice.

4. Offer some concrete suggestions about leadership to a police chief, using one of the theories of leadership examined in this chapter as a model.

5. Examine the ideas offered by the leadership institute of the California Department of Corrections. Would these ideas be effective in most criminal justice organizations or just a few?

FOR FURTHER READING

Bass, B. M. (Ed.). *Stodgill's Handbook of Leadership: Theory, Research and Managerial Applications*. New York: Free Press, 1990.

Fiedler, F. A. *A Theory of Leadership Effectiveness*. New York: McGraw-Hill, 1967.

Geller, W. A. (Ed.). *Police Leadership in America: Crisis and Opportunity*. Chicago: American Bar Association, 1985.

Kouzes, J. M., and Posner, B. Z. *The Leadership Challenge: How to Get Extraordinary Things Done in Organizations*. 3rd ed. San Francisco: Jossey-Bass, 2002.

Ouchi, W. *Theory Z: How American Business Can Meet the Japanese Challenge*. Reading, MA: Addison-Wesley, 1981.

Stojkovic, S., and Farkas, M. A. *Correctional Leadership: A Cultural Perspective*. Belmont, CA: Wadsworth/Thomson Learning, 2003.

Wright, K. A. *Effective Prison Leadership*. Binghamton, NY: William Nell, 1994.

CHAPTER 8

Personnel Evaluation and Supervision

LEARNING OBJECTIVES

After reading this chapter, the students will have achieved the following objectives:

- Understand the difficulty in arriving at goal consensus within criminal justice organizations.

- Comprehend the importance of organizational structure to employee supervision.

- Know the differences between the human service approach to employee supervision and the traditional model of employee supervision.

- Understand the difficulty in implementing a human service model of employee supervision within criminal justice organizations.

- Explain the guidelines for performance evaluation and supervision.

VIGNETTE

No type of offender raises the fears of citizens more than the sex offender. How do you effectively supervise such an offender? Driven by a desire to protect society against predatory sex offenders, many states have created sexually dangerous or sexually violent offender statutes providing for the long-term care and supervision of offenders in institutional settings as well as community settings. This raises a question on how to best supervise such a group of offenders.

In addition, the courts have weighed in on state statutes that are directed toward sexually violent persons and their re-institutionalization subsequent to the completion of criminal sentences. Court decisions have supported the notion that communities have the right to civilly commit sexually violent offenders after their criminal sentences have been completed, but they have also reinforced the idea that civil commitment must include some type of treatment as a justification for the re-institutionalization, and, in some cases, the courts have held that a least restrictive environment must exist, as well as a plan for how offenders will transition to community living. For both mental health and correctional officials, this expectation raises many questions of supervision.

As more states grapple with the management of sex offenders in their communities, how important will effective models of supervision be in making sure the community is protected, while simultaneously ensuring a treatment program for offenders? These important questions raise other questions and concerns regarding the effective supervision of the most problematical population under the authority of both mental health officials and correctional authorities.

This chapter examines the topic of supervision and evaluation as it relates to individual performance. As an organizational issue, employee supervision and evaluation has gained heightened importance among criminal justice administrators. In fact, scholars have called into question the basic tenets of personnel supervision and evaluation that have dominated criminal justice organizations for many years (Goldstein, 1990). Most of these traditional efforts focused on "hard measures" of performance (e.g., arrests for police organizations) with very little concern over how these measures in any way related to larger organizational and societal objectives and goals (Bayley, 1994). Current attempts at restructuring police organizations, court systems, and correctional organizations have centered on questions of how employees will be supervised and evaluated, as well as questions about the efficacy of newer methods to maintain control in these organizations (Skolnick and Bayley, 1986). Among criminal justice administrators, the question has become more direct and practical: How do supervisors maintain control of employees so that their behaviors are consistent with organizational goals? A corollary question is the following: What specific changes need to be implemented to enhance the supervision and evaluation of employees? Answering these questions is the focus of this chapter.

In addition, this chapter examines contemporary methods and models of employee supervision and evaluation. The discussion presented will be guided by the goals and expectations we have for criminal justice organizations. Any examination of personnel supervision and evaluation must include an analysis of the goals we are seeking to achieve. We begin the discussion with the idea of multiple goals, goal consensus, and criminal justice administration; move to an examination of structural aspects of criminal justice organizations; explore models of employee supervision and evaluation; and conclude with a discussion on issues pertaining to employee performance evaluation and supervision within criminal justice organizations.

CRIMINAL JUSTICE ADMINISTRATION: THE SEARCH
FOR GOAL CONSENSUS

It is a common and widely held belief that criminal justice organizations are expected to provide multiple services to the community. All components of the criminal justice system have multiple goals and functions. Criminal justice organizations seek **goal consensus**—an agreement regarding purposes. In some cases, these goals contradict one another, and it is difficult to discern the primary direction of the organization. Within police organizations, for example, we not only expect the police to provide community protection but also to maintain community order and respond to multiple calls for service (Goldstein, 1990:11). These calls for service have very little to do with the traditional notion of being a crime fighter.

Egon Bittner (1970) posed the central dilemma faced by police administrators in enforcing the law: How should nonnegotiable, coercive force be exercised in a society that stresses freedom, democracy, and peace? According to Bittner, this is typically accomplished through the development of myths, symbols, and various images that legitimize and, in some cases, conceal the very assumptions upon which police organizations function. Similar views have been offered by critics of the modern community policing ideal. To these critics,

Goal consensus:
Agreement on the purposes of an organization.

community policing represents another attempt to justify and legitimize the central function of police, which is to exercise coercive force (Klockars, 1991).

Others have also suggested that correctional organizations and the courts have operated under similar premises. Stojkovic and Lovell (1997) have argued that myths, symbols, and image maintenance cover fundamental ways in which correctional administrators make decisions. Many of these decisions support the idea that the primary purpose of prison is actually punitive control over large segments of the offender population, with very little concern about rehabilitation or change among prisoners. Given the growth in prison populations, it is uncertain how prisons can do more than simply warehouse offenders (Irwin and Austin, 1997).

Thus, in discussing prison goals, the only consensus to be reached is that there are too many inmates and too few resources to manage them. Lofty assertions about deterrence, selective incapacitation, rehabilitation, and societal protection may be far removed from the operational realities of prisons that are trying to maintain prisoner control under conditions of severe resource shortages. Nevertheless, some research has suggested that the orientations of correctional workers may be more diverse than originally thought. Tewksbury and Mustain (2008) show that the correctional orientations of staff vary by role (position) and gender, yet rehabilitation is viewed by all persons in prisons as being more valuable than deterrence, retribution, and incapacitation.

Such a view is also supported by recent research examining the work of probation and parole officers. To some, given the large number of offenders supervised by probation and parole agents, it is difficult to expect that anything beyond simple surveillance is the primary goal of these organizations. In fact, traditional practices such as presentence reports have come under fire by researchers, who claim that such reports are superfluous because most probationers are "typed" by the officer into specific categories based on offense and criminal history (Rosecrance, 1986). A particular emphasis is placed on the potential threat the probationer or parolee presents to the community. Even so, other research conducted in England suggests that despite the move toward more bureaucratization and efficiencies in probation work, the number one reason people enter the workforce is to assist others; they also cite the importance of relationships to effective change (Matthews, 2009). In fact, for most probation officers, working with people is central to deriving maximum satisfaction from the work.

Horror stories have highlighted the plight that many probation and parole agents face when one of their offenders is caught committing a heinous offense. The reality, however, is that because of limited resources and an unlimited demand for service, probation and parole organizations, like other social service agencies, will always operate under conditions of scarcity (Lipsky, 1980) and will adapt to their situations as best they can. Moreover, the dual tasks of providing supervision and support will always be present and both will have to be addressed by probation and parole workers seeking a balance in work effort that recognizes both as critical to the mission of probation and parole departments.

Similarly, court systems face large numbers of cases with too few resources to process all defendants adequately. Critics of the court system point to the fact that many offenders plea bargain and escape justice, while supporters argue that the mandate of due process requires full constitutional protections for all criminal defendants. Represented as the concerns for crime control and due process, the courts face the dilemma of how to control crime while remaining sensitive to the legal requirements of due process for those suspected of criminal activity.

According to Walker (1994), the criminal courts for the most part process lower-level cases; the sheer volume of these cases is what overwhelms the system. Accordingly, the idea that the courts process cases in an assembly-line fashion makes sense. The real goal is the quick processing and efficient handling of cases. Research has shown that this is true and, in addition, that the process is the punishment (Feeley, 1979).

Because many of the costs of going to court are too high for typical misdemeanant defendants, many will "cop" pleas to lower charges and accept a minimal penalty. To ask for rights, in many cases, would really cost the defendant more money than the penalty of pleading guilty—though the consistency of this finding is questioned by some researchers (Schulhofer, 1985, cited in Walker, 1994:36). Thus, pleading guilty is in the best interests of most defendants.

It is the conflict between assembly-line justice, on the one hand, and concerns of due process on the other hand that poses difficulties for the court administrator (Mays and Taggart, 1986). Like the other components of the criminal justice system, the courts have to function within the context of limited resources. It is simply impossible to guarantee that most defendants will receive due process when finite resources dictate to a large degree how due process concerns can be addressed.

Moreover, larger normative issues of goal consensus overshadow the resource problem in criminal justice organizations. These concerns include how a criminal justice system should look, the degree of fragmentation among system components, and the role diversity plays in its operation. There has been a growing awareness that the criminal justice system as it has been portrayed over the past fifty years (President's Commission on Law Enforcement and Criminal Justice, 1967) is not reflective of most local systems of justice across this country. The documented variety and differences across the organizations of criminal justice within the states and the federal government start to raise a question of whether or not goal consensus is a reality or even a desirable state.

Wright (2004) has argued that the construction of a monolithic system of criminal justice tied together by the activities of its various components does not make sense either organizationally or politically. Attempting to construct a single "system" of criminal justice contradicts commonly held beliefs about the relationship between the people and their government. Fragmentation, or a lack of unification across the components of the criminal justice system, is often viewed negatively by proponents of a systems approach to criminal justice, yet such a view denies the importance of fragmentation to the democratic principles we cherish about diversity of viewpoints as expressed through the criminal justice system. Without fragmentation and diversity across the criminal justice system, it would be difficult for those organizations to deal with their different and varied communities.

In this sense, a lack of coordination and unification within the criminal justice system is desirable because diverse points of interest can be expressed and reflected in local systems of justice. To achieve goal consensus within a criminal justice system could be construed as undemocratic and dangerous. In addition, searching for a singular goal may simply be pointless, given the multiple expectations of communities concerning the operations of their local systems of criminal justice.

Thus, many efforts to integrate local systems of criminal justice into one system are doomed to failure because all of these systems have to respond to local constituencies and environments. This is most true of federal initiatives that mandate specific policies and goals for state and local criminal justice systems. The passage of the Violent Crime Control and Law Enforcement Act of 1994, for example, was an attempt by the federal government to mandate the direction of crime policies in the states; however, critics argue that most crime is local in nature and that these communities should be allowed to dictate how their criminal justice systems will respond to it. Forcing some type of consensus onto the direction and purpose of local systems of criminal justice has always been problematic for legislatures and politicians. The results of such efforts have been questioned by many who have been critical of federal attempts to confront crime (Conley, 1994). Criminal justice administrators have had many organizational difficulties trying to operationally implement plans that are ill conceived and poorly thought out.

The central objective of criminal justice administrators is to determine the goals of their communities and the most efficient ways to meet those goals. For some communities, attaining specific goals may be less cumbersome than for others. In communities with large, diverse populations, arriving at goal consensus on what the local system of criminal justice should be accomplishing is no small task. Equally important are the methods or strategies employed by criminal justice personnel to achieve community goals. It is at the street level that the reality of criminal justice is presented to the community, and this is why the rank-and-file worker, whether that is a police officer on the beat or a correctional officer in a prison, is the most important part of the administration and management of criminal justice organizations. These "street-level bureaucrats" (Lipsky, 1980:5) are the essence of the criminal justice system, and how these employees are supervised and evaluated is one of the most pressing issues facing criminal justice administration in this century.

Organizational structure: The way in which an organization is set up to accomplish its goals, objectives, and tasks. Organizational structure is defined by size, degree of formality, complexity, and purpose.

ORGANIZATIONAL STRUCTURE AND EMPLOYEE EVALUATION AND SUPERVISION

Organizational structure influences employee evaluation and supervision. **Organizational structure** is defined by size, degree of formality, complexity, and purpose. It is clear, for example, that the size of a criminal justice organization affects how employees are evaluated and supervised. Criminal justice organizations with a large number of employees are more complex, and employee evaluation and supervision methods are constrained and limited in comparison to smaller criminal justice agencies. No one would disagree that the mechanisms used to evaluate and supervise employees in the New York City police department, with close to 40,000 police officers, need to be different from those evaluation and supervision strategies found in a police department of fifty officers.

Due to the variations found among criminal justice organizations on various dimensions, criminal justice administrators have to be creative in how they devise evaluation and supervision methods. Other issues besides size that can affect the evaluation and supervision approaches employed by criminal justice administrators are budget, differing goals, and the degree to which the organization is centralized or decentralized in its decision-making processes. We offer some general guidelines on evaluation and supervision of criminal justice employees at the end of the chapter.

Work Perspective: EMPLOYEE SUPERVISION AND EVALUATION—SOME GENERAL THOUGHTS

I have been a Federal Investigator with the U.S. Equal Employment Opportunity Commission (EEOC) for almost twelve years. The mission of the agency is to enforce the federal laws that prohibit discrimination in the workplace and to promote equal opportunity in the workplace. In fiscal year 2010, EEOC had 99,922 complaints filed nationwide, the highest level since its inception in 1965. We also saw a record high of $294 million in relief collected through administrative enforcement and mediation.

As agents of the employer, supervisors and managers are held to a higher standard under the law and their actions have significant liability implications to the employer. Any missteps by a supervisor and/or manager can lead to costly litigation. As an investigator, I have seen the full spectrum of issues that can arise in the workplace. Some of the issues can be attributed to personality conflicts between front-line supervisors and managers. However, many EEO complaints arise due to the employee's perception of unfair treatment in the workplace. Employers could minimize complaints of unfair treatment and discrimination with effective supervision and constructive evaluation of employees. The following are ways that poor supervision and undirected evaluation can lead to employee complaints of unlawful treatment in the workplace.

1. **Lack of clearly communicated rules, policies and procedures.** It is of the utmost importance to get subordinates, middle management, and upper management all on the same page. Failing to clearly communicate rules, policies, and procedures leads to confusion about what the expectations are. Well-written policies ensure consistency and will help guide both subordinates and management. For instance, the procedure for an employee to file an internal complaint of harassment should be clearly defined in an employee handbook. In addition, if the employer has a progressive discipline policy, the policy should be clearly defined and easily accessible for both employees and management.

2. **Inconsistent application of policies and procedures.** In theory, being consistent sounds like an easy practice to follow. However, as I see on a daily basis, inconsistencies in the application of policies and procedures can lead to unlawful treatment of employees. Supervisors and managers need to apply policies and procedures the same way to all employees across the board. While unfair treatment and favoritism are not necessarily unlawful, inconsistent enforcement of policies and procedures oftentimes results in low morale among staff. It also can lead to a lack of respect toward management among front-line staff and lower employee production.

3. **Failure to address problems and concerns.** Supervisors and/or managers need to take immediate corrective action when problems arise. For instance, when management becomes aware of a harassment complaint, they have a legal obligation to take immediate action to investigate and prevent further instances of harassment. If the employer is made aware of the harassment but fails to remedy the situation, the employer may be liable for damages caused by

the continued harassment. Another situation that requires expeditious action is where an employee exhibits poor performance. Management needs to immediately address the employee so that there are no surprises down the road. If later the employer chooses to terminate the employee, then the employee cannot say that they were never counseled about their performance. When management immediately addresses concerns as they arise, it sends a message to all that certain behavior will not be tolerated. Conversely, when managers do not immediately address problems as they come up, it is just asking for problems in the future.

4. **Untimely professional feedback and disingenuous evaluation.** Supervisors and managers sometimes fail to provide negative feedback and evaluation when warranted. It causes problems when management is not upfront and honest with the employee regarding their performance. Managers should give constructive criticism and praise when necessary. However, managers should relate the criticism to the job and not the person. For instance, it is proper for an employer to point out that an employee consistently fails to meet deadlines, but it is not appropriate to characterize the employee as too slow or too old. This may be perceived as direct evidence of discrimination. When giving praise, it is acceptable to say, "has met the office goals," but do not use words like "energetic, vibrant, or youthful." To avoid falling into these traps, it is best to measure performance on objective criteria. Using subjective criteria could lead to discrimination complaints. An employer should also provide rewards to employees that are consistent with the evaluation. For instance, it sends a conflicting message to the employee if an employee is terminated after receiving an outstanding performance evaluation.

5. **Inadequate supporting evidence and lack of documentation.** Ineffective supervisors and managers fail to adequately document performance issues. Without a paper trail of incidents such as memos, performance

evaluations, disciplinary actions, etc., the employer is at a major disadvantage. In cases where employers do not have documentation to support issuing disciplinary action or termination, employees are more likely to perceive the action as discriminatory. Therefore, the employee is more likely to pursue avenues of redress, such as filing an internal complaint of discrimination or filing a complaint with a governmental agency. The problem may be remedied by making it a practice to document employee performance issues to support subsequent adverse employment actions.

6. **Inadequate training and lack of employee development.** Employers need to provide effective training at all levels for front-line, managers, supervisors, and human resources staff. Managers need to view training as an investment. Spend the resources on training staff now to avoid potential legal problems later. Supervisors and managers need to know how to handle difficult situations and the proper steps to take. Failing to be well versed in all policies and procedures can lead to complaints of illegal discrimination.

7. **Management sets the tone in the workplace.** Incompetent supervisors and managers need to be held accountable. If not, subordinates may think the behavior is okay. Supervisors should be treated no differently than their subordinates with respect to disciplinary measures and professional development.

This is not intended to be a substitute for legal advice. These are general issues that, in my experience, have led employees to perceive illegal discrimination in the workplace and take subsequent legal actions against their employer. By taking the aforementioned issues into consideration, supervisors will go a long way to enhance the supervision and evaluation of employees consistent with agency mission and vision and legal requirements that guide and direct pubic agencies.

SOURCE: Monica Lozer, Federal Investigator, Equal Employment Opportunity Commission.

MODELS OF EMPLOYEE SUPERVISION

Models of employee supervision: The ways in which organizations guide and direct their employees.

Models of employee supervision have proliferated over the past few decades (Rainey, 2014). These **models of employee supervision** serve as a guide and direct employees. Public agencies seeking improvement in the quality of employee supervision have attempted to apply the principles and practices of private-sector management to the public sector (see Ouchi, 1981; Peters and

Waterman, 1982). Some applications have been in the criminal justice system. Our objective here is to show how these ideas translate into specific models of supervision. The reader is asked to place these models within the contexts described previously—namely, an organizational goal context and an organizational structural context.

The Traditional Model of Employee Supervision

The **traditional model of employee supervision** stresses centralized authority, clear-cut rules and regulations, well-developed policies and procedures, and discernable lines of authority operationally through a chain of command—in short, high degrees of centralization, formalization, and complexity. Contemporary critics, however, question the effectiveness and appropriateness of this model of supervision to the changing societal expectations of the criminal justice system. We will have more to say on this line of criticism later. For now, it is useful to flesh out the key elements of the traditional model of employee supervision used in most criminal justice organizations.

The traditional model is made up of the following elements: a hierarchy that stresses an identifiable span of control, a precise unity of command, and a clear delegation of authority; rulification; and specialization of services and activities of employees (Gaines, Southerland, and Angell, 1991).

Span of control refers to the appropriate number of employees that can be managed by any one supervisor. What this magic number should be has been part of the debates among scholars and practitioners alike. This concept can be applied both to employees and the people they supervise. For example, span of control is a central question in the delivery of services to probationers and parolees (McShane and Krause, 1993). Concerns over the maximum number of probationers who can be supervised by one agent have plagued community corrections officials for years (Clear and Cole, 1994). For police departments, span of control refers to the number of officers that can be reasonably monitored by a supervisor.

Unity of command refers to the placement of one person in charge of a situation and an employee. The importance of this concept to traditional supervision revolves around multiple and conflicting orders from supervisors. For control and supervision to be maximized, there has to be one supervisor, known by every employee. In this way, confusion about directives and commands is reduced, and the employee is aware of to whom he or she must report. In the words of one correctional administrator, "There have to be one chief and a lot of Indians in prison."

Delegation of authority maintains the integrity of the organization by clearly defining tasks and responsibilities of employees, as well as delegating power and authority to complete required tasks. For police organizations, this means providing employees clear direction on what their responsibilities are, the necessary skills to accomplish tasks, and the requisite authority to achieve objectives. Each employee understands his or her role in the accomplishment of tasks and where they fit into the larger goals of the organization.

Rulification emphasizes the importance of rules and regulations to the organization. Every policy, procedure, and directive must have some specific written

Traditional model of employee supervision: A model that emphasizes clear rules and regulations, division of labor, span of control, delegation of authority, and employee specialization within organizations.

referent. In this way, clarity of organizational tasks and purposes is maintained, as well as documentation concerning appropriate behaviors by employees. As a control mechanism, rules, policies, and procedures are the essential components of the organization. One cannot imagine a police or correctional organization existing and functioning without well-specified rules, policies, and procedures. The rules define the scope and direction of criminal justice agencies.

Specialization involves the division of labor in criminal justice organizations. Each employee knows his or her tasks and is held accountable for those tasks. Specialization enhances employee supervision because it is through exact job definition that employees can be evaluated, disciplined, promoted, and dismissed. In most cases, increases in specialization enable advances in employee supervision because there is an increase in responsibility, yet increased specialization may also create administrative coordination problems (Gaines, Southerland, and Angell, 1991:101).

Through the concepts of span of control, unity of command, delegation of authority, rulification, and specialization, supervisors are presumed to enhance their supervisory capabilities. For decades, training within police departments and correctional organizations has stressed these important concepts for effective employee supervision. Current advocates, such as DiIulio (1987, 1991), argue that the role of effective management should not be downplayed. DiIulio believes that greater attention should be paid to improving the effectiveness of managers and administrators.

Although his ideas were originally presented within the context of prisons, it is clear that they have equal relevance and application to other criminal justice organizations, such as police departments. Recently, however, research has questioned the efficacy, effectiveness, and efficiency of such a model. Critics point out many practical difficulties with the traditional model of supervision such as increased role stress experienced by correctional staff (Lambert, Hogan, and Tucker, 2009) and the perceived unfairness of bureaucratic processes to answer questions of fundamental fairness in criminal justice operations (Tyler, 2004).

One of the most ardent critics of the traditional model of police supervision has been Fyfe (2004a:146–156). In his view, traditional ideas about police supervision and employee performance have been predicated on largely fictionalized accounts of the police role and inappropriate assessments of police work; they are, he says, more often than not based on perceptions of police supervisors with no input from the officers themselves. The traditional model of supervision stresses arrest statistics, for example, as one outcome measure of performance, yet there is no consideration of the relationship between arrest activity and the realization of organizational goals.

As such, Fyfe argues that it is not clear how the elements of the traditional model of police supervision actually enhance the supervisory process and, more important, how the model itself is related to the goals of police organizations. What gets produced instead is a fractured and misleading picture of police as primarily "crime fighters." In addition, critics have argued that the traditional model produces authoritarian supervisors, precludes organizational innovation, stymies information flow, and reduces the motivational levels of officers (see Gaines, Southerland, and Angell, 1991:105–107). Skolnick and Fyfe (1993:117–124) have argued that many police problems can be traced to the paramilitary style that pervades police organizations.

If such criticisms are correct, the utility of the traditional model to the attainment of organizational goals must be questioned. Goldstein (1990:157) suggests that the reason the traditional model of employee supervision has lasted so long relates to the ease with which supervision can be routinized. Under the traditional approach, supervision is rather straightforward and predictable. Asking police supervisors—sergeants and lieutenants, in particular—to supervise through innovation consistent with the changes and demands of the community is a more difficult task.

For example, community policing efforts, while expanding the role of rank-and-file officers through decentralization, create enormous challenges for the immediate supervisor. Supervisors now have to respond to the demands of the community in ways that often defy routinization. Furthermore, supervision defined as control becomes more difficult under arrangements that place individual officer autonomy as a higher organizational imperative. For these reasons, traditional police supervisors are highly suspicious and unaccepting of contemporary attempts to redefine the police role more consistently with community policing or problem-oriented police models. These models of police management accentuate the importance of attending to multiple expectations of the community and, as such, demand new ways of doing business in police organizations.

Similarly, correctional organizations are going through changes that are calling into question the relevance and usefulness of the traditional model of employee supervision when faced with competing and multiple demands from the community (Johnson, 2002; Stojkovic and Farkas, 2003; Wright, 1994). Correctional institutions, parole agencies, and probation departments are all being asked to protect society from criminals; in addition, they are expected to do something productive with offenders so that criminal propensities are reduced. This, too, is no simple set of expectations. Nevertheless, such expectations are altering the context within which correctional agencies, as well as other criminal justice organizations, are functioning. Newer models of employee supervision have been proposed to augment the functioning capabilities of employees to meet these new challenges.

The Human Service Model of Employee Supervision

Unlike the traditional model of employee supervision, which emphasizes monitoring through tight organizational controls, the **human service model** views the supervision process within the context of both individual employee goals and larger organizational goals. The human service model attempts to integrate employee goals into organizational goals.

What do employees want? They want a number of things, with surprising consistency—both to accomplish job tasks and to feel fulfilled within their roles.

Human service model of employee supervision: A model that stresses employee ownership, delegation of authority, and the sharing of power within organizations.

Toch (1978), as one of the first to comment on the traditional assumptions we hold about rank-and-file criminal justice workers, states the following:

> A correctional officer assigned to tower duty is a residue of the dark ages. He requires 20/20 vision, the IQ of an imbecile, a high threshold for boredom, and a basement position in Maslow's hierarchy.

Similar views have also been offered about police officers ("street cops") and their vitriolic attitudes toward administrators ("management cops") (Reuss-Ianni, 1984). The result of such a split is often hostility and a sense of separation between officer and manager. Such a split is directly related to the military-style organization found in most police departments (Fyfe, 2004a:158).

Such a view highlights the tension that is created between rank-and-file employees and administrators when assumptions about employees are less than flattering, and there is no appreciation of the diversity of their role and the job performed. The traditional model of police supervision does not recognize either the importance of this diversity or that organizational control—the single most important goal under the traditional model—is only one goal among many. It is this recognition of diversity in both personal and organizational goals that defines the human service model of employee supervision.

Within the context of a problem-oriented approach to police organization, Goldstein (1990:149) argues that the traditional model of supervision must be supplanted with a model of supervision that fosters a "relationship with management built on mutual trust and on agreement that an officer has the freedom to think and act within broad boundaries." Similarly, Johnson (2002) has shown that effective correctional officers are those who stretch the role of custody to include the delivery of goods and services to prisoners, even though there are very few inducements for such behavior. Why do some officers exhibit such behaviors? The answer to this question, offered by Johnson (2002:256), serves to define the basic assumption of the human service model of employee supervision:

> Why, then, do some [correctional] officers persist in activities that take time and effort, are neither recognized nor rewarded by others, and must be hidden or played down for fear of trouble with administrators, peers, treatment staff, or recalcitrant inmates? The reason … is simply this: *human service activities make the officer's job richer, more rewarding, and ultimately less stressful.*

Recognition of the true nature of the employee's role enables managers and administrators to grasp that supervision must include a rather expansive definition of employee tasks and activities. Less centralization, fewer and more clearly defined rules, and less bureaucracy are central tenets of the human service model of employee supervision. Unlike the traditional model of employee supervision that emphasizes tight controls and limited decision making among employees, this approach stresses the importance of decentralization of authority for greater decision-making capabilities among lower-level members, fewer rules to encumber the enlarged activities of employees, and a breaking down of the traditional hierarchy found in most police and correctional organizations.

Such views are consistent with popular ideas expressed by contemporary management experts, such as Peters and Waterman (1982:150), who stress autonomy and entrepreneurship (less centralization); simultaneous loose–tight properties (less formalization); and simple form, lean staff (less complexity). Such approaches have proven to be invaluable to the corporate world and have equal relevance to criminal justice administration and management. All are consistent with the human service model of employee supervision. Both experts and reformers alike have called for the application of these ideas in transforming the supervision process within criminal justice organizations (see Christopher Commission Report, 1991:242–244).

In addition, the case for humanizing organizational structure has had its strongest support among researchers who investigate the importance of investing in people within organizations and organizational performance. O'Toole and Meier (2009) stress that an investment in people in organizations yields much return relative to cost. Their research, based on a review of evidence for hundreds of organizations in the public sector over a four-year period, showed that even controlling for all performance indicators available, it is still a wise choice to invest in employees for maximum organizational performance:

> The results are convincing; they are found across a wide array of performance measures, and they can even be found for almost all of the measures when controlling for past performance. The evidence provides especially strong support for the proposition that the human side contributes to tangible, measurable results (2009:513).

According to Goldstein (1990:157–172), a new supervision model in police organizations requires a decentralization of authority; a new dimension of supervision that capitalizes on the knowledge of frontline supervisors, such as sergeants and lieutenants; an alteration in the criteria for recognizing and evaluating performance among officers; a change in the recruitment and selection of new officers; a revitalized sense of purpose and direction in training; and the development of new sources of information and new knowledge on how to address crime-related problems within communities.

Similarly, Wright (1994) offers identical prescriptions for correctional administrators and managers. He suggests that correctional institutions can be made more cohesive and can work toward both organizational goals and developing people in the organization. Wright's ideas center around three fundamental concepts associated with the human service model of employee supervision: employee ownership, delegation, and the sharing of power.

Employee ownership refers to gaining a greater voice in the creation of institutional policy. According to Wright, correctional employees who are able to express their concerns within the context of decision making are more productive employees and experience less stress. In his words, "People who 'own' their job and 'own' their organization feel strong, capable, and committed" (1994:48). This ownership is structured within the concept of *delegation*. Delegation allows employees, within prescribed limits, the opportunities to make decisions that affect their ability to perform tasks. As such, delegation is not without structure or undirected participation by lower-level employees; it is the ability to maximize the knowledge and skills of employees in a directed fashion (Lambert, Hogan, and Tucker, 2009). In short, delegation exploits the experiences of the workers.

The *sharing of power* follows nicely from the concept of delegation. Sharing power assumes that power is not a finite entity. Instead, power is viewed as "energy, potential, and competence" (Wright, 1994:51). Power is given to employees in such a way that they are able to enhance their performance levels and adjust to contingencies of the institutional environment. Under such a view, the correctional worker is viewed as an active contributor to the organization, not simply a reactive automaton to institutional policies and procedures.

Taken together, these three ideas generate a work philosophy that seeks to institutionalize greater authority in the hands of employees and respects their intelligence and creativity in a changing correctional environment. Such a philosophy has been the model for the Federal Bureau of Prisons since the mid-1960s and is known as *unit management*. Unit management is an organizational design as well as an operating philosophy for the Federal Bureau of Prisons. Houston (1999) defines unit management as having the following components:

- A small number of inmates (50 to 120) who are permanently assigned together

- A multidisciplinary staff (unit manager, case manager[s], correctional counselor[s], full- or part-time psychologist, clerk typist, and correctional officers) whose offices are located within or adjacent to the inmate housing unit and are permanently assigned to work with the inmates of that unit

- A unit manager who has administrative authority and supervisory responsibility for the unit staff

- A unit staff that has administrative authority for all within-unit aspects of inmate living and programming

- Inmates who are assigned to the unit because of age, prior record, specific behavior typologies, a need for a specific type of correctional program, such as drug abuse counseling, or random assignment

- Unit staff who are scheduled by the unit manager to work in the unit evenings and weekends, on a rotating basis, in addition to the unit correctional officer. Within the institution, the guiding principle is to have a flexible set of rules and regulations that allows staff the discretion and direction to complete tasks.

For advocates of unit management, the advantages far outweigh the disadvantages. Houston (1999:325) suggests the following advantages: a greater sense of cohesion and community between inmates and staff; an increase in the contacts between inmates and staff, which leads to better communication and a positive work environment; a decentralizing of decisions within the correctional units that improves decision making; and greater program flexibility.

Such advantages must be weighed, however, within the context of competing disadvantages. Houston (1999:325–326) offers the following disadvantages to unit management. Unit management is costly and labor intensive, takes much time and resources to implement, and, most telling, threatens the organizational status quo. In particular, it challenges fundamental ways of doing business in the prison. Instead of the traditional hierarchical control found in most prisons, unit management increases the flexibility of subordinates and decentralizes authority at the operational level—in this case, within the housing unit where staff completes the day-to-day functions of the prison.

Wright (1994:54) offers the primary reason correctional administrators have been slow to adopt unit management:

> Some top executives may feel uneasy about giving up control.... They may wonder whether they can depend on line staff to make critical decisions. Yet, most prisons are too large for a few administrators to get to know all the inmates well. Unit management provides for more efficient and informed decision making because the individuals making the decisions spend the most time with inmates.

In this statement, we see the fundamental difference between the traditional model and the human service model. The primary concern of the traditional model is control of the employee, whereas the human service model stresses the completion of organizational tasks. The often tumultuous and uncertain political environment forces criminal justice administrators to stress accountability and control of employees. Employees' concerns, meanwhile, center on task completion. Often there is conflict between the organization's search for control and certainty and the desire to accomplish "soft" organizational objectives and goals. Wilson (2000:168–171) has documented how many public service agencies are what he called "coping organizations." Unlike product-based organizations, these types of organizations cannot observe their own outcomes and outputs. It is often difficult to identify what tasks are actually related to the accomplishment of specific goals in coping organizations.

Given this situation, it will be difficult, if not impossible, for administrators in coping organizations to give up power, decentralize their organizations, and empower employees. They fall back on what they can do well and that usually means hierarchy and other traditional practices that, on the surface, provide greater control of employees as well as measures of output that have a control focus.

Such a view questions the applicability of the human service model to criminal justice organizations. Wright (1994:43–47) discusses how correctional administrators often stress centralization of authority, clear rules, and uncertainty avoidance in their organizations. This means greater bureaucracy and tighter organizational control. Yet advocates of the human service model seek a loosening of the organizational reins by administrators. Is this really possible?

IS THE HUMAN SERVICE MODEL POSSIBLE?

Commenting on the entire human relations movement in organizations, Charles Perrow (1986:94–95) cynically states the fundamental problem in trying to "humanize" organizations:

The search for authenticity and spontaneity should be never-ending, and if it must occur in the guise of better productivity in organizations, let it. The trainees will return refreshed to a world of hierarchies, conflict, authority, stupidity, and brilliance, but the hierarchies and the like probably will not fade away. Most organizations remain highly authoritarian systems; some even use T-groups to hide that essential fact.

For criminal justice administrators, citizens (the consumers of our products), and reformers, such organizational issues as decentralization, employee empowerment, and delegation are significant concerns today and into the future. Yet given the uncertain, conflicting, and multiple goals facing criminal justice organizations, it is not clear how such issues can become relevant to administrators. At the end of the day, criminal justice administrators have to show that adopting more human service principles actually improves their product. It is the product that is important. Polakowski, Hartley, and Bates (2008) argue that the number one predictor of success in a juvenile drug court is the quality of participant experiences in the program. In effect, we expect drug courts to assist people with their drug problems. When program participants feel that the experience is positive and assists them in moving away from a life of drugs and crime, they are more likely to succeed in the program. It is interesting that in this example, drug testing, residential treatment, sanction rate, severity of sanctions, and rewards (days off) made up the definition of the drug court program. How these aspects of the program were organized and delivered affected the outcome or product. As an example of an innovation in criminal justice, drug courts provide an opportunity for criminal justice administrators to organize and deliver their services differently and hopefully with a better outcome. This is a serious organizational issue.

Criminal justice administrators, as we have emphasized in this and other chapters, face many constraints and receive multiple expectations from their constituents, with finite resources. This forces goal ambiguity about their purpose and direction. Because of this, they adopt a structure and system of employee supervision that emphasizes what they can accomplish. More often than not, this means routinization, an overemphasis on employee control, and consistent policies and procedures. Such a structure reduces uncertainty and stabilizes all threats from the environment.

More important, humanistic attempts to reorganize the ways of doing business in criminal justice organizations require greater clarity of purposes (identifying the product), consensus on the purposes (agreement among competing interests about the product), and a well-defined technology or methodology to produce the product (how to make the product). Public service organizations, such as the criminal justice system, possess no such clarity about these issues.

Wilson (2000) argues that issues of accountability, equity, fiscal integrity, and efficiency serve as possible obstacles to innovation in public organizations.

Although Wilson applies these concepts to an analysis of public organizations in general, we can apply them to employee supervision as well. *Accountability* centers on employee performance and issues of supervision and control. *Equity* focuses on fairness and treating similarly situated employees in the same way. *Fiscal integrity* means ensuring that public dollars are spent on the personnel and functions mandated to the organization. Finally, *efficiency* involves employing a sufficient number of employees, not too many nor too few, to accomplish the organization's tasks within the prescribed level of resources.

Taken together, these concerns, along with conflicting goals and missions, serve as constraints on how employees are to be supervised. Police organizations, for example, that attempt to reorganize under a community policing philosophy would find enormous difficulties in trying to decentralize their structures while still being sensitive to public accountability, equity among officers, fiscal concerns about the appropriateness of deploying staff in such a way, and efficiency concerns. Would the creation of mini-stations in police organizations be cost effective? Would they allow accountability to be monitored? What about issues of exercising discretion and monitoring of discretionary acts among officers by supervisors?

Similar questions could be raised about correctional organizations. One state department of corrections lost a major judgment in court on the payment of overtime to probation and parole officers. The department responded bureaucratically and tightened procedures so that overtime was no longer possible for agents, even though it knew that officers required greater time and flexibility to complete tasks, such as home visits of offenders. While attempting to decentralize their decision making for agents, correctional officers were more concerned about the public impression that the department was not being efficient and lacked fiscal integrity in their operations.

These concerns overshadowed treatment and offender supervision issues. The net result was that services were cut back and the department became even more rigid. In addition, the department created mechanisms to control the time and workings of agents to the point where many agents complained that there was no professionalism in the job. Proponents of the humanistic model of employee supervision, consequently, need to address how concerns over accountability, equity, fiscal integrity, and efficiency would be handled outside the traditional structure of criminal justice organizations.

To date, many supporters of the humanistic approach have not moved beyond an abstract discussion of how criminal justice organizations will presumably benefit from the adoption of their principles. What still has to be examined is how these ideals can become real within the context of multiple goals, interests, and constraints. This is a formidable challenge for those who administer criminal justice organizations, yet not an impossible one. Responding to this challenge will be a primary initiative for criminal justice administrators in the new century. In fact, it might be said that the push for increased privatization of criminal justice functions and agencies is rooted in a belief that private organizations can respond more efficiently and effectively to the changing and turbulent environments of criminal justice organizations (Shefer and Liebling, 2008).

GUIDELINES FOR PERFORMANCE EVALUATION AND SUPERVISION

All guidelines for supervision and evaluation of employees require a road map on how to proceed. The supervision and evaluation of employees is no easy task, nor is there any single approach that can be given to criminal justice supervisors to follow. Instead, there are key issues and concepts that can assist and guide criminal justice administrators (see Bennett and Hess, 2007, for a thorough discussion of supervision techniques). Yukl (1981) provides a list of guidelines to aid supervisors in the performance of their jobs. They include the following: defining job responsibilities, assigning work, and setting performance goals. Each of these areas has a number of subareas that define the supervision process.

Within the realm of defining job responsibilities, explaining the important job responsibilities, clarifying the person's scope of authority, explaining how the job relates to the mission of the unit, and, most important, explaining important and relevant policies, rules, and requirements are essential. When assigning work, the supervisor must clearly explain the assignment, explain the reasons for the assignment, clarify priorities and deadlines, and check for comprehension among employees. Similarly, setting performance goals means setting goals for relevant aspects of performance, setting goals that are clear and specific, setting goals that are challenging but realistic, and setting a target date for the attainment of each goal (Yukl, 1981:68).

Oettmeier and Wycoff (1998) offer a model for evaluating and supervising police officers within the context of community policing efforts. This model offers three levels at which evaluation and supervision can be examined. At the first level, the evaluation and supervision efforts focus on individual performance and can include the following elements: traffic stops, arrests, and directed patrols toward specific crimes, to mention a few. At the second level, the evaluation and supervision parameters are focused at the team level within the organization.

The efforts of the team are evaluated on how well specific aims are met and incidents addressed. For example, officers may be evaluated on how well they implement a drunk driving apprehension unit and how many arrests are made. The focus of the evaluation is on team performance, not individual performance. The third level of evaluation examines the organization's internal activities or procedures to address certain problems. At this level of evaluation, the administration is introspectively examining the operations of the organization with a focus on improving a process or procedure. An example is the procedures employed in the disciplinary process. The focus of the evaluation is to move beyond the individual or a team of officers; instead, the purpose is to evaluate the processes and procedures used to realize organizational goals.

This model has been applied to both small and large cities, and research has documented the trials and tribulations associated with this new way of evaluating police performance. In Houston, Texas, for example, application of the model has proven to be challenging and rewarding. Oettmeier and Wycoff (1998:377–391) report that Houston police officials learned new ways to improve their performance evaluation systems and supervision approaches.

These researchers offer the following changes in police performance evaluation to assist police administrators: adopt new assumptions concerning performance evaluation, specifically how and when performance evaluations are conducted; define the purposes of evaluation; identify new performance criteria; measure the effects of officer performance; strengthen the verification of performance among officers; develop new instrumentation to evaluate officer performance; solicit officer feedback about the performance of frontline supervisors, such as sergeants; and, finally, revise rating scales.

The evaluation and supervision of employees will always be problematic. Developing guidelines and specific approaches to evaluation and supervision will always be questioned. Nevertheless, personnel supervision and evaluation are a major task for criminal justice administrators. How this is accomplished is, in part, the test of an administrator's skill level. The twenty-first-century criminal justice administrator will be pressed to provide more credible information and ways to assess employee performance. It will be one of the continuing challenges facing criminal justice administrators.

To meet this challenge, a number of writers have suggested that a 360-degree model of employee supervision be employed. This model of supervision recognizes the importance of multiple views on employee performance. It is a rather expansive model of supervision that envisions greater input from all those who are affected by an employee's actions. The dominant stakeholders in this approach are both internal and external to the department. The Sacramento Police Department, for example, uses four sources of information for police officer performance appraisals: *input from departmental personnel*, such as peers who know the officer, *personnel files*, which may include commendations and complaints, *officer performance within the unit* as assessed by a supervisor, and an *officer's self-appraisal*. Taken together, these sources of information provide a comprehensive review of an officer's performance (Scrivner, 2001:115).

In addition, it is highly recommended that criminal justice organizations conduct performance appraisals on various dimensions that gauge employees' success on the job. This means there are operationally defined performance appraisal dimensions. Scrivner (2001:111–114) identifies nine specific dimensions to police officer performance appraisal: *communication skills, interpersonal skills, integrity, commitment to service, work ethic, problem solving, safety, demeanor, and operation of a motor vehicle*. By taking a comprehensive look at an officer's performance, it is possible to conclude how successful the officer is in achieving the stated objectives and goals of a specific unit within the organization.

What about employee supervision? Are there prescriptions that can be offered to criminal justice supervisors to be more successful? The answer to this question is not simple because it is difficult to delineate supervision from management and what benchmarks are used to gauge success. Research suggests that for most managers, work can be divided into four basic functions: *traditional management*, including decision making, planning, and controlling; *communication*, exchanging information and completing paperwork; *human resource management*, motivating, disciplining, managing conflict, staffing, and training; and *networking*, socializing and politicking with outsiders.

Criminal justice supervisors have to perform all these functions to be successful in the supervisor role, yet the research also suggests that there is a difference between being an *effective* manager (performs well and gets things done) and a *successful* manager (speed of promotion within an organization). (See Robbins and Judge, 2007:8–9, for a more thorough discussion of this topic.) Moreover, the research on effective models of supervision within criminal justice organizations suffers from a dearth of empirically based findings. More often than not, we perform as supervisors within criminal justice organizations based on tradition and informed intuition rather than sound prescriptions from research, even though this is changing in many criminal justice organizations (see the case study in Chapter 15).

Nevertheless, there is some research to guide our thinking. Engel (2004) provides some interesting findings regarding styles of supervision among police supervisors (sergeants). She found four styles of supervision among police sergeants. The **traditional supervisor** is the person who expects measurable outcomes from subordinates and aggressive law enforcement activities. This type of police supervisor expects officers to produce many arrests and written citations. There is a particular emphasis on rule enforcement and expecting officers to comply with orders and commands.

A second type of supervisor is the **innovative supervisor**. This person encourages officers to be less concerned about measurable outcomes and more concerned about solving problems within their assignments. Engel (2004:209) argues that this type of supervisor holds values more consistent with a community policing approach to police work. The role of the supervisor is to provide support to officers so they can perform their jobs well.

The **supportive supervisor** is a person who seeks to support officers in the performance of their jobs and to serve as a potential buffer between officers and management. The supportive supervisor provides praise and rewards to officers and seeks to inspire them to perform their jobs. In addition, the supportive officer, according to Engel (2004:211), may be open to criticism when support serves as a shield against inappropriate behavior among officers and diminishes accountability.

Active supervisors exhibit behaviors that are consistent with positive views of subordinates and high activity for themselves. Active supervisors work with officers in the field. They spend much of their time working with officers and less time in the district or precinct. They are not overly concerned with global issues of crime and disorder. They are more concerned with doing, not talking or being inspirational. Officers view such supervisors as getting involved in their work and supporting them in their assignments when possible.

Which style is most common and most preferred? Engel (2004:13) found that the styles are equally distributed across the departments she surveyed, but when separating the departments, she found differences in the types of supervision styles found among police sergeants. No one style, according to Engel (2004:216) is preferred because we do not know which style leads to what outcomes. This research highlights what we have said before in this chapter:

Traditional supervisor: A supervisor who expects measurable outcomes and aggressive activities.

Innovative supervisor: A supervisor who encourages problem solving over measurable outcomes.

Supportive supervisor: A supervisor who supports employees and serves as a potential buffer between employees and management.

Active supervisors: A supervisor whose behaviors are consistent and predictable with positive views of employees and high activity for himself or herself.

You cannot think about supervision styles among criminal justice supervisors without thinking about what organizational goals you are trying to achieve. Engel (2004:216) states the following:

> Police administrators who wish to establish particular policies and procedures within their departments need to recognize the differences in first-line supervisors. None of the four supervisory styles identified in this research should be considered the "ideal" standard for police supervisors. Each style was associated with both benefits and problems. The appropriate supervisory style for departments will differ based on their *organizational goals* (our emphasis). Police administrators should recognize the need for better training of first-line supervisors to achieve these organizational goals.

For now, we can conclude that effective supervision occurs within criminal justice organizations when supervisors exhibit **technical skills** (specialized knowledge or expertise), **human skills** (the ability to work with and motivate people), and **conceptual skills** (the ability to analyze and diagnose complex situations) to complete the supervision function (Robbins and Judge, 2007:7), and these activities are linked to specific organizational goals. Further research will have to test and assess these competencies to provide prescriptions of value to criminal justice supervisors. These empirically based prescriptions will have value to all components within the criminal justice system: police, courts, and corrections.

Technical skills: Specialized knowledge or expertise exhibited by a supervisor.

Human skills: The ability of a supervisor to work with and motivate employees.

Conceptual skills: The ability of a supervisor to analyze and diagnose complex situations.

RIGHTS OF CRIMINAL JUSTICE EMPLOYEES

As public employees, criminal justice employees are guaranteed rights as defined by law. In addition, oftentimes these rights are also expressed through labor agreements with unions. It is not our intention to provide a thorough discussion of employee rights, but instead to provide the basic rights guaranteed to criminal justice employees by virtue of their employment. These rights directly impact the supervision and evaluation of employees. It can be said that these rights define, in part, the context in which criminal justice administration occurs. Every criminal justice administrator has to consider these rights in the day-to-day management and leadership of their organizations.

Most employee rights come from specific pieces of legislation designed to address a specific concern. The major pieces of legislation that are central to criminal justice organizations include the following:

Fair Labor Standards Act: This act defines minimum salary provisions for both public and private employees. It even has specific sections for police officers and firefighters. The intent of this piece of legislation is to make sure employees have access to additional pay and benefits when they work more than the standard 40 hours per week. This act has additional provisions that define how and when pay and benefits must be increased to match the service provided.

Section 1983: This piece of legislation provides opportunities for employees to sue employers for any deprivation of constitutional rights. It has been employed by police officers and corrections officers in lawsuits filed against police departments and correctional organizations.

Equal Pay Act: This act provides compensation to employees who believe their wages and benefits are not the same for similar type of work. It has been used by women in both police and correctional agencies who believe they are paid less even though their work activities are the same as their male counterparts.

Age Discrimination in Employment Act: This act is directed toward employees who are older than 40 and protects them in all phases of their employment: hiring, firing, receiving benefits, and other general conditions of employment.

Americans with Disabilities Act (ADA) of 1990: This major piece of legislation defines and provides similar opportunities for those persons with disabilities as those persons without disabilities. This piece of legislation has made a profound impact on criminal justice organizations because it now requires affirmative actions on the part of criminal justice administrators to remove barriers from employment within their agencies. One of the major impacts of this piece of legislation has been increased public accessibility to police departments and correctional institutions.

Family and Medical Leave Act (FMLA): This act provides an employee, under certain conditions, the right to take up to 12 weeks of unpaid, job-protected leave in a 12-month period to address family and/or medical concerns. The law stipulates the conditions under which FMLA can be used by employees and affects not only the employee but family members as well. It provides leaves of absences to care for oneself and those in the immediate family. It is most commonly used by women who have recently given birth, but it can be used under any condition that makes the employee unable to work or perform assigned duties.

Taken together, these pieces of legislation define, in part, the context within which criminal justice administrators perform their duties. These legislatively created laws do not cover the full panoply of rights and benefits that are provided to criminal justice employees, but they do reveal the major or primary laws that impact criminal justice administration. In addition, it must be stated that much of what guides the personnel and evaluation of employees is not only found in these laws but in labor agreements that take on the full force of law as well. It is easy to see within this context the importance of legislation and employee rights in the evaluation and supervision of criminal justice employees.

SUMMARY

Understand the difficulty in arriving at goal consensus within criminal justice organizations.

- Criminal justice organizations have many goals and these goals oftentimes contradict and conflict with one another. This makes it difficult for goal consensus within criminal justice organizations.

Comprehend the importance of organizational structure to employee supervision.

- Organizational structure plays a major role in how employee evaluation and supervision will occur.

Know the differences between the human service approach to employee supervision and the traditional model of employee supervision.

- The two primary models of employee supervision within criminal justice organizations are the traditional model of employee supervision and the human service model of employee supervision.

- The traditional model of employee supervision stresses the importance of rules and regulations and organizational control, while the human service model of employee supervision emphasizes both employee goals and organizational goals with less centralization, fewer and more clearly defined rules, and less bureaucracy.

Understand the difficulty in implementing a human service model of employee supervision within criminal justice organizations.

- Criminal justice administrators will face multiple challenges when trying to implement a human service model of employee supervision within criminal justice organizations, for example, conflicting goals, competing interests, and fiscal and organizational constraints.

Explain the guidelines for performance evaluation and supervision.

- Guidelines do exist for effective employee supervision within criminal justice organizations and they must fit the needs, goals, and structures of those organizations.

- Research has identified the primary work functions of criminal justice managers and the work roles of employees. In addition, some research has examined the styles of supervision found among criminal justice supervisors, but no one style is correct; it all depends on the types of organizational goals being pursued by the organization.

Know the major pieces of legislation that define employee rights.

- The major pieces of legislation that define employee rights are the following: Fair Labor Standards Act, Section 1983, Equal Pay Act, Age Discrimination in Employment Act, Americans with Disabilities Act, and the Family Medical Leave Act.

- These pieces of legislation define, in part, the context for criminal justice administrators as they evaluate and assess the performance of their employees.

Case Study: THE CORRECTIONAL SERGEANT'S DILEMMA

Correctional Sergeant Craig Rick was a seasoned veteran of the department of corrections. He had begun his career shortly after his discharge from the military. After spending his first ten years on the "line" and in various prisons as a correctional officer, he was promoted. Gone were the days of working back-to-back shifts as an officer and being forced to take overtime when other officers phoned in sick. His family was feeling the strain of him working as an officer, so he looked forward to the days when his shift schedule was more regular and predictable.

Sergeant Rick began his supervisory career on nights at the old Sampson Correctional Institution (SCI). SCI was one of the older prisons in the department of corrections. Sergeant Rick knew he was going to have to work nights for the first few years, given that he was a new sergeant in the institution. He didn't mind this; he was glad that he was not going to have to experience any more double shifts, and the routine was very predictable. What he didn't know was what the expectations of officers were on how he was to supervise them and what expectations his boss, the lieutenant, had for him as a supervisor.

In his first week on the job, he realized the difficulty of being a sergeant. He knew some of the officers from other prisons during his career as an officer. Some of these officers never got promoted and resented the fact that he got promoted, even though he had ten years of line experience in various prisons within the department. There were other officers who had fewer than five years as a correctional officer but were still promoted. Those officers caught more grief than other sergeants with more experience. The problem for the new sergeant was how to supervise someone he considered to be a friend.

This question became an issue for Sergeant Rick when he had to tell one of his close friends, Officer Johnson, that he could not have a day off outside the regular sequence of days off for officers. He tried to explain to his friend that the policy was there for a reason; if Rick violated it for Johnson, he opened himself up to criticisms of showing favoritism and would "catch shit" from his boss, Lieutenant Murray, with whom he'd had a difficult relationship in the short time he had been a sergeant. "But Craig, my kid is playing in the state baseball championship. How do I explain it to him that I can't make the game?" Sergeant Rick said if he could get someone to switch days with him, then there would be no problem. The fact was, however, that Officer Johnson had already made numerous requests to other officers for a switch in days off, even to the point of sweetening the pot by offering to pay $100 extra to the officer who switched with him.

Despite all his attempts, no one was going to switch with him, so his final appeal rested with Sergeant Rick. For Sergeant Rick, the decision was tough, but he stood his ground, not allowing Johnson to take the day off. When Officer Johnson did not show up for work, it was assumed that he had taken a sick day, but department policy required that a visit be made to the homes of officers who had "abused" the sick leave policy. Johnson was categorized as a sick leave abuser based on his previous year's usage of sick leave. If he was not home during the visit, he faced disciplinary charges for not reporting to work and for filing a fraudulent sick leave request form.

Sergeant Rick knew that if he went to the officer's home he would not be there. What should he do? He empathized with the officer because he had experienced similar issues with his children when they were growing up. However, Rick knew that his integrity and ability to effectively supervise all officers was being called into question. He also knew that other officers were watching how he was going to react in this situation; his boss, Lieutenant Murray, could be brought into the situation. As Rick expected, Officer Johnson was not at home when he visited, so when he did show up for work on his next working day, Sergeant Rick confronted him.

He informed Johnson that he was going to recommend that disciplinary action be taken against him by Lieutenant Murray. The officer, upon hearing the news, was infuriated and filed a union grievance against Sergeant Rick, stating that his actions were to "single" him out and that it was common practice in the prison to give people days off for "special circumstances." The lieutenant got involved in the dispute only as the person who would have to formally react to the allegations and mete out discipline to Johnson if justified. The lieutenant decided in favor of Officer Johnson and recommended no action be taken against him. Sergeant Rick was dismayed by the decision; he approached Murray to determine why his recommendation for discipline of Johnson was overturned. Rick felt he was being undermined by his immediate supervisor. He also felt that he was being tugged by two different loyalties: one to his former officers and one to his new supervisor. The lieutenant ended the matter by stating to him in confidence, "If you knew how to supervise officers you would not have gotten into this trouble. Before you bring this type of bullshit case to me again and it blows up in your face, like this one did, think of the consequences you will pay."

This experience made Sergeant Rick consider whether or not being a supervisor was worth all the

CASE STUDY—continued

hassles. He had spent days documenting how his actions were correct and consistent with departmental policy, only to have it all fall apart when reviewed by the lieutenant. He learned from the experience that keeping a low profile is what needed to be done. Don't rock the boat and don't make the lieutenant look bad. Supervision was about "covering your ass" and not holding line officers accountable.

Sergeant Rick rose to the rank of correctional lieutenant and retired under a cloud after serving twenty years with the department. He never was able to resolve the dilemma of serving two sometimes-competing interests as a correctional supervisor. Other supervisors labeled him as "mushroom Rick." Similar to a mushroom, he wanted to be kept in the dark, especially regarding officer improprieties. This supervision style finally blew up on him when some officers were caught holding "gladiator games" among rival gangs in the prison and betting huge sums of money, all on his watch. An external investigation by the state's watchdog group for prisons found that mismanagement and poor supervision were at the heart of problems in SCI prison. They recommended that all first-line supervisors be given more training on how to supervise and that accountability standards be implemented. Sergeant Rick's supervisory practices were offered as examples of how not to supervise correctional officers.

CASE STUDY QUESTIONS

1. Was Sergeant Rick wrong in referring the correctional officer for discipline? How could he have handled it differently?
2. What type of training would have assisted Sergeant Rick in his supervision of the officer?
3. Is there such a thing as supervisor burnout? If so, what would you do to address it?

 # Think like an Administrator

There has been an appeal to more objective and performance-based evaluation of employees within criminal justice organizations since 2000. For criminal justice administrators, the task of employee evaluation is wrought with many challenges, especially the evaluation of a difficult employee. As noted in the Work Perspective in this chapter, consistency and fair applications of policies and procedures are critical to effective employee supervision. How does this play out with a difficult employee?

Take the following example of a correctional employee who works in a jail setting. This is an employee who is indifferent to being a correctional officer, transferred to the jail due to poor performance on the road as a deputy sheriff, has had disciplinary problems in the past, and has stated he dislikes working in the jail. As a jail administrator, this employee can be assessed based on his adherence or nonadherence to basic principles of "direct supervision," which is how all employees are evaluated in the jail. Direct supervision is based on the premise that the management of jail prisoners is best when there is an active participation of correctional officers within housing units. It is a management style that promotes greater interaction between the officer and prisoners to make the jail safe and secure. This means interacting with prisoners and being present in and around the inmate population during the shift. This also means getting to know the particulars and nuances of prisoners and being proactive with them. Yet, the officer under

---

THINK LIKE AN ADMINISTRATOR—continued

question is oftentimes observed following none of these principles and practices. In fact, he is most often seen sitting at his control desk with his feet up and having limited or no interactions with prisoners.

1. Will there be an impact on officer morale if poor performance of the officer is not corrected?
2. How will prisoners react to the officer's poor performance?
3. How will the safety and well-being of staff and prisoners be affected by the officer's poor performance?
4. What immediate steps should be taken by the jail administrator?
5. How would progressive discipline be addressed in this case?
6. In this example, a distinction is being made between deputy sheriff ("on the road") and being a correctional officer in the jail. The placement in the jail was a punishment for poor performance on the road. What do you think about this as a practice in jails among sheriffs?
7. How does the union and labor agreement affect the decision making in this example?

FOR DISCUSSION

1. Will goal consensus in criminal justice organizations ever be possible? What are the major obstacles and disadvantages to having goal consensus in criminal justice organizations?

2. This chapter discusses the importance of structure to the delivery of criminal justice services. Can police organizations or prisons, for example, be less formal and more decentralized in their structures? Why or why not?

3. What are some major problems with implementing the ideas of a human service model of employee supervision in criminal justice organizations?

4. Given the nature of criminal justice organizations is the traditional model of employee supervision the best possible choice?

FOR FURTHER READING

Bayley, D. H. *Police for the Future.* New York: Oxford University Press, 1994.

Bennett, W., and Hess, K. *Management and Supervision in Law Enforcement.* 5th ed. Belmont, CA: Thomson Publishing Company, 2007.

Bolman, L., and Deal, T. *Reframing Organizations: Artistry, Choice, and Leadership.* 3rd ed. San Francisco: Jossey-Bass, 2003.

Fyfe, J., Greene, J., Walsh, W., Wilson, O., and McLaren, R. *Police Administration*. 5th ed. New York: McGraw-Hill, 1997.

Oettmeier, T. N., and Wycoff, M. A. *Personnel Performance Evaluations in the Community Policing Context*. Washington, DC: U.S. Department of Justice, 1998.

Peak, K. J., Gaines, L. K., and Glensor, R. W. *Police Supervision and Management: In an Era of Community Policing*. 2nd ed. Upper Saddle River, NJ: Prentice-Hall, 2004.

Peak, K. *Justice Administration: Police, Courts, and Corrections Management*. 5th Edition. Upper Saddle River, NJ: Prentice-Hall, 2007.

Trojanowicz, R., Kappeler, V. E., Gaines, L. K., and Bucqueroux, B. *Community Policing: A Contemporary Perspective*. 2nd ed. Cincinnati, OH: Anderson, 1998.

Wilson, J. Q. *Bureaucracy: What Government Agencies Do and Why They Do It*. Glenview, IL: Basic Books, 2000.

Part III

Group Behavior in Criminal Justice Organizations

Criminal justice organizations employ people, but people work in groups. Group behavior is fundamental in all organizations. Criminal justice organizations are no different. In fact, some of the best research in criminal justice organizations has been done on group behavior. This part of the book examines three aspects of group behavior: occupational socialization, power and political behavior, and organizational conflict.

Occupational socialization within criminal justice organizations is examined in Chapter 9. The socialization of police officers has been the topic of many research efforts and it is revealing and powerful. Implications from this research directly affect how police administrators lead and manage their organizations. An analysis of occupational socialization reveals the reality of the work situation and both the strengths and limitations of criminal justice administrators.

Power and political behavior are examined in Chapter 10. The saying, "It is all politics," has a double meaning for public agencies like criminal justice organizations. On the one hand, the political process is how criminal justice administrators accomplish things, having both internal and external meanings. Too often, politics is understood as dirty word, but in the world of the criminal justice administrator, it is just a process that moves agencies forward.

In addition, politics understood this way also refers to relationships with others outside the organization, for example, elected officials and other interested parties. On the other hand, politics is also understood as favoritism, cronyism, and misuse of authority. This is the "bad side" of politics as applied to criminal justice administration. Many criminal justice employees understand this definition of politics as a reality they face every day, yet its prevalence may not be as common as they might think.

The final chapter in this section explores organizational conflict. Organizational conflict is examined as inevitable, given the complexity and diversity of criminal justice employees and their organizations. Chapter 11 highlights the importance of managing organizational conflict. Criminal justice administrators seek to manage organizational conflict, not to eradicate it. Well-led and well-managed criminal justice organizations have acceptable levels of organizational conflict.

CHAPTER 9

Occupational Socialization

LEARNING OBJECTIVES

After reading this chapter, the students will have achieved the following objectives:

- Understand occupational socialization.
- Understand the basic precepts of organizational culture.
- Understand the socialization process as it applies to criminal justice agencies.
- Be able to discuss the problems in the socialization process in criminal justice agencies.
- Understand the basic strategies for socialization.

VIGNETTE

Socialization is a natural process that takes place with all of us from infancy. We learn social rules, attitudes, and appropriate behaviors from our parents, extended family, and friends and later from social institutions such as schools and churches. Our early social learning may direct us to go on to college, join the military, or, at the other extreme, may direct us to a career in crime. In college, you may have chosen a major based in part on your earlier social learning. As a student, you will have your beliefs, attitudes, and social behaviors altered through your interactions with professors and fellow students. After college, most students will enter an occupation.

Values: Desirable group goals that are set because of a shared group; measured by the investment of resources toward the goals.

The occupation one enters is, in part, a function of prior social learning. You will likely choose a profession that seems to be in line with your **values** and beliefs. After entering your chosen profession, you will be further socialized by formal training, on-the-job training, and your interactions with coworkers. If you are successful in your chosen profession, it is because you have met the expectations of the profession—you have been socialized properly. But here is where it all gets murky. To be considered a success, you have to meet the expectations of bosses and peers, which are often in conflict. If you are successful, it will be due, in part, to your ability to balance the socialization processes of more than one group within your work environment. Oddly enough, this may be the most important life skill you will learn while attending college.

In the criminal justice system, practitioners have a great deal of autonomy and a great deal of power. A significant problem for criminal justice executives is to assure that the practitioners in their agencies work within the scope of their legitimate authority—that is, they perform their duties by the rules and within ethical boundaries.

Staff members work without much direct supervision, so executives have little choice but to hope that the staff members are socialized in accordance with the dominant values of the organization. In fact, most criminal justice agency executives make a great effort to impose desirable beliefs, attitudes, and practices on agency members. We have seen in earlier chapters that criminal justice practitioners who work directly with clients have different perspectives on how to get the job done compared to the managers who write policy. In the real world, differences in activities are ignored if the outcomes benefit organizational goals or image. If the outcomes harm the organization and/or manifest in corrupt activities, agency executives are forced to take punitive actions against rule breakers as a formal socialization mechanism. In the end, the socialization process is management's most important tool to promote a professional culture throughout the organization.

Almost all organizations have processes for converting people into organizational members with appropriate attitudes and behaviors. The most common formal methods of occupational socialization include recruiting individuals who will "fit" into the organization, formal education and training, and forms of on-the-job training. For example, almost all states require local and state law enforcement recruits to attend a lengthy police academy before entering the service. All federal law enforcement and federal bureau of prison agents are subjected to intensive preservice training. In a growing number of states, preservice academies are required for correctional officers in state and local service. In addition, supervision—the process that governs the activities and behaviors of organizational members—is a process of ongoing occupational socialization. However, when recruits leave their respective academies and begin their jobs, they are subjected to an informal socialization process imposed by peers attempting to perpetuate the culture of their work world.

Lawyers, prosecuting attorneys, and judges, however, are not subject to rigorous preservice training and are socialized primarily through the judicial culture. All organizations have cultures that rely on the beliefs, activities, and behaviors of their members. Forces located in the culture impose the process of informal socialization. In this chapter, we begin by discussing organizational culture and its impact on members. We then discuss the process of formal occupational socialization in criminal justice agencies. We also cover the methods by which agency administrators can manage and lead the development of the agency's culture in order to impose some degree of influence over the informal socialization process.

OCCUPATIONAL SOCIALIZATION

Occupational socialization is the process by which a person acquires the attitudes values, and behaviors of an ongoing occupational social system. It is a continuous process that includes both intentional influences, such as training, and unintentional influences, such as locker room or work group cultures. The attitudes, values, and behaviors acquired as a result of occupational socialization can include those regarded as appropriate and legitimate for the job, as well as those that are illegitimate and even illegal. Thus, judges may learn appropriate sentence lengths for offenders, but judges convicted in the 1986–1988 Greylord investigations in Chicago argued that they also learned to accept bribes because of the shared view that they were underpaid compared with their lawyer peers.

Occupational socialization: The process by which a person acquires the attitudes and behaviors of an ongoing occupational social system.

Similarly, police learn how to enforce the law, but even "good" cops learn to bend or reinterpret the rules to perform their duties. Also, correctional professionals bend the rules to, in their view, get the job done. The practice of bending the rules with impunity can lead to **corruption** for personal gain and profit. When Officer Robert Leuci (whose story was told in the movie *Prince of the City*) was collecting evidence on police corruption in New York City for the Knapp Commission in the early 1970s, he also testified about giving drugs to addicted informants in exchange for information, and some believe he committed many more serious crimes (Dershowitz, 1983).

Corruption: Violating rules, policies, and ethical considerations for personal gain.

Habitual behaviors of individuals in organizations, both good and bad, persist as long as the attitudes, beliefs, perceptions, habits, and expectations of organizational members remain constant. This consistency is particularly evident in criminal justice organizations where the practices of police officers and prison staff, for example, often seem unchanging and even resistant to change efforts. One common assessment of legal efforts to change criminal justice organizations is that the courts seem more efficient at bringing about procedural rather than substantive change. Prison discipline hearings, for example, continue to be characterized as dispositional rather than adjudicatory despite case law requiring impartial, trial-like hearings. How can we account for the fact that almost all inmates are found guilty by prison disciplinary boards? Although inmate behavior is probably the most important determining factor, part of the explanation may also be found in the concept of organizational role. Katz and Kahn (1978) give the social-psychological concept of role a central place in their theory of organizations. For them, organizations are best understood as systems of roles. These roles link the individual to the organization and assure its continued stability.

ORGANIZATIONAL CULTURE

The behaviors of individual members of an organization, as well as of the organization itself, are a product of the organization's culture and also create its culture. An **organizational culture** can be described briefly as a set of assumptions and beliefs shared by members of an organization. Moreover, the assumptions and beliefs create language, symbols, and folklore and ultimately serve to direct the behaviors of the organizational members, especially in response to work-related problems. Edgar Schein (2004) summarizes common meanings of organizational culture, which include observed behavioral regularities, such as language, patterns of interactions, rituals, and norms that evolve in working groups; dominant goals espoused by an organization, such as rehabilitation and crime prevention, as well as the philosophy of the organization toward employees or clients; rules of the game for getting along in the organization's social system; and the feeling or climate created in an organization by the way employees are managed or interact. Arguing that these common meanings may reflect an organization's culture but are not the essence of the culture, Schein (2004:17) defines organizational culture as a pattern of basic assumptions—invented, discovered, or developed by a group as it learns to cope with its problems of

Organizational culture: A set of assumptions and beliefs shared by the members of an organization.

external adaptation and internal integration—that has worked well enough to be considered valid and, therefore, to be taught to new members as the correct way to perceive, think, and feel in relation to those problems. In other words, the process of socialization in an organization serves to impose the organization's patterns of basic assumptions on its new members.

Understanding an organization's culture and its socialization process, especially in a large or complex organization, is a difficult task. It is therefore instructive to begin by reviewing the basics of culture in the broadest sense. *Culture* is often defined as the complex whole of a society and includes knowledge, belief, art, laws, morals, customs, and other capabilities and routines acquired by the society's members (Tylor, 1958). This is a rather standard definition of culture —one, however, that does not provide an understanding of its essence. An alternate view describes culture (much like Schein does) as problem solving, a pattern of basic assumptions invented by a group as it learns to cope with problems of external adaptation and internal integration:

> Whenever people face recurring problems, cultural patterns evolve to provide a ready-made solution. This does not mean that it is the best or only solution, merely that the culture develops a set of standard patterns for dealing with common problems.... The more frequently a society relies upon its ready-made solutions, the more deeply entrenched the culture (Brinkerhoff and White, 1991:58).

Societies develop language to solve the problem of communicating, and language thus becomes the framework for culture. Groups also have desirable goals that are expressed as values. **Norms** evolve specifying what people should or should not do. Also, **folkways** (standard ways of doing things), **mores** (strong views of right and wrong), and *laws* (**codified mores** enforced by the group) develop. Once a society or group has developed its culture—a set of ready-made answers or established patterns, language, beliefs, behaviors, to solve its problems—it attempts to perpetuate the culture. The process of perpetuating conformity to the established culture, *social control*, provides a series of *sanctions*—rewards and punishments—for individual conformity or nonconformity to established behavioral patterns, language, mores, folkways, and laws. Most sanctions are informal because they are not codified and are applied in daily interactions between individuals. Social or informal sanctions can be more powerful than legal sanctions. *Formal sanctions* are abstract and stem from impersonal sources. **Social or informal sanctions**, such as peer pressure, however, can be personal and evoked by sources valued by an individual receiving sanction. Rewards from supervisors, such as the "corrections officer of the month" for meritorious performance, will not have the same influence on officers in general as the immediate day-to-day and often subtle pressures from peers. In spite of attempts at social control, societies generally have *subcultures,* groups that have their own beliefs and norms while sharing those of the dominant culture. *Countercultures,* groups whose shared beliefs and values differ substantially from those of the dominant culture, typically exist within any large society.

Norms: Specify what group members should or should not do.

Folkways: Established ways of doing things, how things have always been done, or common practice.

Mores: Strong views of right and wrong, not necessarily codified.

Codified mores: Rules and laws that are written and published, such as in memos or policy manuals, or union contracts.

Social or informal sanctions: Peer disapproval of a group member manifested by some form of social punishment, such as being subjected to gossip, verbal reprimand, being ignored, or being excluded from social activities.

Organizations can be considered micro-societies within which distinct cultures emerge. The mixture of individuals who belong to any organization create —through their attempts to solve organizational and personal problems or achieve organizational or personal goals—sets of ready-made solutions, a shared language, folkways, and mores unique to the organization. The pivotal question for an organization is how the culture is formed, what forces are critical in forming the culture, how the cultural arrangements impact the organizational goals, and how and to what extent administrators can influence the cultural arrangement of their agency.

The culture of an organization is first impacted by problems of external adaptation—problems imposed by demands, constraints, and pressures from its environment (Schein, 2004). If those problems are recurring ones, the organization will attempt to develop ready-made solutions to meet them. Organizations, however, face more problems than those explicitly identified as their mission. For example, all organizations also strive to acquire status and respectability, grow and garner resources, set and expand boundaries, control environmental forces, and, when the chips are down, survive.

Police, for example, are dramatized as crime fighters, but the duties of law enforcement officers include crime prevention, traffic and parking regulations, and a host of other problems that the public faces and expects law enforcement agencies to solve. Courts attempt to process criminal offenders efficiently while seeing that rules of justice and fairness are followed. Corrections carry out the role of criminal punishment while meeting the basic physical and social needs of offenders. The criminal justice system has been assigned aspects of social control that society feels it cannot solve directly. The criminal justice system attempts to meet three missions: crime control, justice, and provision of forms of social service (Gains and Kappler, 2005; Sherman and Hawkins, 1981). Each component of the criminal justice system attempts to solve a different aspect of the overall problem-solving mandate, but it also shares to a greater or lesser extent the burden of all three functions. Each component has developed its unique set of ready-made solutions and patterns of basic assumptions to cope with or solve its problems, along with its language, norms, mores, and the like. In other words, each component of the system has its own unique culture.

Likewise, each member of an organization also attempts to meet personal goals and needs (solve problems) within the framework of the organization. For example, each member shares, to a greater or lesser extent, an economic need and the needs to belong and be respected, to acquire status and power, and to be considered successful. Although individuals can meet their needs directly through the formal structure of the organization by carrying out its objectives, they often fulfill these needs through the informal structure or social system that develops within the organization.

Large organizations have hierarchies and a range of component agencies. Each component agency and level of the hierarchy has a different set of problems to solve, which in turn requires the development of a set of ready-made solutions and assumptions. Therefore, each component or hierarchical level of an organization will be a subculture of the greater organizational culture. Because each component of a large organization faces different problems of external adaptation, the process of internal integration evolves under a different set of conditions. In Chapter 3, for example, it was argued that large organizations decouple because top administrators and work process functionaries exist in different environments and face different sets of demands and constraints. In short, administrators and operational staff have different sets of problems to solve; each group, therefore, creates its own set of ready-made solutions and acceptable patterns, resulting in different subcultures of the organization.

There are many subcultures within the criminal justice system and its component agencies. Within correctional systems, some degree of conflict usually exists between the treatment and custody staffs. An important component of the conflict is the cultural difference that arises from the different set of problems each group has been assigned to solve. Detective work is usually viewed as having a higher-order status because detectives do not deal with typical street-cop problems. Rather, the problems they solve are cerebral in nature—they investigate, interact directly and often with members of the prosecutor's staff, are assigned office space, and wear suits and ties to set them apart. Judges as well as prosecuting and defense attorneys work in a world almost foreign to most criminal justice practitioners. Sophisticated legal-based expertise and knowledge symbolized by the legalistic language set this subculture apart from other criminal justice system subcultures. Currently, most large law enforcement agencies have divisions dedicated to homeland security that are responsible for antiterrorism efforts. Homeland security units have duties and require expertise that sets them apart from other units in their agency. The administrative/management culture is identified by the constant search for numbers and statistics. Administrators must solve the problem of "accountability" to the public and political systems, and numbers provide the solution. To the "street-level bureaucrats" (Lipsky, 1980)—the correctional officers, police officers, probation and parole officers who carry out the work—numbers may have little value and are viewed as "red tape." The intentional filtering of communication upward and downward through the chain of command (discussed in Chapter 4) is an artifact of organizational culture. Middle managers screen and reinterpret directives to make them "fit" into the established routines developed to solve problems. Conversely, information in reports on activities sent upward through the chain of command is often slanted to provide the appearance of conformity to management directives by the street-level bureaucrats. This practice is a common artifact of most organizations, especially criminal justice agencies, where organizational members believe that rules must be violated to get the job done.

The cultural milieu of an organization is also impacted by the mix of cultures imported by its personnel. Relatively small organizations, such as small local jails, courts, or police departments, may hire staff from the local community with a homogeneous culture. In this case, it is likely that the agency's organizational culture will be similarly homogeneous and cultural conflict will be minimal. However, large agencies that recruit personnel from urban areas with heterogeneous cultures will absorb a mix of individuals from different ethnic groups, socioeconomic groups, and a growing number of women who may bring with them somewhat different mores and established patterns of problem solving that create misunderstandings and conflict with the male-dominated system. The mix of cultures can also conflict with a traditional and well-established formal structure that is supported by and is congruent with the prevailing management culture. With the influx of women into the criminal justice system, management is held responsible via regulations evolving out of federal equal opportunity guidelines that address organizational hostilities toward women and minorities. The implications clearly make management responsible for controlling and impacting the culture of the organization to create an accommodating or nonhostile culture for women and minorities.

The major role of top-level administrators is to define the organization's mission and identify the problem or problems it has been mandated to solve. Moreover, lower-order problems must be assigned to levels of the hierarchy, line and staff functionaries, and subcomponents of the system. Management then requires that the problems and means to solve the problems be identified and spelled out with clarity and that the ready-made solutions or routines be followed. In other words, the task of management is to perpetuate its version of the organizational culture: the assumptions about the organization's role, the sub-roles of individual members, and how the roles are to be carried out. Role giving and taking include the organization's philosophy, norms, laws, expected observable behaviors, and language. Managing the culture is, for most administrators, a hidden agenda (often from themselves as well) as they attempt to direct and control the organization by directing and controlling the behaviors of its members.

Administrators typically attempt to control the behavior of agency staff through the structural frame of their systems (Bolman and Deal, 2003). Control efforts are based on training, policies and procedures, supervisory structures, and formal sanctions that can be imposed to ensure conformity. Again, the example of integrating minorities and women into the organization clearly manifests the administrator's reliance on the formal structure to impact cultural variables. Policies, procedures, rules, and regulations are typically written to protect the interests of women and minority staff. For example, a police agency hired several women and minorities; these new employees broke through the "glass ceiling" as the result of a court order that imposed changes in hiring and promotional practices. A number of women were appointed to administrative posts within the structural frame of the agency (King, 2005).

Rules usually attempt to control, if not ban, behaviors, such as offensive language, that would make life in the agency difficult for women and minorities. One state department of corrections in the Midwest defines any statement, comment, or communication that can be construed to have sexual content as sexual harassment. Formal sanctions are also created to prevent organizational members from violating policies, rules, and regulations that were created to protect minority groups. Currently, the formal occupational socialization process includes hiring women and minorities and providing diversity training to sensitize staff to ethnic and gender differences to promote positive relationships across ethnic and gender lines.

Clearly, administrators do impact an organization's culture through formal administrative mechanisms. However, the informal structure of an organization also impacts powerfully on its culture. First, staff may develop methods that differ from the formally prescribed methods to solve the problems assigned to them. The informal methods of achieving the agency's objectives may be viewed by staff as a better way to operate. The frontline police or corrections officer, acting as a street-level bureaucrat (Lipsky, 2002), creates his or her own unwritten policies and procedures in response to the immediate problems he or she faces in the task environment. Corrections officers may ignore illicit activities on the part of inmate leaders who, in return, will help maintain order in their cell blocks, and police officers develop methods to circumvent rules of evidence to solve and favorably prosecute a criminal case. The informal methods adopted may also fit the staff's own skills, personal needs, value preferences, and the need for behavioral expression. While new staff members are indoctrinated into the formal culture through mechanisms provided by the organization, the new staff members are also subjected to informal socialization and role giving by veteran staff. Newly trained staff are commonly told to "forget everything they learned at the academy" because the real training takes place in the field. Rites of passage await the rookie or the "new fish" employee. They serve to both test and sanction the newcomer to begin the informal socialization process.

Hence, an organization's culture results from pressures from the formal structure to solve organizational problems in ways prescribed by administrators and well-established patterns of problem solving developed by staff that differ from the formal prescriptions and also meet the personal needs of the staff. For organizations with a long history, such as the agencies of the criminal justice system, the cultural pattern found in both the informal and formal structures is deeply entrenched. The pattern of problem solving and assumptions about the world in which the organization is immersed are not easily altered without perceived dramatic changes such as a prison riot or a public investigation into corruption charges. A deeply entrenched organizational culture and its powerful socialization process will cause behavior in organizations to remain remarkably stable despite the frequent turnover of personnel.

Role behavior is the visible outcome of cultural constraints. Katz and Kahn (1978) define role behavior "as the recurring actions of an individual that are appropriately related to the repetitive activities of others so as to yield a predictable outcome." In addition, they view *role behavior* as a function of social setting rather than the individual personalities of people in organizations. Role theorists, therefore, suggest that workers engage in both formal and informal learning processes to become aware of and committed to behavioral norms that are seen as appropriate for their jobs.

Work Perspective: SO YOU WANT TO BE A TRAINING DIRECTOR

After working for eighteen years as a deputy sheriff in many assignments—road patrol, criminal investigations, street crime units, undercover narcotics, and organized crime—and also serving as a supervisor over those same units as a sergeant, lieutenant, and captain, the sheriff promoted this writer to the position of training director. I accepted the position even though I considered being out on the street more fun and interesting. However, what the training director's job lacked in fun was made up by its complexity and challenges.

The challenges facing a training division of a large agency (over 6,000 employees) that had decided to change the legalistic style or culture to a community policing service approach were tremendous. The strategic planning for such a complex set of objectives was a continuously evolving process. Conflicts escalated to open warfare on a monthly basis due in part to a complicated data-driven accountability process to direct and manage department personnel. The public safety responsibilities included policing and fire contracts in fifteen cities, a major ocean port, an international airport, civil process servers, court services, and five detention facilities that, on average, housed over 5,000 inmates daily. The county had a very diverse population of over one million full-time residents and several million visitors annually. The conflicts that arose created many training paradoxes.

The executive officers wanted to push the decision making about crime-prevention techniques down the chain of command to the sergeants and deputies, but they were not willing to allow failure. The monthly accountability meetings required the district commanders to review their efforts, both successful and unsuccessful, on crime prevention, case clearance, and community issues before the sheriff and the senior staff. The pressure was enormous and intentional. When asked why a particular operation failed to achieve the desired result, many times the commanders, rather than placing the blame on planning or a lack of supervision, would suggest that it was a training problem. Regardless of whether it was a deputy training deficiency, a planning deficiency, or a supervision breakdown, all of the circumstances had training ramifications. Clearly, one of the major training needs in this environment was the executive officers' new role in mentoring as well as motivating the people in their line of authority to be creative in their approach to problem solving. The true training officers in any police agency are the sergeants, and many agencies do not devote enough time or funds to train them. Typically, newly promoted sergeants get one week of training in transition to their new duties. The new ser-

geants attempt to learn their new policy responsibilities from other senior sergeants; hence, their effectiveness is dependent on these informal relationships. Sergeants are the key to socializing new employees and are central in any attempt to change the culture of an agency.

Two significant problems emerged in corrections during this writer's first year as training director. First, the sheriff requested recommendations about how the agency could reduce the violence problems in the jails. The level of violence was high in two categories: inmate-on-inmate and inmate-on-officer. This was scrutinized in our data analysis because of the excessive overtime, sick leave health care costs due to injuries, and civil lawsuits. The jails were being monitored by the federal courts due to an earlier overcrowding problem, and the assigned monitors were openly critical. After reviewing several large jail systems' efforts to control the problems and evaluating our jail's event reports of the prior two years, I concluded that the majority of the confrontations leading to injury had occurred in the mental health unit. Based on these findings, I made a series of recommendations for policy changes, including training requirements, equipment, and protocols to reduce the injuries.

A significant recommendation was made that pepper foam should be utilized in the jail in the use of force continuum to reduce injuries to both inmates and staff. It was also recommended that any corrections deputy bidding for a job in the mental health unit must be certified in mental health custodial techniques. These recommendations started another full-scale war in our monthly accountability meetings. The corrections commander stated that as long as he was at the agency, there would be no use of pepper foam in "his" jail. Also, the commander raised another major hazard in that the jobs were bid by union contract seniority, and it would take negotiations to get the union on board. This writer had his executive staff review the research results of several studies indicating that multiple large jail systems had successfully reduced their number of violence injuries by up to 50 percent by including the use of pepper foam in their use of force continuum. The policy was implemented, and the results were better than had been reported around the country. The use of pepper foam was extensive in the initial stage of its use but it was used more judiciously in the latter stages of the program. The high initial use of pepper foam was anticipated because the research had shown this trend nationwide. Also, after the initial use of pepper foam, inmates became compliant and the rate of violence decreased. The rate of violence in our jail system quickly fell below the national average.

WORK PERSPECTIVE—continued

The primary reason the results were better than the national average was the required certification program in mental health designed by consultants in mental health, corrections, in cooperation with the training division, and members of the School of Criminology at the local university. The program consisted of forty hours of intense training on managing and supervising mentally ill inmates. The program was offered to other corrections agencies in the South Florida area. The department followed the progress of the detention deputies and surveyed corrections deputies' perceptions of the merits of the mental health training. They stated that the regular academy training was very good but that it did not in any way prepare them to manage mentally ill inmates. However, the deputies felt that the certification program helped them better understand mental illness and to supervise mentally ill inmates. The training was expensive to offer initially but it has reimbursed the agency many times over with reduced liability and greater safety for inmates and employees.

The preceding vignette gives examples of problems the training director faces. To help give a more complete picture of the responsibilities of the training director, the following list spells out an abbreviated set of director's objectives:

1. Designing the socialization and training processes for new employees in all of the positions: deputy sheriff, correction deputy, dispatcher, civil process server, fleet control personnel, victim advocate, clerical personnel, child protection officers, and so on. These new hires must be trained in the policies and procedures of the agency as well as any state or accrediting agency requirements for the position.

2. Monitor the renewal dates and requirements of certification for each specialized category of employee, such as bomb squad, SWAT, and CPR training. Each district commander must be notified of the pending dates in order to plan for the employee replacement during the required training.

3. Certify that State of Florida requirements have been met by each sworn officer completing mandatory retraining in high-liability areas, such as firearms, driving, and so on. The state also requires retraining in ethics, human diversity, changes in traffic statutes, and Florida criminal law.

4. Provide training in the changing federal law, evolving case law regarding search and seizure, asset forfeiture, and so on.

5. Provide training in the new role of local law enforcement (Homeland Security): responding to terrorist events, new protocols regarding sharing intelligence, and joint command training in emergency response to terrorist events.

6. Develop leadership training in all supervision positions.

7. Monitor the trends in policy and procedure noncompliance as sanctioned by the department of professional compliance, and adjust training accordingly.

8. Research the best practices and policies, and review all of the proposed policies prior to the sheriff's review.

9. Evaluate the personnel assigned to the training division and also evaluate any outside consultants or trainers that were utilized.

10. Accommodate special training requests from other commanders, when possible. For example, internal affairs wanted training to place emphasis on Truthfulness in Ethics training because many deputies were losing their jobs over minor violations of policy because they lied or withheld the truth when questioned under oath. Police officers may lose their State of Florida Certification for untruthfulness.

11. Prepare the annual training budget.

12. Assume any other duties as assigned by the sheriff.

SOURCE: Dr. James Chinn, Director of Training, Broward County, Florida, Sheriff's Department, Retired. Presently, Dr. Chinn is an Instructor at the School of Criminology/Criminal Justice, at Florida Atlantic University.

This socialization hypothesis, however, is not the only explanation for the shared sets of behaviors that appear to be associated with some occupations. Some researchers have suggested that occupational behaviors are a function of personality rather than socialization—that is, some occupations may attract certain types of people. Research on the working personality of the police has been influenced by this perspective.

Some researchers have argued that the personality traits of individual police officers differ from those of the general public prior to their entering the police field (Rokeach, Miller, and Snyder, 1971). Police work has been said to attract recruits who are more authoritarian, more cynical, and more oriented toward excitement than the public at large. This explanation of police behavior is, however, currently out of favor. A number of studies have failed to find significant differences in the attitudes of police officer recruits and the general public, and the original research has been criticized for methodological shortcomings (see Bennett, 1984). Researchers continue to utilize the socialization model that focuses on the nature of police work itself and the process by which novices are recruited from the general public and become experienced officers. More current research suggests that ethnic and gender backgrounds may make a difference in the decision to make arrests. White officers were more likely to make arrests under similar circumstances (Brown and Frank, 2006), whereas African Americans and women correctional officers were less control-oriented than their white male counterparts (Gordon, 2005).

THE SOCIALIZATION PROCESS

A study of judges illustrates the process of socialization within the federal judiciary. Through in-depth interviews with federal judges, Carp and Wheeler (1972) were able to describe the process by which a lawyer becomes an experienced trial judge. Legal training itself is a lengthy and intense socialization experience. Still, the authors found that novice judges were ill prepared for the problems they faced. The problems encountered by new judges fell into three categories: legal, administrative, and psychological. The first of these problems arose because of the limited legal experience of the judges. Most had come from firms dealing primarily with civil suits, and the most common problem of these judges was ignorance of criminal law. The second complaint was heavy caseloads and difficulty in preventing backlogs. Finally, the judges complained of the psychological stresses of loneliness, of maintaining judicial bearing on and off the bench, and of local pressures in decision making.

The research described a variety of formal and informal mechanisms for addressing these problems. The most conspicuous source of formal socialization is the new judges' seminars sponsored by the federal judicial center in Washington, DC. Although the purpose of these seminars is formal education through speakers and workshops, the judges noted that their primary benefit was informal discussions with other judges. Although less obvious, the most potent source of socialization for new judges was practicing judges in the same court, as well as court staff.

Carp and Wheeler highlight the distinctive local nature of judicial socialization and its resulting perpetuation of local and regional differences in the judiciary. Senior judges perpetuated local procedures and attitudes by providing their junior colleagues with legal information, administrative advice, and personal reassurances. Likewise, local attorneys with particular specialties often influenced novice judges with limited knowledge in these areas.

One judge described the net result of the socialization process as membership in a fraternal organization characterized by mutual respect and a feeling of brotherhood. (There were no female judges in the study.) Similarly, Neubauer (1996) describes the "courtroom work group" that forms around the judge as the dominant figure and is influenced by the remaining key actors, such as the district attorney, bailiff, defense attorneys, and so forth. While the judge is the dominant figure in the work group, all members impose the work group culture on new members.

STAGES OF SOCIALIZATION

The case of judicial socialization calls our attention to several factors important in the transmission of organizational roles. In particular, socialization is a *process*. A model of socialization, therefore, must deal not only with the substantive dimension of the roles but also with change over time and the nature of the influences producing change. The literature on socialization generally divides the process of change into three distinct stages: anticipatory, formal, and informal.

The socialization process begins before an individual enters an occupation. In this stage of *anticipatory socialization*, those considering a particular field look forward to the demands and expectations of their future job. They begin to adopt attitudes and values they believe are consistent with the occupation, and they come to view themselves as members of a group. During this stage, individuals are influenced by two main reference groups. First, those tangential to the occupation, such as friends and family, may transmit their views of the job. For example, a lawyer seeking to join the judiciary may be influenced by family members' views of the job's status. Second, members of the occupation may directly transmit information about the job. Lawyers working with judges gain insight into what is perceived as appropriate or inappropriate behavior for a member of the judiciary. Along with these sources of influence, both the amount of time in the anticipatory stage and the accuracy of information received affect the adoption of organizational roles.

Most organizations are cognizant of anticipatory socialization and attempt to recruit individuals who "fit" into their systems by setting standards and qualifications for new recruits. For example, many law enforcement agencies prefer or require a two- or four-year college degree and will give preference to individuals who have served successfully in the military. It is assumed that the higher education creates a pool of applicants who have had the discipline to complete a degree and have the basic intellectual skill to carry out their prescribed duties. A term in the military is assumed to have produced disciplined individuals and conditioned them to "fit" into the paramilitary structure of large correctional or law enforcement agencies. Also, agencies typically do extensive background checks on applicants and often subject them to rigorous interviews and psychological screening to ensure the candidates for positions are physically, morally, and psychologically fit for a law enforcement or correctional career. Moreover, the interviews and background checks attempt to identify individuals who have a normative commitment to the profession (Jones, 2006). The major qualification for practicing law or becoming a prosecutor or judge is a law degree and the ability to pass a state bar exam. This effort presumes a basic knowledge of law and sufficient intellectual skills to practice.

When a person joins a particular occupation, the second stage, *formal socialization*, usually occurs. This is generally a period of formalized training. Training that is designed, implemented, and delivered well can have a strong effect on the socialization process (Salas et. al., 2012). For law enforcement and, to some extent, correctional officers, new recruits are subjected to preservice training academies. The academies attempt to provide recruits with basic job-related skills as well as a degree of indoctrination about their expected behaviors. For judges, the formalized training period is shorter and less powerful than that for many other occupations within criminal justice. The new judges' seminars are the primary means of formal socialization. In police work and corrections, the training academy immerses recruits into an occupational role. Aside from providing important information about doing a job, the formal training process serves a variety of other functions through exposure to experienced veterans. This reference group provides normative prescriptions for the attitudes and behaviors of the recruits. In doing so, it also creates feelings of belonging and acceptance. The new judges' seminars are valued not only for imparting technical knowledge but also for fostering relationships that provide membership in a group. Here, the origins of the judicial fraternity can be found.

The third and ongoing stage is *informal socialization*. In this stage, the relevant reference groups are peers, managers, and even clients to whom a worker is exposed on a daily basis. Here, the routine of the job shapes the role of the criminal justice worker. Leaders who are insensitive to their organization's culture will have little success in impacting the informal socialization process (Stohr et. al., 2012).

It is important to consider that most informal socialization takes place through small groups. New members learn the rules and expectations and learn to conform in order to be accepted into the group. Conversely, a new member will also have some degree of influence over group norms (Moreland and Levine, 1982). For criminal justice work groups, new members are received with caution. Individuals outside the system are rarely welcomed to the group. The formal side of an organization can provide new staff with skills through training and impose some level of socialization on them. However, informal socialization is essentially a process that molds individuals to the organizational culture. The culture of a criminal justice agency may not establish beliefs and rules for member behavior that are congruent with the organization's prescribed beliefs and behavioral rules. For example, police officers, whose peer group may place a high value on aggressiveness, are more likely to base their decision to arrest on extralegal factors, whereas officers working in low aggressive peer groups will rely primarily on legal factors (McCluskey, Terrill, and Paoline, 2005). Also, it has been common within police culture to stigmatize community police officers as social service workers rather than real cops (Garcia, 2005). Exacerbating the perceived role differences are the different informal socialization processes for traditional and community police officers. For traditional police officers, their expectations and roles are sent from within their groups, which are tightly bound and with which they have attempted to seal themselves off from the public. Community police officers, however, receive a significant part of their expectations and role from the public with which they constantly interact. The informal socialization process is a force that is much more powerful than the formal socialization process. Informal association is a product of the day-to-day interactions of organizational members, clients, and even offenders in the context of organizational constraints. For judges, daily associations with their staff and with lawyers influence the uniquely local nature of their roles. For some police and corrections officers, the positive attitudes gained at the academy may give way in the informal stage to cynicism, alienation, and even corruption.

A MODEL OF INFLUENCES

Although the stages of socialization illustrate the process of change, a specific model is needed to explain the manner in which socializing influences affect the individual. A theoretical model of the process of taking organizational roles has been detailed by Katz and Kahn (1978). The **models of influences** include a social-psychological model of *role taking*, which relies on four key concepts, as shown in Figure 9.1. *Role expectations* are the standards by which the behavior of an organizational member is judged. Supervisors, peers, clients, and even the general public may hold different and even conflicting expectations. The *sent role* is the communication of those expectations to the member. The *received role* is the person's perception and understanding of the sent role. Finally, *role behavior* is the person's response to the complex information received. According to this model, then, the behavior of an organizational member is the result of expectations communicated by significant others and filtered through his or her own psychological processes. The role-taking model thus calls our attention to key variables that may help explain role behavior.

The model also indicates that a person's behavior affects expectations through a feedback process—that is, conformity or lack of conformity to role expectations may influence the sent role over time. In her study of parole, Studt (1978) describes **escalation episodes**, in which parolees dramatically altered the role of parole officers. Ordinarily, parole officers viewed their role as one of helping within a context of casual surveillance. This role was sustained by the lack of information about a parolee's misbehavior. When officers did receive information about even minor transgressions, however, they escalated their surveillance role.

In one example, an agent arranged for the release of a parolee who had been arrested for an unpaid traffic ticket. The agent set up a meeting with the parolee that afternoon, but the parolee was late. His common-law wife was at home with her new baby; she took this occasion to tell the agent that she was considering leaving the parolee because he was sometimes physically rough with her.

Model of Influence: Key concepts include role expectation, role sent, role received, and role behavior in response to expectation and sent role.

Escalation episodes: A process of increasing hostility between police and citizen(s) that causes citizen(s) to act out aggressively against police. This aggression serves to cause the police to make an arrest and to take control.

FIGURE 9.1   A Theoretical Model of Factors Involved in the Taking of Organizational Roles.

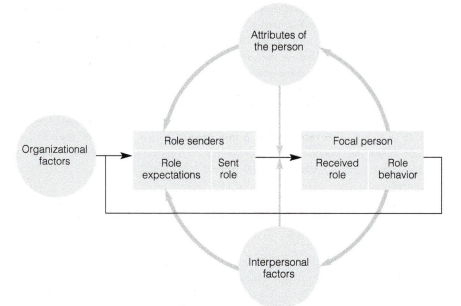

SOURCE: From D. Katz and R. L. Kahn, *The Social Psychology of Organizations*, 2nd ed. Copyright 1978 by John Wiley & Sons, Inc. Reprinted by permission.

The rest of the afternoon was largely devoted to activities that ranged from searching the extensive case record for evidence of previous violence to investigating the possibility that the parolee's aged parents could provide housing for him temporarily, pending the results of further investigation. By the end of the afternoon, although the parolee had not yet been interviewed, the agent and the supervisor were outlining the case for revocation (Studt, 1978:80–81).

Katz and Kahn (1978) also point out that the process of role taking does not occur in isolation and is shaped by several other factors in the model, including organizational, interpersonal, and individual factors. Studt (1978) points out, for example, that organizational concerns are a strong factor in the decision to revoke parole. The important question in this case was the extent to which the parolee's conduct could expose the organization to criticism. Other organizational factors that may affect role taking include organizational size and level of bureaucratization. Large, bureaucratized organizations, for example, may support impersonal attitudes among staff. Finally, evidence indicates that position in the organizational hierarchy influences role taking.

Even when supervisors are recruited from the frontlines, they may take on new roles widely different from those of their former colleagues. Some managerial orientations are the result of position rather than individual character, as illustrated in a study of corrections staff by Duffee and O'Leary (1980), in which frontline officers viewed their activity as centering on order maintenance and restraint, but supervisors were supportive of rehabilitation goals. Another moderator of the role-taking process is interpersonal relationships. The relationship between parole officer and parolee, for example, appears to affect the parole agent's role. It takes time for a parolee to understand an officer's expectations. Once those expectations are understood, surveillance may be deemphasized. Even a "good" relationship, however, can be disrupted by the parolee's behavior causing the relationship and roles expectations to change.

Finally, roles are also influenced by individual differences in approach to the job. Studt (1978) found that some agents were "just doing the job," while others seemed most interested in catching offenders for rule violations. Some emphasized treating parolees with a modicum of respect; some emphasized predictability in their supervision relationships. The general model of role taking can still accommodate such individual orientations.

PROBLEMS IN THE SOCIALIZATION PROCESS

Evidence for the power of the role-taking model can be found all around us in the patterned behavior of organizational members. Still, there is abundant evidence that the process of role taking is not as straightforward as the model may imply. In criminal justice, the most often discussed problem is that of role conflict. In the model, **role conflict** is the occurrence of two or more role expectations in such a way that compliance with one makes compliance with another difficult or impossible. Conflicting expectations may come from two or more role senders or may emanate from a single role sender. These problems are endemic in all street-level bureaucracies and particularly in criminal justice. Lipsky (1980), for example, argues that one of the defining characteristics of all street-level bureaucracies is competing goals. This competition is expressed in the conflicting expectations of frontline workers. Police officers are charged with controlling crime as well as meeting due process constraints. Probation and parole officers must provide surveillance of their caseload to prevent crimes and assure compliance with rules, but they must also provide a supportive atmosphere and services to assist in adjustments to the community. In addition to conflicts over substantive goals, all human service workers are sent conflicting messages about the process of their work. Although the importance of providing custodial or helping services is stressed, these services are to be provided to large caseloads of clients. Probation and parole officers may supervise an average of seventy clients. Demands on time thus accentuate conflicts in the role.

Perhaps the literature on institutional corrections best illustrates the problem of role conflict. In his study of a Rhode Island maximum security prison, Carroll (1974:52) described the basis for role conflict:

> Prior to 1956, the officers were "guards" and their role was precisely defined. The sole functions of the guard were to maintain security and internal order.... Today, the official title of the custodial staff is "correctional officer," a title that both incorporates and symbolizes the conflicting and ambiguous definitions of their current role. As the term

Role conflict: The members of an organization are faced with contradictory and conflicting expectations.

officer connotes, the custodians remain organized in a military hierarchy, the function of which is to ensure security and order. But the adjective *correctional* connotes an additional expectation of equal priority—that of changing offenders.

Also, scholars considered the role of the guard to have evolved to meet the professional standard required to work in correctional centers as opposed to traditional prisons (Gray and Mayer, 1997; Stinchcomb, 2005). However, custody and control remain central concerns to so-called correctional facilities.

In his study of corrections officers at the Auburn, New York, penitentiary, Lombardo (1981) found a similar sort of role conflict. Although the security role of officers required a high degree of social distance from the inmates, the informal counseling roles adopted by some officers demanded low social distance. About one-third of the officers studied found conflict between these roles. One officer provided the following illustration of the conflict:

> There's been times I could have done something for a guy, but I couldn't because of the rules. In one situation where they'd gassed a whole section, the guys [inmates] were vicious. They [other officers and supervisors] wouldn't help them. I opened the windows and turned on the water. One guy was vomiting. I called the medical authorities. The guy wanted air, and I wanted to give him a cup of milk. The medical personnel says no. So there was nothing I could do (Lombardo, 1981:138).

Research into the effects of role conflict indicates that it results in low job satisfaction and poor performance. Role conflict has been found to be a principal cause of stress among corrections officers. It has also been suggested that the conflict "immobilizes" officers and makes them ineffective in both their roles. Other research suggests that conflict over roles causes staff to emphasize their most clearly defined tasks. In their study of Illinois prison guards, Jacobs and Retsky (1975:27) found that "guards are most likely to fall back on their security and maintenance role because it is the only role on which they can be objectively evaluated." *Role ambiguity* means uncertainty about what the occupant of a particular office is supposed to do—that is, the sent message is unclear. This problem often manifests itself because there is a lack of clear performance criteria, a common complaint among police and corrections staff and a major source of stress on the job (Terry, 1983:162). Wilson (1968), for example, notes that the police have been given tasks that cannot all be performed to the satisfaction of society. Police are destined to be viewed as either ineffective or overly repressive. In their maintenance function, for example, differing expectations about what constitutes a just resolution of a dispute between two parties often leave police officers with great discretion and little direction.

In his classic essay *The Society of Captives*, Gresham Sykes (1958) describes the ambiguity in the role of the corrections officer. He points out that the goals of punishment and rehabilitation provide little direction. Questions of what is appropriate punishment remain unanswered, and the technology for changing offenders' behavior is uncertain. The corrections officer is, therefore, left with

an uncertain mandate. The officer must gain compliance from inmates and maintain control within the prison. This mandate is accomplished through accommodations, which Sykes describes as the corruption of the guard's authority. Officers
allow inmates to violate some minor rules to gain cooperation when such violations serve to maintain order in the cell blocks (Kalinich, 1984). Others also note
that the corrections officers who are regarded as good by their superiors are the
ones who get the best compliance without having to resort to formal disciplinary
procedures. General performance prescriptions provide little concrete advice for
officers. As with role conflict, officers may seek additional direction. After a survey of maximum security guards, Poole and Regoli (1980) concluded that *role
stress*, defined as perceived uncertainty about job expectations, was positively
associated with custodial orientation—that is, those officers experiencing role
ambiguity were most likely to define their job in narrow custodial terms.

Lee and Visano (1981) discuss a special case of role-related problems in criminal justice. These authors focus on the concept of *official deviance*, which they
define as "actions taken by officials which violate the law and/or the formal
rules of the organization but which are clearly oriented toward the needs and
goals of the organization, as perceived by the official, and thus fulfill certain
informal rules of the organization" (1981:216). Thus, official deviance does not
benefit the individual as corruption may, but is aimed at furthering the perceived
goals of the organization. In most cases, role senders regard official deviance as
expected and thus as part of their job. For example, law enforcement officers
may allow informants to violate the law if the informants, in turn, provide crucial information on significant cases. Also, officers may effect traffic stops for the
sole purpose of searching a vehicle that they think is occupied by "probable
cause" individuals, even though they have no evidence that indicates criminal
activity on the part of the occupants. Some investigators are also skilled at con-
triving information to help them get a search warrant for a dwelling that they
feel certain holds key evidence for a case. Official deviance can stretch beyond
skirting the rules to achieve a legitimate end. In one recent case in Chicago, citizen Noel Padia was arrested and held in custody for nine months on what were
proven to be trumped-up charges. Blumberg (1967) illustrates official deviance
among public defenders. Defense lawyers, and particularly public defenders, are
expected to maintain ongoing relationships with judges and prosecutors. Relationships with most clients are transitory. As a result, defense attorneys often
pressure clients to plead guilty in order to process cases efficiently. They may
even conspire with other courtroom personnel to increase punishments for
seemingly guilty clients who insist on going to trial (also see Neubauer, 1996).

The pressures supporting official deviance were also revealed in investiga-
tions of the security service of the Royal Canadian Mounted Police (RCMP).
Members of the RCMP are formally bound through law and the rules of the
RCMP organization to uphold the laws of Canada. But they are informally
instructed that they must engage in such "dirty tricks" as illegal break-ins, wire-
tapping, kidnapping, theft of documents, faking documents, and even arson.
Superior officers of the RCMP have admitted, during a federal inquiry on
RCMP wrongdoing, that members of the security services who refused to

engage in dirty tricks because they were illegal would be punished by transfers, denial of promotions, and so forth. At the same time, Mounties were warned that if they were caught, the RCMP would deny any knowledge of their activities and leave them to defend themselves as best they could (Lee and Visano, 1981:218). The cases of public defenders and Mounties clearly show differences in the severity of official deviance, but both suggest responses to conflicting demands in criminal justice. Neither example can be explained by viewing individual actors as bad apples; instead, all are responding to expectations.

Corruption goes well beyond "official deviance" because the sole purpose of corrupt activity is to benefit the individual. In 1998, it was discovered that a number of New York City police officers were protecting a brothel in exchange for services (Gains and Kappeler, 2005). On December 5, 2006, seven Chicago police officers were charged with burglarizing homes. The officers broke open safes and took money, jewelry, and other valuables. The bad-apple theory has also been rejected as a useful explanation for corruption that results in personal gain. One can argue that the seven Chicago police officers are "bad apples." However, in its investigation of police corruption in New York, the Knapp Commission (1972:114) went so far as to note that the elimination of bad apples was a "proven obstacle to meaningful reform." The explanation of corruption as the product of a few aberrant individuals ignores organizational structures and operational codes that establish norms and expectations that permit corruption to grow and spread through organizations. As the Knapp Commission noted, "even those who themselves engage in no corrupt activities are involved in corruption in the sense that they take no steps to prevent what they know or suspect to be going on" (1972:114). In other words, being on the take—using the power of position to accept bribes and so forth—is part of the culture; new officers will either be socialized into accepting this as "normative" behavior for that culture or they may be driven out of the agency.

No aspect of criminal justice is immune to corruption. Investigations into corruption in the Cook County, Illinois, courts between 1986 and 1988 resulted in nearly sixty federal indictments for case fixing and payoffs. Probation officers have been known to exact sexual favors from clients who sought to avoid revocation; corrections officers have been prosecuted for smuggling drugs into prisons and even for aiding in prison escapes. Most of the research on corruption, however, has focused on the police. Studies of police corruption have investigated behavior ranging from accepting an occasional free meal to participating in burglary rings. Much of the research has examined the sources of support for corrupt practices. Sherman (1974), for example, argues that a rookie police officer's work group exercises considerable influence. The likelihood of new officers' accepting bribes is related to the extent to which such practices already occur in the work group. In fact, failure to indulge in corrupt practices may not be sanctioned by an officer's peers. Sherman reports that officers who rejected peers' invitations to receive payoffs to overlook illegal gambling often transferred to different jobs. Rejection of solidarity left officers isolated from their peers.

Aside from the influence of peers, there may also be supervisory support for corrupt practices. In 1967, the President's Commission on Law Enforcement and the Administration of Justice pointed to administrators as having a direct influence on the ethical standards of frontline officers. Police executives can contribute much to a department's tolerance of or intolerance for corruption and the establishment of departmental norms for behavior through their influence on organizational roles. Corrupt police officers, however, do not view themselves as corrupt. They view the role imposed on them by their peers as legitimizing their behavior as nondeviant. Thus, corruption is shared with other officers who provide open support to each other (Reiss, 1971:171), and such support is accomplished through the legitimization of corruption. Wilson (1968) points out that police justify some types of corruption by pointing to declining moral standards in the general community. They note the hypocrisy in the desire to have police officers who will not take bribes when even prominent citizens may wish to bribe them. Skolnick (1966) also explains that police officers legitimize some corrupt practices by distinguishing between practices that will or will not harm the public. In the study, graft associated with bookmaking was regarded as acceptable in a West Coast police department, but bribes associated with drugs were not.

Others have also indicated that the same role-sending process that supports corruption also sets its limits. Thus, officers may differentiate between clean graft (acceptable) and dirty graft (unacceptable) (see Sherman, 1974), or they may distinguish between accepting a bribe and extorting money from someone. Extreme forms of corruption appear to be rare and require an explanation that looks at factors beyond the occupational socialization model.

We have discussed both the stages in which socialization occurs and the specifics of the process itself. In the following sections, we examine the content of socialization, which varies according to different occupations. We look at socialization among the police and among corrections officers, areas where sufficient research exists to describe occupational socialization. These generalizations, however, are not meant to downplay the significance of the moderators of role taking, discussed in the earlier section, A Model of Influences.

SOCIALIZATION AND THE POLICE

The suggestion that large numbers of recruits are attracted to police work because they have authoritarian and violence-seeking personalities is not supported by research. Instead, novice police officers seem drawn to the task by a variety of motives. One early study found that nearly one-third of recruits were "always interested in being a policeman"; others were attracted by prestige, working with people, and the variety in the work (Reiss, 1967). For these officers, anticipatory socialization was a powerful influence. These interests, however, have not generally been confirmed in other studies. Although most recruits may possess an accurate impression of police work prior to selection, the nature of the job is not necessarily what draws them. Motivations are complicated, but the stability of civil service employment and economic benefits attract a significant number of officers (Harris, 1973; Niederhoffer, 1969). Female officers, however, are likely to be attracted to the job by the "interesting" nature of the work (Ermer, 1978). Regardless of the motivation, anticipatory socialization leads a police officer candidate to certain expectations about the job.

Veteran officers also have expectations of the candidates. In a study of the Fort Wayne, Indiana, police, Charles (1986) discovered that in the past, officers in the department were given a list of potential police candidates and asked to vote on whether an applicant should be accepted or rejected. Now, objective and subjective exams define whether a candidate is "good police material," but that assessment still depends heavily on the candidate's image of police work that is gained through anticipatory socialization. "Good police material," in general, "portrays an individual who is pro-police, highly motivated to become a police officer, willing to remain in the department for at least twenty years, accepting of an authoritarian atmosphere, and interested in fighting crime" (Charles, 1986:37).

Anticipatory socialization determines the ease with which the recruit fits into the social systems found in the formal and informal stages of socialization. The formal socialization process is perhaps more elaborate in policing than in any other occupation within criminal justice. Academy training can last 16 weeks, with candidates living together and spending only weekends at home. Life at the academy is characterized by "absolute obedience to departmental rules, rigorous physical training, dull lectures devoted to various technical aspects of the occupation, and a ritualistic concern for detail" (Van Maanen, 1985:73). Although the curriculum includes subjects from report writing to hand-to-hand combat, the lessons of the academy go far beyond the technical information imparted by instructors. Bennett (1984) summarizes four main functions of academy training for the police. First, it provides prescriptions for attitudes and behaviors. Second, it provides opportunities for recruits to evaluate their own behavior and performance against the behavior and performance of their peers. Third, the academy reference group—trainers and fellow trainees—provides a sense of belonging, acceptance, and being rewarded by the group. Fourth, the reference group acts as a controlling influence by withholding acceptance in the face of inappropriate attitudes or behavior.

The basis for identification with the police reference group was examined in a study of a training academy. Harris (1973) found that three structural factors strengthened the ties between individual recruits and the police peer group. First, police work is depersonalizing. Officers are stereotyped by administrators and by the public, and their views are oversimplified. They find themselves stripped of individuality. Behavior that was previously accepted is no longer permitted. Drinking in public may bring criticism from the public and from police officials. Similarly, the officer's newly acquired authority often structures interactions with the public. The police officer finds that his or her social identity is equated with the occupation. In or out of uniform, a cop is a cop. Thus, isolated from the community, the recruit turns to peers for support. In fact, a study of resignations from a police academy found that recruits were most likely to resign when they felt police solidarity did not adequately compensate for social isolation (Fielding and Fielding, 1987).

A second factor in police solidarity can be found in the drive toward police professionalism. Harris (1973) argues that this drive is in some ways an effort to cover feelings of isolation, fear, and disappointment with the hostile reaction of the public. Professionalism assumes that only other police are qualified to judge police behavior, and thus there is support for secrecy, distance from the public, and close bonds to one's peers. A third source of solidarity is the ambiguous nature of police work. The unpredictable routine and lack of appreciation from politicians, the press, and other groups breed defensiveness and contribute further to the ingrown nature of police groups. The informal and continuing stage of socialization involves learning to cope successfully in the real world. In policing, this initiation into reality is done through field training officers (FTOS), who supervise the novice officers on the street. Experienced veterans, including the FTOS, often provide an insightful summary of the academy experience for the new officer. One mentor cautioned a new officer:

> I hope the academy didn't get to you. It's something we all have to go through. A bunch of bullshit as far as I can tell.... Since you got through it all right, you get to find out what it's like out here. You'll find out mighty fast that it ain't nothing like they tell you at the academy (quoted in Van Maanen, 1985:20).

The rookie's evaluation of the academy is thus confirmed, and the new officer continues to learn that peers are the people who can and must be trusted. The FTO or other experienced officers provide continuous coaching of the novice. Westley (1970:157–158) vividly describes it:

> Eight hours a day, six days a week.... They talked with their partners. Long hours between action have to be filled; and the older men, hungry for an audience, use them to advantage. Here, the experienced man finds an opportunity to talk about himself as a policeman, about his hardships and happiness. Here is someone to whom he is an expert.... Thus, amidst an increased barrage of warnings as to silence, the recruit is initiated into the experience of the man, the history of the department, the miseries of police work, the advantages of police work, and the gripes and boasting of a long series of men.... This is the training and the initiation.

A critical moment in that training and initiation is what Van Maanen (1985) has identified as the enforcement encounter. The first enforcement-related contact of an officer's probationary period demonstrates the hostility between police and the public. Continued encounters make for a reality shock that highlights the discrepancy between "idealistic expectations and sordid reality" (Niederhoffer, 1969:52).

Perhaps the most extreme description of informal socialization of the police is presented in Westley's (1970) study of a Midwestern police department. The officers Westley studied formed a distinct subculture marked by clear norms of conduct. These norms included secrecy—a strong prohibition against discussing police business with outsiders—and the use of violence. Many of the officers supported the use of violence in the form of roughing up suspects simply when disrespect to the police was shown or to obtain information. Nelson (1986) found the same characteristics and beliefs with Boston police officers in his study on police culture. According to

Nelson, the media was considered the number one enemy of the Boston police department by its officers. The roots of this morality, this subculture ethos, lay in the perception of hostility from the public. In response to public criticism, police solidarity grew, and officers protected their comrades even to the extent of excusing beatings and graft. Such extreme cases are less likely today because approval of corruption has been moderated by police organizations' internal investigation divisions and the threat of personal civil suits against abusive police tactics.... At a minimum, however, police officers seem to resolve their conflict with the public and with police administration by relying on advice to "lie low, hang loose, and don't expect too much" (Van Maanen, 1985:212).

SOCIALIZATION IN CORRECTIONS

Although the reasons for taking up any occupation are complex and varied, the attraction for corrections officers seems less complicated than that of the police. In a study of new corrections officers in Canada, Willett (1977) described the motivations of recruit officers as "prosaic." Lombardo's (1981) study of New York guards came to a similar conclusion. Most of the new recruits were attracted to the job mainly by the promise of regular pay and job security. Many officers come to corrections from periods of unemployment or insecure jobs. In northern Michigan, for example, communities lacking job opportunities lobby hard to have new prisons built "in their neighborhoods." In addition to the jobs and funds generated by construction of the new prisons, secure, high-paying jobs in the prisons as corrections officers are made available to local individuals. As a logger turned corrections officer stated to one author, he missed working in the forest next to nature, but he needed steady employment to provide for his family. For most corrections officers, the nature of the work is not the attraction; in fact, recruits do not know much of the nature of corrections work prior to entry into the field. Anticipatory socialization for corrections officers is thus marked by incomplete and inaccurate information. Potential recruits acquire their images of prison from the popular media long before they decide to become guards.

Stereotypes from television portrayals of prison violence and police encounters with violent offenders on the television show *Cops* mingle to create the impression that the job of corrections officer is one of watching (at a distance) over a melange of dangerous subhumans. As one recruit put it, "I thought a prison guard was like a turnkey, and inmates were fierce monsters standing around looking at you" (quoted in Willett, 1977:430). Even recruits who have friends and relatives working in the prison may have little accurate information about the job. One officer in Lombardo's (1981:23) study noted the following:

> I had some help having a cousin down there. He got me a copy of some old rulebooks and some other things. Even these didn't give a full understanding of what you're getting into. Again, just ideas from the movies. Guards, not pushing inmates but still the bad guys. But I knew some guards and knew they weren't like that. I was willing to take a chance.

Just as the rookie police officer may be jolted on first contact with a hostile public, the rookie corrections officer experiences a significant reality shock on first contact with inmates. New officers learn that they will be in close contact with inmates, and the stereotype of the dangerous convict dissolves. Officers begin to see inmates as a diverse group, many of whom are "no different from the run of guys on the street" (quoted in Willett, 1977:433). As anticipatory socialization dissolves under the weight of real experience, the informal and formal processes begin.

Corrections officers often attend the training academy only after weeks or even months of on-the-job training at an institution. This schedule is the result more of necessity than design. Officers are usually available and needed in the institutions well before a training academy class is scheduled. This arrangement does, however, expose the recruits to the reality of prison work, and many officers quit shortly after this exposure. In Jacobs and Grear's (1977) study of officers who were fired or quit at Stateville Prison in Illinois, 41 percent of resignations and 60 percent of terminations occurred during the first six months on the job. Current studies show turnover rates for corrections officers remain high. Roughly 37 percent of custody staff will leave prison work, and the average turnover rate is approximately 14 percent (Stinchcomb, 2005). Such high rates of turnover taking place soon after initiation are indicative of the power of the socialization process. Officers who are not responsive to it leave.

The informal socialization process for new guards is often marked by mistrust and often hostility from their experienced peers (Conover, 2000). At the same time that recruits are learning that inmates are human like anyone else, their preconceptions of other officers as "pretty good guys" dissolve. This change in perceptions usually relates to strong prohibitions against normalizing relationships with inmates. Although the rookies are taught to be firm but fair, only formal contact with inmates is expected. In fact, the informal socialization process in some institutions has been described as going so far as to support and even demand unnecessary violence against inmates (Marquart, 1986b). Older officers seem particularly concerned that recruits maintain considerable social distance from inmates. The irony is, however, that such distance is difficult to maintain in light of the constant contact between officers and inmates, and even the older officers generally do not maintain that distance.

The field training officer (FTO) programs common among the police are generally not as formally organized in corrections. Although there is some effort to pair rookies with experienced officers on job assignments, these efforts often break down because of staff shortages. Not infrequently, new officers find themselves alone on job assignments, surrounded by inmates, and poorly supervised. In such cases, rookies often turn to inmates for help in carrying out assignments. Lombardo (1981) points out how inmates provide some of the most significant training for officers. They even offer instruction on procedures such as searches and shakedowns. One officer noted the following:

An inmate broke me in. Inmates trained officers. Really! He told me to stand back and he showed me how and where to frisk. He hit the table to sound it out. Rap the bars to see if they were solid (quoted in Lombardo, 1981:321).

As the informal socialization process for corrections officers begins, then, conflicting role expectations are sent to the rookie. Veterans and supervisors emphasize the guard's formal role, while at least some inmates send expectations of reasonableness, dependence, and friendship. The officers thus see themselves caught in the middle. Such confusion is often accentuated by the formal training process. Whatever the curriculum, the corrections academy is often viewed much the same as the police academy, and experienced guards counsel recruits to "listen carefully, give it back at the exams, then forget it and do as we do. Treat the course as a good holiday from the real work" (quoted in Willett, 1977: 433).

The first corrections academy opened in 1859 with the goal of training guards who would have a good influence over inmates (Sellin, 1934). It was not, however, until the 1960s, with financial incentives from the Law Enforcement Assistance Administration (LEAA) and the urging of the Joint Commission on Correctional Manpower and Training (1969), that academy training gained wide support. That support has continued from the Commission on Accreditation for Corrections, which has established minimum training requirements. The American Correctional Association (ACA) recommends a minimum of 160 hours of entry-level training during the recruit's first year, with at least 40 hours before being assigned to a post and 40 hours a year thereafter (American Correctional Association, 2004). In practice, the length of correctional officer training across the states fluctuates. Some academies may meet for a few weeks, while more progressive states try to conform to ACA standards. Curricula generally include technical information, such as firearms training and emergency procedures, and a smattering of behavioral sciences. As with the police, however, the informal lessons of the academy are also significant. Corrections academies often employ the same model of regimentation as the police in an effort to create unity and professionalism among the recruits. Without the anticipatory socialization characteristic of the police and with constant manpower shortages, however, corrections academies often have difficulty enforcing regimentation. In Lombardo's (1981) study, the academy's failure to dismiss rule violators increased recruits' cynicism.

The novice officers' expectation that the academy experience is of little relevance to the actual work may also be confirmed. Officer cadets often complain that subjects are too academic, and even instructors are sometimes seen as teaching one thing while believing another (Willett, 1977:438). Frequently, the impression of the academy as irrelevant is reinforced once a new officer is back in the institution (Liebentritt, 1974). Through the informal socialization process, officers learn the rules of their subculture, which include concepts such as don't rat on fellow officers, always support a fellow officer in a dispute with an inmate, and maintain officer solidarity in dealing with outside groups (Kauffman, 1988) that cannot be taught in the formal training sessions. Moreover, the informal socialization process will change officers' attitudes over time. New officers tend to be relatively naive with low levels of cynicism and generally positive attitudes. The oldest officers show a similar disposition, perhaps accepting their fate. In the group between these two, however, negative attitudes are high.

Although the concept of a subculture has been useful in studies of the police, its appropriateness in describing corrections officers is debatable. Evidence indicates that officers share some basic concerns about security and appropriate social distance from inmates (Crouch and Marquart, 1999), but studies indicate that corrections officers vary considerably in their attitudes toward inmates. Lombardo (1985) also notes that the processes needed for the formation of a subculture are not present among corrections officers: corrections officers are not attracted to the field by some shared sense of mission; they generally do not work together; they do not share in the decision-making process; and there is limited communication among them. Relations among officers are often characterized by suspicion rather than solidarity.

Rather than describing corrections officers as a subculture, some authors have used the concept of **pluralistic ignorance**. Under conditions of pluralistic ignorance, individuals falsely believe that their own opinions are not widely shared. Thus, Klofas and Toch (1982) found that corrections officers reported themselves as being less punitive and less custodially oriented than their peers. Some officers were effective opinion leaders, and they convinced the majority that their view was widely shared. In reality, the officers greatly exaggerated the punitiveness of those peers; only a small group of officers could accurately be described as primarily custodially oriented. The subculture was a myth. In this regard, King (2008) argues that a perception of potential violence in high-security prisons may become a self-fulfilling prophecy. Officers' work group norms will be affected by the prophecy, and they will act out their part and create unnecessary conflict between officers and inmates.

Pluralistic ignorance: A condition in which individuals falsely believe that their own opinions are not widely shared.

SOCIALIZATION AND COMMUNITY EXPECTATIONS

Anticipatory socialization sets the context for many employees in the criminal justice system. Their perceptions and expectations about the job are strong influences throughout their careers. Yet another influence centers on public expectations of people in the criminal justice system. These public expectations affect how criminal justice personnel perceive support from the community. Surveys and research on public perceptions and attitudes toward the criminal justice system and its employees are numerous (see the U.S. Bureau of Justice Statistics, 2000b). Most paint a flattering picture of criminal justice professionals. Perceptions and attitudes toward the police are the most common. Research on public confidence in the police is the most positive: close to 90 percent of people surveyed in one national opinion poll have a great deal/quite a lot and some confidence in the police. Almost two-thirds (62 percent) in the same national survey believe the police can either do a great deal or quite a lot in protecting them from violent crime. Similar findings are found with respect to the public's perception of the Supreme Court, with over 80 percent of those surveyed expressing confidence in the court. Although the Supreme Court's activities are not representative of the duties performed by other lower courts, there is still wide consensus that these courts perform their functions in a satisfactory way. Where public confidence may be questionable is in the area of corrections, specifically in the ability of correctional officials to rehabilitate criminals and protect prisoners and correctional staff from harm in prisons. Nevertheless, the socialization of police officers, court personnel, and correctional officers is affected to a great degree by how the public views them as being capable and competent in the performance of their jobs. The only profession related to the criminal justice system where public attitudes are fairly low is that of lawyers. The legal profession receives uniformly low scores from the public on the dimensions of honesty and ethical standards (*Sourcebook*, 2000:114). For criminal justice administrators, these findings are encouraging and puzzling.

Although, on the one hand, public confidence is high for many criminal justice organizations, there is, on the other hand, a perception among criminal justice professionals that they are viewed negatively by the public. Addressing this apparent contrast is where many criminal justice administrators focus their efforts. For the new recruit in policing or corrections, knowledge that the public is behind you in your efforts is critical and affects job performance and commitment to a career in the criminal justice field. The socialization process through formalized training, for example, is directly influenced by how the public supports criminal justice organizations with resources for training and education required to perform the duties of the profession.

This is most evident in the increases in training and education requirements for both police and corrections professionals. Unlike the legal profession, where a four-year college degree as well as three years of law school is required, many police and correctional organizations have until recently had minimum education and training requirements for new employees. Yet the trends in both the police field and the corrections profession are for major increases in both entry-level requirements and in-service requirements. Camp and Camp (2000), for example, report steady increases in both preservice and in-service training requirements for entry-level correctional officer positions since 1990. In some states, due to budgetary constraints, these requirements have slipped, but across the country, there has been a general increase in both educational and training requirements for entry-level positions in police and correctional agencies. With higher levels of education and training for criminal justice personnel, there is a concomitant increase in both the public's expectations concerning job performance and the expectations of personnel who demand more from their organizations on many work dimensions: recruitment, promotion, and discipline, to mention a few. For criminal justice administrators in these organizations, the expectations influence the ways in which they structure the work environment, how they supervise employees, and how they manage to deliver services to the public.

STRATEGIES FOR SOCIALIZATION: IMPLICATIONS FOR ADMINISTRATORS

The process of socialization is not immutable. By deliberate design or by their failure to design, managers continuously influence the socialization process. In this section, we examine the ways in which managers affect the process of socialization in criminal justice. As discussed, the socialization process begins with the anticipation of occupational roles. Administrators have little control over anticipatory socialization. The media and movie industries portray a system based on ratings rather than reality. Positive images of the profession can be made through successful community policing and programs like Drug Abuse Resistance Education (DARE), in which officers inform schoolchildren about the problems associated with drug use. Also, selecting candidates who acquire criminal justice degrees may be instrumental in recruiting individuals with a clearer picture of the profession. However, proper socialization into the profession is squarely on the shoulders of agency administrators.

A direct influence on socialization occurs during recruitment and selection. The determination of job titles and qualifications is the first step in this process. Some communities, for example, use the words *police agent* rather than *police officer* to convey a sense of professionalism. The change in title from *prison guard* to *corrections officer* was also meant to connote a different role for frontline prison staff. Likewise, *campus security* carries a different set of expectations than *campus police*, and *state trooper* conveys its own images. Job qualifications also directly influence socialization. Experience, education, and even fitness requirements determine the paths that candidates must take. In 1969, the Joint Commission on Correctional Manpower and Training noted that age requirements affected organizational roles by creating a generation gap between workers and clients in criminal justice. At the time, the gap was regarded as detrimental.

Presidential commissions have long been concerned with educational requirements (National Advisory Commission on Criminal Justice Standards and Goals, 1973a, 1973b). In the 1960s and 1970s, the Law Enforcement Education program provided funds for the education of criminal justice employees. A college education, now required for most social service positions, is regarded as beneficial for almost all entry-level positions in criminal justice (Waldron, 1984).

An obvious influence on organizational roles is exerted in the selection process itself. During this process, a variety of criteria, often intuitive, sometimes systematic, is used to weed out candidates. A common approach was described by Willett (1977) in his study of Canadian corrections officers. The selection process involved informal interviews without standardized guidelines. The interviewers possessed no particular skills and were given no particular instructions but focused on maturity and intelligence, ability to supervise, ability to organize, and ability to communicate. In policing, hiring practices are often elaborate and include civil service tests, physical fitness evaluations, character investigations, and even polygraph examinations in addition to oral interviews.

Efforts to introduce psychological assessments into the selection process are still more sophisticated but not necessarily more successful at discriminating between good and bad employees. Standardized tests, such as the *Minnesota Multi-phasic Personality Inventory* (MMPI) and the *Cattell 16pf*, have been used, but a review of the research determined that, for corrections officers, the empirical studies are not of sufficient quantity or quality to warrant conclusions (Wahler and Gendreau, 1985). Research, however, continues. Psychological screening has become common in policing (Territo, Swanson, and Chamelin, 1985) and is beginning to be utilized in corrections. New York state requires psychological screening of all corrections officer candidates (Morgenbesser, 1984). These tests are used in the hope of identifying highly unusual psychological profiles rather than making subtle distinctions among candidates.

A different approach is found in behavioral-skills assessments as a basis for selection. These assessments are based on job analyses and focus on the ability to perform specific tasks or the potential to acquire necessary skills through training. Some criminal justice organizations are developing assessment centers that use simulations of on-the-job performance (see Byham and Thornton, 1982).

The formal stages of training provide significant opportunities to influence socialization. Here, the process as well as the training content influences role taking. Van Maanen (1982) describes some variables or strategies in the training process that influence socialization. Managers should be aware of the ways in which manipulation of these variables can affect socialization. The *degree of formalization* is the extent to which training is segregated from the ongoing context of work. In criminal justice, the police academy represents a highly formalized process, while most probation officers undergo a much less formalized process of on-the-job training. Formalization has several important consequences. The more formalized it is, the more the training will stress adoption of appropriate attitudes and beliefs and the more new employees will be stigmatized in the organization, usually by segregation in a rookie class. At the same time, formalized training is often technical in nature and its relevance for day-to-day work is likely to be questioned by both rookie and experienced employee, regardless of content.

Collective socialization strategies involve the training of new members as a group. Individual strategies involve an apprenticeship approach to socialization. Collective strategies inevitably create feelings of comradeship and peer support because trainees feel they are in the same boat. Among the police, for example, collective strategies may be useful because officers must often depend on each other in the field. The cost, however, may be that these strategies create distance from supervisors and enhance subculture supports. *Individual socialization* strategies depend on the affective bonds between individuals; they breed dependence on mentors or on established ways of doing things. The new probation officer who shares a mentor's caseload may get individualized attention but may be slow to gain autonomy. In probation, where close supervision of frontline staff is difficult, this dependence in the training phase may be desirable.

In *sequential socialization*, a trainee passes through discrete stages on the way to becoming a fully accepted member of an organization. Police, for example, go through a sequence of academy training, field training, and a probationary period, whereas corrections officers frequently begin with on-the-job training prior to entry into the academy. When training is divided into these relatively separate steps, coordination of those stages becomes important. Lack of coordination may mean that the material is contradictory or that trainees can disregard material learned in one stage, as is often the case in the transition from the training academy to on-the-job training. This lack of continuity can lead to cynicism among the recruits.

Serial socialization relies on experienced veterans to groom newcomers in organizations. Criminal justice organizations frequently rely on serial practices. Experienced police officers, for example, often get academy instructor assignments and FTO jobs. Similarly, novice judges turn to experienced judges for advice. Such practices ensure that organizations will change only slowly.

Established attitudes and practices are passed on, and new ideas gain little support. Such stability may not always be beneficial, however, and disjunctive practices may be useful in introducing change. University faculty, for example, may be called on to discuss police–community relations or offer training in new procedures for classifying probationers. *Investiture strategies* make membership in organizations easy by accepting the recruit's credentials as the major entrance requirement. Education and the practice of law grant entry to the judiciary and form the foundation for a professional identity. However, *divestiture strategies* strip away certain characteristics before entry is allowed. Academy training requires regulation haircuts, special uniforms for the novitiate, and separation from friends and family. Although perhaps mild compared with the experience of a U.S. Marine recruit, this experience is designed for similar reasons: to dismantle the identity of the newcomer and replace it with an appropriate organizational identity. This process binds the rookie to the organization and promotes a strong sense of fellowship among those who have traveled the same path.

Socialization is more prevalent during the early, rather than later, stages of a career (Schein, 2004), and thus recruits are more susceptible than experienced workers. Nonetheless, managers must be aware of the socializing influences that continue to confront staff. Personnel practices, such as shift assignments or bidding procedures for job assignments, may influence socialization. For example, Klofas and Toch (1982) found that anti-inmate attitudes among young corrections officers received support when the rookies were clustered on the 3:00 to 11:00 PM shift. The officers lacked the seniority to bid on assignments that would have integrated them with their experienced peers on desirable shifts. Assignment to vice divisions or repeat-offender programs may expose employees to additional subculture influences. Technological changes may also influence socialization. Continued training may alter expectations or relationships between employees and clients. And the dynamic of the new generation of correctional architecture, with its emphasis on direct supervision of inmates, may alter assumptions about inmates (Menke, Zupan, and Lovrich, 1986). Although socialization influences may be most prominent at the beginning of a career in criminal justice, those influences should not be neglected at any time.

ETHICAL CONSIDERATION IN THE SOCIALIZATION PROCESS

"Ethics concerns the study of right and wrong, duty, responsibility, and personal character" (Close and Meier, 1995:3). The formal socialization process is a mechanism for the organization to impose its dominant belief system and rules on its members: right and wrong, duty, responsibility, and personal character required by the organization on its members. At the formal level, agency members are trained and supervised based on agency policies, proce-dures, and written rules and regulations. Because there is a great deal of lati-tude for discretion and autonomous decision making by practitioners, most training programs also dedicate time for several hours of lectures based on applied ethics to guide practitioners when making ethical decisions that rely on their discretion.

It is probable that, like most of us, the majority of police, correctional, and court officers make ethical decisions most of the time. However, ethical breaches are a common occurrence in the system as witnessed by cases of corruption, perjury, falsely obtained confessions, and so forth. Nolan (2009), for example, exposes an incident in which an off-duty police officer was mis-taken for a suspect in a homicide who was attempting to avoid arrest. The off-duty officer was severely beaten and left for dead by several of his fellow officers. The officers involved in the beating wrote false reports stating that they saw nothing happen, hoping to protect themselves from punitive action. The brutalized officer understood that his beating was a mistake and held no personal grudges, but, nonetheless, he reported the incident. As a result, he was considered a rat by his fellow officers and received threatening phone calls, death threats, and had his tires slashed. Nolan, who served in the Bos-ton Police Department for twenty-five years, uses this as an example of the department's institutional culture of deception that, he argues, is common in most law enforcement agencies. He describes police culture as embracing tribal culture because it is steeped in ritualism, militaristic code, weaponry, power, and a chain of command that "literally and metaphorically binds the warrior tribe" (251).

From a socialization perspective, the view the author gives us is one in which the group's culture comes from a tradition of police as tribal warriors. This traditional belief is imposed indirectly—and perhaps unconsciously—by the command staff. In passing on "traditional" policing, they are also passing on the expectation of masculine toughness. To the extent that this is the subtle message of command staff, the informal socialization process will read-ily impose tribal warrior practices on police officers. Ethics for police will be determined by the needs of the tribe and will often differ from official dicta that are based on higher-order beliefs, such as federal and state constitutions, rule of law, due process, and so forth. In effect, police command staff that pass on a culture of toughness and masculinity directly support the informal socialization process and impede their own agency's formal socialization pro-cess that would seek to impose civil behavior and a public service mission on their officers.

Corruption, deceit, and violence among correctional officers are found in prison settings. Corrupt officers take bribes and favors from inmates and their fam-ilies and are prone to use violence to control inmates. Souryal (2009) argues that autocratic management, which is endemic to prison administration, applies puni-tive measures to control corruption. The application of punitive measures serves to distance officers from management staff. What is needed, he argues, is a form of civil management under which staff members are somewhat free to discuss corruption. Under an autocratic system, staff members tend to form a "code of silence" to protect themselves from punitive sanctions by administrators. In other words, autocratic management and the traditional militaristic style of organizing police and prison organizations may cause police and correctional officers to form group norms that protect the unethical behaviors of some of their members through deception and a code of silence. Officers will falsify facts or stand silent to protect themselves, as did the officers who participated in or witnessed the off-duty police officer being beaten by his fellow officers after mistaking him for a murder suspect. In addition to formal mechanisms to socialize criminal justice practitioners, the argument here is that management philosophy of command staff has to move to a more civil and democratic style to eliminate the need for work groups to develop informal mechanisms to shield and protect themselves from management.

SUMMARY

Understand occupational socialization.

- A process by which a member of an organization acquires the attitudes and behaviors of an ongoing occupational social system. This process may include formal training and will include social interactions with work peers.

Understand the basic precepts of organizational culture.

- Organizational culture is a set of assumptions and beliefs shared by members of an organization. This includes language, symbols, and folklore that direct the behavior of the organization's members.

Understand the socialization process as it applies to criminal justice agencies.

- Anticipatory socialization is often based on media, movies, and television programs and is inaccurate. Formal socialization is often weak, and informal socialization is usually strong.

Be able to discuss the problems in the socialization process in criminal justice agencies.

- Criminal justice practitioners face role conflict, role ambiguity, conflicting expectations, and murky and contradictory goals. Hence, the socialization process presents conflicting stimuli.

Understand the basic strategies for socialization.

- Managers continuously influence the socialization process. Organizational socialization begins with recruiting and selection. Formal socialization is accomplished through the orientation and training process. Supervision provides a continuous impact on formal socialization.

Case Study: REFLECTIONS ON A CAREER

I struggled through all of the crap in law school to join the noblest of professions, I thought. I had a belief in the system of justice, that through the adversarial process, the truth would be discovered and justice would be served. I knew about plea bargaining, but I was totally naive about the legal system and how the "old boys" ran things. I passed the bar exam and joined a decent law firm. I was intent on being a defense attorney. The state had a skilled staff of prosecuting attorneys and the power of skilled detectives to work with to get convictions. To have a balanced adversarial process, skilled and dedicated defense attorneys were important. Then I got my first case. The court appointed my firm to represent an individual who had earned a solid criminal record and was indigent. My boss was happy to assign the case to me—to prime the pump, as he put it. Negotiate the best plea you can for your client, was his advice. The defendant had served time and did not seem troubled by the possibility of returning to prison. However, he maintained his innocence and was opposed to accepting a plea. I discussed the case with the prosecutor assigned to it and asked to look over the file. I was treated well, but clearly as a beginner. As I perused the file, I noted and commented on several discrepancies in the case. The tone of our conversation changed, and the prosecutor became somewhat miffed about my analysis. I patiently pressed my point of view. However, the chief prosecutor, who was in earshot of our conversation, intervened. She made it strikingly clear that this was a plea-bargain case.

She firmly explained that my client had committed a string of burglaries over the years, that this offense fit his pattern, that everyone knew it was his job, and that we did not need to expend time and money agonizing over discrepancies in the case. She further explained that I was assigned the case as a personal favor to allow me to get some experience with the system and make a few easy bucks. By this time, she was in my face, lecturing me about waking up and forgetting all of the crap I had learned in high school civics or law school. This put me over the

edge. I asked for my copy of the file and told her and her assistant that I would see them in court.

To make a long story short, I took the case to a jury trial and obtained a not guilty verdict. Along the way, I embarrassed the investigating detective, who was not well prepared for the obvious plea-bargain case; angered the judge, who, as I later found out, thought my client was guilty as sin; and completely alienated the chief prosecutor and her assistant who tried the case.

My boss attempted to mend the few fences I broke and asked me to apologize and be gracious with the people I had beat up in the process. I was stunned and outraged. The jury found my client not guilty; therefore, in my mind, that was the truth. The adversarial process should prevail over egos or convenience, I thought. I stood my idealistic ground and refused to apologize to anyone. A month after the acquittal, my client committed another burglary, was appointed another attorney, although he requested I represent him, pleaded guilty to a lesser offense, and was sentenced to prison. Two months later, I was asked to resign from my law firm and was advised to practice on my own.

Well, I still do criminal defense work, and the thieves and convicts love me. But they usually cannot pay their fees. I have to pay the rent and my bills, so I developed a pretty good divorce practice. But the real truth is that most of my domestic relations clients cannot afford to go to court and have their case reviewed through the adversarial process. So we bargain and settle.

CASE STUDY QUESTIONS

1. Describe the occupational socialization process illuminated in the case study.
2. What major weaknesses appear to exist in the stages of socialization?
3. What appear to be the real rules of the game, and how does the legal system benefit from these rules?

Think like an Administrator

You have just been elected to the office of County District Attorney (DA). You spent your earlier years in the profession as an Assistant District Attorney (ADA) and later as a criminal defense attorney. You ran for the DA position because you saw the need to upgrade

---

THINK LIKE AN ADMINISTRATOR—continued

the professionalism and effectiveness of that office. You found the ADAs to be cynical and hostile toward defendants, defense attorneys, and, even in some cases, victims. Also, the ADAs were permitted to take civil cases to supplement their low state wages.

However, many of the ADAs were reputed to be spending more time and energy on their civil cases than the state criminal cases. As a result, they were rushing to get criminal cases off their desks by giving out generous pleas to criminal defendants. It was also suspected that criminal defense attorneys getting favorable pleas for their clients were referring civil cases to the ADAs. The former DA tried to rectify this situation by hiring a couple of young zealots as ADAs in the hopes they would have a positive influence on the work group. However, the zealots were soon alienated from the work group and seemed determined to take as many cases as possible to trial rather than plea bargain. It is clear that you have to change the behavior and work values of the ADAs to improve the effectiveness and professionalism of the office.

1. What is the first thing you should do the first day at the office?
2. What beliefs and values on the part of the ADAs need to be addresses?
3. How would you go about writing new policies for the DA's office?
4. What is the first formal policy that needs to be addressed?
5. What unofficial (informal) practices on the part of the ADAs need to be changed?
6. Can the energy of the zealots be harnessed and used to affect the cynical ADAs in a positive manner?
7. How can a DA affect some stages of anticipatory socialization?
8. What new forms or methods of formal socialization would you implement?
9. How can you impact the informal socialization process among your staff?

FOR DISCUSSION

1. Describe the content of the role of a probation officer. What are the norms associated with this work? Include those that can be regarded as legitimate as well as those regarded as not legitimate. What are the sources of these norms? How do education, training, and the work experience influence them?

2. How can you distinguish between corruption and official deviance in policing? What socialization processes support each of these? Design an in-service training program whose chief goal is to combat the organizational processes you describe.

3. If you were selecting volunteers to work in a maximum-security prison, what attitudes would you find desirable and why? What attitudes would you like to see transmitted in the formal socialization process and in the informal stage of socialization?

4. Your job is to develop a program for training corrections officers for a special internal affairs unit. They will investigate problems of contraband and violence in prison while working as regular officers. Whom would you recruit and how would you structure the process of training? What would be the content of training? What problems with the socialization process do you anticipate?

FOR FURTHER READING

Conover, T. *Newjack: Guarding Sing Sing*. New York: Random House, 2000.

Katz, D., and Kahn, R. L. *The Social Psychology of Organization*. 2nd ed. New York: Wiley, 1978.

Lombardo, L. X. *Guards Imprisoned: Correctional Officers at Work*. New York: Elsevier, 1981.

Schein, E. H. *Organizational Culture and Leadership*. 2nd ed. San Francisco: Jossey-Bass, 2004.

CHAPTER 10

Power and Political Behavior

LEARNING OBJECTIVES

After reading this chapter, the students will have achieved the following objectives:

- Understand a definition of power as being both an individual construct and an organizational construct.

- Distinguish among the various types of authority and power.

- Comprehend the consequences of power relations within criminal justice organizations.

- Grasp the importance of expressing power and political behavior among criminal justice administrators.

- Describe effective types of power within criminal justice organizations.

VIGNETTE

"After 16 years Behind Bars for an $11 Robbery, the Scott Sisters Will Be Freed at Last"
   By James Ridgeway

The following announcement was issued today by Haley Barbour, governor of Mississippi, regarding Jamie and Gladys Scott.

Dec. 29, 2010

Governor Barbour's Statement Regarding the Release of the Scott Sisters

Today, I have issued two orders indefinitely suspending the sentences of Jamie and Gladys Scott. In 1994, a Scott County jury convicted the sisters of armed robbery and imposed life sentences for the crime. Their convictions and their sentences were affirmed by the Mississippi Court of Appeals in 1996.

To date, the sisters have served sixteen years of their sentences and are eligible for parole in 2014. Jamie Scott requires dialysis, and her sister has offered to donate one of her kidneys to her. The Mississippi Department of Corrections believes the sisters no longer pose a threat to society. Their incarceration is no longer necessary for public safety or rehabilitation, and Jamie Scott's medical condition creates a substantial cost to the State of Mississippi.

The Mississippi parole board reviewed the sisters' request for a pardon and recommended that I neither pardon them nor commute their sentences. At my request, the parole board subsequently reviewed whether the sisters should be granted an indefinite suspension of their sentences, which is tantamount to parole, and have concluded with my decision to suspend their sentences indefinitely.

Gladys Scott's release is conditional on her donating one of her kidneys to her sister, a procedure that should be scheduled with urgency. The release date for Jamie and Gladys Scott is a matter for the department of corrections.

I would like to thank Representative George Flaggs, Senator John Horne, Senator Willie Simmons, and Representative Credell Calhoun for their leadership on this issue. These legislators, along with former Mayor Charles Evers, have been in regular contact with me and my staff while the sisters' petition has been under review.

From Solitarywatch.com/2010/12/29

This vignette vividly demonstrates how gubernatorial power influenced the release of two sisters from prison under some unique circumstances. The decision to release the sisters raises serious questions regarding whether that power should have been used in this case. It is the expression of power and political behavior that we seek to address in this chapter. Power is expressed in different forms in the various arenas of the criminal justice system as well. The sentencing judge, the police sergeant, the prisoner, or the corrections administrator all rely on power to gain compliance from others and are affected in turn by power relationships. A police supervisor may wish to exercise control over the beat cop, or a prisoner may desire to control another prisoner. Expressions of power are ubiquitous in criminal justice organizations, and who has the power and how they acquire it are further variables.

Moreover, power and politics are inseparable in the criminal justice system. To the chagrin of some criminal justice employees, that power often seems to be used inappropriately and to the detriment of their organization. The consequences of such perceptions can be injurious to the organization, something we examine later in the chapter. Suffice it to say that expressions of power—and the consequences of these expressions—are ubiquitous in criminal justice organizations.

Police organizations, for example, employ different types of power to gain compliance from officers. The types of power used depend on the tasks and functions of the particular unit. Supervisors in the vice unit do not use the same types of power as those in the detective unit because each unit has its own duties and responsibilities. In correctional systems, the types of power used by supervisory personnel are often constrained by a number of factors inherent in the prison structure. As an example, we know that pure coercive power rarely works in prisons, in part because inmates significantly outnumber staff. As a result, corrections administrators and officers use other types of power to gain compliance from prisoners.

Our purpose in this chapter is to review the literature on power and apply this material to criminal justice organizations. As some scholars suggest, the investigation of power in organizations is not new. Few studies, however, have examined the complexity of the issue (House, 1984), and many researchers have suggested that measurement of a quantity like power is extremely difficult (Podsakoff and Schriesheim, 1985). More important, we have few studies of the exercise of power in criminal justice organizations.

Nevertheless, in this chapter, we seek to identify the types of power and authority employed in criminal justice bureaucracies by examining the major research available. We also discuss the consequences of power relations in organizations, emphasizing the political nature of power in organizations and the strategies criminal justice officials can employ to maintain their power positions. We begin, however, with a definition of power, and we distinguish this concept from authority.

POWER DEFINED

Power: A construct that underscores the importance of how compliance among subordinates is achieved. It can be understood at both the individual level and the organizational level.

Power is one of the most difficult concepts to define, as witnessed by the multiple definitions found in the literature on organizations. Hinings et al. (1967), for example, believe that power is analogous to bureaucracy. Some authors have viewed power in only one dimension—that is, as purely coercion (Bierstedt, 1950; Blau, 1964). Dahl defines power in this way: "A has the power over B to the extent that he can get B to do something B would not otherwise do" (1957: 43).

Although this somewhat simple definition has been accepted by many scholars who are interested in power in organizations; still others have seen power as being much more complex and have defined it more broadly. They look at power at the organizational level and include the role of social systems in organizations (Crozier, 1964; Dubin, 1963; Emerson, 1962; Lawrence and Lorsch, 1967)—that is, the interactions of people and units. If we view organizational power as a product of exchange relationships in organizations, we can see how the interdependent nature of organizational tasks creates power for some people.

Perrow (1970) has demonstrated that sales departments within industrial firms are much more powerful than other units within the organization. He argues that specific units within an organization are able to exhibit what is known as "interdepartmental power" and that any investigation of power must be able to discern those units, which are critical to the operation of the organization. If some sectors of an organization are more powerful than others, what within these units makes them powerful and central to the organization? One possible answer is that these units are effective in dealing with uncertainties in the organization's task environment. In effect, they are able to absorb the uncertainty created by an often turbulent and unstable environment (March and Simon, 1958).

Criminal justice organizations, however, often do not operate in unstable environments, and they are not influenced greatly by market concerns. They generally operate in consistent and predictable ways. Power acquisition, therefore, among subunits in these organizations is typically not based on how well they can deal with uncertainties in their task environments. What is important to criminal justice organizations is that they accomplish their tasks in an efficient manner while simultaneously meeting the demands of the public, yet we will see that the important distinction between individual power and organizational power is very relevant to comprehending how compliance is gained within criminal justice organizations (Smith, Applegate, Sitren, and Springer, 2009).

Thus, some have suggested that it is not the interaction with the environment that is important for understanding organizational power. More critical is how units operate to accomplish tasks that are crucial to the organization's survival. Hicksen et al. (1973) have demonstrated that organizational units that cannot be replaced in an organization (substitutability), that have a pervasive and immediate relationship to the work flow of the organization (centrality), and that deal with contingencies effectively are usually powerful in organizations.

This assertion is borne out by evidence gathered in institutional corrections and in police organizations. Early research by Sykes (1958) demonstrated how the help of inmates is required to run prisons. In the words of Sykes, there is a "defect of total power" in our correctional institutions among the custodial staff. Because inmates are crucial or central to the operation of the prison, are not likely to be replaced by other workers, and can deal relatively well with the various contingencies of prison life, it is easy to see how they would have power within the institution. This observation is equally applicable to police officers. Research has documented how certain police positions are more powerful than others and that the types of power used by police are constrained by the task required and the police hierarchy (Tifft, 1978:104).

Sergeants in tactical units, for example, have high rewards and coercive power available to them. They make the determinations, in most cases, of who will come and go into the unit. Moreover, many sergeants have high expert power. Their knowledge of the activities in the unit makes them hard to replace and critical to the police organization. Before we continue, however, we need to summarize the key aspects of power in organizations. First, power denotes that "a person or group of persons or organization of persons determines, that is, ... affects, what another person or group or organization will do" (Tannenbaum, 1962:236). Second, power exists among the units of an organization as well as at the interpersonal level. Much of the research has emphasized the interpersonal aspects with little regard for the organizational level, thus obscuring the importance of departmental power in the organizational setting. Third, power in an organization depends on how subunits deal with uncertainty and on whether they meet the criteria of substitutability and centrality. A hypothesis in the literature is that units that meet these criteria are able not only to influence the direction of the organization but also to solidify themselves in power positions (Michels, 1949).

Finally, we must differentiate between power and authority. Many have considered these terms interchangeable, yet, as Pfeffer (1981) suggests, doing so is not helpful to an understanding of the process of power acquisition in organizations. He posits, therefore, that the two can be best understood by examining the extent to which employees "legitimize" their use. He further argues that the use of authority seems legitimate to those being supervised or controlled in an organization. Power, however, especially purely coercive power, is not a form of compliance that sustains organizational life. Power that is legitimized over time becomes characterized as authority. This view of power and authority has many ramifications for organizations. Ultimately, organizations seek the expression of authority rather than power. Pfeffer (1981:4) states the following:

By transforming power into authority, the exercise of influence is transformed in a subtle but important way. In social institutions, the exercise of power typically has costs. Enforcing one's way over others requires the expenditure of resources, the making of commitments, and a level of effort that can be undertaken only when the issues at hand are relatively important. On the other hand, the exercise of authority, power that has become legitimated, is expected and desired in the social context. Thus, the exercise of authority, far from diminishing through use, may actually serve to enhance the amount of authority subsequently possessed.

For our purposes here, we want to know the types of power and authority employed in criminal justice organizations. In addition, it is equally important to match types of power and authority with tasks. Police, for example, may require specific types of authority or power or both to perform their jobs. The same is true for corrections. As a result, the issue becomes identifying those types of power or authority that enhance the ability of a component of criminal justice to successfully complete its objectives. Some types of power and some types of authority are more suitable than others.

TYPES OF POWER AND AUTHORITY

Any discussion of the types of authority must begin with the work of Weber (1947). From his earliest writings, Weber distinguished authority and power, with authority denoting compliance with particular directives essential for achieving a common or shared goal. Power is based on coercion, not compliance, and is used in organizations that emphasize strict obedience, for example, slave-labor camps and some prisons.

Traditional authority: Authority vested in a position that a person holds and that has a long tradition in a culture or organization.

Weber delineated three types of authority: traditional, charismatic, and legal. **Traditional authority** is authority that is vested in the position a person holds and that has a long tradition in a culture or organization. This type of authority can be found in countries with traditional monarchies. Within organizations, one can say that old and well-tested methods of operation are part of the organization's tradition or, equally important, may reflect the interests of those who run the organization in maintaining the status quo. As Hall and Tolbert (2005) suggest, traditional authority is expressed in the saying, "The old man wants it that way." The second type of authority is **charismatic authority**. This type is founded in the personal attributes or actions (or both) of a particular individual in an organization.

Charismatic authority: Authority found in the personal attributes or actions (or both) of a particular individual in an organization.

President John F. Kennedy, for example, wielded tremendous amounts of charismatic authority, largely because many people found attractive qualities in him. An example in the criminal justice field is the veteran police officer. Many officers who have spent a long time on the streets adopt a "police personality" that they are able to turn into charismatic authority. The flamboyant police officer described in many novels expresses this type of authority.

Finally, there is **legal authority**. This type of authority is based on an appeal to the formal rules and regulations of an organization. In addition, legal authority is rooted in the hierarchy of the organization. It is predicated on the belief that subordinates are expected to follow the orders and commands of those above them in the formal chain of command. Much of the authority exercised within criminal justice agencies is of this type. Corrections officers are organized in a chain of command, and officers assume that those above them in the institutional hierarchy have the right to impose rules and regulations. We will see, in later chapters of this book, how this type of authority breaks down under the strain of day-to-day activity.

Although Weber's ideas regarding authority have been widely adopted by those who seek to explain compliance mechanisms in organizations, his concept of power has not found as much acceptance. Current research has fostered an increased awareness of power in organizational settings, but most of this research has focused on power at the interpersonal rather than the organizational level and, in addition, is open to criticism on the grounds of validity and reliability. This is equally the case for research done on power distribution in the criminal justice system. These problems aside, we can still identify bases of power found in organizations and discuss them in light of what we know about criminal justice administration.

According to French and Raven (1968), there are five bases of power in all organizations. These bases (or types) of power are used to gain the compliance of subordinates. We will see that some are akin to the types of authority described by Weber. Others, however, match the traditional definition of power given previously in this chapter. The five types of power are reward, coercive, legitimate, referent, and expert. Although these bases of power were originally meant to explain the behavior of subordinates and supervisors at the interpersonal level, they may also be used to analyze power at the organizational level (Hall and Tolbert, 2005: 138). Moreover, these types of power are meant to be explored as interactions and relationships among individuals in organizations.

In short, there is no power unless it is expressed by one person and received by another. The person who expresses the power is called the **power holder**, and the receiver is called the **power recipient**. **Reward power** is based on the power recipient's perception that the power holder can grant some type of reward or remuneration for compliance with orders or commands.

An example of this type of power is the piecework system found in many factories. Workers do what the supervisor tells them in order to get paid. Without the reward by the supervisor or the company the supervisor represents, workers will not perform as ordered. It is the reward, in the form of a salary or hourly rate, that makes workers comply with the supervisor's directives.

Coercive power is based on the power recipient's perception that failure to follow orders will bring the threat of punishment or punishment itself. This type of power has been associated with traditional prison structures, where it is widely believed that an inmate who does not comply with the wishes of corrections officers will be punished. This is not always the case, however, and the belief in coercive power as the primary compliance mechanism in prison organizations

Legal authority: Authority rooted in the rules and regulations of an organization.

Power holder: One who has power in an organization.

Power recipient: The receiver of an expression of power from a power holder.

Reward power: The use of a reward by a power holder to gain the compliance of a power recipient.

Coercive power: The use or threat of punishment or actual punishment to gain compliance in an organization.

remains somewhat problematic given the nature of institutionalization today and the other forms of power available to corrections officers.

Legitimate power:
The use of power based on the internalized beliefs of a power recipient to gain compliance.

Legitimate power is exercised when a power holder is able to influence a power recipient to do something based on the power recipient's internalized belief. This type of power is most closely aligned to Weber's concept of authority. The internalized norm can be traced to many sources: cultural values, social structure, or a designated and legitimized informal leader. French and Raven (1968) suggest that an individual in an organization may follow the directives of a superior because the superior's power is legitimized by another, informal leader in the organization. Police officers may follow the commands of the shift sergeant not totally because of the traditional authority the commander has, but because an informal leader, such as a veteran police officer who is viewed as their legitimate representative, follows those commands. In this way, legitimate power can be expressed not only by those in the organization's chain of command but also by those in its informal sector. Problems arise when orders and commands made by those in the formal sector of the organization (police sergeants, for example) are not consistent with the expectations and demands of leaders exhibiting legitimate power at the informal level who are respected by rank-and-file workers (police officers). Such problems are a direct consequence of power relations in organizations, which we address in another section of this chapter.

Referent power:
The identification of a power holder with a power recipient to gain compliance.

Power based on the identification of the power holder with the power recipient is known as **referent power**. This fourth type of power is predicated on the power recipient's attraction to the power holder. French and Raven state: "In our terms, this would mean that the greater the attraction, the greater the identification and consequently the greater the referent power" (1968:265). This type of power can be seen in correctional institutions. In many instances, inmates view officers in a positive light and may even attempt to emulate a favored officer's attitudes and beliefs. An important difference among referent power and reward and coercive power is the mediation of rewards and punishments. In both reward and coercive power, the power holder is able to control rewards and sanctions. Referent power depends on the power recipient's identification with the power holder, regardless of the consequences of the relationship, positive or negative. An individual, for example, may have an opinion on a subject but will go along with the group because of a desire to be like other members of the group. The group in this case is exhibiting a strong form of referent power over the individual.

The literature on police socialization is full of examples of individual officers who, because of intense peer pressure, go along with the demands of their group even though this behavior violates police rules and regulations. Research on this topic has suggested that to understand the power of the group, we must understand the socialization process of police officers and how it reflects the expectations of society (Manning and Van Maanen, 1978; Stoddard, 1983). Chapter 9 discusses occupational socialization within criminal justice organizations.

Expert power: The power recipient's belief that the power holder has specialized knowledge in a specific area that allows compliance to be gained.

The final power base offered by French and Raven is expert power. **Expert power** is based on the power recipient's belief that the power holder has a high level of expertise in a given area. Based on the power recipient's "cognitive structure," expert power fosters the dependence of the power recipient on the power holder, although this dependence may lessen over time. In the social system of U.S. courts, for example, both defense and prosecuting attorneys undeniably exercise tremendous amounts of expert power over their clients, who rely on their attorney's special knowledge and comply with their wishes. Besides the French and Raven typology, other forms of power identified in the research literature are applicable to criminal justice administration. Bacharach and Lawler (1980) discuss information as an important source of power in organizations.

Individuals or groups may have power because of their ability to control information flow in the organization. Most important is the ability to control information essential for maintaining operations (Pfeffer, 1977a). This power can be distinguished from expert power because it is derived from position in the organization rather than knowledge. For example, inmates who understand the legal system exhibit expert power, whereas inmate clerks have access to information (such as knowing whose cell will be searched by corrections officers) that allows them to manipulate the prison structure to their advantage.

A final type of power is based on the ability to acquire and provide needed organizational resources. Research has shown how certain subunits in organizations become powerful because of their ability to acquire critical resources (Salancik and Pfeffer, 1977:3–21). Another work by Pfeffer and Salancik (1974) has suggested that subunit power is contingent largely on the ability of the subunit or department to gain outside grants and contract funds. This ability enables the subunit to have more prestige than the other subunits and to gain a lasting position of power in the organization (Lodahl and Gordon, 1973).

CONSEQUENCES OF POWER RELATIONS

Research on the effects of varying types of power in organizations is plentiful (see Hall, 1987:136–139). Using the French and Raven typology, Warren (1968) has shown that on the dimensions of **behavioral conformity** (conformity without internalization of norms) and **attitudinal conformity** (conformity and internalization of norms), schoolteachers showed high levels of attitudinal conformity when they were subject to expert, legitimate, and referent power, but they displayed behavioral conformity when they were subjected to reward and coercive power. It is important to recognize that differing kinds of power exist in organizations and that behavioral output changes noticeably when different types of power are employed.

This interpretation is further supported by Lord (1977), who analyzed the relationship between types of social power and leadership functions. Lord concludes that legitimate power is highly related to the leadership functions of developing orientation (providing direction to employees), communicating, and coordinating, whereas coercive power is most highly related to facilitating evaluations, proposing solutions, and total functional behavior. He maintains that various types of power have different impacts on the organization and its members. In a study of power in hospitals, Julian (1966) concludes that,

Behavioral conformity: Conformity without internalization of norms.

Attitudinal conformity: Conformity with internalization of norms.

depending on the type of hospital, different types of power are utilized. Voluntary hospitals, for example, rely on a legitimate power system with talks and explanations provided to patients. In contrast, veterans' hospitals employed methods of coercion to gain compliance.

By using sedation and the restriction of activity, workers were able to get compliance and, at the same time, fulfill their primary organizational goal: control of patients. An implication from this research is that differing organizations use diverse types of power to accomplish their organizational goals, and the type and amount of power used are variable and contextual.

The same is true of criminal justice organizations. Tifft (1978:90), in his analysis of control systems and social bases of power in police organizations, attempted to examine the "structural conditions" that affect the location of power. In addition, he was interested in exploring how these conditions affect the exercise of power, how they can be altered to increase organizational control, and what the consequences of these structures are on the people within the organization. He concludes (1978:104) that there are structural factors within police organizations that contain the bases of power available to police sergeants. He further suggests that differing policies would have to be implemented within different police units for the effective exercise of police sergeant power. Detective units, for example, would be best suited if sergeants had previous experience in the unit because expert power or knowledge is critical to the sergeant role. Knowledge of the methods and operations of burglars and robbers provides the sergeant with requisite information that is respected and valued by subordinate detectives. Because expert power is so critical to the sergeant's role in a detective unit, it would be prudent for police administrators to place people in the unit who have had some experience as detectives. In this way, organizational control is enhanced.

The consequence of such a policy would be greater effectiveness and efficiency within the unit. Tifft further states that the various functional units of a police force allow differing types of power to be developed. He mentions that a patrol sergeant has coercive and legitimate power because of that unit's specific tasks, whereas a tactical unit exhibits high levels of referent, legitimate, and expert power because of its own unique structural design and activities.

Traffic sergeants are not able to develop referent and expert bases of power because of the nature of the unit's tasks, the rapid rotation of officers out of the unit, and the minimal types of expertise required to conduct routine traffic investigations. Thus, we would expect that legitimate, reward, and coercive power are the primary tools of compliance available to the traffic sergeant. In addition, as Tifft (1978:100) states, even coercive and reward power may be circumscribed by the ideology, intraorganizational conflicts, and size of the unit.

Stojkovic (1984, 1986) reports similar findings on the expression of power in correctional institutions. He found five types of social power among prisoners: coercive, referent, legitimate, provision of resources, and expert. Coercive power was employed by prisoners in the inmate social system to gain "respect"; referent power was the mechanism of compliance used by various religious groups; legitimate power rested with those inmates who were older and had longer periods of confinement; provision-of-resource power was exhibited by those inmates who could distribute contraband materials, often illegal narcotics; and expert power was found among those prisoners who were knowledgeable about the legal system and could provide legal assistance to other prisoners.

Stojkovic concluded that the social bases of power are much more circumscribed for corrections administrators than for inmates. He found only three types of power among corrections administrators: coercive, reward, and access to information. These bases of power were easily eroded, however, and had limited effectiveness in gaining the compliance of inmates and corrections officers. Prisoners, for example, perceived access-to-information power as the result of active "snitch" recruiting on the part of corrections officials and thus pernicious and destructive to the institutional environment. This finding obviously raises questions about which types of power are more conducive to organizational stability.

Both Stojkovic (1987) and Hepburn (1985) report interesting findings on the power of corrections officers. Hepburn (1985) found that because of significant changes in the administration of prisons and the demographics of prisoners, corrections officers are required to do their jobs much differently today from in the past. Interestingly enough, he does not depict prison guards as solely concerned with punishing or coercing prisoners. He found that both legitimate and expert power were used by corrections officers; that referent and reward bases of power were weak; and that although it was not as prevalent as other types of power, coercive power was used by some guards.

These findings contrast with those of Stojkovic (1987:6–25) in his analysis of power among corrections officers. Although Hepburn (1985) found reward power to be weak among the officers he surveyed, Stojkovic found the reliance-on-reward power to be strong among corrections officers in his study. This finding is consistent with previous research that suggests that "accommodative relationships" are at the core of the relationship between corrections officers and prisoners (Sykes, 1958:40–62; Sykes and Messinger, 1960). In addition, although Hepburn found that many corrections officers he studied relied on coercive power less than other forms of power, later research suggests that, at least in some parts of the country, this method of gaining compliance among prisoners is still strong (Marquart, 1986b). Future research will have to be conducted to accurately assess the bases of power among corrections officers.

In addition, others have suggested that earlier research on correctional organizations was premised on *perceptions* of power and did not examine how power is *manifested*. Smith, Applegate, Sitren, and Springer (2009: 246–47) found that the distinction between perceived power and manifest power is critical and important. Unlike earlier research that focused on prisons, these researchers examined how the bases of power affected probationers' compliance to the conditions of their sentences. It is interesting that a high perception of power did not result in manifest power. While probation officers in this study were perceived by probationers to have many differing bases of power available to them, this did not affect whether or not they complied with the conditions of their sentences. Further, the researchers suggest that it may be that officers are not utilizing the power they have appropriately to gain compliance among probationers and that power may be more influential at the organizational level and not the individual level, something we noted earlier in the chapter. In fact, the emphasis on individual power of officers masks the important role that criminal justice managers and administrators play in influencing power relations across units and departments within the criminal justice system.

In summary, we have seen that the social bases of power vary from organization to organization and that certain structural characteristics affect the types of power within an organization. The important question becomes: Under what conditions and with what tasks are specific types of power more appropriate than others? We have found that depending on the police unit and function, different types of power are required. Within the institutional corrections system, we have seen how the bases of power differ from group to group. For criminal justice administration, then, the key issue is recognizing the correct type of power for the situation while being aware of the structural constraints of the organization. Moreover, we need to understand that perceived power may not translate into manifest power or actually produce more compliant subordinates. Obviously, certain types of power are not going to be useful within many criminal justice organizations. Gaining compliance in correctional institutions through purely coercive methods, for example, is doomed to failure because of the nature of the institutional groups. In fact, this type of response was attempted and failed miserably in many correctional institutions (Jacobs, 1977). This same argument can be applied to the police field. Employing coercive methods of compliance among rank-and-file officers, usually through strict rules and regulations, is no longer satisfactory because many officers are averse to such strategies.

In fact, many have called for a loosening of the police organizational structure to make it receptive not only to the changing nature of the police officer but also, and more important, to the role of the police in society. External groups and demands from these groups have also had a tremendous impact on the operating methods of police departments. In essence, some traditional methods of compliance in criminal justice agencies may not be perceived as legitimate by many criminal justice employees and the general public. Because legitimacy is crucial to effective criminal justice administration, several important management questions remain: What types of power are perceived as legitimate by those who perform criminal justice functions? If improper types of power are employed by criminal justice administrators, what are the end results? We have seen, again, the importance of distinguishing perceived power from manifest power, with the latter stressing outcomes of power relations. These questions and concerns lead us to the topic of the next section of this chapter: the connection between the legitimacy of power and political behavior in criminal justice organizations.

Work Perspective: POLITICS AND PUBLIC SAFETY

Politics is the art of looking for trouble, finding it whether it exists or not, diagnosing it incorrectly, and applying the wrong remedy.

—Ernest Benn

In my view, the leader of a correctional agency has two primary functions. The first is to administer the existing system in a safe, effective, and fiscally responsible manner—a challenging but not impossible task. The second is to analyze the existing system, diagnose the changes necessary to improve it, and then utilize the political system to effectuate those changes. This is made particularly difficult in a corrections agency because both politicians and prison systems are extremely risk averse. As the Secretary of the California Department of Corrections and Rehabilitation, I have spent much of my time and energy over the last three years focused on three fundamental challenges: addressing prison overcrowding, reducing the department's $10 billion budget, and lowering the system's 70 percent recidivism rate. Of course, the quickest way to reduce overcrowding and spending is to reduce the number of offenders in prison and on parole. This is turn would allow the system to focus its precious rehabilitation resources on the remaining offenders, thereby lowering recidivism over time. The problem for me was, and to a degree still is, how to convince elected officials to take the steps necessary to get the job done?

The first answer is to educate policy makers. It seems straightforward, but it is actually more complex than one would suspect. One must obtain both a thorough understanding of the systemic problems at hand and the best possible solutions available. For example, it helped immensely to be able to speak with authority concerning how other jurisdictions have reduced crowding in their prisons by giving inmates additional credits for earning a high school diploma or GED. Once legislators and the governor understood we could reduce overcrowding, lower costs, and reduce crime through this simple change, most got on board.

Another effective technique is to utilize one crisis to solve another. In California, the fiscal crisis became so severe that policy makers had no choice but to seek new approaches to reduce costs. In the prison setting, for example, that meant conservative politicians were willing to vote for parole reform in order to reduce the state's deficit. It helped that some liberal politicians would only agree to cut funding for social services if prison spending was cut. Simply put, I don't believe that many of the recent changes to California's criminal justice laws would have passed absent the current fiscal crisis.

But perhaps the most important job of a government leader is relationship building. The decision to work constructively with the department rather than criticize it is often based on whether a personal relationship with the elected official has been established. As with every occupation, it is more difficult to attack people we know. In the world of politics and public safety, where criticism is the norm, making a few friends is the key to getting things done.

SOURCE: Matthew L. Cate, Former Secretary, California Department of Corrections and Rehabilitation.

THE LEGITIMACY OF POWER AND POLITICAL BEHAVIOR

According to Tosi, Rizzo, and Carroll (1986:527), "when legitimate authority fails, political behavior arises." **Political behavior** may be defined as any action by a criminal justice worker that promotes individual goals over organizational goals. In their opinion, political behavior exists in organizations when there is (1) a lack of consensus among members about goals, (2) disagreement over the means to achieve goals, or (3) anxiety about resource allocation. Because each of these problems exists within many criminal justice agencies, political behavior among criminal justice employees is inevitable. Let us examine these three problems within correctional institutions, beginning with the lack of goal consensus among corrections staff. Before we proceed with this discussion, however, we need to clarify that not *all* political behavior is inappropriate or bad.

Political behavior:
An action by a criminal justice employee that promotes individual goals over organizational goals.

Political process: The method by which things are addressed both inside and outside criminal justice organizations.

When we examine how things are accomplished within criminal justice organizations, we see that the **political process** is the accepted mechanism to address matters. For many, politics is a dirty word. Our presentation here is that without a political process nothing would get done within criminal justice organizations. The political process is used, both legitimately and illegitimately, by criminal justice officials; it is the essence of the democratic process. Our concern is when inappropriate behaviors occur such that criminal justice organizations lose sight of their mission and/or purpose and the political process leads us toward outcomes that are not in our best interests. Take, for example, the drug war over the past twenty years. Both police agencies and correctional systems took from the various levels of governments *in the political process* billions of dollars to confront the nation's drug problem, maintaining they were the primary institutions in society that could stem the tide of illegal drug usage. After twenty years of expanding criminal justice organizations—that is, more police and more prisons—what have we delivered regarding an impact on illegal drug usage?

Critics of criminal justice agencies have expressed dissatisfaction with criminal justice officials regarding their strategies to address the nation's drug problem. For these critics, investments of limited tax dollars into public education and treating drug abuse as a health problem and not a criminal justice problem would be a more prudent course of action. Criminal justice organizations became aligned with *political positions and interests* that produced questionable outcomes, with enormous costs for the citizenry and those who were brought into the criminal justice system. In this example, we played into the irrational fears and interests of politicians who were pandering to citizens' fears regarding crime, especially drug-related crime and violence. Very few people as criminal justice leaders spoke truth to power when decisions were being made on supporting criminal justice functions and services during the 1980s, 1990s, and the beginning of the twenty-first century. In addition, very few criminal justice leaders were asking whether a singular focus on criminal justice activities really aids us in addressing illegal drug usage. Instead, through the political process, many criminal justice officials took the money and ran and lost sight of their fundamental missions and purposes. At one level, they lost their souls. Marion and Oliver (2009) provide a fascinating account of the relationship between crime and the budgetary responsiveness of Congress. Arguing that earlier research had shown that from 1935 to 1975, Congress was very responsive to what they perceived to be rising crime rates, yet this all changed in the 1980s and 1990s and beyond when crime appropriations were skyrocketing but crime rates had reached a plateau or dramatically dropped. What explained this disjuncture? Marion and Oliver argue that crime legislation and appropriations had become part of a symbolic attempt to show that legislators are tough on crime and reinforce a perception of toughness through the passing of harsh laws, even as misdirected as those perceptions might be. Marion and Oliver (2009:132) state: "Congress is no longer responsive to official crime rates but are rather responsive to what policies sell well and help them obtain both public support and legislative victories. Because crime sells and sells well, crime policy has become more symbolic, even to the extent of the budgetary process."

The net result of such political behavior was that expectations of citizens became jaded, criminal justice workers were left with impossible mandates to fulfill, and limited tax dollars were being spent on entities and activities that had only a marginal relation to any desirable outcome, in this case a reduction in illegal drug usage. For criminal justice administrators, the fall is beginning and becoming hard as budgets are cut and personnel are let go due to new political processes that define criminal justice organizations not as problem solvers but as the *problem*. Moreover, funding that was targeted in the past for criminal justice activities is now being redirected to other organizations, such as schools, transportation, and health care, that are competing for limited tax dollars to support their efforts.

The important point is that politics is a process and cannot simply be viewed in pejorative terms. We function as criminal justice organizations in a political process. How we work that process is important in defining who we are and where we are headed. For the political process to be useful to criminal justice administrators, they need to know who they are (mission), where they want to be (vision), and how the political process is central to defining these important issues. It is when the political process is pursued with no clear sense of mission and purpose that the bad side of politics can rear its ugly head. Regarding the drug war, too many criminal justice agencies took the money at the expense of redefining their missions and visions to their long-term detriment. In this example, and for the critics of criminal justice agencies, the political process produced limited beneficial outcomes that clearly, in the long run, hurt the legitimacy of criminal justice operations and devastated the lives of many citizens. Having said this, we now turn back to a discussion of the genesis of political behavior within criminal justice organizations.

Regarding goal consensus, research in correctional institutions since the 1950s has indicated that disagreement over goals among corrections staff has created not only political behavior but also ineffective operations. This disagreement essentially concerns treatment versus punishment. Is the purpose of correctional institutions primarily to punish offenders, to rehabilitate them, or both? This debate has not only created conflict about the purpose of imprisonment but, in addition, has raised the issue of whether such conflicting goals can realistically be met within the prison setting. Research has clearly indicated the variability of attitudes among corrections employees about the real purpose of imprisonment (Klofas and Toch, 1982). This research has also questioned whether there is any public consensus about the primary purpose of our correctional institutions. Lack of agreement, both internally and externally, has created a situation conducive to political behavior. Without the legitimacy engendered by agreement on goals among corrections workers and acceptance of these goals by the public, prescriptive recommendations about the appropriate types of power to be employed in these organizations are of little or no value. The only value in suggesting specific types of power within criminal justice organizations is if they are able to create legitimacy and acceptance among those who work in these organizations.

A similar issue arises in discussing the proper means to attain the agreed-upon goals. For years, for example, police organizations have debated the issue of what types of patrolling are the most appropriate, efficient, and effective in achieving the generally accepted goals of crime prevention and societal protection. Whether the debate is over foot patrol versus motorized patrol or one-person cars versus two-person cars, the lack of agreement among police administrators, the general public, and officers on the beat regarding the appropriate means to achieve these goals raises questions regarding their legitimacy. This, in turn, has created a climate in which political behavior flourishes. Once again, prescribing proper methods of obtaining compliance within criminal justice organizations becomes pointless when legitimacy is absent. Moreover, in recent times, there have been questions about the appropriate measures to accomplish the goals of crime reduction and community safety.

Both supporters and ardent critics of police have debated what the most effective organizational structure is for police departments. Supporters have suggested that reinforcing the paramilitary structure within police organizations and providing greater resources for aggressive patrol strategies are the most effective ways to guarantee crime reduction and community safety (Bratton, 1996). Others, however, question the long-term utility of such an approach and seek reorganization of police departments to be more consistent with decentralized organizational structures (Fyfe, 2004b; Goldstein, 1990; Trojanowicz and Bucqueroux, 1990). These critics suggest that more community-oriented and problem-oriented approaches would be more effective in the reduction of crime and the enhancement of community safety. The debate between these two schools of thought on police structure has caused much opportunity for political behavior to flourish within police departments. In addition, it has produced a situation in many departments where differences among officers, supervisors, and administrators are split along various dimensions, including but not limited to race, educational level, experience level, and gender. This same political behavior occurs within community corrections agencies as well.

Schlager (2009) provides a fascinating essay on how organizational politics can undermine the most effective methods of supervising offenders in the community. She provides a detailed account of how organizational politics can work toward the lack of adoption of risk assessment methodologies to supervise large numbers of offenders in the community. Risk assessment is a technique that can be used by community corrections professionals to enhance their possibilities of protecting the community and changing offender behavior, yet the ideal of risk assessment and the reality of implementation can often lead toward a mire of organizational politics and ultimately no or limited application within community correctional agencies. Without the clear support of administrators, a commitment to a new paradigm, and increased professionalism among community corrections personnel, the chances of implementation of risk-assessment tools is highly unlikely. The point is that no new approach to criminal justice operates in an organizational vacuum. Politics are part of the process of implementation. Minimizing negative politics is one of the primary roles of criminal justice administrators.

Finally, because criminal justice agencies rely on the public budgeting process and must compete with other social service agencies for funds, it is inevitable that political behavior results. Political behavior, in this instance, may not be bad in and of itself because it can be useful in acquiring resources for the organization. In fact, political behavior is a very necessary skill for an effective criminal justice administrator to possess. In this case, appropriate political behavior may be viewed as legitimate not only by employees but also by others in the political arena. When the expression of political power is viewed as illegitimate by employees, the public, and significant political figures in the community, it can have a deleterious effect on the organization. Paparozzi and Caplan (2009) raise the issue of legitimacy among paroling authorities in their review of parole authority professionalism across the fifty states. They found that most departments of correction do not require professional qualifications as a prerequisite to serve on a parole board. The authors question whether such an important task—deciding who gets released from prison—should be left to persons who do not have relevant professional qualifications. Again, the concern is the erosion of trust that may occur among many in the public if they do not believe the efforts of a criminal justice agency are legitimate.

Our purpose in this section is not to speak pejoratively about political behavior in criminal justice organizations, especially as it relates to budgeting. Our purpose is rather to propose some bases of power conducive to the development of legitimate authority in criminal justice organizations that prevent the perpetuation of political behaviors that do not contribute to the effective and efficient operation of these agencies. We begin with an examination of the political processes of criminal justice organizations.

Dalton (1959) suggests that the diffusion of types of power in organizations produces a concomitant rise of powerful cliques or coalitions. These cliques defend their members in response to various threats to organizational autonomy. Pfeffer (1981:36) points out that such cliques and coalitions are highly political, relying on various strategies to advance their own purposes and causes over those of other coalitions in the organization. The political nature of coalitions and their power configurations are relevant to decision-making processes in organizations (Allison, 1969; Kaufman, 1964; March, 1962; Pandarus, 1973). More important, these political behaviors erode employees' sense of legitimacy and may lead to a number of dysfunctional behaviors in the organization.

Such results are nowhere more apparent than in the agencies of criminal justice. Prisons, for example, have been fragmented along interest-group lines for many years, both internally and externally (Stastny and Tyrnauer, 1982). Because inmates, corrections officers, and administrators have been traditionally alienated from one another, prisons have been ineffective in accomplishing many of their goals. This observation is consistent with our previous observation that lack of consensus among groups in an organization reduces legitimacy and engenders political behavior. Only by obtaining consensus can the issues of means to achieve goals and resource allocation be resolved.

Many similar observations can be made in police organizations. Much research has been done since the 1960s on management models for effective police supervision; volumes of research have discussed how police supervisors should manage their subordinates. Yet much basic disagreement remains about what police should be doing and what methods are the most effective for the accomplishment of their goals. We can speculate that because of a lack of consensus on goals, disagreement over what means should be applied to achieve those agreed-upon goals, and uncertainty over resource allocation, police organizations are prime places for political behavior to occur. In fact, much of the research on police socialization is, in effect, research on the political actions or behaviors of police officers, for example, police corruption.

Similarly, organizational behavioral research has demonstrated how competition for scarce resources among both employees and departments within organizations inevitably leads toward political behavior, but it also suggests that where great uncertainty exists about decision-making procedures and performance measures among employees, there is a high probability that political behavior will flourish (Beeman and Starkey 1987). Again, criminal justice organizations tend to have both of these characteristics. These organizations are, therefore, fertile ground for political behavior.

Is political behavior only a function of situational or structural characteristics of criminal justice organizations? Hellriegel, Slocum, and Woodman (1995) suggest that certain personality traits make some people more prone to exercising political behaviors in organizations. These four personality traits are the need for power, Machiavellianism, locus of control, and risk-seeking propensity. The *need for power* is a common trait among both effective and ineffective leaders. Depending on what the leader desires, this may or may not be an effective trait. Leaders who seek simply to dominate others through expressions of power will create climates where political behavior is more likely than those leaders who seek power to move employees toward some identifiable and acceptable levels of performance.

Machiavellianism is predicated on the ideas of manipulation and deceit. Administrators who exhibit this trait view political behavior as a prerequisite to effective leadership. Such a trait accentuates manipulation of employees for specific ends and, in the long run, perpetuates greater division among employees and between employees and administrators.

Locus of control refers to an individual's ability to control his or her fate within an organization. Persons with a high *internal locus* believe they are able to control and influence other people and their surroundings. Political behavior is simply an expression of that high internal locus, willfully expressed.

Similarly, individuals with a high propensity for **risk taking** are much more likely to engage in political behavior than those individuals with a low risk-taking propensity. These persons view risk taking as a necessity within a politically charged organization. They enjoy taking the risks and acting out the political behavior that is a necessary element of taking risks.

These four personality traits, again, are not necessarily bad, yet more often than not they can produce deleterious political behavior. Such traits must be assessed as effective or ineffective dependent on what the person exercising them is seeking. In criminal justice administrators, political behaviors can be evaluated on the basis of whether or not they are directed toward the long-term interests of the organization or the narrow interests of the supervisor,

Machiavellianism: The use of manipulation and deceit to gain a favored position within a criminal justice organization.

Locus of control: The ability of an individual to control his/her fate within a criminal justice organization.

Risk taking: Taking chances as part of a personality style to achieve goals within criminal justice organizations.

manager, or administrator. If the latter is the predominant perception among employees, then they will view their superior's political behavior in a negative light. If, however, the political behavior is understood as unifying employees toward legitimate objectives and goals of the organization, then employees will interpret the political behavior as positive for the organization. The leader's personality traits and concomitant political behaviors must be understood within this context. In some cases, being able to control those personality traits that lead toward adverse political behaviors is a true test of a criminal justice administrator. In other cases, the proper exercising of these traits is useful and desirable within criminal justice organizations and is viewed as legitimate by criminal justice employees.

EFFECTIVE TYPES OF POWER

The critical question becomes: What types of power are criminal justice employees most likely to consider legitimate? Borrowing from the work of Tosi, Rizzo, and Carroll (1986:540–542), we can identify the psychological effects of specific types of power on individuals, as represented in Figure 10-1. In this model, the five bases of power correspond to the French and Raven (1968) typology, examined previously in the chapter. (Charismatic power is analogous to French and Raven's referent power.)

These types of power have three possible effects: (1) the exercise of legitimate, charismatic, and expert power leads to employee acceptance, (2) reward and coercive power may lead to acceptance if the power is used for some legitimate purpose, or (3) reward and coercive power may lead to two dysfunctional effects—learned helplessness and resistance—if the power is used for illegitimate purposes. For example, when a police sergeant employs coercive power to motivate an officer, the officer perceives this use of power as having a legitimate purpose and therefore accepts it.

This model also stresses ancillary effects of power exercised in organizations, all of which are relevant to criminal justice administrations. Although legitimate, charismatic, and expert bases of power lead to acceptance from employees, this acceptance leads to the rationalization and justification of the behavior. In short, the power recipient legitimizes, understands, and accepts the directives of the supervisor. When learned helplessness and resistance are the effects, increased psychological dependence, psychological withdrawal, attempts to modify power relationships, and possible physical withdrawal from the organization occur. These effects may be manifested through appeals to reason by the power recipient to the power holder, minimal compliance, sabotage, development of a counterforce, and departure from the organization. All are common reactions to power expression in criminal justice organizations, and their frequency may decrease the efficiency and effectiveness of these organizations.

Many researchers have suggested that prisons are prime breeding grounds not only for the political behavior mentioned previously but also for the dysfunctional behaviors associated with coercive and reward types of power. It

FIGURE 10.1   The Psychological Effects of the Use of Power in Organizations.

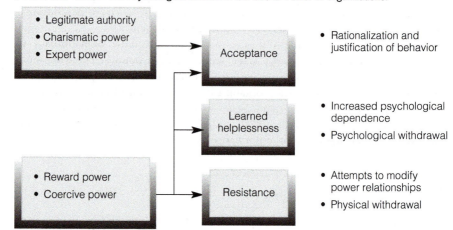

SOURCE: From H. L. Tosi, J. R. Rizzo, and S. J. Carroll, *Managing Organizational Behavior*. Copyright 1986 by Pitman Publishing Company. Reprinted by permission of Harper & Row Publishers, Inc.

is all too common in the literature on prisons to see that both inmates and corrections staff, suffering from learned helplessness, ultimately withdraw from the institution in either a psychological or a physical sense. In fact, stress among correctional employees is a central concern for prison administrators (Owen, 2006). Many of these characteristics may be, in part, reactions to the exercise of coercive power by supervisors in these organizations. More directly, much of what we know about social systems in prisons can be tied to the illegitimacy of current types of power exercised by both corrections administrators and officers. The inmate social system may represent a counterforce to the power of those in command of the organization.

These effects of the use of power are seen equally in police organizations. Much current research has explored the problems associated with the traditional police structure. We are arguing here that the types of power traditionally associated with that structure are, in part, the cause of resistance, most notably the development of a police counterforce and departures from the organization. The research literature has documented the development of subcultures in police organizations that may oppose the formal structure. In addition, the high turnover in many police departments can be tied to the types of power exercised by supervisors.

However, if legitimate, charismatic, and expert bases of power lead to acceptance among employees, as shown in Figure 10.1, then it would seem logical to attempt to employ these uses of power in our criminal justice organizations. A body of research supports this position. Etzioni (1961) suggests that organizations enjoy a high level of commitment from members if they are involved in the organization, which they cannot be if coercive and reward power are used. Current research reports similar findings. The amount of control exhibited by employees in their organization is directly related to compliance with organizational rules and regulations (Houghland, Shepard, and Wood, 1979; Houghland and Wood, 1980; Styskal, 1980). In effect, as the organization is legitimized by subordinates, it gains compliance from them.

Much can be said about the value of instilling a sense of legitimacy in criminal justice employees. As we have seen, negative political behavior tends to surface in organizations where legitimacy is not present. Such seems to be the case in many criminal justice organizations; to suggest otherwise would be naive. The future of criminal justice administrations hinges to a great degree on how legitimacy will be gained from both subordinates and the general public. The use of other methods of compliance in these organizations is just one avenue that deserves attention by those who administer our agencies of social control. The traditional types of power employed in these agencies no longer promote effective administration. Other bases of power would seem to be conducive to criminal justice management.

We can only speculate about what these other bases would be. It is easy to say that legitimate, expert, and referent bases of power need to be developed, yet this statement assumes that we have goal congruity, methods to achieve goals, and certainty about budget allocations in these organizations.

Attention must be given to these problems if effective compliance structures in criminal justice organizations are to be created. We can then develop bases of power that are consistent with our objectives and, more important, are perceived as legitimate by the lay public and by those who perform the day-to-day tasks in criminal justice agencies. Moreover, we must concern ourselves with the role that political behaviors play in criminal justice administration. Some criminal justice employees and administrators believe that "everything is politics." This cynical view exists at two levels within criminal justice organizations. At the first level, it is understood as part of a larger political process that dictates and directs how criminal justice organizations will function. For many criminal justice administrators, political behavior means playing politics with legislators, public interest groups, governor's staff, unions, and other interested parties. This type of activity comes with the territory of being a criminal justice administrator, yet as we proceed into the twenty-first century, many criminal justice administrators express the concern that politics and political interests have too much influence on the daily operations of their organizations.

Such a view of politics suggests that it is too invasive and pervasive in criminal justice organizations and negatively affects the ability of administrators and managers to do their jobs effectively. (See Lehr and O'Neill, 2001, for a fascinating account of how "bad politics" influenced the FBI in its dealing with Boston organized crime figures.) This is a legitimate concern among criminal justice administrators, yet it is not clear how this situation can be altered. Given the public nature of criminal justice organizations, political influences will always shape how these entities perform their duties. At this level, the criminal justice administrator will have to develop and hone his or her political skills in such a way that protection of organizational turf is possible while simultaneously attending to their concerns. This means becoming more politically astute and active in the determination of their fates. Too often, criminal justice administrators have shown passive attention to political detail. Such a strategy will no longer attend to either the needs of the organization or the concerns of individual employees. As a consequence, playing politics may not be a bad thing for criminal justice administrators at this level. In fact, it is a necessity. At a second level, however, political behavior within criminal justice organizations may be detrimental to long-term stability and functioning if that behavior is too removed from the concerns of employees who perform the routine tasks of the organization.

Herein lies a fundamental disjuncture between the interests of employees (typically centered on accomplishing tasks) and administrators (centered on the political concerns of their bosses or significant others). At the administrator level, employees view playing politics as a dirty process. A common sentiment among employees is that their interests are often sacrificed for larger political interests. At this level, the expression of power is most felt by criminal justice workers. Not only must administrators display effective uses of power that are legitimized by subordinates, but these expressions of power must also be understood as having a political dimension. Effective criminal justice administration means being sensitive not only to the political demands of external interests but also showing concern for the constraints and difficulties experienced by subordinates. Exercising differing forms of power provides clear examples of where priorities lie for criminal justice administrators. Not to recognize the importance of the way expressions of power fall along these two dimensions is a critical error commonly made by those who administer criminal justice organizations. Criminal justice administrators, supervisors, and managers must stay aware of this two-dimensional perspective on power. Only through such awareness will they fully appreciate the effective use of power.

Moreover, most criminal justice subordinates are public employees with significant rights as defined through labor negotiations and contracts. In some cases, as civil service employees, they are accountable to a host of public regulations that make management and administration more cumbersome and difficult. For the criminal justice administrator, it is essential to make sure that the political process is used correctly to define what can and cannot be pursued. Administrators have an obligation to promote the best possible strategy to achieve their missions and visions, both being constrained and directed by civil service requirements and labor contracts. This process is inherently political and is an expression of political power. Many criminal justice administrators have fared poorly when it comes to working with their political leaders to define and direct labor agreements consistent with their missions and visions. (See an interesting discussion by Rainey, 2014, on how there was an attempt to limit civil service protections to employees in the Department of Homeland Security. Ultimately, a compromise was reached that addressed both increased flexibility in the hiring, firing, and termination of employees and provided employee protections.)

SUMMARY

Understand a definition of power as being both an individual construct and an organizational construct.

- Power has been examined on the individual level and the organizational level.
- Power and authority have been understood as being interchangeable, but this is not the case.

Distinguish the various types of authority and power.

- There are three types of authority according to Max Weber: traditional, charismatic, and legal.
- There are five types of power according to French and Raven: coercive, reward, legitimate, referent, and expert power. In addition, the literature has identified two other bases of power: control of information and access to resources.

Comprehend the consequence of power relations within criminal justice organizations.

- Consequences of power relations within organizations are along two dimensions: behavioral conformity and attitudinal conformity.
- Differing types of expressions of power will have different impacts on organizations, including attitudinal changes and behavioral changes among employees.

Grasp the importance of expressing power and political behavior among criminal justice administrators.

- There is a relationship between legitimacy and political behavior in criminal justice organizations. The political process is not an inherently bad process for criminal justice administrators. Political behavior can exist in organizations as a result of lack of consensus regarding goals, disagreement over the means to achieve goals, and anxiety about resource allocations.
- The political process is how things are accomplished by criminal justice organizations. The political process, in part, defines both mission and vision for criminal justice organizations.

Describe effective types of power within criminal justice organizations.

- Legitimate, charismatic, and expert power may lead to greater employee acceptance.
- Coercive and reward bases of power may lead to acceptance if the power is used for some legitimate purpose.
- Coercive and reward bases of power may lead to two dysfunctional effects— learned helplessness and resistance—if the power is used for illegitimate purposes.

Case Study: DOES KNOWLEDGE MATTER IN THE FACE OF POLITICAL POWER? THE CASE OF CHECK-CASHING ESTABLISHMENTS AND CRIME

This case study is based on the actual experience of a criminal justice colleague of the authors. This person was asked to provide an opinion on the incidence and prevalence of crime in a section of an affluent city in a Midwestern state by an attorney who was representing a private company that was in the loan and check-cashing business. The request seemed quite odd to our colleague until he was able to sit down with the attorney to discuss the particulars of the case. The facts of the case are fascinating and have implications for criminal justice administrators who have to deal with the political realm on a daily basis to perform their duties.

The attorney was suing the city for what he believed was an unreasonable and illegitimate ordinance passed by the city's common council to keep loan and check-cashing establishments from operating between the hours of 9:00 PM and 6:00 AM. The city has an outstanding reputation as one of the best cities in America, as rated by *Forbes* magazine, and has a flagship university with an impeccable reputation. Residents work for state and local governments and the university. In addition, the community has many small to moderately sized businesses, and the crime rate is very low. By all assessments and accounts, the community is an idyllic place to live.

The business, which was open twenty-four hours a day, was told to cease operations during the hours of 9:00 PM and 6:00 AM. The rationale for the proscription was that crime, especially robbery and other violent crime, would result. The primary rationale of the common council's decision was based on the fear of increased crime that such an establishment would bring to the community. Our colleague was asked to comment on the incidence and prevalence of crime at and surrounding the business for six months prior to its opening and six months after its opening when the business ceased the nighttime operations. The attorney wanted to know if there was an empirical basis for the rationale behind the ordinance.

Our colleague collected the crime incident data from the police department by police sector. In addition, he not only examined traditional crime data, such as the eight major index crime categories but also examined civil tickets issued by police for such minor crimes as disorderly conduct, trespassing, damage to property, and other property-related crimes. His analysis revealed, to the chagrin of the common council, that the business had very little crime in or around its location for the time period examined. In fact, the business that did have the most criminal activity was a nearby Taco Bell, largely due, he suspected, to the late

hours that it served food to college students and others who frequented taverns around the restaurant. The news sounded good for the attorney who represented the loan and check-cashing establishment.

When confronted with these facts regarding the incidence and prevalence of crime at and surrounding the business, the common council still upheld the ordinance, again citing concerns over crime and the possible influx of undesirables to the community. The attorney had no choice but to sue the city, claiming it was illegally denying his client the right to pursue his commercial interests with no legitimate justification. The claim found its way into federal court, where our colleague provided an affidavit regarding his analysis of the location of the loan and check-cashing business and the incidence and prevalence of crime. The affidavit affirmed that there was no empirical basis, at least found in the crime statistics, to deny the business the ability to operate at night because the amount of crime at or around the business was very small. No crime was directly related to the business, and there were no secondary effects.

The judge in the case listened intently and issued his opinion. Regardless of the analysis provided by our colleague, the judge ruled that the "evidence concerning crime incidence and prevalence didn't matter," and, moreover, that the council is imbued with an inherent right to govern. Through its normal powers as a governmental entity, the city could do whatever it deemed appropriate, even if they were uninformed, in error, or their theory was incorrect. For the city, this decision reaffirmed the ordinance. For the attorney, although he was disappointed with the decision, it still left open the opportunity to appeal to a higher court, even the U.S. Supreme Court.

For our colleague, the decision reflected something he suspected all along: when knowledge and power collide, power usually wins. It was a bit disconcerting to learn firsthand that "facts" and evidence have so little influence when it comes to the raw power of a court. This is not the first time that a court has blatantly disregarded the facts offered by social scientists. The *McCleskey v. Kemp* (1987) decision, for example, dismissed the scientific evidence on the disparate treatment of defendants who kill Whites compared to defendants who kill Blacks in death penalty cases. In this particular case, the Supreme Court ruled that Mr. McCleskey had to prove as an *individual* that he was discriminated against and that aggregate group data is not legally sufficient to show discrimination. For many social scientists, this decision served to, in part, question

---

CASE STUDY—continued

scientific inquiry as a means to determine the truth in a court of law.

For criminal justice administrators, speaking truth to power with facts and evidence can be difficult and sometimes pointless. This does not mean that facts and evidence don't matter, but they must be understood within the context of political interests and the power that people have to influence criminal justice administration and management. In fact, and somewhat ironically, this same colleague has written about how the use of knowledge in criminal justice organizations serves both symbolic and instrumental purposes of criminal justice administrators and reflects certain values and preferences. Understood this way, it is easy to see why knowledge acquisition will always be subservient to

political interests, both internal and external to criminal justice organizations.

CASE STUDY QUESTIONS

1. What role, if any, should empirical evidence play in criminal justice decision making and policy making? What role should politics play in the same processes?
2. Do you agree or disagree with the judge's ruling in this case study, and what are your arguments for the position you hold?
3. What is the role of social science research in criminal justice administration? How best can criminal justice researchers speak truth to power?

 ## Think like an Administrator

How does a criminal justice administrator speak truth to power? What if he or she knows, for example, that a particular activity or program does nothing to actually improve the organization or address crime in any way? Take, for example, the influence of the Drug Abuse Resistance Education (DARE) program on police activities and its acceptance among police administrators as an effective strategy to keep young people off drugs. Yet, there is no evidence that the DARE program does anything in relation to long-term drug usage among young people. (We will examine particulars of the DARE program in Chapter 15.) The program may have other benefits that were unintended and positive, such as pulling communities together to address other issues of significance, for example, vacant buildings and gang activity.

1. At the end of the day, how do we speak to others, especially influential community members, about programs that are not effective, even if they are well liked by them?
2. Do we as criminal justice administrators have both a moral and legal obligation to speak out against something we know does not work?
3. How does politics influence the adoption or deletion of an activity or program in a criminal justice organization?
4. Is politics always a "dirty" word, or should we separate the negative connotations of politics from the political process as a way things get done in criminal justice organizations? Is this distinction noteworthy and valuable to criminal justice administrators?
5. Can you envision the political process ever not being a part of criminal justice administration?

FOR DISCUSSION

1. Of the types of power described in this chapter, which do you think is the most relevant to a specific agency of the criminal justice system? Are the types of power exhaustive, or can you think of others besides the French and Raven typology presented here? Describe the strengths and weaknesses of this typology in criminal justice organizations.

2. What do you believe is the role of power in criminal justice administration? Is power important to agencies of criminal justice? What kind of power? Is it critical to have power as a criminal justice manager, and, if so, should this power be internally or externally based? Finally, describe instances where criminal justice administrators have abused their power, and offer suggestions about how we can control these individuals.

3. Distinguish between power and authority. Do you believe the foundation of criminal justice organizations is power or authority? Why? Give examples of everyday criminal justice that reflect the differences among these concepts.

4. Discuss the role of politics in criminal justice organizations. Is politics critical to these organizations, and, if so, how should it be controlled? Is it true, as Norton Long said years ago, that "politics is the lifeblood of administration" (1949:257) in public agencies like criminal justice organizations? Comment on the relevance of power to criminal justice administration and the survival of criminal justice organizations.

5. Is political behavior too pervasive within criminal justice organizations? Do legislatures, public interests, and private interests have too much influence on the organizations of criminal justice? If so, what would you recommend to alter such a situation? Provide some suggestions.

FOR FURTHER READING

Culbert, S. A., and McDonough, J. J. *Radical Management: Power Politics and the Pursuit of Trust.* New York: Free Press, 1985.

Kotter, J. P. *Power and Influence.* New York: Free Press, 1985.

Lehr, D., and O'Neill, G. *Black Mass: The True Story of an Unholy Alliance between the FBI and the Irish Mob.* New York: Harper Collins, 2001.

Mintzberg, H. *Power In and Around Organizations.* Englewood Cliffs, NJ: Prentice-Hall, 1983.

Pfeffer, J. *Power in Organizations.* Marshfield, MA: Pitman, 1981.

Srivastva, S. (Ed.) *Executive Power: How Executives Influence People and Organizations.* San Francisco: Jossey-Bass, 1986.

CHAPTER 11

Organizational Conflict

LEARNING OBJECTIVES

After reading this chapter, the students will have achieved the following objectives:

- Understand the definition of conflict.

- Know the major types of conflict in organizations.

- Define intra-organizational conflict.

- Know the types of intra-organizational conflict.

- Define interorganizational conflict.

- Describe the stages of a conflict episode.

- Know conflict behaviors.

- Define conflict management.

- Describe process interventions and structural interventions.

- Understand the limits to conflict management and their application to criminal justice organizations.

- Understand the role of conflict in organizations.

VIGNETTE

The Milwaukee *Journal-Sentinel* reported on January 6, 2011, the possible existence of a rogue element in the Milwaukee police department that operated under a set of norms that treated criminal suspects very harshly and outside the pale of departmental policies and procedures and existing laws. Known as the "Punishers," the group was named after a mythical character in a comic book. The purpose of the group was to mete out punishments to suspects outside the normal review of criminal justice processes. The article even reported that officers who were affiliated with the group had a skull insignia that could be found on some squad cars, departmental uniforms, and other clothing. The police chief was quoted as saying the group never really existed and was only an unsubstantiated rumor that, for the most part, predated his tenure as police chief. Internal investigations, however, revealed a different story.

An investigation as to whether or not the group actually existed began in earnest in 2007 after a highly visible police beating occurred in the city. As part of the initial investigation, one commander began a parallel investigation into the existence of the group. He filed a report in December 2007, stating, "This is a group of rogue officers within our agency who I would characterize as brutal and abusive." Subsequent investigations in 2008 through 2010 by this commander and others in the department's professional performance division could not substantiate the existence of the group, and only a small number of incidents were tied to specific police officers. Nevertheless, how does even a rumor of the existence of such a group create conflict for police administrators?

Even if the claims regarding the group's existence were assumed to be not true, what conflict would a police administrator face? Clearly, disagreement may exist among rank-and-file officers regarding the existence of the group, but, more important, how could the perception of the existence of such a group create conflict within the police department? How should this be addressed by police administrators? In addition, consider the differential fallout among community groups and citizens. As evidenced on the paper's blog subsequent to the story's release, a range of perspectives regarding police were expressed as a result of the story. Do you attempt to manage these perceptions? If yes, how do you manage these perceptions? Where is the greatest conflict going to occur?

Oftentimes, criminal justice administrators simply dismiss these types of events, assuming there is, in essence, nothing to manage. The chief in this case did what most police chiefs have done under similar circumstances—deny the individual specifics of the situation and avoid any further comment regarding the existence of a rogue element in the police department. Is this the best way to manage this conflict? What about police legitimacy in the eyes of the public? Is a do-nothing strategy a strategy at all? Does inaction actually raise the ugly side of politics into the equation? In other words, will police officials be perceived as covering up the problem?

The answers to these questions should assist us in understanding conflict and conflict management from the perspective of a criminal justice administrator. As you read the chapter and absorb the information, think about how you would respond to the conflict described in this vignette. For some of you, the issue may not be a conflict at all. For others, however, this has the potential to become a huge conflict for a police organization. After reading the chapter, you should be able to articulate why you hold the view that you do regarding this incident.

This chapter addresses a subject that many academics, practitioners, and policy makers interested in criminal justice find perplexing—the process of conflict in criminal justice organizations. We have all worked in organizations and have experienced conflict, whether it is a disagreement with the boss about our work assignment or about the overall direction of the organization. Conflict is endemic to all organizations, including those in the criminal justice system. This chapter examines conflict in criminal justice organizations by exploring several topics.

First, we define conflict in organizations and examine the stages in a conflict episode. We describe what conflict in criminal justice organizations means and, more important, the process of conflict. We should then be able to understand why conflict exists in criminal justice organizations and the complex dynamics associated with the conflict process.

Second, we explore the types of conflict behavior exhibited by people in organizations. In this section of the chapter, our discussion focuses on existing knowledge from the literature on organizational behavior about the process of conflict in organizations and then applies these ideas to the operations of criminal justice organizations.

Third, we examine the topic of conflict management, suggesting various interventions and exploring the dimensions of conflict outcomes. We suggest also that a proper analysis of conflict and its resolution must consider how conflict reaches well beyond the borders of individual criminal justice organizations.

Finally, the chapter concludes with a discussion of the role of conflict in criminal justice organizations and how conflict management can enhance the effectiveness of these organizations.

CONFLICT DEFINED

Like other topics this book has explored, the idea of conflict is one that is intuitively understood yet technically difficult to assess or measure. For this reason, researchers interested in conflict in organizations often employ a number of different conceptualizations.

Conflict is defined as a dynamic process in which two or more individuals in an organization interact in such a way as to produce "conflict episodes" that may or may not lead to hostile behaviors (Pondy, 1985:383). Pondy, for example, suggests four ways in which conflict can be understood in organizations. First, researchers often explore the antecedent conditions of conflict, such as resource scarcity, policy differences, and disagreements concerning preferred outcomes for the organization. When, for example, a treatment specialist does not agree with an immediate correctional supervisor on inmate supervision, the disagreement may be a precursor to conflict between subordinate and supervisor. This is the classic goal conflict that occurs within correctional institutions. In this example, the treatment specialist may believe that the primary goal of the institution should be the treatment of offenders, whereas the correctional supervisor may hold that security concerns of the institution override treatment programming.

Second, conflict in organizations can be understood as producing affective states in workers, such as stress, hostility, or anxiety. In our example, a corrections officer who is upset by what she perceives as an incorrect policy choice by the immediate supervisor may experience a great deal of stress as a consequence and may ultimately become dysfunctional to the organization. Much of the research on stress in criminal justice organizations may reflect the worker's inability to deal effectively with a conflict situation in the workplace. The examination of stress among criminal justice employees may thus require an exploration of the conflict process in those organizations. For this reason, perhaps, criminal justice organizations have introduced conflict-management seminars for their employees.

Third, conflict can be viewed from the individual employee's cognitive states. Once again, in our corrections officer example, the officer may or may not be aware of the conflict she has with the supervisor. Researchers interested in conflict processes in organizations have examined employees' awareness of conflict in their organizations and the degree to which it influences their behavior. We may, for example, survey corrections officers and ask them whether they perceive conflict situations in their work and how they deal with these situations. Corrections officers are, in fact, good at adapting to or accommodating the conflict inherent in their roles. As Lipsky (1980) suggests, much of what street-level bureaucrats, such as police officers and corrections officers, accomplish is done through a series of accommodations (Stojkovic, 1990). There have been similar findings among criminal justice administrators (Stojkovic, 1995). We would add that these accommodations may be in reaction to the conflict situations they face.

Fourth, conflict in organizations has been examined by exploring the conflict behavior itself, whether it is passive resistance or outright confrontational or aggressive behavior. Many researchers interested in correctional institutions can understand this form of conflict research because of the voluminous material on the nature of disturbances or riots in correctional institutions. Much of the research has examined the etiology of these riots (Barak-Glantz, 1985; DiIulio, 1987; Useem and Kimball, 1989).

We also can examine conflict at multiple levels. This approach to defining and examining conflict attempts to comprehend it as having many antecedents (something we discuss later) and is engendered at the intra-individual level, the dyadic level, and the group level. Much of the early twenty-first-century research on conflict has especially focused on these levels and has not examined them simultaneously while employing a multilevel strategy (Korsgaard, Jeong, Mahony, and Pitariu, 2009). This level of complexity makes conflict management even more difficult. At the end of the day, as criminal justice administrators, we have to comprehend the sources of conflict in our agencies and propose interventions that address them in useful and practical ways.

TYPES OF CONFLICT

We can identify four types of conflict in organizations, each of which requires a different adjustment mechanism. They are personal conflict, group conflict, intra-organizational conflict, and interorganizational conflict. (See Chapter 8 for a discussion of goal conflict.)

Personal Conflict

Personal conflict exists within the individual and usually is some form of cognitive conflict. Typically, this form of conflict results from failed expectations. For example, a young police officer who holds certain ideals about the police profession may find that many of them are not consistent with the reality of the police role or the police organization. The officer may feel a great deal of personal conflict because he cannot reconcile his own expectations with those of his superiors. In short, the officer may feel what Festinger (1957) refers to as "cognitive dissonance." To deal with this conflict, the young police officer may change his expectations to bring them in line with the organization's expectations, or he may seek to understand the conflict and thereby reduce its impact. Whatever the decision, it will affect his future behavior. In the extreme case, the officer may decide to leave the organization because he cannot resolve his

Personal conflict:
Cognitive dissonance within an individual.

personal conflict. For this reason, conflict-management programs, which we discuss later in the chapter, are critical to criminal justice organizations.

Group Conflict

Group conflict: Individual members of a group disagree on some common point of interest.

Group conflict occurs in organizations when individual members disagree on some point of common interest. The resolution of the conflict is essential to the survival of the group and may even enhance the effectiveness of the group in the long run. Take, for example, a group of police officers who work in a patrol unit. A conflict arises because of a disagreement over writing tickets. The department has formal expectations about the number of tickets the group is supposed to issue, but the officers have their own norms, which are different. Conflict occurs because some officers in the group believe that the expectations of their superiors override the group's informally derived expectations. The ensuing conflict can improve the coordination and communication processes of the group by forcing them to be cohesive and coordinated in determining an acceptable level of ticket writing. Obviously, if the conflict escalates too far, possibly because proper conflict-resolution techniques are not employed, then the group may disintegrate. Group conflict can also be healthy and productive if it is properly handled by the immediate supervisor. In our example, the sergeant can use certain techniques to benefit the group in the long term.

Task conflict: Disagreements regarding the content of tasks being performed by group members.

In addition, research has suggested that the nature and scope of group conflict can be broken down into two types: **task conflict** and **relationship conflict**. The former refers to disagreement among group members about the content of the tasks being performed, while the latter refers to "interpersonal incompatibility" among members of the group (Tekleab, Quigley, and Tesluk, 2009). Current research has examined the relationship among task conflict and relationship conflict and team cohesion, suggesting that as task conflict and relationship conflict vary, there are differential effects on the cohesion of the group. In other words, it is not clear that conflict management (a topic we explore later) has clear beneficial effects when addressing task conflict and relationship conflict in organizations.

Relationship conflict: Disagreements rooted in interpersonal incompatibility among group members.

Intergroup conflict: Groups within an organization compete for valuable and limited resources.

Another form of group conflict is **intergroup conflict**, in which groups within an organization compete for valuable and limited resources. If we look at police organizations and examine the multiple groups within them, we can see why intergroup conflict exists. Many police departments are composed of functional units—patrol, detective, vice, juvenile, and traffic—each with its own objectives and tasks. Given differing tasks and finite resources, it is common for conflict situations to arise. If, for example, the detective unit is favored by the chief and given the most resources, conflict is likely to ensue. The other units may perceive the chief's favoritism toward the detective unit as an unfair advantage and may request increased allocations for their own units. In this example, the chief may resolve the conflict by providing good reasons for allocating more resources to the detective unit than to the other units. However, if the other units believe that the explanation is inadequate, the conflict may escalate. When the conflict among the competing units does escalate, the police chief can use the competition among the groups as a mechanism to engender improved performance.

Thus, intra-group conflict may be healthy for the organization. An example of this type of administrative use of competition was documented by Arthur Schlesinger (1958) in his analysis of the presidency of Franklin Delano Roosevelt. Roosevelt was able to use the conflict generated by competing governmental units to control information about the workings of the federal bureaucracy while simultaneously generating improved levels of performance among subordinates. This method of conflict management may be effective, but if particular units continually fail in the process, they may become demoralized and assume a defeatist attitude that will be detrimental to the organization in the long term. If it escalates too far, intergroup conflict can be counterproductive. In our example, the competition among the different police units must be monitored to ensure that it remains effective and beneficial.

Intra-Organizational Conflict

Although group conflict deals with the relationships within and between groups in organizations, **intra-organizational conflict** is generated by the structural makeup of an organization—that is, by formal authority in the organization and how it is delegated. There are four major types of intra-organizational conflict: vertical conflict, horizontal conflict, line-staff conflict, and role conflict (Hellriegel, Slocum, and Woodman, 1995).

Vertical Conflict   **Vertical conflict** exists between workers at different levels in an organizational hierarchy. Within a department of corrections, for example, corrections officers sit below sergeants, sergeants sit below lieutenants, and so forth; this paramilitary model makes vertical conflict an inevitable event as superiors try to control the behavior of officers. The relationship between corrections officers and prisoners is so tenuous that conflict usually ensues whenever superiors try to tell officers how to supervise inmates. This perceived encroachment by supervisors on officers' jobs is the antecedent condition for conflict. In fact, a body of knowledge about corrections work supports the vertical nature of conflict in correctional institutions, not only between supervisor and subordinate but also between inmate and officer (see Crouch and Marquart, 1989; Johnson, 2002; Lombardo, 1981). Whatever the location, it would be fair to say that vertical conflict is ubiquitous within correctional institutions. Similar research findings support widespread vertical conflict in police organizations (Angell, 1971:19–29; Mastrofski, 1991).

Moreover, the conflict that is produced may be more pronounced for some subordinates and less pronounced for other subordinates in the vertical hierarchy of organizations. Schieman and Reid (2008), for example, found that the interpersonal effects (conflict) of a higher authority position in an organization are different along the dimensions of age and gender. Younger workers tend to have more stress and experience more interpersonal conflict than older workers, especially younger male workers. While gender cannot be totally negated in the

Intra-organizational conflict: Disagreements generated by the structural makeup of the organization and connected to its formal authority system.

Vertical conflict: Disagreements at differing levels of authority within an organization.

relationship between interpersonal conflict and job authority, it is much more dynamic and felt more acutely by younger, male workers. This may be due to their striving for higher positions within an organization and the concomitant stress that is associated with that pursuit. It is interesting that older workers, in general, experienced less interpersonal conflict when compared to their younger colleagues. This is not necessarily just because they have more authority, but they also may be perceived as more experienced and legitimate by others in the organization, thereby minimizing the level of interpersonal conflict they experience. When applying this finding to criminal justice organizations, it is clear that respect and deference are oftentimes granted to "older" workers due to their years of tenure on the job. Thus, the impact of vertical conflict on them may be minimal or irrelevant at this point in their careers when compared to younger employees who are still striving for higher positions in the organization.

Horizontal conflict:
Disagreements among employees who work on the same hierarchical level of an organization.

Horizontal Conflict   **Horizontal conflict** is exhibited by units that are at the same hierarchical level in an organization. Our previous example of conflict among the various units in a police department can also be understood as an example of horizontal conflict. If the multiple police units are of equal rank, then the conflict is horizontal. If, however, they are not at the same hierarchical level in the organization, the conflict is vertical.

Horizontal conflict is most evident when there is too much concern for task accomplishments within one unit. If the juvenile unit, for example, seeks increased resources for its investigation of gang-related activities and the arrests of gang members, granting the request may work against the larger purpose of the unit and the department—to maintain order in society. This overemphasis on gang-related activity may produce conflict with other units because they perceive the activities of the juvenile unit to be counter to their own goals—for example, the public relations unit or the crime prevention unit may be trying to establish positive ties with gang members—or because they feel the activity wastes finite departmental resources.

Line-staff conflict:
Disagreements between employees who perform the basic functions of the organization and personnel who support those employees.

Line-Staff Conflict   **Line-staff conflict** is readily apparent in public organizations, where staff personnel are used to augment and supplement the work of line managers. Criminal justice agencies also have support personnel who work with line managers to accomplish the objectives of the organization. Such people as legal advisors in police organizations or treatment and medical personnel in correctional institutions are good examples. The line-staff distinction in correctional institutions is noteworthy because it has generated much conflict between traditional security personnel and those whose goals are treatment and physical care.

Like correctional institutions, police organizations experience a lot of conflict between line personnel and staff. The most notable causes of these conflicts are the line personnel's perception that staff workers are trying to assume authority over basic line functions; the inability of the two groups to communicate effectively; the claim that staff people take the credit for successful programs yet are quick to point the finger of blame at line personnel when something goes wrong; and the claim that line personnel do not believe that staff people see the big picture of a specific program (Swanson, Territo, and Taylor, 1997).

Role Conflict   **Role conflict** is probably the most common in criminal justice organizations. Role conflict occurs when an individual is not able to comprehend or accomplish assigned tasks. The source of the conflict may be faulty communication between subordinate and supervisor; disagreement between the subordinate and the supervisor about the tasks required; conflicting expectations from differing supervisors; or differing expectations and differing roles among the groups to which the subordinate belongs. Regardless of its causes, role conflict as a form of intra-organizational conflict has been documented extensively in the criminal justice literature. (See Philliber's [1987] review of the literature on role conflict among corrections officers.)

Role conflict: Disagreement regarding the assigned tasks and responsibilities of a position.

Role conflict and role ambiguity are not the same. *Role ambiguity* occurs when a subordinate perceives that information about the required tasks of the job is unclear and inconsistent, whereas role conflict occurs when a subordinate perceives incompatible expectations about how the tasks should be performed. In other words, role ambiguity denotes inconsistencies in the knowledge needed to complete a job, and role conflict denotes inconsistencies about what is expected of the subordinate. It would be fair to say that criminal justice employees frequently experience both role conflict and role ambiguity in their jobs.

Finally, we must comment on the effects of role conflict in criminal justice organizations. Research has suggested that role conflict in both correctional institutions and police departments is not only widespread but may also lead to many other problems experienced by both these organizations, including high turnover, absenteeism, and low morale. (See Alpert, Dunham, and Stroshine [2005] for a good review of these problems in police organizations.) In particular, role conflict can be traced to stress found in police organizations. We know, for example, that people can react in a number of ways to role conflict, including being aggressive toward superiors, attempting to reduce conflict by communicating effectively with superiors, and withdrawing from the organization. Withdrawal is a reaction that is seen too often in criminal justice organizations. Thus, future research needs to provide concrete suggestions about how role conflict can be reduced.

Interorganizational Conflict

Interorganizational conflict occurs when different organizations share a common purpose but disagree about how that purpose will be achieved. This type of conflict arises when one organization (such as one component of the criminal justice system) perceives its goals and objectives to be in conflict with those of other organizations. Take, for example, the jail and its links to other components of the criminal justice system. The jail has as its central task the control of two offender populations: pretrial detainees (people awaiting trial because they could not make bail and those who have committed serious crimes and are being preventively detained) and those who have already been convicted of a crime and are serving a sentence.

Interorganizational conflict: Organizations that share a common purpose but disagree on how that purpose will be achieved.

Although these are the two primary groups housed within the jail and its central purpose is to maintain a safe and secure environment for them, the jail is also used by prosecutors, police, and probation and parole personnel for other purposes. Prosecutors use the jail to coerce recalcitrant inmates to plea bargain.

The threat of staying in jail encourages the defendant to "cop a plea" and relieves the pressures of the prosecutor's overcrowded caseload. The jail thus serves the organizational interests of prosecutors because it ensures a smoothly operating system of plea bargaining and caseload reduction; it serves similar interests of both the police and probation and parole personnel. The police use jail as a repository for the "rabble" (Irwin, 1986; Irwin and Austin, 2002) who are found on the streets of our major cities or as an inducement for defendants to confess to a crime or to serve as witnesses against other suspects (Rottman and Kimberly, 1975). Probation and parole officers use jail as a convenient place for offenders who are suspected of committing either a technical violation or a new crime. In many large urban jails, a sizable number of people are awaiting revocation hearings, and jail in this case gives probation and parole personnel control over their clients. In short, jail serves all these components of the criminal justice system and helps them all meet their goals (Kerle, 1998).

However, although the jail can be critical for the accomplishment of these goals, it can equally be a place of interorganizational conflict. We can examine, for example, the links between jails and other correctional agencies. Commonly, jails house offenders who cannot be placed in state prisons or detention settings because they are overcrowded. Data from the U.S. Bureau of Justice Statistics (2006a) indicate that many local jails are holding inmates for federal, state, and local authorities. An estimated 5 percent of all jail inmates are prisoners held for state or federal authorities. This situation creates much conflict between the jail and correctional institutions. Typically, the conflict is resolved through a feedback process between the jail and other correctional institutions. In effect, jails have communicated directly with correctional institutions, saying they will not or cannot receive more state prisoners into their facilities. In many cases, this interorganizational conflict can be resolved only by the jail's refusing to take inmates from other jurisdictions until the overcrowding problem is resolved.

As another example, jail overcrowding can be caused by the refusal of judges to implement rational bail guidelines for those suspected of a crime. Many jails are overcrowded with individuals who could be bailed out and pose no threat to the community. The question becomes: Why won't judges institute rational bail guidelines if overcrowding is a problem in the jail? The answer lies in the fact that the jail is not of primary importance to judges. What is important is that some type of punishment be given to people who have violated the laws. A little jail time reminds the suspect that the court is serious about the crime committed. Judges may feel even more strongly about using the jail in this way when the person has been before the court in the past and behavior has not changed. In this example, the judge may have goals that differ from those of the sheriff who runs the jail, and the disagreement about the relative importance of each goal leads to interorganizational conflict in the system. This same type of interorganizational conflict can be seen in correctional institutions with respect to the delivery of services, such as education and medical attention (see Duffee, 1986:274–276), specifically when the provision of these services is the responsibility of another state bureaucracy, such as a state department of public health or education (Henderson, 2006).

Clearly, interorganizational conflict is common in criminal justice. The resolution of such conflict depends on the ability of separate organizational units to coordinate their efforts and increase their level of communication to ensure long-term preservation of their links. The resolution of interorganizational conflicts, both among the components of the criminal justice system and between those organizations and other state bureaucracies, may be the single most important issue facing administrators of the criminal justice system today.

Stages of a Conflict Episode

Although this typology helps us define and categorize conflict in criminal justice organizations, Pondy (1985:382) believes that it does not add to our understanding of the process of conflict. To understand the conflict process, he suggests that research must consider conflict episodes. More important, Pondy (1985) emphasizes that not all conflict situations lead to overt aggression or hostility. In other words, the conflict situation may never come to fruition. In fact, the purpose of conflict-management programs in organizations is to prevent the escalation of events that lead to actual aggressive or hostile behavior by employees. In addition, however, not all conflicts are resolved with conflict-management techniques; some, for example, may disappear because one of the parties does not perceive the situation as a conflict situation. It is critical, therefore, to identify the various stages of a conflict episode, as Pondy (1985:383–386) suggests.

The five **stages of a conflict episode** are presented in Figure 11.1. The stages are latent conflict, perceived conflict, felt conflict, manifest conflict, and conflict aftermath. These stages are affected by both environmental and organizational factors, as Figure 11.1 shows. Consistent with the idea that a conflict episode is dynamic, we can see that the entire episode evolves from the aftermath of a preceding conflict episode. In this way, all conflict episodes are interrelated and have a degree of continuity. Conflict in organizations must thus be understood beyond the immediate situation.

Latent Conflict   This stage of the conflict occurs when the conditions that are the underlying sources of the conflict are present. According to Pondy (1985:383), **latent conflict** is typically rooted in competition for scarce resources, drives for autonomy, or divergence of subunit goals. Each of these roots can be seen in the organizations of criminal justice. In the typical police department, scarcity of resources produces fierce levels of competition among the various subunits when, for example, the juvenile unit demands increased resources to combat gang activity or the vice unit seeks additional officers to arrest drug dealers. Drives for autonomy can also create conflict in police organizations. When immediate supervisors attempt to control the behavior of officers and the officers, as a group, seek autonomy or control over their work environments, conflict is inevitable. Finally, divergence of subunit goals occurs "when two parties who must cooperate on some joint activity are unable to reach a consensus on concerted action" (Pondy, 1985:383). Patrol officers, for example, who must work together and cannot agree on how to complete their tasks will have much latent conflict.

Stages of a conflict episode: The various steps in which disagreement is felt, perceived, and reacted to by disagreeing parties in an organization.

Latent conflict: The stage of a conflict episode in which the sources of the conflict are present.

FIGURE 11.1   The Dynamics of a Conflict Episode.

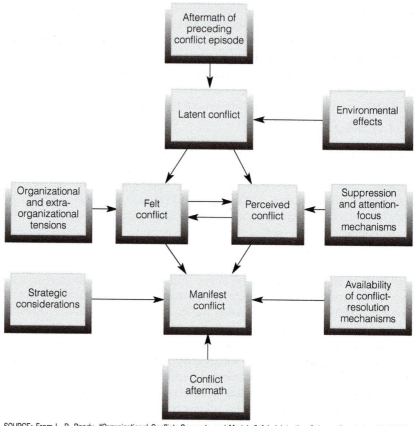

SOURCE: From L. R. Pondy, "Organizational Conflict: Concepts and Models," *Administrative Science Quarterly*, 12, 1967. Adapted by permission of *Administrative Science Quarterly*.

All three components of latent conflict are present in prison settings. Scarcity of resources is evidenced by limited space, overcrowding, and minimal attention to such areas as treatment programs. Subunits in the prison organization—such as treatment personnel and security personnel—compete for these limited resources, each believing that its goals are most critical to the prison. And we see drives for autonomy in correctional institutions among both corrections staff and prisoners. Corrections staff seek additional input into how institutions are run, while prisoner groups demand control over their lives and prison conditions.

Perceived conflict: The stage of a conflict episode when at least one party recognizes that a conflict situation exists.

Perceived Conflict   The stage of the conflict episode known as **perceived conflict** occurs when at least one of the two parties recognizes that a conflict situation exists. When they do, they may seek to escalate the conflict episode or choose to deflect it. A police officer, for example, may have a perceived conflict with her partner; she can decide to suppress the conflict because she doesn't believe it to be a major issue, or she can decide that the issue is important to her. The officer may decide to suppress the perceived conflict with her partner regarding who will drive the squad car, yet she may want to push the perceived conflict to the next stage over the issue of handling recalcitrant suspects. The important point is that once we consciously recognize the conflict between ourselves and another individual, we have control over whether the conflict episode will proceed into the next stage. Kennedy and Pronin (2008) interject an interesting perspective on the importance of bias and the escalation of perceived conflict. Our perceptions of a conflict episode are structured by biases that we carry regarding the other party's intentions in our interactions. These biases only escalate conflict. Kennedy and Pronin (2008:845) state: "[A] common perceptual tendency (involving our inclination to impute bias to those who see things differently from us) leads us to take competitive approaches toward those with whom we disagree— approaches that escalate conflict rather than encourage its resolution." Later in the chapter, we discuss how to manage these biases to deescalate conflict situations.

Felt Conflict   **Felt conflict** occurs when a party personalizes the conflict situation. For example, Officer A may be aware of a conflict between herself and her partner, but she doesn't allow the conflict to upset her. However, Officer B may be so upset by a perceived conflict that it now affects his relationship with his partner. Once personalized, the conflict not only is felt by the individuals concerned but may also become dysfunctional for the organization. This stage of the conflict episode is critical to organizations; proper handling of the conflict situation in this stage is extremely important to the long-term stability of any organization, including those in the criminal justice system.

Felt conflict: When disagreeing parties personalize the conflict situation.

Manifest Conflict   After the conflict situation has been perceived and felt by a party, it may move into **manifest conflict**. This stage of the conflict episode is characterized by overt or covert behavior to bring out the conflict. In prisons, for example, manifest conflict may be expressed in riots or disturbances. These types of overt situations are rare, however, even for prisons. More often than not, manifest conflict takes the covert form of deliberate blockage by one party of the other party's goals.

Manifest conflict: The stage of a conflict episode characterized by overt or covert behavior.

Going back to our police officer example, if Officer B knowingly frustrates his partner in such a way that she cannot attain her goals, then manifest conflict is surely present. At this point, tension between the two may be the greatest. More important, at this juncture, managers must step into the conflict situation to diffuse it before it becomes dysfunctional to the organization. As a result, it is critical that immediate supervisors be able to recognize manifest conflict among their subordinates. Supervisors must also recognize that they may be the source of manifest conflict in the organization. In fact, it is all too common in criminal justice for frontline supervisors to be perceived as facilitators of manifest conflicts instead of diffusers. Even worse, often the conflicts in criminal justice organizations are not among employees but between the employees and their supervisors or administrators. In all these cases, the superior must take care not to escalate the manifest conflict but instead must facilitate its resolution.

Conflict Aftermath   At this point in the conflict episode, if the antecedent conditions (competition for scarce resources, drives for autonomy, and divergent subunit goals) are dealt with in a satisfactory manner, the conflict will dissolve. Such a resolution is the hope of those who are interested in keeping organizational conflict to a minimum and who want to learn from the conflict episode. If, however, the antecedent conditions are not addressed but are only suppressed for the short term, then the conflict will continue to surface like a wound that has not been properly attended to. If the conflict continues, we enter the stage of **conflict aftermath**. The danger of this stage of the conflict episode is that it may become serious or, worse yet, weaken the relationship between the two actors so that it can never be fully repaired. In this way, conflict episodes become part of a dynamic process. We can see how the conflict aftermath occurs in the components of the criminal justice system. In prisons, where the antecedent conditions of conflict (as described previously) are never resolved, the conflict is allowed to fester until another disturbance occurs.

> **Conflict aftermath:**
> Continued disagreement with little or no attention to the antecedent causes of the disagreement.

Conflict Behaviors

Awareness of **conflict behaviors** helps us understand the role that conflict plays in criminal justice organizations. Moreover, it enables us to develop and implement effective **conflict management** programs in these organizations.

Conflict behaviors can be understood by examining a model proposed by Thomas (1985). The model has two dimensions, each representing an individual's intention in a conflict situation. The two dimensions are cooperativeness —attempting to satisfy the other party's concerns—and assertiveness—attempting to satisfy one's own concerns. Different combinations of these two dimensions, according to Thomas, can create five conflict behaviors: competing behavior, accommodating behavior, avoiding behavior, collaborating behavior, and compromising behavior.

Competing behavior (assertive, uncooperative) occurs when one person is willing to place his or her own concerns above the concerns of the other person. Typically, force and even violence can occur in this conflict situation. In addition, competing behavior seeks the resolution of the conflict in a fashion that maximizes the person's own interests. A common example of this type of conflict behavior in police organizations is a disagreement over an arrest between a citizen and a patrol officer. The officer may feel an obligation to arrest a citizen in a particular situation, whereas a citizen may not feel the arrest is legitimate or the correct course of action in the situation. The arrest may involve a physical confrontation where the officer is pitted against the citizen. It is for this reason that police training emphasizes a continuum of force when subduing an individual and involves the officer providing justification to an arrestee as to why the arrest is occurring (Fyfe, 2004b).

> **Conflict behaviors:**
> Responses to the conflict situation.
>
> **Conflict management:**
> Approaches designed to address conflicts within organizations.
>
> **Competing behavior:**
> When one party places his/her concerns over the concerns of another in a conflict situation.

Accommodating behavior (unassertive, cooperative) satisfies the concerns of the other individual rather than one's own concerns in a conflict situation. This behavior may be rare in organizations because it is difficult to understand why one would neglect one's own interests and maximize another's, yet we all know this happens in everyday life. Accommodating behavior occurs, for example, among prosecutors who attempt to come to resolution with defense attorneys and suspects due to large caseloads. The prosecutor accommodates and fulfills the demands of the defendant (a plea bargain) due to the pressure of increased caseloads and finite resources to address them.

Avoiding behavior (unassertive, uncooperative) neglects both the person's own concerns and the concerns of the other person. People who exhibit avoiding behavior want a minimal amount of friction in their interactions and do everything in their power to make sure no problems occur between themselves and others. This type of conflict behavior is very common in prisons where prisoners and correctional officers avoid confrontation. Issues may arise that require the attention of officers, but for whatever reason, they decide not to address matters. Avoidance behavior occurs, and, in some cases, the situation may escalate and create even more serious and violent episodes at a later date. An extreme example is when correctional officers avoid dealing with gang issues in the prison until it is too late and violence occurs.

Collaborating behavior (assertive, cooperative) attempts to satisfy the demands and concerns of both parties in a conflict situation; it is a type of conflict behavior that few possess yet many desire. Collaborating behavior occurs within criminal justice organizations when parties involved see the benefits of collaboration. Drug courts, for example, have been touted as a win-win for criminal defendants and prosecutors and judges. The defendant is given an opportunity to address drug dependency issues while prosecutors and judges satisfy their demands for justice. Research shows that drug courts are a successful bridge, in addition, between criminal justice organizations and health service providers (Wenzel et al., 2004).

Finally, **compromising behavior** (intermediate in both assertiveness and cooperativeness) seeks the middle ground. People who exhibit this type of conflict behavior realize that they cannot always get what they want and further recognize that conflict resolution demands some give-and-take by both sides. Sacrifice, in other words, is part of this type of conflict behavior. This type of conflict behavior is common in the courtroom work group where participants —that is, prosecutor, judge, and defense attorney—come to a common understanding of how justice is to be meted out to criminal defendants. This understanding is a compromise between the demands of justice and the operational realities of the court system. There are too many cases, too little time, and too few resources to devote to every case individually. The compromise represents the best decision given the realities of the court system (Walker, 2006).

Individually, no conflict style is bad or good. Whether a conflict behavior is appropriate depends on the context and situation. Accordingly, Thomas (1985:399) suggests that in some situations, specific conflict behaviors are better than others. For example, it has been said that conflict management is at the

Accommodating behavior: When one party addresses the concerns of another party but does not address his/her concerns in a conflict situation.

Avoiding behavior: Neglect of another person's concerns and his/her concerns in a conflict situation.

Collaborating behavior: Attempts to address the concerns of both parties in a conflict situation.

Compromising behavior: Attempts to seek the middle ground between disagreeing parties in a conflict situation.

heart of running a modern police department. How chiefs respond to various conflict situations is critical to perceptions about their effectiveness as leaders. When chiefs believe that their way of doing things is correct, it may be appropriate for them to take a stand and compete on the issue. When an emergency arises and a quick response is needed, the competing form of conflict behavior may also be the most appropriate, though we do not want to say it is always the best choice.

As another example, a citizen group that demands a different form of patrolling in its neighborhood has an understanding of and perspective on the allocation of police officers within the community. The group may also have some knowledge of how and when police resources can be used to combat crime in its neighborhood. This type of information may be valuable to the chief in a number of ways, from creating positive relationships with the community to getting important feedback from residents on how police resources can be distributed in the community. If the police chief's intention is to gain ideas about crime control from the community, then the collaborating form of conflict behavior may be most appropriate.

If, however, the chief believes that this issue of community input into police operations is trivial or unimportant to the department, he or she may perceive that avoiding the conflict is the appropriate response. If the chief's perception is incorrect, however, this type of conflict behavior may prove to be deleterious to the department. For this reason, selecting the correct conflict behavior for the situation is critical to organizations today and to criminal justice organizations in particular.

This example describes a conflict situation between a police chief and a group outside the police organization. Conflict situations, however, can also occur within organizations, and it is equally important for criminal justice administrators to select the correct conflict behavior in such situations.

Work Perspective: INTERORGANIZATIONAL CONFLICT: THE HIDTA EXPERIENCE

When the High Intensity Drug Trafficking Area (HIDTA) program was developed in the early 1990s, the core construct was a partnership between local, state, and federal law enforcement agencies focusing resources on investigating, disrupting, and dismantling violent drug trafficking organizations (DTOs). Over the next twenty years, the program matured as agencies found the value of close cooperation, leveraging of resources, and information sharing to have maximum impact on DTOs. As one can imagine, there were numerous challenges in bringing very disparate organizations with varied cultures together and the resultant conflict that it caused.

While federal, state, and local law enforcement agencies work together on a regular basis, pulling agents from their home agencies and putting them together in a facility (HIDTA) that is not their home agency is unique. Providing investigators with opportunities not available in their home agencies is exciting, intriguing, and fraught with the constant challenge of conflict. This conflict can manifest itself in a variety of forms from personality issues, agency "best practices," and feelings of inferiority based on inexperience in highly complex investigations that may stretch over six months or more.

Experience has shown that a clear operational strategy with agreement by the executive board (agency heads set the operational priorities of each HIDTA) is the single best way to reduce the impact of conflict, followed closely by the administration staff listening more than talking, ongoing education for the teams of investigators on innovative ways of enhancing investigations, and massive amounts of humor to diffuse issues at the minor irritant level.

Because the HIDTA program encourages out-of-the-box thinking on how to structure investigations, the potential for conflict is constant; the energy generated by this environment must be channeled. Through education, numerous meetings, and best practice demonstrations from other HIDTAs, energy is channeled toward building better investigative techniques and tools.

The role of the HIDTA director is one of coach and cheerleader, referee, and idea salesperson. Each operational initiative is led by a law enforcement supervisor, and getting everyone to agree on general parameters takes a great deal of "sales expertise." However, the job is most challenging and rewarding due to organizational conflicts.

Successful directors have a "tool bag" of interventions that they can use to defuse and refocus conflict.

These strategies could be as simple as direct communication between combating employees or more complicated discussions on how to resolve disagreements and conflicts among participating agencies. Regardless of strategy employed to manage conflict, the fact of the matter is that conflict is ubiquitous within criminal justice organizations, and a good criminal justice administrator recognizes that it is neither good nor bad. It is just something you have to address to get the maximum effort out of employees and the diverse and varied organizations they represent. At the end of the day, HIDTA effectiveness is assessed by the number of DTOs we disrupted and/or dismantled. Along the way, conflict will be engendered. My job as the director of the local HIDTA is, in large part, about conflict management and resolution. How well I accomplish this task will reflect on our success to attain our mission and vision, something that both the public and Congress focus on when allocation decisions regarding scarce financial resources are made.

SOURCE: Director Ed Polachek, Milwaukee High Intensity Drug Trafficking Area.

CONFLICT MANAGEMENT

Thomas (1985:405–411) identifies two ways of dealing with conflict situations: process interventions and structural interventions. **Process interventions** attempt to "become directly involved in the ongoing sequence of events" (Thomas, 1985:405) that result in the conflict. *Structural interventions* attempt to alter the conditions in an organization that influence the direction of conflict episodes. Each intervention aims for conflict resolution. Using both strategies allows us to deal with conflict in criminal justice organizations. Although these interventions are designed for intra-organizational conflict, they can also be partially applied to interorganizational conflicts.

Process Interventions

Process interventions fall into two categories. First, *consciousness-raising interventions* attempt to change the "internal experiences of the parties" that shape their behaviors. This type of intervention requires that the manager or supervisor intervene indirectly in the conflict, suggesting how the competing parties can reconceptualize their perceptions and thus remove the conditions that created the conflict. Sluzki (2010) provides a six-stage process whereby conflict can be minimized and reconciliation made possible. This model is predicated on an evolutionary

Process interventions: Ways to intervene in a conflict situation by altering the internal experiences of the disagreeing parties. There are two types: consciousness-raising interventions and interaction-management interventions. Conditions that must be manipulated during a process intervention include the following: personal characteristics, informal rules, constituent pressure, conflict of interest, power and status, and organizational policy.

Confrontation: Two parties in a conflict assume that any act of the other is based on ill intent.

Truce: Disagreements between two parties are controlled by powerful third parties.

Collaboration: Assumes moderate ill will between disagreeing parties, but common activities are still pursued.

Cooperation: Assumes neutral intent between disagreeing parties and common activities are pursued.

Interdependence: Disagreeing parties agree to move toward a common good.

Integration: A common ground is found with the intent of supporting growth and change for both parties.

Interaction management: When a supervisor intervenes directly in the conflict situation between two subordinates, suggesting how the two parties resolve this conflict and avoid future conflicts.

approach to addressing conflict and, while meant for addressing interpersonal and international conflict, may have some relevance to organizational conflict. The six stages are the following: **confrontation**, each party assumes ill intent by the other party; **truce**, the parties are forced to end confrontation by a third party; **collaboration**, ill intent still remains between the parties but certain activities are accepted between them; **cooperation**, neutral intent of parties while activities in common are planned and carried out; **interdependence**, both parties become active toward a common good; and **integration**, active projects develop that support the common good and other party growth. As conflicting parties evolve along the various stages, the role of a "third party," in our case a manager or administrator, is critical to continued evolution to a "harmonious coexistence" (Sluzki, 2010:55).

As a potential process intervention, criminal justice administrators would have to devote much time and effort to implement and sustain this evolutionary process in their organizations. A key role for the administrator would be to facilitate a different "narrative" on what the conflicting parties understand as the conflicting situation. Sluzki (2010:66) states: "One valuable, perhaps key, task of a mediator, facilitator, or consultant [administrator or manager in our case] consists in destabilizing and transforming the stories brought forward by the parties in a conflict, in favor of a 'better' story, and facilitating the consensual adoption of this new narrative by all the parties." As a process intervention, this method to manage conflict has the potential to assist criminal justice administrators. For it to have relevance, however, the pathway to institutionalizing this evolutionary process must be more clearly understood by criminal justice administrators. This necessary pathway is not well understood; a methodology to train others in facilitation requires development and refinement.

Second, **interaction management** occurs when a supervisor intervenes directly in the conflict situation between two subordinates, suggesting how the two parties can change their behaviors to resolve this conflict and avoid future conflicts. Both types of process interventions thus require active participation by supervisors for the conflict to be reduced. Next, we review some of the organizational conditions that can be altered by process interventions from administrators and managers. Our examination of these conditions includes criminal justice examples.

Personal Characteristics   Conflict episodes in organizations are a result of multiple factors, including the personalities of those involved in the conflict. Our personalities affect how we deal with conflict. As Thomas (1985:406) puts it, individuals in organizations have "repertoires" in dealing with conflict that are rooted in their personalities, and these repertoires can be difficult to deal with. Sometimes an individual's position in an organization cannot be altered even though that person may have a poor conflict repertoire. More often than not, other employees try to adapt to this type of personality in hopes of minimizing conflict. For example, if a police sergeant has a competitive repertoire, we often tell subordinates that they are going to have to live with this person and learn to accept the situation. Obviously, if the situation becomes nonproductive, then actions must be taken by those supervisors above the sergeant to deal with the conflict. In this example, interaction management has been a tool used by police managers to deal with personality differences among subordinates. Usually, the police manager attempts to get the conflicting parties to focus on job responsibilities and how those cannot be hindered by personality differences.

Informal Rules   All organizations have written and unwritten rules about employee behavior. These rules are critical to the operation of the organization. For example, when there is a conflict between officers, going to the sergeant or the lieutenant may not be approved by the informal code among officers. Dealing with conflict episodes in police organizations, therefore, may require an understanding of the role the informal code plays in such situations.

The informal code may accept reasonable attempts by police administrators to resolve the conflict. Although such activities as serving as an arbitrator or "referee" between two disputants may prove helpful, the police administrator must always be aware that such an interaction management strategy could be limited by an informal code and interactions should, therefore, proceed with caution.

Constituent Pressure   All organizations experience pressure and competition among groups, known as *constituent pressure*, that typically force cohesiveness within the groups. Examining a correctional organization highlights this concept. The treatment-versus-custody debate that has raged for years is a good example of how groups become cohesive when they feel threatened. Prison administrators have been unable to deal with the conflict that ensues from constituent pressures, but they could do so by using process intervention—as in getting both groups to realize the benefits to the organization of resolving their conflicts. In this example, the prison administrator could show how the dual functions of treatment and custody serve the purpose of maintaining prison order and also help each group accomplish its goals. In this way, the administrator is trying to raise the consciousness of members in both groups.

Conflict of Interest   According to Thomas (1985:407), the precursor of *conflict of interest* exists in organizations when the concerns of two parties in an organization are incompatible. Such conflict is escalated when both parties are competing for limited resources. In prisons, for example, we know that limited funds are available for all programs, particularly treatment programs. Satisfying custodial concerns invariably leads to a reduction in resources for those groups in prisons who are interested in treatment. Unless there is some "organizational slack," as Thomas (1985:407) states, it will be difficult for the prison organization to meet the objectives of both groups, thereby increasing the likelihood of conflict.

This conflict episode in prison organizations has existed for many years, and unless further resources are granted these organizations, it is unlikely to diminish. If nothing else, this situation has forced prisons to define the objectives and purposes of their organizations given their limited funds and resources. Moreover, it may not be apparent how process interventions resolve conflicts resulting from conflicts of interest. Actually, interactive management can resolve the conflict between treatment workers and custody personnel by clearly stating the central purpose of the prison. Once parties recognize that, for example, custody concerns are supposed to override treatment goals, the conflict could be resolved. Treatment employees may recognize that the demands, and therefore more resources, should be given to the custody function.

Thomas (1985:408) says that the degree of competition among conflicting interests in an organization is determined by the stakes involved (the degree to which the issue at conflict is important) and the interdependence among the competing parties (the relative connection between the groups when competing for high stakes). For example, corrections officers may compete with the treatment staff for scarce resources in the prison independently (*parallel striving*), or they may seek to block the possibility of a treatment group achieving its goals (*mutual interference*). Thomas (1985:409) suggests that parallel striving may increase the efforts of groups to work toward organizational goals, whereas mutual interference disrupts each group's attempt to accomplish organizational goals.

Power and Status   Power and status play an important part in the conflicts that occur in organizations and also affect their level of intensity. Obviously, because of the power differential between them, a police officer does not seek to enter into conflict-laden relationships with an immediate supervisor. In fact, avoidance as a conflict behavior is common in situations where large power differentials exist between the parties. Moreover, some organizational units have greater status and levels of power than others. As a result, departments have to be conscious of their relative power and status before making requests of other departments. Although treatment personnel in prisons, for example, do not have much power, they may believe they have higher status than guards, both in prison and society. This belief may be part of the reason for the high level of conflict between treatment staff and custodial staff, though we would not want to reduce the explanation of all conflict between the two groups to status differentials.

Another possible process intervention is the prison administration's making both treatment personnel and custodial workers aware of their relative importance to the prison. Indeed, proper prison administration involves educating workers in the role they play to achieve organizational goals. This awareness in both groups may lead to the reduction of conflict between them.

Organizational policy:
An organization's set of rules, guidelines, and procedures used to guide actions and decisions.

Organizational Policy   An **organizational policy** is often created to minimize a conflict. However, if rules are nothing but the result of "political struggles" (Thomas, 1985:410), we would expect that rules and organizational policies are only a short-term response. Opinions among groups in police departments on the types of enforcement action to be taken may vary considerably; therefore, we may make a policy that states when and how an arrest will be made. This policy, however, will not resolve the issue but only take it temporarily out of the forefront of organizational business. We would, therefore, expect that once the issue arises again, another rule will be created to deal with the situation and appease the competing parties. Making a new policy that attempts to eliminate conflict between two parties in an organization can be perceived as a process intervention.

Structural Interventions

Whereas process interventions are concerned with conflict episodes, **structural interventions** are designed to reduce conflict by examining and altering preexisting conditions of the organization that promote conflict. These conditions are ongoing and part of the structure within the manager's system. Thomas (1985:410–411) describes two types of structural interventions that can be employed: selection and training interventions and contextual-modification interventions.

Selection and Training Interventions   *Selection interventions* use screening procedures to choose the people best suited for the organization and the job. Both police organizations and corrections departments attempt to select the most favorable candidates for positions within their organizations. They hope that they have chosen the people who can perform the tasks of the job and with whom they can work. In addition, they attempt to train people to work in the way they believe is most conducive to accomplishing organizational objectives. Administrators hope that through such interventions they can minimize conflict and increase the effectiveness of the organization.

Contextual-Modification Interventions   *Contextual-modification interventions* attempt to change the context within which parties interact. Such changes typically require forceful management and leadership in the policy-development process. For example, conflicts of interest in correctional organizations between treatment staff and custodial groups can be reduced, in part, by reducing competition for scarce resources between the groups. If a manager can acquire increased resources for both groups, there is no longer any reason for competition. Through this contextual modification, the manager has increased the likelihood that each group will be able to meet its own needs while fulfilling the needs of the organization. Yet accomplishing this modification is easier said than done. In fact, contextual modifications in criminal justice organizations require great awareness of interorganizational conflict, a topic we examined previously in the chapter.

Limits to Conflict Management

Although conflicts requiring contextual modification may be resolved, other conflicts are more intractable because managers have even less control over their resolution. For example, conflicts escalate in correctional settings when there is limited space for housing prisoner populations. Overcrowding produces conflict between and among inmates and staff, but corrections administrators do not have the resources to add space. A possible solution to the conflict is to build additional prisons, yet this may be a short-term solution because further resources are not going to be available when prison space again becomes limited.

Instead, a satisfactory solution to the problem may require attention to non-incarcerative mechanisms for dealing with offenders. Given the reality of limited resources in prison settings, the conflict may require solutions that reach well beyond the boundaries of the organization to both the interorganizational and

Structural interventions: The alteration of preexisting conditions of the organization that produce conflict. There are two types of structural interventions: selection and training interventions and contextual-modification interventions.

the societal level. Many organizational conflicts in criminal justice are thus not satisfactorily addressed because it is beyond the scope of these organizations to resolve the latent conditions that perpetuate these conflicts.

Administrators must accept that sometimes they will not be able to handle a conflict situation; sometimes they will fail in their attempts to deal with conflicts both internal and external to the organization. This failure, however, does not relegate administrators to doing nothing. The reasonable position is to learn from mistakes and go forward to resolve similar conflicts in the future with the knowledge gained from past experiences.

Is Conflict Management Possible in Criminal Justice Administration?

According to Thomas (1985:412–415), successful conflict management deals with all three dimensions of conflict outcomes. The first is *goal attainment* by conflicting parties. In the conflict between treatment staff and custodial personnel, goals must be attained by either one group or the other or both. In an optimal sense, both parties should gain something from the conflict. Although desirable, such an outcome is highly improbable in this case. Thomas even states that one would not want to grant every party equal weight in the conflict. Custodial functions, for example, may be more important to the prison organization than treatment programs, or vice versa. If the conflict does resolve anything, it may be the priority of one function over the other.

For this reason, effective criminal justice administration requires communication of the priorities in an organization. Once subordinates understand these priorities, the number of conflicts in the organization may decrease. This same line of reasoning can be extended to conflict at the interorganizational level. Clear communication among the components in the criminal justice system will reduce the likelihood of long-term conflict among them. If an administrator perceives that the parties in conflict are of equal value, however, then the optimal strategy is some type of compromise so that each believes that it received a portion of what it sought in the conflict.

Second, administrators in the criminal justice system must be aware of the *consequences* of a conflict episode for the people involved. If, for example, treatment staff perceive that they have been treated unfairly by the administration of the institution in resolving a conflict, this perception may adversely affect their productivity and outlook toward the job. Such long-term effects on performance can also be the result of interorganizational conflict. Because the parts of the system are so interdependent, it is crucial that administrators understand the importance of maintaining stable relationships with each other, as this chapter's case study demonstrates. These relationships may be the most pivotal aspect of effective criminal justice administration today. Here, collaboration seems to be the best possible method for dealing with conflict. The collaboration strategy enables conflicting parties to see that their concerns are being recognized even though they may not get what they want.

Third, conflict management in the criminal justice system must be *economical of time and effort*. A tremendous amount of effort is put into dealing with conflicts both within criminal justice organizations and outside their boundaries. Energy used to deal with conflicts could be used for constructive activities within the organization. Good criminal justice administrators understand, therefore, the importance of efficient conflict management in their organizations.

This point leads us to a question: Is conflict management possible in criminal justice organizations? We think that it is not only possible but essential. The key lies in improving communication both within and among the components of the system. At present, communication is fragmented at both levels. For conflict management to work, this problem of poor communication must be resolved. Improving communication will require some structural changes, including more specific lines of communication in the organization. At the interorganizational level, this would mean raising the consciousness (process intervention) of criminal justice administrators to help them see that improved communication is essential to their effectiveness.

THE ROLE OF CONFLICT IN ORGANIZATIONS

A number of views have been advanced over the years about the role that conflict plays in organizations. Our position is that conflict in criminal justice organizations can be both beneficial and harmful. Much of the conflict that occurs is good in the sense that it promotes change in those organizations; conflict makes the system responsive to the demands of a changing environment (Wright, 2004). Assume, for example, that a police organization is viewed as unresponsive to demands from the community for changes in the way police services are delivered. In this situation, conflict may arise not only between community groups and those who run the department but also between department administrators and the officers. If the department does become responsive to the community, rank-and-file officers may feel that the department is trying to appease the community groups to their detriment. Conflict in this situation may be good because it forces the department to rethink its relationship with the community and its own officers, a task that can be beneficial to the organization's operations and delivery of services. The ultimate goal of conflict management in the system of criminal justice should be an increase in organizational effectiveness. This view is supported by research that suggests that when it comes to task conflict, it is not automatic that a reduction in it is desirable. Instead, moderate amounts of task conflict may actually provide a greater voice to those in the group who would not otherwise be heard, and, until their views are heard, the level of group cohesion might be less than optimal (Tekleab, Quigley, and Tesluk, 2009:176).

Conflict can also be harmful. If, in the previous example, conflict between the officers and the department over the role of the community escalates to the point that the functioning of police units is jeopardized, then conflict has become detrimental to the long-term operation of the department. Management has failed to control the escalation of conflict, and, as a result, the effectiveness of the organization may be diminished.

Conflict in criminal justice organizations is, however, a normal process, and eliminating it is not only unrealistic but also counterproductive to their long-term health. In short, conflict serves a useful function. Although long-term and deeply entrenched conflict is of no value to any organization, conflict enables an organization to grow and adapt successfully to its environment. Because conflict in criminal justice organizations seems inevitable given the fact of frequently incompatible goals, managers have to learn how to live with, adapt to, and cope with it. Conflict-management programs need to be developed to train managers and administrators how to do so effectively.

SUMMARY

Understand the definition of conflict.

- Conflict is a dynamic process.
- Conflict does affect workers differentially.
- Conflict can be viewed from an employee's cognitive state.
- Conflict behavior can be understood.

Know the major types of conflict in organizations.

- Personal conflict
- Group conflict
- Intra-organizational conflict
- Interorganizational conflict

Define intra-organizational conflict.

- Intra-organizational conflict is the type produced by the structural makeup of an organization, including how formal authority is delegated.

Know the types of intra-organizational conflict.

- Vertical conflict
- Horizontal conflict
- Line-staff conflict
- Role conflict

Define interorganizational conflict.

- Interorganizational conflict is when differing organizations share a common purpose but disagree on how that purpose will be achieved.

Describe the stages of a conflict episode.

- Latent conflict
- Perceived conflict
- Felt conflict
- Manifest conflict
- Conflict aftermath

Know conflict behaviors.

- Competing behavior
- Accommodating behavior
- Avoiding behavior
- Collaborating behavior
- Compromising behavior

Define conflict management.

- Conflict management is a series of steps involving both process interventions and structural interventions to manage conflict.

Describe process interventions and structural interventions.

- Process interventions are personal characteristics, informal rules, constituent pressure, conflict of interest, power and status, and organizational policy.
- Structural interventions are selection, training, and contextual modifications.

Understand the limits to conflict management and their application to criminal justice organizations.

- Goal attainment by competing parties
- Consequences of conflict episodes
- Conflict management must be economical of time and effort

Understand the role of conflict in organizations.

- Conflict within criminal justice organizations can be both beneficial and harmful.
- Conflict may be beneficial to the long-term health of criminal justice organizations. Eliminating it may not be practical or possible and could be counterproductive to these organizations.

Case Study: MULTI-JURISDICTIONAL DRUG UNITS

Warren County was a thriving municipality that enjoyed a broad base of political and economic support due to its manufacturing growth, diverse population, and low crime rate. In fact, the low crime rate was attributed to stable families, steady employment, and, for the most part, a good school system. The county had over fifteen cities, each of which had fairly stable communities. This positive perception of the county changed with the introduction of crystal methedrine (crystal meth) and its proliferation in the county through secret laboratories. County officials, in coordination with city officials, decided to pursue a strategy to combat this new drug and its production and distribution.

The plan involved the creation of a multi-jurisdictional drug unit specifically directed toward crystal meth.

The unit was to be composed of officers from all fifteen municipalities in the county, yet problems surfaced at initial discussions and deliberations on how the unit was to be organized. Some cities did not like the ways the unit was going to be supervised and budgeted. Others felt that the bigger cities were forcing themselves onto the small cities and sought greater control over the unit. The three largest cities in the county did desire a much larger role in how the unit was to operate, and this was due, in large part, because they had more immediate resources to devote to

CASE STUDY—continued

the unit, and they were promised more federal pass-through monies that were being distributed to the state as part of a larger joint collaboration between the federal government and the state government directed toward drug enforcement.

In spite of some initial organizational problems, the unit began its work in earnest, resulting in ten cities agreeing to be part of this collaborative approach to drug enforcement. Early in the deliberations among the municipalities, there were many issues on which agreement was difficult to achieve. One issue that did not raise the concerns of governmental officials was the operation of the tactical unit. It was decided that if raids were going to be conducted on homes within the county, they would be done by a coordinated use of officers from each city. Each city was to designate two to three officers who would be part of a tactical response team, only to be used under specific circumstances. The supervisors learned from their experiences that raids were not that common and pulling the team together at short notice would not be difficult to accomplish.

For eighteen months, the multi-jurisdictional unit functioned with full authority to investigate, apprehend, and arrest drug suspects. The original purpose of the unit to "seek out and destroy laboratories producing crystal meth and arrest perpetrators" became a difficult mission to achieve. One problem was that most officers really did not have the kind of training to understand what was involved in a laboratory and how the crime scenes were to be managed. Only after some costly errors and mistakes did the unit's command realize that to properly raid these types of laboratories there was a need to coordinate with fire departments and their hazardous materials personnel. As one of the officers realized early in their raids, the police were becoming the "blue canaries" for the fire department.

To facilitate communication with the many fire departments within the county, the unit's commander suggested that the police chiefs represented in the collaboration approach their respective fire chiefs to begin a dialogue on how best to accomplish the mission of pursuing crystal meth laboratories. For the police chiefs, this meant opening up communications with other city departments with which they had, at best, limited relations. In fact, in some cases, the police were in direct competition with their fire departments for resources, and many of the police chiefs did not want to begin discussions with the fire chiefs due to a long history of complaints and disagreements. In addition, the unit was getting bad commentary from the local press.

The major paper in the county produced data to show that the unit was actually doing very little investigation and arrests for crystal meth production and distribution in its first eighteen months of operation. Instead, most of the arrests were for simple possession and distribution of small quantities of marijuana among teenagers. The paper jokingly suggested that if this was going to be the purpose of the unit it would be better served by simply paying police to attend high school dances! Moreover, the unit was responding to more and more crimes that were clearly outside its mandate. Not only were they investigating drug-related criminal activities, albeit in small numbers, but in addition, they were being asked to back up other specialized units that were effectuating home search warrants for violent criminals. This mission "creep" brought out even more critics. Some even called for the disbanding of the unit because it really served no useful purpose. Rumblings also were heard among the unit's members who thought they were pursuing crystal meth laboratories but now became adjuncts to their own departments. Many considered going back to regular patrol in their home communities.

The issue came to a head when the unit executed a search warrant for a suspect involved in crystal meth production and raided the wrong establishment, killing the owner of the house. To compound matters, the owner was an elderly gentleman who was a veteran and the former coach of a local high school football team. As soon as the tragedy unfolded, the collaborative cities each pulled their officers from the unit and admitted no wrongdoing in the tragedy. An ensuing investigation by the district attorney's office found no criminal responsibility on the part of the officers but did comment on what it viewed to be a poor organizational structure to accomplish its mission. The investigation revealed poor supervision of officers, the lack of a clear chain of command, the tendency for officers to listen to their "home" supervisors as opposed to unit supervisors, and poor definition of authority in the memorandum of understanding that created the unit regarding roles and responsibilities.

The decision by the district attorney's office to not prosecute anyone for the killing did not resonate well with the family of the victim and many members of the community. The family brought forward a multimillion-dollar lawsuit against all ten municipalities involved in the collaboration and functioning of the unit. The lawsuit claimed gross negligence by those in charge of the unit leading to the wrongful death of an innocent citizen. Each municipality sought to fight the lawsuit by separating itself as the primary agent

CASE STUDY—continued

responsible for the unit's management, supervision, and operations, even though there was clear evidence that specific persons made management decisions on behalf of the unit. A jury awarded the victim's family $200,000 in compensatory damages and $1,000,000 in punitive damages, citing what they believed to be poor communications among the cities on how the unit was to be managed and administered. The jury, somewhat begrudgingly, placed the blame for the wrongful death on the municipality whose officer actually shot the citizen. The jury foreman told a reporter that jurors could not believe how the cities did not clearly define the roles and responsibilities of the unit in the beginning. In the words of the jury foreman, the "unit spent more time bickering and fighting among themselves and between themselves and other law enforcement agencies; it is a wonder that they accomplished anything."

CASE STUDY QUESTIONS

1. What type of conflict is described in the case study?
2. Multi-jurisdictional drug units are common across the country. What issues should be discussed and by whom before such a unit is created? How much of the impetus for the creation of these units can be attributed to increased federal funding and the irrational fear of drugs?
3. Suggest ways in which the conflict described in this case study could have been managed more effectively. Should the unit have ever existed?

Think like an Administrator

Conflict is common within criminal justice organizations. Criminal justice administrators have recognized that the best they can do is manage conflict; eradication of organizational conflict is not only impossible to achieve, it also may be counterproductive. So, the best strategy is to appropriately manage conflict within organizations. Because we know that eradication of conflict is not possible within criminal justice organizations, how do we best manage organizational conflict?

1. Can you harness conflict by encouraging competition among groups within the organization?
2. How much conflict centers on the distribution of resources in the organization?
3. How does the desire for critical information create an atmosphere of conflict across criminal justice organizations?
4. How does a poor reward system create conflict within criminal justice organizations?
5. Describe "de-confliction" within police agencies, especially those agencies focused on multi-jurisdictional drug investigations.
6. How can conflict be used to initiate change within criminal justice organizations?
7. How do you know when conflict is both productive and/or nonproductive?

FOR DISCUSSION

1. Describe a potential conflict situation in a criminal justice setting. Suggest possible ways this conflict could be managed. Also, describe what you believe the role of a criminal justice administrator should be in such a situation, and why. Is there a specific conflict behavior that would be useful to deal with this conflict situation, and what is it?

2. Choose a conflict situation in one of the components of the criminal justice system and describe its various stages. Identify the stage at which you think the conflict could be managed and the supervisor's role in the management process. Moreover, are there conflict situations beyond the control of the immediate supervisor? If so, mention a few and discuss why they cannot be dealt with effectively by management personnel in that component of the criminal justice system.

3. Interorganizational conflict is common in the criminal justice system. Suggest methods that administrators can employ to decrease this conflict. Is interorganizational conflict in the criminal justice system inevitable?

4. Invite the local police chief to class to discuss the conflicts that arise in his or her department. Ask the chief to describe the methods employed to decrease conflict. Finally, ask about the department's position on the role of conflict-management programs in policing. Do you think such programs are useful in reducing conflict?

FOR FURTHER READING

Alpert, G., and Dunham, R. *Understanding Police Use of Force: Officers, Suspects, and Reciprocity.* New York: Cambridge University Press, 2004.

Jenn, K., and Mannix, E. "The Dynamic Nature of Conflict: A Longitudinal Study of Intragroup Conflict and Group Performance." *Academy of Management Journal*, April, 2001, 238–251.

Pondy, L. R. "Organizational Conflict: Concepts and Models." *Administrative Science Quarterly*, 12, 1967, 296–320.

Robbins, S., and Judge, T. *Organizational Behavior.* 12th ed. Upper Saddle River, NJ: Pearson/Prentice-Hall, 2007.

Thomas, K. W. "Conflict and Conflict Management." In *Handbook of Industrial and Organizational Psychology,* edited by M. D. Dunnette, pp. 889–935. Chicago: Rand McNally, 1976.

Part IV

Processes in Criminal Justice Organizations

P rocesses define the actions of criminal justice administrators. How criminal justice administrators move their organizations forward is largely dependent on the processes they put in place. In this part of the book, we examine four distinct processes within criminal justice organizations: decision making, organizational effectiveness, change and innovation, and the application of research findings within criminal justice organizations.

Decision making is examined in Chapter 12. No other process has been more scrutinized within criminal justice organizations than decision making. Both critics and supporters of the criminal justice system look at how criminal justice administrators and their subordinates make the daily decisions that define criminal justice in America. Whether it is the beat cop on the street, the judge during sentencing, or the parole board regarding release decisions, these actions define criminal justice agencies.

Another interesting process involves the question of organizational effectiveness. Chapter 13 notes the difficulty in trying to assess the actions of criminal justice organizations and their administrators. The concept is quite simple: Do criminal justice organizations accomplish what they say they do? No simple answer to this question exists. In fact, as a way of assessing criminal justice organizations, goal-attainment questions are quite sticky and only one way to assess organizational effectiveness.

Chapter 14 examines change and innovation within criminal justice organizations. It has been stated that "change for change's sake makes no sense," yet there are many who believe that you have to be changing to meet the multiple and conflicting changes in the environment. How do we assess when change does make sense, and how do we know when we have achieved a positive state? How does innovation create tension, conflict, and resistance within criminal justice organizations? Can you think of innovation within criminal justice organizations without thinking about conflict and disagreement among subordinates?

The final chapter of the book explores the topic of research in criminal justice organizations and its value to criminal justice administrators. The entire book is predicated on applying research findings to what we do as criminal justice administrators. What role should research play in what we do as criminal justice administrators? Why does an appeal to "evidence-based practices" and "best practices" exist as a moniker for those who want to change criminal justice organizations? Is research really that important to criminal justice administration? Will the twenty-first-century criminal justice administrator have to become a consumer of research findings as crime becomes more sophisticated and complex? These are questions to ponder as you read the chapters in this section of the book.

CHAPTER 12

Decision Making

LEARNING OBJECTIVES

After reading this chapter, the student will have achieved the following objectives:

- Be able to define decision making.

- Understand the basis for decision-making rules of criminal justice practitioners.

- Understand the "garbage can" theory of decision making.

- Be able to briefly discuss the four types of criminal justice decision makers.

- Understand the major themes to improve criminal justice decisions.

VIGNETTE

On January 16, 1919, the Eighteenth Amendment to the Constitution of the United States was ratified. U.S. citizens, through the representative government of their state legislative bodies, decided to impose a national ban on the manufacture, sale, or transportation of intoxicating liquors. This decision began the decade of *prohibition* and with it a series of governmental decisions and individual decisions that created the era of the illegal manufacturing, sale, and transportation of intoxicating liquors.

Consuming beer, wine, and whiskey was a major pastime for Americans. The Eighteenth Amendment, prohibition, did not limit the taste for alcohol on the part of the American people. They did not decide to obey the law and discontinue in their indulgence. Although major distilleries and breweries closed, alcoholic beverages were soon smuggled into the United States from Canada, Cuba, Jamaica, and other contiguous countries. In addition, alcohol production was picked up by small-scale producers in response to the demand. The distribution and retail sales of alcoholic drink were soon run by organized crime. Providing alcoholic beverages to the thirsty public, although criminal, was a business decision, a response to market demands. Organized criminals had to learn how to operate as a business. To a great extent, the power and skill of organized crime today is a result of our national decision to ban alcoholic beverages.

Local law enforcement agencies had the authority to enforce prohibition, but most local agencies were reluctant to do so. In fact, local officials frequently chose to take bribes from distributers of illegal alcohol rather than enforce the law. They made this choice easily because, like most Americans, they were not opposed to the consumption of alcohol and most were probably practicing drinkers. The federal government created an enforcement bureau within the Internal Revenue Service (IRS) to enforce the Eighteenth Amendment. The special IRS agents, referred to as revenuers, were dramatically underpaid. They received an amount that would equate to around $20,000 at today's pay levels. Of course, the decision to pay the revenuers so poorly made them easy targets for corruption.

The decision to prohibit the manufacturing, sale, or transportation of intoxicating liquor did not happen overnight. Religious groups long argued that the root cause of violence, crime, spousal abuse, and other social maladies could be found in the American habit of consuming alcoholic beverages. Prison reformers of the 1890s argued that most penitentiaries and jails could be closed if we would impose a national ban on alcohol consumption. It was a long time in coming. January sixteenth was celebrated by the "drys" as the day of the great reform. Fourteen years later, the Eighteenth Amendment was revoked, and the great experiment came to an end. The experiment in social engineering was considered a failure and created disastrous side effects. Prohibition encouraged crime, corruption, and violence among criminal gangs that marketed illegal alcohol. Did we learn from that decision?

It is valuable to note that prior to the passage of the Eighteenth Amendment, approximately 70 percent of the federal budget was funded by taxes on the sale, transportation, and consumption of alcoholic beverages (Okrent, 2010). As an alternative to the loss of revenue, the federal government created our national income tax system. In effect, the federal income tax system we have today can be seen as an unintended consequence of the Eighteenth Amendment. However, it can be argued that the decision to create the income tax system fits into the "garbage can" theory. The idea of an income tax had been simmering among political actors for decades. The loss of revenue due to prohibition was the perfect opportunity for interest groups to put forward the income tax as a timely solution to the problem of lost revenue.

Decision making is one of the most important concerns for managers in all organizations. Managers make decisions with long-term consequences by reviewing and altering their agency's mission, establishing long-term goals as a result of formal planning, or changing the agency's philosophy and operations. For example, the shift from traditional to community policing is, in effect, a decision to alter the agency's purpose, structure, and the activities of its police officers. Managers also make decisions on budget allocation, policies, and operating procedures that constrain the decision making of its subordinates (Houston and Parsons, 2006). Having made the higher-order decision just outlined, managers also oversee the decisions of their subordinates. Subordinates regularly decide what policies and procedures apply to a particular situation and often ignore policies and procedures when making operational decisions.

Hindsight provides us with examples of good and bad decision making at all levels of an organization. During the late 1970s, legislators across the country decided to roll back crime by lengthening criminal sentences for offenders. Proponents thought the strong general deterrent would cut crime dramatically and reasoned that prison population would decrease as a result. They therefore ignored predictions that prison populations would increase as a result of tougher sentences. As is now apparent, prison populations have soared and the percentage of state budgets allocated to departments have similarly soared. In this case, legislators who dismissed predictions of an increasing prison population were committed to their cause-and-effect belief about the power of the general deterrent effect on would-be offenders.

In 1984, the police decision to drop an incendiary bomb on the roof of a house to evict a cult in Philadelphia ultimately resulted in the burning of some sixty homes and created a costly political firestorm. In the late 1970s, the U.S. government's decision to spray the herbicide paraquat on Mexican marijuana led to reduced supplies of the drug but also created concerns about the possible health effects of tainted supplies. This concern ultimately stimulated domestic production of the illegal crop (Brecher, 1986).

In criminal justice, countless decisions are made about the clients of the system. Decision making often begins with legislative decisions that alter the mandates or processes of the criminal justice system. Legislated sentencing guidelines, for example, severely limited judicial discretion in sentencing convicted offenders. Civil and appellate court decisions often impact the operations of criminal justice agencies. The most striking example is the U.S. Supreme Court decision of 1966 that created the infamous Miranda warning that police officers must read to individuals who are charged with a felony. Decisions take place in the administrative hierarchy of criminal justice agencies when policies are developed or procedures are changed. Difficult decisions have to be made about an agency's budget. Budget priorities have to be established and budget allotments have to be anticipated (Lee, 2012). Decision making also takes place beginning with reporting a crime to the police through the final discharge of an offender; each step in the criminal process is marked by a decision made by workers in the criminal justice system. Figure 12.1 is a partial list of such decisions. Lipsky (1980) indicates that these decisions, often made by frontline staff, are more important than executive decisions in determining organizational policy. In fact, some scholars have argued that the conglomeration of different criminal justice agencies with different jurisdictions can only be understood as a system by recognizing that the disparate organizations are linked by the decisions made about offenders (Newman, 1986).

In this chapter, we examine the process of decision making in criminal justice. We turn first to issues of theory and the growing recognition of the limits of rationality. Next, the focus is on two issues in criminal justice decision making that appear to represent extremes in our assumptions about rationality. First, we investigate discretion in decision making, a topic often criticized by those seeking rational processes. Second, we study prediction, a topic often assumed to be linked to high degrees of rationality. These two issues have engendered more discussion in criminal justice organizations than have other decision-making topics. Finally, we consider the ways managers can influence the decision-making process in criminal justice in an effort to increase rationality.

WHAT IS A DECISION?

A decision is a judgment, a choice between alternatives (Houston, 1999). The decisions you made when you opened your closet this morning and the parole board's decision whether or not to parole an offender may seem to have little in common. Your choice of clothing and a parole board's decision, however, both

FIGURE 12.1 A Partial List of Decisions Made about Criminal Cases.

1. Has a crime occurred in the eyes of a victim or a bystander?
2. Should a crime be reported to the police?
3. Should police be dispatched to the scene?
4. Should police regard the event as a criminal offense?
5. Should investigators be called in?
6. Should an arrest be made?
7. Should search warrants be issued?
8. Should arrest warrants be issued?
9. Should a police officer fire at a suspect?
10. Should an alleged offender be detained in jail?
11. Should a citation be issued?
12. Should bail be set and at what amount?
13. Should release-on-recognizance be allowed?
14. Should an alleged offender be prosecuted?
15. Should an alleged offender enter a diversion program?
16. With what priority should prosecution be undertaken?
17. Is an alleged offender competent to stand trial?
18. Should motions be granted?
19. Is an alleged offender guilty?
20. Is an alleged offender not guilty due to insanity?
21. Should an offender be incarcerated or allowed to remain in the community?
22. How long should the sentence be?
23. Should there be special conditions to the sentence?
24. What level of security does an offender need?
25. When and how should the levels of security change?
26. Should an incarcerated offender be transferred?
27. Should disciplinary reports be written?
28. Is an offender guilty of disciplinary infractions?
29. What are appropriate sanctions for disciplinary violations?
30. To what program should an offender be assigned?
31. Should an offender be transferred or committed to a mental hospital?
32. Should an incarcerated offender be paroled?
33. Should parole or community release be revoked?
34. Should an offender be discharged?

FIGURE 12.2   Elements of a Decision.

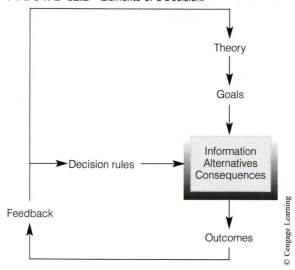

resulted from processes that share some basic elements. Those elements are shown in Figure 12.2.

In general, some *theory* or broad framework guides most decisions. As you examine your wardrobe, your selection of what to wear may simply be based on your beliefs about what looks good on you, but complex decisions may involve sophisticated theories. In his study of parole board decision making, for example, Hawkins (1983) found that broad support of *classicalism* or *positivism* frames board members' decisions—that is, some members of the parole board place great importance on whether an offender has been punished for a suitable time, whereas others are concerned with evidence of rehabilitation or change in the offender's outlook.

Wilson's (1968) styles of policing may also be seen as broad frameworks within which police officers make decisions to arrest or not arrest. Officers in departments characterized by the *watchman style*, with its primary focus on maintaining order, may be reluctant to arrest if less drastic means will control a disturbance. Officers in *legalistic* departments, however, may invoke their power to arrest based solely on whether a statute has been violated. More recent research, however, suggests that organizational structure or styles of policing only partially predict arrest rates, and factors such as crime rates or violent crime rates may be a stronger determinant (Chappell, MacDonald, and Manz, 2006).

Goals in the decision-making process are specific to each decision, and they refer to what a decision maker would like to achieve. In a decision to prosecute a particular case, the prosecuting attorney's goal may be to gain a conviction; in the decision to dispatch a police car to a burglary scene or to schedule an appointment, a dispatcher's goal may be the efficient use of personnel. Goals may not always be so obvious, however. In his study of probation officers' sentencing recommendations, Rosecrance (1985) concluded that "ball park recommendations" serve the goal of maintaining credibility with the judge and may have little to do with particular cases. However, plea bargaining, mandatory minimum sentences, and sentencing guidelines have reduced the role of probation officers' recommendations in sentencing decisions (Stinchcomb and Hippensteel, 2001).

Decision makers also need three kinds of information. First, they must be aware of alternatives, or choices. If there are no alternatives, no decision must be made. Second, they must also be aware of the possible consequences of the alternatives. If consequences do not differ or if there are no expectations regarding consequences, an alternative can be selected only at random. Third, some information is needed about the subject of the decision in order to guide the selection among the alternatives. A judge's sentencing decision can illustrate the importance of information. Evidence of a convicted offender's crime and criminal history provides a basis for selection among the sentencing alternatives as provided by statute. All of this information is considered in light of the expected consequences of each possible sentence. Among these consequences may be danger to the public if an offender remains in the community, the possible brutalizing effects of a prison term on a youthful offender, and public dissatisfaction if a substantial penalty is not imposed.

The availability of the information, however, does not necessarily produce a decision. That information must be processed. Processing occurs through the **decision rules**, which govern how the elements of the decision are combined. In criminal justice, many decisions rely on essentially *clinical* decision rules that are based on education, training, and experience. Arrest decisions, sentencing decisions, and classification decisions usually rely on the clinical judgments of individuals. At the other extreme are *quantitative* decision rules, involving the assignment of **numerical weights** to pieces of information. Those weights are added to produce a sum that dictates the decision. Scales based on these principles have been developed for use in prosecution, bail, sentencing, and parole decisions.

The processing of information according to decision rules produces *outcomes*. People are arrested, sentenced, transferred between prisons, or paroled. Policies are implemented, changed, or dismantled. The outcome is the result of the decision. In many but not all cases, the decision process is not completed with the outcome. Many types of decisions are repeated again and again. Police officers soon face new decisions about whether or not to arrest, and judges continue to sentence convicted offenders. In a **cybernetic**, or self-correcting, **decision model**, the outcome of prior decisions provides feedback to influence future decisions. Cybernetic decision processes are based on mechanical models similar to the thermostat in a house. When the heat is turned on, the temperature rises until the preset temperature high is reached; then the thermostat turns off the heat until the preset low temperature is reached, at which point the heat comes on again. Criminal justice feedback is not nearly so simple, but the same principles apply. Police officers' arrest practices are influenced by prosecutors' decisions to pursue prosecution or dismiss charges. Parole board decisions are influenced by information about the failure of some parolees.

Decision rules: Rules, guidelines, or criteria that filter and prioritize information and help choose alternatives. The rules may be cognitive and apparent or unconscious and subjective.

Numerical weights: Indicate the relative importance of information by placing a weight on the data. This can be seen as a mathematical method to prioritize information.

Cybernetic decision model: Self-correcting decision-making model in which the outcomes of prior decisions provide feedback to influence future decisions.

Feedback may affect future decisions through its influence on theory, decision rules, information, or all three. For example, corrections decision making has been greatly affected by feedback from research in the mid-1970s that suggested that treatment programs had little effect (see Cullen and Gilbert, 1982). Theoretical frameworks supportive of treatment were replaced by the principle of just deserts—that is, punishment proportionate to the crime committed—and decision goals focused on equity in sentencing and time served. In parole, for example, information about participation in prison programs became less important than it had been, and some parole boards all but abandoned clinical decision rules and adopted numerical scales to assist in decision making.

Feedback about police intervention in spousal abuse cases has also influenced arrest decisions. Increasingly, police departments are encouraging or requiring arrest in domestic disputes, especially if there is some sign of physical violence (Morash, 1986). In the past, police and prosecutorial decisions were greatly influenced by feedback showing that many women did not pursue prosecution of husbands or boyfriends in domestic violence cases. Police officers were encouraged to negotiate settlements at the scene, counsel the participants, or make referrals to social service agencies. Feedback with a different content was generated by several well-publicized cases of continued abuse and even homicide and by research studies showing that arrest is most likely to prevent further violence (Sherman and Berk, 1984). That feedback has altered the decision-making process in favor of arrest over mediation. Yet even this finding is not uniform because some research has also shown pro-arrest policies to be ineffectual in deterring future violence among offenders (Sherman, 1992; Walker and Katz, 2002).

DECISION-MAKING THEORY: FROM RATIONALITY TO THE GARBAGE CAN

At first glance, the diagram of decisions in Figure 12.2 appears to be a model of perfect rationality. The goals of a specific decision are identified and needed information is processed according to agreed-on decision rules and is considered within some theoretical framework. The diagram also suggests directions for improving the decision-making process. Increasing **consistency in theory**, increasing agreement on goals and decision rules, and improving the quality of information will produce increasingly rational decisions. In criminal justice, as in other fields, rationality in decision making may be assumed to be a requirement for effectiveness and efficiency. As Gottfredson (1975) points out, however, although we may strive for rational decisions, achieving rationality is unlikely and probably impossible.

At one time, scholars of decision making believed the process could best be understood as a rational one that could produce optimal results or "correct" answers for given situations (Hall and Tolbert, 2005; Murray, 1986). This view assumed, for example, that an obviously correct answer existed to the question of whether a given suspect should be arrested or paroled. It was assumed that a

Consistency in theory:
The need to have a decision-making theory apply to all decisions, hence, it is used consistently.

specific policy on the deployment of patrol cars or the choice of a site on which to build a prison could be objectively regarded as the best solution to the problem.

In an influential book, March and Simon (1958) first questioned the rationality of the decision-making process. They pointed out that decisions were made on the basis of **bounded rationality**, partly because decision makers are incapable of collecting and handling the kinds of information needed for completely rational decisions:

1. Rationality requires a complete knowledge and anticipation of the consequences that follow each choice. In fact, knowledge of consequences is always fragmentary.

2. Because these consequences lie in the future, imagination must supply the lack of experienced feeling in attaching value to them. But values can only be imperfectly anticipated.

3. Rationality requires a choice among all possible alternative behaviors. In actual behavior, very few of these possible alternatives come to mind.

Perrow (1981:2) outlines the thesis of bounded rationality:

> We cannot process large amounts of information but only limited bits, and those slowly. We tend to distort the information as we process it. We cannot gather information very well even if we could process it: We do not always know what is relevant information, inasmuch as we do not understand how things work. Above all, we cannot even be sure of what we want the information for because we cannot be sure what our preferences are. We have trouble discovering what we want. We also have contradictory preferences, or contradictory goals, and are unable to fulfill all of them at once. As a consequence, we do not look for the optimal solutions: we have to settle for "satisfycing," taking the first acceptable solution that comes along.

A good example of **satisfycing** that students can readily understand is the decision process they followed to select a university to attend. A rational decision would have required that prospective college students have an accurate view of their career goals and precisely what university offered the major and/or classes they would need to direct them toward their careers. Also, students would need a good grasp of the various reputations universities have in general and would have with prospective employers. Students also would have to factor in all costs (tuition, living expenses, costs relating to living various distances from home, and so on). This approach is followed partially by some students. But most prospective college students do not have clear career goals to guide their decision-making process. More important, it is impossible for prospective students to have all the information suggested on all of the colleges and universities across the country, or even their home state. Most likely, the student's choice of what university or college to attend is a process of "satisfycing"—that is, students get available information from high school counselors, blend that information with

Bounded rationality: Absolute rational decision making requires all information necessary and as much time as necessary to process the information. In organizations, rationality is bound by limited time to make decisions and by incomplete information.

Satisfycing: The attainment of acceptable rather than optimal results; a realistic description of decision making with limited access to information and a limited time frame in which to make a decision.

what they hear from their friends and family, consider a cost range that is roughly affordable, and select a number of colleges and universities to consider. Some students choose to attend a local community college because of the cost and convenience. The major goal of most of us—to get a college degree—will be met. The point is that deciding on what university or college to attend is not purely rational but also can be sensible.

Working under conditions of bounded rationality is common to all organizations and, therefore, is the nature of decision making within the criminal justice system. Many decisions, especially those regarding offenders, are characterized by volumes of information about their history and background. It is important to recognize that the information is selectively collected and interpreted based on past practices and the experience of decision makers and that satisfycing, or the attainment of acceptable rather than optimal results, is also a useful concept in criminal justice. Sound management decisions can be made, however, with limited, incomplete information. For example, in New York City, detectives will not investigate burglaries in which less than $10,000 in property is taken. This policy is clearly not optimal, but it is regarded as a minimally acceptable compromise between investigation goals and the efficient use of employees' time. In the courtroom, the extent to which home detention is used as a response to jail crowding may reflect satisfycing between concerns for punishment and concerns about overcrowding. Overcrowded prison systems, in turn, will often force decision makers to lower the classification of higher-risk inmates in order to find available bed space. For example, in a northern state, a high-risk inmate was classified as a low-risk inmate and moved to a low-security facility. The inmate escaped and shot and killed a local citizen during his escape attempt.

An extension of the concept of bounded rationality also merits our attention. Cohen, March, and Olsen (1972) use the analogy of the garbage can to describe one model of decision making. Decision makers handle problems of ambiguity by developing sets of **performance programs**, or standardized methods of responding to problems. Organizations thus possess a repertoire of responses, or a garbage can full of ready-made answers in search of problems. The link to bounded rationality, however, is the idea that the garbage can must also contain the problems—that is, a decision maker will not think a situation needs action until that situation is defined in terms of solutions available (see Pinfield, 1986). When necessary, organization members modify their perceptions of problems to justify their actions (Staw and Ross, 1978). Hall and Tolbert (2005) suggest that individuals also possess garbage cans of solutions and problems. Westley (1970) found preprogrammed responses in his classic study of the police. He reported that a major justification for the use of violence was that a suspect was considered guilty. However, research indicates that police use excessive force in only 0.3 percent of their encounters with citizens (Adams, 1971).

Although the garbage can analogy may not help us understand all decisions in criminal justice (Mohr, 1976), some research suggests the usefulness of the model. Sudnow's (1965) examination of a public defender's office describes a process by which public defenders' decisions about defense strategies are the

Performance programs: Decision makers handle ambiguous problems by developing a set of performance programs, or standard methods, to respond to problems.

results of defining clients by using existing categories rather than considering the individual merits of each case. Public defenders have set practices of encouraging defendants to plead guilty as soon as possible if their cases have the hallmarks of a typical offense, or, as Sudnow calls it, a "normal crime." A young male arrested for burglary who has a prior record for burglary, for example, is encouraged to plead guilty even if he insists on his innocence. Atypical defendants get the benefit of a close examination of the strengths and weaknesses of their case. But typical defendants who resist pressures to plead guilty as soon as possible may find themselves defined as recalcitrant. As the garbage can model would suggest, the existing solution for such cases involves proceeding to trial with a public defender who assumes the defendant is guilty. The trial then takes on the characteristics of a ritualized conspiracy against the defendant.

In a study of police investigations, Waegel (1981) argues that research strategies that focus on the decision-making processes of individual investigators have severe limitations. It is fruitful, rather, to study the existing shared categorizations of cases. In other words, he supports studying the garbage can of solutions to which police investigations (the problems) will be applied. Much of police investigation, then, involves "mapping the features of a particular case onto a more general and commonly recognized type of case" (1981:265). The most basic categories into which investigations are placed are routine versus nonroutine cases.

Characteristics of the victim, the offense, and the suspects figure into the categorization of cases, and these characteristics trigger different levels of investigation. In some cases, the distinction between routine and nonroutine is obvious, while in others the detective forces a fit. In either case, assumptions about the nature of the incident and the parties involved guide case handling. The ability to type cases quickly is important in investigations. Waegel points out that the necessity to report on the status of cases influences whether or not a case is regarded as routine. Cases can be open, closed, or—if leads have been unproductive—suspended. We can observe the other side of this process of applying problems to existing solutions in case skimming. A steady stream of arrests is produced by working on only those cases that appear potentially solvable from information in the original patrol officer's report and summarily suspending the remainder of the cases.

The garbage can analogy has its appeal as a means of understanding some decision making in criminal justice. We need to be careful, however, not to let the cuteness of the imagery confound our analysis. Solutions and problems in the garbage can are not collected in some random fashion, after all. The approach to problems, as well as the problems themselves, represents the interests and history of the organization and its members. Thus, little in the way of entirely new material is likely to enter into the decision-making process (Hall and Tolbert, 2005).

Thus, stability and even routinization of decision making are products of bounded rationality. In this organizational perspective, the boundaries determine the context of decision making, and those boundaries are the product of organizational processes, such as limiting the kinds of information available or viewed as relevant, establishing procedures, and requiring reports, as well as less obtrusive controls (see Perrow, 1986:128). Another important contribution of the concept of bounded rationality is recognition of the cognitive limitations of individual decision makers. Not only must decision makers deal with multiple goals and possibly conflicting theories, and not only are they controlled by organizational practices, but they can also effectively handle only small quantities of information. Research has demonstrated, for example, that people can recall only seven or eight bits of information without developing some process or shorthand method for recalling the data (Burnham, 1975). This finding suggests that studying the ways people process information is important to understanding their decisions. In the following sections, we examine the influence of culture on decision making, the role of politics in decision making, characteristics of the decision makers, and finally, the characteristics of the information used in decisions.

The use of the garbage can theory can also be seen as decision makers possessing solutions that are waiting for problems to emerge and offering opportunities to put the favored solutions into action. It seems that a good example is the extension of sex offender controls, such as mandatory registering as a sex offender, to incidents of statutory rape. In application, if two young individuals, one just recently earning adult status by virtue of his or her age and the other still a minor by virtue of his or her age, have sexual relations, the adult will be guilty of statutory rape. If convicted, the young adult will be labeled a sex offender and lumped into a category that includes repulsive child molesters. The fallacy of such practices is evident. However, the crackdown on sex offenders gave proponents of limiting or preventing young citizens from indulging in sex an opportunity to impose a harsh set of circumstances on youthful offenders in an attempt to deter sexual activity on their part.

Organizational Culture and Decision Making

Satisfycing and garbage can decision making are both processes bound by organizational culture. Defining problems and recognizing acceptable and workable solutions—whether it is assigning parking, prescribing procedures, or developing long-term strategic planning—are framed within the context of an organization's culture (Sever, 2008). For our purposes here, **organizational culture** is defined as ready-made answers to problems (March and Simon, 1958) or a set of basic assumptions and beliefs shared by organizational members that are taken for granted (Schein, 2004). Hence, agencies now have a prevalence of such common proverbial wisdom as, "We have always done it that way," "It worked in the past," "If it ain't broke, don't fix it," and the like. Assumptions and beliefs are learned responses to problems that are valued enough to pass on to new members through both the formal and informal socialization processes. Specifically, assumptions about who makes decisions and at what level of the organization and what information is utilized in decision making are not necessarily based on rational thought or reflection on mission or goals. Rather, the "decisions on who makes decisions, when and how" are based on past practices, routines, and assumptions about who is best suited to make decisions and what information is

Organizational culture: A collection of ready-made answers to problems or a set of basic assumptions and beliefs shared by organizational members that are taken for granted.

considered reliable. For example, in traditional hierarchical agencies, decision making is, in theory, centralized because the classic assumption is that wisdom, and the "big picture" is to be found at the organization's apex. If experience is highly valued, information from the organization's memory bank, usually anecdotal in nature, is readily accepted, and information that contradicts past beliefs would tend to be rejected.

Organizations tend to define problems and identify solutions to problems based on deeply rooted values and beliefs. For example, a deeply rooted value in corrections is that inmates must be subject to staff control. Inmate autonomy in this framework is viewed as a problem, and inmate participation in governance, a solution proposed by some prison reformers (Murton, 1976), as anathema—in part because it is contrary to these basic values. Sparrow (1999) suggests that moving from traditional policing to community policing will require a major shift in the organizational culture of police agencies. The shift would impact the framework for decision making because information that would drive decisions, long and short-term, would derive from community members' problems, needs, and satisfaction with police services rather than from traditional statistics, such as crime, arrest and conviction rates, and response time. In addition, decisions would be made in coordination with community members rather than at the chief's desk.

In a classic article, Rosecrance (1999b) challenges the "myth" of individualized decisions on criminal sentences and questions the value of the information accumulated on criminal defendants in presentence investigation reports (PSI) for sentencing decisions. Rosecrance sees the presentence investigation as more ceremonial than instructive. Many internal agency reports are ceremonial. One author reports that, while he was a district supervisor for a state parole authority, he discovered, quite by accident, that the lengthy monthly reports supervisors were required to submit were not being read. Seeing this as an opportunity, he retrieved old monthly reports and, every month, placed a new cover page on the old report and then submitted it through the chain of command. Of course, all subsequent reports were submitted on time, and he was complimented by his boss for routinely meeting the deadlines for submission.

Criminal sentencing is likely to be based on an accumulation of past practices framed within a heuristic assessment that classifies identified groups of offenders as either deserving of incarceration or more lenient dispositions. Court work groups, in effect, predetermine criminal sentences, and most of the rituals that surround sentencing serve to legitimize ready-made solutions (Neubauer, 1996). Walker (1994) further explains this process by using the analogy of thermodynamics in organizations, which describes a social process wherein courtroom work groups—judges, prosecuting and defense attorneys, probation officers—blunt, evade, and circumvent any proposed changes in existing philosophies, principles, or operations. In effect, equilibrium is set and protected by a deeply entrenched courtroom culture with long-standing beliefs, values, assumptions, and legitimizing rituals.

The entrenched beliefs, values, assumptions, and legitimizing rituals frame and perpetuate the decision-making process. To the extent that decisions on criminal sentencing are bound by culture, the PSI will serve to provide information crucial to fitting the decision to incarcerate or release an offender to the community within accepted but implicit, culturally determined informal guidelines. For this reason, recommendations written by probation officers as members of the culture generally correlate with sentencing decisions. Hence, the cultural context within which decisions are made is crucial to an understanding of decision-making processes among criminal justice practitioners. This implicit decision-making process can be explained more directly. Over time, the court work group reaches a consensus on offenders who clearly deserve probation or lenient sentences and, at the other end of the continuum, offenders who deserve imprisonment or tougher criminal sentencing. Placing offenders somewhere along this sentencing continuum will be based on facts, such as the offender's criminal history, circumstances of the crime, and so on. The important point is that an unwritten consensus or agreement evolves over time on what facts and circumstances dictate the sentence criminal offenders will receive.

Politics and Decision Making

The political scientist Norton Long once noted that power is the lifeblood of politics. Possessing power becomes important, therefore, to decision making, but it also is critical to understand that power influences decision making. No effective criminal justice administrator or manager underestimates the power and influence of politics, both internal and external, on decision making. *Internal politics* are the processes by which interested parties within the organization express their concern and seek implementation and acceptance of their ideas and practices. Bolman and Deal (2003) suggest that political behaviors within organizations are not all bad, but that for politics to be constructive, leaders and managers must understand the importance of agenda setting, working and forming coalitions, and bargaining and negotiating. With these ideas as decision rules, administrators can focus their energies on directing political influence toward productive ends.

External politics: Forces outside the organization that influence decision making.

    External politics consist of the influence that outside parties exert on the organization's definition of mission, the appropriate types of operations the organization exhibits, and the directions it takes. Outside groups constantly put pressure on organizations to move in directions that are favorable to their interests. For example, the establishment of the Amber Alert that posts public information about child abduction is the result of public pressure for law enforcement to make a greater and coordinated effort to secure the safety of an abducted child. These pressures serve as constraints for decision makers, as well as increase the ambiguity about which decisions are relevant, which should receive priority, and when they should be made. A confluence of external interests shapes the ways decisions will be made, and administrators are often left with too many demands, too few resources, and too little time to make effective decisions. Nowhere is this truer than in the sphere of decision making within public organizations, especially criminal justice organizations.

Internal Politics and Decision Making   The role of **internal politics** on decision making cannot be understated. Criminal justice organizations are made up of multiple and conflicting individuals and groups. The interests presented by various individuals and groups form internal political behaviors that seek to advance particular interests and concerns along identifiable dimensions.

Police departments, for example, are fraught with internal politics along the dimensions of race, gender, veterans and rookies, relative levels of education, management style of administrators, the development of cliques, the power of informal leaders and unions, and so forth. Recently, a reform-minded police chief was fired after a no-confidence vote was rendered by the local police union. The reason for the no-confidence vote was that he ordered the release of a local wealthy businessman who had a distant relationship with the chief. The man released was charged with a misdemeanor, was bleeding profusely as a result of the struggle he had with the police, and had had a number of recent heart attacks. The decision to release the offender seems reasonable. However, the underlying reason the chief was fired was that he had a poor relationship with the union as a result of his attempts to impose close accountability measures on his officers. Young, highly educated, inexperienced police officers have very different interests from more seasoned, older, less educated police officers. Informal leaders may not buy into formal policies. Unions will strive to have power over policy as well as wages and benefits. The internal struggles that ensue can sometimes be vicious and can produce a tremendous toll on officers, their supervisors, police administrators, and even the public at large. Coalescing these multiple interests into a unified group working toward identifiable objectives and goals is a major challenge for police administrators (Fyfe et al., 1997).

Decision making within a context of diverse interests among employees becomes a problematic activity, particularly for supervisors and administrators who are expected to be sensitive to these interests and, in some cases (such as sexual harassment), are mandated by law. Also, the compartmentalization of organizations into, for example, treatment and the custody components of corrections systems and specialized units in police organizations create competition for resources and influence over significant policy decisions. There is a view that participative decision making can have positive effects on organizations by making politics a more transparent game (Reeves et al., 2012).

External Politics and Decision Making   External politics influence decision making in ways that become difficult for administrators to address. Concern for external interests can become a central activity among criminal justice administrators. Departments of corrections, for example, have been under tremendous pressures since the early 1990s to respond to perceptions of ever-growing crime problems. Proponents of incarceration strategies have suggested that sending more offenders to prison has a direct effect on crime rates (Mitchell, 1997), even though evidence is scant to suggest that an increase in incarceration will have an effect on crime rates. For corrections administrators, however, the pressure to accept more offenders has been unprecedented, and correctional leadership and management have become extremely difficult as a consequence. Succumbing to the demands of these external groups, most notably legislators

Internal politics: Forces within the organization that influence decision making.

and governors, departments of corrections have been receiving record numbers of offenders as prison incarceration rates have grown over 60 percent since 1980 (U.S. Bureau of Justice Statistics, 2007).

The most direct effect of these pressures has been on decision making among corrections officials. The dramatic increase in governmental budgets for corrections has also awakened legislator interest in their now large and visible investment; a tendency for legislators to micromanage the system has become apparent. Currently, legislation to ban recreational activity in prisons is taking hold across the states. Legislators in Ohio and Michigan have also prescribed the addition of gun towers to prisons following escapes and disturbances and have added officer positions to prisons beyond departmental requests. Behind such legislation are correctional officer union lobbyists who attempt to influence administrative policy through pressure on legislators.

The most pronounced effect has been the degree to which politics influences the practices of departments of corrections. Top correctional officials have seen a greater degree of invasiveness in their decision making as political concerns of external groups have taken precedence over the operational concerns of administrators and managers in running their facilities. Correctional administrators, however, have been unable to marshal enough external political support to get politics out of the decision-making process and to develop appropriate political technologies to help them do this (Baro, 1988). One director of a large correctional department resigned largely over what he viewed to be an overly aggressive court system, coupled with a meddling legislator and an entirely political governor who sought to micromanage his department.

With politicians making unrealistic demands on correctional officials, such as the abolition of parole, no good time, and "three strikes and you're out" initiatives, correctional administrators are left asking what exactly do they administer and under what conditions. Also, Mississippi required inmates to wear striped uniforms with the word *convict* written on the back of the uniforms, and Alabama, Arizona, and Florida attempted to reinstate forms of chain gangs (Stinchcomb, 2005). For many corrections officials, external politics has had an adverse effect on their decision-making capabilities. Short of keeping politics entirely out of corrections—an unrealistic goal—administrators need the ability to function in the political arena so that desirable outcomes for corrections are possible.

Flanagan, Johnson, and Bennett (1996) report that, based on their survey of 648 correctional administrators across the country, many support activities and routines that assist prisoners in their treatment and development. Yet the current political environment, which emphasizes a get-tough posture, precludes them from publicly advocating for such amenities, even if these activities actually improve administrators' capabilities to manage correctional institutions (Stinchcomb, 2005). The surveyed correctional administrators suggested that prisons would be more efficient and effective places if external politics could be kept to a minimum, but that outcome is highly unlikely. Similar concerns have been expressed by police chiefs (Gardner, 1997). Attempts have been made by legislators to control police discretion (Gains and Kappeler, 2005), parole commissioners (Husz, 1996), and community-based corrections officials (Dickey, 1996).

CHARACTERISTICS OF DECISION MAKERS

Although organizational and political factors are important in understanding the notion of bounded rationality, some research in criminal justice has focused on the decision makers themselves. In studying parole decision making, Wilkins (1975b) uncovered fundamental differences in the way people process information. He first asked decision makers to make interim decisions after reviewing only limited items of information. Some of the decision makers, however, found it impossible to make decisions based on the limited information, even when they were told that they could indicate a low level of confidence in the decision. These decision makers would not consider making a decision without information they regarded as "sufficient." From this line of research, Wilkins described four types of decision makers. This typology is relevant to a large number of criminal justice decisions that are characterized by uncertainty and a relatively large amount of available information. These decisions may concern intensity of investigation, sentences, or classification or transfer of prisoners.

Decision makers described by Wilkins as *sequentialists* use their experience to determine what items of information are most important. Then they consider items in a sequential fashion, one at a time, based on their view of each item's importance. These decision makers are able to make interim decisions, and each additional item of information adds to or lowers their level of confidence in the decision. Wilkins compares this decision-making process with the logic of the statistical procedure known as *stepwise regression*, in which the most important information is considered first, followed by information that contributes less and less to the end result.

A second type identified by Wilkins is the *ah yes! decision maker*. Instead of employing a sequential search strategy, they collect large amounts of information and search for patterns in that information. Only after they find a pattern with which they are familiar do these decision makers exclaim, "Ah, yes, this is the typical such-and-such!" Then they make a decision. If the data do not fit precisely into existing patterns, "ah yes! decision makers" reinterpret the data to fit those patterns. Although the most pronounced distinctions are between people who process information sequentially and those who do not, Wilkins also identifies two additional types of decision makers. The *simplifier* reduces complex problems to their simplest form. On a parole board, the simplifier asks questions like, "Anything negative known about this person?" or "What are the problems with this case?" Finally, Wilkins describes the *ratifiers*, whose information search strategy is to wait for comments by someone else and then associate themselves with that person's viewpoint. These decision makers may review the case file to agree with comments from a caseworker, probation officer, or warden, or they may look to another member of the parole board for direction.

In his observation study of parole board decision making, Hawkins (1983) also considered the boundaries of rationality. Rather than focusing on types of decision makers, however, he discusses processes by which "a structure is imposed on the knowledge available in any case." Hawkins indicates that decision makers often use a few master categories in deciding what is relevant. For example, a parole board member may regard the facts of an offense and the criminal record as central. All board members may not agree; however, some, for example, may find a person's record during incarceration the most important piece of information. Decision makers in criminal justice also often make certain assumptions about the people involved.

When a convict's story varies from the official record, for example, conflicts are often resolved in favor of the record. This decision is made not by clarifying the facts but by viewing the convict with suspicion because of his or her status. Finally, Hawkins indicates that decision makers often structure their data by resorting to precedent. They categorize cases in ways that allow the cases to be "handled in the usual way." Significantly, for both Wilkins and Hawkins, the categories used and the structure given to information are *not* evident in the content of the information; they are imposed by the decision maker.

DECISION-MAKING STYLES

Decision makers in organizations take on differing styles of decision making (Kinicki and Kreitner, 2006). Individuals who are *directive* make decisions and announce them, are highly task oriented, and have a low tolerance for ambiguity. Individuals who have a more open decision-making style might nonetheless be directive if subordinates are inexperienced, not committed to the goals of the organization, or reluctant to participate in the process.

Decision makers with an *analytical* style have a high tolerance for ambiguity and tend to overanalyze situations. They take time to make decisions and seek as much information as possible. Given an analytic decision maker is carefully invested in a decision, he or she will be direct and autocratic in implementing the decision.

Conceptual decision makers work well with people and rely on discussions with others to consider the problem and possible solutions. They also consider several options as well as future possibilities. Conceptual decision makers take risks and find creative solutions. However, they tend to be idealistic and indecisive.

Behavioral decision makers like to interact with others and welcome open discussions. They are receptive to ideas, but tend to avoid conflict. This type of decision maker tends to waffle on decisions and making tough decisions. Most decision makers do not fall neatly into each category. The style they choose is a function of the decision maker's personality and the circumstances in which the decision is being made.

Decision-making styles can also be seen on a continuum from autocratic, or boss-centered, in which the boss makes decisions and announces them, to laissez faire, totally subordinate-centered, in which subordinates are given total control. At the midpoint in the continuum, we can conceptualize a balance in which the administrator frames problems and actively seeks input from subordinates. Or subordinates can be given the problem and are allowed to analyze, frame, and develop solutions to the problem. This type of decision making is considered participative or a "democratic" style of decision making. Entering into participative management requires a leader or manager who is comfortable with exchanging ideas and debating with subordinates and is not using the process to sell ideas. Second, participative management requires that subordinates be organizationally mature, seeking the goals and overall good of the agency. The advantages include a free flow of information about the problems and state of the organization, and typically, subordinates who share in decision making are more likely to support subsequent decisions. The downside is that it requires time and can result in conflict, lead to power struggles, and exacerbate internal organizational politics.

Police chiefs and wardens have a historic reputation of being directive and autocratic, relying on traditional beliefs and assumptions to guide them in their decisions. Further, reference to police and prison organizations as paramilitary in nature also suggests that their executives tend to be directive and autocratic in their decision making. Police officers who work on the streets or corrections officers who patrol cell blocks must often make dichotomous decisions on which action to take, such as to arrest or not to arrest. Although information and analysis is important to all such decisions, typically, they must be made in a short time. In the event of a crisis situation, such as in the decision to shoot or not to shoot, a decision must be made in an instant without waffling, consulting with others, or extensive analysis. Training police and corrections officers attempts to program them with the conditions, circumstances, and contingencies of crucial situations they will probably face to help them reach the proper decision in the short time available. At times, mid-level managers and top executives are confronted with crisis situations, such as civil unrest, riots, or prison riots, and must make quick decisions and impose those decisions on subordinates in an autocratic and directive manner.

CHARACTERISTICS OF INFORMATION

Our society is in a state of constant change and becoming more complex, especially as we enter the era of globalization. Every decade, public organizations and the criminal justice system seem to become more legalistic and rule bound; thus, decision making is more cumbersome and complicated. Large police agencies and most departments of corrections have their own lawyers to help in the decision-making process. As we become a more complex, rule-bound society linked closely to the rest of the world, the breadth and depth of information needed to make reasonable decisions become more important. However, no agency can possibly gather all of the information needed to make a rational decision. Yet computers allow organizations to gather reams of information in a short time. The problem becomes our ability—or inability—to make sense of or use all of the information now available to decision makers. Decision makers must find some way to structure information in order to use it. Having knowledge of some characteristics of information contributes to that process.

Work Perspective: DECISION MAKING IN HUMAN RESOURCE MANAGEMENT

I served as a director of human resources for twenty years in various public agencies. For three years of my career, I managed the human resource department for one of the largest law enforcement agencies in the country. The agency had approximately 1,500 law enforcement personnel and 2,000 jail deputies as well as a cadre of "civilian" personnel.

Every law enforcement agency's goal is to hire, promote, and retain the best possible personnel. However, the process of making personnel decisions is bound by a myriad of local, state, and federal rules and regulations, as well as personnel management rules laid out in union contracts. The director of human resources for a law enforcement agency also seeks to recruit high-quality personnel but is also responsible for setting up personnel policies and procedures that are in compliance with the rules that constrain agency personnel policies. To the human resource director, a rational decision is one that conforms to all of the external laws and constraints on hiring and promoting personnel. A brief overview of the external rules and regulations that constrain the personnel process will give students a notion of the complexity of personnel decision making in large law enforcement agencies.

An interesting set of problems is posed by the Americans with Disabilities Act (ADA), a federal statute passed in 1990 to protect individuals with disabilities from discrimination. The act requires potential employers to find ways to accommodate individuals with disabilities in order to give them an opportunity to compete with nondisabled individuals. The question is how far we should go to accommodate a person's disability so they can be law enforcement officers or jail deputies. Most law enforcement and jail personnel have a narrow view and don't think most disabilities can be accommodated. But we have an obligation to seek some accommodation. For example, we had an applicant whose hand had been injured and did not function in a normal manner. We did place him in training and gave him work-simulation scenarios to see if he could perform crucial tasks with his disabled hand. Unfortunately, he was not able to perform a number of tasks that fall upon law enforcement officers rather routinely. As a result of the exercises, our decision was to drop this individual from further participation in training and not to offer him a position as a law enforcement officer or jail deputy.

Affirmation action issues can also make personnel decisions complicated. We are obligated to ensure that our selection process does not create artificial barriers to protected groups. In other words, we must do our best to ensure members of all ethnic, religious, and racial groups—and genders—can compete on a level playing field. One of our approaches is to develop broad-based qualifications (decision criteria, if you like) that broaden the selection pool of minorities. For example, we do not attempt to hire or promote the individual with the top test scores, scores, for example, based upon written tests,

interviews, or training academy results. What we try to do is create a band based upon a range of scores that allows a number of highly qualified people to be considered. Thus, the chances of having a member of a minority group being considered increases. An interesting anomaly exists with individuals who are fluent in a second language, such as Hispanic or Cresol, as they are extremely valuable in law enforcement. Hence, the decision to hire individuals who are bilingual is due to their language skills and not because of their minority status.

Considering the spirit of affirmative action, decisions to promote individuals cannot be based primarily upon seniority. Minority groups have been entering law enforcement in recent years and have not had an opportunity to accrue seniority. Considering only seniority would eliminate affirmative action candidates from the promotion pool. The problem becomes exacerbated when going up the ranks because significantly fewer minorities are available in the candidate pool for each subsequent promotion. Historically, union contracts required that seniority play a prominent role in promotions. However, affirmative action requirements have caused that aspect of union contracts to be revisited and softened during management–labor negotiations. Presently, seniority is less of a key decision criterion in a decision to promote individuals.

Human resource directors play an active role in disciplinary action decisions of most employees.

However, for disciplinary actions for law enforcement personnel, there are a number of internal and external panels that review an officer's actions and advise on proper sanctions. One of the challenges the human resource director has is to instill reasonable and progressive disciplinary standards into the disciplinary process for law enforcement officers and jail deputies and to see that standards are applied consistently. There are times when an internal disciplinary panel is more tolerant of some offenses by officers and deputies than an objective third party would be. Some of these decisions are based on personal sentiment toward fellow officers rather than by applying decision standards within which factual knowledge surrounding an incident is considered.

Human resource directors need to be diligent in establishing quality communication, particularly with command staff, to ensure that command staff understands the challenges and issues that surround personnel decision making. The director must also be diligent in learning about the special environment and challenges that law enforcement and jail staff face on a daily basis. If the human resource director does not create a good working relationship and establish credibility with law enforcement and jail staff, his/her role in establishing guidelines for personnel decision making will be ineffective.

SOURCE: Ronald P. Clare, Human Resource Director, City of Lake Worth, Florida.

Clearly, the most important characteristic is accuracy. The point that improved decisions can be made with accurate information may seem simple, but accuracy of information is a major problem in criminal justice for several reasons. First, case files and other collections of information used by decision makers are compiled from numerous agencies and officials along the way. They often contain incomplete or incorrect information that may be repeated and given inappropriate weight by decision makers as an offender moves from the police through the courts and to corrections. The information also resurfaces if a person is rearrested.

Second, much of the information needed in criminal justice decisions is collected from people who have an interest in the outcomes or the process. Victims want arrests to be made, and convicts want to be paroled. McCleary (1977) has shown that parole officers' records are compiled for purposes that may include threatening a parolee or justifying revocation. Probation officers also write presentence investigations to court the favor of judges (Rosecrance, 1985), a process called "slanting" the report. As an example, a consultant developed a quantitative matrix for a probation department to use to arrive at recommendations. He was, in his words, shocked to discover that the probation officers were manipulating the numbers they inputted into the matrix to reach their desired conclusion. Also, this interest in decision outcomes does not necessarily mean that reports are fabrications or that information is intentionally skewed, but it may mean that the data subtly reflect the range of the collector's purposes.

A third problem of accuracy in criminal justice information lies in the need for decision makers to use summary information about people. Because criminal histories, personality assessments, and records of adjustment are often presented in summary fashion, distortions are difficult to avoid. Remington et al. (1969:697) found these examples in presentence investigations:

> He is a nice-looking, clean-cut, all-American-appearing young man. Beneath this, however, he is as cold as ice. He is an expert manipulator, playing one person against another, with an amazing ability to say just what he thinks you want to hear. He is a loser plain and simple. He is sexually inadequate, vocationally inadequate, and mentally inadequate. He has failed in everything—schools, jobs, military service, with his family, and with his wife. He has even failed as a crook. There is absolutely no reason to think that he can make it on probation and probably prison won't help him much. The only thing I can recommend is incarceration for as long as possible and then hope for the best.

Because legislation and case law now allow disclosure of presentence investigation reports to most defendants, such generalizations would be rare today. Most probation officers are trained to write less opinionated and more factual reports.

But factual reports do not necessarily eliminate the problem of using summary information. The quest for accuracy is partly responsible for the proliferation of standardized information-collection devices that assign numerical weights to factual data. The addition of the weights creates a score that summarizes the information. Such devices are frequently used in bail, sentencing, and parole decisions. The devices appear to report information with high degrees of accuracy. Assigning a score of 0 if a person is employed or a 1 if unemployed certainly has the appearance of being more accurate than describing an offender as "vocationally inadequate." But the devices can also distort the information. For example, if the offender is a seasonal worker, is she to be classified as employed or unemployed? Should criminal histories be based on charges made at the time of arrest or at conviction, when plea bargains may have been struck? Often, lengthy and complex instructions are needed to address these and similar problems. In addition, a basic question of accuracy is raised by the fact that the information presented in narrative sentences or numerical scores is often gathered from the offender himself.

Another characteristic of information is the order in which it is presented. Research indicates that because many decision makers use sequential methods to search for and analyze information, the first pieces of information are likely to be more influential than later pieces. This *order effect* (Burnham, 1975) is important in criminal justice because often the first information used by decision makers is the facts of a crime or an offender's prior record. This order contributes to cautious decision making. Because of the order effect, new information—that is, information introduced after a tentative decision has been reached—does not have the same influence as if it were introduced earlier. Decision makers using sequential strategies become invested in their decisions and tend to devalue new information. Wilkins (1975b) found that decision makers often continue to ask for items of information long after a tentative decision has been made. In his experience, however, additional items never changed the decision.

Information about the availability of alternatives can also influence decisions. In criminal justice, many decisions are perceived as resulting in one of only two possible solutions. These dichotomous outcome choices include such things as to arrest or not arrest, to prosecute or not prosecute, to parole or not parole. Dichotomies like these often support **minimax** *strategies* by decision makers. These strategies are designed to minimize the maximum loss that could result from a given decision outcome, and they produce very conservative or low-risk decisions. A police officer, for example, may arrest a juvenile vandal if the only alternative is doing nothing, or a parole board may deny parole if outright release is the only other option. However, the introduction of alternatives, such as diversion programs, prerelease options, or even shortening a convict's parole review date, may alter decision outcomes in a less conservative direction.

It is important to appreciate the boundaries of rationality in decision making. We have examined the origins of those boundaries and have discussed how they function in organizational processes, the cognitive limitations of decision makers, and the nature of information itself. In the next sections, we examine two important topics in criminal justice decision making—discretion and prediction—and focus on the limits of rationality in these areas.

Minimax: Strategies designed to minimize the maximum loss that could result from a given decision outcome.

DISCRETION

In a significant collection of works on the subject, Atkins and Pogrebin (1981:1) define discretion as applying to "a situation in which an official has latitude to make authoritative choices not necessarily specified within the source of authority which governs his decision making." Lipsky (1980) points out that latitude in decision making by frontline staff is one of the defining characteristics of human service organizations. In criminal justice organizations, staff has broad discretionary powers to invoke the criminal process or to send a suspect or offender onto the next stage in the criminal justice process. For police, the power is to arrest or not to arrest. Prosecutors exercise broad discretion in the charging decision, and judges have wide latitude in managing the judicial process and in sentencing. In corrections, probation officers, prison staff, and parole officials exercise discretion over program placement, penalties for rule infractions, and release.

Critics of discretionary decision making argue that it often amounts to a total lack of control: "decision making unfettered by constraints of law or policy" (Gottfredson and Gottfredson, 1980:350). A classic statement of this position is provided by Goldstein (1960), who studied police discretion. Goldstein argues that police have a legal mandate to pursue full enforcement of the law. To his regret, however, circumstances, such as limitations of time and money as well as ambiguities in the definitions of laws, make full enforcement unrealistic. In being forced to adopt selective enforcement practices, the police make decisions that determine the level of law enforcement throughout the criminal process, but no clear guidelines constrain those decisions. Goldstein points out that the decision not to arrest is one that often escapes public scrutiny but one that controls the gate to the entire criminal justice system. Low-visibility decisions, such as police bargains not to seek charges in exchange for information or not to arrest if an assault victim will not sign a complaint, therefore, undermine "a major criminal law objective of imposing upon all persons officially recognized minimum standards of human behavior" (1960:38). Further, discretionary decisions made by police can be based on the race of the officer as well as the race of the offender (Eitle, Stolzenberg, and D'Alesso, 2005). Also, Corsianos (2003) suggests that the discretion of detectives becomes limited in high-profile, visible cases. Moreover, discretion can be abused if it is used to harass or intimidate individuals because of their ethnicity or race, outside the purview of the justice system (Walker and Katz, 2002).

In corrections, the American Friends Service Committee (1971) takes an extreme position on discretion in their classic critique of the rehabilitation model. They argue that the discretion inherent in indeterminate sentences and requirements for program participation often serve illegitimate custodial rather than legitimate treatment aims. They feel that discretion permits prison administrators to use release or denial of parole as a carrot-and-stick control mechanism. Discretion even supports such practices as using offender attitudes or characteristics, for example, hair length or race, as a basis for criminal justice intervention, from arrest through parole. Sentencing guidelines attempt to limit discretion in the judicial process. However, research suggests that for drug offenders, a disparity in sentencing exists when comparing jurisdictional locations (Kautt, 2002). In addition, Native Americans may be sentenced more harshly for misdemeanor offenses than other offenders (Munoz and McMorris, 2002). Also, in the New York criminal courts, Black and Hispanic females received harsher sentences than their White counterparts, a phenomenon likely due to their unfavorable socioeconomic status (Brennan, 2006), and women were subjected to gender role stereotypes in probation decision making (Mullany, 2002). In sum, the application of discretion may well allow subjective, if not subconscious, forces to drive decisions.

Thus, critics of discretion in criminal justice have argued that the latitude given frontline staff has led to uncontrolled decision making that results in illegitimate and even corrupt practices. They see a solution to these problems by imposing increased control on decision makers. Thus, the American Friends Service Committee strongly supports determinate sentencing, and Goldstein (2002:80) states that "the ... ultimate answer is that the police should not be delegated discretion not to invoke the criminal process." His first recommendation is that legislatures should write statutes to reduce or eliminate ambiguity and to make police decisions visible and thus subject to review. These reforms, it would seem, are designed to increase the rationality of decision making by severely restricting or eliminating discretion. Under this view, then, wide discretion is inconsistent with a rational model of organizational decision making. However, the application of discretion may be necessary in a system that relies on satisfycing.

A somewhat different perspective on discretion is also present in the literature. In their seminal work on bounded rationality, March and Simon (1958) suggested there is room for discretion in their theory. When a general goal in decision making is specified but the means remain unspecified, the decision maker, they say, is left with supplying the means–ends connection. The choice of a means–ends connection, however, is not completely unconstrained. Discretion can involve, for example, following guidelines that can be triggered only after additional information is obtained, as when a police officer must decide whether violence has occurred in a domestic dispute before deciding whether an arrest is to be made. Discretion may also involve deciding on a course of action based on expectations about others' decisions, as when police officers decide not to arrest in minor cases because they believe the cases will not be prosecuted. Or discretion may involve drawing on memory or experience, as when a police officer does not make an arrest because similar arrests in the past have not led to prosecutions.

This view of discretion, then, is based on the idea that the goals of decisions are often general and complex and that discretionary decisions are not completely unregulated. Three significant implications follow from this perspective. First, discretion can be viewed as necessary and useful. Second, the boundaries or regulations of discretionary decisions can be studied and understood. And third, because they can be understood, these regulations can be influenced without eliminating discretion.

The belief that discretion is necessary is now common in criminal justice. An accepted argument is put forth by Lipsky (1980), who suggests that discretion in the human services is needed because of the complexity of the task. In policing, for example, whether an assault and battery has occurred can be a complex question requiring police discretion. As in all decisions, some order must be imposed on the information available. Questions about the amount of force needed, the level of injury, and the relationship between the parties are complex. This complexity means that discretion is useful. Newman (1981), for example, argues that the discretionary process of plea bargaining can promote fairness by addressing the variability and complexity of offenses. Gottfredson et al. (1975) argue that parole board discretion fulfills the same purposes.

A bounded rationality model of discretion also provides direction for the study and reform of decision making. Implicit in the work on sentencing and parole guidelines by Wilkins, Gottfredson, and Kress (Kress, 1980) is the view that such decisions are not completely uncontrolled or lacking in rationality. When they studied sentence disparity in courts, these authors found that the vast majority of these discretionary decisions could be explained by a small set of information items. An example of these items and the scale used to summarize them is presented in Figure 12.3.

Items providing information about a defendant, such as prior criminal record, and items about the crime, such as degree of violence or injury to the victim, accounted for 85 percent of sentencing decisions. The remaining 15 percent of sentences could not be explained by the small list of items and would need to be studied as individual cases.

The recognition that discretionary decisions can be highly predictable also suggests methods of affecting those decisions. Wilkins, Gottfredson, and Kress all describe a method of *structuring* judicial discretion without greatly restricting or eliminating it. Sentence averages or narrow intervals based on sentences that have already been handed down by judges can be constructed for all the combinations of offense and offender scores. The resulting guidelines reflect sentencing policy in the court because they are based on sentences actually given out. Sample guidelines are presented in Figure 12.4. Judges are given the guidelines and are told that they can issue sentences outside the guidelines (while remaining inside statutory limitations) but must provide explicit written reasons for the deviation. The guidelines are then updated at regular intervals so that they continue to reflect current court policy.

By structuring rather than eliminating discretion, this process recognizes that sentencing is a complex process in which judicial discretion is useful and beneficial. Instead of viewing discretionary decisions as unconstrained by law or policy, this approach is based on identifying and building on implicit constraints. The patterns of previous decisions reveal those constraints, and studying those patterns provides a productive method for influencing discretion while still noting its importance. The bounded rationality perspective can thus provide a useful method for addressing problems of discretion.

PREDICTION

Although some authors have considered discretionary decision making as nearly devoid of rationality from an organizational perspective, the opposite assumptions seem common in discussions of **prediction**. Although recent advances

Prediction: Attempts to predict the outcomes of alternative choices. Predictions are based on experience, clinical predictions, or statistical predictions.

FIGURE 12.3 Sample Sentencing Guidelines Worksheet.

Offender _____ Docket number _____

Judge _____ Date _____

Offense(s) convicted of: _____

_____

_____

Crime score

A. Injury
   0 = No injury
   1 = Injury
   2 = Death   _____   +

B. Weapon
   0 = No weapon
   1 = Weapon possessed
   2 = Weapon present and used   _____   +

C. Drugs
   0 = No sale of drugs
   1 = Sale of drugs   _____   =

Crime score

Offender score

A. Current legal status
   0 = Not on probation/parole, escape
   1 = On probation/parole, escape   _____   +

B. Prior adult misdemeanor convictions
   0 = No convictions
   1 = One conviction
   2 = Two or more convictions   _____   +

C. Prior adult felony convictions
   0 = No convictions
   1 = One conviction
   2 = Two or more convictions   _____   +

D. Prior adult probation/parole revocations
   0 = None
   1 = One or more revocations   _____   +

E. Prior adult incarcerations (over 60 days)
   0 = None
   1 = One incarceration
   2 = Two or more incarcerations   _____   =

Offender score

Guideline sentence _____

Actual sentence _____

Reasons (if actual sentence does not fall within guideline range):

SOURCE: From J. Kress, *Prescriptions for Justice*. Ballinger © 1980. Cambridge, MA.

F I G U R E 12.4   Sample Felony-Sentencing Grid.

Crime score	0–1	2–4	5–7	8–10
4–5	4–6 years	5–7 years	6–8 years	8–10 years
3	3–5 years	4–6 years	6–8 years	6–8 years
2	2–4 years	3–5 years	3–5 years	4–6 years
1	Probation	Probation	2–4 years	3–5 years
0	Probation	Probation	Probation	2–4 years

Offender score

SOURCE: From J. Kress, *Prescriptions for Justice* Ballinger © 1980. Cambridge, MA.

have involved mathematical models, whether decisions are made by highly trained experts employing clinical methods or by statisticians applying complex formulas, the prediction of human behavior is generally thought of as a highly rational scientific process. Even when nonexperts make predictive decisions, their lack of expertise is generally not viewed as detracting from the rationality of the process. In this section, we examine the extent to which such assumptions of rationality are justified.

Many decisions in criminal justice involve the prediction of future behavior. After reviewing studies of decision making in the field, Gottfredson and Gottfredson (1980:334) describe prediction as "omnipresent" in the criminal justice system. Bail decisions, sentencing decisions, and parole decisions obviously involve predictions, but so do many other decisions made by workers in the criminal justice process. Classification into risk categories for probation involves prediction. Prediction figures into sentencing recommendations by probation officers, into corrections caseworkers' reviews of inmates for transfer, and into assistant prosecutors' determinations of charges and priorities for prosecution. Even police officers' decisions to arrest, issue a citation, or use a diversion program involve predictions.

In considering the usefulness of a pure rationality theory of these decisions, let us first consider the methods used in prediction. Two broad categories exist: clinical methods and statistical methods. *Clinical methods* involve assessments that focus on such factors as personality variables, situational variables, and the interaction of these variables. They may or may not involve the use of standardized tests, such as personality assessments, and they may or may not involve personal interviews. In death penalty cases in Texas, for example, psychiatrists make predictions about the likelihood of future violence by relying on hypothetical descriptions of the criminal record and the character of convicted murderers. The heart of clinical methods, then, is the use of expertise in selecting and interpreting data from a variety of sources.

By contrast, *statistical methods* of prediction specify precisely what information is to be used and how it is to be interpreted. These methods use mathematical formulas that incorporate information about individuals to produce **probability**

Probability estimates: Prediction models, or chances of outcomes, estimated in terms of probability and stated as the percent chance of various outcomes to occur.

estimates of behavior. To make these estimates, information on the individual whose behavior is being predicted is compared with information on a large sample of individuals whose behavior in similar situations is known. For example, the information items that were originally found to be the best predictors of whether a convicted offender would continue to offend at a high rate and, therefore, should receive a long prison sentence (Greenwood, 1982:50) are the following: was convicted before for the same type of offense; was incarcerated more than 50 percent of the preceding two years; was convicted before age sixteen; served time in a state juvenile facility; used drugs in the preceding two years; used drugs as a juvenile; was employed less than 50 percent of the preceding two years. The scale produced with these items was used in support of a policy of selective incapacitation.

Statistical prediction methods were first used in criminal justice in 1928, when Burgess produced expected rates of failure for parolees by developing a scale that assigned a point for each characteristic of an individual that was correlated with parole failure in a large sample of previously released offenders. The higher the total score, the more likely a person was to fail on parole and, therefore, the stronger the argument for denying parole. Since then, sophisticated methods have been developed that use multivariate models to account for differences in the importance of some predictor items and the interaction effects of the items. Computerized decision making has been implemented and includes the following: web-based systems that allow litigants who represent themselves to have access to family law and legal aid systems (Zeleznikow, 2002); the creation of computerized identification systems to supplement eyewitness identification of defendants in criminal cases (Bromby, 2002); and programs to aid in resolution and judicial decision making (Zeleznikow, 2000). However, courts have been reluctant to implement the use of data-driven systems and tend to rely on traditional methods of decision making (Baker, 2013). The prediction instruments used with this method resemble the instrument in Figure 12.3, but all the variables are selected for their strength in predicting some specific behavior, such as parole failure or failure on pretrial release.

Currently, much of the literature in criminal justice reveals a preference for statistical methods of prediction. An authoritative volume on the subject of prediction and classification in criminal justice does not even mention clinical prediction methods (Gottfredson and Tonry, 1987). Clinical approaches to classification are mentioned only as a stage in the development of more sophisticated models in Brennan (1987). Much of the pessimism surrounding clinical prediction may be related to questions of accuracy (which we take up later in this section) and to the negative publicity surrounding some cases. In the 1980s, for example, a national newsmagazine dubbed Dr. James Grigson "Dr. Death" after he testified, as an expert witness in the death penalty hearing of Thomas Barefoot, that he was 100 percent certain in his prediction of future dangerousness. Psychologists and psychiatrists give expert testimony in "not guilty by reason of insanity" cases based on their clinical evaluation of the defendant. Invariably, the defense brings in an expert who claims, based on his or her clinical evaluation, that the defendant did not know right from wrong at the time of the criminal act, while the prosecutor brings in his or her expert to testify to the contrary.

In an amicus curiae brief to the Supreme Court in the Barefoot case, the American Psychiatric Association (APA) (1982) maintained that such predictions cannot be made with accuracy and that psychiatrists should not be permitted to testify in death penalty proceedings about predictions of future dangerousness. The court, however, viewed prediction as integral to criminal justice and ultimately rejected the APA's position. The case in support of statistical methods as well as the criticisms of clinical methods can, however, be overstated. The American Psychiatric Association rejected only long-term clinical predictions and even questioned the statistical predictions in these cases. There is support for short-term clinical predictions, especially when informed by statistical data and when attention is given to unique conditions in an individual's environment (Monahan, 1981). It is equally true, however, that incompetent clinical assessments have their parallels in sloppy statistical procedures, which may involve improper sampling or unreliable measurement.

These points notwithstanding, clinical predictions may be unavoidable. Adequate databases for statistical methods do not exist for many decisions made in criminal justice. There may be little data on the characteristics of those who succeed in a diversion program or on those who fail to adjust in one particular medium security prison. Even where statistical data do exist, clinical processes remain relevant. A juvenile vandal's motives will continue to be relevant to a prosecutor deciding on charges, and racist attitudes and the tensions they produce will be relevant to prison placement.

On this subject, Monahan (1981) presents a sensible argument that statistical data may be most useful within a context of clinical decision making. It follows, then, that examining the assumptions about rationality that underlie both clinical and statistical predictions can be productive. Toward that end, we examine several factors important to all predictions of behavior. First, all decisions based on prediction involve a *criterion*, such as dangerousness, repeat offending, failure on parole, or failure on pretrial release. Defining the criterion variable, however, can be difficult. Monahan (1981) discusses the difficulties in defining dangerousness.

What specific behaviors entail dangerousness? Must they be overt acts? Must they cause injury? At first, these questions may seem relevant only to clinical predictions, in which no objective measurement of the criterion is made. With statistical methods, however, equally difficult problems arise. Should predictions about future criminality be made based on official arrest records or on self-report studies of offenders? These two criteria may produce different results (Farrington, 1987). Likewise, success on parole may involve anything from upstanding citizenship to drug-addicted fringe lifestyles in which arrest is avoided. Failures may range from a repetition of major violations to revocation for technical violations (Glaser, 1969). Clearly, viewing prediction as a purely rational process requires an unambiguous criterion variable. In clinical prediction, the failure to define the criterion in unambiguous terms is a problem, whereas with statistical methods, the need for precise measurements may mask the ambiguities.

Predictor variables are used to predict the criterion. In clinical prediction, they may differ from case to case but can include, for example, assessments of stability and subjective views of adjustment. With statistical methods, the predictors are the same for all cases and may include variables such as age at first arrest and number of juvenile convictions. With either method, appreciating the limits of rationality remains relevant. It is impossible to know all the variables that may be pertinent, and information may arguably be different for different cases. Another difficulty is that often only the variables available in an official record make it into statistical processes.

Perhaps the most difficult problem in prediction relates to the *base rate* of the criterion variable. The base rate is the proportion of individuals in a population who exhibit the criterion. For example, the base rate for parole failure is the percentage of all paroled inmates who fail. For predictions to be useful, then, they must improve on the base rate. If, for example, 20 percent of all parolees fail on parole, then parolees released based on predictions must fail at a rate below 20 percent for the predictions to be useful. If predictions produced failures of more than 20 percent, the parole board would be better off simply releasing everyone because that would produce a failure rate of only 20 percent. Of course, no parole board would abdicate responsibility in this way, but the point illustrates the importance of understanding the base rate.

Base rates are problematic in criminal justice predictions for two reasons. First, the base rate is frequently unknown by decision makers. This is particularly true in clinical predictions, where studies to determine base rates may not have been undertaken.

Not knowing the base rate may lead to dramatic overpredictions of such things as parole or pretrial release failures. Base rates, however, also present problems in statistical predictions. For example, because the base rates for parole failure have generally been based only on the behavior of people released by parole boards, the rate for all potential releases is not known. The rates as well as the predictors have not been calculated on a representative sample of parole-eligible inmates. Second, base rates are often low—that is, much of the behavior we seek to predict is rare. For example, in his development of statistical predictions in bail decision making, Goldkamp (1985) found that only 12 percent of pretrial releasees failed to appear in court. For the predictions to be useful, then, they must improve on a 12 percent failure rate. The rub is that for statistical reasons, as base rates get farther and farther from a proportional distribution of 50/50 in a population, it becomes increasingly difficult to predict. Behavior that is statistically rare, such as violent crime, dangerousness, or parole failure, is very difficult to predict.

An additional issue is relevant to our discussion of the rationality of prediction: the consequences of predictions and our view of their accuracy. A parole board would certainly be well regarded if only 10 percent of its parolees were rearrested. Although at first glance the board's predictions seem highly accurate, a closer examination is required. Figure 12.5 reveals that there are, in fact, four possible consequences to the parole decision as well as other predictions. Those predicted to succeed will be released and will either succeed or fail. Those predicted to fail, however, will continue to be incarcerated and could succeed or fail but are not given the chance.

FIGURE 12.5 Hypothetical Outcomes from Parole Predictions.

Predicted outcome

	Success	Failure
Success	Accurate 90% Paroled True negative	Inaccurate 60% Parole denied False positive
Failure	Inaccurate 10% Paroled False negative	Accurate 40% Parole denied True positive
Column total	100%	100%

Actual behavior

© Cengage Learning

In our example, the 10 percent of parolees who fail are known as *false negatives*: the prediction that they would not fail was incorrect. By considering only these, however, it is clear that a parole board that releases few inmates will always be regarded as more accurate than a parole board willing to take more risks. To complete the assessment of accuracy, then, we must also consider the *false positives*, or the percentage of inmates whom the board predicts would fail and who would, in fact, actually not fail if they were released. In the example in Figure 12.5, we see that 60 percent of those predicted to fail would actually succeed. Of course, there is a problem with this rate. If the board predicts that inmates will fail, the board will not let them out. In reality, the false positive rate is rarely known.

Only if our parole board is willing to release the inmates who they expect to fail can we completely evaluate the success of the predictions. Although such releases rightly do not occur, in some instances courts have required the release of offenders who had been predicted to be violent based on clinical prediction methods. Subsequent studies of these offenders have found that approximately 60 percent of them did not engage in violence (see Monahan, 1981). Overall, these studies have prompted the conclusion that clinical predictions of violence are incorrect in approximately two out of three cases. Studies of statistical predictions use statistical procedures to estimate false positive rates. These studies have revealed only slightly better results than the other studies, generally with false positive rates of around 40 percent to 50 percent.

The issue of false positives raises two questions relevant to the rationality of prediction. First, as we already mentioned, the false positive rate is rarely known in terms of actual predictions. Decision makers, then, often do not have information critical to the prediction process. Second, the tolerance of different rates of false positives is a policy determination that has nothing to do with scientific methods. Even with some idea of its rate of false positives, a parole board must decide how many offenders it is willing to keep in prison in order to prevent criminal offenses. The lower the acceptable percentage of false positives (i.e., those denied parole who would not fail), the higher will be the percentage of false negatives (that is, released offenders who commit crimes); the more we are concerned with reducing the number of false negatives, the higher will be the rate of false positives. It may be appropriate, for example, for the board to release only extremely low-risk candidates while still knowing that 60 percent (but not knowing which 60 percent) of those they reject for parole would not commit offenses. Whether decision makers should accept false positive rates of 60 percent or higher is a policy question distinct from the prediction process itself.

All of this analysis suggests that even under the best circumstances, claims about the rationality of prediction can be overstated. In considering the highly technical aspects of prediction, we should not overlook the conceptual problems connected with specifying the criterion, identifying appropriate predictors, appreciating the base rate, and determining the tolerable ratios of false positives and false negatives. Understanding these aspects of prediction can be productive in guiding decision studies and improving prediction. In the final section of this chapter, we consider the ways managers can influence and improve the decision-making process in criminal justice.

IMPROVING CRIMINAL JUSTICE DECISIONS

Early in this chapter, we noted that improvement in criminal justice decision making means making rational decisions. Although completely rational decision making may be an unattainable goal, the process can be moved in the direction of being more rational than it is now from an organizational perspective. The question remains, however: What is rational from an organizational perspective? From a theoretical viewpoint, this is a complex question, but the matter may be simplified by identifying recurrent themes in the literature on criminal justice decision making. These themes can guide the improvement of decision making.

One important theme in criminal justice decision making is equity. *Equity* in criminal justice processing means that similar offenders in similar circumstances are treated in similar ways. It does not mean that all offenders are treated alike, but it does mean that differences in treatment should be based on some meaningful distinctions among the offenders. Legal and ethical arguments support the goal of equity in decision making.

A second theme is *accuracy*. It is obvious that we should strive to see that persons not guilty of crimes are not arrested and that those released on parole do not commit additional crimes. It is equally important to strive to see that guilty persons are subject to arrest and that those denied parole based on prediction would, in fact, fail.

Equity and accuracy, however, provide only limited direction for decision makers. Sentencing guidelines, for example, may iron out inequities across judges, but the guidelines themselves say little about the purpose of sentencing an offender to prison. A third theme, then, is *consistency with theory*. Many theories exist about such issues as the purpose of police intervention, prosecution, or the punishment and treatment of offenders. Decision makers should strive to articulate the theories that underlie their decisions and to make future decisions consistent with those theories. We must appreciate, however, that the theories may be inconsistent with concerns for equity and accuracy. Deterrence theory, for example, may require arrest and prosecution, as well as long sentences, for only a few people accused of crimes such as tax evasion or failure to register for the draft (see Morris, 1982).

A fourth theme of decision making in criminal justice is *consistency with resources*. While we strive for consistency with theory, we must also consider pragmatic interests. The decision to arrest or issue a citation should be influenced by the availability of jail space (see Hall et al., 1985). Prosecutors need to be sensitive to court backlogs, and even if there is a disproportionately high number of maximum security prison cells, classification officers must find ways to distinguish between those who will and will not fill those spaces. Although long-term planning can change available resources, decision makers must also confront short-term necessities.

Finally, a fifth theme in the literature of criminal justice is that *decisions should contribute to future decisions*. Both the process and the outcome should help to improve decision making in the future. This theme implies a cybernetic approach to improving decisions, which recognizes that all future decisions are affected by previous decisions. Decision making should be guided by continuing assessments of equity, accuracy, and consistency with theory and resources. In this way, improving decision making becomes an ongoing, evolutionary process (Gottfredson and Gottfredson, 1980).

The five general themes we have just discussed also provide us with specific ideas for influencing the decision-making process. Those ideas involve the development of decision-making policies, concern for the people who make decisions, and concern regarding what information is used in decision making. When similar decisions are made time and time again, as many criminal justice decisions are, organizations need to formulate explicit policies about them. Those policies must address the theories underlying the decisions and the goals of particular decisions, as well as the types of information to be used and the decision rules for processing information. Without such policies, no guidelines exist for examining the consequences of decision making and no basis exists for systematically studying and increasing the effectiveness of decisions. Policymakers, however, should appreciate the complexity of criminal justice decisions and the potential uniqueness of individual cases. Decision policies should provide for flexibility. The use of sentencing guidelines illustrates one approach to flexibility. The guidelines allow judges to go outside the expected sentence range but require a written explanation of the reasons for the deviation.

In improving decision making, attention must also be paid to the decision makers themselves. Decision processes should be structured to deemphasize personality variables and subjective confidence levels. When possible, group, rather than individual, decisions should be encouraged. Groups tend to be more willing to take risks than individuals. Group decisions, then, lessen the conservative influences of minimax criteria. Group discussion about what information is considered relevant and how information is processed also encourages consistency in both the process and outcome of decisions.

Decision makers should also be encouraged to frame their decisions as probability estimates (Burnham, 1975) for two reasons. First, the accuracy of those estimates can then be checked against actual behavior; and second, policy can dictate the outcome of decisions when probability estimates are made explicit. For example, parole board policy should dictate whether an offender should be released when that individual is regarded as having a 60 percent chance of succeeding. In addition, decision makers should be trained and retrained by examining both the process and the results of previous decisions. Attention should also be paid to the information used in decision making. Efforts should be made to ensure that the information used is reliable and valid. For example, information on the seriousness of the offense, the length of criminal history, or adjustment to incarceration should be recorded and measured consistently by all decision makers. And decision makers should be encouraged to use information that research has demonstrated is relevant to the results of the decision. Along with reliability and validity, format is important. Information should be presented to decision makers in sequential as well as summary form to accommodate the variety of search processes among decision makers. Efforts should also be made to avoid the influences of order effects and to assure adequate consideration of new information. Information on alternatives must also be used during decision making.

When possible, dichotomous outcomes should be avoided because they increase the likelihood that minimax strategies will be invoked. Intermediate steps—such as citation as an alternative to arrest, or release and revised parole or classification dates as an alternative to denial—should be encouraged.

Finally, to make the improvement of decision making an evolutionary process, decision makers should have feedback about decisions they have made in the past. This information is most useful when presented in the form of correct-answer feedback that provides decision makers with correct or best answers to past decisions (Burnham, 1975). Correct-answer feedback not only tells decision makers whether past decisions were correct but also provides information about why some decisions were correct while others were not. For example, correct-answer feedback to a parole board would report the percentage of parolees who failed and would also provide information about the characteristics of offenders who are most likely to fail. This feedback, then, can influence the information that decision makers regard as relevant, how the information is combined, and even the theories underlying the decision process. With modern computing and statistical capabilities, even decision makers in small organizations and agencies should have access to correct-answer feedback.

The National Institute of Corrections developed a model for decision making called *a framework for evidence-based decision making in criminal justice agencies* (2010). This model for decision making incorporates the five themes for improving decision making discussed earlier. Evidence for decision making is defined in the proposal as "findings from empirically sound social science research" (2010:7). The creators of the document propose that evidence exists to support programs that reduce crime and recidivism. For example, it is posited that recidivism can be reduced by 30 percent by applying correct programs to appropriate offenders, suggesting there are a number of proven methods to reduce recidivism. What is needed is decision making that applies these particular evidence-based methods instead of traditional unsystematic parole decision making and offender supervision. This approach has four underlying principles. First, it is proposed that the judgment of criminal justice decision makers will be enhanced when informed by evidence. Second, every decision and interaction within the system is an opportunity to reduce harm to society. Third, the system will achieve better outcomes through collaboration—that is, key decision makers need to be indentified and the formal and ongoing process of collaboration between decision makers needs to go on. Fourth, decision making will continually improve when professionals make decisions based on collected and analyzed data and applying the analysis to decision making. The report also calls for clear and specific performance measures, the establishment of baseline measures, and a commitment to view results showing that goals have not been met as an opportunity to improve.

ETHICAL CONSIDERATIONS IN DECISION MAKING

Procedural and administrative decisions are made as a matter of daily business in criminal justice organizations. This chapter shows, however, that decision making is far from perfect. A number of factors contribute to imperfect decision making, such as limits on information and a lack of objective decision-making methods. Time is also scarce because criminal justice practitioners face a steady stream of work under rigid time constraints (Waegel, 1981). Decisions are also framed by conflicting internal and external preferences of constituents manifested by power struggles referred to as organizational politics. Personal biases of individual decision makers also lessen the likelihood of consistently good decisions. The Innocence Project (2011), for example, reports that wrongful convictions and incarcerations have commonly taken place due to false confessions, unreliable or dishonest informants, eyewitness misidentification, and improper application of forensic sciences. Exposés on corrupt criminal justice practitioners are common news stories, as is the occasional video recording of random police violence.

While the system continues to try to improve its decision-making process, decision making will ultimately be in the hands of individuals who are subject to system and personal flaws that will always limit objective and rational decision making. In other words, bad decisions and mistakes will be part of the process.

The pivotal question is: Are the mistakes of the heart mistakes of the head? Are the mistakes due to the lack of information or miscalculation, or are they due to personal or agency bias, greed, egoism, or another mechanism that would justify harmful acts? Applying an ethical framework to decision making can help reduce mistakes of the heart as well as encourage consequential thinking as part of the decision-making process (Ruighaver, Maynard, and Warren, 2010).

Close and Meier (1995) pose four questions that provide an ethical checklist decision makers can follow to ensure ethical decisions. First, will the decision lead to a violation of an individual's constitutional rights? Second, does the decision or the resulting action cause individuals to be treated instrumentally or as a means to an end? Third, does the decision violate the organization's goal of civic duty—is it illegal? Will the decision ultimately produce more social harm than good as a final outcome? Fourth, does a decision violate departmental policies or a professional code of conduct? When considering these four principles, it is important to keep in mind that published mission statements or policies and procedures are visible and almost always will conform to the ethical principles. Decisions made by the application of street level **discretion** of criminal justice practitioners or managers are not always subject to public scrutiny and are more likely to cross ethical lines (Atkins and Pogrebin, 1982). Even visible decisions may cross ethical lines if they are made under extreme pressure from public or personal outrage. For example, civil rights protesters have often been subjected to public beating at the hands of police officers sent to disperse demonstrations. Finally, decision makers often justify their decisions by using the utilitarian argument that the ends justify the means. Unfortunately, the means–ends justification for a decision is often an argument of convenience for decision makers. If the means to an end is morally wrong, the end result will be tainted by the process and also be morally wrong.

Discretion: The latitude practitioners have to choose alternative decisions outside of written procedures and rules, for example, a decision to not make an arrest or not to prosecute.

SUMMARY

Define decision making.

- Decision making is based on goals and is the process of making a choice between alternative paths leading toward the goals. The consequences of a decision can be estimated.

Understand the basis for the decision-making rules of criminal justice practitioners.

- For most criminal justice practitioners, decisions rule, are clinical in nature, and are based on their education, training, and experience.

Understand the garbage can theory of decision making.

- Decision makers keep a repertoire of solutions in a "garbage can," and they pull a solution out, seeing it as the answer to a problem that matches their own solution.

Briefly discuss the four types of criminal justice decision makers.

- Sequentialists make decisions based on experience; "ah yes" decision makers search for patterns within large amounts of information; the simplifier reduces complex problems to their simplest form; the ratifier waits for comments and feedback from others before making a decision.

Understand the major themes to improving criminal justice decisions.

- The important themes for improving criminal justice decision making include *equity*, similar disposition across similar cases; *accuracy*, separating guilty from the innocent; and *consistency*, applying the same rules over time. Improved decision making should contribute to future decisions.

Case Study: THE OLD BOYS DON'T LIKE PLEA BARGAINING

Marvi Rivera had served as the county prosecuting attorney for over six years. The job had its stressful moments, but she had a good staff and a set of routines to handle most cases. She and her staff had a habit of stopping at the local tavern on Friday evenings to cool off and debrief the week's work over a drink. Most of the other patrons were lawyers and members of the business community. Most also had supported her in previous elections and even donated funds to her campaign.

This particular evening, a local banker approached her and was vociferous about a couple of cases her staff had disposed of that week. Both cases involved mortgage fraud to some extent. The banker demanded to know why she gave them a "slap on the wrist." His view was that if we gave these cretins severe punishments, the fraud would stop. She explained that in one case the defendant was sentenced to six years. He replied that she had reduced his charges and, had she stuck to her guns, he would be serving fifteen years in prison. Moreover, the second defendant was given probation, which he and his fellow bankers thought was an outrage.

What these ordinary citizens were unaware of were the demands placed on the prosecutor's office to mete out justice within the constraints of the law and the budgets they had available. District Attorney Rivera explained that in this particular case, determining the guilt of all parties involved required that they work one defendant against another to get a conviction. The bar patron listened intently, but it was clear that they wanted no part of her explanation.

"Why should any of them get a deal?" responded one. "If they are guilty of the crime, then they should face the music."

Rivera understood their view, but she responded, "My job is to determine *if* they are guilty and in many cases that is not easy to do. It is one thing to think someone is guilty, but

it is another to prove it in court." She attempted to describe the reality of prosecuting cases where evidence is scant and proof is often elusive. "Because we don't have all the evidence of wrongdoing, we usually work one defendant against another to get information, and, in return, we offer reduced-sentence agreements, what you guys call plea bargains."

One citizen responded, "This is like *Law and Order*, the television show."

She responded that in some cases that is the outcome. But she wanted to say more.

The banker interjected, "Well, why didn't you at least use the guy you turned, as you call it, to testify against the other in a trial?"

"Because he would have been a lousy witness, and we might have lost the case," Rivera replied. "These are the decisions we have to make on a case-by-case basis."

"The reality of criminal prosecution is that it takes time and costs money, and every time I meet someone who is critical of our decision making, I always refer back to the Martinez case. Do you remember that case?"

One patron responded yes, he did remember. "So, what was so unique about that case?" She responded that the defendant had been acquitted by a jury after the county spent close to a million dollars on the case. The case took almost three months, involved a sequestered jury, five prosecutors, and a host of staff to process all the court documents and evidence. "We tried to bargain with the defendant, but frankly we had a weak case, and some of my staff felt that he might have been innocent."

"Why didn't you cut him a deal then?"

She responded: "We tried; he turned us down.

"In the end, we spent all that money, invested all that time, and still lost the case." She continued to describe the

CASE STUDY—continued

process and how all decisions must be understood in the context of limited resources and finite expectations.

"So, do we plea bargain? We sure do, because we know two things: The cops always report every possible criminal violation with the arrest so the defendant thinks we can throw the book at him. This is a routine part of the process. We are now in a position to drop some charges as an incentive to plead guilty to a specific charge. We simply can't take everyone to criminal trial and don't want to. We have to make decisions that allow us to use our limited resources in a way that maximizes justice, and plea bargaining allows us to do that. You guys understand efficiencies. You are businessmen and you can't work outside of your budget. If we did, I wouldn't be a prosecutor for long because guys like you would vote me out."

"I guess I understand, but I don't like it anyway," responded one of the bar patrons as he finished his drink.

CASE STUDY QUESTIONS

1. What was the banker's agenda? Would you have agreed with him if you were a banker?
2. Do you find Rivera's response to his criticism sufficient? What else might you tell the banker if you were in her position?
3. What were the organizational decisions that went into the plea-bargained disposition of the case?
4. To what extent do resources impact the decision making of the prosecutorial system?
5. If the prosecutor's budget were doubled, how would this affect the decision-making process for the prosecutor's office and police decision making? How would the judiciary in this jurisdiction be affected by an increase in the prosecutor's budget?

 Think like an Administrator

Parole decision making may be one of the most difficult decision points in the criminal justice process. Making decisions on who gets released early from prison is always controversial, especially when it is someone who has committed a serious offense. Persons put in charge of parole commissions oftentimes work at the pleasure of the governor of the state. In addition, parole commissioners receive heavy pressure from many different sources to be very conservative in making parole decisions. A significant concern is the perception of the victim or the victim's family regarding the offender and his/her possible release from prison. While confronted with these pressures, there also is a current emphasis on releasing low-risk offenders to reduce prison overcrowding and the cost of incarceration. It is within this context that parole decision making occurs.

1. Given your relationship with the governor, at what point is your parole decision making influenced by political concerns?
2. How can statistical risk-prediction models ameliorate political considerations?
3. How would you factor political influence into your statistical prediction model?
4. What role do other criminal agencies have in your decision making?
5. What weight do you give to victims and their advocates regarding a parole decision?
6. What role should the legislature have in parole decision making via the sentencing process?
7. Should parole decision making mitigate the effects of sentencing practices concerning racial, ethnic, and gender bias?
8. Should family and community conditions of the offender affect parole decision making?

FOR DISCUSSION

1. What made you decide to go to college? What was your goal or goals? What information did you seek to help you pick a college or university that would help you meet your goals? List some of the information you would have needed to make a purely rational decision.

2. Consider a probation officer contemplating a decision to seek revocation of a client's probation. What theories might underlie such a decision? What are the goals? What kinds of information should the officer seek? What kinds of feedback might the probation officer want in order to influence later decisions?

3. What are some of the biases that would underlie a police officer's discretionary decision whether or not to make an arrest? What biases or beliefs do you possess that would impact your decision to make an arrest or to release the offender?

4. Cover the pros and cons of participative decision making. From what you know about the criminal justice system, under what circumstances would participative decision making be effective and under what circumstances would it be counterproductive? State your reasons.

5. Design a process for determining, on a case-by-case basis, which juveniles should be diverted from court processing. Is this a predictive decision? What is being predicted? How should the decision process be structured? Who should make the decisions? What kinds of information should be used? How should it be presented? How would you evaluate the decisions?

FOR FURTHER READING

Atkins, B., and Pogrebin, M. *The Invisible Justice System: Discretion and the Law.* Cincinnati, OH: Anderson, 1981.

Gottfredson, D. M., and Tonry, M. (Eds.) *Prediction and Classification: Criminal Justice Decision Making.* Chicago: University of Chicago Press, 1987.

Gottfredson, M. R., and Gottfredson, D. M. *Decision-Making in Criminal Justice: Toward a Rational Exercise of Discretion.* Cambridge, MA: Ballinger, 1980.

Murray, M. *Decisions: A Comparative Critique.* Marshfield, MA: Pitman, 1986.

Walker, S., and Katz, M. C. *Police in America.* 4th ed. Boston: McGraw-Hill, 2002.

CHAPTER 13

Organizational Effectiveness

LEARNING OBJECTIVES

After reading this chapter, the students will have achieved the following objectives:

- Be able to define organizational effectiveness.

- Understand the issues underpinning measuring organizational effectiveness.

- Discuss the difficulties of the goal model.

- Be able to briefly discuss the three significant elements of the process approach.

- Understand variable analysis.

- Understand why ethical problems arise out of attempts to measure effectiveness.

VIGNETTE

How well does an agency do its job? Are police really protecting society or having an impact on crime? How can we answer these questions? Can we judge—or measure by some yard-stick—how effective our local police department is in reducing or preventing crime? Finally, if we develop a method to evaluate the effectiveness of our local police department, can we use the measure to improve effectiveness? These questions are addressed in this chapter. But we need to start with a brief exposé on how agencies can easily misuse efforts to track productivity and how society can reap harmful consequences.

A large city recently went to a data-driven method to measure the effectiveness of their crime-fighting efforts. Each district was responsible for driving down crime by getting tough on criminals and increasing the arrest rate in the district. This is a simple approach dictated by a commonsense belief that making more arrests will act as a deterrent. Because the expectation is that increasing arrests would deter crime, crime rates should decrease. Cutting down crime rates is the program goal, and the measure for success is an observable measure of a reduction in reported crime rates. The program was imple-mented in a district plagued with high rates of poverty, drug use, and gangs. After a few months, it appeared that the arrest rate increased and reported crime rates fell accord-ingly. To the distant observer, city council members, the mayor, the chief of police, and other constituents, the get-tough program is a raging success. Not so fast, my friends!

Most criminal justice practitioners will tell you they can generate numbers and data almost at will. In policing, if a district commander treats the troops well, they will try and protect the commander. If a respected district commander is subjected to pressure to produce numbers, the line officers will find a way to produce the numbers. Going back to our example, it was discovered that, indeed, the police officers working in the field were getting the numbers their district commander needed. First, it is not difficult to increase the number of individuals arrested per time period (the arrest rate), especially in the crime, drug, and gang-ridden area described. It is psychologically easy to arrest young people with whom the police have always had a conflict relationship and who are considered on the margins of criminality. The justifications for arrest are also bountiful and range from suspicion of drug dealing, resisting arrest, assault of a police officer, obstruction of justice, and consuming alcohol in public to a host of—the independent variable, as it were.

Altering the crime rate is a bit more complicated. In this case, the reported crime rate was being used. To contrive a decrease in reported crime, the district personnel found ways of making it more difficult for citizens in their district to report crimes. There are a number of ways of doing this. One method is to require individuals to travel to the district center station to report crimes. Once there, citizens reporting crimes can be made to wait in lines and fill out lengthy documents. Worse, citizens reporting crimes can be subjected to subtle hazing by officers at the district center. A former offender from the area, for example, came in to report that his car was stolen. As the story goes, the officers at the district mocked the ex-offender, suggesting that a thief had a lot of nerve complaining to the police that he had been robbed. Another accused him of stealing his own car for insurance fraud and threatened to arrest him. The ex-offender withdrew the complaint and left the district offices. Not all hazing and harassment was this harsh, but overall the number of individuals from the district who came in to report a crime went down over time. In other words, as a result of the district's unethical and rude treatment of the local citizens, the willingness of inhabitants in the district to file complaints went down and so did the reported crime rate. Here, we have it: Police behavior changed to increase arrest rates. The reduction in the reported crime rate was also a result of a change in police behavior and activities. The community members within the district suffered disrespectful treatment by their police officers, crimes were not investigated, and offenders committing the unreported crimes were not apprehended. One might argue, however, that if the aggressive increase in arrests served to reduce the actual crime rate, the law-abiding member of the district benefited. But did the actual crime rate in the district go down as a result of the more aggressive policing? There is no way to tell if the actual crime rate was reduced or, for that matter, increased using the contaminated data contrived in this case.

For many people, the very concept of organization implies purpose, and the question of how well purposes are met is central to understanding organizations. *Organizational effectiveness* is thus a central theme in both the pragmatically oriented literature on management and the theoretically oriented literature of organizational behavior. For many managers, determining effectiveness involves identifying the criteria with which to assess effectiveness, measuring these criteria, and weighing the various outcomes. Implicit in these steps, however, are important theoretical questions, such as: Effectiveness for whom? How are outcomes to be measured? What is a good outcome? Such inescapable questions illustrate the complexity of the concept of organizational effectiveness.

That complexity is evident in most discussions of organizations (see Peters and Waterman, 1982). For example, Tayloristic managers might cringe at a policy that 3M Company finds central to its effectiveness. At 3M, some employees are expected to steal company time and material for their own creative enterprises in the hopes that this theft will produce marketable innovations. (Those sticky Post-It™ notes illustrate the potential for success in this approach.) Managers at Ford also grappled with definitions of organizational effectiveness when, in the late 1970s, they allegedly used a cost-benefit analysis to decide not to recall Pintos, even though they knew the faulty gas tank design was linked to fires and the subsequent deaths of some of their customers (Cullen, Maakestad, and Cavender, 1987).

In criminal justice, the question of effectiveness is equally complicated. For example, what criteria for effectiveness should drive prison policies on overcrowding? In the mid-1980s, the Illinois Department of Corrections granted massive numbers of "good-time" deductions, thus permitting the early release of thousands of prisoners before the courts intervened to stop the policy. Although the department argued that the policy was necessary for the effective management of the prison population, prosecutors argued that it violated corrections' fundamental purpose of protecting the public from convicted criminals (Austin, 1986).

The Florida Department of Corrections faced a similar situation when it retroactively rescinded good-time credits for prisoners, thereby delaying the release of some offenders and reincarcerating others when it was found that they were let out too soon. Some offenders went to court, and the Supreme Court ruled that such a policy of rescinding good-time credits was in violation of the Constitution's ex post facto clause prohibiting, in effect, retroactive punishment. The result was the release of hundreds of felons, some of whom were serious offenders. Arguing from a public protection perspective, some politicians advocated that a constitutional amendment be passed to prevent the provision of good-time credits to prisoners on the basis of advancing public protection as the primary purpose of criminal sentencing (CNN, 1997).

The complexity of the effectiveness issue is also seen in then-federal prosecutor Rudolph Giuliani's support of a three-year prison sentence in the largest case of insider stock trading. In late 1987, after an investigation lasting nearly two years, Ivan Boesky was convicted of illegally making hundreds of millions of dollars by trading stocks based on insider information not available to the public. Giuliani defended the sentence, which made Boesky eligible for parole after one year, by pointing out that Boesky had cooperated with the investigation and had provided information useful in several other cases. He argued that cooperation is necessary in such complex cases and that a stiffer sentence may have sent the wrong message to other stock traders considering cooperating with the prosecution.

Who is the final arbiter of an organization's effectiveness? In a large industrial and commercial city, the city council members threatened police executives and the union with across-the-board wage reductions if the downtown shopping area was not cleared of what the merchants considered a crime wave that was driving custo-mers away. The goal for the police was not particularly clear, but police were expected to drive the criminal element from the downtown area. However, the goal for the merchants was to see more customers; for the city council, their goal was to receive fewer complaints from the merchants. The city council also wanted more businesses to open in the downtown area to increase the city's tax base. These are not goals that police executives would articulate, but they were imposed upon the police department by economic and political forces. Consider Chapter 3 on the envi-ronment, and you can easily understand how external entities can determine organi-zational mandates and goals and assess effectiveness separate from the goals and priorities of the organization. Moreover, public groups such as local merchants can also declare criminal justice organizations effective or ineffective without having any knowledge about the actual performance of criminal justice agencies on which they depend. In this chapter, we examine the questions posed by these examples. We begin by defining effectiveness and noting the political consequences of this definition. We then focus on theories of organizational effectiveness, paying special attention to the limitations of the models used frequently in organizational assess-ments. After examining a variety of methods for assessing effectiveness, the chapter ends with a discussion of key issues to consider in determining the effectiveness of criminal justice organizations.

WHAT IS ORGANIZATIONAL EFFECTIVENESS?

In the literature on organizations, the term *effectiveness* has been used in many ways. Most commonly, effectiveness refers to the degree of **congruence** between organi-zational goals and some observed outcome. This definition, however, masks many complicated concerns. For example, some have argued that organizational survival is the best indicator of effectiveness (Hannan and Freeman, 1977). Others have focused on adaptability to the environment rather than simply on survival. Most scholars focusing on organizational goals have also argued that effectiveness is a mul-tidimensional concept and have advocated the use of multiple measures to assess it. The literature on public administration argues that social indicators, such as quality of life, an increase in a community's ascetic values, the potential for growth, sustainabil-ity, and so on, are ultimate goals for all public organizations (Lee, Johnson, and Phil-lips, 2008). To complicate the picture further, postmodernists argue that effective policing should be victim centered and judged by the quality and quantity of service rendered to victims (Clark, 2005). In the literature on organizations, then, effective-ness remains a largely ambiguous and ill-defined concept. Some scholars have even questioned the value of the concept in the scientific study of organizations (Pfeffer, 1977b). Few scholars, however, would doubt the value of the concept for management.

    Cameron (1981) identifies three reasons that the concept of organizational effectiveness remains muddled. First, there are important differences in the way scholars have conceptualized organizations. Some have suggested that organizations

Congruence: Matching, pertaining to effectiveness; goals and outcomes match.

are best viewed as rational entities pursuing goals. In this view, a police department may be viewed as attempting to control all crime. An organization, however, might also be viewed as responding to strategic constituencies. In this view, police managers may be most concerned with their impact on property crime in a business district. Or police organizations may be viewed as primarily meeting the needs of their members through pay schedules or shift and holiday assignments.

A second but related reason for the confusion surrounding the concept of effectiveness is the complexity of organizations. To the extent that organizations pursue goals, those goals are often complex, multiple, and conflicting. This complexity prohibits the identification of specific indicators of effectiveness that can be applied across organizations.

Third, the confusion has been enhanced by the fact that researchers have often used different, nonoverlapping criteria, thus limiting the accumulation of empirical evidence about organizational effectiveness.

Scholarly discussions of effectiveness do make one thing clear. Effectiveness is not a single phenomenon. Organizations can be effective or ineffective in a number of different ways, and these ways may be relatively independent of one another. There is, however, little agreement on the specific criteria that should be considered in examining organizational effectiveness. In a review of the research, Campbell (1977) identified thirty different criteria that have been seriously proposed as indices of organizational effectiveness. The list includes productivity, efficiency, employee absenteeism, turnover, **goal consensus**, conflict, participation in decision making, stability, and communications. In criminal justice, it is easy to imagine as long a list of idiosyncratic measures: crime rates, arrest rates, conviction rates, sentences, victim satisfaction, incapacitation, recidivism, humaneness, attention to legal rights, worker satisfaction, and increasing budgets. Obviously, such measures may often be independent or even conflicting.

In light of ambiguities about a general definition of organizational effectiveness, perhaps the best approach is to first address the question of why we try to assess the effectiveness of organizations. Scholars give many answers to that question. They may be interested in accounting for the growth or decline of organizations; they may want to investigate interactions between organizations and their environments; or they may seek to understand the antecedents of effectiveness.

For managers, however, the answer is straightforward. Beliefs about effectiveness influence how organizations are managed. Notions of effectiveness undergird many management decisions, and effectiveness studies can have direct and tangible consequences for organizations and their members.

In criminal justice organizations, those consequences may be felt in a variety of areas, including budget, personnel, and even mission. Treatment programs may be dismantled if they do not lower recidivism rates. Civilian staff may replace sworn officers in traffic control and other assignments when cost effectiveness is considered (Harring, 1982). Managers or their subordinates may be fired in the face of indicators of ineffectiveness. Prison wardens may resign following disturbances or escapes; police chiefs may be forced out by dissatisfied officers (Mastrofski, 1991). Managers may even redefine their goals in response to effectiveness studies. In the mid-1970s, treatment came to be regarded as

Goal consensus:
Agreement by internal and external constituents on the goals of an organization.

ineffective, and departments of corrections redefined their mission by emphasizing incapacitation and punishment. Prompted by the same research, probation agencies took on responsibilities for victim services, pretrial supervision, and increased surveillance of offenders (Petersilia and Turner, 1993). Some have suggested the relevance of a crime-control approach to making probation and parole more effective (Petersilia, 1995).

Concern with effectiveness, in short, can often lead to the redistribution of resources within and across organizations. In a completely rational model of organizations, changes in budget, personnel, or mission may appear to be logical consequences of efforts to assess and improve effectiveness. As we pointed out in Chapter 12, however, rationality has its limits within organizations. Conflicting goals, inadequate information, and the need to satisfyce rather than optimize limit organizational rationality. Under these circumstances, effectiveness can be viewed as being subject to the same bounded rationality as decision making. Effectiveness, therefore, might best be understood as a normative, value-laden concept used to distribute resources between and within organizations.

For many criminal justice organizations, conflicting goals and inadequate information are no small concerns. Take, for example, the microscope under which many prisons are now viewed. During the 1990s, many states saw massive expansion and growth in the number of prisons they managed. Prison expansion became the norm for many states trying to get control of a bourgeoning prison population, yet at the same time both critics and supporters were raising questions about the effectiveness of such efforts. Some states, California, for example, passed laws that required the Department of Corrections to take aggressive steps in its treatment of drug offenders. Under pressure from multiple interests, the rational pursuit of public safety through imprisonment was questioned by some. And efforts to redirect the effectiveness question toward what was actually being done to assist offenders and away from simply warehousing them became important. Societal protection is still important, but treatment expectations became normative as well. Prison effectiveness was being assessed on how prisons fit into the larger picture of changing criminal behavior.

This question became so significant in the state of California that the Department of Corrections was renamed the Department of Corrections and Rehabilitation in 2005, reflecting a changed expectation that prisons were to do more to rehabilitate criminals. Questions of whether or not this was possible in prison settings were raised by some critics who thought that departments of corrections were biting off more than they could possibly chew and that when prisoners were not rehabilitated, the departments would be held responsible (Stojkovic, 2005). Similar concerns have been raised by those who question police strategies on how they fit into the larger question of societal protection and community well-being (see Oettmeier and Wycoff, 1998).

Effectiveness studies, like all evaluation research, take place within a political context. According to Weiss (1972), this context intrudes in three ways. First, the organizations, programs, or offices are the creatures of political decisions. They have been proposed, created, funded, and staffed through political processes. Second, the results of effectiveness studies feed into the political processes that sustain or change the organization. Third, the studies are political themselves because they involve implicit statements about the legitimacy of goals and interests within the organization (Lovell, 2004). In this regard, McCann (2004) suggests that a systems model of effectiveness requires understanding that environmental and political constraints ultimately define effectiveness. A paroled child molester, for example, who recidivates may cause heated criticism of the system while other forms of recidivism may go unnoticed.

Appreciation of the complexity of organizations and the political context of evaluation highlights one important question that undergirds all discussions of organizational effectiveness: effectiveness for whom? Regardless of the theory of effectiveness under consideration and regardless of how data may be gathered and analyzed, this question remains relevant.

Many studies of effectiveness adopt the perspective of the organization's dominant coalition by reflecting the interests of those in power. As Hall and Tolbert (2005:288) note, effectiveness "lies in the eye and mind of the beholder, with the important qualification that some beholders are more powerful than others." Police managers, for example, may argue that arrest rates are the best indicator of effectiveness. Corrections managers may regard low levels of inmate violence and few escapes as indicators of effectiveness. Other constituencies, however, may have alternative views. Internal constituencies led by union stewards may base an assessment of effectiveness on working conditions. This was the case in 1979 in the largest prison guard strike in history. New York corrections officers had to be replaced by the National Guard when they walked off the job to protest a perceived lack of control over inmates and their low status within the organization (Jacobs and Zimmer, 1983). Similar views have been expressed by the California Correctional Peace Officers Union about the safety and welfare of their members, who work in a highly volatile and tense environment where overcrowding and inmate violence have escalated and the Department of Corrections has been unable to convince the public that additional monies should be set aside to build more prisons (Gomez, 1996).

One of the most significant cases in the history of prisoner litigation also illustrates the importance of the question of effectiveness for whom and the importance of power in determining whose view prevails. Prior to the case of *Ruiz v. Estelle* (1980), the Texas Department of Corrections (TDC) was widely regarded as highly effective based on its low costs, low incidence of reported violence, and the general cleanliness of its institutions. A combination of internal and external constituents, however, saw the matter differently. Inmates, prison reform lawyers, and the federal court came to regard the TDC as grossly ineffective. As one lawyer noted, "While corrections in Texas may be cheap in some senses, the system exacts intolerable costs to the human rights of the citizens in its custody, and its unlawful practices must be remedied" (quoted in Martin and Ekland-Olson, 1987:111). These differing views figured prominently in the longest and most expensive prisoners' rights trial to date, a case that, after long and bitter battles, led to the near-total reorganization of the TDC. The case was finally resolved when the presiding judge, William Wayne Justice, threatened to impose fines of up to $24 million a month against the Department of Corrections for contempt and failure to comply with court orders. The case was settled between the judge and the TDC after progress had been made to rectify the unconstitutional conditions within Texas prisons. Judge Justice's ruling suggested that the Texas prisons were effective to the extent to which inmates received proper food. The importance of the question of perspective is also demonstrated in a study of the use of telephones to arrange bail for pretrial inmates. Here, another powerful external constituency was involved. An experiment in the Tombs, a detention prison in Lower Manhattan, proved that many inmates could raise bail money simply by being given access to telephones. The social scientists conducting the study felt that increased availability of telephones not only would benefit inmates but would also increase organizational effectiveness by reducing crowding and saving large sums of money on pretrial detention. Implementation of increased access to telephones was resisted, however, when prosecutors intervened. This external constituency opposed the policy because it was seen as weakening their position in plea bargaining. Because detained arrestees are more likely than released arrestees to plead guilty, the prosecutors attempted to block increased access to telephones (Lenihan, 1977).

These examples illustrate varying perspectives on organizational effectiveness. Dominant coalitions, powerful internal constituencies, and powerful external constituencies may all have different ideas as to what makes for an effective organization. Because those perspectives may lead to different distributions of resources in organizations, it is critical to understand whose perspective underlies any discussion of the effectiveness of an organization. Often discussions on organizational effectiveness within criminal justice organizations frame the debate on how measures of organizational activity are limited and provide no new insights on how effectiveness can be addressed. Where there has been improvement in examining organizational effectiveness within criminal justice organizations, it has been led by the police field.

Sparrow (1999) discusses how issues of police effectiveness can be examined by posing different questions concerning police operations. Take, for example, the question of police efficiency. Sparrow suggests that the traditional police department responds to this question by examining detection and arrest rates as the measures of police performance. Sparrow offers an alternative view by framing the question differently. Under a community policing model, this question would be answered by examining the degree to which the community is free from crime and disorder. Effectiveness, therefore, is dependent on the perspective offered and what questions of interest are advanced. For some, arrest rates reflect some measure of activity among police; for others, unless this activity is tied to larger concerns, such as the absence or presence of public disorder, it has limited utility when discussing organizational effectiveness (Oettmeier and Wycoff, 1998).

Similarly, Dalton (2004) argues that reconceptualizing police strategies can be effective in the reduction of homicides. Based on an initiative entitled Project Safe Neighborhoods (PSN), the operating strategy is to get police, community organizations, and academic researchers working together to analyze how they can effectively address the homicide question. The idea is to ask the right questions about homicides. For example, how big an impact do we expect in our efforts? How long will it take to see a measurable impact on homicides through directed efforts? Can we really accomplish a significant reduction of homicides? Do we really want to reduce homicides and what does that actually entail? Answers to these questions reveal how we understand police effectiveness.

Police organizations are not the only criminal justice entities where these questions are being asked. Changing the nature of questions and answers concerning organizational effectiveness can be found in probation and parole organizations, prison systems, and court operations as well.

Writers and researchers during the 1990s began to raise questions on how organizational effectiveness can be assessed differently. The emphasis has been on changing the way in which we understand and gauge performance measures and organizational effectiveness within criminal justice organizations (see U.S. Bureau of Justice Statistics, 1993; High Intensity Drug Trafficking Area (HIDTA), 2006b). A particular emphasis has been on distinguishing organizational outputs (e.g., arrests) from organizational outcomes (e.g., crime reduction), with the goal of improving employee performance evaluations and organizational effectiveness. Virtually all state and federally funded projects now require some attention to how an agency will measure effectiveness, with a heavy reliance on outcome measures. Only when outcomes are assessed will we be able to answer if organizational efforts are effective.

THEORIES OF ORGANIZATIONAL EFFECTIVENESS

Hannan and Freeman (1977) point out that some theoretical perspective must underlie any discussion of effectiveness. Even the question of whether an organization is regarded as succeeding or failing will depend on theory. In this section, we review the major theoretical perspectives on the assessment of organizational effectiveness.

The Goal Model

The goal model is the most common theoretical perspective on effectiveness and, as Hall and Tolbert (2005) suggest, it is both simple and complex. In its simplest form, the goal model defines *effectiveness* as the degree to which an organization realizes its goals (Etzioni, 1964:8). The model posits that organizations can be understood as rational entities. In using this perspective, evaluators assume that an organization's goals can be identified, that organizations are motivated to meet those goals, and that progress toward them can be measured. Evaluating companies by their profits is, perhaps, the most obvious example of this approach. In criminal justice, such measures of effectiveness as arrest rates, conviction rates, and recidivism all reflect the goal model.

There are some difficulties with this model. As we noted in Chapter 12, research has revealed the limitations of the rational model of organizations. Many commentators have also noted the difficulties involved in defining an organization's goals (Etzioni, 1960; Simon, 1964); most organizations have multiple and, frequently, conflicting goals. Even manufacturing firms must balance quantity with quality goals and concern for short-term profits with long-term considerations. The situation is still more complicated in criminal justice. Police departments are charged with controlling crime but must also ensure due process. They also generate revenue through enforcement practices, reduce fear of crime, maintain order, and satisfy their employees, as well as pursue many other goals. Identification of some primary goal or goals is clearly a difficult task and one that again raises the question of effectiveness for whom.

Nevertheless, all public organizations have numerous goals (Hannan and Freeman, 1977:111). In his study of street-level bureaucracies, Lipsky (1980) considered the impact of these goals on effectiveness. He argues that one of the characteristics of public organizations is that their conflicting goals reflect conflicts absorbed by the organization from society at large. For example, the public generally supports services for welfare recipients, but the same public argues for reductions in welfare rolls and cutbacks in services. The public also wants to see offenders rehabilitated but at the same time wants prison to be, at least, uncomfortable. One implication of Lipsky's argument is that public organizations are designed to be ineffective when effectiveness is ascertained by a broad-based goal model.

A second problem with the goal approach also relates to the question of what goals should be considered but poses that question differently. Perrow (1961) distinguishes between official goals and operative goals. **Official goals** are generally for public consumption and can be found in annual reports and broad policy statements. Such goals as "to serve and to protect," however, provide little guidance for what goes on in an organization on a daily basis. **Operational goals** are generally derived from official goals but tell us exactly what the organization is trying to do.

Official goals: Goals based upon formal mandates; generally written in manuals and promulgated by agency executives.

Operational goals: Goals established by work process members seen as congruent with goals of immediate clientele.

The difference between official and operative goals is illustrated in Sykes's (1958) study of Trenton Prison. He argues that because we know little of the technology needed to "treat" offenders and because punishment must be tempered with humaneness, prison cannot accomplish either official goal. Instead, the regimen of incarceration reveals an operative goal of simply retaining custody through benign means. The Texas prison system confronted the same dilemma that Sykes describes but apparently resolved it in a different fashion. Although neither treatment nor punishment were actively pursued, the TDC did follow a strict and sometimes brutal regimen directed at maintaining order (see DiIulio, 1987). Considering only official goals invokes unrealistic standards and ignores goals that are actually being pursued. Considering only operative goals, however, makes it impossible to compare effectiveness across organizations.

A third problem with focusing on organizational goals relates to the consequences of measuring goal attainment. On one hand, this approach means that behavior that is not viewed as relating to goals is not measured and, therefore, is not viewed as contributing to effectiveness. Police officers' compassion toward victims of crime or a judge's exhortations to an impressionable juvenile go unrecognized if effectiveness is measured by arrest statistics or cases processed. On the other hand, the effectiveness criteria selected may go further and actually alter desirable behavior that is not recognized in the measurement process. While studying an employment agency, Blau (1964) observed that the choice of evaluation criteria had a dramatic effect on behavior within the organization. When the agency was evaluated on its job placement rate, employment counselors shifted their focus from clients who were difficult to place to clients who were the most likely to find work and who may even have been successful without the agency. Measuring goal attainment, then, not only leaves some activity within an organization unrecognized but may also narrow activity so that only those goals whose attainment is measured are met.

A final concern about the goal model of effectiveness deals with the relationship between goal attainment and consequences for the organization. In public organizations, this relationship is not at all straightforward. Lipsky (1980:35), for example, suggests that the demand for services in street-level bureaucracies will always increase to meet (or exceed) supply. He illustrates the point with the example of a health care clinic forced to move out of a poor neighborhood in an effort to control the demand for services. The more successful the clinic was at providing services, the greater was the demand. The evidently bottomless demand necessitated either cutbacks in the quality of services or making services difficult to obtain by increasing transportation problems for clients. The attainment of goals thus led to drastic changes for the organization. Similarly, Wilson (2000) argues that the question of effectiveness is always a sensitive issue for public bureaucracies because much of what they do cannot be understood from a purely "market perspective." Whereas goal attainment may have negative consequences for some organizations, failure may not only have negative consequences; it may, in fact, also have some positive consequences. For example, it is unlikely that a police department's budget will actually be reduced while crime rates are increasing! Likewise, when Martinson (1974) and others declared correctional treatment a failure in the mid-1970s, prison populations and resources for prisons began to soar. When some goals are considered, then, prisons may look ineffective, but the consequences may be positive for the organization.

Despite the complexities of the goal model, a goal-model-based program considered successful, called Compstat (computer + statistics), was initiated by the New York City Police Department in 1995. Compstat is considered a management tool that imposes responsibility for crime analysis and crime reduction upon district commanders and clarification of mission and goals at the district level. The system also forces clarification of the mission and operational goals within each district. District commanders are required to analyze crime patterns and reallocate resources to reduce crime by some percentage estimate. What is taking place is a management method to improve the effectiveness of police work and measure effectiveness on the basis of the extent to which set goals are achieved. For example, crime analysis may reveal that burglaries peak at certain times of day or during certain months and in particular geographical areas. District commanders then assign more resources to the area identified at the time and dates burglaries spiked the past year as shown by analysis. Based upon the analysis, estimates of how many burglaries can be prevented with appropriate planned strategies are made. The estimate becomes the measurable goal through which effectiveness of the program is estimated. Scholars have argued that Compstat is an effective management tool that does alter police structures and practices such that police operations can measure reduced crime (Willis, Mastrofski, and Weisburd, 2003). However, the drop in crime in New York City was accompanied by a similar drop in crime rates in big cities across the country during the time period that Compstat was being applied.

The goal model, then, is a complex framework in which to consider organizational effectiveness. Despite its limitations, however, the assessment of effectiveness continues to be largely a process of identifying goals, measuring them, and comparing the results against some standard. The reader, however, should be aware of the problems and limitations of this perspective.

Some Alternatives to the Goal Model

The goal model is a broad and complex means of examining organizational effectiveness. In response to problems with this goal approach, several other models have been developed that view effectiveness differently. One of these, the *internal process* model, is consistent with human relations perspectives in organizational analysis (see Likert, 1967; Perrow, 1986). It argues that effective organizations are those in which there is little internal conflict, where information flows easily both horizontally and vertically, and where internal functioning is smooth and characterized by trust and benevolence toward individuals (Cameron, 1981). To the extent that this model is concerned with morale within an organization, it may be seen as simply focusing on a limited set of goals. Such a narrow focus, however, is not without its benefits, especially in fields like criminal justice, when agreement on other goals may be difficult to reach.

Another perspective has been described as the **counter-paradigm** to the goal model (see Hall and Tolbert, 2005). **Participant-satisfaction** or **strategic-constituency** models are not concerned with questions of morale as the names may suggest. Instead, they view effective organizations as serving the interests of key constituencies (see Cameron, 1981; Hall, 2002), which may include resource providers, suppliers, users of an organization's products, or even clients in social service agencies. Effective organizations are able to maintain the contributions of these constituencies. For example, this model might highlight the importance of good relations between the police and the prosecutor's office or might explain why public defenders often maintain good relationships with their supposed adversaries in the courtroom. The model may also explain why some organizations fail. The Willowbrook School on Staten Island, a school for the mentally challenged, was closed in the late 1970s after failing to satisfy parents and the courts (Rothman and Rothman, 1984). An investigative reporter had sneaked into the school and revealed deplorable conditions on the local television station. Eventually, a parents' group was organized, and it successfully fought the institution.

Another view of organizational effectiveness incorporates many of the elements in the approaches already discussed. Steers (1977) describes this *process approach*. Under this model, effectiveness is described as a process rather than an

Counter-paradigm: A new way to conceptualize organizations, goals, and outcomes that contradicts existing thinking.

Participant-satisfaction: Serving interest of key agency to their satisfaction.

Strategic constituency: Meeting the needs of important constituents as a major goal.

Systems perspective: Being sensitive to changes in demands and constraints within the environment.

Goal optimization: The need to balance goals and thus to optimize multiple goals rather than to fully achieve a particular one.

System resource model: The primary goal of an organization is to obtain resources in order to ensure its survival.

end state, as might be the case under the goal model. The process approach consists of three related components: goal optimization, a **systems perspective**, and an emphasis on behavior within organizations. **Goal optimization** refers to the need to balance goals and thus to optimize multiple goals rather than to fully achieve a particular one. A *systems view* incorporates concerns for changes in an organization's environment. The *behavioral emphasis* suggests attention to the possible contributions of individual employees to organizational effectiveness. Under this model, then, the effective organization is one in which goals are responsive to the environment, optimization of multiple goals is pursued, and employees all contribute to meeting those goals. Bolman and Deal (2003) refer to the value of such a perspective as providing multiple views, or "frames," from which the question of organizational effectiveness can be addressed.

One last important theory of organizational effectiveness is a substantial deviation from the others. Yuchtman and Seashore (1967) developed the **system resource model** from an empirical investigation of the effectiveness of seventy-five independent insurance agencies. In this model, organizations are not assumed to possess goals, nor is goal accomplishment a relevant consideration. Instead, an organization is effective to the extent that it can obtain needed resources from its environment. As Yuchtman and Seashore note, the effectiveness of an organization can be defined as the "ability to exploit its environment in the acquisition of scarce and valued resources to sustain its functioning" (1967:893). Thus, whereas the goal model emphasizes output, the system resource model is concerned with inputs.

This difference in orientation can produce useful insights in areas where the goal model may lead to confusion. For example, under the goal model, the failure of probation agencies to rehabilitate clients may be regarded as ineffectiveness. The system resource model, however, would lead to the conclusion that these same agencies have been highly effective because they were able to change their mission and attract resources for custody-oriented surveillance programs, such as intensive supervision or electronic home monitoring. Likewise, if running safe and humane prisons was a goal of the Louisiana Corrections Department, then a 1975 court decision ordering sweeping reforms indicates that the organization was ineffective. However, then-Corrections Secretary C. Paul Phelps said that "the court order was the best thing that ever happened to corrections in [the] state" (cited in Rideau and Sinclair, 1982:47). Such a proclamation is understandable from a system resource perspective because the court order gave the department considerable political power and financial resources to make needed improvements (Wilkinson, 2006). Similar conclusions have been generated by those involved in local corrections and the management of jail facilities (Artison, 1996). This may be true because organizational cultures—beliefs, values, and unwritten rules—will work against methods of measuring performance and staff behaviors that may require any cultural changes. Staff may simply produce numbers and reports needed to satisfy the evaluation process without making any substantive behavioral or outcome changes (the saying used to describe this process is "give to Caesar what is Caesar's"). Therefore, it is important to create a culture that supports productivity. Moreover, business organizations whose cultures are both consistent and adaptable are high performers (Kotrba et. al., 2012).

METHODS OF ASSESSING EFFECTIVENESS

Reviewing a variety of theoretical perspectives on effectiveness is useful because it not only points out the limitations of the goal model but also provides alternative ways of considering organizations. In examining studies of effectiveness, however, it is clear that the goal model dominates efforts to assess organizations. Studies based on this model involve the identification and measurement of some goal or goals. Most frequently, this type of study has used a method referred to as *variable analysis*. Sophisticated studies of this type try to examine causal links in the attainment of some goal. For example, they may examine the contribution of training or supervision style to job satisfaction. Before discussing some of the pragmatic uses of this design, it is important to note that other types of effectiveness studies are possible.

Perrow (1977) describes two alternatives to variable analysis. In *gross-malfunctioning analysis*, the target of inquiry is failed or failing organizations. The analysis may examine the reasons behind a commercial bankruptcy, the disappearance of a social service program, a police department reorganization, or a major prison riot. Perrow describes gross-malfunctioning analysis as reflecting a "primordial" concern with effectiveness because it deals with basic questions of outcome. He argues that the subtleties of complex goals or goal displacement become irrelevant when organizations fail dramatically. Gross mismanagement, Perrow suggests, is easy to spot, and understanding it is a useful guide to improving organizations.

One example of gross-malfunctioning analysis can be seen in the report of the National Advisory Commission on Civil Disorders (1968), also known as the Kerner Commission. The group was formed to investigate the causes of the urban riots that occurred in 1967 in major cities across the country, including Los Angeles, Newark, Detroit, and New York. The commission found that African Americans in each of the cities complained of police misconduct— harassment, brutality, and even the improper use of deadly force. Although many causes of the riots were cited in the report, these practices, along with aggressive patrol practices in urban ghettos, were seen as major contributing factors to the unrest. Law-and-order candidates for the presidency rejected its conclusions (Cronin, Cronin, and Milakovich, 1981:66), but the Kerner Commission maintained that at the height of the civil rights movement, police organizations continued to rely on enforcement strategies reflecting policies of racism and neglect. Similar findings have been offered by subsequent commissions examining the role the police played in urban disturbances (Christopher Commission Report, 1991; Fire and Police Commission, 1991).

The history of Texas prisons also illustrates the potential benefits of gross-malfunctioning analysis. Texas prisons, too, failed to adapt to a changing environment. Prisoner litigation cost millions of dollars, was associated with increased violence and instability, and ultimately led to the reorganization of the prison system. Martin and Ekland-Olson's (1987) history of the litigation makes it clear that the policies of harassing inmate litigants and their lawyers and of ignoring or violating court orders exacerbated problems for the prison system. In addition, Baro (1988) argues that much of the poor performance of the Texas Department of Corrections can be tied to the inadequate development of "political technologies" to cope with changing environmental conditions, notably the growing influence of the courts in the day-to-day operations of the Texas prisons.

Perrow's (1977) second alternative to variable analysis is called *revelatory analysis*. Whereas variable analysis seeks to answer the question of how well some goal is being met, revelatory analysis asks who is getting what from an organization. In other words, revelatory analysis directly addresses the question of effectiveness for whom by investigating how organizations are used by groups inside and outside those organizations. Prisons, then, may be effective by virtue of the employment opportunities they provide in rural areas. This fact explains why many rural communities have actively sought to attract these institutions, which seem relatively ineffective by a simple variable analysis. Likewise, Perrow suggests that organizations can be effective at meeting the individual needs of employees. A police department, for example, may be regarded as effective by some because it offers a work schedule of four ten-hour days per week, which allows officers to maintain second jobs or engage in their favorite hobbies. In a variable analysis, employee morale may be seen as significant because of its assumed effect on goals such as productivity. In a revelatory analysis, however, morale may be regarded as significant in and of itself.

VARIABLE ANALYSIS IN CRIMINAL JUSTICE

In the assessment of organizational effectiveness, *variable analysis* refers to research designs that attempt to measure the attainment of some goal. Measurement of some outcome variable is often accompanied by investigation of the relationship between that outcome and independent variables. These studies, then, not only lead to general statements about effectiveness based on goal attainment but also provide information on what may contribute to effectiveness and thus on how effectiveness may be enhanced. For example, studies using crime rates as measures of police effectiveness may examine the relationship between that dependent variable and independent variables, such as police expenditures, the numbers of personnel, or the intensity of investigation (Rosenfeld, 2006; Wycoff, 1982).

Variable analysis is the most common approach to studying effectiveness in criminal justice. In this section, we examine five issues critical to these assessments and reveal the complexity of this approach.

What Domain of Activity Is the Target of the Assessment?

This question recognizes that organizations have multiple goals and that an assessment of effectiveness may not deal with all of them. As with all organizations, we could assess the effectiveness of criminal justice organizations in providing a safe and comfortable working environment for workers or managers, or we could assess their effectiveness at garnering or spending budgetary resources.

There are also many activities unique to criminal justice organizations. For example, Wycoff (1982) focuses on the effects of crime control activity by the police. Vanagunas (1982), however, argues that only a small amount of police activity deals with crime-related events and that, for the "consumer" of police services, problems unrelated to crime are more frequent and more important than criminal problems. He suggests using a human services model in the evaluation of the police, which would include evaluating conflict-reduction efforts and emergency services. Mastrofski and Wadman (1991) argue that a distinction must be made between *performance appraisal* and *performance measurement*. The former refers to the processes central to the evaluation of an individual's performance, whereas the latter refers to the relationship between performance and actual goal accomplishment. The latter determination is often difficult for criminal justice administrators to make. Again, the central issue is what goal(s) is/are being assessed in the evaluation process.

Oettmeier and Wycoff (1998) propose a three-dimensional model to performance measurement within police organizations under a community policing model. This model suggests that the community policing model can evaluate along individual, group, and organizational dimensions to ascertain how well the community policing model is achieving its objectives and goals. In addition, Oettmeier and Wycoff employ the imagery of a cube to describe how these three dimensions can also be addressed by examining the incidents, patterns, and problems in the community and how the department responds through activities, programs, or strategies. Taken together, the model offers twenty-seven different cubes that reflect the goals and responses of the department when operating under a community policing model.

Such questions about the activity or activities being assessed are central. Assessments of courts may focus on efficiency in the processing of cases or equity in the dispensation of sentences (see Goodstein and Hepburn, 1985; Hardy, 1983). Likewise, corrections programs have often been assessed on their ability to change offender behavior through rehabilitation, but some observers have suggested focusing on fairness (Fogel and Hudson, 1981; Logan, 1993; Stojkovic, 2005). Attention in the 1980s turned to deterrence (Phillips, McCleary, and Dinitz, 1983), incapacitation (Greenwood, 1982), and crime control (Petersilia, 1995). The National Institute of Justice released a cost-benefit study that analyzed the financial savings brought about by crime reductions due to imprisonment (Zedlewski, 1987), even though many have questioned the primary assumptions associated with the findings (Zimring and Hawkins, 1995). In addition, the complexity of the variables must be assessed. In the case of prisoner rehabilitation, it is difficult to assess the long chain of antecedents that are related to individual change in an offender. Many activities that affect personal rehabilitation, such as employment and family relations, for example, reach well beyond the scope of correctional institutions (Stojkovic, 2005).

The selection of the *domain of activity* is a significant step in the evaluation of effectiveness. That selection bears directly on many of the issues we have discussed—most notably, the question of effectiveness for whom, the fact that goals often conflict, and the tendency for effectiveness criteria to influence behavior within organizations.

What Do the Variables Mean?

After some domain of activity is selected, the next important consideration is validity, or finding variables that actually provide measures of effectiveness in the selected domain of activity. The problem is not a simple one. For example, recidivism rates have often been used as a measure of the effectiveness of rehabilitation programs. In fact, Martinson's (1974) famous critique of correctional treatment was based on the programs' failure to reduce recidivism rates. As he summarized his findings: "With few and isolated exceptions, the rehabilitative efforts that have been reported so far have had no appreciable effect on recidivism" (1974:49). That summary influenced the move away from a rehabilitation model and toward a just desserts, or punishment, model.

Work Perspective: PERSPECTIVES IN UNDERSTANDING ORGANIZATIONAL EFFECTIVENESS

I was a Special Agent in Charge (SAC) for over a decade for the U.S. Environmental Protection Agency (EPA), Office of Criminal Enforcement Criminal Investigation Division (CID). Here, we have a blending of two agencies. The EPA was concerned with promulgating regulations that would be imposed upon businesses in order to minimize the disposal of pollutant emissions to protect the environment. The EPA was made up of scientists and attorneys. My branch, the Criminal Investigation Division, was the law enforcement branch of the EPA. We were a bunch of cops, and our job was to investigate possible criminal violations of EPA regulations, make arrests, and get convictions—pretty standard stuff that cops are good at doing. Just as any other law enforcement agency, CID special agents began their careers in law enforcement under the tutelage of a field training officer (FTO) who was responsible for showing new agents the ropes. The FTO's duty is to advise new agents of the many land mines a new special agent could encounter if he/she was not made aware of the dos and don'ts contained in what became known as the "Agents' Manual." This was our Bible, our road map to success as law enforcement officers. Do everything the manual advised; you would be considered a good agent and promised longevity in your career. As you can imagine, the Agents' Manual was a compilation of instructions on everything from drafting affidavits for the application of a search warrant, surveillance techniques, use of body wiretaps and phone-monitoring systems, how to write reports, rules surrounding the discharge of firearms, proper procedures for arrests, and an almost endless list of instructions. The FTO was with you until he/she thought you had mastered the tools necessary to perform your duties as outlined in your job description as a Government Service level five Agent (GS-5). These job descriptions outlined the requirements up through the higher pay grade of GS-13. Ordinarily, you started as a GS-5 or GS-7 and spent an average of two years with the FTO. Your organizational effectiveness during these early years was assessed by your FTO based on his/her opinion of your performance and upon your compliance with instructions in the Agents' Manual. Your FTO's assessment of your performance was reported up through the chain of command.

However, for the journeyman agent, his/her effectiveness was measured by success in the field. This simply meant the number of active cases you were carrying, how many cases had been opened and then closed, number of cases not prosecuted, the number of defendants, convictions, fines, restitution, and probation. While not readily measurable but still of major significance, was the size and complexity of the cases. This meant something in those early years. Even though you can't realistically put a numerical weight on complex cases, we all knew that complex cases take more time and effort than routine cases, and complex cases were subjectively weighed more heavily than routine cases when considering the effectiveness of an agent.

WORK PERSPECTIVE—continued

So we counted activities, but we also allowed for subjective measures, if you will, regarding the complexity of cases; frankly, when judging the effectiveness of an agent, we considered such things as if the agent showed up, showed up on time, showed up prepared, and was a team player. But, as time moved on, numbers gained paramount importance, "bean counting" encroached more heavily in the process, and the way we gauged effectiveness changed. We were required to report all of the activities that could be easily reported with numbers. Based on the numbers, statistics would be compiled, forwarded to Washington, DC, tabulated and compared with the other fifteen regions within EPA\CID, and given to the director of CID, who would pass the numbers further up the chain of command. The level of effectiveness of EPA\CID would now be compared with all of the other entities within EPA, one of the largest federal agencies. In CID, we could have lived with just counting any and all activities to satisfy the new demands for numbers. If I may be sarcastic for a moment, we would have had no problem including just how many sheets of paper it would take to write a report—or how many typos there were in the average report. The problem was that we were now being asked to include in the individual effectiveness reports of each agent the extent to which their activities protected the environment from pollutants. We understood that the public and Congress had a right to know—in addition to the arrest and prosecution of individuals who were poisoning our environment—the extent to which we were keeping pollutants from the environment with our police activities. This new component of effectiveness would also reflect upon CID as well as individual agents.

This, of course, was not good news for CID agents and managers. We were cops, not scientists. Measuring pollution, which often is stated in parts per million or billion, was not something agents had been trained to do. Law enforcement agencies know about search warrants, arrests, convictions; we can identify and record most hazardous substances that are recovered, such as barrels of toxic materials. However, we did not have a clue about translating all of that into a set of numbers to reflect the impact of our police activities upon the environment. This is the work of a person with a strong scientific background. The agency recognized this and hired scientists to work with CID agents and mid-managers. The scientists created a form for us to fill out to explain how much pollution was kept from the environment as a result of our policing activities. Even with the help of the scientists and the form, the process was confusing and chaotic; often the form was filled out with such wild estimates because accuracy was not possible. We all knew that the information provided on the form was probably not valid. What we did accomplish was to create a system that always showed positive estimates on the impact our activities had on the environment.

We, in the CID, had no problem understanding the need to report more abstract results to Congress and the public. The EPA/CID was charged with keeping the environment clean and safe, after all. All of the members of CID took great pride in making arrests and convicting individuals that were criminal in the way they managed pollutants. But the agency's top management lapsed on this issue. In my experience, effective management requires a top-down, bottom-up approach in which top managers establish the mission, set priorities, compose general operating principles, obtain resources, etc. The general plan of top managers is passed to middle managers who have the autonomy to implement and carry out the mission within their district and the context of their field work. Poorly run agencies are top down only—that is, direct orders for field agents are composed and communicated from the top without regard to the realities of the field. This is what happened with the rise of numerical accountability and the imposition of scientific outcome measures on our rather traditional law enforcement agency. Had the leaders of EPA in Washington told us about their need to provide estimates or data on the effectiveness of our law enforcement efforts to protect the environment, we could have worked out a system that might have been of real value.

SOURCE: Ricky Langlois, Instructor, School of Criminology/Criminal Justice, Florida Atlantic University; Special Agent Criminal Investigation Division, Environmental Protection Agency, retired.

In fact, however, there is every reason to question the use of recidivism as a satisfactory measure of rehabilitation. As Maltz (1984) points out, without paying attention to how programs are expected to affect recidivism, it is impossible to tell just what recidivism rates measure. They may also be measuring the effects of punitiveness and, therefore, special deterrence rather than rehabilitation. In other words, "it may not be possible to disentangle the effects of the carrot (rehabilitation) from those of the stick (special deterrence)" (Maltz, 1984:11).

The situation is equally complex with other measures of criminal justice effectiveness. For example, Chicago police and prosecutors were criticized for failing to successfully prosecute a large number of people arrested for drug offenses. It was later reported that the primary motive for the drug possession arrests was to get gang members off the streets for brief periods of time. The police were using the charges in much the way they had once used charges of public intoxication. It was argued, therefore, that successful prosecution was not an appropriate criterion for effectiveness because failure to prosecute did not mean what the critics suggested (*Chicago Tribune*, 1987). (Whether arrests should be used in this way raises a completely different question about effectiveness criteria.) Reported crime, arrest rate, and clearance rate are the most frequently employed outcome measures in assessments of the police. Problems with the validity of these measures, however, have been well documented (see Wycoff, 1982). In one series of case studies, McCleary, Nienstedt, and Erven (2004) demonstrated that official crime statistics may sometimes be the result of organizational behavior that has little to do with effectiveness. In one of the cases, the authors explained a major drop in Uniform Crime Reports (UCR) burglary rates in one city by a significant change in investigation and recording procedures. The city changed procedures to require investigation of burglaries before they were recorded by the UCR clerks rather than have investigations follow the official recording. With the change in procedures, many events that would have been recorded as burglaries based on the initial patrol officers' reports were not viewed as meeting UCR definitions by the investigating detectives.

In a second case study, a "crime wave" coincided with the retirement of a police chief of long tenure. The study argues that the chief had "wished" crime rates down by rewarding district commanders who produced low UCR rates. That "wish" was then passed down through the ranks. With the chief's retirement, the hierarchical authority patterns within the department disintegrated, and crime rates rose.

Finally, McCleary, Nienstedt, and Erven found another unsuspected source of a crime wave. In one city, the task of directly supervising police dispatchers was removed from shift sergeants. Without the experience and protection of the sergeants, dispatchers began to send police officers to respond to many calls that otherwise would have been handled informally. Department statisticians experienced the increased dispatching of officers as a crime wave.

One final example illustrates the political issues inherent in defining effectiveness criteria. Morash and Greene (1986) report two studies that came to radically different conclusions about the effectiveness of female police officers. The curious thing is that both studies were done by the same consulting firm in the same city (Philadelphia) in the same year. In the first study, criteria for effectiveness were developed by using sophisticated techniques to find consensus among police administrators. In that study, resolving problems without arrests was an indicator of effectiveness, and female officers were found to be as effective as their male counterparts. Later, as a response to court proceedings and the city administration's concern with violent confrontations, a second study was conducted in which the decision to arrest was viewed as an indicator of effectiveness. By this criterion, women were not found to be as effective as male officers. The studies illustrate that not only do organizational factors influence outcomes but also that the way those outcomes are viewed is the result of value judgments and political decisions.

How Are the Variables Measured?

The problems just discussed relate to how effectiveness criteria are conceptualized and understood. Another aspect of the problem involves the measurement of the variables. The question is not necessarily one of inaccurate measurements. Although computational errors do occur, the significant problem is the choices made among measures that may all be mathematically correct. Some measures may be more suitable than others to the specific effectiveness problem being addressed. For example, in calculating crime rates in an urban area, considering only the number of crimes per 100,000 residents ignores the fact that many potential victims (and offenders) commute into the city every day.

The literature on measuring recidivism provides many illustrations of the importance of knowing how outcome variables are measured. Although there are many examples of inappropriate models and formulas used in recidivism research, even mathematically correct equations may produce widely different results. Recidivism can be defined as the proportion of some specified group of offenders who fail, according to some criteria, within some specified time. At a minimum, then, measuring recidivism for some group of offenders requires the identification of a failure criterion and a follow-up period. Failure may involve anything from rearrest to a return to prison with a new sentence, and the follow-up period may be anything from a few months to many years. *Recidivism* rates can thus vary greatly according to the failure criterion and the length of the follow-up period. The easier it is to fail and the longer the follow-up, the higher will be the recidivism rate. To illustrate the point, Hoffman and Stone-Meierhoefer (1980) computed recidivism rates on a sample of released prison inmates using various failure criteria and follow-up periods. When return to prison was the criterion for failure and a one-year follow-up was used, the recidivism rate was 8.7 percent. When arrest was used as the failure criterion with a six-year follow-up, the same sample produced a recidivism rate of 60.4 percent.

An inquiry into effectiveness by Wilkins (1976) also demonstrates the complexity of using recidivism measures. The Maryland Institute for Defective Delinquents at Patuxent, a well-known treatment facility, reported a recidivism rate of 7 percent using rearrest with a one-year follow-up. This rate was well below the 65 percent reported by similar facilities. When Wilkins examined the data, he found that the institute had used a unique way of figuring recidivism. The treatment program involved a period of institutionalization followed by three years of outpatient supervision and services. The institute counted an offender as a recidivist only if the juvenile was not returned to the institution during the three-year outpatient phase and was later arrested. Those who were returned to the institute during their period of outpatient services were not counted among the recidivists. Wilkins showed that the likelihood of anyone from any program failing after three years was about 7 percent and that Patuxent did no better than other institutions when the three-year outpatient period was included in the analysis.

Petersilia and Turner (1993) also found very high rates of failure among offenders on intensive probation and parole due to the nature of the interaction between offender and agent. Increased surveillance and supervision of offenders led to an increase in "technical violations," which caused many offenders to be sent back to jail or prison. The authors suggest that different ways of assessing intensive probation and parole supervision be developed in addition to the traditional measure of recidivism. The research underscores two important points about the measurement of variables. Those conducting studies of effectiveness need to be aware of the implications of selecting different ways of measuring outcomes, and the reader of reports on effectiveness must understand precisely how the outcome variables were measured.

Alternatives to Outcome Measures

Until now, our discussion has focused primarily on outcome variables as indicators of effectiveness. Crime rates, arrest rates, convictions, and recidivism are all measures of the outcome of organizational activity in criminal justice. There are, however, many limitations to such variables. They are complicated and expensive to measure. They can often be assessed only long after some activity has taken place. And many factors outside the organization may influence them. It is easy to see, for example, that police can have only a limited impact on crime rates and that many factors other than prison may contribute to an ex-offender's return to crime (Stojkovic, 2005).

In response to the problems of outcome measures, many managers and researchers have turned to measures of process or structure as indicators of effectiveness (Scott, 1977). *Process measures* are measures of the activities assumed to cause effectiveness within organizations. For example, assessments of probation and parole agencies have incorporated variables, such as the length of time probation/parole officers spend in supervision of each case or the length of time they spend in face-to-face contact with parolees. Judges might examine the length of time a case takes to go from indictment to final disposition, and police managers often examine numbers of traffic stops made by officers. The advantage of these measures is that they are easy to collect and are likely to be easier than outcome measures to influence directly. A disadvantage lies in the fact that they may not be as highly related to outcome measures as is often assumed.

Structure measures are still further removed from outcomes. These variables measure organizational features or participant characteristics that are presumed to have an impact on effectiveness. Courts have used the ratio of corrections officers to inmates as a measure of inmate safety in prison. Likewise, the level of training among staff has been used in assessing the effectiveness of many criminal justice agencies. One way of viewing these measures is to regard them as measures of organizational inputs that serve as surrogate measures for outputs.

Using Multiple Measures of Effectiveness

There has been considerable criticism of evaluation efforts that use single measures as indicators of effectiveness (see Chen and Rossi, 1980). Whether structure, process, or outcome variables are used, single measures have often been regarded as too simplistic and often uninformative. Single-variable measures assess achievement of only one goal and are, therefore, based on a lack of appreciation of the complexity of multiple goals within organizations. Furthermore, single-measurement analyses inevitably conclude that a goal either has been reached or has not been reached. A program is thus regarded as a success or as a failure. Such a conclusion provides a static, one-shot view of effectiveness and little information on how an organization might change or improve.

Multigoal/multimeasure designs give a more comprehensive view of organizational effectiveness than do single measures. These designs utilize a variety of measures to assess the achievement of multiple goals. In doing so, they permit examination of the effectiveness of different domains of organizational activity and examination of the relationship between the achievement of various goals. These models can also view effectiveness as an ongoing activity and thus provide information about how an organization can improve. Research measuring the effectiveness of a multi-jurisdictional drug task force considered arrest rates and quality cases brought to prosecutors as goals (Smith et al. 2000). One may argue, however, that arrests are a process measure to an ultimate goal of reducing the rate of drug use.

Blomberg (1983) provides an example of the multigoal/multimeasure approach in assessing the effectiveness of juvenile diversion programs. These programs have often been evaluated from a single-goal perspective. They also have often been regarded as failing because the goal of diverting nonserious offenders from the criminal justice system has been displaced as the diversion programs became an add-on intervention rather than an alternative. In other words, through net widening, diversion programs have sometimes come to serve clients who would not even have been arrested if the diversion program did not exist. Where evaluations have focused on rearrest data, these single-outcome measures have also not shown these programs to be effective.

Blomberg is critical of the simplicity of such evaluations. As an alternative, he suggests a multigoal/multimeasure approach that incorporates at least three broad measurements. First, measures of structure identify the types of youth served by the diversion programs, including such variables as age, ethnicity, social status, and offense history. Second, measures of services provided by the programs can distinguish between various types and intensities of programs. Finally, outcome measures, such as rearrest data, should be included. Taken together, these variables recognize that different types of programs may serve different types of youth. The evaluation, therefore, addresses the question of what works for whom and thus provides information for program improvement.

Another model of multigoal/multimeasure evaluation is an assessment of the juvenile corrections system in Massachusetts (Coates, Miller, and Ohlin, 1978). Researchers from the Harvard Center for Criminal Justice carried out the evaluation of the community-based system that replaced juvenile institutions after they were closed by Jerome Miller, the commissioner of youth services, in the early 1970s. The study incorporated a variety of structure, process, and outcome variables.

The assessment began with a theoretical model of community-based corrections as running along a continuum from institutionalization to normalization. Variables such as the types of relationships between staff and inmates and the types and extent of links to the community, were used to distinguish between facilities that created social climates more like traditional correctional institutions and facilities that created social climates that were more open and approximated normal life. The researchers found that some of the programs had social climates and links to the community that nearly duplicated those of institutions. Most often, these programs focused on changing offenders' values rather than reintegrating them into the community. This structural dimension was then examined to see how it related to process and outcome variables.

The process variables were decisions made to place youth in the various types of programs. The researchers found that youth with more extensive records were more likely to be placed in the less open programs. Thus, many youth did not benefit from the new treatment programs and those most needing the innovative programs were least likely to get them.

The study also incorporated a variety of outcome measures. Cost and recidivism outcomes were examined, as were a variety of attitudes in the short and long term. Attitudes were examined at release from the program and again at six months after release. The evaluation revealed that the open, or normalized, programs had the most positive effects but that these modest program effects diminished when the youth returned to their homes.

The complex design of the Massachusetts evaluation permitted conclusions that went far beyond commenting on the success or failure of the community-based programs. The study showed that most youth offenders could be handled in the community-based system. Another finding was that "community based" was an inadequate description and masked a wide range of programs. Yet another finding was that the more open programs were more likely to be successful. The evaluation also produced significant recommendations for program improvement, which ranged from increasing links to the community to strengthening advocacy work and follow-up in the community.

These five issues illustrate the complexity of variable analysis in the assessment of organizational effectiveness. At first glance, these issues may appear to deal with narrow technical problems. Careful consideration, however, reveals that they get to the heart of understanding organizational effectiveness under the goal model. Attention to these issues will require that decisions be made about what goals are relevant to effective organizations, how attainment of those goals can be assessed appropriately, and what benefits their assessment can have for members of the organization.

Attention to the issues will also suggest that the assessment of effectiveness can be an ongoing activity that provides information for the continuing change and improvement of organizations. Skogan (1996) suggests that any evaluation of a program must have a basic understanding of the "logic model of the program." This logic model has four specific components: *intervention* (level of effort involved), *context* (surroundings and circumstances where the intervention is being placed), *mechanism* (how the program is to affect the outcome), and, finally, *outcomes* (anticipated outcomes of the program). By following this logic model, it is possible to make more definitive statements concerning program effectiveness. Other researchers have noted how assessments of program effectiveness have become critical for criminal justice administrations; they no longer are simply a luxury but a requirement. (See Fyfe et al. [1997] for a discussion of program effectiveness as it relates to police performance issues.)

ETHICAL CONSIDERATIONS IN ASSESSING ORGANIZATIONAL EFFECTIVENESS

We began and now end this chapter by thinking about the potential for abuse in efforts to measure effectiveness. As any practitioner can testify, numbers and data can be produced to give the appearance of compliance to rules or to achieving organizational goals. The motivation to fudge data exists in practitioners if they are cynical about the value of attempts to evaluate their work, mistrust the evaluation process or evaluators, or fear that they will somehow be made to look bad or harmed in some manner as a result. Moreover, most experienced practitioners know better than most of us the complexity of their world and the gulf between official and operational goals. As a result, they will doubt that they can be evaluated fairly. Hence, to protect themselves, they may feel it necessary to manipulate data or the process to their benefit. Real or perceived competition among practitioners or supervisors if fostered through an evaluation process can also give rise to fudging data or altering reports. Moreover, because criminal justice practitioners work outside the immediate purview of their supervisors, they have the freedom to play out their roles in such a manner to produce the appearance of "good results." Police officers, for example, have unfettered opportunities to avoid making arrests or to make an arrest when it is not necessary. Corrections officers may choose to report or not report drug use on the part of inmates depending on longer-term consequences to them or their warden if formal records indicate increasing or decreasing incidents of drug use by inmates. Hence, the motivation to contaminate an official feedback loop is potent, and the opportunity is endemic to the structure of criminal justice agencies. Hence, these issues must be addressed before the initiation of any formal effectiveness evolution is implemented.

First, any evaluation process must be seen as making sense to those who will eventually be judged. Including the rank-and-file in designing planned effectiveness research can help in this regard as well as increase credibility toward the evaluators. Also, executives or evaluators need to set realistic goals by which to judge effectiveness. Being measured against unrealistic goals will justify falsifying data in the minds of many. Next, organizational members need to feel that heads are not going to roll and egos are not going to be bruised—at least badly—as a result of the process and outcomes. In addition, organizational members need to believe that they are being judged within their domain and that the set of circumstances unique to those domains is being considered. But the major consideration for agency members will be how the results of the evaluation will impact their careers or affect their professional reputations.

SUMMARY

Define organizational effectiveness.

- Organizational effectiveness is the degree of congruence between organizational goals and some observed outcomes.

Understand the issues underpinning measuring organizational effectiveness.

- Organizations are complex and have complex and conflicting goals.

Discuss the difficulties of the goal model.

- It assumes that organizational goals can be identified, that members work toward the goals, and that goal attainment can be achieved.

Briefly discuss the three significant elements of the process approach.

- Multiple goal attainment must be optimized, changes in the organization's environment and goals will change, and the contribution of employees will be considered.

Understand variable analysis.

- Variable analysis is electing separate domains and finding variables that provide measures of success within each domain and are specific to effectiveness within each domain.

Understand why ethical problems arise out of attempts to measure effectiveness.

- It is relatively easy to produce numbers to make an individual or a group look good—as if goals have been attained.

Case Study: COMMUNITY PERSPECTIVE ON EFFECTIVE ENFORCEMENT

This is a true story that took place in a "big" city in the Midwest, the heartland of America. A group of successful professionals purchased a row of old statuesque homes in an inner-city neighborhood. They worked together to restore the homes to their almost historical quality. The homes were stunning and the yards were immaculate. All of the owners were proud of their achievement. Their success was also written up in the local newspaper's home and garden section, which portrayed them as owners with a vision. But, they had an ongoing problem that severely blemished their investments, hard work, and sense of accomplishment. It seems that the street directly in front of their houses had been a strip where prostitutes would meet with their johns for sex. The johns would arrive at 5:00 ... in their lavish new BMWs, Lincoln Town Cars, and even an occasional Bentley. After the sexual encounter, the participants would throw condoms, paper towels, napkins, and other residual paraphernalia on the lawns and street in front of the houses.

The owners reported the problem to the police. Initially, a police officer met with the owners and took a detailed report. However, the prostitution continued. The residents continued to call the police and were told their problem was not a high priority, but the police would look into the situation. A few owners resorted to throwing eggs on the fancy new cars, but that was not much of a deterrent. The owners finally insisted that they talk to the shift commander to report their problem, hoping to get some results. The shift commander listened politely and explained that the police would get to the matter, but at 5:00 ... the time of the commercial romances, the police were always busy with other activities and just could not get to their problem. He tried to explain that "real law enforcement" meant going after the robbers and murderers. He even indicated that the crime analysis section of the department had issued a report that the greatest threat was from burglars who operated from 3:00 to 5:00 a.m. in their neighborhood and not those involved in prostitution and petty drug dealing. To be effective, they had set goals to reduce the number of burglaries in their neighborhood and meeting their goals would make it a safe place to live. The owner talking to the shift commander stated that he appreciated the commander's objectives, but he had discovered a number of police cars parked at the local Dunkin' Donuts at 5:00 a.m. every day for the last week. He sarcastically asked if they were preventing the donut shop from being burglarized. This got the shift commander's attention as the conversation ended.

The owners, represented by a probation and parole agent who lived in the neighborhood, took the shift commander's explanation as inadequate. The agent knew that other things could be done to improve their neighborhood and that, for the owners, the presence of prostitutes and pimps in the morning was unacceptable. He also knew that his employer, the department of corrections, was implementing a new program whereby probation and parole agents would work with police officers to detect and apprehend probation and parole violators. He suspected that many of the prostitutes were on probation and parole and in violation of their conditions, thereby giving him a new tool to remove them from the streets and in particular from their street. At a subsequent face-to-face meeting, the agent suggested to the shift commander that he work with the department of corrections to pursue the prostitutes for being suspected of violating the conditions of their probation and parole.

The shift commander, of necessity, thought the idea was a good one because he would not have to devote his limited resources to the problem and could work with probation and parole agents to address the problem. Probation and parole officials could administratively revoke the probation and parole statuses of the prostitutes without having the police arrest them. In addition, the only police resources that would be needed involved the actual taking into custody of the prostitutes when called by a probation and parole officer. This arrangement satisfied both parties, but it also raised questions regarding what we mean when we say an organization is effective or ineffective. For the police, effectiveness was gauged by a reduction in burglaries relative to available resources; for residents, organizational effectiveness meant their neighborhood would be free of petty crimes that affected their quality of life.

CASE STUDY QUESTIONS

1. Whose definition of effectiveness is correct? Are they both correct? Explain.
2. Should crime analysis be done in consultation with community residents?
3. To what extent should effectiveness be evaluated by community residents or other groups external to the police?
4. Which model of organizational effectiveness presented in this chapter would you use to assess this police organization?

Think like an Administrator

The former deputy commissioner of the New York City Police Department, James Fyfe, had written that police effectiveness is best gauged by those among the rank and file of police departments. In other words, if you want to know what a good cop is, then ask cops. For the police, effectiveness is defined within a culture that values certain things, such as loyalty to fellow officers, arresting those who pose the most danger to the community, and most important, the protection of your partner. The latter point includes standing up to administrators, and in some cases, even lying to protect themselves. Author David Simon has stated that lying is expected among witnesses and suspects in murder cases, but how much lying occurs among police themselves is left up to debate.

Regarding effectiveness, police administrators often are searching for "objective" criteria to offset the impact of the police culture and its practices. In the last few decades, the age of accountability has taken hold in human service organizations, like police agencies, where the expectation is that tangible results are provided and accountability ensured. Yet, at the end of the day, how is this accountability guaranteed by police administrators? Police administrators know how objective measures can be offset by police subordinates rather easily.

1. How would you create an objective effectiveness system within the police culture?
2. What barriers would you have to overcome to introduce effectiveness measures within police organizations?
3. How would you introduce an effectiveness assessment procedure that would address possible ways data could be manipulated in a police organization?
4. Do you think it is practical to set goals for police agencies focused on arrest rates and crime rates?
5. Is it politically feasible not to use arrest rates and crime rates as a measure of police effectiveness?
6. Discuss the value of process evaluation as opposed to outcome evaluation in police organizations.
7. How can "quality of life" measures in the community impact police effectiveness?
8. What kind of response from the union would you expect as a result of implementing new effectiveness measures in a police organization?

FOR DISCUSSION

1. Local jails are complex organizations with multiple goals. Consider how you might assess the effectiveness of your local jail. What internal and external constituencies exist? How might their views of effectiveness differ from that of the jail administrator?

2. Describe the goals of a local police department. How do official and operative goals compare? What variables would you suggest using to measure achievement of those goals? Is the meaning of the variables clear?

3. Consider the effectiveness of a drug court using a variety of theoretical perspectives. Would you reach similar conclusions using a goal, strategic, constituency, and system resource model of effectiveness? Under what circumstances might the theories lead to different conclusions about the court's effectiveness?

4. Develop a plan for a multigoal/multimeasure evaluation of a prisoner reentry program. What kinds of structure, process, and outcome variables would you measure? How would you use the evaluation procedure to provide information for the ongoing assessment and improvement of the program?

FOR FURTHER READING

Bolman, L. G., and Deal, T. *Reframing Organizations: Artistry, Choice, and Leadership.* 3rd ed. San Francisco: Jossey-Bass, 2003.

Dalton, E. Targeted Crime Reduction Efforts in Ten Communities: Lessons for the Project Safe Neighborhoods Initiative. *United States Attorneys' Bulletin*, Vol. 50, No. 1, January, 2002.

Flemming, R. B. *Punishment before Trial: An Organizational Perspective of Felony Bail Processes.* New York: Longman, 1982.

Fyfe, J., Greene, J., Walsh, W., Wilson, O., and McLaren, R. *Police Administration.* 5th ed. New York: McGraw-Hill, 1997.

Oettmeier, T. N., and Wycoff, M. A. *Personnel Performance Evaluations in the Community Policing Context.* Washington, DC: U.S. Department of Justice, 1998.

CHAPTER 14

Change and Innovation

LEARNING OBJECTIVES

After reading this chapter, the students will have achieved the following objectives:

- Understand why change occurs.

- Be familiar with the process of organizational change.

- Discuss four significant elements of a planned change.

- Understand the basic ingredients of planning in criminal justice.

- Understand personal resistance to change.

- Understand organizational resistance to change.

- Discuss the characteristics of organizations that readily facilitate change.

- Describe the processes to overcoming resistance to change.

- Understand organizational development.

- Describe unintended consequences of change.

- Be aware of ethical pitfalls resulting from organizational change.

VIGNETTE

Mental health courts dedicated to processing mentally ill offenders are finally a reality. The advent of criminal courts for offenders who are mentally ill is a major step in bridging the gap between the criminal justice system and mental health systems (Redlich et al. 2006). Beginning in the early 1970s, criminal defendants who suffered from mental illness were becoming a problem for law enforcement, courts, local jails, and prisons because they were released en masse from state mental institutions. Prior to the late 1960s until the 1970s, mentally ill citizens who became a behavioral problem for families, communities, or law enforcement ended up fairly routinely in state mental institutions. The problem of managing mentally ill citizens began to shift from state mental hospitals—often referred to as insane asylums—to a system of community mental health. The shift was a result of our collective observation during the previous decade that citizens placed in "insane asylums" had few civil rights and would be kept in the asylum until they were diagnosed as "sane" by staff psychiatrists. Individuals were sent to insane asylums by criminal courts if it was determined that the individual was incapable of standing trial due to their illness, and the person was to be returned to the courts after they were cured. Offenders considered criminally insane— not guilty by reason of insanity—were also sent to asylums by criminal courts. People also ended up in asylums through a civil commitment by a family or a probate court if it was determined they were sufficiently mentally ill as to require institutionalization.

In the 1960s—the decade in which individual civil rights were being emphasized—all public institutions were being scrutinized. It became clear to civil rights activists that inmates in our mental institutions were being managed in an arbitrary and capricious manner, often kept in custody for years beyond a sentence for a "sane" criminal offender. Further investigations revealed that the conditions in the institutions were abysmal, often leading to cruel treatment of inmates. The law changed as a result of our changing view of mentally ill citizens as well as our emphasis on civil rights, and it became more difficult to place individuals into mental institutions and almost impossible to keep them there for any length of time. This solution basically closed mental institutions and released patients/inmates back to their communities. But we then had mentally ill individuals in our communities rather than kept away from us in an asylum. Now what?

A community mental health system was created to provide treatment and assistance to the mentally ill now living in their communities. However, the system was dramatically underfunded and mental health workers, unlike criminal justice professionals, were never trained to work with criminal offenders who also suffered from mental illness. In addition, criminal justice practitioners were trained to work with criminal offenders but did not have a clue about working with individuals who suffered from mental illness. Hence, we had a classic *performance gap*: Mental health workers would not provide services for criminal offenders who were mentally ill. They considered this group of individuals as the responsibility of police and the criminal justice system. Conversely, police who encountered mentally ill individuals as offenders, whether the individuals were acting out their delusions in public or committing serious crimes, had no idea how to manage them and received little help from the experts, the mental health workers.

Individuals with mental illness were a real problem for jail personnel. They had no idea how to handle individuals who were acting bizarrely—talking to God or other invisible contacts, for example. The days when a mentally ill arrestee or inmate could be easily transferred to a mental institution were over. As a result, mentally ill offenders and inmates received very little mental health treatment, and jail officers coped the best they could. And, of course, more and more, mentally ill citizens found their way into the criminal justice system and became a major problem for those managing local jails and prisons. Gradually, changes in the system began to take hold. Cross-training between criminal justice practitioners became common; large jails and prisons gradually established a mental health treatment process for inmates. In an odd way, jails and prisons took the place of the old asylums, certainly an unintended consequence of earlier changes. Finally, the system has established courts that deal exclusively with mentally ill offenders. The courts and their probation staff are all trained to deal with mentally ill individuals and find the best path to deal with their problems in the long term rather than resorting to traditional probation services or confinement to jails and prisons. Change happens—especially after a problem gets everyone's attention and it becomes apparent to decision makers that we are not expending our resources wisely.

This chapter focuses on organizational change within the criminal justice system and its organizations. It is suggested that readers review the first several pages of Chapter 3, The Criminal Justice System in its Environment, before reading this chapter. Organizational change and its attendant concepts and theories cover minor procedural changes within an agency as well as sweeping reforms that change the philosophy and operations of an entire system. At one extreme, changes can take place in an agency because of internal decisions; at the other extreme, major system-wide change is typically the result of reform movements that emanate from cohesive groups in society at large. Historically, such organizational change takes place within the context of general social changes that create, or are created by, new perspectives, ideas, or paradigms that force the organization to adapt to the external forces (Schein, 2004). Henry (2007:78) suggests that public agencies staffed by professionals change when there is a perceived loss of status. Public agencies protected by patrons—such as lobbyists or legislators—change when they lose their patrons' support. However, routinized public agencies that have followed the same processes and routines for years on end have little capacity for change, and they change only after "expectations about what they should be doing increase in a sustained way over time." For better or worse, it seems that the criminal justice system and its agencies often fall into this category. However, change has occurred in the criminal justice system, at times as a result of the need to adapt. In addition, change is more likely to occur in the face of a crisis that affects an agency or the system (Rochet, Keramidas, and Bout, 2008).

The criminal justice workforce is rapidly becoming more diverse with the inclusion of minorities and women. This change, which itself will impact the system, has its roots in the earlier civil rights movement that, in turn, produced legislation ensuring minorities and women an equal right to employment opportunities, which again led to affirmative action requirements and programs. Rothman (1980) argues that the prison reforms that took place at the beginning of the last century were the natural consequence of the Progressive era of 1890 to 1920, during which all social institutions were being questioned and changed. The perceived need for reform and change in the criminal justice system, however, preceded the Progressive era; attempts to bring reform to the criminal justice system began at least as early as the mid-1800s, when prison reform was pursued in New York and Pennsylvania. In essence, our present parole system, which is now being challenged and has been eliminated in some states, was developed in the late 1800s to emulate the "successful" system of penology developed by Sir Walter Crofton in Ireland (Barnes and Teeters, 1959). In 1870, penologists from across the United States met in Cincinnati at the National Congress of Penitentiary and Reformatory Discipline. The goal of this congress's dedicated members was to reform and reorganize the existing American penal system. In 1931, the National Commission on Law Observance and Enforcement published the fourteen-volume Wickersham Commission Report, which provided recommendations to improve the ability of our criminal justice system to manage crime and delinquency.

The President's Commission of 1967 was followed in 1973 by massive volumes from the National Advisory Commission on Criminal Justice Standards and Goals on recommendations to improve police, courts, corrections, and the juvenile justice system. The commission was provided with $1.75 million through the Law Enforcement Assistance Administration (LEAA), which had been created in the 1960s to respond to increasing crime, civil and racial disturbances, and looting during riots. The unrest, both civil and political, shed doubt on the ability of criminal justice institutions to impose law and order, rehabilitate and control offenders, and, in general, impose social control in a just and efficient manner.

Because change and innovation were seen as desperately needed throughout the system, millions of dollars in grants were provided to state and local criminal justice agencies through LEAA to assist them in making their operations effective and efficient, in the hope that the standards and goals promulgated by the National Advisory Commission would be implemented.

The effectiveness and practices of the criminal justice system are continually being challenged by society or the political and legal systems. During the 1980s, successful civil rights litigation in federal courts left the corrections systems unprotected by the traditional "hands-off" policy of federal courts and opened the prison system to an avalanche of inmates' rights litigation (Bailey and Hayes, 2006). Passage of the *Violence against Women Act* in 1994 and antidrug legislation during the 1980s not only created a more direct federal response to crime, it also led to significant changes across the components of the criminal justice system. Police agencies are being restructured through the implementation of foot patrol units or team policing. The practice of indeterminate sentencing and parole has been challenged by both liberal and conservative members of the public (Cullen and Gilbert, 1982; Tonry, 2004), and traditional judicial sentencing practices have been changed dramatically by legislated sentencing guidelines that are being challenged by court appeals and pressure groups that oppose the harshness the guidelines imposed on selected cases. Currently, change is being sought in the juvenile justice system by academics and practitioners who favor the concept of restorative justice for juvenile offenders (Bazemore and Schiff, 2004). In short, the perceived need for reform within the criminal justice system is an ever-present constant, and both substantive and symbolic changes have been made over time to meet that need. During the last decade, private sector services and private prison corporations have sprung up and the system is still struggling to adapt to the intrusion of market forces into the primarily exclusively public sector operations of criminal justice agencies (Mills et al., 2012; Taxman et al., 2009). Change manifested in simple agency alterations or in major reforms may be purposive or crescive (Warren, 1977). **Crescive change** is inadvertent or unplanned, independent of an organization's control, and may come about in spite of organizational efforts at self-direction. Crescive change can result from environmental influences on an organization or from internal organizational conflict (see Chapters 3 and 11 on organizational environments and conflict). As suggested earlier, what we refer to as crescive change is often imposed upon criminal justice agencies only after a long period of sustained doubt about what

Crescive Change:
Change imposed on an organization, usually by external forces.

the system should be doing (Henry, 2007). The striking example of crescive change being imposed upon aspects of law enforcement agencies stems from the 9/11 Commission Report in response to the destruction of the World Trade Center in New York City on September 11, 2001. The commission discovered what was well known by law enforcement practitioners and criminal justice academics: Law enforcement agencies, especially intelligence-gathering agencies, such as the FBI and CIA, kept crucial information to themselves and had informal policies not to share information with other agencies. The commission recommended that such practices be immediately altered for the sake of national security. In addition, the Department of Homeland Security (the *Homeland Security Act*, 2002) was formed, in part, to impose a coordinated, intelligence-gathering effort on federal agencies. Also, as a result of the commission's recommendations, the *Intelligence Reform and Terrorism Prevention Act* was passed in 2004 in an effort to create an information-sharing environment for data on terrorism (Henry, 2007). However, policies, routines, and attitudes of agencies will have to change to meet the new demands.

Purposive change:
Change that results from conscious, deliberate, and planned efforts by organizational members, typically managers.

Purposive change results from conscious, deliberate, and planned efforts by organizational members, typically managers. It may be a response to changing environmental conditions or pressures, to internal conflict, or to organizational members' perceived needs to change or improve aspects of their system. Crescive and purposive changes are obviously not mutually exclusive processes. Purposive change represents an "intervention into a flow of events that will in any case result in change.... Consequently, the decision is not whether or not there will be change, but rather what one's part will be in shaping or channeling inexorable change" (Warren, 1977:10). The *Patriot Act* is a current example of a mix of crescive and purposive changes and fits into our discussion on the national response to terrorist threats. It is beyond the scope of this chapter to consider every possible change within an organization. We are concerned here primarily with purposive, or planned, change as it applies to the agencies of the criminal justice system. Change can take place at every level of an organization and in every nook and cranny. We discuss organizational change as a general phenomenon rather than its innumerable specific applications in every facet of a criminal justice agency or system. As we have seen in moving from the twentieth century into the twenty-first century, many changes have occurred within criminal justice organizations. All of these changes have altered, to some degree, how criminal justice agencies are responding to crime.

WHY CHANGE OCCURS

As we have said, change can emanate from inside or outside an agency's environment. To the extent that members are aware of environmental changes or internal conflict that may affect the agency's operations or outputs, the agency may enter into deliberate or planned change efforts. Before executives actively make some form of change effort, however, they must first perceive a need for change—that "something is broke and needs to be fixed." When an agency is performing improperly or below capacity, it is suffering a **performance gap** that may be recognized by agency executives, personnel, clients, or other constituencies (Downs, 1967:191): "Whenever an official detects some performance gap between what he is doing and what he believes he ought to be doing, he is motivated to search for alternative actions satisfactory to him." Therefore, a change effort will usually be initiated in an agency only after officials perceive a performance gap or are convinced that a performance gap exists. The need for change may also be a result of environmental changes, such as changes in public perceptions of what agencies should be doing or how agencies should carry out their mission or duties. As discussed in Chapter 3, environmental forces, such as technological changes, demographic changes, or social or political pressures, may impose on agencies at least a need for change. For agencies of the criminal justice system, their task environments—new legislation, court decisions, and so on—will have the strongest impact (Henry, 2007) on the need to change. A performance gap may also be produced internally by employee turnover, internal structural or technical changes, or repercussions from an agency's performance (Downs, 1967).

External or internal forces taken separately or collectively can cause disequilibrium in an agency (Chin, 1966). Turnover of personnel will lead to differences in the collective behaviors of organizational members, regardless of official agency goals. New employees may have different goals, values, or work ethics from older employees. They may also view the mission of the agency differently. Newly appointed executives may cast the agency in a new role and ascertain that existing policies do not match that role. For example, younger corrections officers are less concerned with inmate use of marijuana than older officers (Kalinich, 1984). The change in prison composition from traditional inmates to street gangs has also affected operations (Irwin, 1980). New organizational members with different values and ethics become primary forces for internal change (Steers, 1977).

Advanced communications and recording technology supplied by computer systems have created a clear performance gap in the criminal justice system. Although computer technology provides the potential for increased efficiency in communication and record keeping, most criminal justice practitioners must be trained to work with this advanced technology before it can be useful to them. In addition, computer crimes are on the increase, and criminal justice agencies must learn new techniques to prevent this kind of white-collar crime, as well as to solve computer crimes and prosecute the sophisticated computer fraud criminal (Hinduja, 2004, 2006).

The use of bridging strategies "presumes the presence of decision makers who survey the environment, confront alternatives as well as constraints, and select a course of action" (Scott, 1987:200). Organizations modify their internal workings to adapt to external environmental pressures and constraints. The adaptation process is a form of purposive change in response to a perceived performance gap. Expansion of the use of community mental health services in county jails is a response to the increase in the number of mentally ill jail inmates and to contemporary standards of care for inmates imposed on corrections systems (Embert, 1986; Swank and Winer, 1976). Physical and mental health care standards for prison inmates resulted from court cases requiring a standard of care for inmates on par with community standards (Schmalleger and Smykla, 2007).

Unexpected and unintended consequences following a routine agency performance may create repercussions that make a performance gap evident. Such routine activities often have the potential to upset the agency's dynamic equilibrium (Chin, 1966; Downs, 1967). For example, the discovery of police corruption will upset the balance and stability of a police agency. Also, prisons may be replete with brutality and corruption or may be managed by inmate gangs, but this corruption or lack of control by the prison staff may not be apparent until it becomes manifest in a riot or an inmate disturbance. The recent discovery, through the application of DNA testing, that several Illinois inmates on death row were in fact innocent has led to a moratorium on the application of the death penalty in that state. Moreover, this discovery also questions the reliability of criminal investigations in capital crimes. In effect, more reliance will be placed on "scientific-based evidence" in future investigations and prosecutions of murder and rape. If agency directors perceive a performance gap in their organization, they must first determine whether the gap is a short-term, or situational, phenomenon or if the gap is a long-term problem relating to some fundamental aspect of the agency (Kalinich, Stojkovic, and Klofas, 1988; Spiro, 1958). If the performance gap is viewed as a short-term phenomenon, agency executives may choose to ignore it. If it cannot be ignored, they may enter into "sales," or persuasive, tactics to convince their critics that no problem exists (Downs, 1967). If such persuasion is not effective, the agency executives may placate critics by making limited changes in the bureau's "window dressing" (Wilensky, 1967) or symbol structure (Kalinich, Lorinskas, and Banas, 1985). Organizations that passively adapt to pressures for change typically take this as a first step without analyzing the scope of the problems they are facing. They routinely seek the least diverse and least costly change that will most readily satisfy its members or external constituents (Downs, 1967; Sharkansky, 1972). Criminal justice agencies are skilled at altering symbols to placate pressure groups. If, however, the agency executives themselves perceive the performance gap as a fundamental organizational problem, they may attempt to bring about substantial change.

THE PROCESS OF ORGANIZATIONAL CHANGE

Planned change: A conscious effort to bring change to an agency by careful analysis of the mission, goals, and problems; forecasting; and seeking alternative paths.

The optimal approach to creating substantial change in an agency is to enter into a deliberate and rational process of **planned change**. A behavioral view suggests, however, that most organizational change is not purely rational or deliberate. Planned change requires that decision makers come to rational decisions. To do so, they must possess all pertinent information and must not be constrained by time or other resource limitations in the planning and decision-making process. However, decision makers, at best, operate under conditions of *bounded rationality* (March and Simon, 1958), in which they have limited knowledge and a finite amount of time and resources to dedicate to the decision-making process. An extension of the concept of bounded rationality is the *garbage can theory*, which suggests that organizational change is typically less than a deliberate, rational process. (See Chapter 12 on decision making.) For example, the garbage can theory posits a model of organizations in which problems become receptacles for people to toss in solutions that interest them. Thus, agency decision makers have favorite solutions stored away that are searching for problems (Perrow, 1986). As competition ensues among organizational members and decision makers over which solution to choose, the original problem may get lost or take on a new form or a life of its own (Cohen, March, and Olsen, 1972). As a consequence of competition among agency decision makers, unintended outcomes no one considered at the beginning of the process may be created. Solutions that lead to unintended outcomes can be "fatal remedies," which we will discuss later in this chapter, when the outcomes are harmful to the agency's mission (Sieber, 1981). Diversion programs created to limit the flow of offenders into the criminal justice and juvenile systems have broadened rather than reduced the number of offenders the system encounters officially and thus increased the intake of offenders (Decker, 1985; Doleschal, 1982). Critics of diversion programs also argue that the process requires individuals to accept guilt and governmental control over them without the benefits and safeguards of due process (Schmalleger and Smykla, 2007).

Planned organizational change consists of "a set of activities designed to change individuals, groups, and organization structure and process" (Goodman and Kurke, 1982; Kinicki and Kreitner, 2006). Planned change requires innovation and accepts problems as opportunities to pursue real improvement in an agency's performance. Conversely, planned change is not a passive adaptation to environmental pressures or a minimal attempt to reduce organizational tensions (Warren, 1977). Examples of passive change in response to tensions abound in criminal justice. The cliché that criminal justice administrators are reactive rather than proactive suggests that a passive, adaptive approach to change may dominate the criminal justice system. Units to improve police–community relations sprang up after the civil disturbances of the late 1960s in a weak attempt to give police agencies the appearance of being sensitive to minority needs (Radelet, 1986). These units were typically funded poorly and were not much more than a token attempt to respond to a fundamental problem (Block and Specht, 1973). Corrections is famous for changing labels: from guards to corrections officers, convicts to prisoners to inmates, and, in some states, to residents. Henry (2007) suggests that governmental agencies overreact to small changes in their task environment, making planned change difficult.

Planned change requires first overcoming organizational decision-making routines, such as garbage can solutions, seeking knee-jerk quick fixes, confusing symptoms with problems, overzealously protecting boundaries, and using least-cost solutions and methods to placate external pressures. Planned change also requires the ability to predict at least obvious contingencies and unintended consequences of proposed change as well as having a view to the future rather than merely adapting to immediate pressures and problems. In short, the process of planned change requires an open systems view of an agency and its environment. Leadership and vision are required to overcome poor organizational habits that quietly subvert planned change (Yukl, 2002). Kotter (1996) argues that leaders play a pivotal role in the change process.

Leaders establish the direction and develop a vision of the future. They align people, influence the creation of teams and coalitions that accept or acquire a shared vision, and provide people with an understanding of the path or strategies to achieve that vision. Leaders are also motivators who inspire and energize people to overcome obstacles and resistance to change. To the extent that obstacles to achieving a vision are found in the organization's structure, habits, or routines, leaders are antithetical to managers, whose role is to protect the existing structure, routines, and practices. In short, leaders create change (Kotter, 1996; Stojkovic and Farkas, 2003). Vision is the process of looking to the future for challenges that will impact an organization and looking inward for a better way of meeting the organization's mission (Nanus, 1992). Implicit in this statement is the need to identify present and future changes, which requires looking to the future using demographic projections—a technical chore—and understanding subtle current trends that may, for example, influence the future. Consider the corrections officers who predicted many of the future demands and changes that would be imposed upon corrections in the near future (see Chapter 3); they had a vision but were not in a leadership position to make the changes necessary to meet the new set of challenges. Identifying present and future changes also requires a judgment on the degree to which the organization or system can influence the future. Simply informing political leaders about the predictions may have sensitized legislators to the need for change. Looking internally, the visionary leader constantly seeks ways of changing the formal and informal structures and the culture of his or her system to improve the product or service quality.

W. Edwards Deming (1986), recognized for developing total quality management (TQM) and credited with turning Japanese industry into the world's leading competitor, argues that American leaders in industry and government need to make a commitment to quality and to think of success as a long-term effort as opposed to quarterly profits, number of arrests, court backlogs, or today's problems. Challenging the existing operating principles, organizational philosophy, values, excessive reliance on accountability, judgments by numbers, and other sacred cows of American management, Deming's primary advice is to make a commitment to quality (1986). He is a model for visionary leaders who want to create both change and sensitive systems responsive to change. Meaningful change begins with visionary leaders who use the techniques and tools for planning but are not subverted by the formal planning process, which in turn is routinely held hostage by tradition, structure, culture, and organizational politics.

Planned change requires routine and continuous examination of the agency's operations, including the expectations and demands of its clients and constituents, to discover existing and potential problems that will create performance gaps. Problems must be examined comprehensively and identified as substantive or mission problems, fundamental or policy-related problems, procedural problems, or circumstantial problems. After the problems are understood with some clarity, then solutions can be developed and ultimately implemented. Planned change requires an ongoing examination and a continuous restructuring of goals, policies, procedures, practices, and behaviors. An occasional discovery of a performance gap or a single look at a problem is insufficient; doing this creates a *ridged* system of decision making; familiar problems recur and are met with traditional and familiar solutions. Moreover, the traditional decision-making routine views symptoms as problems, and a thorough analysis does not take place. The basis of successful analysis for decision making and, hence, for planning is a "continuous cycle of formulating the problem, selecting objectives, designing alternatives, collecting data, building models, weighing costs against performance, testing for sensitivity, questioning assumptions and data, reexamining the objectives, … and so on, until satisfaction is achieved or time or money forces a cutoff" (Quade, 1977:157). Bryson (1995) suggests that a systems model of planned change requires planners to examine the organization's strengths and weaknesses, desired goals, structure, and the abilities and culture of its members, as well as the methods used to create its outputs. Considering all these factors provides a big-picture view of the agency to planners and allows consideration of the best manner to move the organizational pieces to create the desired change.

From our general discussion of planned change so far, it becomes clear that deliberate and extensive effort is required in the process. Typically, organizational members expend their energies pursuing established goals, performing internal maintenance activities, adapting to environmental pressures (Selznick, 1949), and protecting agency routines. Planned change requires a break from these routines.

Work Perspective: WHAT IT WAS LIKE BEING THE FIRST WOMAN CORRECTIONS OFFICER

In 1973, I became the first woman corrections officer at a medium security prison. This facility was located in a rural area, with rolling hills, flowers, and beautiful landscaping that you seldom see at prisons any more. Our prison provided many job opportunities for the local inhabitants of this small community. It had six buildings for housing prisoners, and every inmate had his own room. Prisoners were even allowed to wear their own clothing, and if they couldn't afford clothes, they wore a dark blue, state-issued uniform. What was it like to work there? Except for the low wages ($4.10/hour) and the hour-long commute, it was a wonderful experience. At that time, we were in the era of rehabilitation where it was felt that by attending school, learning a trade, etc., a prisoner could change. This rehabilitative philosophy was embedded in the institutional culture, where prisoners were called students and the warden was the superintendent. Even the design of the prison looked like a college campus where every inmate had his own room. Years later, I took my three children there so they would learn the consequences of poor choices and they thought it was a "nice school"! There was even a gym and a physical education teacher who wore a whistle and carried a clipboard! I immediately embraced the institutional philosophy because this is what I had learned at Michigan State from Professor Bob Trojanowicz (who later created the concept of Community Oriented Policing).

Our warden was very strict, but he was fair and treated everyone equally. One morning I came to work in a blizzard and was one minute late. I was written up by my sergeant, who told me that if I came late again, I would be fired. I had always prided myself on being punctual and resolved to never be late to work again. And I haven't been. I recently told a warden this story and he laughed and said it was unfortunate, but if he did this today, he wouldn't have enough employees to manage the prison!

The inmates were very respectful to me and so were most of the staff. I was known for being very strict, and as a member of the Institutional Disciplinary Board, I often voted for the inmate to be transferred to maximum security. That is because our prison was designed for young, first-time offenders who averaged in age between 18–25 years. Inmates were often in prison court for serious offenses, such as selling drugs and fighting. One day, an inmate came to court and when he saw me, he tried to leave, complaining that he wouldn't come to court if I was there. The captain and the inspector said that this was the era of equal rights and as a woman, I had every right to be there. The inmate stated that wasn't the problem. He was concerned that I would vote the maximum sentence of five days in lockdown and a transfer to maximum security. (The prisoners called this "five and a ride.") Since this individual bashed another prisoner on the head with a lead pipe for having his

---

WORK PERSPECTIVE—continued

music on too loud, all of us felt that he no longer merited medium security status. I can still hear this young man saying, "I told you she was going to do this," as he was being led away to a maximum security prison.

I can only think of two obstacles I faced from staff. The first one occurred when I was promoted to Prison Classification Director. One of the sergeants, who had always been friendly and helpful, stopped speaking to me. Teamwork is especially important in an institutional setting because your safety and ultimately your life can depend on a coworker. And of course, communication is a key component to getting along. Therefore, I asked this individual what was wrong. He stated that I had "taken his job and he was supposed to be the Classification Director." He added that he had worked at the prison much longer than I had and was more experienced. I remembered that the position required a bachelor's degree and asked him whether he had one. Everyone in the room laughed but the sergeant. Although he never had lunch with me again, we were able to maintain a good working relationship after this discussion.

The other situation involved a supervisor who refused to let me come into his unit to classify prisoners. Initially, this person told me that I couldn't come in because the inmates were taking showers. When I later returned, he told me he would never allow me to come into "his" building. (This individual believed that women should not be working in men's prisons and had expressed this view publicly many times. It was not an uncommon viewpoint during this era, either.)

I went to the warden who had assigned me with this task and explained the situation. The warden immediately called "Counselor White" and ordered him to allow me into his building now. I never had a problem with this individual again, either, and we remained on good terms.

Most of the inmates were very immature and came from abject poverty and abusive environments. This is true today, too, where studies show that 70 percent of prisoners have suffered from some form of abuse. Unfortunately, as years passed and the inmate population increased, many of

the trades were eliminated to make room for more beds. As more people became victims, the rehabilitation perspective shifted to one of "crime control," where society put the emphasis on punishment instead of treatment. It is interesting to note that despite longer sentences and three strikes and you're out laws, etc., the crime rate, particularly the violent crime rate, is rising in many cities across the nation.

Recently, I checked the status of some of the inmates at our facility on the department of corrections "inmate locator." With a few exceptions, most of the prisoners had stayed out of trouble. I believe this was due to the rehabilitative philosophy of our warden where it was felt that if the prisoner learned a trade, graduated from high school, and received counseling for any personal or substance abuse issues, he would have the tools needed to be successful upon reentry into society.

I still adhere to this philosophy today, and because it was often successful, I believe we will one day return to it. It was truly wonderful to see inmates learn auto body and then to see their "tricked-out car" win first place in the state fair! It was most rewarding to see them leave prison and become law-abiding citizens. Conversely, it was disheartening to see a former prisoner, who had learned a skilled trade, dealing drugs on the streets of Detroit. However, this is also reality and someone can only change if they want to. Unfortunately, this individual's criminal lifestyle led to his violent death at the age of 25.

In closing, I feel that the experience of being a corrections officer was very enlightening and paved the way for other corrections positions. Although I was the first woman, many others have followed, and I recently learned that over half of the corrections officers at my prison are now women. It is especially nice to be recognized and thanked by women who are currently corrections officers for "paving the way." Finally, this opportunity has also provided me with many interesting stories to tell my criminal justice students!

SOURCE: Nancy Oesch, Retired Administrator, Michigan Department of Corrections.

PLANNING IN CRIMINAL JUSTICE

Planning has been defined as "any deliberate effort to increase the proportion of goals attained by increasing awareness and understanding of the factors involved" (Dahl, 1959:340). More simply, planning is a process that precedes decision making, that gives explicit consideration to the future, and that seeks coordination among sets of interrelated decisions or actions (Bryson, 1995; Hudzik and Cordner, 1983). Planning ideally allows the achievement of ends and the making of rational choices among alternative programs (Davidoff and Reiner, 1962). The planning process is the first step in developing and implementing planned change. It is a process of "lining up the ducks" by identifying the immediate and future needs of an agency and the goals that must be met and then devising a systematic way in which to meet these needs and goals. In short, the tasks of planners are identifying agency goals and problems, **forecasting**, and generating and testing alternatives (Hudzik and Cordner, 1983). Each of thcese tasks deserves additional discussion.

Forecasting: Making estimates of future challenges, opportunities, and contingencies, often by projecting past trends forward.

The basic purposes of the agency for rational planning must be reviewed consistently to gain a clear understanding of its mission or goals as well as the values implicit in the agency's purpose. Often, the agency mission may be ignored in favor of day-to-day routines or lost in agency folklore about its social role. Hence, frequent reviews of an organization's purpose can remind administrators of the basic mission and goals and facilitate the promulgation of policies and procedures that are congruent with the agency's basic purpose as well as assist in long-term planning.

The mission of jails, for example, has changed dramatically over the years. Traditionally, the major purpose of prisons and jails was security or to prevent inmates from escaping or rioting. This was seen as contributing to the public safety mission of the criminal justice system. The health, safety, and welfare of inmates were a low-level concern. Although security remains an important function, the health, safety, and welfare of inmates is now equal to the security objective (Schmalleger and Smykla, 2007). Hence, planning for correctional institutions that does not consider the health and welfare of inmates will be, at best, inadequate. Correctional institutions house a growing number of mentally ill inmates, inmates who are HIV positive, inmates with drug addictions, and a growing number of homeless citizens. Professionals in the field report that homeless or poor parolees often violate their parole to return to prison for refuge or needed medical or dental treatment. Corrections systems need to face these realities to understand and redraft their real mission, goals, and objectives before entering into any major planning efforts.

Police agencies often focus on crime fighting as their major or even sole mission and ignore the vast service aspect of policing (Adams, 1971; Mastrofski, 1991). In one recent study, it was discovered that more than 86 percent of performance evaluation criteria in police agencies made no mention of service and less than 8 percent pertained to citizens' assistance (Lilley and Hinduja, 2006a).

Planning that is based on crime-fighting folklore and that excludes crime prevention and the vast array of services provided by police agencies will obviously miss the police system's broader mission. Thus, examining agency goals in the planning process may force agencies to adjust their missions and goals in light of contemporary social demands and expectations rather than simply in conformity with traditional values or agency folklore.

The identification of problems is crucial to planning. Planners who perceive a performance gap need to analyze the root causes of the gap or problem. This process involves looking through a layer of possibilities to extract the probable basic causal factors. For example, we often hear that low morale in a given police agency is causing a low level of productivity. However, morale and productivity are not necessarily causally related (Perrow, 1986). It is more likely that workers with set goals are productive (Hiam, 1999) and will have high morale.

It is most important to locate and examine the basic organizational problems that create both low productivity and low morale. It may be discovered that low levels of productivity and morale both relate to employees' lack of certainty about their role (March and Simon, 1958), which may relate to the agency's failure to identify its goals with clarity. A lack of clarity about the organization's mission and goals will make it difficult for the agency to promulgate policies and procedures and provide training that relates to current constraints on and expectations of its operational personnel (Lilley and Hinduja, 2006b). Police officers are often publicly criticized for their behaviors, and jail personnel are made responsible for inmate deaths through civil litigation.

Forecasting is obviously an important aspect of planning, especially long-term planning. Assumptions about the future are implicit in any decision. However, it is often assumed that the future will replicate the present. Forecasting requires planners and decision makers to project into the future to understand prospective problems and to estimate the impact decisions will have on the agency or its constituents. Predicting crime rates is a common procedure and can be utilized in assessing the future needs of criminal justice agencies. In retrospect, the overcrowding in prisons could have been predicted, and, in fact, some people within the formal political structure did predict overcrowding and attempts to expand the prison system. Again, the impact of deinstitutionalizing the mentally ill has led to an increased number of mentally ill individuals in our nation's prisons and jails, where they are not provided with adequate treatment (Petrich, 1976). It is estimated that we have between 300,000 and 3 million homeless individuals living on the streets and in the parks of our cities. The homeless have become a public nuisance by panhandling, aggressive begging, and the commission of minor crimes (Peak and Glensor, 2004) and, inadvertently, they have become the responsibility of the criminal justice system. Local jails serve as temporary quarters for the homeless and vagrant alcoholics (Stinchcomb, 2005). Systematic and formal forecasting of the impact of deinstitutionalization might have led to a secondary set of decisions and plans to improve the abilities of correctional institutions to treat mentally ill inmates.

Generating and selecting appropriate alternative solutions to problems is another crucial step in planning. Planners must construct a series of possible alternative solutions for the problems that have been identified. These solutions must take into account present and future constraints. Typically, the generation of alternatives begins with past strategies or ideas that seem to fit within the agency's philosophy, structure, knowledge–technology core, or resource limitations. If alternatives generated within these limitations are not deemed satisfactory, more creative or innovative alternatives need to be found (Hudzik and Cordner, 1983). As overcrowding continues to plague prisons and jails, alternative solutions are being sought. Efforts have been made to control the influx of offenders into institutions by creating sentencing guidelines for judges (Kratcoski and Walker, 1978). However, sentencing guidelines with strict sentences have evolved and have, in effect, increased the number of inmates in prisons and worsened the problem. Other efforts include using appearance tickets in lieu of arrests for certain offenses and creating special bail-bond programs for indigent offenders (Harris and Hartland, 1984; Schmalleger and Smykla, 2007).

In spite of these efforts, the problem of overcrowding continues. Hence, alternatives to incarceration are being sought. New forms of community corrections place incarcerated offenders in work-release programs, weekend or day parole, or community centers prior to their eventual release from confinement. Other innovative alternatives have been utilized to address overcrowding, including emergency release (parole consideration for inmates ninety days away from their minimum sentence date); early release of sentenced, nonviolent jail inmates; and court orders that require jails to refuse arrestees in certain crime categories when those jails are overcrowded.

Home confinement and electronic monitoring with computer-linked offender tracking have been used to limit the placement of offenders into jails (Schmalleger and Smykla, 2007; Schmidt, 1989). But such innovative approaches often prove to be politically unpopular. In fact, the governor of Michigan discontinued the use of emergency release in 1986 in reaction to public criticism. Others, however, have emphasized how framing community correctional alternatives as enhancing public safety and crime control efforts is a useful strategy to deflect public criticism (Petersilia, 1993). In law enforcement, an alternative to traditional policing has been the development of Community Oriented Policing and Problem Solving (COPPS). The program remains a critical part of the traditional role of crime fighting, but it also has crime prevention and dealing with community problems as its goals (Peak and Gensor, 2004).

It is important to point out that the application of these alternatives to institutional overcrowding is not necessarily the result of any long-term planning or planned change. Rather, these alternatives were created in reaction to a desperate state of affairs and, in many respects, exemplify the garbage can approach to change. Legitimate planning would have considered the possibility of overcrowding before the fact, and alternatives would have been implemented in time to meet the crisis. Forecasting overcrowding, understanding the reasons overcrowding would occur, and creating alternatives to deal with overcrowding would have been a good example of rational planning. Had the innovative alternatives been implemented, planned change would have occurred.

Purely rational planning may be especially difficult for criminal justice agencies. *Rational planning* requires that an agency's goals are congruent rather than contradictory, are clear and known to agency members or decision makers, and that means–ends relationships are understood (Hudzik and Cordner, 1983). However, goals for criminal justice agencies are often vague and conflicting. Means–ends relationships and methods to achieve agency goals are often unknown or uncertain. Rehabilitation of criminal offenders, for example, can take on several meanings and is but one of many goals of corrections. To the extent that rehabilitation requires a degree of freedom from prison routines for inmates, it may come squarely into conflict with security concerns of the custodial staff. Further, reliable means of achieving some form of long-term behavioral change in offenders do not exist. In fact, empirical evidence to date suggests that most rehabilitation programs have not had any long-term effect on offenders' post-release behavior (Lipton, Martinson, and Wilkes, 1975). At best, therefore, planning for rehabilitation programs is a disjointed, incremental process in which programs may be developed and then tested for acceptability, effectiveness, and unintended consequences (Lindblom, 1959). The planning process has the potential of clarifying goals or at least prioritizing agency objectives. Further, means–ends relationships can be developed through agency research and development efforts.

It is theorized, for example, that prison classification programs can identify inmates who are amenable to particular types of rehabilitation programs (Austin, 1983). Hence, rehabilitation goals and means can be offender specific and designed to take into account the constraints and conflicting goals of the prison system. However, changing an institution's classification system and developing an array of treatment programs that can coexist with security needs will take a great deal of organizational skill and energy beyond the formal planning process. Planning is the initial and perhaps the simplest step in organizational change. The creation of desired planned change throughout an agency may require its members to replace old values, habits, relationships, and routines with a new repertoire of behaviors. New ways of thinking about goals or performing tasks, therefore, will typically meet with resistance. Understanding and overcoming resistance and obstacles to change are, perhaps, the most important and difficult aspects of planned change.

RESISTANCE TO CHANGE

Innovation: Pertaining to change, organizations that value innovation change readily, and organizations that do not value innovation tend to become rigid.

Resistance to change: A response of organizational members and their established structural factors and routines that cause pressure against attempts to create change.

Planning is the technical aspect of planned change. Implementing change is the human and more difficult aspect of planned change. The human side requires that agency members change their work behaviors and possibly their values, depending on the breadth or depth of the prescribed change. Change may also require restructuring of routines, and particular characteristics of **innovations**, such as cost, may create obstacles for their implementation. Hence, a natural **resistance to change** exists in almost all organizations. The prison system in Texas under director George Beto is a good case of concerted resistance to change imposed by federal courts of the time. Beto, for example, launched a judicial counterattack, and used political connections to recruit allies (Ekland-Olson and Martin, 1988). External obstacles to change abound and are often difficult to identify in planning: "Reformers have ignored the surrounding political, social and ideological context in which reforms occur" (Austin and Krisberg, 1981, cited in Doleschal, 1982:137). Obstacles and sources of resistance to change must be identified and eliminated or controlled if planned change is to be successful. If obstacles to change are beyond the control of an agency or its planners, plans may have to be tailored within those constraints.

In this section, we discuss the major sources of resistance to change. Steers (1977) posits the sources of resistance to change are found in the psyche of the organization's members and the structure and management of the organization itself. Personal sources of resistance to change, for example, can include one's fear of his or her loss of status and vested interest in the way things are being done. Members may also fail to see the need for any changes or have not been included in the change or planning process. Organizational sources would include sunk costs in present operations, an agency's reward system, or long-term rituals and beliefs that may have to be changed. Personal and organizational sources that cause resistance to change are discussed in the context of criminal justice agencies in the following sections. Resistance to change may also stem from potential role change, unit boundary changes that cause role conflict, and change of information networks (Greeson and Campbell, 2012).

Personal Sources

Agency employees may resist change for any number of personal reasons. Corrections officers, for example, may resist the use of due process for inmate discipline because it may necessitate a loss of their power and discretion. Corrections officers may also perceive that this loss of power could lead to a dramatic change in their relationships with inmates. From a broad perspective, changing guard–inmate relationships may interfere with the norms of the corrections officers' subculture (Lombardo, 1985; Stinchcomb, 2005). In some cases, the fear of loss of control over the inmate population has led to an actual loss of control, perhaps as a self-fulfilling prophecy. In community corrections, probation officers have resisted utilizing neighborhood-based supervision programs, fearing they would be subject to civil suits for harmful or criminal actions (Drapela and Lutz, 2009).

In the police area, effecting better police–community relations through programming or training officers to interact in new ways with civilians has been resisted by police officers who see the world as divided into "us and them" and regard community relations as an appeasement program that weakens police authority (Skolnick and Bayley, 1986). Personal resistance is especially apparent in areas where community policing or foot patrols are being implemented. Community policing officers who walk the beat are viewed by other officers as "social workers" and are "not real cops" (Trojanowicz and Carter, 1988). Many traditional police officers and administrators view the role of the community police officer as being in conflict with their traditional role.

They also believe that community policing will bring loss of power because it requires police to associate and identify with civilians who have traditionally been viewed as the recipients of coercive control by law enforcement personnel (Mastrofski, 1996; Skolnick and Bayley, 1986). Police officers given a foot patrol assignment must also leave the comfort and security provided by the well-armed patrol car and its communication system. Peak and Glensor (2004) suggest that police agencies are rooted in the paramilitary command style and will attempt to block shifts to community policing. Also, unions opposed to the shift can petition the city council or even use the media to get public support against the move to community policing.

For courts, the establishment of sentencing guidelines also has the potential of taking discretion and power away from judges, prosecutors, and probation officers, all of whom have a vested interest in criminal sentencing (Tonry, 2004). Utilizing court administrators to manage court procedures and case flow has been accepted in principle. However, court administrators deal with judicial personalities and egos that resist administrative control, which is the substance of such programs. Prosecutors may resist the creation of community corrections programs or liberalized bail bond systems, seeing these programs as contrary to their role of protecting the community from criminal offenders. In good conscience, prosecuting attorneys have often expressed the fear that reducing confinement in favor of community programs would cause an increase in crime and delay case processing because offenders on liberalized bail bond programs are likely to fail to appear for their court hearings. This fear of liberalized bond systems, however, has not proven realistic (Vetter and Territo, 1984).

Organizational Sources

An agency's traditional practices, values, structure, or leadership can influence the success or failure of its attempts to implement change. A case study of a local jail illustrates resistance to change as a consequence of organizational climate and major investments (sunk costs) in past decisions and routines. A consent decree —in which the defendant in a civil case agrees to terms set up by the court— promulgated by a federal district court ordered a local jail to modify the existing facility and provide contact visitations and other services to inmates (Schafer, 1986). Immediately following the consent decree, a steering committee, consisting of local jail and criminal justice officials, was formed to plan the change and provide guidance for its implementation. In spite of the decree and the show of good faith signaled by the formation of a steering committee, county governmental officials and the sheriff actively dragged their feet on compliance. Much of the system's energy was focused instead on attempting to circumvent and renegotiate the consent decree. Jail administrators along with the local political leaders created a negative climate within the jail and the community that greatly slowed the process of change, which did not begin until five years after the original consent decree (Schafer, 1986). A current example of organizational resistance to change is apparent in the attempts by local police agencies in a county in the Southeast to standardize communication systems among the county-wide police agencies. The chiefs of the thirty-six agencies, along with the sheriff's department, hoped to implement a new radio system that would have allowed each user to be in contact with multiple individuals simultaneously rather than with one individual per call. The new technology also could be made compatible with state and federal agencies' communication systems. Despite the obvious benefit the new system would have for law enforcement, the county resisted the change to the new system because it had a deep cost sunk in the old system that linked all of the county agencies, such as fire, roads and highways, parks and recreation, and so forth. In short, the change to the new system was seen as excessive by the county government.

An inappropriate reward–punishment system may hamper desirable change. Since the 1970s, attempts have been made to upgrade the quality of corrections officers in local jails. In many jurisdictions, however, corrections officers receive a lower wage than road patrol officers within the same agency, which motivates corrections officers to strive for a transfer to the road patrol. In addition, corrections officers who perform well in jails are typically rewarded by being transferred to road patrol, leaving the less talented or motivated personnel to continue as corrections officers. There are, of course, other advantages to working in a police department rather than in a correctional facility. However, the reward system described here clearly retards the best efforts of jail administrators to upgrade their staff (Kerle, 1998).

Organizations with rigid structures are typically those with well-established traditions, belief systems, routines, and practices, as well as little history of change. Williams (2003) points out that attempts at change in police agencies need to be accompanied by changes in aspects of the department's structure to be successful. Large, powerful organizations that are capable of influencing their environments also typically place more effort into resisting change than into conforming to pressures for change (Scott, 1987). Organizations that readily facilitate change also have several characteristics in common. Besides having a history of change, Burnes and Stalker (1961) and Hage and Aiken (1970) found that change-ready organizations share the following characteristics:

1. High complexity in terms of professional training of organizational members
2. High decentralization of power
3. Low formalization
4. Low stratification in differential distribution of rewards
5. Low emphasis on volume (as opposed to quality) of production
6. Low emphasis on efficiency in cost of production or service
7. High level of job satisfaction among organizational members

Although these characteristics may be antithetical to change resistors, many are also antithetical to criminal justice agencies, which tend to be centralized and highly formalized. Job satisfaction, especially among corrections officers, tends to be low (Toch and Klofas, 1982). Police agencies and often courts tend to emphasize volume, with police agencies often resorting to arrest rates as a benchmark for success and courts placing emphasis on efficient case flow (Grau, 1980).

Organizational change requires altering the organization's routines. Routines develop in all organizations that survive for an extended period of time and provide certainty and purpose to organizational members. Of equal importance is that routines are the skills that govern all aspects of organizations, from formal record keeping and daily work practices to the ongoing truce between management and subordinates. It is management's job to maintain routines (Nelson and Winter, 1982). To the extent that routines are altered, the basic skills of an organization, the guideposts for its members' behavior, are being challenged, and management's role in maintaining routines must be set aside. An organization and its members face uncertainty with the elimination of well-established routines and therefore will resist their elimination.

The criminal justice system has a rich tradition of established routines (Atkins and Pogrebin, 1981), many of which relate to important values in society in general. A proposed change for the criminal justice system—one, for example, that limits police authority—could also be viewed as a threat to law and order, an important belief of the general public and the law enforcement community. Moreover, the routines in community policing are much different from the routines found in traditional policing. Rather than working at a distance from community members while riding in a patrol car, community police officers deal actively with community members and seek their assistance and input.

More specifically, many criminal justice routines are imposed by statute and case law, and subroutines are created within the organization to establish conformity—or the appearance of conformity—to prevailing laws. The court system performs extensive rituals that are considered significant in protecting the rights of defendants. For example, defendants appear in a formal courtroom for sentencing. At a criminal sentencing hearing, the defense attorney pleads for leniency, and the prosecuting attorney may counter by requesting the court to impose a harsh sentence to "protect the public." This process is honored and acted out even though sentencing decisions are typically decided well in advance of the formal hearing. The formal hearing is symbolic of the court's duty to protect the rights of the offender. The suggestion that the formal sentencing hearing be dispensed with in cases where a clear decision has been made to place an offender on probation—a suggestion that would save the court time and expense—has not been well received (Robin, 1975). The routine has historical ritualistic value and is difficult to set aside. A recent change in the judicial system is the co-joining of civil and criminal sentencing for sex offenders (Uggen, Manza, and Thompson, 2006). When sex offenders are released from their criminal sentence, civil courts are being petitioned by the prosecutors' office to civically commit the sex offender to a treatment facility. This serves primarily to extend the time the offender will be incarcerated. However, many states are attempting to build treatment centers for the sex offenders and are being met with severe resistance from the communities in which they plan to locate the centers. Local community members do not want institutions for sex offenders in their backyards.

Large police agencies and correctional systems are organized along bureaucratic lines and are often considered to be paramilitary organizations. They have a clear chain of command and a hierarchy of authority supported with formal rules and regulations. The rigid formality of such agencies requires and creates a set of routines, often seen as a statement of organizational purpose, that are difficult to eliminate or alter; hence, agencies are resistant to change. The extent to which change will be resisted is thus, in part, a function of the rigidity or flexibility of an organization and its members.

Resistance to change is also a function of the magnitude and depth of the change being proposed. A proposed change that focuses on a single aspect of the behavior of a few agency members or on a limited number of procedures that are not frequently used will be met with much less resistance than change in fundamental aspects of an organization. Fundamental change often requires a shift in agency ideologies, a major shift in operations and programming, and a dramatic shift in the role of the line or service delivery personnel (Duffee, 1986; Peak and Glensor, 2004). Fundamental change, therefore, encounters a great deal more resistance than attempts to create circumstantial or procedural change. It is easier to create special units within a police agency to focus on police–community relations or crime prevention than to change the policies and procedures of the entire agency. The practices, behaviors, and attitudes of most agency members do not have to be altered if special functions are assigned to a few members included in the specialized units. Similarly, it is easier to use short-term measures to alleviate overcrowding, such as emergency release procedures (described previously), than to build new correctional facilities or expand the use of community corrections.

A change as fundamental as creating community corrections centers may run into resistance from the public. Organizations whose members are unionized face another potentially powerful constraint on change. Management–labor contracts often call for specific behavior on the part of both management and labor. These agreements reinforce particular routines and make them unalterable for the duration of the contract. Police unions have had a significant impact on policy decisions in many jurisdictions and have eroded the power and discretion of police administrators to make changes (Swanson, Territo, and Taylor, 1997). Corrections officers' unions have also been on the increase across the nation, and they will ultimately have a powerful impact on corrections policies historically reserved for management. When unions and administrators share the same objectives, the union can be a powerful ally in planning and implementing change. If they are not in accord, unions can become a major obstacle to the implementation of planned change. We must consider, however, that unions ideally represent the interests and views of the rank-and-file. If the critical mass of the rank-and-file is opposed to it, a planned change is unlikely to be implemented, regardless of whether or not personnel belong to a union. In this regard, a police agency that wishes to move from traditional policing to community-oriented policing must change basic organizational structures and practices as well as activities of police officers in order to institutionalize the change (Williams, 2003).

Finally, forces in the environment can thwart an organization's attempts at innovation. Successful innovation within an organization is dependent on the positive association between external pressures for change and an internal, perceived need for change (Griener, 1967). Public support is, therefore, important to effect planned change. Conversely, public opposition to change or support for the status quo will hinder major change or change visible to the public. Attempts to establish corrections centers in communities, for example, have typically been vociferously challenged by community members (Smykla, 1981). Innovation in police agencies often faces criticism from community members who have a preference for traditional police operations (Skolnick and Bayley, 1986).

Characteristics of Innovations

Previously in this chapter, we suggested that the nature of innovation itself would affect resistance to change. For example, we stated that fundamental change would require greater effort than altering the procedures of a system because resistance to a fundamental change would be greater than resistance to a circumstantial change. In this section, we discuss the characteristics of innovations that affect resistance to change (see Zaltman, Duncan, and Holbeck, 1973).

Innovations with a higher price tag will be implemented with greater reluctance. An innovation that creates a high return on the initial investment or improves an agency's efficiency will be more attractive than one that does not. For example, the initial cost of implementing substantive and comprehensive rehabilitation programs throughout a corrections system may be extremely high. If, however, recidivism could be cut by such programs, the long-term savings to corrections and the criminal justice system may pay off the initial investment. The establishment of comprehensive rehabilitation programs would also be attractive if they had the potential of making inmate management efficient.

The extent to which organizational change creates risk or uncertainty will also affect the likelihood of innovation. Less complex innovations that are compatible with the existing organizational structure will pose less risk and uncertainty to an agency than incompatible, complex innovations. Also, change that is reversible creates less apprehension and has less potential for causing risk and uncertainty. Moving from well-established, traditional indeterminate sentencing and parole to determinate sentencing will be difficult to reverse (Cullen and Gilbert, 1982). Hence, most states have resisted such a sweeping change.

Plans for innovations that emanate within organizations and are timely have a better opportunity for acceptance than externally imposed or poorly timed innovations. Timeliness suggests that innovative ideas are put forward to meet a need when consensus about the problem and its source exists among organizational members. Timely ideas have a stronger chance of survival in an organization than ideas that must be sold to or forced on agency members. The concept of house arrest or home confinement coupled with the use of electronic monitoring techniques of offenders is timely. First, overcrowding has created a desperate situation. Second, monitored home confinement may be more acceptable than traditional forms of community corrections from the public's point of view because it is more punitive, restrictive, and secure. Finally, the larger the mass of people involved in the change process, the more implementation will be impeded. If innovation is likely to affect the general public or external groups, more individuals will be involved in the process of change than if these groups are not affected. Moving from traditional policing and institutional corrections to community policing and community corrections will ultimately involve community members who will also be part of the decision-making and innovation process.

Overcoming Resistance to Change

As we have seen, resistance to change seems to be a natural characteristic of most organizations and their members. Efforts to create change within an organization require overcoming its natural resistance to assuming a new or modified mission, creating and implementing new goals and procedures, and ultimately altering the arrangement of its activities (Katz and Kahn, 1978). A chief of police or a director of a corrections system cannot simply decree change by issuing a memo or a direct order through the chain of command. Because a degree of alienation exists between administrators and line staff in criminal justice agencies (McCleary, 1978; Stojkovic and Farkas, 2003; Toch, Grant, and Galvin, 1975), it is likely that decrees from administrators to subordinates may increase resistance to change rather than lead to the implementation of innovations. Change ultimately requires a set of strategies for **unfreezing**, changing, and **refreezing** the behavior of an organization's members to overcome resistance to change (Lewin, 1947). Change also requires leadership that understands the threats and opportunities that exist in the political environment.

The responsibility for overcoming resistance to change within an agency typically falls on change agents—usually management and leadership within the organization (Bennis, 1966; Yukl, 2002). The extent to which managers have a commitment to change and are capable of overcoming change-resistant staff is an important determinant of successful implementation of planned change (Bennis, 1966; Skolnick and Bayley, 1986; Sparrow, 1999; Yukl, 2002; Zaltman, Duncan, and Holbeck, 1973). Strategies for change can be aimed at individuals in an agency, the agency's structure and system, the organizational **climate** (the interpersonal style of relationships), or combinations of these targets (Huse, 1975; Steers, 1977). Porter, Lawler, and Hackman (1975) offer three approaches to promote organizational change. First, organizational members must be reoriented through education or training. Second, the structure of the organization—practices, policies and procedures—must be altered. Third, it may be necessary to alter the organization's climate. These strategies are applied to criminal justice agencies in the following sections.

Unfreezing: Pulling apart organizational structures and routines in order to create change—unfreezing the logjam.

Refreezing: Putting an organization back together at a point where desired change is accomplished.

Climate: A good place to work as judged by feelings about relationships, trust, clear reward systems, and/or competent bosses and coworkers.

Individual Change Strategies

The assumption underlying this approach is that individuals or groups of individuals within an agency must modify their attitudes, skills, and behaviors. For example, corrections officers had to relearn certain aspects of their work to implement the due process model of corrections; officers who were accustomed to almost complete discretion in disciplining inmates had to adapt to a process that allowed inmates their "day in court" (*Wolff v. McDonnell, 1974*). Consequently, shifting corrections officers into the new disciplinary process required some resocialization because they no longer had total discretion in disciplining inmates. It also required a new set of skills for officers, who were now required to prepare their cases thoroughly, write a complete report, and testify in a formal hearing. Ideally, corrections officers should have been provided with a clear explanation of their new role, training programs to provide new knowledge, skills commensurate with the new tasks, and programs to help them accept the liberal approach to inmate management (Duffee, 1986). Similarly, law enforcement officers moving from traditional to community-based policing must relearn their roles (Carlson, 2005). In addition, juvenile probation officers need to relearn their roles in the event their systems take on a restorative justice model (Bazemore and Schiff, 2004). If agency managers attempt to impose the new roles upon staff by decree, resistance to the new roles by staff and the change desired by the agencies will be the inevitable reaction.

Structural and Systems Change Strategies

Realizing improved methods may require a rearrangement of an organization's policies, procedures, and reward–punishment system. Before workers' behaviors can change, basic structural aspects of the system that constrains their behaviors must be changed. For example, a major performance gap exists in jails. Typical jail operations are not geared to provide the range of care and services to which jail inmates are presently entitled (see Kalinich and Klofas, 1986). It has been argued that physical structure is a major constraint that limits jail corrections officers from sufficient contact with inmates to provide adequate supervision and management (Nelson, 1986). Therefore, new jail facilities constructed across the nation, known as "new-generation jails," allow corrections officers to readily observe all inmates for whom they are responsible. In addition, policies and procedures congruent with the contemporary mission of jails must be introduced in the new facilities as well as in traditional facilities. Corrections officers are required to take an active role, interacting with inmates and identifying problems before they take on crisis proportions, rather than a passive role of intervening in crises with coercive force (Fischer, 2005; Zupan, 1991).

Similarly, moving from traditional to community policing, controlling sentencing disparity with sentencing guidelines, and expanding the methods and availability of community corrections all require restructuring various aspects of the respective systems. In all the examples, old routines must be set aside in favor of new routines; and old roles of many of the key actors must be set aside for new ones. Because change in routines and roles often curtails the authority and discretion of the actors, they may require some philosophical reorientation. Providing organizational members with training and making structural changes may not, therefore, be sufficient strategies in themselves to bring about desired change. The core of an organization—its culture, behavioral regularities, rituals, norms, dominant values, and climate—may have to be modified to facilitate the adoption of new routines and member role behaviors required to complete the change process (Schein, 2004; Steers, 1977).

Organizational Climate Change Strategies

The assumption behind attacking organizational climate to initiate change is that the behaviors in an organization are largely a product of the organization's culture (Schein, 2004). An organization's routines and its members' work behaviors are constrained by the collective value structure and the emotional and social interaction among its members. An organizational climate also has the following dimensions (Steers, 1977:102):

1. Task structure: the degree to which the methods used to accomplish tasks are spelled out by an organization.

2. Reward–punishment relationship: the degree to which the granting of additional rewards, such as promotions and salary increases, is based on performance and merit instead of other considerations, such as seniority, favoritism, and so forth.

3. Decision centralization: the extent to which important decisions are reserved for top management.

4. Achievement emphasis: members' desire to do a good job and contribute to the performance objectives of the organization.

5. Training and development emphasis: the degree to which an organization tries to support the performance of individuals through appropriate training and development experiences.

6. Security versus risk: the degree to which pressures in an organization lead to feelings of insecurity and anxiety in its members.

7. Openness versus defensiveness: the degree to which people try to cover their mistakes to look good rather than communicate freely and cooperatively.

8. Status and morale: the general feeling among individuals that the organization is a good place in which to work.

9. Recognition and feedback: the degree to which employees know what their supervisors and management think of their work and the degree to which management supports employees.

10. General organizational competence and flexibility: the degree to which an organization knows its goals and pursues them in a flexible and innovative manner. This includes the extent to which it anticipates problems, develops new methods, and develops new skills in members before problems become crises.

The task at hand is to create a climate within an organization that facilitates change in its culture and simultaneously affects traditional agency practices and habits to allow changes in the values, attitudes, and personal interactions of its members. For example, if organizational members tend to be defensive and insecure, they will be reluctant to venture into new roles, even if dictated by management. Returning to our example of new-generation jails, corrections officers are being asked to interact with inmates rather than simply keep them locked up. Moreover, a growing number of inmates are mentally ill and require special treatment (Stinchcomb, 2005). This change poses a new set of risks for corrections officers. If they feel they will be "burned" by the bosses if they make mistakes, they will attempt to delegate many of their responsibilities back up to their supervisors and allow their supervisors to take the blame for mistakes. In effect, they will cling to their old roles and routines. In addition, if communication is poor or decision making is centralized, it will be difficult to gain the active participation of organizational members in the change process (Duffee, 1986; Yukl, 2002). If corrections officers are not involved in the transition from a traditional jail to a new-generation jail, they are not likely to have complete knowledge of the change process or to identify with the purpose of the new system. Conversely, management will have, at best, a contaminated feedback loop from the line staff and will not be able to assess accurately the efficacy of the transition. With a contaminated feedback loop, even incremental change will not be successful (Lindblom, 1959). Creating an organizational climate that is conducive to cooperative change can be an overwhelming task, especially if the change is prompted by extreme conflict within an agency. However, any change within an agency that goes beyond the alteration of simple procedures or consensual change will probably face impediments from the environmental and cultural dimensions of the system. Therefore, steps for dealing with an agency's climate should be considered in the early phases of planned change. In the next section, we examine a series of human relations techniques and training programs for improving an agency's climate that have been utilized with some frequency. The approaches fall loosely into the category of organizational development.

ORGANIZATIONAL DEVELOPMENT

Organizational development (OD): A process, usually led by an outside consultant change agent, that attempts to alter an agency's values, routines, and structures to minimize obstacles to change.

Organizational development (OD) focuses on the environmental influences of an organization. The process attempts to alter simultaneously a system's values, routines, and structures in an attempt to create an atmosphere in which obstacles to change can be identified and minimized (French, 1969). Also, OD is a planned change effort that involves a total system strategy with the goal of making the organization more efficient (Beckhard, 2006). Traditionally, OD programs have been the responsibility of a single change agent, an individual whose sole role is to promote change within a system. The *change agent* may come from within an agency—usually from management—or may be a consultant from outside the agency. Some of the objectives of OD programs (French, 1969:24) are the following:

1. To increase the level of trust and support among organizational members
2. To increase the incidence of confronting problems rather than ignoring them
3. To create an environment where authority is based on expertise as well as title
4. To increase the level of personal satisfaction among organizational members
5. To increase open communication within the organization

OD focuses on agency practices and social–political systems. As a field of social and management science, OD relies on a multidisciplinary approach and draws heavily on psychology, sociology, and anthropology, as well as on information from motivation, personality, and learning theory and on research on group dynamics, leadership, power, and organizational behavior (Hellriegel,

Slocum, and Woodman, 1995). The techniques used in OD are based, in part, on theory Y assumptions that individuals are responsible and can be motivated most readily when they are given responsibility (see Chapter 5 on motivation). Hence, the techniques are aimed at getting organizational members' active contributions in identifying agency problems and developing solutions rather than leaving that task to a few of the management elite.

In effect, OD requires active participation of organizational members in the process of management, and especially change. Criminal justice agencies, however, are typically bureaucratic, paramilitary organizations in which communications flow predominantly downward. Upward communication, while theoretically possible, is severely limited (see Chapter 4 on communication). Lateral communication is contrary to organizational structure and practices. The preponderance of traditional routines precludes the quality and quantity of member participation in organizational decision making that is requisite to the practice of OD. The management style of corrections administrators, for example, is often autocratic and, therefore, does not allow for corrections officers' participation in change (Duffee, 1986; Stojkovic and Farkas, 2003). Thus, utilizing change agents—outside consultants or internal specialists—on an ad hoc basis when change seems to be inevitable will have limited value. The outcome of ad hoc attempts at change within rigid systems that do not routinely facilitate open communication and participation among members will be changes in written policies and procedures that will be passively resisted by the line staff. Planned change is the optimal approach to meeting public demands in an effective way; however, in criminal justice agencies, these plans often produce unintended consequences or fatal remedies. Simply put, the whole notion of planned change is based on a series of attitudes and practices of organizational administrators and managers that run contrary to the traditional attitudes and practices of criminal justice administrators. This concept is discussed briefly in the next section.

UNINTENDED CONSEQUENCES OF CHANGE

The final outcomes of a change effort may be different from those desired by change agents or planners. At times, change may be harmful either because the outcomes are unintended or the remedies are "fatal." Fatal remedies are the result of the natural regressive effects of social engineering (Sieber, 1981). Earlier scholars, including Weber, Marx, and Engels, have written about regressive effects.

More recently, sociologists have studied the fatal remedies of governmental programs (Banfield, 1974). However, the prescriptive literature on organizational change does not address this phenomenon. In brief, Sieber (1981) advises that social interventions fail because policymakers and planners fall into regressive traps for several reasons. (We cover only a few of Sieber's principles here.) First, the multiplicity and priority of goals of target groups may not be understood thoroughly, if they are understood at all. It may be of little value, for example, to provide minimum-wage jobs for teenagers who make large sums of money selling drugs. Interventions also may be exploited by undesirable groups. It was unfortunately common for federal grants provided for improvement of inner cities during the War on Poverty to end up in the pockets of fraudulent contractors.

In addition, goals may be displaced by the bureaucratic emphasis on process rather than outcome. For example, when the Drug Enforcement Administration (DEA), whose mission is to protect the public from health-threatening drugs, sprayed paraquat, a toxic herbicide, on marijuana crops in Mexico in an attempt to eliminate a major supply source, the poisoned crop harmed consumers.

During the 1970s, reformers led the way to decriminalize a number of victimless crimes. When two states abolished public drunkenness laws, arrests for public drunkenness were eliminated and public inebriates were taken off the streets at a high rate by law enforcement officers under the rubric of "protective custody." Gallup, New Mexico, with a population of 18,000, checked drunken persons into its jail for protective custody 26,000 times (Doleschal, 1982:141). The protective custody cases were held in a large drunk tank, void of mattresses and basic amenities. The drunk tank was considered exempt from jail standards because protective custody did not rise to the level of criminal arrest. (See Doleschal, 1982, for an excellent review of criminal justice reforms that not only failed but also exacerbated the problem they were intended to solve.) Unintended consequences can be positive as well as negative. Lambert and Hogan (2010) point out that innovative programs in a prison setting can have the effect of lowering job stress and increasing job satisfaction on the part of correctional officers.

Program evaluation needs may also pervert the desired ends because agencies may evaluate program outcomes that are readily measurable or show favorable results rather than the program's original goals (Hoos, 1983). Providing a program for one group or creating a change may provoke opposing groups into action to thwart interventions and create their own. In California during the early 1970s, for example, liberal groups unhappy with what they considered the unfair, indeterminate sentencing system fought for the establishment of determinate sentences. Liberals viewed this change as a just and humane system and a benefit to offenders and inmates. The inmates' union joined the liberal factions. Once the issue was made public, conservative law-and-order groups also joined the reform movement in favor of the determinate sentencing system. This coalition of groups felt the existing system was excessively lenient and did not provide sufficiently long sentences for inmates. The conservative element of the coalition became more influential than the liberals, and determinate sentences were established. However, the sentence structure implemented provided longer sentences for inmates than the indeterminate system it replaced, contrary to the liberals' original intent (Holt, 1998; Travis, Latessa, and Vito, 1985). Other fatal criminal justice remedies are widespread. The evidence suggests that diversion programs actually widen the criminal justice net instead of diverting offenders (Decker, 1985; Doleschal, 1982). In addition, decriminalization of victimless crimes seems to increase arrest for related misdemeanors; community corrections programs that survive become, in effect, small prisons within the community (Doleschal, 1982). Doleschal argues: "The highly disturbing findings of evaluations show that well-intentioned humanitarian reforms designed to lessen criminal justice penalties either do not achieve their objectives or actually produce consequences opposite [to] those intended" (1982:133).

We frequently fall into the trap of promoting regressive intervention strategies because of our myopic vision. The intended outcomes of "sting" operations, for example, are to reduce crime by enticing thieves into the operation and making quick and solid arrests. However, the "street" vision of police officers allows them to predict the unintended consequences: increases in theft and the crime rate during the tenure of the sting operation. Such anecdotal predictions are often verified in studies of sting operations (Langworthy, 1989). However, policy-level innovators are compelled to overlook such contingencies. Why? The answer lies in traditional management practices, styles, and philosophies that promote and protect the formal structure of the organization, along with its values, operating principles, and assumptions. The successful change agent needs to be free of traditional organizational paradigms to possess the vision to look for future contingencies. The visionary leader needs to have an understanding of the cultural forces within his or her own organization that limit vision (Stojkovic and Farkas, 2003).

ETHICS AND ORGANIZATIONAL CHANGE

Organizational change is a sequence of management decisions and actions, whether planned or inadvertent. Every management decision and action has ethical implications. Change will cause some degree of pain and conflict on the part of an organization's members, clients, and stakeholders. In other words, the professional lives of organizational members, clients, and stakeholders will be affected as a result of change. Ignoring this reality is per se unethical. Even at its best, organizational change may require a rearrangement of functions and stature of its members, clients, and stakeholders, many of whom will become dissatisfied. At its worst, organizational change can be accompanied by ugly political warfare based upon deceit, misinformation, and salacious gossip in which winners and losers are created. Winners are agency members that stand to gain materially, obtain an increase in power and influence, or get a corner office with windows as a result of changes, and losers are those who will have fewer goodies when the dust settles.

To paint a drearier picture, winners are often agency members who are skilled at political wars but who are not necessarily excellent or productive workers. As a result, good employees who foresee they will become losers may take early retirements, change jobs, or continue to accept their paychecks while opting out of the productive process. Moreover, mediocre employees with friends in high places may find rewarding niches in the system within new organizational arrangements as a result of their allegiance (sucking up) to the "friends." At least it will seem that way to members who are losers in the process. In the "worst-case scenario" being painted here, change can be harmful to the organization, its clients, and its stakeholders, at least in the short run, as well as decrease the organization's ability to achieve its goals and objectives. In other words, change, whether imposed by environmental forces or through careful planning, can be harmful if not done within a clear ethical framework.

Organizational leaders—acting as change agents—need to create an ethical framework to guide the organization as they initiate and facilitate the process of change. To accomplish this goal, they have to be aware that the change process is going to affect the lives of individuals within the organization as well as the lives and well-being of external constituents. Moreover, leaders need to place the good of the organization above their eventual benefit. Leaders also need to distinguish between the means to create change and the ends—the desired outcomes. Focusing primarily on the desired outcomes can create a framework of unethical values and practices throughout the change process. Leaders and change agents will be instrumental in their treatment of organizational members, clients, and stakeholders and will treat these significant individuals as objects that need to be manipulated by some method. It is all too easy to resort to deceit, threats, and other forms of manipulation and coercion to accomplish one's goal; therefore, creating an ethical framework for change is to articulate as an operating principle that for the ends to be ethical, the means to the end must also be ethical. This principle should apply to management in general. Organizational leaders and change agents must map out an ethical means to restructure their organization and its practices and culture.

A key step in creating an ethical means is a commitment to honesty and clarity on the part of the change agents or leaders. Unethical leaders like to keep people in the dark or keep them guessing. Withholding information is unfortunately a common temptation for authority figures to use in deceiving and manipulating people. Subordinates can see when this is going on and will become resistant and even combative to the process. A similar temptation is to withhold communication from members that may dissent or ask hard questions but to share information with more compliant members. In effect, an old boys' network is created by doing this and the seeds of political warfare are being sown. In this regard, it is essential to develop clear, routine, and consistent methods to manage the flow of information regarding the substance and process of plans and to preempt rumors and disinformation. The second consideration is to bring as many people as possible into the process. The participation of agency members and others who will be affected by change will provide participants with some degree of confidence in the change process.

A more subtle ethical consideration is how to frame the past and present in discourse regarding the need for change. As discussed earlier, performance gaps, noted failures, and/or public pressure may lead to efforts to bring change to an organization. As a general precept, it is unethical to lay the blame for failure on individuals or groups within the organization. Failure is a systems problem that all organizational members share to some degree. Conversely, ethical rhetoric that accompanies change should honor traditions, past accomplishments, and the organization's contributions to the social good. In this regard, an ethically bound change process will seek ways to compensate losers—individuals who are diminished materially or who lose status or stature as a result of the changes—symbolically or materially.

As a final consideration, organizational leaders will have the opportunity to decide to what extent change will be substantive and address its perceived performance gap, or to what extent things will change just enough to stay the same. Will this change make symbolic adjustments, or will it put up new window dressings to make it appear that things have changed in the hope that pressures for substantial change will decrease? This can be done intentionally or just as a matter of past habits, decisions, and practices. Chappel (2009) suggests that the philosophical acceptance of *community* has spread almost universally. However, there is often a gap between the philosophical acceptance of community policing and the actual practice—allowing some agencies to adopt the pretense of having implemented progressive programs.

IMPLICATIONS FOR CRIMINAL JUSTICE MANAGERS

Managers seek stability, order, and certainty. Planning and budgeting are completed within a context for stability and control. Managers and administrators police the organization's boundaries to keep out disruptive influences and provide the organization with stability. They also enter into calculated exchange relationships with the agency's task environments to acquire resources and support (see Chapter 3). By virtue of their tasks, their view is narrow, and planning serves to solve problems that threaten stability. We know that change comes slowly to public organizations, often at a creeping pace. The early prison reformers would be disappointed to see how little the essence of corrections has changed in over 100 years (Gies, 2004). Change requires leadership and vision coupled with an urgent sense that new paradigms are needed—the set of rules and assumptions that guide us in inputting and processing information and lead us to conclusions, decisions, or understanding. The rules and assumptions of an organization are typically ingrained in the formal and informal structures, routines, and culture, and they often go unchallenged. Developing new paradigms requires recognizing and setting aside the assumptions that dominate the organization. Change is also most likely when internal and external constituents of an agency share the urgency for new ways of doing business. Urgency portrayed as a state of crisis is an even stronger motive for change and can be used by managers to develop internal and external consensus on the need to change (Rochet, Keramidas, and Bout, 2010). Change that is viewed as urgent to external constituents but not urgent to agency managers may lead to external constituents taking steps to correct macro problems. For example, privatization is a response to the growing costs of the justice process. Standards for privatization, for example, have been implemented by legislators to facilitate the transfer of tasks from the public to the private sector (Schloss and Alarid, 2007).

Sparrow (1999) offers an excellent description of the paradigm shift required to move from a traditional police agency to community policing. Table 14.1 provides a succinct summary of the profoundly different assumptions about purpose, process, and relationship with the community that are implied in traditional and community policing, respectively (Sparrow, 1999). The new set of assumptions required to move to a community policing system necessarily affect the organization's structural, human resource, political, and symbolic frames (Bolman and Deal, 2003; Carlson, 2005; also see Peak and Gensor, 2004). This implies that leaders who would be change agents must have an understanding of the four organizational frames and the ability to create strategies to impact each frame. It is doubtful that any one

TABLE 14.1   TRADITIONAL VS. COMMUNITY POLICING: QUESTIONS AND ANSWERS

	Traditional	**Community Policing**
Who are the police?	A government agency is principally responsible for law enforcement.	Police are the public, and the public are the police. The police officers are those who are paid to give full-time attention to the duties of every citizen.
What is the relationship of the police force to other public service departments?	Priorities often conflict.	The police are one department among many responsible for improving the quality of life.
What is the role of the police?	Focusing on solving crimes.	A broader problem-solving approach.
How is police efficiency measured?	By detection and arrest rates.	By the absence of crime and disorder.
What are the highest priorities?	Crimes that are high value (e.g., bank robberies) and those involving violence.	Whatever problems disturb the community the most.
What, specifically, do police deal with?	Incidents.	Citizens' problems and concerns.
What determines the effectiveness of police?	Response times.	Public cooperation.
What view do police take of service calls?	Deal with them only if there is no real police work to do.	Vital function and great opportunity.
What is police professionalism?	Swift, effective response to serious crime.	Keeping close to the community.
What kind of intelligence is most important?	Crime intelligence (study of particular crimes or series of crimes).	Criminal intelligence (information about the activities of individuals or groups).
What is the essential nature of police accountability?	Highly centralized; governed by rules, regulations, and policy directives; accountable to the law.	Emphasis on local accountability to community needs.
What is the role of headquarters?	To provide the necessary rules and policy directives.	To preach organizational values.
What is the role of the press liaison department?	To keep the "heat" off operational officers so they can get on with the job.	To coordinate an essential channel of communication with the community.
How do the police regard prosecutions?	As an important goal.	As one tool among many.

SOURCE: Sparrow, Malcom K., *Perspectives on Policing*. Monograph 9, National Institute of Justice, and the Program in Criminal Justice Policy and Management, John F. Kennedy School of Government, Harvard University, November 1988.

individual will have such a complete knowledge of an organization. However, individuals throughout an organization have knowledge in the various pieces of the puzzle and should be recruited to participate in the leadership and the change process (Cooperrider and Sekera, 2006). Without participation from organizational members, long-term planning will be nothing more than a high-tech exercise, lacking any holistic understanding of the organization.

The importance of leadership and a holistic approach is demonstrated by Skolnick and Bayley (1986), who identify four factors crucial to change and innovation in police agencies attempting to become crime-prevention oriented. First, they cite "the chief's abiding, energetic commitment to the values and implications of a crime-prevention-oriented police department" (1986:220). They argue that the chief must be more than an advocate of new programs; he or she must infuse the entire organization with a sense of purpose that supports the logic of new programs or innovations. In addition, Peak and Glensor (2004) suggest that leadership must create a stimulus for change. The stimulus can be as simple as recognizing an obvious performance gap. They also suggest that change must be logical and defensible to internal and external constituents.

Second, the chief must promote the values and programs he or she is advocating by motivating and even manipulating departmental personnel into accepting those values. A series of tactics used to motivate or manipulate personnel was identified (Skolnick and Bayley, 1986:222–223) and includes influencing younger members, speeding up retirements, and enlisting seasoned officers into the plans.

Third, once a program is established, conscious efforts must be maintained to keep it in place and protect its integrity because the natural tendency for a police agency is to fall back on old routines. Fourth, "innovation is unlikely to happen without public support" (Skolnick and Bayley, 1986:223; see also Chapter 4).

Public support is needed at least to obtain resources for new programs, and it may come in the demand for better services from a criminal justice agency. A critical public can be an opportunity for a change-oriented executive because creating new programs to deliver services to a critical public can garner public support. However, criminal justice agencies have traditionally been insular and often subjected to criticism over spurious, highly visible incidents. The public may also be suspicious of new programs developed by criminal justice agencies. Nonetheless, public support is crucial and can be obtained only when leadership possesses "an abiding, energetic commitment" to change.

Leaders need to develop a high level of sophistication about the organization's political and task environments to be successful change agents. Potential stakeholders, allies, threats, and opportunities must be recognized. Criminal justice officials, for example, see the media as a threat and rarely attempt to cultivate support through the media. Also, criminal justice administrators typically have limited abilities to influence the political system and rarely have lobby groups to support them.

In addition, high-ranking criminal justice administrators are appointed by and work at the will of governors, mayors, and other political bodies. They are not in a position on their own to speak publicly or freely without fear of reprisals. What is needed is the development of coalitions with citizen groups and individuals who can influence the political system. For example, unions, which are usually viewed as a threat, can be utilized as a powerful political arm of an organization.

Administrators may attempt to create change to improve the organizational climate or to increase productivity. Decisions to improve the quality of services require leaders to be responsive to changing demands from their constituencies as well as internal assessments of quality. Ideally, changing conditions, constraints, or demands should be anticipated, and changes made within the agency should be congruent with environmental shifts. If the ideal is not achieved, performance gaps should be recognized and steps taken to close them—which is easier to say than to do. As we have discussed, many of the obstacles to change lie within the traditional folklore, routines, and structure of criminal justice agencies themselves. The rank-and-file become infected with their agency's past, perhaps making them less likely to find change desirable than their bosses, who may develop some degree of environmental sensitivity as a function of their position.

Purposive rather than crescive change in an organization requires a commitment to responsiveness and innovation, at least at the administrative level. Proactive responsiveness requires systematic methods of gathering input from constituents, the work environment, and agency members as well as useful methods of evaluating service delivery and programs. Purposive change also requires that organizational members identify with the goals of the agency and be committed to personal as well as organizational success. This again requires that agency members have an opportunity to participate actively in decisions at every level and, therefore, commit themselves to change. To the extent that criminal justice agencies are paramilitary bureaucracies or are managed from the top down, agency members will be discouraged from any form of participation in planned change. The "view from the street" will never be integrated into planning. Change will not come about through decrees from the top. Updated policy and procedure manuals may do no more than gather dust. Requiring staff to "read and sign" new memoranda will not change their work-related behavior. Ideally, staff must be involved at all levels of the change process. Staff involvement will allow planners to tap staff expertise and improve the likelihood that staff will accept change. Finally, organizational members must have a fairly clear sense of their new roles and possess the knowledge, skills, and tools to carry out the new tasks involved.

In sum, planned change in criminal justice depends on agency administrators' alertness to the need for change and innovation, readiness to set aside traditional management styles, and ability to create a climate within their agencies that fosters communication and criticism from the ranks. Managers and administrators can be important catalysts for the change process (Fernandez and Rainey, 2006). Finally, they must be willing to expend the resources required to implement change. In general, criminal justice managers who would themselves be change agents must free themselves and their personnel from firmly rooted organizational values that contain major obstacles to change.

SUMMARY

Understand why change occurs.

- Changes in agencies take place after external groups—citizens, legislators, clients, and so on—believe that the agency is underperforming. Change can also occur from pressure from internal constituents, such as unions.

Be familiar with the process of organizational change.

- Change can take place by careful planning or because of forces beyond an organization's control. For example, successful civil litigation against an agency can force it to make changes.

Discuss four significant elements of a planned change.

- A set of activities with four significant elements is one that is designed to change individuals, groups, organizational structure, and process.

Understand the basic ingredients of planning in criminal justice.

- Basic ingredients are identifying agency goals and problems, forecasting contingencies, creating alternative opportunities, making clear the means–ends relationship.

Understand personal resistance to change.

- Personal resistance can include fear of loss of income or status, need to protect territory, lack of trust with management or the change agent, or prescribed change, fear of new challenges, uncertainty, and a host of other issues.

Understand organizational resistance to change.

- Organizational traditions, ideology, past practices, deeply sunk costs, change of large magnitude, and ridged organizational culture can all be a part of resistance to change.

Discuss the characteristics of organizations that readily facilitate change.

- The characteristics include compatibility with current organizational structure and ideology, professional organization rather than hierarchical organization, and culture of innovation and creativity.

Describe the processes to overcoming resistance to change.

- The processes are unfreezing, changing, and refreezing organizational members. Management is primarily responsible for change. Strategies are aimed at individuals, structure and systems, organizational climate and culture.

Understand organizational development.

- It is a process that attempts to alter systemic values, routines, and structures to eliminate obstacles to change. Such development also increases the level of trust among members and creates an environment in which authority is based on expertise.

Describe unintended consequences of change.

- The final outcome of change may be different from what was intended. As a result, change often creates a new set of problems.

Be aware of ethical pitfalls resulting from organizational change.

- Change can create winners and losers, harmful organizational politics, and can dishonor past efforts and successes.

Case Study: ORGANIZATIONAL CHANGE: ACCOUNTABILITY VS. CULTURE

John Bolder became the police chief of Largeland City after only fifteen years in the department. The former chief had a practice of assigning new officers to districts that were considered productive and professional to ensure that the new officers would receive a healthy informal socialization. The former chief also transferred his burnout cases and problem officers into districts that were considered unproductive and populated with cynical veteran officers to keep his problem officers away from the new recruits. John Bolder was a criminal justice major; he enjoyed his membership in a math club and was a former club president. During his tenure as a police officer, he consistently received public recognition for his good work. He considered himself a dedicated professional and did not approve of some of his fellow police officers who took a casual approach to their work. He approved of the former chief's practice of assigning new recruits to productive districts. Shortly before being promoted to chief, he completed a master's degree in criminal justice. The course work had been challenging, and he excelled in statistics and research methods. His master's thesis applied statistical measures to evaluate police productivity. He was especially interested in innovative police programs, such as crime mapping and Compstat. He placed high value on community policing and thought that the application of Compstat could be the tool that would bring radical change to his department. He reasoned that Compstat would cause the cream to rise to the top. His highly professional officers would easily conform to the Compstat operating principles of seeking accurate and timely intelligence, setting crime-reduction goals based on the analysis, and creating the rapid development of programs and tactics to meet the goals they had developed as a result of the analysis. Bolder reasoned that giving officers measurable goals and holding them accountable would force a behavioral change in his unproductive officers. This change, he thought, would be supportive of his productive officers and coerce the unproductive officers to get out and do their jobs or suffer embarrassment for their failure to perform.

Chief Bolder required all district commanders to implement Compstat. The district commanders were responsible for reporting the results of their agency in a public forum of fellow commanders, members of the city council, and community leaders. At the meeting, Districts 1, 2, and 3 reported first. These districts were composed of a critical mass of new recruits and highly motivated veterans. The district commanders of 1, 2, and 3 offered detailed and well-organized presentations that showed they had completed a great deal of analysis, set crisp goals, and developed smart strategies to meet the goals. However, all three districts failed to achieve their goals. The chief was

pleased with the excellent presentations but was somewhat disappointed that they did not reach their goals. District 4, composed of officers and a command staff made up of the cynical veterans, was poorly prepared and seemed almost indifferent to the process. The command staff of District 4 tried to answer a barrage of questions from the audience about their poor effort. Many of the questions were personal in nature, which led to an intense shouting match between the command staff and the audience. The District 4 command staff became embarrassed and eventually walked away from the podium.

District 5, which, in the chief's opinion, was his worst district, gave a shabby presentation, but showed that they had set measurable goals and had reached their goals. District 5 indicated that they had a drug-related criminal problem with youth gangs hanging out on street corners in residential communities. After their implementation of a high arrest program in that area, reported crimes went down and residents wrote letters to the district commander praising her for cleaning up their neighborhoods. Chief Bolder was skeptical. The high arrest program was nothing new and had failed to achieve any results in the past. He suspected something was rotten in District 5, as usual.

CASE STUDY QUESTIONS

1. What are some of the possible unintended consequences of assigning a new officer to the districts the chief considered more professional and transferring officers considered to be unproductive into districts reputed to be populated by officers who manifested low levels of productivity over the years?

2. Based on your knowledge of police operations and management, speculate on how District 5 pulled off their success. Something is rotten in District 5. What do you think it is?

3. To what extent do you think the public embarrassment suffered by District 4 will break down their resistance to implementing Compstat? How will their public embarrassment affect the behavior of other districts?

4. Districts 1, 2, and 3 did a thorough job of instituting Compstat, but failed to reach the goals that were set. To what extent will the failure to achieve goals set through the utilization of Compstat affect its long-term implementation? To what extent might Compstat be valuable to the department if goals are not achieved? What advice might Chief Bolder offer to the commanders of Districts 1, 2, and 3 on establishing goals in the future?

Think like an Administrator

You are the warden of a medium security prison. Because of turnover and prior year budget cuts, you do not have a full complement of correctional officers and many positions could be filled with additional funding. Prior year budget cuts also caused you to eliminate your educational program and much of your recreational activities for inmates, such as arts and crafts and physical fitness programs. You do have a full complement of medical staff and mental health staff. Your statistics show that violence between inmates and attacks on guards has increased with the budget reductions and cuts in staff and programming. However, you can't glean from your statistics if the rise in violence is due to the lack of planned activities or the reduction in correctional staff. You suspect that lack of structured activities and programming may be the root cause of any inmate unrest. You believe that boredom is a major stressor. A small budget increase for corrections has been announced, and you have to decide how to allocate the new funds. In the past, filling correctional officer positions has been the fairest order of business with budget increases. However, you have had contact with an accredited educational firm that will provide online courses for your inmates at a very low rate. An initial investment has to be made in a server for the prison and laptop computers to rent to the inmates for them to access the program. The initial investment for the program will take up almost 40 percent of the budget increase. You would like to add the online educational opportunities for inmates in spite of the initial cost involved. You decide to form a committee to consider your plan on allocating the budget increases.

1. Who would you appoint to the committee? Why?
2. How would you structure the committee's agenda?
3. What issues/questions would you give the committee to consider?
4. You believe that the increase in violence is due primarily to lack of structured activity and inmate programs. What is the logic of the argument? Is there any research that would support this argument?
5. Would you frame the online education program as a major change or just a minor shift to one that keeps the system up with current technology? What are the advantages and disadvantages of framing the change as major or minor?
6. What obstacles will you face in implementing the online educational program in your prison?
7. Develop and then describe strategies to overcome resistance to change.
8. Identify the internal and external constitutions that will have a stake in implementing the educational program.
9. Correctional officers are notoriously cynical. How would you sell the educational program to the officers?
10. By what metric will you know that the new educational program has been implemented as planned?

FOR DISCUSSION

1. To what extent does an agency's reliance on its folklore to enhance its self-image impede planned change? Police agencies, for example, may see themselves as fighting a war on crime, or corrections administrators may see the primary role of their institutions as rehabilitation.

2. A growing number of entry-level criminal justice practitioners have college degrees. Will the advanced education of these practitioners create greater or less resistance to change from within criminal justice organizations?

3. What must a corrections administrator consider in deciding whether to protect the agency's boundaries or succumb to pressure for change?

4. Define a criminal justice agency problem with which you are familiar and understand in some depth. Discuss why the problem exists, develop alternative solutions, decide which solution is the most feasible, and, finally, consider what negative or unintended consequences might result from implementing your selected alternative solution.

5. To what extent does the classic paramilitary structure of police and corrections organizations create a climate that is not conducive to change?

FOR FURTHER READING

Duffee, D. *Correctional Management: Change and Control in Correctional Organizations.* Prospect Heights, IL: Waveland, 1986.

Hudzik, J., and Cordner, G. *Planning in Criminal Justice Organizations and Systems.* New York: Macmillan, 1983.

Muraskin, R., and Roberts, R. R. *Visions for Change: Crime and Justice in the Twenty-First Century.* 4th ed. Upper Saddle River, NJ: Prentice-Hall, 2005.

Peak, K. J., and Glensor, R. W. *Community Policing and Problem Solving: Strategies and Practice.* 4th ed. Upper Saddle River, NJ: Prentice-Hall, 2004.

Sieber, S. *Fatal Remedies: The Ironies of Social Intervention.* New York: Plenum, 1981.

Skolnick, J. H., and Bayley, D. H. *The New Blue Line: Police Innovation in Six American Cities.* New York: Free Press, 1986. Stojkovic, S., and Farkas, M. A. *Correctional Leadership: A Cultural Perspective.* Belmont, CA: Wadsworth Press, 2003.

Yukl, G. *Leadership in Organizations.* Upper Saddle River, NJ: Prentice-Hall, 2002.

CHAPTER 15

Research in Criminal Justice Organizations

449

LEARNING OBJECTIVES

After reading this chapter, the students will have achieved the following objectives:

- Know the difference between "basic research" and "applied research".

- Understand the ways knowledge is utilized by criminal justice organizations.

- Describe the nature of social science research and knowledge utilization.

- Describe the limitations of data within criminal justice organizations.

- Define "in-house research" and how it can be useful to criminal justice organizations.

- Know the various ways of conceptualizing and applying knowledge.

VIGNETTE: PROJECT DARE AND RESEARCH

One of the most popular programs ever initiated within police organizations has been the Drug Abuse Resistance Education (DARE) program. This effort was heralded by supporters and police departments as an effective way for local schools to reduce the incidence of illegal drug usage among young people. Since its inception in 1983 in Los Angeles, thousands of DARE programs have been implemented across the country aimed at addressing drug usage among the young. For some, the DARE program became a blessing and a response to a presumed drug epidemic among schoolchildren. For others, DARE represented another example where aspiration never matched reality. In fact, the numerous research studies that have evaluated the DARE initiative over the past fifteen years have generally come up with the same conclusion: It does not reduce drug usage among the young, and, in some cases, the program actually increases usage of illegal drugs by youth (Rosenbaum, 2007). So, why does it still exist as a popular drug abuse program within police departments?

The DARE program and the evaluation of it actually reveal some interesting and important issues about the use of research by criminal practitioners. Berman and Fox (2010) suggest that the goal of DARE to reduce illegal drug usage among young people did not fare well when evaluated using rigorous research designs. Most academic researchers simply dismissed DARE as a misguided effort that had little or no credibility. For police professionals committed to the DARE program, the research results did not matter. For some vocal supporters, DARE was a good program, no matter what the research indicated. The scale and scope of the DARE program was enormous: by the early 1990s, the program was in 60 percent of all school districts across the country and reached over 5 million students, even though the scientific research regarding DARE's effectiveness was mounting (Berman and Fox, 2010).

So why did DARE continue to exist in light of significant controversy regarding its effectiveness? Berman and Fox (2010) note that for local communities, DARE was more than just a drug-reduction program for youth. On another level, DARE served many important functions for communities that oftentimes were lost in the evaluations. The DARE program provided an opportunity to address other concerns of communities and their schools. Parental involvement, for example, has always been a key variable to successful schools. The DARE program, in some communities, fostered greater parental involvement in the school, although focused on the issue of illegal drug usage among students. The presence of parents in schools provided other benefits to students, such as better attendance, more involvement in school programming, and, for some, better school performance. The DARE program was not created with these ambitions in mind, but it had these effects in some communities. Similarly, for police organizations, the DARE program provided benefits as well: increased morale and satisfaction among DARE officers and greater awareness of the difficulties that students face.

Berman and Fox (2010) note that if DARE were to be evaluated solely on its drug-reduction effectiveness among the nation's youth, it would be an abysmal failure, but DARE had many more benefits than originally understood, and if those outcomes were used to evaluate DARE's effectiveness, then we might say it was a very effective program.

So, what is your outcome variable? As we suggested in Chapter 13, organizational effectiveness is a tricky subject. The same is true for applying research findings regarding criminal justice efforts. As you read the chapter, remember to consider how research can be understood and used by criminal justice administrators. It is not that criminal justice research is always right; criminal justice research may be valuable, but it also has limitations in the contexts of criminal justice organizations.

To today's students of management in criminal justice, the 1967 President's Commission on Law Enforcement and the Administration of Justice may seem to deserve little more than a historical footnote. But the commission's contributions to contemporary criminal justice have been far greater than such a brief mention would suggest. And its projections for the field in the year 2000 were even grander. Emphasizing that criminal justice was best thought of as a system rather than disconnected agencies and organizations, the commission envisioned a system governed by a process of rational planning. Although the commission found little empirical research to guide its recommendations at the time, research was to play a central role in the future. In the commission's vision, empirical research "would provide a powerful force for change in the field of criminal justice" (President's Commission on Law Enforcement and the Administration of Justice, 1967: 203).

Historically, research has also had many other champions who might have been expected to influence the management of criminal justice. From Frederick Taylor, who sought statistical definitions of a good day's work, through Kurt Lewin, whose "action research model" was driven by the dictum, "Research that produces nothing but books will not suffice" (1947:203), generations of management models in business and industry have regarded the collection and analysis of data as critical. In today's widespread "quality" movement in industry, research plays a central role in the management process.

In this chapter, we examine the role of research in criminal justice organizations. We begin by considering the impact of social science research of the kind envisioned thirty years ago by the President's Commission. We then look more closely at the nature of research in the organizational context, considering such varied types as basic, applied, evaluation, and action research.

"KNOWLEDGE FOR WHAT?"

In a classic work published in 1939, Robert Lynd asked the question: "Knowledge for what?" in considering the role of social sciences in American culture. The debate over the appropriate relationship between social science research and public policy continues today (see Postman, 1992).

One distinction relevant to that debate can be made between basic and applied research. **Basic research** seeks to understand fundamental issues of process and structure in ways that may not immediately be useful to practitioners. In education, for example, basic research has examined such issues as the process of learning or the developmental stages through which children pass (see Miller, 1986). In criminal justice, basic research examines the causes of crime, the nature of social control, and the social structure of correctional institutions. The primary purpose of **applied research**, in contrast, is to develop knowledge that is directly useful to practitioners. In education, that has included testing the effectiveness of various educational methods or programs and gathering other data that can be of use to decision makers.

The debate over the relative value of basic and applied research in the social sciences centers on several issues. Some authors have argued that basic research is more important than applied research because it influences practitioners' fundamental understanding and views of reality and, therefore, influences practice in the long term; they also point out that there is little evidence suggesting that applied research has significantly influenced practice. Others contend that basic research produces axioms that are too general to be useful and are sometimes even trivial. Proponents of applied research argue that methodologically sound studies, particularly studies that evaluate current practices, can have a significant impact. Still others argue that a respect for both applied and basic research is the best way to advance useful knowledge (Miller, 1986).

Some researchers and managers have also envisioned a different relationship between research and practice. Although they insist that useful research should not compromise methodological soundness, they also note the importance of a team approach. Managers and, ultimately, frontline workers must appreciate the value of research, and social scientists must be able to respond to the needs of practitioners. They argue that working together emphasizes both process and product and is most likely to produce useful knowledge.

For many researchers, criminal justice is an applied field in which studies should be designed in a way to influence practice. There are certainly many

Basic research: To understand fundamental process and structure in ways that may not immediately be useful to practitioners.

Applied research: To develop knowledge that is useful to criminal justice practitioners and addresses specific issues and problems.

examples of sound and significant applied research in this field, and some of the work has involved strong partnerships between researchers and practitioners. For example, scholars such as James Fyfe and Lawrence Sherman have conducted research that has been influential in policing; Todd Clear has completed valuable research in probation and parole supervision; and Hans Toch and James Jacobs have done important research in the field of corrections.

Despite these examples, however, it is widely acknowledged that the practice of criminal justice has not been directly affected by social science research to the degree the President's Commission predicted. And this problem is not limited to criminal justice. In reviews of the utilization of research findings in public policy, the general conclusion has been that academic research has had relatively little influence on policy decisions (see Lester, 1993), at least in the short run. On the other hand, the evidence is not universally negative. In fact, Weiss (1987) reported that although only a small percentage of specific recommendations of research are followed, a much larger percentage are used to influence how policy makers think about issues.

One thing is clear: Although practitioners often report that greater exposure to social science research would be helpful and researchers report an interest in producing studies that will be used in policy discussions, the link between these interests has often not been successful. In fact, an entire field of study, known as dissemination and utilization of knowledge (Havelock, 1979), has developed to help understand and improve this process. These interests are also being reflected more directly in criminal justice. The National Institute of Justice (NIJ) (1995), the agency that funds the majority of government-supported research on crime and criminal justice, has begun emphasizing the importance of partnerships between academics and criminal justice agencies. A great example of a significant collaboration between researchers and practitioners has been the creation of the Community Oriented Policing Services (COPS) in the Department of Justice (U.S. Department of Justice, 2001). The COPS office was specifically created to work through issues of applying the principles of community policing to police organizations using research as the basis for decision making.

CRIMINAL JUSTICE ORGANIZATIONS AND KNOWLEDGE UTILIZATION

One example of efforts to understand knowledge utilization is provided by Rick Lovell (1988), who examined the use of research in a state corrections department. When Lovell interviewed top administrators, including research staff, to see how research information was used in the agency, he found little "instrumental" use of research data—that is, studies seldom directly influenced decision making. **Symbolic use**, or the use of research findings as justification of budgets, for example, was a more common practice. More common, although still fairly infrequent, were claims of **conceptual use** of research. In those cases, managers claimed to have been informed or enlightened by research but cited no specific use of findings in decision making.

Lovell also found that certain characteristics of the organization and its management influenced how information was used. The absence of any coordination of research utilization efforts combined with the functional division of the

Symbolic usage: Use of research to justify a specific decision, such as a budget.

Conceptual usage: Data used to enlighten and inform, yet not used in decision making.

organization to limit use of research information. Subunits were left to solve problems on their own, with no expectation that research would be a necessary part of that process. Furthermore, management was seen as crisis oriented and the solution of immediate problems was seen as precluding the examination and use of research information. Research was perceived as a luxury the organization didn't have time for.

Other studies have also shown that organizational structure and management influence the use of research in organizations. A study of social work practice in schools (Chavkin, 1986), for example, found that formalization and centralization affected the likelihood that some research findings would influence practice. Specifically, the authors examined the implementation of research-based recommendations that social workers change their activities from traditional casework management to organizational and community change activities. The more that social workers' tasks were governed by formal rules and the more decision-making power was centralized in the head of the organization, the less likely research findings were to be implemented. In schools with fewer rules and less central control, social workers were better able to utilize research findings to change their activities.

In his corrections study, Lovell also described another reason that research findings may not influence practice in some organizations. Police departments, courts, and corrections agencies all exist in highly political environments. At the upper levels of organization management in those environments, many questions of policy are strongly tied to questions of value and preference. No matter how defensible a practice may be on research grounds, no one can afford to be seen as insensitive to community standards—whether that means being seen as soft on crime or as excessive in the use of force or other forms of social control. Facts may play a secondary role when decisions are driven by such political considerations.

THE RESEARCHER AND KNOWLEDGE UTILIZATION

There is also another side to understanding the utilization of research in public policy. Although we have considered organizational impediments to the use of research, researchers can also contribute to problems in the research–practice relationship. One reason researchers and practitioners may see the world differently is that, in fact, they see different worlds. Many practitioners may never be exposed to available research at all. Lovell, for example, found that although corrections managers had access to research in journals, magazines, and other publications, that information was not coordinated or organized in any systematic and accessible way. The most important source of information for managers appeared to be the word of trusted colleagues or staff members.

Meanwhile, the common method of dissemination of the results of social science research in criminal justice and other fields is still through the specialized journal literature of the field. There, in the language of their disciplines and in the conventions of scientific research, academics communicate, largely with one another. The writing style and narrow dissemination of academic research have been identified as major reasons that some administrators report that research findings are of little use in their decision-making process (Light and Newman, 1992). Decision makers in organizations may have little time or ability to digest research findings directly but may instead rely on people with whom they have direct relationships.

There have been significant efforts in recent years to improve the dissemination of research findings and, in the process, to improve the relationship between researchers and practitioners. A program for police executives held regular sessions at Harvard University, for example, in which practitioners and researchers gathered regularly over several years to review research and practice in the area of community policing. The National Institute of Corrections has successfully used academics and practitioners in providing technical assistance for prisons and jails. The National Council on Crime and Delinquency (NCCD) has also formed effective relationships between researchers and practitioners as states have struggled to find ways to project prison population growth and address crowding.

These examples go beyond simply addressing problems of dissemination and reveal a second common problem: that of mutual understanding. Academic researchers and practitioners may have different views on the value of data. Expertise in methodology and statistics gives researchers confidence that conclusions based on the analysis of data are technically sound and rational; the better the methodology, the greater confidence they have in their conclusions. For practitioners, however, additional expectations may need to be met.

Practitioners must be convinced first of all that research findings are relevant to the problems they face. National studies or research done in other jurisdictions may seem too distant to them, despite the soundness of the methods. Furthermore, because even the best studies must acknowledge their limitations, policy makers may be hesitant to accept their conclusions. Practitioners may be far less comfortable than academics with notions of probability, confidence levels, and statistical significance. Thus, academics need to do a better job communicating the meaning and value of such ideas.

Another factor enters into the sometimes-different views of practitioners and researchers: Practitioners and researchers may emphasize different aspects of data. Researchers are trained to value what is typical or average; mean, median, and mode—measures of central tendency—are their bread and butter. When the strength of relationships is considered, the unusual case may be seen as an outlier and may sometimes even be excluded from correlation or regression studies, but it is always denigrated for its atypical character.

For the practitioner, however, it is the outlier rather than the typical case that often demands attention. Researchers may be surprised to find administrators who are sometimes wildly inaccurate in their estimates of some data. Parole board members may overestimate recidivism; some police, prosecutors, and judges may know little of crime rates or actual time spent in prison for average inmates. But they will all know the details of the extreme outliers. Those are the unusual but sensational cases that shape public sentiment. Their recidivism ends furlough programs, closes halfway houses, or leads to defeat in bids for reelection. In the language of the statistician, central tendency may be the focus of researchers, but variance will always be a concern for the practitioner.

Researchers must come to appreciate that the outlier is more than a statistical anomaly in the real world. And practitioners must appreciate that the unusual case cannot be allowed to obscure our understanding of the ordinary. Like technical issues of probability and significance, these issues also may best be addressed through closer working relationships.

THE NATURE OF SOCIAL SCIENCE RESEARCH
AND KNOWLEDGE UTILIZATION

A still more basic problem has been raised by some academics, who question whether social science research has reached a level of sophistication sufficient to merit influencing public policy. Elliot (1990) responded to a call for greater influence (see Petersilia, 1993) by sounding a note of caution. He argued that criminologists should be more hesitant to offer advice to policy makers. Although experimental design research of the highest quality has become more common, Elliot notes that such studies are still few in number and that little data on criminal justice have been collected over a long enough period of time to ensure confident conclusions.

One example of research that Elliot suggests should temper academics' enthusiasm for influencing policy is the studies of police response to domestic violence. The Minneapolis domestic violence experiment (see Sherman and Cohn, 1989) was a well-designed and well-executed study in which responses to domestic violence calls were randomly assigned to responses of arrest and non-arrest with counseling, respectively. The research demonstrated that arresting suspects of domestic violence could reduce recidivism, as measured in repeated police calls to the same address. Those conclusions were regarded as support for a movement reflected in state statutes and departmental policy calling for mandatory arrest when there was evidence of any injury or physical confrontation in domestic violence calls.

Although mandatory arrest policies have been widely adopted, even the authors of the research later cautioned policy makers about moving too quickly to implement policy based on their findings. In the meantime, other research failed to replicate the Minneapolis findings. Replication, or retesting experiments in different settings and at different times to see if the same or similar results are found, should be a standard research procedure. In this case, the Minneapolis findings were not only not replicated in other cities, but also there was some support for the opposite conclusion. Some evidence, for example, suggested that social class makes a difference; arrests in middle- and upper-class cases could be successful, but in lower- and working-class families, arrests could actually increase the chances of future violence in the home.

The Minneapolis example raises important questions about the relationship between research and public policy. Should the initial findings have been released and promoted before they had been subjected to the replication test? If not, at what point and how do we judge the readiness of research to influence policy? How many replications are sufficient? One answer, of course, is that as long as the research design is sound and appropriate limitations are discussed, the release and use of research is appropriate. The fact that future research may alter findings is simply part of the process of scientific exploration.

The experience with the Minneapolis research, however, suggests that even that answer may be insufficient. One reason the original research may have been so influential was that it supported policies that were already favored for other reasons. Many victims' advocates and feminists had supported policies of arrest because these policies were seen as fair and just. It is reasonable to wonder how widely implemented the research would have been if its original findings did not support arrest decisions. A hint may lie in the fact that the revised findings have not reversed the course of public policy.

The domestic violence studies raise one additional issue about the relationship between research and policy. The original finding—that arrest worked—was regarded as an unambiguous conclusion for policy makers to act on. But as the replication attempts showed, research does not always yield such tidy findings. What, for example, could be the policy implications of findings that arrests may reduce violence in middle-class households but increase it in others? Wouldn't a policy that overtly treated people differently based on their social class conflict with other values? Although the effectiveness of certain policies may be a comfortable subject for researchers to address, other problems are not solved by increasing methodological rigor.

Domestic violence research and policy provide one illustration of the potential complexity of the research–practice relationship. Although it may seem straightforward to many that objective analysis of data should guide public policy, the situation is much less clear when we examine specific issues. That lack of clarity suggests that research can be, and perhaps should be, only one of a variety of factors considered in policy making and in the decisions of practitioners. Research, then, can contribute to policy but is not likely to be the only, or even the primary, basis for it.

Although domestic violence research provided some interesting findings relevant to both theory and practice, there are also examples of where research should be done and it is not. The most telling example of this is in the programmatic impact of three initiatives touted as stellar examples of criminal justice successes. They are the Ceasefire, Compstat, and Exile projects. Each initiative made bold claims, addressing the problem of homicide with innovative approaches and aggressive police practices. Each program operated during the 1990s and was credited with leading toward the significant reduction in homicides in three cities: Boston, New York, and Richmond, Virginia. In New York, for example, Compstat was credited with assisting police in reducing the homicide rate from 27 per 100,000 in 1990 to 8 per 100,000 in 2000 (Rosenfeld, Fornango, and Baumer 2005). In the midst of all the hype and self-congratulation among police officials, there was never a systematic evaluation of how significant these programs actually were in the reduction of homicides.

Rosenfeld, Fornango, and Balmer (2005) applied advanced statistical analyses to data from the decade of the 1990s and from the ninety-five largest cities in the country and controlled for conditions known to be associated with violent crime rates. Their assessment of the data offers a more sobering portrayal of the impact of Ceasefire, Compstat, and Exile. With project Compstat in New York, the researchers found that the overall reduction in homicide did not differ significantly from those of other large cities during the same period; with project Ceasefire in Boston, the drop was significant but the small number of incidents precluded any definitive statement on the impact of the program on homicide rates; and finally, there was a program effect found in Richmond with project Exile, but the total effect was small.

This research highlights the importance of holding criminal justice officials accountable when bold claims are made regarding program effects, and, as noted by the researchers, this research should serve as a departure point for researchers working in tandem with practitioners to come up with common evaluation criteria when assessing program effects and multiple interventions. This same thought can be applied to many other areas of interest in the criminal justice system, such as parole reentry efforts and prison-based rehabilitation programming.

This conclusion does not suggest an inferior role for research in the public policy or administrative process. Quite the opposite is true. A major consequence of taking research seriously is that doing so opens up the policy process for critical examination. Data take policy out of the realm of simple preferences or untested assumptions. A commitment to research is a commitment to defending policy choices as rational. Research may not be the only rational influence in decision making, but taking it seriously means that other influences should be subjected to the same scrutiny as the research findings.

These issues are typically not covered in undergraduate or graduate research courses. Instead, researchers' training may lead them to expect that quality research will drive rational policy choices; that research will have an authoritative role. They may expect their work to direct, rather than simply influence, decision making. These misunderstandings of the policy-making process can sometimes be at the heart of researchers' complaints that even their best efforts are not directly used by policy makers. Similar misunderstandings may also lead researchers to underestimate the long-term and indirect effects of their work.

DATA AND THE UTILIZATION OF KNOWLEDGE

We have examined the potential for barriers to applying knowledge in the context of organizations, researchers, and the research process. Another obstacle may arise from the nature of the data themselves.

Uniform Crime Reports:
Official measures of crime; highly unreliable for research purposes.

When the 1967 President's Commission made its recommendations, the **Uniform Crime Reports (UCR)** provided the only major source of information on crime, and there was skepticism about the accuracy of those reports. Since then, the UCR have improved, and an incident-based reporting system is being implemented that will provide even more valuable data. Other sources of data have also been developed, including the National Crime Victims Survey and surveys of jail and prison inmates.

Although these data may be useful for some research purposes, such as describing national trends, they are often much less useful for management purposes. Surveys that use national sampling frames and scientific methods do not often permit comparisons at the local level. Even the UCR, which record all reported crime, may be of limited use. The aggregation or combination of data at the national, statewide, and even city level will mask great differences within the jurisdiction. Furthermore, crime and other rates depend on population estimates for their accuracy, and such estimates are less accurate for local levels. The irony is that, although there is some reason for confidence in some of the measures used in criminal justice research, those measures are the least reliable at the local level, and that is where data can be the most influential in the decision-making and management processes.

Developing useful and reliable data has been a particular concern in the area of drug policy. There, too, national surveys of drug use can be informative but provide little data to direct drug treatment or intervention at the local level. Reuter (1993) has described the problems with estimates of the prevalence of drug use as well as measures of expenditures on drugs. These measures should be important for drug policy but remain little used because the estimates often suffer from a perceived lack of credibility (in the case of self-reported drug use) and because the politics of drug policy has not placed a premium on the use of data. Reuter also points out that although prevalence estimates are the cheapest and easiest at the national level, local estimates remain the most useful. The high cost of accurate local-level data, however, may mean that they are little used in the policy process.

It is critical, then, that data be valid and reliable if it is to be part of the decision-making or policy-making process. But validity and reliability must be considered in the context of the decisions being made. And because most criminal justice services are provided at the local level, that is the level at which we need accurate data. That is also why, as we shall discuss later, some researchers have placed a high priority on involving consumers of research in the development of the measures and methods they use.

IN-HOUSE RESEARCH

In-house research refers to the development of the capacity within organizations to address their own data and research needs. This capacity is often provided through separate units or research offices within the organizations. Frederick Taylor's development of a managerial class trained in time and motion studies was an early example of a manager's interest in increasing the research capacity of his organization. Now research offices report directly to the highest executives in most large companies and many public organizations.

In-house research: The development of organizational capacity to gather data and conduct research.

In policing, crime analysis units track crime trends and evaluate policy choices. In courts, sophisticated management of information systems has been developed to track cases and control backlogs. In corrections, in-house research units monitor objective classification systems, track population movement and disciplinary procedures, and, in some cases, regularly measure the social climate of institutions.

There is great potential for in-house research efforts to overcome some of the problems discussed here. In-house research units can establish credibility and gain the support of managers to overcome organizational resistance to research. They can also integrate researchers into the fabric of organizations, thus overcoming the limitations associated with outside researchers and the research process. The potential strength of in-house research is found in the potential for close partnerships between managers and researchers. That is the relationship described by Toch and Grant (1982) in their review of in-house research at General Motors under manager Howard Carlson. Under Carlson, the role of researchers was to help solve problems as they affected the line organizations. That meant that researchers could not be isolated in their offices in front of their computers but instead had to work with frontline staff in defining problems appropriately, collecting and analyzing the necessary data, and helping staff respond to the results of analyses.

The "quality" movement in industry today emphasizes the importance of in-house research. Although he disliked the term, W. Edwards Deming has been seen as the founder of **total quality management (TQM)**. He taught statistically based quality-control measures in Japanese industries before leading the quality movement in this country in the 1980s and early 1990s. Deming's vision of management, however, went well beyond statistics and technical methods. He emphasized the need for organizations to develop the capacity for problem solving (Deming, 1986).

Because knowledge is a key component of that capacity, total quality management has emphasized the knowledge-building process. The heart of that process has been reliance on data-based analysis and teamwork that brings managers, workers, and researchers together to define and solve problems. Total quality management with an emphasis on customer orientation, research, and participation has been a significant movement in major companies, including AT&T, Kodak, and many others.

As with many innovations that take hold in the private sector, public organizations have also begun to utilize TQM principles. Although there is room for debate about the precise definition of customer and the fit between TQM in the private and public sectors may not be perfect, TQM has had some success in criminal justice management. In Monroe County, New York, the county executive hired a TQM manager out of retirement from a major company to apply the TQM principles to local government. As in many counties, there was strong political pressure to build an addition to the jail. The TQM consultant, along with the director of public safety, assembled a team of managers and staff from across the criminal justice system. The judges, police chiefs, prosecutors, and defense attorneys oversaw the collection and analysis of data on jail population.

Total quality management:
Developing the capacity to solve problems in organizations through the active involvement of management and the use of statistics and technical methods; collaborative responses to specific problems or issues.

They discovered that the jail was filled with people detained for minor offenses, almost all of whom would be released from jail in a short time anyway. (They even found that misdemeanor suspects were staying in jail longer than their felony suspect counterparts!) In their report (Monroe County, New York, 1994), the team noted, "This data clearly shows that a system processing problem exists in Monroe County.... Based on an extensive review of the available data, the Team came to the conclusion that jail expansion was not an appropriate response to the current jail overcrowding problem."

The most interesting point of this experience is that many members of the team had worked together for years in an ineffective attempt to coordinate efforts in the local criminal justice system. The TQM requirement—that the team respond to the data—seemed to make an important difference. The team now faces new challenges, however. The resignation of the county executive and a subsequent election have once again put jail expansion on the agenda. And the new executive is less enamored of TQM methods or of research in general.

If those TQM efforts hold and the process of considering data continues over time, it will be a model of rational planning. There are also other examples of successful in-house research efforts. For many years into the 1980s, innovative and important research was done through the research division of the California Youth Authority. The research office of the New York State Department of Mental Hygiene conducted important studies of mental illness and crime. Today, however, these studies are perhaps best seen as examples of successful efforts by dedicated and creative researchers and research-oriented managers and not necessarily of institutionalized practices.

Significant criticism has also been directed against in-house research efforts. Sometimes those critics have highlighted the tendency of in-house research to amount to little more than counting and accounting procedures. Police department research units may be consumed by the process of counting reported crimes or recording the characteristics of persons arrested. In corrections, what passes for research may simply be tracking prisoners throughout the prisons and logging levels of education or mental health histories. In many agencies, a primary function of research may be to justify program budgets.

One study provides insight into the circumstances under which in-house research may have little impact on management in criminal justice organizations. Lovell and Kalinich (1992) examined the role and potential for in-house research in a large nonprofit organization that provided a variety of criminal justice services, including diversion and treatment programs. Researchers, administrators, and program managers all indicated that there was minimal use of research despite the existence of a separate research office staffed by competent researchers.

A variety of factors contributed to the lack of use of research in this organization. Chief among them was the ambiguous role of the research department despite its high level of activity. Top administrators had failed to clarify the research role to program managers, who often saw potential conflict between research findings and their own expertise. For their part, the researchers tended to claim credibility based on technical expertise rather than on position and influence in the organization.

Clearly, problems in the research–practice relationship can persist when the research function is moved in-house. But there are also lessons to be taken from the experience of others. Administrative support for the research function is critical. If top administrators do not have a clear role for their research office, managers underneath them may view research as irrelevant or perhaps even as conflicting with their own expertise. Researchers must also strive for fuller integration into the organization; they must actively seek an integral role in the main functions of the organization. To stand aside, aloof but ready to offer expertise to the trenches, is a position that dooms researchers to limited influence. And part of the researchers' efforts must include more effective communication in all phases of the research process, from the development of research problems through the design and implementation of studies and the reporting and interpretation of results (Stojkovic, 2007).

Work Perspective: LINKING RESEARCH TO PRACTITIONERS

Most people who do research on issues of public policy would very much like to have their research reflected in improved policy. Unfortunately, however, much too often we see research results that could be very useful in the shaping of policy remain totally ignored. This is much more a problem with social-science research than with biomedical research. Physicians, throughout their training, are taught about research and research methods and are inculcated with an obligation to keep up with research developments by following research findings and incorporating new ideas and methods—and particularly new drugs that have been tested and approved—directly into their practice. Understanding the scientific method is an inherent aspect of their training and of the skills they bring to their practice. That background is very different for people who engage in public policy research and those who set the policy, many of whom come out of a political or lawyerly culture, neither of which is typically characterized as having a close connection to science and research.

One of the key issues in communicating research results to practitioners is that of language. Academics tend to talk to each other in "journalese," a style that conforms more closely to academic jargon than to plain English; the style thrives on technical terms and often abstruse terminology invoking methodological constructs that serve as convenient descriptors to the relatively few who have been initiated, but constructs can also be totally baffling and perhaps off-putting to the uninitiated. The "initiated," who understand a particular jargon, may well be a small subset even among the academics, but they are virtually nonexistent among the practitioners. One of the skills

one learns as an academic is how to quickly find out the essential features of some technical idea or perhaps to gloss over some terminology that may at first be unintelligible, but could be figured out from the context. Most practitioners are more likely to discard any such document as merely representing academic gobbledygook and pass over what may be an important finding.

In many domains, one can find articulate academics who can read and understand such documents and then translate them into straight English for professional publications, such as *Criminology and Public Policy* or IEEE *Spectrum*, for practitioners in a particular field or for the general public in publications, such as *The Atlantic* or the *New York Times Magazine*. With increasingly complex methodologies, fewer and fewer people are able to fill this role, and so the gap between the academic researchers and the practitioners has been widening. Sometimes, we find academics who have crossed the bridge to become practitioners, at least on occasion, and who have established credibility in interpreting their own findings and those of others because they have learned to understand and speak in both languages. The numbers tend to be few, but they fill an important role.

Another feature of the academic–practitioner dialogue that tends to get in the way of trust and understanding is the need to maintain a sufficiently clear distinction between findings and values. Anyone who does research in public policy brings a scientist's perspectives that will teach us something about the phenomenon; that knowledge could well lead to policy implications. Perhaps he or she could see some policies and find them flawed and then develop

---

WORK PERSPECTIVE—continued

some knowledge that highlights those flaws in a more targeted and understandable way. For example, my own research on criminal careers has involved estimating the duration of individual criminal careers and I have found those to be relatively short, thereby arguing against very long prison terms, at least from the perspective of incapacitation. The knowledge about career duration is an appropriate scientific finding, whereas its invocation to argue against long sentences reflects a value consideration. That finding ignores other values such as retribution, which may be important to a particular judge. I would argue that the retribution calling for very long sentences is reasonable but should be reserved for the most heinous offenses. Such a dialogue should certainly find room for mutual accommodation, but the value choices of the policy maker will ultimately prevail.

In another context, I have been concerned about the exponential growth of the U.S. prison population over the past thirty years. Some research with Allen Beck found that changes in crime rates and in arrests per crime have been negligible contributors to that growth, but it has been predominantly a result of increased commitments per arrest and longer time served, with longer time served being especially important recently. Also, a major contributor to that growth has been the incarceration of drug offenders, largely as a result of a simplistic solution (increasingly long mandatory-minimum sentences) to a complex problem that has done little good to avert the drug transactions that had been of concern. In contrast to incarceration of a rapist, whose rapes are taken off the street, incarceration of a drug seller serves simply to recruit a replacement to respond to the demand. Here, I have not been railing against incarceration, but rather trying to bring some documented knowledge to the table in the hope that such knowledge will increase the likelihood of rational decision making. Unfortunately, the political benefit of being "tough on crime" has overcome that wish for rationality. Recently, however, the fiscal distress faced by most states as a result of the Great Recession has led to an astonishing convergence of the left (which is generally against punitiveness) and the right (which is generally for fiscal restraint), leading to an increasing adoption of more rational incarceration policies.

SOURCE: Alfred Blumstein, Heinz College of Public Policy and Information Systems, Carnegie Mellon University.

KNOWLEDGE AS POWER

The power of knowledge may contribute to rational processes within organizations, processes that can promote or resist change based on empirical evidence. **Knowledge as power** is the use of knowledge to coerce a particular point of view on others. But that power may also be used in change strategies that Chin and Benne (1969) have described as power–coercive strategies. Under these strategies, research is a source of coercive power. An example can be found in the housing testing programs that take place in cities around the country. Field researchers follow up on advertisements for rental housing or work with realtors; White and minority couples present similar records of employment and assets and are trained to standardize their approaches with landlords or realtors. Evidence of differential treatment based on the race of the couples is then used to make legal cases against landlords and realtors. Another example involved identifying and changing biased treatment of restaurant customers around the United Nations building in New York (Selltiz, 1955). When couples were treated differently based on their race, legal action wasn't necessary. Showing the data to owners and managers with the threat of continued "study" of their discrimination was sufficient to change practices.

Consumer advocate Ralph Nader has also effectively used research to influence organizations. Nader began his career with a review of automobile accident

Knowledge as power:
The use of knowledge to coerce a particular point of view on others.

data published in *Unsafe at Any Speed* (1965). That research contributed to General Motors's decision to take the Corvair out of production. Since then, the consumer movement has often made use of research by people unaffiliated with the organizations they seek to influence.

In criminal justice, outside groups have also used research to provoke change. The movement to stiffen penalties against drunken driving, for example, was led by court watch efforts that recorded and publicized judges' sentencing practices. An important part of the strategy of the grassroots organization Mothers Against Drunk Driving (MADD) was to pressure judges and politicians by revealing the facts about how drunk drivers were being treated by the criminal justice system (see Jacobs, 1989).

Concern over the use of knowledge in this way may be what causes some managers to resist research. In some cases, fear of knowledge from outside sources can reach a level of organizational paranoia that breeds distrust and isolation from others (Havelock, 1979). It may lead managers to resist evaluation studies for fear that the results will be interpreted in a thumbs-up or thumbs-down manner. When evaluation is done in that way, the research may be interpreted as determining that a program is a failure instead of simply suggesting approaches to program change and improvement (Stojkovic, Lovell, and Brandl, 2001). Fearing the power–coercive use of data by others, managers may be particularly concerned about research conducted by people who are not directly affiliated with their organization.

Managers themselves can use data in a power–coercive manner, however. It is not uncommon for researchers to be approached to do evaluations because managers are under pressure to show how well their program works. In one recent example, program managers sought an evaluation of a transitional housing program for welfare mothers in an effort to attract funding. The staff had initially selected people to participate in the program and then selected those they regarded as "graduates" from all those who had been through the program. An "independent" researcher was asked to follow up on the graduates. Not surprisingly, the researcher offered the conclusion that the program was successful in helping women get off welfare services. Of course, a research design with two layers of nonrandom selection and no control groups does not justify such conclusions. Whether based on naiveté or deliberate manipulation, such evaluations are not likely to be helpful in the long run.

KNOWLEDGE AS UNDERSTANDING

Knowledge as understanding: The use of knowledge to develop a fundamental awareness of an issue, concept, or problem.

For many years, U.S. agricultural researchers worked with West African farmers to increase crop yields. But often their research bore little fruit. Many recommendations, such as delaying spring planting to first plow and fertilize the fields of this semiarid savanna area, were not acted upon. It was not, however, until the researchers collaborated more closely with farmers, demonstrating **knowledge as understanding**—using knowledge to develop an awareness of the issue—that they realized their mistake. Farmers did not plow and fertilize their fields because fertilizer prices were relatively high compared to the costs of using more land. It was more economical to get low yields from large plots than to increase production on small plots. As a result of the research, farmers and researchers turned their attention to building an agricultural infrastructure that could produce cheaper fertilizer.

In the preceding example, knowledge of ways to increase crop production provided neither compelling insight nor the power to bring about change. Indeed, the problems faced by the farmers were not even what the researchers had presumed they were. Instead, it was only through the collaborative efforts of farmers and researchers that advancements could be made.

Chin and Benne (1969) describe a category of change strategies that they call **normative-reeducative strategies**. These strategies emphasize that understanding is a transactional process in which information is taken in, interpreted, and acted upon according to the consumer's values and experiences. The impetus for change comes not from the expert's analysis but rather from collaboration and experience-based learning.

To describe normative-reeducative strategies that are based in the collection and analysis of data, Kurt Lewin coined the term **action research**. He developed the model in studies focused on changing consumer behavior during shortages of meat and other commodities during World War II (see Lewin, 1947). Lewin stressed the need for strengthening the relationships among research, training, and action. And he emphasized the need for collaborative relationships in organizations in which managers, workers, and researchers came together to understand the need for change, to develop the knowledge base necessary to bring about change, and to monitor the process of change. For Lewin, action research was never to be less scientific than other research efforts, but it was to engage many new participants in the process of formulating the research problem and in identifying and interpreting data that would be seen as valid and potent. In fact, the action research model data could serve the very powerful function of testing and sometimes disconfirming the biases and prejudices of the participants.

In one famous example, the manager of a pajama factory employed a student of Lewin's to deal with middle managers' concerns about the productivity of older female workers. The managers designed a study to investigate how much the company was losing as a result of the limited productivity of this workforce (Marrow and French, 1945). They developed the measures of effectiveness and were closely questioned so as not to leave out any important issues. The involvement and commitment of these managers to the research made the findings—that the older female workers were among the most productive—all the more powerful in influencing their hiring and supervision decisions.

In discovering the productivity levels of the female workers and disconfirming their own biases, the pajama factory managers demonstrated a key role for data in Lewin's action research model. Change, Lewin argued, comes about when the status quo cannot hold, when forces supporting change outweigh those resisting it. The power of self-generated knowledge is the power to unfreeze the status quo. Involvement in research has the potential to unfreeze

Normative-reeducative strategies: Change based on a collaborative approach that involves transactions between researchers and consumers.

Action research: Research based on the involvement of both researchers and those being researched in defining problems and offering solutions.

managers by disconfirming their expectations and undermining their prejudices. Here, research does not simply chronicle the need for change or record its consequences. Instead, action research is itself a strategy for bringing about change.

A variety of methods have been developed to support collaborative research efforts. One approach is to incorporate data feedback to those involved in the process of change. In the preceding example, managers received feedback about older workers' performance. Wilkins (cited in Kress, 1980) has also used data feedback to influence judges' sentencing decisions. Under his approach, sentencing guidelines are based on average sentences handed out for specific offenses. Judges can then consider whether any particular case warrants sanctions more or less severe than the average.

Data feedback methods have also been supplemented by the use of employee and client surveys. Survey feedback methods pioneered in the 1950s by Floyd Mann (1950) and his associates have been used widely in the private sector. The procedure includes the systematic collection of data from organization members on a wide range of topics, including supervisory styles, communication patterns, and worker satisfaction. In some cases, standardized surveys developed and tested in other settings have been used to measure organizational climate, management style, and other variables, with the results fed back to members of the organization. The Federal Bureau of Prisons now routinely measures the social climate of its institutions using such survey methods.

The use of standardized measures may enhance the validity and reliability of the data, but there is also value in having members of the organization develop the instruments to measure what they regard as important and, in some cases, carry out the research themselves. Such participation in research has been advocated by Chris Argyris (1957), who sees "organic research" as a way of drawing on the expertise of people, increasing their competence, and avoiding the dependency or resistance that may result from noninvolvement.

Involvement in research can enhance the meaningfulness and sense of ownership of the data. In one example, jail officers developed a survey of inmate program preferences during the planning and construction of a new jail. The officers, who shared responsibility for program planning for the facility, presumed inmates would rank recreational programming as most important and would have little interest in education or vocational training. In fact, their interests were just the opposite. The officers, surprised to learn of the inmates' priorities, eventually invited inmates to participate in planning educational programming for the facility.

In a classic example of participatory research in criminal justice, Toch, Grant, and Galvin (1975) involved police officers in studying the use of force. Police administrators in the agency recognized that some officers had high rates of reported complaints from citizens and high rates of reported uses of force. Toch and Grant recruited the officers with the worst records for a research project on the use of force. The officers tape-recorded and analyzed their interactions with citizens; their goal was to identify the dynamics of incidents that produced undesirable exchanges. As the officers' own interactions with citizens changed in response to their new knowledge, they went on to train others in managing police–citizen encounters. The study continues to serve as a model of problem solving that uses the expertise of frontline staff to address important problems in policing (Skolnick and Fyfe, 1993).

In another example of criminal justice practitioners collaborating with academic researchers, Dalton (2004) discusses the role of research in assisting police to address the problem of homicide. Known as **homicide review**, this approach applies the techniques of social science to determine demographic patterns and behavioral patterns of both *potential* victims and perpetrators of homicide. By using this data, researchers are able to work with police, community leaders, social service agencies, and citizens to confront the homicide problem, each group having a role in preventing future homicides (see this chapter's case study).

Homicide review: The use of collaborative research techniques to identify potential victims of violent crime as well as perpetrators of violent crime.

These examples illustrate the potential contributions of research to a process of organizational change. They take research beyond the collection and analysis of data that is separate and apart from the participants. These efforts emphasize a process of self-study in which not only facts but also how they are understood and how they motivate action are important. Self-study makes it possible for participants to supplement their intuition and unsystematic knowledge based on experience with externally gathered facts. As Toch and Grant have described: "The process translates staff hunches into research questions and defines arenas for experimentation: It also leads to expanded personal horizons, learning and growth" (1982:166).

KNOWLEDGE AND RESEARCH PARTNERSHIPS

In recent years, and primarily through the support of the federal government, there has been an increasing interest in local research partnerships in criminal justice. **Knowledge and research partnerships** are the collaboration among government agencies, public agencies, and private entities to address specific problems, such as crime. There is a growing body of evidence of the value of such partnerships in the development of strategic interventions and in criminal justice planning. There has been little study of the variety or details of these partnership arrangements. Research arrangements can be seen as ranging from traditional in-house models to models of separate university-affiliated or research-center-affiliated researchers. A hybrid model between these extremes can be very valuable. A detailed case study is one such hybrid research arrangement.

Knowledge and research partnerships: The collaboration among government agencies, public agencies, and private entities to address specific problems, such as crime.

There can be little doubt as to the power of the information revolution in the lives of Americans over the past two decades. Grocery stores now routinely record their customers' buying habits to focus advertising as narrowly as possible.

Advertisers predict a day not far away when personalized ads will pop up before shoppers as they walk through malls or busy downtowns. Prescription records are shared among pharmacies to ensure that vacationers can maintain their medication schedules. Even the repair history on one's automobile is available in full on the Internet.

The criminal justice system has also been dramatically influenced by that revolution. That system has long been described as a system for processing information (Wilkins, 1975a). The chairman of the 1967 President's Crime Commission Task Force on Technology, Al Blumstein (1994:148), has noted the use of computers for processing information has been the single most significant technological change in society. In its report, the task force called for broadly expanded use of that technology so that research can guide criminal justice practice. Increases in the sophistication of criminal justice databases and in the sophistication of leaders in criminal justice has dramatically increased the interest in research in ways beyond those even anticipated by the President's Crime Commission.

KNOWLEDGE AND FAILURE

It may seem rather intuitive that organizations seek knowledge and conduct research to, in part, not commit mistakes, at least not mistakes that are so deleterious to their missions and purposes. Nevertheless, all organizations make mistakes and those mistakes may lead to failure. Yet, failure may or may not be a bad thing, as we have mentioned earlier in other chapters. The point is that through the knowledge-creation process we may learn from our mistakes, and, as such, failure, in the long run, may actually be beneficial to an organization.

Criminal justice organizations are replete with failure: police initiatives that engender ambiguous results, sentencing reforms that do not alleviate injustices, courts that operate under conditions of scarce resources with little notion of individualized justice, and correctional organizations that do not rehabilitate offenders, to mention a few. If we had to assess the effectiveness of these organizations based on their ability to meet stated goals, we would have a very dismal view of them (see Chapter 13). So, what does this have to do with knowledge creation and application to criminal justice organizations? It is easy to see that for many criminal justice administrators, asking tough questions regarding their operations can be very difficult and possibly lead toward unacceptable failure. No one wants to be viewed as ineffective, or at least told that they are ineffective, because such revelations are costly to the long-term future of administrators and even their agencies (Wilson, 2000).

Nevertheless, knowledge creation, and even failure as a result of acquiring knowledge, may actually be very beneficial to criminal justice administration. Berman and Fox (2010) provide valuable points of advice to criminal justice administrators concerning knowledge creation, failure, and even reform. Anyone who has been around long enough in criminal justice organizations knows that knowledge can be dangerous, yet as administrators, criminal justice managers and leaders have a responsibility to take the good with the bad. Knowledge creation through acceptable research regimens can be very valuable, but as a consequence of seeking out knowledge regarding criminal justice operations, mistakes will be made. Learning from these mistakes is what is pivotal. Berman and Fox (2010) suggest that all reformers, including administrators who seek change in criminal justice organizations, become cognizant of what we have learned from our failures over the years. These authors offer the following suggestions.

First and foremost, criminal justice administrators need to be self-reflective and introspective regarding their practices and activities. Too often, we are overly critical and negative when something does not work as well as we had hoped. Being more introspective about research findings and their application to operations requires some good judgment and self-reflection. We are too often willing to throw the baby out with the bathwater. We need to learn why something does not work, utilizing knowledge generated from our research, and then make appropriate changes to see what happens.

We should define success more broadly. If we primarily define criminal justice effectiveness in terms of crime reduction, we will truly fail. Criminal justice efforts do more than reduce crime; they may help communities in other ways. As mentioned in the opening vignette of the chapter, the DARE project has been a questionable program in reducing illegal drug usage among the nation's youth, but it has had discernable benefits to communities in working with police and promoting positive feelings between young people and the police, not to mention the benefits to police officers regarding job satisfaction. If research has taught us anything, it is that what is both beneficial and harmful in criminal justice organizations is not readily apparent. Only through good research do we see what is really going on within our organizations. The impact on criminal justice agencies, both good and bad, must be understood relative to broadly defined goals that have crime reduction as only one possible outcome.

Being purely rational and seeking out "evidence-based" solutions to crime problems is probably never going to happen in a linear fashion. Research shows us that the world is not linear and that solutions to crime problems may not be as easily discernable as we think. Berman and Fox (2010) note this point relative to Operation Ceasefire in Boston. It is certain that homicides went down significantly in Boston during the program, but researchers cannot say without equivocation that it was the program that led toward the homicide reductions. Our best practices and activities may be useful, but they do not explain with absolute certainty what works and does not work when it comes to a specific crime problem. We can be only "intentionally rational" in what we do, and we must expect the limitations of being rational in a highly irrational world (Simon, 1957). We must still use our best judgment on how to proceed when we do not have definitive answers to a problem.

Modesty regarding program impact can be virtuous within criminal justice organizations. Berman and Fox (2010) note that many criminal justice reform efforts are too ambitious. Too often, we inappropriately pander to the fears of a concerned public when crime seems out of control, or, worse yet, we use one horror story to construct a solution that is oftentimes disconnected to the problem we are trying to address. Many of the efforts, for example, of tough sentencing practices to deal with drug offenders never really dealt with the fact that the supply of illegal drugs was too large and suppliers would always provide the product due to significant rewards associated with distributing it. Our practices of pursuing, apprehending, convicting, and severely sentencing illegal drug dealers created worse problems than the drugs themselves: overcrowded correctional facilities, burgeoning and nonaffordable police and prosecution components, overcrowded court dockets, and, in many cases, decimated communities and families. What we should learn from our mistakes as criminal justice administrators is that being modest in understanding our role in managing crime may be more useful. Research tells us to step slowly and deliberately in our efforts toward crime reduction.

Politics and criminal justice reform and practices cannot be separated. We have stressed in this book that the political process is enormously important to criminal justice administrators. We must understand that as public administrators we interact and work with elected leaders through a political process to make things happen in criminal justice. Both the politician and the criminal justice administrator can be very vain and narrow, however. Berman and Fox (2010) suggest that as reformers or as administrators there must be an acceptance that there is plenty of praise when it comes to successful criminal justice programs. The failure to recognize this as a criminal justice administrator can be devastating. There are many examples of where internecine warfare occurred over who should receive the credit for a successful initiative. Berman and Fox (2010) mention that when reformers or administrators do not care who gets the credit for a successful program, it is more likely to have a positive impact for everyone involved.

Planning in isolation is a mistake. There is much value to collaboration and identifying key stakeholders, but caution must be expressed when trying to invite too many to the table. Criminal justice reform efforts and even daily practices require *strategic* alliances to have any meaningful impact on a specific crime-related problem. Research can be used to identify key stakeholders and how they fit into a specific program. If we have learned anything over the past twenty years in criminal justice, it is that crime is not solely a criminal justice issue or problem. The twenty-first-century criminal justice administrator is more open to other public agencies, constituent groups, and relevant third parties as a way to accomplish organizational goals and manage crime. The trick is to be inclusive enough to promote effective practices, but not to be overly inclusive, making any effort impossible to manage and monitor (Berman and Fox, 2010).

Program implementation and context matter in criminal justice. Research has convincingly shown that what works in one community may be a failure in another community. This is why research within the community context is so important. Not recognizing context will bring abject failure to programs. As criminal justice administrators, we know that the devil is in the details. Paying attention to details, assigning work to appropriate people and units, and holding them accountable for specific tasks is what administration is all about. Too many programs are doomed to failure because of the lack of attention to these details and the importance of context in the creation and perpetuation of program efforts.

Involving line personnel in the creation and adoption of new programs is more effective and increases the chances of having an impact. Criminal justice organizations are replete with examples of top-down initiatives being conceived, only to fail once received by rank-and-file personnel. Research can be useful to identify what ordinary line personnel think about various new programs. It is usually helpful to include everyday workers into the process of program selection and program implementation. We have suggested through various chapters that frontline personnel have enormous power in how criminal justice organizations function. They can kill a good idea quickly, especially if they feel no involvement in the development and implementation of the idea. Berman and Fox (2010) state: "It is difficult to achieve positive results without belief—the people charged with implementation must have some faith that what they are being asked to do makes sense."

ADVANCES IN RESEARCH IN CRIMINAL JUSTICE

At least three interwoven threads currently give form to the increased interest in research-guided policy in criminal justice. These include (1) growing use of data in the field, (2) growth among academics in interest in outcome research in criminal justice and developments in the methods used to consider the efficacy of that research, and (3) federal, and some state, support for data-based decision making.

Evidence of the growing use of data in criminal justice organizations is easy to find. Problem-oriented policing, for example, describes a broad movement that incorporates the use of data in problem analysis and solution (Goldstein, 1990). Compstat under Chief William Bratton (1998) in New York and now in Los Angeles has offered a model of data use that has been widely emulated around the country. Crime analysis is also a growing field with a foundation in geospatial data analysis and presentation methods (Clarke and Eck, 2005). Most recently, concepts such as "information-led policing" or "intelligence-led policing" have crept into the lexicon to describe new uses of data (McGarrell, 2006a). Outside of policing, these developments have been paralleled by concepts such as "evidence-based practice." These approaches call for selecting best practices based on available outcome research.

Simultaneous with these developments has been a growing interest among social scientists who study crime in the process of documenting the effects and outcomes of crime reduction efforts. Meta-analysis has become one popular approach that considers program effects (Glass, McGaw, and Smith, 1981). More powerful still, there has been an increase in studies using experimental and quasi-experimental designs. These methods have found strong advocates in researchers like David Weisburd (2000). On the other hand, there has also been a resurgence of interest in "action research" models that involve close partnerships between researchers and practitioners in the field (Toch, 1982).

The growth in interest in research in criminal justice cannot be separated from growing support for that research that has come from the Bureau of Justice Assistance and the National Institute of Justice. Beginning with the Boston Gun Project (Braga, 2004), there has been federal support for new approaches to research that have fostered partnerships between researchers and criminal justice practitioners. In Boston, researchers from the Kennedy School teamed up with police and community members to study gang problems and then design and evaluate interventions. The National Institute of Justice then funded an expansion of the research model through its Strategic Approaches to Community Safety Initiatives (SACSI) that was implemented in ten cities (Dalton, 2003). Project Safe Neighborhoods (PSN) built on the SACSI experience by supporting researcher partners in nearly all U.S. court districts (Bureau of Justice Assistance, 2004).

In New York state, the Division of Criminal Justice Services (DCJS) followed the example of the federal government by providing support for crime analysis, intelligence analysis, and data-based strategic planning under a program called Project Impact. The continued adoption of this research model beyond the specific programs supported by the federal government seems likely and provides further evidence of the expanding role of research in the practice of criminal justice. Support for that proposition can also be found in a set of recent publications jointly produced by the National Institute of Justice and the International Association of Chiefs of Police (IACP) (2006a, 2006b). The companion volumes, one for police leaders and one for researchers, address practical problems in the research partnership.

Fostering research and the use of data in strategic planning would seem to be worthy and practical objectives. To this point, the successes have largely come through the fortuitous pairings of researchers and practitioners. There has been little in the analyses of these relationships that informs us about the elements of those pairings that contribute to or may thwart successful research partnerships. It would appear that the next obvious step in building on the existing foundation is to examine the nature and character of relationships. But instead of focusing on idiosyncratic characteristics of these relations or the personalities in them, it may be valuable to consider what structural or organizational characteristics foster productive research relationships. This suggests the need to build a knowledge base on the advantages and disadvantages of various organizational arrangements.

Despite the groundbreaking work of the President's Commission Task Force on Technology, there has been little systematic discussion of the placement of research responsibilities in criminal justice organizations. Some existing models, however, may have applicability. Research and development (R&D) departments in manufacturing organizations have a history of creativity that separates them from many other organizational units (Stojkovic, Kalinich, and Klofas, 2003). In some cases, however, "in-house research departments" have been seen as focusing on counting, accounting, or other organizational maintenance functions rather than on research. Even Compstat units, despite their use of data, are probably not best thought of as research offices.

When the organizational affiliation of the researchers is considered, we may see the university-affiliated or research center-affiliated researcher as a model juxtaposed with the in-house research model. Although it may be best to avoid the label of "out-house researcher," university-affiliated or research center-affiliated researchers have made significant contributions to criminal justice research while working outside organizations. The recent IACP/NIJ publications describe the potential difficulties in such relationships and approaches to overcoming them.

Between in-house research and outside research models, it is possible to describe a third broad type, the hybrid research model. This model involves university-affiliated or research-center-affiliated researchers who work with their local criminal justice organizations in long-term working relationships. These hybrid-type organizations may be able to avoid the weakness of the previously described research arrangements—that is, they may be able to avoid expectations of serving the maintenance functions of organizations, and they may be able to gain sufficient understanding of the context of local criminal justice to assure validity and reliability of results. Of course, that level of intimacy may also raise questions of conflict of interest that must be addressed, if indeed a level of intimacy can be achieved by these partners in the first place. It is easy to see potential strengths and potential pitfalls in each of the models.

Case study research has a long tradition in organizational analyses. Yin (2002), perhaps the best-known methodologist in the area, suggests this method is most appropriate when contemporary phenomena are to be studied in their real-life context, particularly where the boundaries between what is studied and its context are blurred or unclear. That is certainly the case with organizationally linked researchers. With one foot in academic traditions and one tied to organizational goals, the balance of roles becomes a major focus of study. Likewise, case studies can be especially useful when one goal is to thoroughly describe some phenomenon in a way that will permit further analyses and comparisons as the knowledge base grows.

When examining the utility of the case study research approach to criminal justice organizations, it is important to clearly define relevant questions and issues that require the attention of administrators. For example, what are the key constituencies in the research relationship? Are there conflicts or differences in expectations among the key constituencies? Are there public expectations, and, if so, how do those relate to those of the key constituencies? Second, are there research questions that are easily addressed and others that either cannot be addressed or are addressed with difficulty due to local concerns? How does the ability to address some topics, as well as expectations about addressing them, change or mature over time? What is the effect of various patterns of support? What kinds of products are and can be produced by the research? Are there limitations? What is their impact?

Questions also arise regarding the impact of research. How are the needs to produce research that will be useful in the near term balanced with traditional academic concerns for the quality of research? How do traditionally trained faculty members respond to the action research and experiential learning environment of criminal justice organizations? Finally, questions regarding the impact of the research on criminal justice operations must be addressed. What is the impact of the research on the local criminal justice system and the community? Are program and policy changes implemented as a result of research? Are there lasting effects on faculty as a result of their connection to the research? Are there lasting effects on students as a result of their connection to the research? Is the interest in and capacity for researching local criminal justice agencies increased as a result of the work? Are the expectations and involvement of the community in research-based processes increased over time?

Through a serious discussion with criminal justice administrators, questions such as those raised here can be answered, and the long-term value of research can be understood and incorporated into the operations of criminal justice organizations. For criminal justice administrators, the link with academic researchers provides an opportunity to add to their repertoire of responses to crime. For the researcher, collaborations with criminal justice organizations provide rich data to test theory and to assess criminal justice operations. Such collaborations can only advance the intellectual pursuits of criminal justice and criminology and assist criminal justice administrators in addressing crime.

KNOWLEDGE AND THE FUTURE OF CRIMINAL JUSTICE ADMINISTRATION

The purpose of this book has been to provide an examination of the major dimensions that affect and influence criminal justice administration. Whether we are discussing the workings of police departments, correctional agencies, prosecutors' offices, or court systems, there is much benefit in analyzing them as organizations. Through an organizational analysis, criminal justice agencies are better understood, and it is possible to create useful prescriptions for criminal justice administrators.

We stated in the preface that we had themes we sought to address in this edition of the book. First and foremost, we wanted to focus on what we know about criminal justice organizations from the perspective of many disciplines: political science, sociology, psychology, and, in addition, the burgeoning research conducted by those academically trained in criminal justice. Second, we wanted a systemic focus when viewing criminal justice administration. Very few texts even discuss the interrelatedness and interdependence found among criminal justice organizations. We have sought to discuss these issues in the context of various organizational and administrative dimensions. Whether the topic is decision making, conflict, structure, or job design, to mention a few, we were interested in issues and research across the components of the criminal justice system—that is, police, prosecution, courts, and corrections. Finally, we sought an understanding of criminal justice administration through the integration of theory, research, and practice. We felt, through proper integration of these elements, our understanding of criminal justice administration would be more complete.

We conclude the book by discussing how these three themes are predicated on knowledge, information, and the systematic collection, analysis, and application of data to improve criminal justice administration. The twenty-first century is upon us. The expectations for criminal justice administrators are much higher in this new century than in the past, largely due to limited resources, increased visibility, and constant review by groups with conflicting interests and thoughts on how criminal justice organizations are to be administered. With the availability of more sophisticated technologies, criminal justice administration stands on the brink of a new world. This new world reflects a guarded optimism on how criminal justice organizations will be led and managed by administrators incorporating these newer technologies.

The United States has experienced a direct terrorist attack on its own soil, the magnitude of which is unprecedented in the history of the country, and the country has pursued a war with a country that posed no direct threat to us. Criminal justice administrators have been asked to respond with newer and more sophisticated strategies to combat crime and criminals, including terrorists. The foundation for these twenty-first-century crime strategies will be how well we integrate knowledge, data, and information into the conceptualization of the crime problem, a response to it, and a redirection, if needed, of our efforts predicated on data-informed decision making. Yet, decision making is not the only issue amenable to this process. The entire operation of criminal justice organizations and the actions of their administrators will rely more on quality data, information, and knowledge. We have discussed many of these issues in the context of the organizational topics and dimensions presented in this book.

For the criminal justice administrator, informed intuition and experience will not be enough. Complex systems of data collection, data analysis, and strategic assessment will become the norm for administrative actions and behaviors. Knowledge, data, and information will become critical and essential for effective criminal justice administration. Whether criminal justice administrators are addressing issues of structure, conflict, strategies to motivate employees, organizational effectiveness, the environment, or any other topic the chapters in this book have addressed, knowledge, information, and data will be the foundation upon which future criminal justice administrations will be understood and assessed.

What does the twenty-first century hold for criminal justice administration? We believe that across the components of the criminal justice system, a greater emphasis will be placed on the creation of appropriate knowledge, data, and information to address crime. There will be expectations by public groups, private concerns, and the government itself that criminal justice administrators do things in a different way. Criminal justice administration has evolved as society as evolved. The Internet, integrated data systems and files, more invasive surveillance technologies, and ways to train and supervise employees electronically, will become the mainstream of criminal justice operations. With these changes will come the possibility of greater review of the operations of their criminal justice systems by communities. Concerns about accountability will become more pronounced, and criminal justice administrators will have to justify their requests for increased dollars and personnel to combat crime. With this increased accountability will come more concern for how criminal justice administrators are recruited, selected, and retained. At the core of these activities will be the search for knowledge, data, and information. Unlike his or her predecessors in the twentieth century, the twenty-first-century criminal justice administrator will have more expectations placed upon him or her, resources will be tighter, and questions of effectiveness and efficiency will be recurrent. How these new criminal justice administrators respond to these concerns will be the essence of criminal justice administration into the future.

SUMMARY

Know the difference between "basic research" and "applied research."

- There are two types of research: basic research, concerned with fundamental uses of process and structure to understand a phenomenon; and applied research, the use of knowledge that directly impacts practitioners and policy.

Understand the ways knowledge is utilized by criminal justice organizations.

- Criminal justice organizations can utilize research knowledge in three ways: instrumental, symbolic, and conceptual. Researchers and criminal justice practitioners understand and use research for differing purposes. The former is concerned with statistical averages as a way to comprehend the typical, while the latter emphasizes the atypical in understanding organizational responses to crime.

Describe the nature of social science research and knowledge utilization.

- Researchers must be careful how they influence criminal justice policy because definitive answers to crime issues may be ambiguous and not readily apparent. For the practitioner, research must inform policy but not be totally driven by it.

Describe the limitations of data within criminal justice organizations.

- Criminal justice data, typically as expressed through the Uniform Crime Reports and other crude measures, is not reliable. Researchers and practitioners need to develop both reliable and valid sources of data regarding crime and the criminal justice response to crime.

Define "in-house research" and how it can be useful to criminal justice organizations.

- In-house research means the capacity of an organization to develop its own data and research needs.

Know the various ways of conceptualizing and applying research knowledge.

- Knowledge as power, knowledge as understanding, knowledge and research partnerships, knowledge and failure, advances in research in criminal justice, and knowledge and the future of criminal justice administration are ways to conceptualize and apply research knowledge.

Case Study: HOMICIDE REVIEW

Knowledge for What? is the title of the provocative book in which social scientist Robert Lynd (1939) proposed the thesis that knowledge creation must have some value and utility to society. Knowledge for its own sake is good, but to better the world, we need knowledge that will assist in addressing society's most pressing and perplexing problems. To this end, we see that much can be learned from the methodologies of the social sciences to advance our understanding of crime and criminal justice and to aid criminal justice administrators in managing crime. One such advance that has recently taken hold is the concept of homicide review. Homicide review is the application of social-science techniques to assist police departments and other social service agencies to tackle the difficult crime of homicide.

Begun in the city of Rochester, New York, by the researcher John Klofas, this technique brings together a number of differing organizations to confront the problem of homicide. It is based on a theoretical model that suggests homicide, like any other social behavior, follows a pattern. Through scientific investigation, academic researchers, in collaboration with police and other criminal justice components and other human service organizations, can develop a comprehensive strategy to target potential homicide victims. The homicide review initiative in Rochester began by compiling data on homicide victims over a specified time period. Through such an analysis, patterns or common characteristics of victims were discerned. It was found, for example, that many of the victims were young, African American, male, and had previous involvement with the criminal justice system. In addition, many lived in the same neighborhoods and frequented similar locations in the community. Moreover, the analysis revealed that some places were more dangerous than others, and specific places—that is, emerging crack houses—were particularly dangerous.

With this information, researchers were able to work with other agencies, both criminal justice and noncriminal justice organizations, to develop a strategy of identifying *future* homicide victims. In addition, the roles of the various components of the criminal justice system changed under such a model. So, for example, criminal prosecution and courts developed a strategy in Rochester to work with the research team to identify potential homicide victims.

The identified participants were required to meet with officials and others from the community to discuss the likelihood of them being a homicide victim and the penalties if they continued to pursue criminal activities. The intention of such a meeting was to show a response by the criminal justice system, and to inculcate among the participants that if they continued their current behaviors they would receive harsh responses by the criminal justice system. Although homicide prevention is the primary aim of the homicide review process, a secondary aim is the reduction of high-risk criminal behavior.

A second part of the homicide review process is to inform participants of services that can help them deal with their life situations. The role of social service agencies is to offer other alternatives to a high-risk lifestyle that might lead toward violence and death. At this point in the process, the person has numerous agencies working with him, including churches, schools, and employment agencies. The hope is that through an identification of would-be homicide victims and an active intervention strategy, potential violence can be averted and people can be directed toward a more positive, prosocial lifestyle. Future research will have to assess whether homicide review has value to communities and to criminal justice administrators across the criminal justice system.

So, what does the homicide review research reveal? To date, we have had no systematic evaluation of the efficacy of homicide review. The potential of such an effort is, however, tremendous. Criminal justice administrators are able to use information collected by researchers and others to inform their practices. The valuable point is that research information can have instrumental value to criminal justice administrators. By correctly conceptualizing a problem, collecting good information, and analyzing data, criminal justice administrators are able to use research and direct their practices in a way that potentially has much use in how they do business. In the end, for criminal justice administrators, the value of research is to improve practice and to legitimize the implementation of programs.

CASE STUDY QUESTIONS

1. What are some key organizational constraints that would inhibit the application of research or research findings?
2. What organizations external to the criminal justice system might be opposed to homicide review? What external organizations would be supportive of homicide review? What is the role of criminal justice administrators in working with external groups to facilitate homicide review?
3. Do you believe criminal justice administrators are receptive to research? Why or why not?
4. What specific crime problem do you think is ripe for research and application?

Think like an Administrator

What role does research play in making decisions about how a criminal justice agency responds to crime? Differing criminal justice agencies have differing expectations, resources, and political wherewithal to integrate research findings into policy making in their agencies. It has been demonstrated that the integration of research strategies and findings into criminal justice organizations can be very beneficial. Yet, what does a criminal justice agency give up by relying more heavily on research findings in its day-to-day operations? At one level, a criminal justice organization could more effectively "speak truth to power" regarding an issue or practice under question by having research results available.

1. Because criminal justice organizations are political entities, how important would political concerns be when trying to support or not support a particular program or effort based on research findings?
2. How does the creation of specific research and evaluation division within a criminal justice organization benefit that organization?
3. How influential should research findings be in a criminal justice organization?
4. To what extent can research form a union between differing political perspectives regarding a crime issue?
5. How is research used to advance a specific political agenda?
6. When assessing individual performance and relying on objective assessment procedures, how will the union react to these approaches?
7. By seeking more college-educated employees in criminal justice organizations, what is the likelihood that more emphasis on research findings will occur?

FOR DISCUSSION

1. How do you think research has influenced the criminal justice system since the President's Commission in 1967? What examples can you give of research findings that have had a direct or indirect bearing on practice in the field?

2. Critique the major sources of data about crime in the United States. What are their strengths and weaknesses? How should they be used in research, and how should that research influence management and policy? What cautions would you suggest?

3. How has research been used in your own experience studying criminal justice? In your education, has research generally been viewed as offering facts and truth? Have you seen examples in political campaigns or other circumstances where research has been used as a source of coercive power? Have any of your assignments reflected a participatory or self-study approach? If not, what would such assignments look like?

4. Follow your local paper or online news or talk with criminal justice officials in your community to identify a problem area facing criminal justice. Now design a research project to address it. In fact, design three: one reflecting a rational–empirical approach, one based on power–coercive uses of data, and one based on normative-reeducative self-study methods. Which strategy do you think would be most effective, and why?

FOR FURTHER READING

Berman, G., and Fox, A. *Trial and Error in Criminal Justice Reform: Learning from Failure.* Washington, DC: Urban Institute Press, 2010, 121–122.

International Association of Chiefs of Police (with the National Institute of Justice). *Establishing and Sustaining Law Enforcement Partnerships: Guide for Law Enforcement Leaders: Final Report.* Washington, DC, 2006a.

International Association of Chiefs of Police (with the National Institute of Justice). *Establishing and Sustaining Law Enforcement Partnerships: Guide for Researchers: Final Report.* Washington, DC, 2006b.

Toch, H., and Grant, J. D. *Reforming Human Services: Change through Participation.* Beverly Hills, CA: Sage, 1982.

U.S. Bureau of Justice Statistics. *Performance Measures for the Criminal Justice System.* Washington, DC: U.S. Government Printing Office, 1993.

U.S. Department of Justice. *National Evaluation of the COPS Program: Title I of the 1994 Crime Control Act.* Washington, DC: U.S. Government Printing Office, 2001.

References

Adams, T. F. *Police Patrol: Tactics and Techniques*. Englewood Cliffs, NJ: Prentice Hall, 1971.

Agrawala, M., Li, W., Berthouzoz, F. "Design Principles for Visual Communication." *Communications of the ACM*, 2011, *54*(4), 60–69.

Allen, R. "Changing public attitudes in crime and punishment." *Journal of Community and Criminal Justice, Probation Journal*, 2008, *55*(4), 389–400.

Allison, G. T. *Essence of Decision*. Boston: Little, Brown, 1969.

Alpert, G. P., Dunham, R., and Stroshine, M. S. *Policing: Continuity and Change*. Long Grove, IL: Waveland, 2005.

American Correctional Association. *Performance-Based Standards for Adult Local Detention Facilities*. 4th ed. Lanham, MD: American Correctional Association, 2004.

American Friends Service Committee. *Struggle for Justice*. New York: Hill and Wang, 1971.

American Psychiatric Association. *Brief Amicus Curiae in the Case of* Barefoot *v.* Estelle. Washington, DC: American Psychiatric Association, 1982.

Angell, J. E. "Towards an Alternative to Classical Police Organizational Arrangements." *Criminology*, 1971, *19*, 19–29.

Archambeault, W. G., and Archambeault, B. J. *Correctional Supervisory Management: Principles of Organization, Policy and Law*. Englewood Cliffs, NJ: Prentice Hall, 1982.

Archambeault, W. G., and Wierman, C. L. "Critically Assessing the Utility of Police Bureaucracies in the 1980s: Implications of Management Theory Z." *Journal of Police Science and Administration*, 1983, *11* (4), 420–429.

Archbold, C. A. "Police Legal Advisors in the USA: Past, Present, and Future." *Police Practice and Research*, 2006, *7*(1), 61–76.

Argyris, C. *Personality and Organization*. New York: Harper & Row, 1957.

Argyris, C. *Interpersonal Competence and Organizational Effectiveness*. Homewood, IL: Dorsey Press, 1962.

Artison, R. Personal communication, September 1996.

Asgarkhani, M. "Digital Government and Its Effectiveness in Public Management Reform: A Local Government Perspective." *Public Management Review*, 2005, *7*(3), 465–487.

Atkins, B., and Pogrebin, M. *The Invisible Justice System: Discretion and the Law*. Cincinnati, OH: Anderson Publishing Company, 1981.

Austin, J. "Assessing the New Generation of Prison Classification Models." *Crime and Delinquency*, 1983, *29*, 523.

Austin, J. "Using Early Release to Relieve Prison Crowding: A Dilemma for Public Policy." *Crime and Delinquency*, 1986, *32*, 404–502.

Austin, J., and Krisberg, B. "Wider, Stronger and Different Nets: The Dialectics of Criminal Justice Reform." *Journal of Research in Crime and Delinquency*, 1981, *18*(1), 165–169.

Auten, J. H. "Police Management in Illinois." *Journal of Police Science and Administration*, 1985, *13*(4), 325–337.

Babalhavaeji, F., and Farhadpoor, M. R. "Information Source Characteristics and Environmental Scanning by Academic Library Managers." *Information Research*, 2013, *18*(1).

Bacharach, S. B., and Lawler, E. E. *Power and Politics in Organizations*. San Francisco: Jossey-Bass, 1980.

Bailey, A., and Hayes, J. "Who's in Prison? The Changing Demographics of Incarceration," Public Policy Institute, 2006, *8*(1), 1–14.

Baker, K. M. "Decision Making in a Hybrid Organization: A Case Study of Southeastern Drug Court." *Law and Social Justice*, 2013, *38*(1), 27–54.

481

Baker, T. J. "Designing the Job to Motivate." *FBI Law Enforcement Bulletin*, 1976, *45*(11), 3–7.

Banfield. E. *The Unheavenly City*. Boston, MA: Little, Brown, 1974.

Barak-Glantz, I. L. "The Anatomy of Another Prison Riot." In *Prison Violence in America*, edited by M. Braswell, S. Dillingham, and R. Montgomery, Jr., pp. 47–72. Cincinnati, OH: Anderson Publishing Company, 1985.

Barefoot v. *Estelle*. 103 S. Ct. 3383 (1983).

Barnard, C. *The Functions of the Executive*. Cambridge, MA: Harvard University Press, 1938.

Barnes, H., and Teeters, N. *New Horizons in Criminology*. Englewood Cliffs, NJ: Prentice Hall, 1959.

Baro, A. "The Loss of Local Control over Prison Administration." *Justice Quarterly*, 1988, *5*(3) 127–143.

Baron, R., and Greenberg, J. *Behavior in Organizations: Understanding and Managing the Human Side of Work*. Boston, MA: Allyn and Bacon, 1990.

Bass, B. M. (Ed.). *Stodgill's Handbook of Leadership*. New York: Free Press, 1981.

Bayley, D. *Police for the Future*. New York: Oxford University Press, 1994.

Bazemore, G., and Schiff, M. *Juvenile Justice Reform and Restorative Justice: Building Theory and Policy from Practice*. Cullompton, UK: Willan Publishing, 2004.

Bazemore, G., Leip, L., and Stinchcomb, J. "Boundary Changes and the Nexus Between Formal and Informal Social Control: Truancy Intervention as a Case Study in Criminal Justice Expansionism." *Notre Dame Journal of Law Ethics and Public Policy*, *18*(2), 521–570.

Beckhard, R. "What Is Organizational Development?" In *Organizational Development*, edited by J. V. Gallos, pp. 3–13. San Francisco: Jossey-Bass, 2006.

Beeman, D. R., and Starkey, T. W. "The Use and Abuse of Corporate Politics." *Business Horizons*, 1987, March-April, 1–15.

Belknap, J. "The Economics-Crime Link." *Criminal Justice Abstracts*, 1989, *21*(1), 140–157.

Bennett, B. "Motivation Hang-Ups of the Police Mystique." *Police Human Relations*, 1981, *1*, 136–146.

Bennett, R. R. "Becoming Blue: A Longitudinal Study of Police Recruit Occupational Socialization." *Journal of Police Science and Administration*, 1984, *12*, 47–58.

Bennett, W., and Hess, K. *Management and Supervision in Law Enforcement*. 5th ed. Belmont, CA: Thomson Publishing Company, 2007.

Bennis, W. "Leadership in Administrative Behavior." In *The Planning of Change*, edited by W. Bennis, K. Benne, and R. Chin, pp. 62–79. New York: Holt, Rinehart & Winston, 1966.

Benton, W., and Silberstein, J. "State Prison Expansion: An Explanatory Model." *Journal of Criminal Justice*, 1983, *11*, 121–128.

Berman G., and Fox, A. *Trial & Error in Criminal Justice Reform: Learning from Failure*. Washington, DC: Urban Institute, 2010.

Bierstedt, R. "An Analysis of Social Power." *American Sociological Review*, 1950, *15*(6), 730–738.

Bittner, E. *The Functions of the Police in Modern Society: A Review of Background Factors, Current Practices, and Possible Role Models*. Chevy Chase, MD: National Institute of Mental Health, 1970.

Blake, R. R., and Mouton, J. S. *The Managerial Grid*. Houston, TX: Gulf, 1964.

Blanchard, K. H., and Hersey, P. *Management of Organizational Behavior*. Englewood Cliffs, NJ: Prentice Hall, 1977.

Blau, P. *The Dynamics of Bureaucracy*. Boston, MA: Little, Brown, 1955.

Blau, P. *Exchange and Power in Social Life*. New York: John Wiley, 1964.

Block v. *Rutherford*. USSC, 104 S.C. 3227 (1984).

Block, P. B., and Specht, D. *Neighborhood Team Policing*. Washington, DC: U.S. Government Printing Office, 1973.

Blomberg, T. "Diversion's Disparate Results and Unresolved Questions: An Integrative Evaluation Perspective." *Journal of Research in Crime and Delinquency*, 1983, *20*, 24–38.

Blumberg, A. "The Practice of Law as a Confidence Game." *Law and Society Review*, 1967, *1*, 15–39.

Blumstein, A. "The Task Force on Science and Technology." In *The 1967 President's Crime Commission Report: Its Impact 25 Years Later*, edited by J. A. Conley, pp. 145–158. Cincinnati, OH: Anderson Publishing Company, 1994.

Boba, R. *Crime Analysis Mapping*. Thousand Oaks, CA: Sage Publishing, 2005.

Bohm, R. M. "'McJustice': On the McDonaldization of Criminal Justice." *Justice Quarterly*, 2006, *23*(1), 127–144.

Bolman, L. G., and Deal, T. E. *Reframing Organizations: Artistry, Choice, and Leadership.* 2nd ed. San Francisco: Jossey-Bass, 1997.

Bolman, L. G., and Deal, T. E. *Reframing Organizations, Artistry, Choice, and Leadership.* 3rd ed. San Francisco: Jossey-Bass, 2003.

Book, C., Terrance, A., Atkin, C., Bettinghaus, E., Donohue, W., Farace, R., Greenberg, B., Helper, H., Milkovich, M., Miller, G., Ralph, D., and Smith, T. *Human Communication: Principles, Context, and Skills.* New York: St. Martin's Press, 1980.

Booth, W., and Harwick, C. "Physical Ability Testing for Police Officers in the 80s." *Police Chief,* January 1984, 39–41.

Bopp, W. J. "Organizational Democracy in Law Enforcement." In *Administration of Justice System: An Introduction,* edited by D. T. Shanahan, pp. 84–102. Boston, MA: Holbrook Press, 1977.

Bowditch, L. L., and Buono, A. F. *A Primer on Organizational Behavior.* 4th ed. New York: John Wiley & Sons, 1997.

Braga, A. A. *Gun Violence among Serious Young Offenders.* Washington, DC: U.S. Department of Justice, Office of Community Oriented Policing Services, 2004.

Bratton, W. "New York Crime Rate Down Forty-Five Percent." *New York Times,* February 12, 1996.

Bratton, W. *Turnaround: How America's Top Cop Reversed the Crime Epidemic.* New York: Random House, 1998.

Brecher, E. M. "Drug Laws and Drug Law Enforcement: A Review Based on 111 Years of Experience." *Drugs and Society,* 1986, *1,* 1–28.

Brennan, P. K. "Sentencing Female Misdemeanants: An Examination of the Direct and Indirect Effect of Race." *Justice Quarterly,* 2006, *23*(1), 60–95.

Brennan, T. "Classification: An Overview of Selected Methodological Issues." In *Prediction and Classification: Criminal Justice Decision Making,* edited by D. M. Gottfredson and M. Tonry, pp. 201–248. Chicago: University of Chicago Press, 1987.

Brief, A. P., Munro, J., and Aldag, R. J. "Correctional Employees' Reactions to Job Characteristics: A Data Based Argument for Job Enlargement." *Journal of Criminal Justice,* 1976, *4,* 223–230.

Brinkerhoff, G., and White, L. *Sociology.* Minneapolis, MN: West, 1991.

Britton, D. "Perceptions of the Work Environment Among Correctional Officers: Do Race and Sex Matter?" *Criminology,* 1997, *35*(1), 85–106.

Brodeur, J., and Dupont, B. "Knowledge Workers or 'Knowledge' Workers?" *Policing and Society,* 2006, *16*(1), 7–26.

Bromby, M. "To Be Taken at Face Value? Computerized Identification." *Information & Communication Technology Law,* 2002, *11*(1), 152–164.

Brown, D. C. *Civilian Review of Complaints Against the Police: A Survey of the United States Literature.* Research and Planning Paper 19. London: Home Office, 1983.

Brown, R. A., and Frank, J. "Race and Office Decision Making: Examining Differences in Arrest Outcomes Between Black and White Officers." *Justice Quarterly,* 2006, *23*(1), 96–125.

Brown, W. J. "Operation Citizen Participation: A Report on Public Perceptions of Police Service Delivery." *Journal of Police Science and Administration,* 1983, *1*(2), 129–135.

Bryson, J. M. *Strategic Planning for Public and Non-Profit Organizations.* San Francisco: Jossey-Bass, 1995.

Bureau of Justice Assistance. *Recruiting and Retaining Women: A Self-Assessment Guide.* Washington, DC: U.S. Department of Justice, 2001.

Bureau of Justice Assistance. *Project Safe Neighborhoods: America's Network Against Gun Crime.* Program brief. Washington, DC: U.S. Department of Justice, 2004.

Bureau of Justice Statistics. *Performance Measures for the Criminal Justice System.* Washington, DC: U.S. Department of Justice, 1993a.

Bureau of Justice Statistics. *Prisoners, 1992.* Washington, DC: U.S. Department of Justice, 1993b.

Bureau of Justice Statistics. *Correctional Populations in the United States.* Washington, DC: U.S. Department of Justice, 2000a.

Bureau of Justice Statistics. *Sourcebook of Criminal Justice Statistics, 2000.* Washington, DC: U.S. Department of Justice, 2000b.

Bureau of Justice Statistics. *Jail Statistics.* Washington, DC: U.S. Department of Justice, 2005a.

Bureau of Justice Statistics. *State and Local Law Enforcement Statistics.* Washington, DC: U.S. Department of Justice, 2005b.

Bureau of Justice Statistics. *Jail Statistics.* Washington, DC: U.S. Department of Justice, 2006a.

Bureau of Justice Statistics. *Prisoners in 2005.* Washington, DC: U.S. Department of Justice, 2006b.

Bureau of Justice Statistics. *Prisoners in 2006.* Washington, DC: U.S. Department of Justice, 2007.

Burgess, E. W. "Factors Determining Success or Failure on Parole." In *The Workings of the Indeterminate Sentence Law and the Parole System in Illinois*, edited by A. Bruce, E. W. Burgess, and A. J. Harno, pp. 47–60. Springfield, IL: Illinois State Board of Parole, 1928.

Burnes, T., and Stalker, G. *The Management of Innovation.* London: Tavistock, 1961.

Burnham, W. R. "Modern Decision Theory and Corrections." In *Decision-Making in the Criminal Justice System: Review and Essays*, edited by D. M. Gottfredson, pp. 93–103. Rockville, MD: National Institute of Mental Health, 1975.

Burt, R.S. "Network-Related Personality and the Agency Question: Multirole Evidence from a Virtual World." *American Journal of Sociology*, 2012, *118*(3).

Bush, G. W. Eulogy given at the National Cathedral to the Country. September 2001.

Buzawa, E. S. "Determining Patrol Officer Job Satisfaction." *Criminology*, 1984, *22*, 61–81.

Byham, W. C., and Thornton, G. C. *Assessment Centers and Managerial Performance.* New York: Academic Press, 1982.

California Department of Corrections. *Crime in California.* Sacramento, CA: California Department of Corrections, 1994a.

California Department of Corrections. *Leadership Training Institute Curriculum.* Sacramento, CA: California Department of Corrections, 1994b.

Cameron, K. "The Enigma of Organizational Effectiveness." In *Measuring Effectiveness*, edited by D. Baugher, pp. 200–249. San Francisco: Jossey-Bass, 1981.

Camp, C. G., and Camp, G. M. *The Corrections Yearbook 2000: Adult Corrections.* Middletown, CT: Criminal Justice Institute, 2000.

Campbell, J. "On the Nature of Organizational Effectiveness." In *New Perspectives on Organizational Effectiveness*, edited by P. S. Goodman and J. S. Pennings, pp. 13–55. San Francisco: Jossey-Bass, 1977.

Capowich, G. *Police Communication Systems and Boundary Spanning: An Exploratory Case Study of Information Distortion.* Paper presented at the Academy of Criminal Justice Series, 1998.

Carlisle, H. M. *Management: Concepts and Situations.* Chicago, IL: Science Research Associates (SRA), 1976.

Carlson, D. P. *When Cultures Clash: Strategies for Strengthening Police Community Relations.* Upper Saddle River, NJ: Prentice Hall, 2005.

Carp, R., and Wheeler, R. "Sink or Swim: The Socialization of a Federal District Judge." *Journal of Public Law*, 1972, *21*, 359–393.

Carroll, L. *Hacks, Blacks and Cons: Race Relations in a Maximum Security Prison.* Lexington, MA: Lexington Books, 1974.

Carroll, S. J., and Tosi, H. L. *Management by Objectives: Applications and Research.* New York: Macmillan, 1973.

Carter, D., Sapp, A., and Stephens, D. *The State of Police Education: Policy Directions for the 21st Century.* Washington, DC: Police Executive Research Forum, 1989.

Carter, R. M., and Wilkins, L. T. "Caseloads: Some Conceptual Models." In *Probation, Parole and Community Corrections*, edited by R. M. Carter and L. T. Wilkins, pp. 211–232. New York: John Wiley, 1976.

Center for Assessment of the Juvenile Justice System. *Youthful Gangs and Appropriate Police Response*, 1982.

Center for the Study of Mass Communications Research. *Media Crime Prevention Campaign.* Denver, CO: University of Denver, 1982.

Chappell, A. T., MacDonald, J. M., and Manz, P. W. "The Organizational Determinants of Police Arrest Decisions." *Crime and Delinquency*, 2006, *52*(2), 287–306.

Chappell, A. T. "The Philosophical Versus the Actual Adoption of Community Policing: A Case Study." *Criminal Justice Review*, 2009, *34*, 5–25.

Chapper, J. "Oral Argument and Expediting Appeals: A Compatible Combination." *Journal of Law Reform*, 1983, *16*(3), 517–526.

Charles, M. T. *Policing the Streets.* Springfield, IL: Charles C. Thomas, 1986.

Chavkin, N. F. "The Practice-Research Relationship: An Organizational Link." *Social Service Review*, 1986, *60*, 241–250.

Cheek, F., and Miller, M. *Prisoners of Life: A Study of Occupational Stress Among State Corrections Officers.* Washington, DC: American Federation of State, County, and Municipal Employees, 1982.

Cheek, F., and Miller, M. "The Experience of Stress for Corrections Officers." *Journal of Criminal Justice*, 1983, *11*, 105–120.

Chen, H., and Rossi, P. "The Multi-Goal, Theory-Driven Approach to Evaluation: A Model Linking Basic and Applied Social Science." *Social Forces*, 1980, *59*, 106–120.

Cherniss, C. *Staff Burnout: Job Stress in the Human Services.* Beverly Hills, CA: Sage, 1980.

Chicago Tribune. "The Court Retorts…." August 10, 1987, p. 2.

Chin, R. "The Utility of System Models and Developmental Models for Practitioners." In *The Planning of Change*, edited by W. Bennis, K. Benne, and R. Chin, pp. 297–313. New York: Holt, Rinehart & Winston, 1966.

Chin, R., and Benne, K. D. "General Strategies for Effecting Changes in Human Systems." In *The Planning of Change*, edited by W. Bennis, K. D. Benne, and R. Chin, pp. 32–56. New York: Holt, Rinehart & Winston, 1969.

Chisholm, J. Personal communication with author Stan Stojkovic, 2010.

Christopher Commission Report. *Report of the Independent Commission on the Los Angeles Police Department: Summary.* Los Angeles, CA: City of Los Angeles, 1991.

Choo, C.W. "Environmental Scanning as Information Seeking and Organizational Learning." *Information Research*, Vol. 7 No. 1, October 2001.

Clark, M. "The Importance of a New Philosophy to the Post Modern Policing Environment." *Policing*, 2005, *28*(4), 642–654.

Clarke, C. "Proactive Policing: Standing on the Shoulders of Community-Based Policing." *Police Practice and Research*, 2006, 7(1), 3–17.

Clarke, R. V., and Eck, J. *Crime Analysis for Problem Solvers.* Washington, DC: Center for Problem-Oriented Policing, 2005.

Clear, T. "Ophelia the CCW: May 11, 2010." In *Crime and Justice in the Year 2010*, edited by J. Klofas and S. Stojkovic, pp. 205–224. Belmont, CA: Wadsworth, 1995.

Clear, T., and Cole, G. *American Corrections.* 3rd ed. Belmont, CA: Wadsworth, 1994.

Clear, T. R., and O'Leary, V. *Controlling the Offender in the Community.* Lexington, MA: Lexington Books, 1983.

Close, D., and Meier, N. *Morality in Criminal Justice: An Introduction to Ethics*, Cincinnati, OH: Wadsworth, 1995, p. 3.

Clynch, E. J., and Neubauer, D. "Trial Courts as Organizations: A Critique and Synthesis." In *The Administration and Management of Criminal Justice Organizations: A Book of Readings.* 3rd ed., edited by S. Stojkovic, J. Klofas, and D. Kalinich, pp. 69–88. Prospect Heights, IL: Waveland, 1999.

Clynch, E. J., and Neubauer, D. W. "Trial Courts as Organizations: A Critique and Synthesis." *Law and Policy Quarterly*, 1981, *3*, 69–94.

CNN. "Florida Releases Prisoners." News report, March 1997.

Coates, R., Miller, A., and Ohlin, L. *Diversity in a Youth Correctional System.* Cambridge, MA: Ballinger, 1978.

Cohen, M. D., March, J. G., and Olsen, J. P. "A Garbage Can Model of Organizational Choice." *Administrative Science Quarterly*, 1972, *17*, 1–25.

Cohn, M. A., Rust, R. T., and Steen, S. "Prevention, Crime Control or Cash? Public Preferences towards Criminal Justice Spending Priorities." *Justice Quarterly*, 2006, *23*(1), 317–335.

Cole, G. *The American System of Criminal Justice.* Pacific Grove, CA: Brooks/Cole, 1983.

Cole, G. (Ed.). *Criminal Justice: Law and Politics.* 8th ed. Pacific Grove, CA: Brooks/Cole, 2002.

Cole, G., Hanson, R., and Silbert, J. "Mediation: Is It an Effective Alternative to Adjudication in Resolving Prisoner Complaints?" *Judicature*, 1982, *5*(10), 481–489.

Cole, G. F., and Smith, C. E. *The American System of Criminal Justice.* 11th ed. Belmont, CA: Thomson/Wadsworth, 2007.

Cole, M. S., Bruch, H., and Shamir, B. "Social Distance as a Moderator of the Effects of Transformational Leadership: Both Neutralizer and Enhancer." *Human Relations*, 2009, *62*(11), 1697–1733.

Conley, J. A. (Ed.). *The 1967 President's Crime Commission Report: Its Impact 25 Years Later.* Cincinnati, OH: Anderson Publishing Company, 1994.

Conover, T. *Newjack: Guarding Sing Sing.* New York: Random House, 2000.

Conser, J. A. "Motivational Theory Applied to Law Enforcement Agencies." *Journal of Police Science and Administration*, 1979, 7(3), 285–291.

Conspiracy Planet. www.conspiracyplanet.com

Cook, C. and Lane, J. "Legislator Ideology and Corrections and Sentencing Policy in Florida: A Research Note." *Criminal Justice Policy Review*, 2009, *20*, 209.

Cooperrider, D. L., and Sekera, L. E. "Toward a Theory of Positive Organizational Change." In *Organizational Development*, edited by J. V. Gallos, pp. 223–238. San Francisco: Jossey-Bass, 2006.

Cordner, G. W. "Review of Work Motivation Theory and Research for the Police Manager." *Journal of Police Science and Administration*, 1978, *6*(3), 286–292.

Cordner, G. W., and Hudzik, J. *Planning in Criminal Justice Organizations*. New York: Macmillan, 1983.

Corsianos, M. "Discretion in Detectives' Decision Making and High Profile Cases." *Police Practice and Research*, 2003, *4*(3), 301–314.

Cowherd, D. M., and Luchs, R. H. "Linking Organization Structures and Processes to Business Strategy." *Long Range Planning*, 1988, *21*(5),47–53.

Craig, M. "Improving Jury Deliberations: A Reconsideration of Lesser Included Offense Instructions." *Journal of Law Reform*, 1983, *16*(3), 561–584.

Crank, J. *Understanding Police Culture*. Cincinnati, OH: Anderson Publishing Company, 1998.

Crank, J., and Langworthy, R. "An Institutional Perspective on Policing." *Journal of Criminal Law and Criminology*, 1992, *83*, 338–363.

Crank, J. P., and Gregor, P. E. *Counter-Terrorism After 9/11: Justice, Security and Ethics Reconsidered*. Cincinnati, OH: Anderson Publishing Company, 2005.

Cronin, T., Cronin, T. Z., and Milakovich, M. *U.S. v. Crime in the Streets*. Bloomington, IN: Indiana University Press, 1981.

Crouch, B., and Marquart, J. *An Appeal to Justice: Litigated Reform of Texas Prisons*. Austin, TX: University of Texas Press, 1989.

Crouch, B., and Marquart, J. "On Becoming a Prison Guard." In *The Administration and Management of Criminal Justice Organizations: A Book of Readings*. 3rd ed., edited by S. Stojkovic, J. Klofas, and D. Kalinich, pp. 266–296. Prospect Heights, IL: Waveland, 1999.

Crozier, M. *The Bureaucratic Phenomenon*. Chicago: University of Chicago Press, 1964.

Culbert, S. A., and McDonough, J. J. *Radical Management: Power Politics and the Pursuit of Trust*. New York: Free Press, 1985.

Cullen, F. T., and Gilbert, K. *Reaffirming Rehabilitation*. Cincinnati, OH: Anderson Publishing Company, 1982.

Cullen, F. T., Maakestad, W. J., and Cavender, G. *Corporate Crime Under Attack: The Ford Pinto Case and Beyond*. Cincinnati, OH: Anderson Publishing Company, 1987.

Cushman, D., and Whiting, G. "An Approach to Communications Theory: Toward Consensus on Rules." *Journal of Communications*, 1972, *22*, 217–238.

Daft, R. L. *Organization Theory and Design*. 10th Ed. Cincinnati, OH: South-Western College, 2010.

Dahl, R. "The Concept of Power." *Behavioral Science*, 1957, *2*(3), 201–215.

Dahl, R. "The Politics of Planning." *International Social Science Journal*, 1959, *11*, 340–353.

Dale, M. P., and Trlin, A. "Leadership and Probation Officer Practice in New Zealand." *Probation Journal*, 2010, *57*, 121–138.

Dalton, E. *Lessons in Preventing Homicide*. East Lansing: School of Criminal Justice, Michigan State University, 2003.

Dalton, E. "Targeted Crime Reduction Efforts in Ten Communities: Lessons for the Project Safe Neighborhoods Initiative." In *The Administration and Management of Criminal Justice Organizations: A Book of Readings*. 4th ed., edited by S. Stojkovic, J. Klofas, and D. Kalinich, pp. 384–398. Long Grove, IL: Waveland Press, 2004.

Dalton, M. *Men Who Manage*. New York: John Wiley, 1959.

Danzinger, S., and Weinstein, M. "Employment Location and Wage Rates of Poverty-Area Residents." *Journal of Urban Economics*, 1976, *44*, 425–448.

Davidoff, P., and Reiner, T. "A Choice Theory of Planning." *Journal of the American Institute of Planners*, 1962, *30*, 258–274.

Decker, S. "A Systematic Analysis of Diversion: Net Widening and Beyond." *Journal of Criminal Justice*, 1985, *3*(8), 207–216.

Dejong, C., Mastrofski, S. D., and Parks, R. B. "Patrol Officers and Problem Solving: An Application of Expectancy Theory." *Justice Quarterly*, 2001, *18*(1), 31–61.

Deming, W. E. *Out of the Crisis*. Cambridge, MA: MIT Press, 1986.

Denhardt, R. B. *Theories of Public Organization*. Monterey, CA: Brooks/Cole, 1984.

Dershowitz, A. *The Best Defense*. New York: Random House, 1983.

DHS/A Day in the Life of Homeland Security, May 7, 2010. www.dhs.gov/xabout/gc

Dias, C.F., Vaughn, M.S. "Bureaucracy, Managerial Disorganization, and Administrative Breakdown in Criminal Justice Agencies." *Journal of Criminal Justice*, 2006, *34*, 543–555.

Dickey, W. *From the Bottom Up: Probation Supervision in a Wisconsin Community*. Madison, WI: University of Wisconsin Law School, 1988.

Dickey, W. *Governor's Task Force on Sentencing and Corrections: Final Report*. Madison, WI: State of Wisconsin, 1996.

Dickinson, G. "Change in Communications Policies." *Corrections Today*, 1984, *46*(1), 58–60.

DiIulio, J. *Governing Prisons: A Comparative Study of Correctional Management*. New York: Free Press, 1987.

DiIulio, J. *No Escape: The Future of American Corrections*. Glenview, IL: Basic Books/HarperCollins, 1991.

Doering. C. D. *A Report on the Development of Penological Treatment at Norfolk Prison Colony in Massachusetts*. New York: Bureau of Social Hygiene, 1940.

Doleschal, G. "The Dangers of Criminal Justice Reform." *Criminal Justice Abstracts*, 1982, *14*, 133–152.

Downs, A. *Inside Bureaucracy*. Boston, MA: Little, Brown, 1967.

Drapela, L. A., and Lutz, F. E. "Innovation in Community Corrections and Probation Officers Fears of Being Sued: Implementing Neighborhood-Bases Supervision in Spokane Washington." *Journal of Contemporary Criminal Justice*, 2009, *25*, 364–382.

Dreisbach, C. *Ethics in Criminal Justice*, p. 20. Boston, MA: McGraw Hill–Irwin, 2008.

Dubin, R. "Power, Function, and Organization." *Pacific Sociological Review*, 1963, *6*(1), 16–24.

Duffee, D. *Correctional Management: Change and Control in Correctional Organizations*. Englewood Cliffs, NJ: Prentice Hall, 1980.

Duffee, D. "The Interaction of Organization and Political Constraints on Community Prerelease Programs." In *The Politics of Crime and Justice*, edited by E. Fairchild and V. Webb, pp. 99–119. Beverly Hills, CA: Sage, 1985.

Duffee, D. *Correctional Management: Change and Control in Correctional Organizations*. Prospect Heights, IL: Waveland, 1986.

Duffee, D., and O'Leary, V. "Formulating Correctional Goals: The Interaction of Environment, Belief, and Organizational Structure." In *Correctional Management*, edited by D. Duffee, pp. 36–56. Englewood Cliffs, NJ: Prentice Hall, 1980.

Duncan, R. B. "The Characteristics of Organizational Environments and Perceived Environmental Uncertainty." *Administrative Science Quarterly*, 1972, *17*, 313–327.

Dupree, M. *Leadership Is an Art*. New York: Brill, 1989.

Eck, J., and Spelman, W. "Who Ya Gonna Call: The Police as Problem-Busters." In *The Administration and Management of Criminal Justice Organizations: A Book of Readings*. 3rd ed., edited by S. Stojkovic, J. Klofas, and D. Kalinich, pp. 97–113. Prospect Heights, IL: Waveland, 1999.

Editorial, "Organizational context, systems change, and adopting treatment delivery systems in the criminal justice system." *Drug and Alcohol Dependence*, 2009, 103S, S1–S6.

Eisenstein, J. *Politics and the Legal Process*. New York: Harper & Row, 1973.

Eisenstein, J., Flemming, R., and Nardulli, P. *The Contours of Justice: Communities and Their Courts*. Boston: Little, Brown, 1988.

Eitle, D., Stolzenberg, L., and D'Alesso, S. J. "Police Organizational Factors, the Racial Composition of the Police, and the Probability of Arrest." *Justice Quarterly*, 2005, *22*(1), 50–68.

Ekland-Olson, S., Martin, S. J. "Organizational Compliance with Court-Ordered Reform." *Law and Society Review*, 1988, *22*(2),359–383.

Elias, S. M. "Restrictive Versus Promotive Control and Employee Work Outcomes: The Moderating Role of Locus of Control." *Journal of Management*, 2009, *35*, 369–392.

Elliot, D. "On Policy Relevance and the Future of Criminology: A Response to Joan Petersilia's 1990 ASC Presidential Address." Unpublished manuscript, 1990.

Ellsworth, R. B., and Ellsworth, J. J. "The Psychiatric Aide: Therapeutic Agent or Lost Potential?" *Journal of Psychiatric Nursing and Mental Health Services*, 1970, *8*, 7–13.

Embert, P. "Correctional Law and Jails." In *Sneaking Inmates Down the Alley: Problems and Prospects in Jail Management*, edited by D. Kalinich and J. Klofas, pp. 63–84. Springfield, IL: Charles C. Thomas, 1986.

Emerson, R. E. "Power-Dependence Relations." *American Sociological Review*, 1962, *27*(1), 31–40.

Emmery, F., and Emmery, M. "Participative Design: Work and Community Life." In *Democracy at Work*, edited by F. Emmery and E. Thorsund, pp. 147–170. Leiden, The Netherlands: Martinus Nijhoff, 1974.

Engel, R. "Supervisory Styles of Patrol Sergeants and Lieutenants." In *The Administration and Management of Criminal Justice Organizations: A Book of Readings*. 4th ed., edited by S. Stojkovic, J. Klofas, and D. Kalinich, pp. 197–222. Prospect Heights, IL: Waveland, 2004.

Ermer, V. B. "Recruitment of Female Police Officers in New York City." *Journal of Criminal Justice*, 1978, *6*, 233–246.

Etzioni, A. "New Direction in the Study of Organizations and Society." *Social Research*, 1960, *27*, 223–228.

Etzioni, A. *A Comparative Analysis of Complex Organizations*. New York: Free Press, 1961.

Etzioni, A. *Modern Organizations*. Englewood Cliffs, NJ: Prentice Hall, 1964.

Fairchild, E. "Interest Groups in the Criminal Justice Process." *Journal of Criminal Justice*, 1981, *9*, 181–194.

Fairchild, E., and Webb, V. (Eds.). *The Politics of Crime and Justice*. Beverly Hills, CA: Sage, 1985.

Farace, R., Monge, P., and Russell, H. *Communicating and Organizing*. New York: Random House, 1977.

Faris, R. *Social Disorganization*. New York: Ronald Press, 1948.

Farrington, D. P. "Predicting Individual Crime Rates." In *Prediction and Classification: Criminal Justice Decision Making*, edited by D. M. Gottfredson and M. Tonry, pp. 52–102. Chicago: University of Chicago Press, 1987.

Fearn, N. E. "A Multilevel Analysis of Community Effects on Criminal Sentencing." *Justice Quarterly*, 2005, *22*(4), 452–487.

Feeley, M. *The Process Is the Punishment*. New York: Russell Sage Foundation, 1979.

Fernandez, S., Rainey, H.G. "Managing Successful Organizational Change in the Public Sector." *Public Administration Review*, 2006.

Festinger, L. *A Theory of Cognitive Dissonance*. Evanston, IL: Row, Peterson, 1957.

Fiedler, F. E. *A Theory of Leadership Effectiveness*. New York: McGraw-Hill, 1967.

Fiedler, F. E., and Garcia, J. E. *New Approaches to Effective Leadership: Cognitive Resources and Organizational Performance*. New York: John Wiley & Sons, 1987.

Fielding, N. G., and Fielding, J. L. "A Study of Resignation During British Police Training." *Journal of Police Science and Administration*, 1987, *15*, 24–36.

Fire and Police Commission. *A Report to Mayor John O. Norquist and the Board of Fire and Police Commissioners*. Milwaukee, WI: Mayor's Commission on Police-Community Relations, October 1991.

Fischer, F., and Sirianni, C. *Critical Studies in Organization and Bureaucracy*. Philadelphia, PA: Temple University Press, 1984.

Fischer, J. E. "Principles for Medical and Mental Health Providers: How Principles of Direct Supervision Relate to Providing Medical/Mental Health Care." *American Jails*, September/October 2005, 25–30.

Flanagan, T., Johnson, W., and Bennett, K. "Job Satisfaction Among Correctional Executives: A Contemporary Portrait of Wardens of State Prisons for Adults." *Prison Journal*, 1996, *76*(4), 385–397.

Flemming, R. B. *Punishment Before Trial: An Organizational Perspective of Felony Bail Processes*. New York: Longman, 1982.

Fogel, D., and Hudson, J. *Justice as Fairness*. Cincinnati, OH: Anderson Publishing Company, 1981.

Frazier, C., and Block, W. "Effects of Court Officers on Sentencing Severity." *Criminology*, 1982, *20*, 257–272.

French, J. R. P., and Raven, B. "The Bases of Social Power." In *Group Dynamics*. 3rd ed., edited by D. Cartwright and A. Zander, pp. 259–269. New York: Harper & Row, 1968.

French, W. L. "Organizational Development: Objectives, Assumptions and Strategies." *California Management Review*, 1969, *12*(2), 23–35.

French, W. L. "The Emergence and Early History of Organizational Development with Reference to Influences upon and Interactions Among Some of the Key Actors." In *Contemporary Organization Development: Current Thinking and Applications*, edited by D. Warrick, pp. 12–27. Glenview, IL: Scott, Foresman, 1985.

Frey, W. "Central City White Flight: Racial and Non-Racial Causes." *American Sociological Review*, 1979, *44*, 435–448.

Fyfe, J. Personal communication on effective supervision strategies within police organizations, 1996.

Fyfe, J. "Good Policing." In *The Administration and Management of Criminal Justice Organizations: A Book of Readings.* 4th ed., edited by S. Stojkovic, J. Klofas, and D. Kalinich, pp. 113–133. Prospect Heights, IL: Waveland Press, 2004a.

Fyfe, J. Personal communication with author Stan Stojkovic, 2004b.

Fyfe, J., Greene, J., Walsh, W., Wilson, O., and McLaren, R. *Police Administration.* 5th ed. New York: McGraw-Hill, 1997.

Gaines, L., and Milleer, R. L. *Criminal Justice in Action.* 3rd ed. Belmont, CA: Thompson Wadsworth, 2005.

Gaines, L., Southerland, M., and Angell, J. *Police Administration.* New York: McGraw-Hill, 1991.

Gaines, L. K., Tubergen, N. V., and Paiva, M. A. "Police Officer Perceptions of Promotion as a Source of Motivation." *Journal of Criminal Justice,* 1984, *12*(3), 265–274.

Gaines, L. K., Worrall, J. L., Southerland, M. D., and Angel, J. E. *Police Administration.* 2nd ed. Boston, MA: McGraw-Hill, 2003.

Gains, L. K., and Kappeler, V. E. *Policing in America,* Cincinnati, OH: Anderson Publishing Company, 2005.

Galbraith, J. *Designing Complex Organizations.* Reading, MA: Addison-Wesley, 1973.

Galliher, J. "Explanations of Police Behavior: A Critical Review and Analysis." In *The Ambivalent Force,* edited by A. Blumberg and E. Niederhoffer, pp. 62–93. New York: Holt, Rinehart & Winston, 1985.

Gandz, J., and Murray, V. "The Experience of Workplace Politics." *Academy of Management Journal,* 1980, *23*, 237–251.

Garcia, V. "Constructing the 'Other' Within Police Culture: An Analysis of a Deviant Unit Within the Police Organization." *Police Practice and Research,* 2005, *6*(1), 65–80.

Gardner, T. Statements made at Crime Trends Workshop, Madison, WI, March 1997.

Geller, W. A. (Ed.). *Police Leadership in America: Crisis and Opportunity.* Chicago, IL: American Bar Association, 1985.

Geva, R., and Shem-Tov, O. "Setting up Community Police Centers: Participatory Action." *Research in Decentralized Policing Services. Police Practice and Research,* 2002, *3*(3), 189–200.

Ghorpade, J., and Atchison, T. J. "The Concept of Job Analysis: A Review and Some Suggestions." *Public Personnel Management,* 1980, *9*, 134–144.

Giacomazzi, A. L., Riley, S., and Merz, R. "Internal and External Challenges to Implementing Community Policing: Examining Comprehensive Assessment Reports from Multiple Sites." *Criminal Justice Studies,* 2004, *17*(2), 223–238.

Gies, G. "Negel K. Teeters (1896–1971) Pioneer in Penology." *Prison Journal,* 2004, *84*(4 Suppl.), 5S–19S.

Gil, P. "Not Just Crossing the Dots but Crossing the Borders and Bridging the Voids: Constructing Security Networks After 11 September 2001." *Policing and Society,* 2006, *16*(1), 27–49.

Glaser, D. *Effectiveness of a Prison and Parole System.* Indianapolis, IN: Bobbs-Merrill, 1969.

Glaser, S. B., and Grunwald, S. Homeland Security Still Without an Image, *Washington Post,* December 22, 2005. www.washingtonpost.com

Glass, G. V., McGaw, B., and Smith, M. L. *Meta-Analysis in Social Research.* Beverly Hills, CA: Sage, 1981.

Glauser, M., and Tullar, W. "Communicator Style of Police Officers and Citizen Satisfaction with Officer/ Citizen Telephone Conversations." *Journal of Police Science and Administration,* 1985, *13*(1), 70–77.

Goffman, E. *Asylums.* Garden City, NY: Doubleday, 1961.

Goldkamp, J. S. *Policy Guidelines for Bail: An Experiment in Court Reform.* Philadelphia, PA: Temple University Press, 1985.

Goldstein, H. "Police Discretion Not to Invoke the Criminal Process." *Yale Law Journal,* 1960, *69*, 33–42.

Goldstein, H. *Problem-Oriented Policing.* New York: McGraw-Hill, 1990.

Goldstein, H. "Police Discretion Not to Invoke the Criminal Process: Low-Visibility Decisions in the Administration of Justice." In *Criminal Justice: Law and Politics.* 8th ed., edited by G. F. Cole, pp. 109–126. Belmont, CA: Wadsworth, 2002.

Gomez, J. Presentation to the first class of graduates of the California Department of Corrections Leadership Institute, Chico, CA, February 1995.

Gomez, J. Presentation to the third class of graduates of the California Department of Corrections Leadership Institute, Chico, CA, January 1996.

Goodman, P. S., and Kurke, L. B. "Studies of Change in Organizations: A Status Report." In *Changes in Organizations: New Perspectives on Theory, Research, and Practice*, pp. 280–315. San Francisco, CA: Jossey-Bass, 1982.

Goodstein, L., and Hepburn. J. *Determinate Sentencing and Imprisonment: A Failure of Reform*. Cincinnati, OH: Anderson Publishing Company, 1985.

Gordon, M. S. "Correctional Officer Control Ideology: Implications for Understanding a System." *Criminal Justice Studies*, 2006, *19*(3), 225–239.

Gottfredson, D. M. *Decision-Making in the Criminal Justice System: Review and Essays*. Rockville, MD: National Institute of Mental Health, 1975.

Gottfredson, D. M., and Tonry, M. (Eds.). *Prediction and Classification: Criminal Justice Decision Making*. Chicago: University of Chicago Press, 1987.

Gottfredson, D. M., Hoffman, P. B., Sigler, M. H., and Wilkins, L. T. "Making Parole Policy Explicit." *Crime and Delinquency*, 1975, *21*, 7–17.

Gottfredson, M. R., and Gottfredson, D. M. *Decision-making in Criminal Justice: Toward a Rational Exercise of Discretion*. Cambridge, MA: Ballinger, 1980.

Granovetter, M. "The Strength of Weak Ties: A Network Theory Revisited," *Sociological Theory*, 1983, *1*, 201–233.

Grau, C. W. "Limits of Planned Change in Courts." In *Misdemeanor Courts: Policy Concerns and Research Perspectives*, edited by J. J. Alfini, pp. 271–300. Racine, WI: Johnson Foundation, 1980.

Grau, J. "Technology and Criminal Justice." In *Vision for Change*, edited by R. Muraskin and A. Brooks, pp. 231–247. New York: Prentice Hall, 1999.

Gray, T., and Mayer, J. "Prison Administration: Inmate Participation versus the Control Model." In *Correctional Context: Contemporary and Classic Readings*, edited by J. W. Marquart and J. S. Sorenson. Boston, MA: Roxbury Publishing, 1997.

Greene, J., Bynum, T., and Cordner, G. "Planning and the Play of Power: Resource Acquisition Among Criminal Justice Agencies." *Journal of Criminal Justice*, 1986, *14*, 529–544.

Greenwood, P. *Selective Incapacitation*. Santa Monica, CA: Rand, 1982.

Greeson, M.R., Campbell, R. "Sexual Assault Response Teams (SARTs): An Empirical Review of Their Effectiveness and Challenges to Successful Implementation." *Trauma, Violence, and Abuse*, 2012, *14* (2), 83–95.

Griener, L. "Antecedents of Planned Change." *Journal of Applied Behavioral Sciences*, 1967, *21*, 51–86.

Griffin, G. R., Dunbar, R. L. M., and McGill, M. E. "Factors Associated with Job Satisfaction Among Police Personnel." *Journal of Police Science and Administration*, 1978, *6*(1), 77–85.

Griffin, T., and Miller, M. K. "Child Abduction, AMBER Alert, and Crime Control Theater" *Criminal Justice Review*, June 2008, *33*(3), 159–167.

Grubb, N. "The Flight to the Suburbs of Population Employment." *Journal of Urban Economics*, 1982, *11*, 348–367.

Guy, E., Platt, J., and Zwerling, S. "Mental Health Status of Prisoners in an Urban Jail." *Criminal Justice and Behavior*, 1985, *12*, 29–53.

Guyot, D. "Political Interference versus Political Accountability in Municipal Policing." In *The Politics of Crime and Justice*, edited by E. Fairchild and V. Webb, pp. 120–143. Beverly Hills, CA: Sage, 1985.

Gyllenhammer, P. "Changing Work Organization at Volvo." In *Perspectives on Job Enrichment*, edited by W. Soujaren, pp. 77–99. Atlanta: School of Business Administration, Georgia State University, 1975.

Hackman, J. R., and Oldham, G. R. *Work Redesign*. Reading, MA: Addison-Wesley, 1980.

Hagan, J. *Victims Before the Law: The Organizational Domination of Criminal Law*. Toronto Ontario: Butterworth, 1983.

Hage, J., and Aiken, M. *Social Change in Complex Organizations*. New York: Random House, 1970.

Hagedorn, J. *Forsaking Our Children: Bureaucracy and Reform in the Child Welfare System*. Chicago, IL: Lake View Press, 1995.

Hahn, H. "A Profile of Urban Police." In *The Police Community*, edited by J. Goldsmith and S. Goldsmith, pp. 109–129. Pacific Palisades, CA: Palisades Publishers, 1974.

Hall, A., Henry, D. A., Perlstein, J. J., and Smith, W. F. *Alleviating Jail Crowding: A Systems Perspective*. Washington, DC: U.S. Government Printing Office, 1985.

Hall, R. A. *The Ethical Foundations of Criminal Justice*. New York: CRC Press, 2000.

Hall, R. H. *Organizations: Structure, Processes, and Outcomes*. 4th ed. Englewood Cliffs, NJ: Prentice Hall, 1987.

Hall, R. H., and Tolbert, P. S. *Organizations: Structures, Processes, and Outcomes*. 5th ed. Englewood Cliffs, NJ: Prentice Hall, 2005.

Halperin, M. "Shaping the Flow of Information." In *Bureaucratic Power in National Politics*. 3rd ed., edited by F. Rourke, pp. 102–115. Boston, MA: Little, Brown, 1978.

Hannan, M. T., and Freeman, J. "Obstacles to Comparative Studies." In *New Perspectives on Organizational Effectiveness*, edited by P. S. Goodman and J. M. Pennings, pp. 106–131. San Francisco: Jossey-Bass, 1977.

Hannan, M. T., and Freeman, J. "Structural Inertia and Organizational Change." *American Sociological Review*, 1984, *49*, 929–964.

Hardy, K. "Equity in Court Dispositions." In *Evaluating Performance of Criminal Justice Agencies*, edited by G. P. Whitaker and C. D. Phillips, pp. 151–173. Beverly Hills, CA: Sage, 1983.

Harring, S. "Taylorization of Police Work." *Insurgent Sociologist*, 1982, *4*, 25–32.

Harris, P. W., and Hartland, G. R. "Developing and Implementing Alternatives to Incarceration: A Problem of Planned Change in Criminal Justice." *University of Illinois Law Review*, 1984, *2*, 319–364.

Harris, R. N. *The Police Academy: An Inside View*. New York: John Wiley, 1973.

Harfield, C. "The Organization of Organized Crime Policing and Its International Context." *Criminology and Criminal Justice*, 2008, *8*(4), 483–507.

Hartwell, S., and Orr, K. "Release Planning and the Distinction for Mentally Ill Offenders Returning to the Community from Jails or Prison." *American Jails*, November/December 2000.

Hatry, H. P., and Greiner, J. M. *How Police Departments Better Apply Management-by-Objectives and Quality Circle Programs*. Washington, DC: National Institute of Justice, U.S. Department of Justice, 1984.

Havelock, R. G. *Planning for Innovation*. Ann Arbor, MI: Institute for Social Research, 1979.

Hawkins, K. "Assessing Evil." *British Journal of Criminology*, 1983, *23*, 101–127.

Hayslip, D. *Can Correction Officers Be Motivated?* Paper presented at the annual meeting of the Academy of Criminal Justice Sciences, Louisville, KY, 1982.

He, N., Zhao, J., and Lovrich, N. P. "Community Policing: A Preliminary Assessment of Environmental Impact with Panel Data on Program Implementation in U.S. Cities." *Crime and Delinquency*, 2005, *51*(3), 295–317.

Hellriegel, D., and Slocum. J. W. *Organizational Behavior*. St. Paul, MN: West, 1979.

Hellriegel, D., Slocum, J. W., and Woodman, R. W. *Organizational Behavior*. 7th ed. Minneapolis, MN: West, 1995.

Henderson, M., and Hollin, C. "A Critical Review of Social Skills Training with Young Offenders." *Criminal Justice and Behavior*, 1983, *10*(3), 316–341.

Henderson, T. Conversation with author Stan Stojkovic, 2006.

Henderson, H., Wells, W., Maguire, E. R., and Gray, J. "Evaluating the Measurement Properties of Procedural Justice in a Correctional Setting." *Criminal Justice and Behavior*, 2010, *37*, 384–399.

Henry, N. *Public Administration and Public Affairs*. 10th ed. Englewood Cliffs, NJ: Prentice Hall, 2007.

Henry, V. E. *The COMPSTAT Paradigm: Management Accountability in Policing, Business and the Public Sector* (with a foreword by William Bratton). Flushing, NY: Looseleaf Law Publications, 2002.

Hepburn, J. R. "The Exercise of Power in Coercive Organizations: A Study of Prison Guards." *Criminology*, 1985, *23*(1), 145–164.

Hernandez, A. P. "Motivation and Municipal Police Departments: Models and an Empirical Analysis." *Journal of Police Science and Administration*, 1982, *10*(3), 284–288.

Hershey, P., and Blanchard, K. *Management of Organizational Behavior*. Englewood Cliffs, NJ: Prentice Hall, 1977.

Herzberg, F. *Work and the Nature of Man*. New York: World, 1966.

Herzberg, F. "Participation Is Not a Motivator." *Industry Week*, 1978, *198*, 39–44.

Herzberg, F., Mausner, B., and Snyderman, B. B. *The Motivation to Work*. New York: John Wiley, 1959.

Hiam, A. *Motivating and Rewarding Employees: New and Better Ways to Inspire Your People*. Holbrook, MA: Adams Media Corporation, 1999.

Hickman, R. Q. Conversation with author Stan Stojkovic, August 2005.

Hicksen, D., Hinings, C., Lee, C., Schenck, R., and Pennings, J. "A Strategic Contingencies Theory of Intraorganizational Power." In *Readings in*

Organizational Behavior and Human Performance, edited by W. J. Scott and L. L. Cummings, pp. 63–96. Homewood, IL: Richard D. Irwin, 1973.

High Intensity Drug Trafficking Area (HIDTA). "Inventory of State Substance Abuse Prevention and Treatment Activities and Expenditures." Washington, DC: Office of Drug Control Policy, 2006a.

High Intensity Drug Trafficking Area (HIDTA). "Memorandum of Understanding with the Helen Bader School of Social Welfare," Milwaukee, WI: University of Wisconsin-Milwaukee, 2006b.

Hill, G. "Correctional Officer Traits and Skills," *Corrections Compendium*, 1997, *22*(8), 1.

Hinduja, S. "Perceptions of Local and State Law Enforcement Concerning the Role of Computer Crime Investigative Teams." *Policing: An International Journal of Police Strategies and Management*, 2004, *27*(3), 341–357.

Hinduja, S. "Computer Crime Investigation in the United States: Leveraging Knowledge from the Past to Address the Future." *International Journal of Cyber Crimes and Criminal Justice*, 2006, *1*(1), 77–86.

Hinings, C. R., Pugh, D. S., Hicksen, D. J., and Turner, C. "An Approach to the Study of Bureaucracy." *Sociology*, 1967, *1*(1), 61–72.

Hoffman, P., and Stone-Meierhoefer, B. "Reporting Recidivism Rates: The Criterion and Follow-Up Issues." *Journal of Criminal Justice*, 1980, *8*, 53–60.

Holmes, M. D., Smith, B. W., Freng, A. B., and Muñoz, E. A. "Minority Threat, Crime Control, and Police Resource Allocation in the Southwestern United States." *Crime & Delinquency*, 2008, *54*, 128.

Holt, N. "Parole in the Future." In *Community Corrections: Probation, Parole, and Intermediate Sanctions*, edited by J. Petersilia, pp. 14–30. New York: Oxford University Press, 1998.

Hoos, I. R. *Systems Analysis in Public Policy*. Los Angeles, CA: University of California Press, 1983.

Houghland, J. G., and Wood, J. R. "Control in Organizations and Commitment of Members." *Social Forces*, 1980, *59*(1), 85–105.

Houghland, J. G., Shepard, J. M., and Wood, J. R. "Discrepancies in Perceived Organizational Control: Their Decrease and Importance in Local Churches." *Sociological Quarterly*, 1979, *20*(1), 63–76.

House, R. J. "Power in Organizations: A Social Psychological Perspective." Unpublished manuscript, University of Toronto, 1984.

House, R. J., and Mitchell, T. R. "Path-Goal Theory of Leadership." In *Organizational Behavior and Management*. 4th ed., edited by H. L. Tosi and W. C. Hamner, pp. 491–500. Cincinnati, OH: Grid, 1985.

Houston, J. *Correctional Management: Functions, Skills, and Systems*. 2nd ed. Chicago, IL: Nelson-Hall, 1999.

Houston, J., and Parsons, W. *Criminal Justice and the Policy Process*. Chicago, IL: Nelson Hall, 2006.

Hudzik, J., and Cordner, G. *Planning in Criminal Justice Organizations and Systems*. New York: Macmillan, 1983.

Huse, E. *Organizational Development and Change*. Minneapolis, MN: West, 1975.

Husz, J. Personal communication with author Stan Stojkovic, December 1996.

Iannone, N. *Police Supervision*. New York: McGraw-Hill, 1994.

Ideus, K. *Staffing and Personnel Management: A Humanistic Look*. Rockville, MD: National Institute of Justice, 1978.

Inbau, F., Reid, J., and Buckley, J. *Criminal Interrogation and Confessions*. Baltimore, MD: Williams, Lippincott, & Wilkins, 1986.

Innocence Project. www.innocenceproject.org

International Association of Chiefs of Police (IACP). *Police Supervision*. Dubuque, IA: Kendall/Hunt, 1985.

International Association of Chiefs of Police (IACP). *Shared Leadership: Can Empowerment Work in Police Organizations?* Alexandria, VA: IACP Center for Police Leadership, 2006.

International Association of Chiefs of Police (with the National Institute of Justice). *Establishing and Sustaining Law Enforcement Partnerships: Guide for Law Enforcement Leaders: Final Report*. Washington, DC: International Association of Chiefs of Police, 2006a.

International Association of Chiefs of Police (with the National Institute of Justice). *Establishing and Sustaining Law Enforcement Partnerships: Guide for Researchers: Final Report*. Washington, DC: International Association of Chiefs of Police, 2006b.

Irwin, J. *Prisons in Turmoil*. Boston, MA: Little, Brown, 1980.

Irwin, J. *The Jail: Managing the Underclass in American Society*. Berkeley, CA: University of California Press, 1986.

Irwin, J., and Austin, J. *It's About Time: America's Imprisonment Binge.* 2nd ed. Belmont, CA: Wadsworth, 1997.

Irwin, J., and Austin, J. *It's About Time: America's Imprisonment Binge.* 3rd ed. Belmont, CA: Wadsworth, 2002.

Ismaili, K. "Explaining the Cultural and Symbolic Resonance of Zero Tolerance in Contemporary Criminal Justice." *Contemporary Justice Review*, 2003, *6*(3), 255–264.

Jacks, I. "Positive Interaction: Everyday Principles of Correctional Rehabilitation." In *Psychological Approaches to Crime and Its Correction: Theory, Research, Practice*, edited by I. Jacks, pp. 424–443. Chicago, IL: Nelson-Hall, 1984.

Jacobs, D. "Dependency and Vulnerability: An Exchange Approach to the Control of Organizations." *Administrative Science Quarterly*, 1974, *19*, 45–59.

Jacobs, J. *Drunk Driving: An American Dilemma.* Chicago: University of Chicago Press, 1989.

Jacobs, J. B. *Stateville: The Penitentiary in Mass Society.* Chicago: University of Chicago Press, 1977.

Jacobs, J. B. *The Unionization of the Guards.* Proceedings of the Thirteenth Interagency Workshop, Sam Houston State University. Huntsville, TX, 1978.

Jacobs, J. B. (Ed.). *New Perspectives on Prisons and Imprisonment.* Ithaca, NY: Cornell University Press, 1983a.

Jacobs, J. B. "The Prisoners' Rights Movement and Its Impacts." In *New Perspectives on Prisons and Imprisonment*, edited by J. B. Jacobs, pp. 33–60. Ithaca, NY: Cornell University Press, 1983b.

Jacobs, J. B., and Grear, M. P. "Drop Outs and Rejects: An Analysis of the Prison Guard's Revolving Door." *Criminal Justice Review*, 1977, *2*, 57–70.

Jacobs, J. B., and Retsky, H. C. "Prison Guard." *Urban Life*, 1975, *4*, 5–29.

Jacobs, J. B., and Zimmer. L. "Collective Bargaining and Labor Unrest." In *New Perspectives on Prisons and Imprisonment*, edited by J. B. Jacobs, pp. 142–159. Ithaca, NY: Cornell University Press, 1983.

James, B. "Computer Assisted Instruction." *American Jails*, 1996, *9*(6), 27–31.

Jaworsky, P. A., Park, Y. "Cause or Consequence? Suburbanization and Crime in U.S. Metropolitan Areas," *Crime & Delinquency*, January, 2009, *55*(1), 28–50.

Johnson, R. "Informal Helping Networks in Prison: The Shape of Grass Roots Correctional Intervention." *Journal of Criminal Justice*, 1977, 7, 53–70.

Johnson, R. *Hard Time: Understanding and Reforming the Prison.* 2nd ed. Belmont, CA: Wadsworth, 1996.

Johnson, R. *Hard Time: Understanding and Reforming the Prison.* 3rd ed. Belmont, CA: Wadsworth, 2002.

Joint Commission on Correctional Manpower and Training. *A Time to Act.* Washington, DC: U.S. Government Printing Office, 1969.

Jones, A. M. "Culture, Identity, and Motivation: The Historical Anthropology of a Family Firm." *Culture and Organization*, 2006, *12*(2), 169–183.

Josephson, E., and Josephson, M. *Man Alone: Alienation in Modern Society.* New York: Laurel, 1975.

Julian, J. "Compliance Patterns and Communication Blocks in Complex Organizations." *American Sociological Review*, 1966, *31*(3), 382–389.

Jurik, N. C., and Winn, R. "Describing Correctional-Security Dropouts and Rejects: An Individual or Organizational Profile?" *Criminal Justice and Behavior*, 1987, *14*(1), 5–25.

Kagehiro, D., and Werner, C. "Divergent Perceptions of Jail Inmates and Correctional Officers: The 'Blame the Other–Expect to Be Blamed' Effect." *Journal of Applied Social Psychology*, 1981, *11*(6), 507–528.

Kalinich, D. *Power, Stability, and Contraband: The Inmate Economy.* Prospect Heights, IL: Waveland, 1984.

Kalinich, D. "Criminal Justice Education: Coming in in the Middle of the Movie." In *The Future of Criminal Justice Education*, Unpublished manuscript, edited by R. Muraskins, pp. 28–43. Brookville, NY: Long Island University Criminal Justice Institute, 1987.

Kalinich, D., and Banas, D. "Systems Maintenance and Legitimization: An Historical Illustration of the Impact of National Task Forces and Committees on Corrections." *Journal of Criminal Justice*, 1984, *12*, 61–71.

Kalinich, D., and Klofas, J. (Eds.). *Sneaking Inmates Down the Alley: Problems and Prospects of Jail Management.* Springfield, IL: Charles C. Thomas, 1986.

Kalinich, D., and Stojkovic, S. "Contraband: The Basis for Legitimate Power in a Prison Social System." *Criminal Justice and Behavior*, 1985, *12*, 435–451.

Kalinich, D., Lorinskas, L., and Banas, D. "Symbolism and Rhetoric: The Guardians of the Status Quo in the Criminal Justice System." *Criminal Justice Review*, 1985, *10*, 41–46.

Kalinich, D., Stojkovic, S., and Klofas. J. "Toward a Political-Community Theory of Prison Organization." *Journal of Criminal Justice*, 1988, *16*(3), 217–230.

Karger, H. "Burnout as Alienation." *Social Service Review*, 1981, *55*, 270–283.

Katz, D., and Kahn, R. L. *The Social Psychology of Organizations*. 2nd ed. New York: John Wiley, 1978.

Katzev, R., and Wishart, S. "The Impact of Judicial Commentary Concerning Eyewitness Identifications on Jury Decision Making." *Journal of Criminal Law and Criminology*, 1985, *76*(3), 733–745.

Kaufman, H. "Organization Theory and Political Theory." *The American Political Science Review*, 1964, *58*(1), 5–14.

Kaufman, H. "Administrative Decentralization and Political Power." *Public Administration Review*, 1969, *29*, 3–15.

Kauffman, K., *Prison Officers and Their World*. Cambridge, MA: Harvard University Press, 1988.

Kautt, P. M., "Location, Location, Location: Interdistrict and Intercircuit Variations in Sentencing Outcomes for Federal Drug-Trafficking Offenses." *Justice Quarterly*, 2002, *19*(4), 633–638.

Kelling, G. "Order Maintenance, the Quality of Urban Life, and Police: A Line of Argument." In *Police Leadership in America*, edited by W. Geller, pp. 296–308. Chicago, IL: American Bar Foundation, 1985.

Kelling, G. L. *Police and Communities: The Quiet Revolution*. Washington, DC: National Institute of Justice, 1988.

Kelling, G. and Moore, M. "The Evolving Strategy of Policing," In *Perspectives on Policing*, No. 13. Washington DC: National Institute of Justice, US Government Printing Office, 1988.

Kelling, G. L., and Coles, C. M. *Fixing Broken Windows: Restoring and Reducing Crime in Our Communities*. New York: Free Press, 1996.

Kelly, J. E. *Scientific Management, Job Redesign and Work Performance*. New York: Academic Press, 1982.

Kelly, L., Mueller, D., and Hemmens, C. "To Punish or Rehabilitate Revisited: An Analysis of the Purpose/Goals of State Correctional Statutes, 1991–2002." *Criminal Justice Studies*, 2004, *17*(4), 333–351.

Kennedy, K. A., and Pronin, E. "When Disagreement Gets Ugly: Perceptions of Bias and the Escalation of Conflict." *Personality and Social Psychology Bulletin*, 2008, *34*, 833–848.

Kerle, K. E. *American Jails: Looking to the Future*. Boston, MA: Butterworth-Heinemann, 1998.

King, D. J. "Separate but Equal: The Introduction and Integration of Policewomen in Bermuda Police 1961–2002." *Police Practice and Research*, 2005, *6*(3), 215–233.

King, K. Conversation with author Stan Stojkovic, September 2006.

King, K., Steiner, B., and Breach, S. R. "Violence in the Supermax: A Self-Fulfilling Prophecy." *Prison Journal*, March 2008, *88*(1), 144–168.

Kinicki, A., and Kreitner, R. *Organizational Behavior, Key Concepts, Skills and Best Practices*. New York: McGraw-Hill, 2006.

Klockars, C. "The Rhetoric of Community Policing." In *Community Policing: Rhetoric or Reality*, edited by J. Greene and S. Mastrofski, pp. 19–36. New York: Praeger, 1991.

Klofas, J., and Toch, H. "The Guard Subculture Myth." *Journal of Research in Crime and Delinquency*, 1982, *19*, 169–175.

Klofas, J., Smith, S., and Meister, E. "Harnessing Human Resources in Local Jails: Toward a New Generation of Planners." In *Sneaking Inmates Down the Alley*, edited by D. Kalinich and J. Klofas, pp. 193–208. Springfield, IL: Charles C. Thomas, 1986.

Klofas, J. M. "Postscript: Teaching the New Criminal Justice." In *The New Criminal Justice: American Communities and the Changing World of Crime Control*, edited by J. M. Klofas, N. Kroovand-Hipple, and E. G. McGarrell, pp. 147–156. New York: Taylor and Francis, 2010.

Klofas, J. M., Kroovand-Hipple, N., and McGarrell, E. F. (Eds.). *The New Criminal Justice: American Communities and the Changing World of Crime Control*. New York: Taylor and Francis, 2010.

Knapp Commission. *Report on Police Corruption*. New York: George Braziller, 1972.

Kohfeld, C. W. "Rational Cops, Rational Robbers, and Information." *Journal of Criminal Justice*, 1983, *11*(5), 459–466.

Kolonski, H., and Mendelsohn, R. *The Politics of Local Justice*. Boston, MA: Little, Brown, 1970.

Kotrba, L. M., Gillespie, M. A., Schmidt, A. M., Smerek, R. E., Ritchie, S. A., and Denison, D. R. "Do Consistent Corporate Cultures Have Better Business Performance? Exploring the Interaction Effects." *Human Relations*, 2012, *65*(2), 241–262.

Kopelman, R. "Job Redesign and Productivity: A Review of the Evidence." *National Productivity Review*, 1985, *4*(3), 237–255.

Korsgaard, M. A., Jeong, S. S., Mahony, D. M., and Pitariu, A. H. "A Multilevel View of Intragroup Conflict." *Journal of Management*, 2008, *34*, 1222–1252.

Kotter, J. P. *Power and Influence*. New York: Free Press, 1985.

Kotter, J. *A Force for Change*. New York: Macmillan, 1990.

Kotter, J. P. *A Force for Change*. 2nd ed. New York: Macmillan, 1996.

Kouzes, J., and Posner, B. *The Leadership Challenge: How to Keep Getting Extraordinary Things Done in Organizations*. San Francisco: Jossey-Bass, 1997.

Kovandzic, T. V., Sloan, J. J., and Vieraitis, L. M. "'Striking Out' As Crime Reduction Policy: The Impact of 'Three Strikes' Law on Crime Rates in U.S. Cities." *Justice Quarterly*, 2004, *21*(2), 85–97.

Kratcoski, P. C., and Walker, D. B. *Criminal Justice in America*. Glenview, IL: Scott, Foresman, 1978.

Kreman, B. "Search for a Better Way of Work: Lordstown, Ohio." In *Humanizing the Workplace*, edited by R. P. Fairchild, pp. 17–41. Buffalo, NY: Prometheus, 1973.

Kreps, G. *Organizational Communication*. 2nd ed. White Plains, NY: Longman, 1990.

Kress, J. *Prescriptions for Justice: The Theory and Practice of Sentencing Guidelines*. Cambridge, MA: Ballinger, 1980.

Kroovand-Hipple, N. "Project Exile Gun Crime Reduction." In *The New Criminal Justice: American Communities and the Changing World of Crime Control*, edited by J. Klofas, N. Kroovand-Hipple, and E. F. McGarrell, pp. 51–58. New York: Taylor and Francis, 2010.

Kuykendall, J. "Police Managerial Styles: A Grid Analysis." *American Journal of Police*, 1985, *4*(1), 38–70.

Kuykendall, J., and Unsinger, P. C. "The Leadership Styles of Police Managers." *Journal of Criminal Justice*, 1982, *10*(4), 311–322.

Lambert, E. G., and Hogan, N. L. "Wanting Change: The Relationship of Perceptions of Organizational Innovation with Correctional Staff Job Stress, Job Satisfaction, and Organizational Commitment." *Criminal Justice Policy Review*, 2010, *21*, 160–184.

Lambert. E. G., Hogan, N. L., and Tucker, K. A. "Problems at Work: Exploring the Correlates of Role Stress Among Correctional Staff." *Prison Journal*, 2009, *89*, 460–481.

Lambert, E. G., Paoline, E. A., and Hogan, N. L. "The Impact of Centralization and Formalization on Correctional Staff Job Satisfaction and Organizational Commitment: An Exploratory Study." *Criminal Justice Studies*, 2006, *19*(1), 23–44.

Landreth, H. *Professoring: A Critique of Higher Education*. Dogear: Indianapolis, 2012.

Langworthy, R. *The Structure of Police Organizations*. New York: Praeger, 1986.

Langworthy, R. "Do Stings Control Crime? An Evaluation of a Police Fencing Operation," *Justice Quarterly*, 1989, *6*(1), 27–45.

Lasky, G. L., Gordon, B. C., and Srebalus, D. J. "Occupational Stressors among Federal Correctional Officers Working in Different Security Levels." *Criminal Justice and Behavior*, 1986, *13*, 317–327.

Lauffer, A. *Understanding Your Social Agency*. 2nd ed. Beverly Hills, CA: Sage, 1984.

Law Enforcement Management and Administrative Statistics (LEMAS). "Local Police Departments." Washington, DC: U.S. Department of Justice, 1999.

Lawler, E. J. (Ed.). *Advances in Group Processes*. Greenwich, CT: JAI, 1986.

Lawrence, P. "Professionals or Civil Servants? An Examination of the Probation Officer's Role." *Federal Probation*, 1984, *43*, 3–13.

Lawrence, P. R., and Lorsch, J. W. "Differentiation and Integration in Complex Organizations." *Administrative Science Quarterly*, 1967, *12*(1), 1–47.

Lawrence, P. R., and Lorsch, J. *Developing Organizations: Diagnosis and Action*. Reading, MA: Addison-Wesley, 1969.

Lee, J. H., and Visano, L. H. "Official Deviance in the Legal System." In *Law and Deviance*, edited by H. L. Ross, pp. 215–250. Beverly Hills, CA: Sage, 1981.

Lee, R. *Public Budgeting Systems*. 9th ed. Burlington, MA: Jones and Bartlett, 2012.

Lee, R. D., Johnson, R. W., and Phillip, G. J. *Public Budgeting Systems*. Boston, MA: Jones and Bartlet, 2008.

Lehr, D., and O'Neill, G. *Black Mass: The True Story of an Unholy Alliance Between the FBI and the Irish Mob*. New York: HarperCollins, 2001.

Leiberg, G. "Computers Then and Now." *American Jails*, 1996, *9*(6), 23–27.

Lenihan, K. J. "Telephones and Raising Bail: Some Lessons in Evaluation Research." *Evaluation Quarterly*, 1977, *1*, 569–586.

Lester, H. "Correctional Facility Architecture: Past, Present, and Future, Part II." *America Jails*, 2004, *18*(4), 21–25.

Lester, J. "The Utilization of Policy Analysis by State Officials." *Knowledge: Creation Diffusion, Utilization*, 1993, *14*, 267–290.

Levinson, R., and Gerard, R. "Functional Units: A Different Correctional Approach." *Federal Probation*, 1973, *37*, 8–16.

Lewin, K. "Group Decision and Social Change." In *Readings in Social Psychology*, edited by E. E. Maccoby, T. M. Newcomb, and E. L. Hartley, pp. 197–211. New York: Holt, Rinehart & Winston, 1947.

Lewin, K. "Action Research and Minority Problems." In *Resolving Social Conflicts: Selected Papers in Group Dynamics*, edited by K. Lewin, pp. 5–100. New York: Harper & Row, 1948.

Liebentritt, D. "The Making of a Prison Guard." Unpublished manuscript, Center for Studies in Criminal Justice, University of Chicago Law School, 1974.

Light, S., and Newman, T. "Awareness and Use of Social Science Research Among Executive and Administrative Staff Members of State Correctional Agencies." *Justice Quarterly*, 1992, *9*, 299–319.

Likert, R. *New Patterns of Management*. New York: McGraw-Hill, 1961.

Likert, R. *The Human Organization*. New York: McGraw-Hill, 1967.

Lilley, D., and Hinduja, S. "Officer Evaluation in the Community Policing Context." *Policing: An International Journal of Police Strategies and Management*, 2006a, *29*(1), 19–37.

Lilley, D., and Hinduja, S. "Organizational Values and Police Officer Evaluation: A Content Comparison Between Traditional and Community Policing Agencies." *Police Quarterly*, 2006b, *9*, 411–439.

Lindblom, C. "The Science of Muddling Through." *Public Administration Review*, 1959, *19*, 79–88.

Lindquist, C. A., and Whitehead, J. T. "Guards Released from Prison: A Natural Experiment in Job Enlargement." *Journal of Criminal Justice*, 1986, *14*, 283–294.

Lippert, R., and O'Connor, D. "Security Intelligence Networks and the Transformation of Contract Private Security." *Policing and Society*, 2006, *16*(1), 50–66.

Lipsky, M. *Street-Level Bureaucracy*. New York: Russell Sage Foundation, 1980.

Lipsky, M. "Toward a Theory of Street-Level Bureaucracy." In *Criminal Justice: Law and Politics*. 5th ed., edited by G. F. Cole, pp. 24–41. Belmont, CA: Wadsworth, 2002.

Lipton, D., Martinson, R., and Wilkes, J. *The Effectiveness of Correctional Treatment: A Survey of Treatment Evaluation Studies*. New York: Praeger, 1975.

Littlejohn, S. W., and Foss, K. A. *Theories of Communication*. 8th ed. Belmont, CA: Wadsworth, 2005.

Lodahl, J., and Gordon, G. "Funding the Sciences in University Departments." *Educational Record*, 1973, *54*, 74–82.

Logan, C. H. "Criminal Justice Performance Measures for Prisons." In *Performance Measures for the Criminal Justice System*. Bureau of Justice Statistics, Washington, DC: National Institute of Justice, 1993.

Lombardo, L. X. *Guards Imprisoned: Correctional Officers at Work*. New York: Elsevier, 1981.

Lombardo, L. X. "Group Dynamics and the Prison Guard Subculture: Is the Subculture an Impediment to Helping Inmates?" *International Journal of Offender Therapy and Comparative Criminology*, 1985, *29*, 79–90.

Long, N. "Power and Administration." *Public Administration Review*, 1949, *9*, 257–264.

Long, S. "Early Integration into Groups: A Group to Join and Group to Create," *Human Relations*, 1984, *37*, 311–332.

Longenecker, C. O., Gioia, D. A., and Sims, H. P., Jr. "Behind the Mask: The Politics of Employee Appraisal." *Executive*, 1987, *1*(3), 183–194.

Lord, R. G. "Functional Leadership Behavior: Measurement and Relation to Social Power and Leadership Perceptions." *Administrative Science Quarterly*, 1977, *22*(1), 114–133.

Lovell, R. "Research Utilization in Complex Organizations: A Case Study in Corrections." *Justice Quarterly*, 1988, *5*, 258–280.

Lovell, R. "Research Utilization in Complex Organizations: A Case Study in Corrections." In *The Administration and Management of Criminal Justice Organizations: A Book of Readings*. 4th ed., edited by S. Stojkovic, J. Klofas, and D. Kalinich, pp. 457–477. Prospect Heights, IL: Waveland, 2004.

Lovell, R., and Kalinich, D. "The Unimportance of In-House Research in a Professional Criminal Justice Organization." *Criminal Justice Review*, 1992, *17*, 77–93.

Lovell, R., and Stojkovic, S. "Myths, Symbols, and Policymaking in Corrections." *Criminal Justice Review*, 1987, *2*(3), 225–239.

Luke, J. S. *Catalytic Leadership: Strategies for an Interconnected World*. San Francisco, CA: Jossey-Bass, 1998.

Lumb, R. C., and Breazeale, R. "Police Officer Attitudes and Community Policing Implementation: Developing Strategies for Durable Organizational Change." *Policing and Society*, 2002, *13*(1), 91–106.

Lynch, R. G. *The Police Manager: Police Leadership Skills*. 3rd ed. New York: Random House, 1986.

Lynd, R. *Knowledge for What?* Princeton, NJ: Princeton University Press, 1939.

Madera, J. "Removing Communication Barriers at Work: What Workforce Diversity Means for the Hospitality Industry." *Worldwide Hospitality and Tourism Themes*, 2011, *3*(4), 377–380.

Madlock, P. E. "The Link between Leadership Style, Communicator Competence, and Employee Satisfaction." *Journal of Business Communication*, 2008, *45*, 61–78.

Maltz, M. *Recidivism*. New York: Academic Press, 1984.

Mann, F. "Putting Human Relations Research Findings to Work." *Michigan Business Review*, 1950, *2*, 16–20.

Manning, P. *Measuring What Matters, Part One: Measures of Crime, Fear, and Disorder*. Washington, DC: U.S. Department of Justice, 1996.

Manning, P. *Police Work: The Social Organization of Police*. Prospect Heights, IL: Waveland Press, 1997.

Manning, P. K. *Organizational Communications*. New York: Aldine de Gruyter, 1992.

Manning, P. K., and Van Maanen, J. *Policing: A View from the Streets*. Santa Monica, CA: Goodyear, 1978.

March, J. G. "The Business Firm as a Political Coalition." *Journal of Politics*, 1962, *24*, 662–678.

March, J. G., and Simon, H. A. *Organizations*. New York: Wiley, 1958.

Marion, N. E. and Oliver, W. M. "Congress, Crime, and Budgetary Responsiveness: A Study in Symbolic Politics." *Criminal Justice Policy Review*, 2009, *20*, 115–135.

Marquart, J. W. "Doing Research in Prison: The Strengths and Weaknesses of Full Participation as a Guard." *Justice Quarterly*, 1986a, *3*, 15–32.

Marquart, J. W. "Prison Guards and the Use of Physical Coercion as a Mechanism of Prisoner Control." *Criminology*, 1986b, *24*(2), 347–366.

Marrow, J. A., and French, J. R. P. "Changing a Stereotype in Industry." *Journal of Social Issues*, 1945, *6*, 33–37.

Marsden, P. V. "Introducing Influence Processes into a System of Collective Decisions." *American Journal of Sociology*, 1981, *86*, 1203–1235.

Martin, S. J., and Ekland-Olson, S. *Texas Prisons: The Walls Came Tumbling Down*. Austin: Texas Monthly Press, 1987.

Martinson, R. "What Works? Questions and Answers About Prison Reform." *Public Interest*, 1974, *35*, 22–54.

Maslach, C. "Burned-Out." *Human Behavior*, 1976, *5*, 16–22.

Maslach, C., and Jackson, S. "Burned-Out Cops and Their Families." *Psychology Today*, 1979, *12*, 59–62.

Maslach, C., and Jackson, S. "The Measurement of Experienced Burnout." *Journal of Occupational Behavior*, 1981, *2*, 99–113.

Maslow, A. H. "A Theory of Motivation." *Psychological Review*, 1943, *50*, 370–396.

Maslow, A. H. *Motivation and Personality*. New York: Praeger, 1986.

Mastrofski, S. "Community Policing as Reform: A Cautionary Tale." In *Community Policing: Rhetoric or Reality*, edited by J. Greene and S. Mastrofski, pp. 314–342. New York: Praeger, 1991.

Mastrofski, S., and Wadman, R. "Personnel and Agency Performance Measurement." In *Local Government Police Management*, 3rd ed., edited by W. Geller, pp. 127–148. Washington, DC: International City Management Association, 1991.

Matthews, J. "People First: Probation Officer Perspectives on Probation Work—A Practitioner Response." *Probation Journal*, 2009, *56*, 61–67.

May, M. E., *The Elegant Solution*. New York: Free Press, 2007.

Mayo, E. *The Human Problems of Industrial Civilization*. Boston: Harvard Business School, 1946.

Mays, G., and Taggart, W. "Court Clerks, Court Administrators, and Judges: Conflict in Managing the Courts." *Journal of Criminal Justice*, 1986, *21*(3), 14–32.

Mays, G. L., and Gray, T. (Eds.). *Privatization and the Provision of Correctional Services*. Cincinnati, OH: Anderson Publishing Company, 1996.

Mazer, J. P. "Validity of the Student Interest and Engagement Scales: Associations with Student Learning Outcomes." *Communication Studies*, 2013, *64*(2).

McCann, J. "Organizational Effectiveness: Changing Concepts for Changing Environments." *Human Resource Planning*, 2004, *27*(1).

McCleary, R. "Correctional Administration and Political Change." In *Prison Within Society*, edited by Lawrence Hazelrigg, pp. 113–154. New York: Doubleday, 1968.

McCleary, R. "How Parole Officers Use Records." *Social Problems*, 1977, *24*, 576–589.

McCleary, R. *Dangerous Men*. Beverly Hills, CA: Sage, 1978.

McCleary, R. "How Structural Variables Constrain the Parole Officer's Use of Discretionary Power." *Social Problems*, 1985, *32*, 141–152.

McCleary, R., Nienstedt, B., and Erven, J. M. "Uniform Crime Reports as Organizational Outcomes: Three Time Series Experiments." In *The Administration and Management of Criminal Justice Organizations: A Book of Readings*. 4th ed., edited by S. Stojkovic, J. Klofas, and D. Kalinich, pp. 292–306. Prospect Heights, IL: Waveland, 2004.

McClelland, D. A. "Toward a New Theory of Motive Acquisition." *American Psychologist*, 1965, *20*, 321–323.

McCluskey, J. D., Terrill, W. and Paoline, E. A. "Peer Group Aggressiveness and the Use of Coercion in Police–Suspect Encounters," *Police Practice and Research*, 2005, *6*(1), 19–37.

McGarrell, E. *"Intelligence-Led Policing."* Draft Paper: Michigan State University, 2006a.

McGarrell, E. *Project Safe Neighborhood*. Unpublished manuscript, 2006b.

McGarrell, E. G. (Ed.). *The New Criminal Justice: American Communities and the Changing World of Crime Control*, pp. 97–102. New York: Taylor and Francis, 2010.

McGregor, D. M. "The Human Side of Enterprise." In *Classics of Organizational Behavior*, edited by W. E. Natemeyer, pp. 12–18. Oak Park, IL: Moore, 1978.

McIntyre, L. *The Public Defender: The Practice of Law in the Shadows of Repute*. Chicago, IL: University of Chicago Press, 1987.

McShane, M., and Krause, W. *Community Corrections*. New York: Macmillan, 1993.

Meisner, S. "Economic Distribution and Societal Homicide Rates: Further Evidence of the Cost of Inequality." *American Sociological Review*, 1989, *54*(4), 579–611.

Melancon, D. "Quality Circles: The Shape of Things to Come?" *Police Chief*, 1984, *51*(11), 54–55.

Melone, A. "Criminal Code Reform and Interest Group Politics of the American Bar Association." In *The Politics of Crime and Justice*, edited by E. Fairchild and V. Webb, pp. 37–56. Beverly Hills, CA: Sage, 1985.

Mengas, J. and Eppler, Martin J. "Understanding and Managing Conversations from a Knowledge Perspective: An Analysis of the Roles and Rules of Face-to-face Conversations in Organizations." *Organization Studies*, 2008, *29*, 1287.

Menke, B. A., Zupan, L. L., and Lovrich, N. P. *A Comparison of Work-Related Attitudes Between New Generation Correction Officers and Other Public Employees*. Paper presented at the annual meeting of the Academy of Criminal Justice Sciences, Orlando, Florida, 1986.

Meyer, J., and Rowan, B. "Institutionalized Organizations: Formal Structures as Myths and Ceremony." *American Journal of Sociology*, 1978, *83*, 340–363.

Meyer, J. P., Becker, T. E., and Vandenberghe, C. "Employee Commitment and Motivation: A Conceptual Analysis and Integrative Model." *Journal of Applied Psychology*, 2004, *89*(6), 991–1007.

Meyers, S., and Simms, M. (Eds.). *The Economics of Race and Crime*. New Brunswick, NJ: Transaction Books, 1989.

Michels, R. *Political Parties*. New York: Free Press, 1949.

Miller, H. T., and Fox, C. T. *Postmodern Public Administration*. Armonk, NY: M. E. Sharpe, 2006.

Miller, Hugh T. and Charles J. Fox. *Postmodern Public Administration:* Revised *edition*. Armonk, NY: M.E. Sharpe, 2007.

Miller, L. "The Application of Research to Practice." *American Behavioral Scientist*, 1986, *30*, 70–80.

Mills, A., Meek, R., Gojkovic, D. "Partners, guests or competitors: Relationships between criminal justice and third sector staff prisons." *Probation Journal*, 2012, *59*(4), 391–405.

Mintzberg, H. *Power In and Around Organizations*. Englewood Cliffs, NJ: Prentice Hall, 1983.

Missonellie, J., and D'Angelo, J. *Television and Law Enforcement*. Springfield, IL: Charles C. Thomas, 1984.

Mitchell, G. *Statements made during a debate on prison expansion*. Milwaukee, WI: Institute for Wisconsin's Future, January 1997.

Mock, L. F. "Action Research for Crime Control and Prevention." In J. M. Klofas, N. Kroovand-Hipple, and E. G. McGarrell, (Eds.). *The New Criminal Justice: American Communities and the Changing World of Crime Control*. New York: Taylor and Francis, 97–102, 2010.

Mohr, L. B. "Organizations, Decisions, and Courts." *Law and Society*, 1976, *10*, 621–642.

Monahan, J. *Predicting Violent Behavior: An Assessment of Clinical Techniques*. Beverly Hills, CA: Sage, 1981.

Monroe County, New York. *Jail Utilization System Team: Proposal for a Comprehensive Community-Based Corrections Program*. 1994.

Moran, T. K., and Lindner, C. "Probation and the Hi-Technology Revolution: Is a Reconceptualization of the Traditional Probation Officer Role Model Inevitable?" *Criminal Justice Review*, 1985, *10*, 25–32.

Morash, M. "Wife Battering." *Criminal Justice Abstracts*, 1986, *18*, 252–271.

Morash, M., and Greene, J. "Evaluating Women on Patrol." *Evaluation Review*, 1986, *10*, 230–255.

More, H. W., Jr. *Criminal Justice Management: Text and Readings*. St. Paul, MN: West, 1977.

Moreland, R. L., and Levine, J. M. "Socialization in Small Groups: Temporal Changes in Individual–Group Relations." In *Advances in Experimental Social Psychology*, edited by L. Berkowitz, pp. 137–192. New York: Academic, 1982.

Morgenbesser, L. "Psychological Screening Mandated for New York Correctional Officer Applicants." *Corrections Today*, 1984, *46*, 28–29.

Morris, N. *Madness and the Criminal Law*. Chicago: University of Chicago Press, 1982.

Morris, N. and Rothman, D. (Eds.). *The Oxford History of the Prison: The Practice of Punishment in Western Society*. New York, NY: Oxford University Press, 1995.

Morse, J. J. "A Contingency Look at Job Design." *California Management Review*, 1973, *16*, 67–75.

Motschall, M., and Cao, L., "An Analysis of the Public Relations Role of the Police Public Information Officer." *Police Quarterly*, 2002, *5*(2) 152–180.

Mullany, J. M., "Special Conditions for Female Probationers: Disparity of Discrimination." *Justice Professional*, 2002, *15*(2), 169–180.

Munoz, E. A., and McMorris, B. J. "Misdemeanor Sentencing Decisions: The Cost of Being Native American." *Justice Professional*, 2002, *15*(3), 239–259.

Murphy, P. V. "The Prospective Chief's Negotiation of Authority with the Mayor." In *Police Leadership in America: Crisis and Opportunity*, edited by W. A. Geller, pp. 30–41. Chicago: American Bar Association, 1985.

Murray, M. *Decisions: A Comparative Critique*. Marshfield, MA: Pitman, 1986.

Murton, T. *The Dilemma of Prison Reform*. New York: Holt, Rinehart & Winston, 1976.

Nader, R. *Unsafe at Any Speed: The Designed-in Dangers of the American Automobile*. New York: Grossman, 1965.

Nanus, B. *Visionary Leadership*. San Francisco, CA: Jossey-Bass, 1992.

National Advisory Commission on Civil Disorders. *Report of the National Advisory Commission on Civil Disorders*. New York: Dutton, 1968.

National Advisory Commission on Criminal Justice Standards and Goals. *Corrections*. Washington, DC: U.S. Government Printing Office, 1973a.

National Advisory Commission on Criminal Justice Standards and Goals. *Police*. Washington, DC: U.S. Government Printing Office, 1973b.

National Commission on Correctional Health Care. *The Health Status of Soon-To-Be-Released Inmates: A Report to Congress*, Vol. *1*. Washington, DC: U.S. Department of Justice, 2004.

National Institute of Corrections. *A Framework for Evidence-Based Decision Making in Local Criminal Justice Systems*. Washington, DC: U.S. Department of Justice, 2010.

National Institute of Justice (NIJ). "Civil Rights and Criminal Justice: Employment Discrimination Overview." *Research in Brief*. Washington, DC: U.S. Department of Justice, 1995.

National Jail Coalition. *Covering the Jail.* Washington, DC: U.S. Government Printing Office, 1984.

National Office of Community Oriented Policing Services. *Community Policing: Leading the Way to a Safer Nation.* Washington, DC: U.S. Department of Justice, 2006.

Nelson, R. "Changing Concepts in Jail Design." In *Sneaking Inmates Down the Alley: Problems and Prospects in Jail Management,* edited by D. Kalinich and J. Klofas, pp. 167–180. Springfield, IL: Charles C. Thomas, 1986.

Nelson, R., and Winter, S. *An Evolutionary Theory of Economic Change.* Boston: Belknap Press, 1982.

Neubauer, D. *American Courts and the Criminal Justice System.* Belmont, CA: Brooks/Cole, 1983.

Neubauer, D. *American Courts and the Criminal Justice System.* Belmont, CA: Brooks/Cole, 1996.

Newman, D. "Plea Bargaining." In *Order Under Law,* edited by R. Culbertson and M. Tezak, pp. 166–179. Prospect Heights, IL: Waveland, 1981.

Newman, D. *Introduction to Criminal Justice.* New York: Random House, 1986.

New York Department of Corrections. *Correctional Officer Position Description.* Albany, New York, 2007.

Niederhoffer, A. *Behind the Shield: The Police in Urban Society.* New York: Doubleday, 1969.

9-11 Commission. *The 9-11 Commission Report: Final Report of the National Commission on Terrorist Attacks upon the United States. Executive Summary.* Washington, DC: U.S. Government Printing Office, 2004.

NIJ Research Report. *Convicted by Juries, Exonerated by Science: Case Studies in the* Use of DNA Evidence to Establish Innocence After Trial, 1996.

Nokes, P. "Purpose and Efficiency in Human Social Institutions." *Human Relations,* 1960, *13,* 141–155.

Nolan, T. "Behind the Blue Wall of Silence." *Men and Masculinities,* 2009, *(12)*2, 250–257.

Nuchia, S. M. "First Amendment Freedom of Speech and the Police Officer's Criticism of Departmental Policy and His Superiors." *Journal of Police Science and Administration,* 1983, *11*(4), 395–401.

Oettmeier, T. N., and Wycoff, M. A. *Personnel Performance Evaluations in the Community Policing Context.* Washington, DC: U.S. Department of Justice, 1998.

Office of Community Policing Services. *Innovations in Police Recruitment: Hiring in the Spirit of Service.* Washington, DC: National Institute of Justice, 2001.

O'Keefe, G., and Mendelsohn, H. *Taking a Bite Out of Crime: The Impact of a Mass Media Crime Prevention Campaign.* Washington, DC: U.S. Government Printing Office, 1984.

Okrent, D. *Last Call, the Rise and Fall of Prohibition.* New York: Scribner, 2010.

Olsen, M. *The Logic of Collective Action: Public Goods and the Theory of Groups.* Cambridge, MA: Harvard University Press, 1973.

Osborn, R., and Hunt, J. "Environmental and Organizational Effectiveness." *Administrative Science Quarterly,* 1974, *19,* 231–246.

O'Toole, L. J., and Meier, K. J. "The Human Side of Public Organizations: Contributions to Organizational Performance." *American Review of Public Administration,* 2009, *39,* 499–518.

Ouchi, W. *Theory Z: How American Business Can Meet the Japanese Challenge.* Reading, MA: Addison-Wesley, 1981.

Owen, S. "Occupational Stress among Correctional Supervisors." *Prison Journal,* 2006, *86*(2), 164–181.

Paker, H. *The Limits of the Criminal Sanction.* Stanford, CA: Stanford University Press, 1968.

Pandarus, P. "One's Own Primer of Academic Politics." *American Scholar,* 1973, *42,* 569–592.

Paparozzi, M. A., and Caplan, J. M. "A Profile of Paroling Authorities in America: The Strange Bedfellows of Politics and Professionalism." *Prison Journal,* 2009, *89,* 401–425.

Parker, D. *Crime by Computer.* New York: Scribner's, 1976.

Parkinson, C. N. *Parkinson's Law.* Cutchogue, NY: Buccanneer Books, 1996.

Parsons, T. *Structure and Process in Modern Societies.* New York: Free Press, 1960.

Peak, J. K., and Gensor, R. W. *Community Policing and Problem Solving: Strategies and Practices.* 4th ed. Upper Saddle River, NJ: Pearson/Prentice Hall, 2004.

Peak, J. K., Gaines, L. K., and Glensor, R. W. *Police Supervision and Management: In an Era of Community Policing.* 2nd ed. Upper Saddle River, NJ: Prentice Hall, 2004.

Perrow, C. "The Analysis of Goals in Complex Organizations." *American Sociological Review,* 1961, *26,* 194–208.

Perrow, C. "Departmental Power and Perspective in Industrial Firms." In *Power in Organizations,* edited by M. Zald, pp. 59–89. Nashville: Vanderbilt University Press, 1970.

Perrow, C. "Three Types of Effectiveness Studies." In *New Perspectives on Organizational Effectiveness*, edited by P. S. Goodman and J. M. Pennings, pp. 96–105. San Francisco: Jossey-Bass, 1977.

Perrow, C. "Disintegrating Social Sciences." *New York University Educational Quarterly*, Winter 1981, 2–9.

Perrow, C. *Complex Organizations: A Critical Essay*. 3rd ed. New York: Random House, 1986.

Perry, J. L. "Measuring Public Service Motivation: An Assessment of Construct Reliability and Validity." *Journal of Public Administration Research and Theory*, 1996, *6*, 5–24.

Peters, T. *Thriving on Chaos: Handbook for a Management Revolution*. New York: Harper & Row, 1987.

Peters, T. *Thriving on Chaos: Handbook for a Management Revolution*. 3rd ed. New York: Harper & Row, 1994.

Peters, T., and Waterman, R. In *Search of Excellence: Lessons from American's Best-Run Companies*. New York: Harper & Row, 1982.

Petersilia, J. "Defending the Practical Value of Criminological Research." *Journal of Research in Crime and Delinquency*, 1993, *30*, 497–505.

Petersilia, J. "A Crime Control Rationale for Reinvesting in Community Corrections." *Prison Journal*, 1995, *75*(4), 497–505.

Petersilia, J. *Community Corrections: Probation, Parole, and Intermediate Sanctions*. New York: Oxford University Press, 1998.

Petersilia, J., and Turner, S. "Intensive Probation and Parole." *Crime and Justice*, 1993, *17*, 281–335.

Petersilia, J. and Snyder, J. G. "Looking Past the Hype: 10 Questions Everyone Should Ask About California's Prison Realignment." *California Journal of Politics and Policy*, 2013, *5*(2), 266–306.

Petrich, J. "Psychiatric Treatment in Jail: An Experiment in Health-Care Delivery." *Hospital and Community Psychiatry*, 1976, 413–415.

Pfeffer, J. "Power and Resource Allocation in Organizations." In *New Directions in Organizational Behavior*, edited by B. Staw and G. R. Salancik, pp. 235–265. Chicago: St. Clair Press, 1977a.

Pfeffer, J. "Usefulness of the Concept." In *New Perspectives on Organizational Effectiveness*, edited by P. S. Goodman and J. M. Pennings, pp. 132–145. San Francisco: Jossey-Bass, 1977b.

Pfeffer, J. "The Micropolitics of Organizations." In *Environments and Organizations*, edited by M. W. Meyer, pp. 29–50. San Francisco: Jossey-Bass, 1978.

Pfeffer, J. *Power in Organizations*. Marshfield, MA: Pitman, 1981.

Pfeffer, J., and Salancik, G. R. "Organizational Decision-Making as a Political Process: The Case of a University Budget." *Administrative Science Quarterly*, 1974, *19*(2), 135–151.

Philliber, S. "Thy Brother's Keeper: A Review of the Literature on Correctional Officers." *Justice Quarterly*, 1987, *4*(1), 9–38.

Phillips, C. D., McCleary, B. W., and Dinitz, S. "The Special Deterrent Effect of Incarceration." In *Evaluating Performance of Criminal Justice Agencies*, edited by G. P. Whitaker and C. D. Phillips, pp. 237–264. Beverly Hills, CA: Sage, 1983.

Phillips, R. L., and McConnell, C. R. *The Effective Corrections Manager: Maximizing Staff Performance in Demanding Times*. Gaithersburg, MD: Aspen Publications, 1996.

Pindur, W., and Lipiec, S. "Creating Positive Police-Prosecutor Relations." *Journal of Police Science and Administration*, 1982, *10*(1), 28–33.

Pinfield, L. T. "A Field Evaluation of Perspectives on Organizational Decision Making." *Administrative Science Quarterly*, 1986, *31*, 365–388.

Podsakoff, P. M., and Schriesheim, C. A. "Field Studies of French and Raven's Bases of Power: Reanalysis, Critique, and Suggestions for Future Research." *Psychological Bulletin*, 1985, *97*(3), 387–411.

Pogrebin, M. R., and Poole, E. D., "The Sexualized Work Environment: A Look at Women Jail Officers." *Prison Journal*, 77, 1997, 41–57.

Polachek, E. Personal communication with author Stan Stojkovic, 2011.

Polakowski, M., Hartley, R. E., and Bates, L. "Treating the Tough Cases in Juvenile Drug Court: Individual and Organizational Practices Leading to Success or Failure." *Criminal Justice Review*, 2008, *33*, 379–403.

Policing and Society. "Intelligence in Policing and Security: Reflections on Scholarship." [Editorial]. 2006, *16*(1), 1–6.

Pondy, L. R. "Organizational Conflict: Concepts and Models." In *Organizational Behavior and Management*. 4th ed., edited by H. L. Tosi and W. C. Hamner, pp. 381–391. Cincinnati, OH: Grid, 1985.

Poole, E. D., and Regoli, R. M. "Role Stress, Custody Orientation and Disciplinary Actions: A Study of Prison Guards." *Criminology*, 1980, *18*, 215–226.

Porter, L. W. *Organizations as Political Animals.* Presidential address to the Division of Industrial Organizational Psychology, 84th Annual Meeting of the American Psychological Association, Washington, DC, 1976.

Porter, L. W., Allen, R. W., and Angle, H. L. "The Politics of Upward Influence in Organizations." *Organizational Behavior*, 1981, *3*, 109–149.

Porter, L. W., Lawler, E. E., III, and Hackman, J. H. *Behavior in Organizations*. New York: McGraw-Hill, 1975.

Postman, N. *Technopoly: The Surrender of Culture to Technology*. New York: Knopf, 1992.

Powers, R. *Secrecy and Power: The Life of J. Edgar Hoover.* New York: Free Press, 1987.

President's Commission on Law Enforcement and Criminal Justice. *The Challenge of Crime in a Free Society*. Washington, DC: U.S. Government Printing Office, 1967.

President's Commission on Law Enforcement and the Administration of Justice. *Task Force Reports: Summary and Conclusions*. Washington, DC: U.S. Government Printing Office, 1967a.

President's Commission on Law Enforcement and the Administration of Justice. *Task Force Report: Corrections*. Washington, DC: U.S. Government Printing Office, 1967b.

Price, B. "A Study of Leadership Strength of Female Police Executives." *Journal of Police Science and Administration*, 1974, *2*, 219–226.

Quade, E. "Systems Analysis Techniques for Public Policy Problems." In *Perspectives on Public Bureaucracy*, edited by F. Kramer, pp. 151–174. Cambridge, MA: Winthrop, 1977.

Quinney, R. *Critique of the Legal Order*. Boston: Little, Brown, 1974.

Radelet, L. *The Police and the Community*. 4th ed. New York: Macmillan, 1986.

Rainey, H. "Public Agencies and Private Firms: Incentive Structures, Goals, and Individual Roles." *Administration and Society*, 1983, *15*, 207–242.

Rainey, H. G. *Understanding and Managing Public Organizations*. 5th ed. San Francisco, CA: Jossey-Bass, 2014.

Redlich, A. D., Steadman, Henry J., Monahan, John, Robinson, Pamela Clark, and Pertilla, John. "Patterns of Practice in Mental Health Courts." *Law and Human Behavior*, 2006, *30*, 347–362.

Reeves, D. W., Walsh, B. M., Tuller, M. D., Magley, V. J. *"The Positive Effects of Participative Decision Making for Midlevel Correctional Management."* Criminal Justice and Behavior, 2012, 39:1361.

Reid, S. *Crime and Criminology*. New York: Holt, Rinehart & Winston, 1982.

Reinsch, Jr., N. L. "Management Communication Ethics Research: Finding the Bull's-Eye." *Management Communication Quarterly*, 1996, *9*, 349.

Reiss, A. J. "Career Orientations, Job Satisfaction and the Assessment of Law Enforcement Problems by Police Officers." In *Studies in Crime and Law Enforcement, by the President's Commission on Law Enforcement and the Administration of Justice*. Washington, DC: U.S. Government Printing Office, 1967.

Reiss, A. J. *The Police and the Public*. New Haven, CT: Yale University Press, 1971.

Remington, F., Newman, D., Kimball, E., Melli, M., and Goldstein, H. *Criminal Justice Administration*. Indianapolis, IN: Bobbs-Merrill, 1969.

Reuss-Ianni, E. *Two Cultures of Policing: Street Cops and Management Cops*. New Brunswick, NJ: Transaction Books, 1984.

Reuter, P. "Prevalence Estimation and Policy Formulation." *Journal of Drug Issues*, 1993, *23*, 167–184.

Ricker, L. "Anatomy of Jail Automation—Case Study: Marion County Department of Corrections." *American Jails*, 1996, *9*(6), 9–19.

Rideau, W., and Sinclair, B. *Inside Angola*. New Orleans: Louisiana Department of Corrections, 1982.

Robbins, S. P., and Judge, T. A. *Organizational Behavior*. 12th ed. Upper Saddle River, NJ: Pearson/Prentice Hall, 2007.

Roberg, R. R. *Police Management and Organizational Behavior: A Contingency Approach*. St. Paul, MN: West, 1979.

Robin, G. D. "Judicial Resistance to Sentencing Allowability." *Crime and Delinquency*, 1975, *21*, 201–212.

Rochet, C., Keramidas, O., and Bout, L. "Crisis as Change Strategy in Public Organizations." *International Review of Administrative Sciences*, 2008, *74*, 65.

Roethlisberger, F. J., and Dickson, W. J. *Management and the Worker*. Cambridge, MA: Harvard University Press, 1939.

Rokeach, M., Miller, G., and Snyder, J. A. "The Value Gap Between the Police and the Policed." *Journal of Social Issues*, 1971, *27*, 155–171.

Rosch, J. "Crime as an Issue in American Politics." In *The Politics of Crime and Justice*, edited by E. Fairchild and V. Webb, pp. 19–34. Beverly Hills, CA: Sage, 1985.

Rosecrance, J. "The Probation Officer's Search for Credibility: Ball Park Recommendations." *Crime and Delinquency*, 1985, *31*, 539–554.

Rosecrance, J. "Probation Supervision: Mission Impossible." *Federal Probation*, 1986, *60*(1), 25–31.

Rosecrance, J. "Getting Rid of the Prima Donnas: The Bureaucratization of a Probation Department." In *The Administration and Management of Criminal Justice Organizations: A Book of Readings*. 3rd ed., edited by S. Stojkovic, J. Klofas, and D. Kalinich, pp. 175–187. Prospect Heights, IL: Waveland, 1999a.

Rosecrance, J. "Maintaining the Myth of Individualized Justice: Probation Presentence Reports." In *The Administration and Management of Criminal Justice Organizations: A Book of Readings*. 3rd ed., edited by S. Stojkovic, J. Klofas, and D. Kalinich, pp. 355–374. Prospect Heights, IL: Waveland, 1999b.

Rosenbaum, D. P. "Just Say No to DARE." *Criminology & Public Policy*, 2007, *6*(4), 815–824.

Rosenfeld, R. Comments made at the annual "Improving Crime Data Symposium." Marietta, GA, July 2006.

Rosenfeld, R., Fornango, R., and Baumer, E. "Did Ceasefire, Compstat, and Exile Reduce Homicide?" *Criminology & Public Policy*, 2005, *4*(3), 419–450.

Rothman, D. J. *Conscience and Convenience*. Boston: Little, Brown, 1980.

Rothman, D. J., and Rothman, S. M. *The Willowbrook Wars*. New York: Harper & Row, 1984.

Rottman, D. B., and Kimberly, J. R. "The Social Context of Jails." *Sociology and Social Research*, 1975, *59*, 344–361.

Rourke, F. *Bureaucracy, Politics, and Public Policy*. 2nd ed. Boston: Little, Brown, 1976.

Rourke, F. *Bureaucratic Power in National Politics*. 4th ed. Boston: Little, Brown, 1986.

Ruiz v. *Estelle*, 503 F. Supp. 1265 (1980).

Ruighaver, A. B., Maynard, S. B., and Warren, M. "Ethical decision making: Improving the quality of acceptable use policies." *Computers & Security*, 2010, *29*, 731–736.

Ryan, E. *A Multidimensional Analysis of Conflict in the Criminal Justice System*. Jonesboro, TN: Pilgrimage, 1981.

Saari, D. J. *American Court Management: Theories and Practices*. Westport, CT: Quorum Books, 1982.

Salancik, G. R., and Pfeffer, J. "Who Gets Power—and How They Hold On To It: A Strategic Contingency Model of Power." *Organizational*, Winter 1977, *5*, 3–21.

Salas, E., Tannenbaum, S. I., Kraiger, K., and Smith-Jentsch, K. A. "The Science of Training and Development in Organizations: What Matters in Practice." *Psychological Science in the Public Interest*, 2012, *13*(2), 74–101.

Sample, L. L., and Kadleck, C. "Sex Offender Laws: Legislators' Accounts of the Need for Policy," *Criminal Justice Policy Review*, 2008, *19*, 40.

Sarrata, B., and Jeppensen, J. C. "Job Design and Staff Satisfaction in Human Service Settings." *Journal of Community Psychology*, 1977, *5*, 229–236.

Schafer, N. "Jails and Judicial Review: Special Problems for Local Facilities." In *Sneaking Inmates Down the Alley: Problems and Prospects in Jail Management*, edited by D. Kalinich and J. Klofas, pp. 127–146. Springfield, IL: Charles C. Thomas, 1986.

Schattschnieder, E. *Two Million Americans in Search of Government*. New York: Holt, Rinehart & Winston, 1969.

Schay, B. "Effects of Performance-Contingent Pay on Employee Attitudes." *Public Personnel Management*, 1988, *17*, 237–250.

Schein, E. H. *The Psychological Contract: Organizational Psychology*. 2nd ed. Englewood Cliffs, NJ: Prentice Hall, 1970.

Schein, E. H. "The Individual, the Organization and the Career: A Conceptual Scheme." *Journal of Applied Behavioral Science*, 1971, *7*, 401–426.

Schein, E. H. *Organizational Culture and Leadership*. 2nd ed. San Francisco: Jossey-Bass, 1997.

Schein, E. H. *Organizational Culture and Leadership*. 3rd. ed. San Francisco: Jossey-Bass, 2004.

Schieman, S., and Reid, S. "Job Authority and Interpersonal Conflict in the Workplace." *Work and Occupations*, 2008, *35*, 296–326.

Schlager, M. D. "The Organizational Politics of Implementing Risk Assessment Instruments in Community Corrections." *Journal of Contemporary Criminal Justice*, 2009, *25*, 412–423.

Schlesinger, A. M., Jr. "Roosevelt as Chief Administrator." In *The Coming of the New Deal*. Boston, MA: Houghton Mifflin, 1958.

Schloss, C .S. and Alarid, L. F. "Standards in the Privatization of Probation Services: A Statutory Analysis," *Criminal Justice Review*, 2007, *32*, 233.

Schmalleger, F. *Criminal Justice Today: An Introductory Text for the 21st Century*. 5th ed. Upper Saddle River, NJ: Prentice Hall, 1997.

Schmalleger, F., and Smykla, J. O. *Corrections in the 21st Century*. 3rd ed. Boston, MA: McGraw-Hill, 2007.

Schmidt, A. K. "Electronic Monitoring of Offenders Increases." *National Institute of Justice Reports*, 1989, *2*(12), 2–5.

Schulhofer, S. "No Job Too Small: Justice Without Bargaining in the Lower Criminal Courts." *American Bar Foundation Research Journal*, 1985, Summer, 519–598.

Schwarzenegger, A. Opening statement made at a press conference announcing the name change in the California Department of Corrections, July 2005.

Scott, E. *Police Referral in Metropolitan Areas: A Summary Report*. Washington, DC: U.S. National Institute of Justice, 1981.

Scott, R. *Organizations: Rational, Natural, and Open Systems*. Englewood Cliffs, NJ: Prentice Hall, 1987.

Scott, W. R. "Effectiveness of Organizational Effectiveness Studies." In *New Perspectives on Organizational Effectiveness*, edited by P. S. Goodman and J. M. Pennings, pp. 63–95. San Francisco: Jossey-Bass, 1977.

Scrivner, E. *Recruiting and Hiring Service Oriented Officers: Innovations from HSS COPS Office Conference*. Office of Community Oriented Policing. Washington, DC: National Institute of Justice, 2001.

SEARCH Group, Inc. "State Law and the Confidentiality of Juvenile Records." *Security and Privacy*, 1982, *5*(2), 1–12.

Selke, W., and Bartoszek, M. "Police and Media Relations: The Seed of Conflict." *Criminal Justice Review*, 1984, *9*(2), 25–30.

Sellin, T. "Historical Glimpses of Training for Prison Service." *Journal of the American Institute of Criminal Law and Criminology*, 1934, 3–27.

Selltiz, C. "The Use of Survey Methods in a Citizens' Campaign Against Discrimination." *Human Organization*, 1955, *14*, 19–25.

Selznick, P. *TVA and the Grass Roots*. Berkeley, CA: University of California Press, 1949.

Selznick, P. *Leadership in Administration*. New York: Harper & Row, 1957.

Sever, M. *"Effects of Organizational Culture on Police Decision Making."* Texas Law Enforcement Management and Administrative Statistics Program, 2008, *15*(1).

Shanahan, D. *Patrol Administration: Management by Objectives*. 2nd ed. Boston: Allyn and Bacon, 1985.

Sharkansky, I. *Public Administration: Policy Making in Governmental Agencies*. Chicago: Markham, 1972.

Sharp, E. B. "Street-Level Discretion in Policing: Attitudes and Behaviors in the Deprofessionalization Syndrome." *Law and Policy Quarterly*, 1982, *4*, 167–189.

Shefer, G. and Liebling, A. "Prison Privatization: In Search of a Business-Like Atmosphere?" *Criminology and Criminal Justice*, 2008, *8*, 261–278.

Sheppard, H. L., and Herrick, N. Q. *Where Have All the Robots Gone?* New York: Free Press, 1972.

Sherman, L. *Policing Domestic Violence*. New York: Free Press, 1992.

Sherman, L., and Cohn, E. G. "The Impact of Research on Legal Policy: The Minneapolis Domestic Violence Experiment." *Law and Society Review*, 1989, *23*, 117–144.

Sherman, L. W. "Becoming Bent: Moral Career Concepts of Corrupt Policemen." In *Police Corruption: A Sociological Perspective*, edited by L. Sherman, pp. 191–208. New York: Doubleday, 1974.

Sherman, L. W. "Middle Management and Police Democratization: A Reply to John E. Angell." *Criminology*, 1975, *12*(4), 363–377.

Sherman, L. W., and Berk, R. "The Specific Deterrent Effects of Arrest in Domestic Assault." *American Sociological Review*, 1984, *49*, 261–272.

Sherman, L. W., Milton, C. H., and Kelly, T. V. *Team Policing: Seven Case Studies.* Washington, DC: Police Foundation, 1973.

Sherman, M., and Hawkins, G. *Imprisonment in America: Closing the Future.* Chicago: University of Chicago Press, 1981.

Shichor, D. "Crime Patterns and Socioeconomic Development: A Cross-National Analysis." *Criminal Justice Review,* 1990, *15*(1), 64–78.

Shipton, H. J., West, M. A., Parkes, C. L., Dawson, J. F., and Patterson, M. G. "When Promoting Positive Feelings Pays: Aggregate Job Satisfaction, Work Design Features, and Innovation in Manufacturing Organizations." *European Journal of Work and Organizational Psychology,* 2006, *15*(4), 404–430.

Sieber, S. *Fatal Remedies: The Ironies of Social Intervention.* New York: Plenum Press, 1981.

Simon, H. A. *Administrative Behavior.* 2nd ed. New York: Macmillan, 1957.

Simon, H. On the Concept of Organizational Goals." *Administrative Science Quarterly,* 1964, *9*, 1–22.

Simpson, R. L., and Simpson, I. H. "The Psychiatric Attendant: Development of an Occupational Self-Image in a Low Status Occupation." *American Sociological Review,* 1959, *24*, 389–392.

Simpson, S. S., Bouffard, J. G., and Hickman, L. "The Influence of Legal Reform on the Probability of Arrest in Domestic Violence Cases." *Justice Quarterly,* 2006, *23*, 297–301.

Skogan, W. "Measuring What Matters, Part One: Measures of Crime, Fear, and Disorder." Washington, DC: U.S. Department of Justice, 1996.

Skolnick, J. H. *Justice without Trial: Law Enforcement in a Democratic Society.* New York: Wiley, 1966.

Skolnick, J. H., and Bayley, D. H. *The New Blue Line: Police Innovation in Six American Cities.* New York: Free Press, 1986.

Skolnick, J. H., and Fyfe, J. *Above the Law: Police and Excessive Use of Force.* New York: Free Press, 1993.

Sluzki, C. E. "The Pathway between Conflict and Reconciliation: Coexistence as an Evolutionary Process." *Transcultural Psychiatry,* 2010, *47*, 55–69.

Smith, A. *The Wealth of Nations,* 1776. London: Methuen & Co., Ltd.

Smith, B. W., Novak, K. J., Frank, J., and Travis, III, Lawrence F. "Multijurisdictional Task Forces: An Analysis of Impact." *Journal of Criminal Justice,* 2000, *28*, 543–556.

Smith, H. P., Applegate, B. K., Sitren, A. H., and Springer, N. F. "The Limits of Individual Control? Perceived Officer Power and Probationer Compliance." *Journal of Criminal Justice,* 2009, *37*, 241–247.

Smith, L. J. "The Organizational Environment and Its Influence on State Criminal Justice Systems within the United States and the Offender Re-Integration Process." *Criminal Justice Studies,* 2003, *16*(2), 97–112.

Smykla, J. D. *Community-Based Corrections: Principles and Practices.* New York: Macmillan, 1981.

Snyder, R., and Morris, J. "Organizational Communications and Performance." *Journal of Applied Psychology,* 1984, *69*(3), 461–465.

Souryal, S. Deterring Corruption by Prison Personnel: A Principle-Based Perspective." *Prison Journal, March* 2009, *89*(1), 21–45.

Sparrow, M. K. *Implementing Community Policing.* Washington, DC: National Institute of Justice, 1988.

Sparrow, M. K. *Perspectives on Policing.* Monograph no. 9, National Institute of Justice and the Program in Criminal Justice Policy and Management, John F. Kennedy School of Government, Harvard University, November 1994.

Sparrow, M. K. "Implementing Community Policing." In *The Administration and Management of Criminal Justice Organizations: A Book of Readings.* 3rd ed., edited by S. Stojkovic, D. Kalinich, and J. Klofas. Prospect Heights, IL: Waveland Press, 1999.

Special Task Force to the Secretary of Health, Education, and Welfare. *Work in America.* Cambridge, MA: MIT Press, 1973, 397–408.

Spiro, H. "Comparative Politics: A Comprehensive Approach." *American Political Science Review,* 1958, *56*(3), 577–595.

Srivastava, V. (Ed.). *Executive Power: How Executives Influence People and Organizations.* San Francisco: Jossey-Bass, 1986.

Stastny, C., and Tyrnauer, G. *Who Rules the Joint: The Changing Political Culture of Maximum-Security Prisons in America.* Lexington, MA: Heath, 1982.

Staw, B. M., and Ross, J. "Commitment to a Policy Decision: A Multi-Theoretical Perspective." *Administrative Science Quarterly,* 1978, *23*, 40–64.

Steadman, H., Monahan, J., Duffee, B., Hartstone, E., and Robbins, P. "The Impact of the State Mental Hospital Deinstitutionalization on United States Prison Populations, 1968–1978." *Journal of Criminal Law and Criminology*, 1984, *75*, 474–490.

Steers, R. M. *Organizational Effectiveness: A Behavioral View.* Santa Monica, CA: Goodyear, 1977.

Stinchcomb, J. B. *Corrections: Past, Present, and Future.* Lanham, NJ: American Correctional Association, 2005.

Stinchcomb, J. B., and Hippensteel, D. "Presentence Reports: A Relevant Justice Model Tool or a Medical Relic?" *Criminal Justice Policy Review*, 2001, *12*(2), 164–177.

Stoddard, E. R. "Blue Coat Crime." In *Thinking about Police: Contemporary Readings*, edited by C. B. Klockars. New York: McGraw-Hill, 1983.

Stohl, C., *Organizational Communication: Connectedness in Action.* Thousand Oaks, CA: Sage, 1995.

Stohr, M., Lovrich, N., Menke, B., and Zupan, L. "Staff Management in Correctional Institutions: Comparing DiIulio's 'Control Model' and 'Employee Investment Model' Outcomes in Five Jails." *Justice Quarterly*, 1994, *11*(3), 471–498.

Stohr, M.K., Hemmens, C., Collins, P.A., Iannacchione, B., Hudson, M., Johnson, H. "Assessing the Organizational Culture in a Jail Setting." *The Prison Journal*, 2012, *92*(3), 358–387.

Stojkovic, S. "Social Bases of Power and Control Mechanisms among Prisoners in a Prison Organization." *Justice Quarterly*, 1984, *1*(4), 511–528.

Stojkovic, S. "Social Bases of Power and Control Mechanisms among Correctional Administrators in a Prison Organization." *Journal of Criminal Justice*, 1986, *14*, 157–166.

Stojkovic, S. "An Examination of Compliance Structures in a Prison Organization: A Study of the Types of Correctional Officer Power." Unpublished manuscript, University of Wisconsin, Milwaukee, 1987.

Stojkovic, S. "Accounts of Prison Work: Corrections Officers' Portrayals of Their Work World." In *Perspectives on Social Problems*, edited by G. Miller and J. Holstein, pp. 211–230. Greenwich, CT: JAI Press, 1990.

Stojkovic, S. Conversation with police chiefs at training workshop on future crime trends, Wisconsin Rapids, WI, October 1995.

Stojkovic, S. Comments presented at the California Department of Corrections Leadership Institute, Chico, CA, January 1997.

Stojkovic, S. Comments made to the former director of the California Department of Corrections and Rehabilitation, Ms. Jeanne Woodford, January 2005.

Stojkovic, S. Conversation with Matthew Frank, Secretary of the Wisconsin Department of Corrections, January 2007.

Stojkovic, S. "*Crime Analysis at UWM.* Helen Bader School of Social Welfare. Milwaukee, WI: University of Wisconsin-Milwaukee, 2013.

Stojkovic, S. and Farkas, M. A. *Correctional Leadership: A Cultural Perspective.* Belmont, CA: Wadsworth, 2003.

Stojkovic, S., Kalinich, D., and Klofas, J. (Eds.). *The Administration and Management of Criminal Justice Organizations: A Book of Readings.* 3rd ed. Prospect Heights, IL: Waveland, 1999.

Stojkovic, S., Kalinich, D., and Klofas, J. (Eds.). *Criminal Justice Organization: Administration and Management.* 4th ed. Belmont, CA: Wadsworth, 2003.

Stojkovic, S., and Lovell, R. *Corrections: An Introduction.* 2nd ed. Cincinnati, OH: Anderson Publishing Company, 1997.

Stojkovic, S., Lovell, R., and Brandl, S. *Evaluation of the Felony Drug Offender Alternative to Prison Project (FDOATP): Final Report.* Madison: State of Wisconsin, 2001.

Stoller, H. E. "*Need for Achievement in Work Output Among Policemen.*" Unpublished doctoral dissertation, Illinois Institute of Technology, 1977.

Stolz, B. "Congress and Criminal Justice Policy Making: The Impact of Interest Groups and Symbolic Politics." *Journal of Criminal Justice*, 1985, *13*, 307–320.

Stolz, B. A. "Congress, Symbolic Politics and the Evolution of the 1994 'Violence Against Women Act'." *Criminal Justice Policy Review*, 1999, *10*(3), 401–428.

Stone, C., and Stoker, R. *Deprofessionalization and Dissatisfaction in Urban Service Agencies.* Paper presented at the 37th Annual Meeting of the Midwest Political Science Association, Chicago, 1979.

Stranton, E. L., Blough, S., and Hawk, K. "Solutions for the Mentally Ill in Jails." *American Jails*, January/February 2004, 15.

Studt, E. *Surveillance and Service in Parole*. Washington, DC: U.S. Department of Justice, 1978.

Styskal, R. A. "Power and Commitment in Organizations: A Test of the Participation Thesis." *Social Forces*, 1980, *57*(4), 925–943.

Sudnow, D. "Normal Crimes: Sociological Features of the Penal Code in a Public Defender Office." *Social Problems*, 1965, *12*, 255–276.

Sutherland, E., and Cressey, R. *Criminology*. Philadelphia: Lippincott, 1978.

Swank, G. E., and Winer, D. "Occurrence of Psychiatric Disorders in County Jail Populations." *American Journal of Psychiatry*, 1976, *133*(11), 1331–1337.

Swanson, C. R., and Territo, L. "Police Leadership and Interpersonal Communication Styles." In *Managing Police Work: Issues and Analysis*, edited by J. R. Greene, pp. 123–139. Beverly Hills, CA: Sage, 1982.

Swanson, C. R., Territo, L., and Taylor, R. W. *Police Administration: Structures, Processes, and Behavior*. 4th ed. New York: Macmillan, 1997.

Sykes, G. *The Society of Captives*. Princeton, NJ: Princeton University Press, 1958.

Sykes, G., and Messinger, S. L. "The Inmate Social System." In *Theoretical Studies in Social Organization of the Prison*, edited by R. A. Cloward, D. R. Cressey, G. H. Grosser, R. McCleary, L. E. Ohlin, G. Sykes, and S. Messinger, pp. 1–34. New York: Social Science Research Council, 1960.

Sypher, D. B., and Zorn, T. E. "Communication Abilities and Upward Mobility: A Longitudinal Investigation." *Human Communication Research*, Spring 1986, 420–431.

Tannenbaum, A. S. "Control in Organizations: Individual Adjustment and Organizational Performance." *Administrative Science Quarterly*, 1962, 7(2), 236–257.

Taylor, F. W. *Two Papers on Scientific Management*. London: Routledge & Kegan Paul, 1919.

Taylor, F. W. *Scientific Management*. New York: Harper & Row, 1947.

Tekleab, A. G., Quigley, N. R., and Tesluk, P. E. "A Longitudinal Study of Team Conflict, Conflict Management, and Team Effectiveness." *Group & Organization Management*, 2009, *34*, 170–205.

Territo, L., Swanson, J. R., and Chamelin, N. "The Police Selection Process." In *Policing Society*, edited by W. C. Terry, pp. 187–196. New York: Wiley, 1985.

Terry, W. C. "Police Stress as an Administrative Problem: Some Conceptual and Theoretical Difficulties." *Journal of Police Science and Administration*, 1983, *11*, 156–164.

Terry, W. C. (Ed.). *Policing Society*. New York: Wiley, 1985.

Tewksbury, R., and Mustain, E. E. "Correctional Orientations of Prison Staff." *Prison Journal*, 2008, *88*, 207–233.

The Economist. The Pursuit of Progress. 1955.

The National Registry of Exonerations, 2013.

Thomas, K. W. "Organizational Conflict." In *Organizational Behavior and Management*. 4th ed., edited by H. L. Tosi and W. C. Hamner, pp. 392–416. Cincinnati, OH: Grid, 1985.

Thompson, J. *Organizations in Action*. New York: McGraw-Hill, 1967.

Thompson, J., Svirdoff, M., and McElroy, J. *Unemployment and Crime: A Review of Theories and Research*. Washington, DC: U.S. Department of Justice, 1981.

Tifft, L. L. "Control Systems, Social Bases of Power and Power Exercise in Police Organizations." In *Policing: A View from the Street*, edited by P. K. Manning and J. Van Maanen, pp. 90–104. Santa Monica, CA: Goodyear, 1978.

Toch, H. "Is a 'Correction Officer' Always a 'Screw'?" *Criminal Justice Review*, 1978, *3*, 19–35.

Toch, H., and Grant, J. D. *Reforming Human Services: Change through Participation*. Beverly Hills, CA: Sage, 1982.

Toch, H., and Klofas, J. "Alienation and Desire for Job Enrichment among Correction Officers." *Federal Probation*, 1982, *46*, 322–327.

Toch, H., Grant, J. D., and Galvin, R. *Agents of Change: A Study of Police Reform*. Cambridge, MA: Schenkman, 1975.

Tonry, M. "The Failure of the U.S. Sentencing Commission's Guidelines." In *The Administration and Management of Criminal Justice Organizations: A Book of Readings*. 3rd ed., edited by S. Stojkovic, J. Klofas, and D. Kalinich, pp. 307–323. Prospect Heights, IL: Waveland, 2004.

Tosi, H. L., Rizzo, J. R., and Carroll, S. J. *Managing Organizational Behavior*. Marshfield, MA: Pitman, 1986.

Travis, L., Latessa, E., and Vito, G. "Agenda Building in Criminal Justice: The Case of Determinant Sentencing." *American Journal of Criminal Justice*, 1985, *10*(1), 1–21.

Trenholm, S., and Jensen, A. *Interpersonal Communication*. 2nd ed. Belmont, CA: Wadsworth, 1992.

Trojanowicz, R. *An Evaluation of the Neighborhood Foot Patrol Program in Flint, Michigan*. East Lansing, MI: National Neighborhood Foot Patrol Center, 1983.

Trojanowicz, R., and Banas, D. *Perceptions of Safety: A Comparison of Foot Patrol versus Motor Patrol Officers*. East Lansing, MI: National Neighborhood Foot Patrol Center, 1985.

Trojanowicz, R., and Bucqueroux, B. *Community Policing: A Contemporary Perspective*. Cincinnati, OH: Anderson Publishing Company, 1990.

Trojanowicz, R., and Carter, D. *The Philosophy and Role of Community Policing*. East Lansing, MI: National Neighborhood Foot Patrol Center, 1988.

Trojanowicz, R., Steele, M., and Trojanowicz, S. *Community Policing: A Taxpayer's Perspective*. East Lansing, MI: National Neighborhood Foot Patrol Center, 1986.

Tullar, W. L., and Glauser, M. J. "Communicator Style of Police Officer and Citizen Satisfaction with Officer/ Citizen Telephone Conversations." *Journal of Police Science and Administration*, 1985, *13*(1), 70–72.

Tully, H., Winter, J., Wilson, T., and Scanlon, T. "Correctional Institution Impact and Host Community Resistance." *Canadian Journal of Criminology*, 1982, *24*(2), 133–139.

Tyler, T. R. "Enhancing Police Legitimacy." *Annals of the American Academy of Political and Social Science*, 2004, *593*, 84–99.

Tylor, E. *Primitive Culture: Research into the Development of Mythology, Philosophy, Religion, Arts, and Customs*. Vol. *1*. London: John Murray, 1958.

Uchida, C. "The Development of the American Police: An Historical Overview." In *Critical Issues in Policing*, edited by R. G. Dunham and G. P. Alpert, pp. 20–40. Long Grove, IL: Waveland Press, 2005.

Uggen, C., Manza, J., and Thompson, M. "Citizenship, Democracy, and the Civil Reintegration of Criminal Offenders." *Annals of the American Academy of Political and Social Sciences*, 2006, *281*.

United States Sentencing Commission. "Report on the Impact of *United States* v. *Booker* on Federal Sentencing." *Federal Sentencing Reporter*, 2006, *18*(3), 190–197.

U.S. Bureau of Justice Statistics. *Prisoners in 1987*. Washington, DC: U.S. Department of Justice, 1988.

U.S. Bureau of Justice Statistics. *Prisoners in 1994*. Washington, DC: U.S. Department of Justice, 1995.

U.S. Department of Justice. *Enforcing the ADA: Looking Back on a Decade of Progress. A Special Tenth Anniversary Status Report from the Department of Justice*. Washington, DC: U.S. Department of Justice, 2000a.

U.S. Department of Justice. *What Is Community Policing?* Office of Community Oriented Policing. Washington, DC: U.S. Department of Justice, 2000b.

U.S. Department of Justice. *National Evaluation of the Community Oriented Policing Services*. Washington, DC: U.S. Department of Justice, 2000c.

U.S. Department of Justice. *National Evaluation of the COPS Program: Title I of the 1994 Crime Act*. Washington, DC: U.S. Government Printing Office, 2001.

Useem, B., and Kimball, P. *States of Siege: U.S. Prison Riots 1971–1986*. New York: Oxford University Press, 1989.

Vanagunas, S., "Planning for the Delivery of Urban Police Services." In *Managing Police Work: Issues and Analysis*, edited by J. Greene, pp. 203–216. Beverly Hills, CA: Sage, 1982.

Van Buren, W. "Computer-Based Training." *American Jails*, 1996, *9*(6): 20–23.

Van Maanen, J. "Observations on the Making of a Policeman." *Human Organization*, 1973, *4*, 407–418.

Van Maanen, J. "Police Socialization: A Longitudinal Examination of Job Attitudes in an Urban Police Department." *Administrative Science Quarterly*, 1975, *20*, 266–278.

Van Maanen, J. "People Processing: Strategies of Organizational Socialization." In *Managing Organizations*, edited by D. A. Nadler, M. L. Tushman, and N. G. Hatvany, pp. 144–157. Boston: Little, Brown, 1982.

Van Maanen, J. "Learning the Ropes." In *Policing Society*, edited by W. C. Terry, pp. 68–88. New York: Wiley, 1985.

Van Zelst, R. "Sociometrically Selected Work Teams Increase Production." *Personnel Psychology*, 1952, *5*, 175–185.

Vetter, H., and Territo, L. *Crime and Justice in America: A Human Perspective*. St. Paul, MN: West, 1984.

Visher, C. "Editorial Introduction on Prisoner Reentry." *Criminology & Public Policy*, 2006, *5*(2), 299–303.

Waegel, W. B. "Case Routinization in Investigative Police Work." *Social Problems*, 1981, *28*, 263–275.

Wahler, C., and Gendreau, P. "Assessing Correctional Officers." *Federal Probation*, 1985, *49*, 70–74.

Waldron, R. J. *The Criminal Justice System*. Boston, MA: Houghton Mifflin, 1984.

Walker, S. *Popular Justice: A History of American Criminal Justice:* New York, NY: Oxford University Press, 1980.

Walker, S. *Sense and Nonsense about Crime: A Policy Guide*. Pacific Grove, CA: Brooks/Cole, 1985.

Walker, S. *Sense and Nonsense about Crime and Drugs*. 3rd ed. Belmont, CA: Wadsworth, 1994.

Walker, S. *Sense and Nonsense about Crime and Drugs: A Policy Guide*. 6th ed. Belmont, CA: Thomson/Wadsworth, 2006.

Walker, S. *The Police in America*. 3rd Edition. New York, NY: McGraw-Hill, 1999.

Walker, S., and Katz, C. M. *Police in America: An Introduction*. Boston: McGraw Hill, 2002.

Walmsley, G., and Zald, M. *The Political Economy of Public Organizations*. Lexington, MA: Heath, 1973.

Walsh, W. F. "Patrol Officer Arrest Rates: A Study of the Social Organization of Police Work." *Justice Quarterly*, 1986, *3*, 271–290.

Waltman, J. "Nonverbal Communications in Interrogation: Some Applications." *Journal of Police Science and Administration*, 1983, *11*(2), 166–169.

Walton, M. *The Deming Management Method*. New York: Perigee, 1986.

Warren, D. I. "Power, Visibility, and Conformity in Formal Organizations." *American Sociological Review*, 1968, *33*(6), 951–970.

Warren, E. "The Economic Approach to Crime." In=*Criminal Justice Studies*, edited by G. Misner, pp. 172–180. St. Louis: C. V. Mosby, 1981.

Warren, R. *Social Change and Human Purpose: Toward Understanding and Action*. Chicago: Rand McNally, 1977.

Weber, M. *The Theory of Social and Economic Organization*. New York: Free Press, 1947.

Weick, K. *The Social Psychology of Organizing*. 2nd ed. Reading, MA: Addison-Wesley, 1979.

Weinberger, L. A. "Emotional Intelligence, Leadership Style, and Perceived Leadership Effectiveness." *Advances in Developing Human Resources*, 2009, *11*, 747–772.

Weiner, J., and Johnson, R. "Organization and Environment: The Case of Correctional Personnel Training Programs." *Journal of Criminal Justice*, 1981, *9*, 441–450.

Weisburd, D. "Randomized Experiments in Criminal Justice Policy: Problems and Prospects." *Crime and Delinquency*, 2000, *46*(2), 181–193.

Weiss, C. "The Circuitry of Enlightenment: Diffusion of Social Science Research to Policy Makers." *Knowledge: Creation, Diffusion, Utilitization*, 1987, *8*, 274–281.

Weiss, C. H. "Evaluation Research in the Political Context." In *Handbook of Evaluation Research*, edited by E. L. Struening and M. Guttentag, pp. 13–26. Beverly Hills, CA: Sage, 1972.

Welch, M. *Corrections: A Radical Approach*. Upper Saddle River, NJ: Prentice Hall, 1996.

Wenzel, S. L., Longshore, D., Turner, S., and Ridgely, M. S. "Drug Courts: A Bridge between Criminal Justice and Health Services." In *The Administration and Management of Criminal Justice Organizations: A Book of Readings*. 4th ed., edited by S. Stojkovic, J. Klofas, and D. Kalinich, pp. 69–90. Long Grove, IL: Waveland Press, 2004.

Westley, W. *Violence and the Police: A Sociological Study of Law, Custom and Morality*. Cambridge, MA: MIT Press, 1970.

Whisenand, P., and Ferguson, F. *The Managing of Police Organizations*. 4th ed. Englewood Cliffs, NJ: Prentice Hall, 1996.

White, J. *Terrorism and Homeland Security*. Belmont, CA: Thompson Learning, 2006.

Whitehead, J. T. "Job Burnout in Probation and Parole: Its Extent and Intervention Implications." *Criminal Justice and Behavior*, 1985, *12*, 91–110.

Whitehead, J. T., and Lindquist, C. A. "Correctional Officer Job Burnout: A Path Model." *Journal of Research in Crime and Delinquency*, 1986, *23*, 23–42.

Wildavsky, A. *The Politics of the Budgetary Process*. Boston: Little, Brown, 1974.

Wilensky, H. *Organizational Intelligence*. New York: Basic Books, 1967.

Wilkins, L. T. "Information Overload: Peace or War with the Computer." In *Parole: Legal Issues/Decision-Making/Research*, edited by W. E. Amos and C. L. Newman, pp. 141–157. New York: Federal Legal Publications, 1975a.

Wilkins, L. T. "A Typology of Decision-Makers?" In *Parole: Legal Issues/Decision-Making/Research*, edited by W. E. Amos and C. L. Newman, pp. 159–168. New York: Federal Legal Publications, 1975b.

Wilkins, L. T. "Treatment of Offenders at Patuxent." *Rutgers Law Review*, 1976, *29*, 45–60.

Wilkinson, R. Comments made at the "Opening Up a Closed World: What Constitutes Effective Prison Oversight" Conference. Austin, TX: April 2006.

Willett, T. C. "The 'Fish Screw' in the Canadian Penitentiary Service." *Queen's Law Journal*, 1977, *3*, 424–449.

Williams, E. J. "Structuring in Community Policing: Institutionalizing Innovative Change." *Police Practice and Research*, 2003, *4*(2), 119–129.

Williamson, O. E. "The Economics of Organizations: The Transactions-Cost Approach." *American Journal of Sociology*, 1981, *87*, 548–577.

Willis, J. J., Mastrofski, S. D., and Weisburd, D. *Compstat in Practice: An In-Depth Analysis of Three Cities*. Washington, DC: Police Foundation, 2003.

Wilson, J. Q. *Varieties of Police Behavior*. Cambridge, MA: Harvard University Press, 1968.

Wilson, J. Q. *Bureaucracy: What Government Agencies Do and Why They Do It*. Glenview, IL: Basic Books, 2000.

Wilson, J. Q., and Kelling, G. I. "Broken Windows: The Police and Neighborhood Safety." *Atlantic Monthly*, March 1982, 29–38.

Witham, D. C. "Management Control through Motivation." *FBI Law Enforcement Bulletin*, 1980, *49*(2), 6–11.

Wolff v. *McDonnell*. 94 S. Ct. 2963 (1974).

Wood, F. Comments made in "Prison Management Trends, 1975–2025," by C. Riveland. In *Prisons*, edited by M. Tonry and J. Petersilia, Chicago: University of Chicago Press, 1999.

Woodford, J. Conversation with author Stan Stojkovic, July 2006.

Wright, K. *Effective Prison Leadership*. Binghamton, NY: William Neil, 1994.

Wright, K. "The Desirability of Goal Conflict within the Criminal Justice System." In *The Administration and Management of Criminal Justice Organizations: A Book of Readings*. 4th ed., edited by S. Stojkovic, J. Klofas, and D. Kalinich, pp. 457–477. Prospect Heights, IL: Waveland Press, 2004.

Wycoff, M. A. "Evaluating the Crime-Effectiveness of Municipal Police." In *Managing Police Work: Issues and Analysis*, edited by J. Greene, pp. 15–36. Beverly Hills, CA: Sage, 1982.

Yeager, M. "Unemployment and Imprisonment." *Journal of Criminal Law and Criminology*, 1979, *75*, 586–593.

Yin, R. K. *Case Study Research, Design and Methods*. 3rd ed. Newbury Park, CA: Sage, 2002.

Yong, E. "Armor Against Prejudice" *Scientific America*, 2013, *308*(6).

Yuchtman, E., and Seashore, S. "A System-Resource Approach to Organizational Effectiveness." *American Sociological Review*, 1967, *32*, 891–903.

Yukl, G. A. *Leadership in Organizations*. Englewood Cliffs, NJ: Prentice Hall, 1981.

Yukl, G. *Leadership in Organizations*. 6th ed. Englewood Cliffs, NJ: Prentice Hall, 2006.

Zaltman, G., Duncan, R., and Holbeck, J. *Innovations and Organizations*. New York: Wiley, 1973.

Zedlewski, E. W. *Making Confinement Decisions*. Washington, DC: National Institute of Justice, 1987.

Zeleznikow, J. "Building Decision Support Systems in Discretionary Legal Domains." *International Review of Law, Computers & Technology*, 2000, *14*(3), 341–356.

Zeleznikow, J. "Web-Based Legal Decision Support Systems to Improve Access to Justice." *Information & Communication Technology Law*, 2002, *11*(1), 15–33.

Zimring, F., and Hawkins, G. *Incapacitation: Penal Confinement and the Restraint of Crime*. New York: Oxford University Press, 1995.

Zupan, L. *Jails: Reform and the New Generation Philosophy*. Cincinnati, OH: Anderson Publishing Company, 1991.

Index

511